2002 CultureGrams™
standard edition

Produced by
CultureGrams™
a division of Millennial Star Network
and
Brigham Young University

Volume I
The Americas and Europe

This book (Volume I) includes CultureGrams™ 2002 Standard Edition cultural reports for The Americas and Europe.

A related volume (Volume II) includes CultureGrams™ 2002 Standard Edition cultural reports for Africa, Asia, and Oceania.

Library of Congress Cataloging-in-Publication Data

CultureGrams™ 2002 Standard Edition /
developed by CultureGrams™, a division of Millennial Star Network and Brigham Young University.

ISBN 0-89434-420-X (v. 1)
ISBN 0-89434-422-6 (2-volume set)

Contents

Endorsements

"CultureGrams's reliance on native writers and reviewers to provide balanced and accurate information for each country is what distinguishes it from most other sources of cultural information. The reports are concise, clearly written, and current."

—Vladimir Wertsman, Chair, Publishing and Multicultural Materials Committee of Ethnic Materials Information Exchange Round Table, American Library Association

"A Croatian theater critic recently visited several American universities, where his hosts showed him, among other things, the Croatia CultureGram™. He was impressed by the precise, coherent, and above all accurate presentation of his native country. Upon his return to Croatia, he described his impressions in an article published in the reputable daily *Novi List*, noting that he had rarely seen a foreign publication giving such a full account of different aspects of Croatia's political, economic, and cultural life. This is the fundamental value of CultureGrams™: each country—and practically all countries are covered—is presented in a way that enables not only the person encountering it for the first time but also the one that already possesses some knowledge about it to approach it easily, with well-chosen and easily understood information concerning the life and specific characteristics of that country. In this way, the CultureGrams™ project spreads the idea of cultural diversity and opens new paths of international communication and cooperation."

—Biserka Cvjeticanin, Ph.D.
Deputy Minister of Culture, Republic of Croatia
Coordinator, Culturelink Network

"CultureGrams™ fits the needs of our students in social studies, foreign language, and foreign culture classes. The simple, concise layout of CultureGrams™ makes it most appealing to students. Large, heavy geographical tomes are quickly avoided by many students, but CultureGrams™ is formatted in a way students find easy to use."

—Clarissa Lowry, Librarian, Franklin Middle School, Wheaton, IL

"As our communities become more and more diverse due to the in-migration of refugees and others from distant countries, it is more important than ever for professionals to better understand the barriers to cultural assimilation. I am very impressed by the scope and breadth of the 177 CultureGrams™ available as individual copies or in sets according to world regions as well as world languages. Each CultureGram™ is well researched and well organized. I highly recommend this product for instructional and training purposes."

—Loren A. Evenrud, Ph.D.
Supervisor of Patrol, Minneapolis Park Police, Minneapolis, MN

"Differences in cultures and customs can make international travel exciting, but they can make it risky, too: no one enjoys getting inexplicable glares at the dinner table or discovering that an innocent remark has been taken as an insult. CultureGrams™ is a simple way to prevent such faux pas."

—TIME Magazine International

Acknowledgments

One year ago, we set lofty goals for the 2002 release of CultureGrams™. Today, we are grateful and pleased we successfully accomplished our goals. We added culturally significant enhancements, including multimedia content, to our electronic products. We created the CultureGrams™ Kids Edition and StateGrams™ Kids Edition products, encouraging cultural understanding for our young readers. We developed the 2002 products with a focus to allow people throughout the world access to this information.

In gratitude, we thank those hundreds of people who provided input for our reports. Living and working in every corner of the world, these contributors lend time and expertise to our educational project, and we appreciate their dedication to helping us fulfill our mission of building cultural understanding.

Closer to home, I humbly respect and thank the many people who have been willing to provide Olympian-type efforts to create this year's publication. Thanks to Andy Bay and our award-winning editorial staff, including Brian Arnell, Kipling Clark, Melissa Humes, and Elizabeth Hutchings. Thanks to our copy editor, Celeste Keele, and proofreader, Aimee Hill. Thanks to the editorial research assistants: Tucker Boyle, Jodee Hortin, Mary Ann Perkins, Rachel Vesterfelt, Patricia Higbee, Marlene Hansen, Ryan King, Elisha Christopher, and Rachel Snell. Credit for organizing and preparing this series goes to our talented production team: Suzy Gerhart, Jason McDonald, Jennia Schwebach, Adam Corey, Andrew Hahn, Cheree Marcov, Morgan Reid, Hadley Soffe, and the staff at Brigham Young University's Print Services. Kristy McEwan leads our marketing and customer service team with a supporting cast of Kimi Moriyama, Joseph Pacini, Jana Lewis, Abby Talich, Rochelle Barton, Charles White, Justin Hemingway, Jill Deagle, Lindsay Ferguson, and Marilee Phillips. Furthermore, we all thank our families for their love, patience, and support as we work to realize our goals.

Of course, we could not produce CultureGrams™ and its related products without the vision, guidance, and support of the directors and employees of Millennial Star Network, a Utah not-for-profit corporation, including CEO Franklin Lewis.

The David M. Kennedy Center for International Studies at Brigham Young University (BYU) was home to CultureGrams™ from 1981 to 1999, and we appreciate continued support from and collaboration with its faculty and staff. We are blessed by their enthusiasm and are thankful for their assistance.

Our sponsoring institution, The Church of Jesus Christ of Latter-day Saints, has provided us with our mission to build cultural understanding, respect for all individuals, and, ultimately, friendship among the world's peoples. We are grateful for our leaders' trust as we work to achieve our mission.

Jim Baird
General Manager
CultureGrams™

Introduction

The CultureGrams™ Standard Edition is unique. In it, we describe a country's people, customs, attitudes, and culture. We are concise. We have enough generality to be useful and enough specifics to be fair and descriptive. And we update our texts yearly and review them regularly for cultural accuracy. No other resource blends brevity, depth, accuracy, and timeliness.

For more than 25 years, the CultureGrams™ Standard Edition has focused both on the peoples it describes and you, the reader. In its evolution from a small local initiative in 1974 to the widely trusted resource it is today, CultureGrams™ has always had a mission to build cultural understanding and friendship among the world's peoples. In all we do, we hope to highlight that which both unites our planet and gives humanity its unique differences.

Quality and accuracy are the backbone of each CultureGrams™ Standard Edition cultural report. Each text has been written by degree-holding professionals (usually a native or longtime resident) whose experience or background allows them to understand different perspectives, regions, and languages in the nation. Native professionals, academics, Peace Corps volunteers, and other qualified persons have reviewed the text, and their suggestions are incorporated for balance, breadth, and strength.

We are committed to building effective tools for teaching cultural understanding. During the last year we spoke with many of you about what you wanted to see in the CultureGrams™ 2002 products. As a result, this year's CultureGrams™ Standard Edition features a new arts category for all of the countries. The electronic version has had major multimedia enhancements to it, including native voice audio files, photos, new maps, and an ambassador's welcome for select countries. We've expanded our offerings to include a colorful Kids Edition of CultureGrams™ and a StateGrams™ Kids Edition for the 50 states and Washington, D.C.

Our goal is to become your first point of contact for accurate cultural information. To do that, we now offer all CultureGrams™ products in print and electronic formats. These ever-evolving products will be produced to the same standards of quality you have come to rely on. In the future, we will continue adding more resources for students, teachers, businesspeople, government officials, volunteers, librarians, and travelers. For all the latest news and information about CultureGrams™ we invite you to explore our Web site at www.culturegrams.com.

Andrew Bay
Managing Editor
CultureGrams™

Republic of
Albania

Boundary representations are not necessarily authoritative.

BACKGROUND

Land and Climate. Albania, covering 11,100 square miles (28,750 square kilometers), is one of the smallest countries in Europe. The terrain is mostly mountainous, with narrow coastal lowlands along the Adriatic and Ionian Seas. Coastal soils are fertile but not well drained for agriculture. Instead, the rocks, forested mountains, and sandy beaches are considered a treasure by Albanians for their tourism potential. Several river valleys carve their way through Albania's mountains, providing spring water and room for towns and cities. Mountain lakes also dot the landscape. Albania's northern Alps feature the nation's highest peak, Korabi (9,026 feet or 2,751 meters), but other ranges also have peaks above 8,000 feet (2,400 meters).

Summers along the Adriatic are hot and dry, while winters are mild and wet. A continental climate prevails inland, with more marked seasonal temperature extremes. Summer readings may reach 95°F (35°C), and winter lows may fall to 0°F (-18°C), especially in the north and southeast.

History. Descended from the ancient Illyrians, Albanians are considered one of the oldest native Balkan peoples. Illyria covered a wide portion of the southern Balkans. It was invaded by the Romans in the second century B.C., and when the Roman Empire divided in the fourth century A.D., Illyria remained with the eastern portion. Many of Rome's emperors had Illyrian ancestry.

A fifth century Bulgar invasion was followed by the Slavs in the sixth and seventh centuries. Slavic attempts to impose their culture and religion on the native population forced Albanians south and into the mountains. A native prince, Progon, established an independent state in 1190 that lasted

less than a century, and Albania was conquered in the 14th century by Serbs. Their empire fell in 1355 and Albania was divided under local feudal lords: the Dukagjinis and Topias ruled in the north, and the Muzakas and Shpatas in the south.

Turkish incursions began in the late 1300s, but Albanian resistance was organized by Gjergj Kastrioti (known as Skanderbeg) in 1444. Skanderbeg is revered by Albanians as a national hero and was even respected by the Ottomans, who could not fully conquer the region while he was alive. But by 1500, the Turks had gained complete control. Thousands of Albanians had fled, and the nation entered a long period under Ottoman rule. A renaissance in the 1870s eventually contributed to a 1911 uprising against the Turks.

In the 1912 London Conference on the Balkans, an independent Albanian state was created. Its disputed borders, finalized in 1913 after the First Balkan War, left some 40 percent of ethnic Albanians outside of Albania. World War I soon engulfed Albania, leading to grinding poverty in the 1920s. Archbishop Fan Noli failed in 1924 to create a Western-style democracy, and he was ousted from power by his rival, Ahmed Bey Zogu. Zogu declared himself King Zog in 1928 and ruled repressively until 1939; he fled when Italy occupied Albania. Italy's rule was followed by a German invasion in 1943. Liberation came in 1944.

After a short civil war, the National Liberation Movement formed a provisional government and named Communist leader Enver Hoxha as president in 1945. Hoxha eventually led Albania down the path of oppression, poverty, and isolation until his death in 1985. Albanians responded to

EUROPE

democratization in Eastern Europe after 1989 by seeking greater freedoms at home or by trying to leave the impoverished country in 1991. Communist leaders won elections in 1991 but soon met with food riots and other turmoil. A second election in 1992 brought the Democratic Party to power with Sali Berisha as president. He began working with international organizations to build a viable economy. Parliamentary elections in May 1996 returned the Democrats to power, although opposition leaders and outside observers reported serious flaws in the voting process. Post-election protests were quelled quickly.

Widespread violence erupted in February 1997 after thousands of Albanians lost their life savings in fraudulent high-risk investment schemes believed to be supported by the government. Public anger fueled weeks of riots; military arsenals were looted and the country rapidly fell into anarchy. A multinational force oversaw elections in June 1997 in which former prime minister Fatos Nano's Socialists soundly defeated Berisha's Democratic Party. Nano resigned in the wake of severe riots, which followed the September 1998 assassination of Berisha's colleague Azem Hajdari. Socialist Pandeli Majko became prime minister. After a November 1998 referendum approved it, a new constitution was signed into law.

The perennial problems of rival gangs, arms smuggling, and lawlessness were eclipsed by fighting between Serbs and independence-seeking ethnic Albanians in the neighboring Kosovo province of Yugoslavia. Violence rapidly escalated in 1998, forcing thousands of refugees into Albania. After failed negotiations, North Atlantic Treaty Organization (NATO) forces began air strikes on Yugoslavia in March 1999; Albania allowed NATO access through its territory. After 78 days of bombing, Yugoslavia agreed to withdraw its forces from Kosovo, but not before systematic killing of and atrocities against Kosovar Albanians forced nearly a million refugees into Albania, Macedonia, and other states. Many have now been repatriated under the protection of a multinational peacekeeping group, but regional tensions remain high.

Socialist Ilir Meta became prime minister in October 1999, with promises to fight government corruption. Legal penalties for corruption have been increased and a civil service board oversees political appointments. In January 2001, Albania and Yugoslavia reestablished diplomatic relations broken off during the Kosovo crisis.

THE PEOPLE

Population. Albania's population of almost 3.5 million is growing by less than 1 percent. Another three to four million Albanians live in neighboring countries; most have lived in those regions for generations. Albania itself is about 95 percent ethnic Albanian. Small groups of Greeks, Serbs, Romany (Gypsies), and Bulgarians live in the country. Only about 38 percent of the population resides in urban areas. Although the populace is educated, opportunities for personal advancement or enjoying prosperity are limited.

Language. Albanians speak *Shqip* (Albanian), an Indo-European language directly descended from Illyrian. In 1908, Albania adopted a Latin script. The alphabet has 36 letters (7 are vowels). Two dialects, Gheg and Tosk, were historically spoken in Albania, but a national language based on Tosk was adopted after 1945. This Tosk-based Albanian is the official language.

Religion. Prior to the Ottoman era, Albanians were mostly Christian. Under the Turks, however, a large percentage of the population converted to Islam and accordingly changed their names. Albanians could practice religion freely until the Communist era, when the country's many mosques, monasteries, and churches suffered damage and destruction under the government's antireligion policy. In 1965, religious practices were outlawed altogether.

Religious freedom was restored in 1990 and religion is again becoming important in people's daily lives. Although official figures are lacking, it is estimated that 70 percent of the population is Muslim (Sunni and Bektashi), 20 percent Orthodox Christian, and 10 percent Catholic. Protestant Christian churches and other denominations are beginning to establish a presence in Albania.

General Attitudes. Albanians value their families and their ethnic heritage. Personal honor is also important. Northern Albanians, particularly the mountaineers, are known to be courageous, resourceful, courteous, and hardy. They honor a traditional institution called the *besa* (sworn truce). Adherence to the *besa*, family honor, hospitality, and a patriarchal order are considered to be the basis for successful relationships. Otherwise, northerners tend to engage in blood feuds, resist governance by others, and distrust outsiders. Southern Albanians are known to be openly emotional and socially more liberal.

Albanians resist appealing to the wisdom and advice of others. Adjusting to a Western system of competition, free speech, capitalism, and materialism has been difficult. Albanians are more accustomed to force and autocracy than to democracy and the rule of law.

Albanians are weary from continued social and economic turmoil. Anger, hopelessness, and poverty have replaced the country's recent optimism, increase in wealth, and progress. Guns now dominate society, particularly in lawless areas where government mistrust is strong. The lack of social order has nearly destroyed community and national values. Some Albanians feel a loss of pride and dignity in not being able to govern themselves. Most people feel discouraged and hopeless about the future.

Personal Appearance. Before 1991, clothing was often homemade but now is usually purchased. Urban professional men wear business suits and ties. Urban women wear dresses and skirts more than pants. They wear Western tops and colorful blouses. The youth like jeans, T-shirts, and sneakers.

Villagers wear traditional outfits, which vary by region. In the north, women wear a head scarf and a *fustanelle* (full, colorful wool skirt) over tights. Men wear cotton or wool pants, heavy cotton shirts, a *xhamadan* (wool vest), and a *qeleshe* (white cap). In the south, such traditional attire is used mainly in ceremonies. Clothing is neat and clean; all Albanians consider cleanliness a personal duty. People prefer natural fabrics (cotton, wool) over synthetic fibers.

CUSTOMS AND COURTESIES

Greetings. Albanians greet with a handshake and add a hug for friends. Greetings between women may also include a kiss to each cheek. Typical phrases include *Si jeni?* (How are you?), *Si keni kaluar?* (How are you doing?), *Ç' kemi?* (What's up?), or *Njatjeta* (Hello). Friends may also greet by saying *Miremengjes* (Good morning). When parting, they say *Mir u pafshim* (Good-bye), *Do te shihemi* (See you later),

Shendet! (Stay healthy!), or *Gjithe te mirat* (All the best). Northern male villagers greet by lifting the cap and saying *Tungjat jeta* (Have a long life). Albanians smile or nod when passing strangers on the street.

Close friends address each other by first name, but Albanians otherwise use *Zonja* (Mrs.), *Zonjushe* (Miss), or *Zoteri* (Mr.) with first or last names. Before 1990, *Shok* (Comrade) was used for introducing someone. Specific kinship terms are important when addressing family members. For instance, an uncle may be called *xhaxha* (father's brother) or *daje* (mother's brother). Likewise, an aunt is either *halle* or *teto* (father's sister) or *teze* (mother's sister). It is common to call an older man *xhaxha* or an older woman *nene* (a term for mother), whether they are related or not.

Gestures. Albanians often move their hands and heads when conversing, although they maintain as much eye contact as possible. To indicate "yes," one shakes the head slowly from left to right. A person indicates "no" either by nodding briefly up and down or by clicking the tongue and nodding the head down once. A "thumbs up" gesture is impolite, meaning "You'll get nothing from me." Placing the left hand over the chest and moving the head slightly shows appreciation.

Albanians use the index finger when they want to make a point, whether expressing an opinion or pointing at another person. Showing both hands with open fingers, palms up, means "Our conversation is over." To pat another person's shoulder means "I am proud of you." Young people might show strong approval by quickly moving the hand horizontally, while at the same time bringing the thumb and index finger together and clicking the tongue.

Visiting. Visiting is considered a joyful event, and Albanian hospitality is a cultural hallmark. Unplanned visits are common. Guests usually are greeted with the phrase *Mire se vini* or *Mire se erdhet* (Welcome). Guests bring gifts for birthdays or special occasions, but not if they are invited for a meal or are just visiting. Gifts, even birthday presents, are opened only after the guests are gone.

In northern villages, people commonly socialize while sitting cross-legged on the floor near the fireplace, a custom that stems from an old tradition of sitting around a low table (*sofra*). Otherwise, people sit on chairs.

After seating guests, the hostess offers the men strong alcoholic drinks such as *raki* or *konjak* and sweet liquors to the women, even during the day. These drinks are accompanied by homemade jam, candies, and Turkish coffee, which is served with biscuits, cookies, or cake. Before drinking, visitors politely say *Gezuar* (Cheers) and *Mire se ju gjeta* (I am glad I find you all well). The host and hostess reply *Mire se erdhet*. Evening visits usually occur between 4 and 8:30 p.m. Visits do not necessarily include a meal, but hosts may extend such an invitation. Albanian hosts traditionally walk their guests a little way down the street when they leave.

Eating. An Albanian breakfast (6:30–7 a.m.) usually consists of milk, eggs, bread and butter, jam, cheese, and Turkish or espresso coffee. A traditional restaurant breakfast is *paçe*, a creamy soup made with a cow or calf head, tomato sauce, garlic, flour, butter, and seasonings. Lunch (3–4 p.m.), usually the main meal, begins with vegetables, rice soup flavored with chicken or veal, and fresh green or tomato salad, followed by the main course of *gjelle* (boiled beans or vegetables with meat) or baked, stuffed eggplants or peppers. Cakes,

fresh fruits, and coffee follow the meal.

Dinner (7:30–9:30 p.m.) consists of light soup or pasta, plain yogurt, bread, and dessert. The mother usually prepares each plate before serving it. For holidays or when guests are present, serving dishes are put on the table and each person chooses his or her portion. When guests are present, hosts serve *meze* (antipasto with boiled eggs, feta and *kackavall* cheese, cold cuts or sausage, onions, tomatoes, and olives) accompanied by *raki*. In the north, *meze* is prepared with cottage cheese and *turshi* (vegetables preserved in saltwater).

Private restaurants reopened after 1990. Albanians eat in the continental style, with the fork in the left hand and the knife in the right. Toasting is common, with the first toast made to everyone's health and friendship. Bills are presented on request and are paid at the table. Tipping is customary.

LIFESTYLE

Family. Urban families generally have one or two children, while rural families have three or four. For the most part, the father heads the family, and women are responsible for cooking, cleaning, and caring for the children. Male children are seen as the future backbone of the family and protectors of the family name. Both parents usually work and send their children to day care. Men and women have equal social rights.

Village homes, shared by two or three generations, usually are built of stone or brick and have two to three bedrooms. City dwellers most often live in apartments with one to three rooms. Due to a housing shortage, unmarried adults often live with their parents, as do married children, usually on the groom's side. These children are expected to take care of their aging parents.

Dating and Marriage. Prior to 1945, most marriages were arranged. This custom came from an early era when northern tribes would announce a girl's engagement at birth. Today, young people make their own choices regarding a spouse, but rural families are still heavily involved in the selection process. Urban youth begin dating around age 16; they go to movies or small café bars to socialize. Men generally marry after they are 26 and women marry in their early twenties.

A civil ceremony is required for a marriage to be legal, but since 1991, many couples also are having a church ceremony. There are usually two wedding celebrations: one on Saturday for the bride and one on Sunday for the groom. At the first party, given by the bride's parents, the groom and his family representatives only appear after 10 p.m., and the bride changes from a white dress to a more colorful one after midnight. The party continues until 3 a.m. The next day around noon, the groom goes with a few relatives to the bride's house to take her to his parents' home. There they receive the congratulations of visitors before having the second dinner party, sponsored by the groom's parents.

Diet. The Albanian diet is influenced by Greek, Turkish, and Italian cuisine. Traditional specialties include *fasule* (boiled dried beans) cooked with onions and tomatoes and flavored with *pasterma* (dried salt mutton); *turshi* salads; *byrek* (a pastry) with vegetables, cottage cheese, or minced meat; and *tave kosi* (meat or liver baked in yogurt). Lamb, veal, and chicken are the most popular meats. Albanians also enjoy pork and seafood. Meat often is boiled together with vegetables such as potatoes, onions, okra, peas, beans, leeks, spinach, or cabbage. In the south, roasted lamb served with fresh vegetables and baked potatoes is considered traditional. Typical dairy

EUROPE

products include homemade yogurt, cottage cheese, and feta and *kackavall* cheeses. Locally grown fruits include apples, pears, peaches, watermelons, plums, oranges, figs, and grapes. *Raki* often is served before the main meal, while wine is served during or after the meal.

Recreation. Men play basketball or soccer. Families gather for religious, historic, and cultural events. Urban families like to picnic or go to the beach in the summer. People like to watch television or attend movies. Western music, especially from the United States, is popular.

The Arts. Under the communist reign, the development of literature, cinema, and theater was limited; however, the current government has made a concerted effort to promote and preserve Albanian culture. Folk dances such as the *valle* and *ajsino oro*, are still frequently performed today, particularly in the smaller villages. Albania also has indigenous music played on unique instruments: a *çiftelia* (type of mandolin with two strings) or *lahuta* (one-stringed instrument played with a bow) in the north, a *gajde* (type of bagpipe) in the central region, and a kind of wailing clarinet in the south. Woodcarvings, woolen rugs, and decorated clothing are common folk arts. The National Archaeological Museum houses the largest Illyrian collection in the world.

Holidays. Official public holidays include New Year's (1–2 Jan.), Easter (Friday–Monday), May Day (1 May), Independence Day and Liberation Day (29 November for both holidays), and Christmas (25–26 Dec.). Muslims celebrate *Ramasan Bairam* (feast at the end of the holy month of *Ramadan*) and *Kurban Bairam* (Feast of Sacrifice). On Memorial Day (5 May), people place flowers on graves and honor fallen warriors. The most popular holiday is New Year's Eve, which Albanians celebrate with big meals (usually a turkey dinner with special desserts in syrup, like *baklava* or *kadaif*), dancing, joking, and singing. They spend the following day visiting and sharing holiday sweets.

Commerce. Businesses are open Monday through Friday, 7 a.m. to 3 p.m. Shops, open-air markets, and private grocery stores are usually open 12 hours a day. Factories and other industrial places operate weekdays from 6 a.m. to 3:30 p.m.

SOCIETY

Government. Albania ratified a constitution in 1998, which provides for rule of law and separation of powers. Executive power rests with the president, who is appointed by parliament. The prime minister is head of government. Socialist Rexhep Mejdani is president. The Socialist Party (former Communists) dominates the 155-seat *Kuvendi Popullor* (People's Assembly). Primary opposition is provided by the Democratic Party, but other parties also have representation. Democracy is not yet strong, and inexperience is a key stumbling block. The voting age is 18.

Economy. Prior to 1997, the country was progressing in its difficult transition towards a decentralized economy. Land was privatized in 1992. Free-market principles were being introduced and the number of small businesses was increasing. Economic growth exceeded 10 percent in 1995. The collapse of the pyramid investment schemes ruined the country's economy in 1997. Albanians lost nearly $1.2 billion in sav-

DEVELOPMENT DATA

Human Dev. Index* rank	94 of 174 countries
Adjusted for women	77 of 143 countries
Real GDP per capita	$2,804
Adult literacy rate	84 percent
Infant mortality rate	41 per 1,000 births
Life expectancy	69 (male); 75 (female)

ings, more than one-half of the country's gross domestic product (GDP).

Though GDP per capita is now higher, most people earn less than six hundred dollars per year. Albania's greatest asset is a skilled and educated workforce. The economy continues to rely on foreign aid, remittances from Albanians working abroad, and revenues from contraband smuggling. Economic growth is around 8 percent and inflation is low. Unemployment is about 18 percent. The government is working to encourage foreign investment and privatization. However, long-term economic progress is unlikely without political reform and stability. Crime remains a serious problem. Exports include asphalt, iron ore, chromium ore, copper, and agricultural produce. The currency is the *lek* (L).

Transportation and Communications. Urban transportation is operated by the state, but private lines provide intercity transport. The number of automobiles (used cars from Europe) has increased since 1991. Bicycles are popular for getting around, as are motorcycles. Albania has a small railway system and one airport at Tirana.

With the end of communism, private newspapers were established. The country's one television station is joined by several radio stations. Phones are not readily available, but televisions and radios are found in most homes.

Education. Education is provided free to all citizens. Children begin school at age six and are required to attend for 10 years (up from 8 before 1994). Parents may be fined if they do not send their children to school for the full period. Education is extremely important to Albanians. At age 16, students can obtain secondary education at vocational and other schools. After four years, qualified students may attend college at state expense. Albania's first university was founded in Tirana in 1957. Other institutions exist, and some students study in other countries.

Health. The government provides free health care at clinics and hospitals, and private clinics are available to those who can afford them. Most medicine is either imported or donated. Facilities are poorly equipped and rely on international aid. The spring water flowing through the pipes is clean, but the pipes themselves render tap water unsafe. Child and maternal care are a high priority.

CONTACT INFORMATION

Embassy of the Republic of Albania, 2100 S Street NW, Washington, DC 20008; phone (202) 223-4942.

CultureGrams™
People. The World. You.

1305 North Research Way, Bldg. K
Orem, Utah 84097-6200 USA
1.800.528.6279; 801.705.4250
fax 801.705.4350
www.culturegrams.com

Antigua and Barbuda

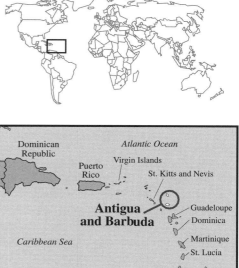

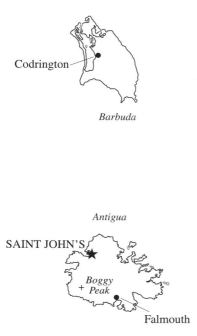

Boundary representations are not necessarily authoritative.

BACKGROUND

Land and Climate. Located 250 miles (400 kilometers) southeast of Puerto Rico, Antigua is relatively low and flat and has a dry, sunny, desert-like climate most months of the year. Boggy Peak, the island's highest elevation at 1,319 feet (402 meters), is located near a small tropical rain forest.

Barbuda, located across shallow water 30 miles (48 kilometers) north of Antigua, is even flatter; its highest elevation is only 207 feet (63 meters). Barbuda is covered by shrubs and brush. It features soft pink-sand beaches, a frigate bird sanctuary, abundant wild deer, and lobster. Including small uninhabited islands, the country covers 170 square miles (440 square kilometers). Hurricanes, such as Georges (1998), José (1999), and Lenny (1999) periodically take a toll on the islands.

History. Called *Wadadli* by the Amerindians who maintained a vibrant culture through the 17th century, Antigua was renamed by Christopher Columbus in 1493 for the Santa Maria de la Antigua Cathedral in Spain. (*Antigua* is pronounced without the *u*.) A lack of water and a thriving indigenous population discouraged European settlement for many years, but English settlers crossed over from Saint Kitts in 1632. Despite attempts to dislodge them, the settlers persisted, cultivating tobacco, indigo, and ginger. The two islands eventually became part of the British Leeward Islands Colony in 1666.

In 1674, Christopher Codrington came from Barbados and established the first large sugar plantation, called Betty's Hope. His success prompted other settlers to turn to sugar, and during the next one hundred years the landscape was cleared of all vegetation to grow this highly demanded cash crop. More than 150 wind-powered sugar mills (the ruins of many

are still standing) soon dotted the island. Antigua was divided into parishes, whose boundaries still remain.

The plantation economy thrived on slave labor, the British having imported thousands of Africans to Antigua. Colonists even used Barbuda as a slave-breeding center. When emancipation finally came in 1834, many of the newly freed Africans began new lives in villages that bear names like Freetown, Liberta, and Freeman's Village. But landowners continued exploitation by charging former slaves for hoe rentals and other services; this kept them working for minimal compensation into the 1930s. Reduced profitability of sugar and growing labor unrest in the 1940s led to the demise of the island's sugar industry, and by 1970 the last sugar refinery on the island had closed. Most light industries were replaced by the steadily growing tourism industry.

When Britain began granting greater autonomy to its colonies following World War II, Antigua's Vere Cornwall Bird was named chief minister. Antigua joined the West Indies Federation in 1958, but that body dissolved in 1962. In 1967, Antigua and Barbuda became a West Indies Associated State. This status granted internal autonomy, with Bird as premier. In 1981, Antigua, with Barbuda as a dependency, achieved full independence under the leadership of Bird's Antigua Labour Party (ALP). Barbuda attempted to remain a British colony, but the request was denied. The ALP consistently won elections, and Bird remained prime minister until he retired in 1994. His son, Lester B. Bird, became prime minister when the ALP won elections in March 1994. Bird was reelected in the March 1999 elections. His administration faces growing national debt.

Antigua and Barbuda

THE PEOPLE

Population. The country's population is 66,422 (1,600 live on Barbuda) and growing slightly. Nearly half of all Antiguans live in the area surrounding the capital, Saint John's. Barbuda is sparsely populated; most people live in Codrington. Despite the island's small size, Antigua's regions are identified with distinct population groups. For example, Old Road prides itself on connections to certain family and West African lines that Freetown may not share.

Barbuda's population consists almost entirely of African descendants. Most Barbudans go to Antigua to shop, work, or live, but many Antiguans have never been to Barbuda. Antigua's population is 96 percent Black African and 3 percent white. One percent is a mixture of Portuguese, Syrian, Lebanese, and other immigrants. Most whites are foreigners engaged in business and tourism.

A crossroads in the Caribbean, Antigua historically has attracted seafaring peoples, so Spanish and French peoples mixed with the African population. The island is also home to more recent immigrants from countries in the region. Although racial disputes are virtually unheard of, the different racial groups do not mix socially. Likewise, while tourism brings thousands of people to the island (especially in winter), contact between tourists and locals is limited mostly to professional services.

Language. Most Antiguans speak English. But they also speak a dialect similar to others in the region; it is a mixture of English and various African and European languages. Commonly used words such as *nyam* (to eat) have African origins. Forms of speech vary among areas and classes. Many upper-class Antiguans look down on those who speak the dialect, but most people appreciate it for its color and expressiveness. Traditional sayings are still popular, such as *No tro way you belly and tek trash tuff um* (Don't lose the substance for the shadow) and *Wah eye no see heart no grieve* (What you don't know won't hurt you). The dialect often is used in casual, friendly situations. *T'all* means "Not at all," and *How!* means "But of course!" *You lie* can mean "You are kidding." Barbudans have their own accent.

Religion. Antiguans are religious people. Women and children attend church regularly, while men go less frequently. Most people belong to various Protestant groups. The Anglican Church, with the island's largest cathedral (St. John's), is the nation's state religion. The Methodist Church has a long tradition in the country as well. A significant Catholic population (mostly non-Africans) also exists. Various other Christian groups have facilities and churches on the island, and there are some followers of Islam, Baha'i, and Rastafarianism.

General Attitudes. The people of Antigua and Barbuda are relaxed, friendly, and warm. They take a casual approach to life, sometimes expressed in the phrase *Soon come*. This is related to the general feeling that life presents or takes care of itself—that it is in God's hands and not necessarily in humankind's. Time also is viewed on a casual basis. People are more important than schedules. They may have things to do on the way to an event or appointment, so it is rarely a problem for them to be late.

Antiguans are extremely proud of their families, homes, and nation. This pride is manifest in the community spirit that surrounds school and church events and displays of local talent. People are especially proud of their international cricket reputation. A number of star players for championship West Indies teams are from Antigua. National pride also emerges during the annual Carnival arts festival, when performers compete in various events.

Personal Appearance. Public dress is neat, sharply pressed, and stylish. Funerals, weddings, and other special events bring out the most elegant and formal clothes in one's wardrobe. Sunday, particularly, is a day for dressing up. At parties or recreational events, Antiguans combine vivid Caribbean colors with international fashions.

Men do not wear shorts at work. Lightweight trousers and pressed shirts with colorful designs are popular. Some men wear ties and a few wear suits. The combination *shirt-jacket* (formal, embroidered, cotton shirt cut square and worn like a jacket) is common in offices. Laborers wear work pants or uniforms. Women wear stylish dresses, high-heeled shoes, and jewelry in offices; for some occupations, they wear dress uniforms.

Around the home, men and women dress in shorts, T-shirts, and athletic shoes or sandals. Women also wear comfortable dresses. In this modest society, people wear bathing suits at the beach, not in town.

CUSTOMS AND COURTESIES

Greetings. Antiguans and Barbudans generally greet one another informally. *How are you?* or *Hi* is common, but friends also use variations like *What's up?*, *How you do?*, or *Alright?* The response to *Alright?* is *Okay, Okay*. The greetings *Good morning*, *Good day*, *Good evening*, and *Good night* are used at specific times; for example, *Good evening* is inappropriate after dark.

Most Antiguans address friends by first name, but they address a boss by a title (*Mr., Mrs., Miss*), and professional exchanges between people (e.g., between a customer and a shopkeeper) are kept on this level. Children and young people address their elders and relatives with *Aunt*, *Uncle*, or an appropriate familial title.

Male friends use various hand-slapping, fist-touching, and thumb-locking handshakes as well as long handshakes. An entire brief conversation might be conducted with hands clasped together. A man waits for a woman to extend her hand before shaking it.

Gestures. Although modest and reserved in appropriate circumstances, Antiguans generally are lively and expressive among friends. A conversation can include a person acting out or demonstrating something with body gestures. People usually point with the index finger, but some situations call for the use of hands, arms, or even the head, eyes, or shoulders. Hand and facial gestures punctuate conversation and often express something better than words. Raising the hand, palm out, and wagging an extended index finger from side to side indicates disagreement. It is usually accompanied with *No, no, no*. A hearty "thumbs up" means things are going well. Sucking air through the teeth (called *chups* or *choops*), expresses exasperation or annoyance (at a flat tire or the store being out of bread, for example). Often, a mild *chups* provokes laughter and is a good release of tension. However, when directed at an individual, the noise is very rude. People do not like to hear their names called out in public, so a discreet "pssst" is often used to get someone's attention. A quick *Hey!* or *Yo!* is also common between friends.

Visiting. Antiguans enjoy socializing with relatives, neighbors, and friends. They use the term *lime* or *liming* for the time spent relaxing and chatting with each other. Most visits occur on weekends or after work. Appointments or plans are rarely made; people sitting in the yard or on the porch usually are willing to chat. Friendly encounters elsewhere can turn into a social visit. For example, much socializing occurs in public, whether among men meeting to repair a fishing net or among women shopping or washing clothes in public areas. Neighbors socialize while preparing meals.

When visiting someone who is inside a home, a person often approaches the gate and shouts *Inside!* The occupant then comes out to greet the person, and the two may spend the entire visit on the porch. Friends or relatives often will be invited inside. It is polite to offer light refreshments, such as fruit juice or herbal tea. Visitors often *walk with* (carry) fresh fruit from trees in their yards to share with hosts. Visits can be of any length, and hosts rarely ask guests to leave. Whole families may visit, especially among relatives. Conversation topics are seasonal, with cricket or calypso dominating, but people also might sit for extended periods without talking. At more formal, invitation events (birthdays, graduations, and holidays), hosts provide food and drink, and guests bring appropriate gifts.

Eating. During the workweek, people start the day with a simple breakfast of fruit, porridge, or eggs. Most workers stop for a full meal at midday, either in the workplace, at restaurants, or at home. Boys and girls usually help with cooking at home. Food often is cooked in *coal pots* (clay ovens) placed outside the kitchen. Saturday is a busy day for chores and errands, so people might buy barbecued chicken or fried fish at the market for the main meal. Evening meals are light if the main meal is eaten at midday.

On Sundays, the family has a large breakfast. Later, grand preparations precede an extended family evening meal featuring roast pork, leg of lamb, or beef. So much food is served that plates generally are sent home with relatives for those who could not come. When fishermen bring in a good catch, a pot of *fish water* (fish stew) usually is cooked up and shared. Church picnics or celebrations bring out many cooks cooperating on a large scale, serving dishes like *goat water*, a spicy stew made with goat meat.

LIFESTYLE

Family. The extended family forms the heart of Antiguan society. Grandparents, aunts, and uncles often raise children for parents who live out of the country for economic reasons. Families are large and living space often is shared among nuclear units. No matter what the living arrangements, families maintain strong ties and gather frequently. In Antigua, people like to joke that everybody is really related to each other if one traces the line back far enough.

Bearing or fathering children is highly valued. The traditional two-parent family is the norm, but it is not uncommon for a young unmarried woman to have children and live with her parents. In such cases, the baby's father provides financial support and is encouraged by both families to be involved in the child's life. Half-siblings live with their mother, and women are not uncommon as heads of households. Men may

have children with different women and never marry, and some women choose to remain single parents.

Dating and Marriage. Boys and girls have many opportunities to socialize and interact, including school parties and dances, church functions, and holiday events. Couples are affectionate, but not in public. At some point in a courtship, the young woman brings the young man home for her family's approval. Parents and churches encourage marriage over other types of relationships. Weddings are lavish, with a decorated church service, formal attire, and plenty of food and dance music.

Diet. People keep small gardens in their yards, but most food is imported. Antigua is subject to drought and supports little agriculture or livestock raising. Tropical fruits (coconuts and mangoes) and vegetables (pumpkins, yams, and potatoes) grow well. There is some fishing, but hotels are expanding increasingly into spawning areas of the mangrove wetlands, threatening future catches.

The basic diet revolves around rice, *peas* (usually red beans or white pigeon peas), and meat (chicken, pork, beef, goat) and fish, plus fruits and vegetables in season. During mango season, when mangoes ripen on trees by the thousands, people commonly *turn their pots down* (cook less) and eat large amounts of the fruit. At Christmastime, the bright red sorrel fruit is mixed with sugar and spices in a delicious tea. Antiguans boast that their local pineapple (Antigua black) is the sweetest in the world.

A popular dish is seasoned rice (rice, peas, vegetables, and meat chunks with seasonings). *Fungee* is a spoon bread made with cornmeal and okra. *Doucana* is coconut, sweet potatoes, flour, sugar, and spices, served with spicy *saltfish* (dried cod). *Pepperpot*, a spicy vegetable stew, varies from home to home. Specialties include *Johnny cakes* (sweet fried dumplings), *souse* (pickled pigs' feet), and blood sausage (called *rice pudding* or *black pudding*). Fast food is making its way into the national diet. Sidewalk vendors sell roasted corn or peanuts as snacks.

Recreation. Antiguans are passionate about sports. Cricket is most popular, with games played during a November-to-May season. Soccer dominates the rest of the year, and basketball is almost as popular. Girls are not as involved in athletics as boys are, but they do compete in netball (similar to basketball) leagues. Other social activities for women usually center on household duties or their children's activities. Dominoes and *draughts* (a form of checkers) are popular with men and boys, who play on tables set up on porches under trees. A direct link to the nation's African heritage is the strategy game *warri*. Complicated stratagems are required to capture the opponent's 24 seeds (4 in each of 6 cups). Water sports remain the domain of tourists and some in the upper class. Most Antiguans do not swim; at beach parties, they *sea bathe* in shallow water.

The Arts. Antiguans love music and dancing; anyone with the right speaker system can get a party going at a restaurant or picnic. Church choirs (mostly female) are numerous and practice regularly. Calypso developed during slavery as an improvisational style for soloists and is now the most popular musical form in Antigua. Calypso music competitions are especially prominent and are long anticipated. Aspiring "calypsonians" perform original songs. Calypsos can carry comical, political, or social messages. Steel drum music appeared when traditional bamboo percussion instruments were replaced by steel pans cut from oil drums. Other popular styles include *soca* (a mixture of American soul and calypso) and reggae. The Antiguan Jazz Festival attracts many West Indians every year in October.

Antiguan crafts developed around traditions brought by slaves from Africa. Folk pottery is still produced, especially in Sea View Farm Village. Harmony Hall in Brown's Bay is a center for the Antiguan arts community, and annual displays include the Artists Exhibition and Craft Fair in November. British influence is evident in the famous St. John's Cathedral, which boasts figurines of John the Baptist and St. John the Divine taken from one of Napoleon's ships.

Holidays. Old Year's Night (31 Dec.) and New Year's Day (1 Jan.) cap off the important Christmas season, which is marked by religious and secular celebrations. Easter (Friday–Monday) is as significant as Christmas. Labour Day (1 May, observed the first Monday in May) is important because of the role labor unions had in gaining independence. Pentecost (50 days after Easter) is a time of spiritual renewal and also coincides with Barbuda's *Caribana* (Carnival). Caribbean Community (CARICOM) Day (4 July) celebrates Caribbean unity. During Antigua's *Carnival* and national arts festival, emancipation from slavery (1 Aug.) is celebrated. This is an important time for Antiguans and Barbudans living abroad to return home. Parades, dancing, and music fill the streets for a week. The climax of *Carnival* is the Calypso King competition. Street dancing at dawn the next day celebrates the first morning of freedom from slavery. Christmas is celebrated on 25 and 26 December. The 26th is Boxing Day, which comes from the old British tradition of giving servants a holiday and boxed gifts. It is now a day to relax and visit.

Commerce. Major shops and businesses are located in St. John's. Most are open from 8 a.m. to 5 p.m. St. John's also has a large open-air market featuring fresh produce. Supermarkets offer a full variety of food.

SOCIETY

Government. As a parliamentary democracy within the Commonwealth, Antigua recognizes Britain's Queen Elizabeth II as head of state. She is represented by a governor-general, currently James Carlisle, who also acts as head of government after elections before a prime minister is named. Parliament has two houses, a Senate and a House of Representatives, each with 17 seats. The senators are appointed and the representatives are elected. The ruling party can amend the constitution. The United Progressive Party (UPP) opposes the ALP, which has dominated Parliament since 1976. The ALP won 12 House of Representatives seats in the March 1999 elections. The voting age is 18.

Economy. Tourism is the primary industry. St. John's is also home to a commercial deepwater harbor. While most revenues from tourism go to foreign developers, Antiguans benefit from jobs and taxes on the industry. The government employs one-third of the labor force, and tourism employs most of the rest. Some manufacturing exists, often related to

DEVELOPMENT DATA

Human Dev. Index* rank	37 of 174 countries
Adjusted for women	NA
Real GDP per capita	$9,277
Adult literacy rate	95 percent
Infant mortality rate	23 per 1,000 births
Life expectancy	68 (male); 73 (female)

the tourist industry (beds, towels, etc.). Unemployment is about 7 percent and inflation is low. The economy is growing at a rate of almost 4 percent. Recent figures indicate that, while poverty persists among some segments of the population, opportunities for personal advancement have expanded. Antigua is a member of CARICOM and the Organization of Eastern Caribbean States (OECS) and uses the East Caribbean dollar (EC$) as its currency.

Transportation and Communications. A number of buses serve the island, although private cars are common and a fleet of taxis cater to tourists. Following the British tradition, traffic moves on the left. Buses leave the station when full and do not follow schedules; they stop on request. Locations in St. John's are accessible by foot, but people avoid long walks in the hot afternoon. Telecommunications systems are modern and extensive. One broadcast television station is supplemented by satellite and cable services. There are two radio stations, and daily and weekly newspapers remain active. Internet access is readily available.

Education. Most Antiguans have had some secondary schooling. The system is modeled after Britain's. Public schools are free; more expensive private schools exist and often are church-affiliated. Schoolchildren are required to wear uniforms; parents purchase textbooks. Mandatory schooling lasts to age 16. Antigua State College provides post-secondary vocational training and college preparatory classes. Qualified students attend universities abroad; many never return home due to the lack of advanced career opportunities. Figures for functional literacy may be much lower than the adult literacy rate.

Health. The country's one hospital is adequate for minor treatment and surgeries, but serious cases may be flown to Puerto Rico. Most people have health insurance, and the government provides medical benefits. Parishes generally have a clinic and a doctor that provide basic care free of charge. Nurse practitioners and nurse midwives play an important role.

CONTACT INFORMATION

Antigua and Barbuda Department of Tourism, 610 Fifth Avenue, Suite 311, New York, NY 10020; phone (212) 541-4117; Web site www.antigua-barbuda.org. Consulate General, 25 SE Second Avenue, Suite 300, Miami, FL 33131; phone (305) 381-6762. The Embassy of Antigua and Barbuda, 3216 New Mexico Avenue NW, Washington, DC 20016; phone (202) 362-5122.

CultureGrams™
People. The World. You.

1305 North Research Way, Bldg. K
Orem, Utah 84097-6200 USA
1.800.528.6279; 801.705.4250
fax 801.705.4350
www.culturegrams.com

Argentina
(Argentine Republic)

Boundary representations are not necessarily authoritative.

BACKGROUND

Land and Climate. With an area of 1,068,296 square miles (2,766,874 square kilometers), Argentina is the eighth largest country in the world; it is one-third the size of the United States. Laced with rivers, Argentina, which literally means "silver," is a large plain rising from the Atlantic Ocean in the east to the towering Andes Mountains in the west along the Chilean border. The Chaco region in the northeast is dry except during the summer rainy season. *Las Pampas*, the central plains, is famous for wheat and cattle production. Patagonia, to the south, consists of lakes and flat to rolling hills that are known for sheep raising. Approximately 60 percent of the land is used for agriculture; another 22 percent is covered by forests.

The nation's landscape varies, containing such wonders as the Iguazú Falls (1.5 times higher than the Niagara Falls) in the north and the Perito Moreno Glacier of Santa Cruz to the south. The Moreno Glacier is one of the few glaciers in the world that is still advancing. Argentina's climate is generally temperate, though hot in the subtropical north and cold in the subantarctic region of southern Patagonia. Cool ocean breezes help keep Buenos Aires relatively smog-free. The seasons are opposite those in the Northern Hemisphere: the warmest month is January, and the coolest is July.

History. Before the Spanish began to colonize Argentina in the 1500s, the area was populated by various indigenous groups, some of whom (in the north) belonged to the Incan Empire.

However, most groups were nomadic or autonomous. Colonization got off to a slow start, but in the 1700s the Spanish established more cities, and indigenous peoples became increasingly marginalized. The British tried to capture Buenos Aires in 1806 but were defeated. This and friction with Spain led to calls for independence. At the time, the colony included Paraguay and Uruguay as well as Argentina.

A revolution erupted in 1810 and lasted six years before independence finally was declared. *Porteños* (coastal inhabitants favoring a centrist government based in Buenos Aires) then fought with those who favored a federal form of government. The actual fighting did not last long, but tensions remained. Argentina finally became a unified nation in 1862. (Paraguay and Uruguay had long since become independent.) Civilian rule, enhanced by the Saenz-Peña suffrage law of 1912, was generally peaceful and stable until a military coup in 1930. After another coup in 1943, Juan Domingo Perón (a key figure in the coup) emerged as the country's leader. He was elected president in 1946 and ruled until he was overthrown in 1955. After a series of military and elected governments, Perón returned to power in 1973 but died in 1974, leaving his wife, Isabel, to rule. She was ousted in 1976 by the military, which then waged a seven-year-long "dirty war" against armed and unarmed civilians to reconstruct the Argentine nation; thousands died or disappeared.

In 1982, Argentina went to war with Great Britain over the *Islas Malvinas* (Falkland Islands). The military's defeat in the war led to 1983 elections that broke military rule and brought Raúl Alfonsín to power. Carlos Saúl Menem (of the *Partido Justicialista*, also known as the Perónist Party) was elected president in 1989, becoming the first democratically chosen Argentine president to peacefully replace a sitting elected president. Menem worked toward containing runaway inflation, privatizing state-held enterprises, and stabilizing democratic institutions.

A new constitution that lifted the ban on reelections and reduced the presidential term to four years enabled Menem to be reelected in 1995. His Perónist Party won a majority in both legislative houses, allowing him to pursue his agenda of economic reform. In December 1999, center-left Buenos Aires Mayor Fernando de la Rúa was elected president on a multi-party reform ticket. De la Rúa's goals have been to spur economic growth and reduce unemployment. Despite his efforts and international loans, Argentina continues to battle a two-year recession, increasing unemployment, and a large government deficit.

THE PEOPLE

Population. The population of Argentina is about 36.9 million (the second largest in South America) and is growing annually by 1.3 percent. About 85 percent of the people live in urban areas. With more than 14 million people, the capital of Buenos Aires is one of the most populated metropolitan areas in the world. Around 85 percent of the people are descendants of European immigrants (Italian, Spanish, German, Welsh, English, French, and Russian). *Mestizos* (Spanish and aboriginal mix), aboriginals, and others make up the remaining 15 percent.

Language. While Spanish is the official language of Argentina, accents vary by region. Perhaps the most distinctive is the *porteño* (Buenos Aires) accent, which has been influenced by Italian. The *porteño* pronunciation of *y* and *ll* as "sh" is particularly distinctive. For example, *llamar* (to call) is pronounced more like "shah-MAHR" than the typical "yah-MAHR." People throughout Argentina also commonly use *vos* rather than the more formal *tú* or *Usted* form of address. Italian, German, and French are spoken by members of the older generation and by some of their descendants. Aboriginals speak indigenous languages, including Quechua, Guaraní, and Mapuche.

Religion. Roughly 85 percent of the people belong to the Roman Catholic Church, which exercises great influence over many social customs and celebrations. Most weddings and funerals follow traditional Catholic norms. Even so, a majority of Catholics are not actively involved with their church, and Argentine society is somewhat more secularized than other Latin American countries.

Non-Catholic Christian churches are gaining popularity. Approximately 7 percent of the people are members of various Protestant churches, another 2 percent are Jewish, and the remaining 6 percent belong to other religious organizations. Religious freedom is guaranteed, as church and state are officially separate.

General Attitudes. Argentines are proud of their nation, which has risen above difficult times to become a modern, democratic, and economically sound state. The days of the "dirty war" are past, and today political problems are solved through democratic institutions rather than coups. People want to improve their economic and social status and provide a better future for their children, but many are concerned prosperity is becoming more elusive. Prosperity, home ownership, and strong personal and family relationships are important to Argentines. Holding or being close to someone who holds political or social power is an indicator of social status. Higher education has a long history in Argentina and is also considered a mark of social status and refinement.

Urban Argentines tend to be cosmopolitan, progressive, and outgoing. Proud of their educational institutions, economic prosperity, and European heritage, they consider themselves somewhat superior to their rural countrymen and even to others in Latin America. Rural Argentines are more conservative and traditional.

Personal Appearance. While dress may differ considerably from region to region, it generally is conservative. Also universal is the desire to be well dressed in public. In Buenos Aires, European and North American fashions are popular. Argentine women consider European designs to be more fashionable than styles from North America. Older women seldom wear pants, but the younger generation prefers dressing more casually. In other areas, dress may reflect regional culture. For example, the *gauchos* (cowboys) of the Pampa region wear traditional clothing, including a wide-brimmed hat, neckerchief, *bombachas* (wide-legged pants), and boots.

CUSTOMS AND COURTESIES

Greetings. When greeting formally or for the first time, Argentines shake hands and nod slightly to show respect. In urban areas, a brief embrace with a kiss on the cheek is common. Both men and women will greet friends, whether male or female, with a kiss on the cheek. A person might wave and smile at an acquaintance who is too distant to greet verbally; it is impolite to call out a greeting. *¡Buenos días!* (Good morning—*¡Buen día!* in Buenos Aires) or *¡Buenas tardes!* (Good afternoon) commonly are used when people pass on the street or greet friends and acquaintances. When one approaches a stranger or an official for information, it is polite to greet the person before asking questions.

When first introduced or in formal situations, Argentines customarily address people by title (*Señor, Señora, Doctor/a*, etc.) followed by the surname, if known. Friends and relatives use given names. Older, respected persons are addressed by first name, preceded by the title *Don* (for men) or *Doña* (for women).

Gestures. Argentines often use hand gestures in daily conversation to supplement verbal communication. They may also use gestures to communicate with others from a distance. For example, to order a cup of coffee from a distant waiter, Argentines hold up an extended thumb and index finger separated slightly, with the other fingers folded in a fist.

During conversation, personal space tends to be small, and individuals might touch each other or stand close; eye contact is important. Passing between conversing individuals is considered rude; if it is necessary, one excuses the action by saying *Con permiso*. Yawning without covering the mouth is impolite, as is placing one's hands on the hips. Pointing with the index finger is considered rude. It is improper for a man and woman to show affection in public. Men remove hats in buildings, elevators, and in the presence of women. Opening doors for and forfeiting seats to women and the elderly are common practices. Argentines generally do not consider it rude to comment on a person's physical characteristics. For example, *negrito* (little dark one) or *gordita* (little fat one) are typical terms of endearment.

Visiting. Argentines often visit friends and relatives without prior arrangement. People enjoy having guests in the home and usually offer them refreshments. Espresso-style coffee is typical. In some regions, friends and relatives commonly share a ritualistic round of *mate* (MAH-tay), a bitter herb tea drunk from a communal cup with a *bombilla* (metal straw). Sharing a round of *mate* is a sign of friendship and acceptance.

Invited guests are not expected to arrive on time, as punctuality is not as important as the individual person. Guests will not offend hosts by arriving up to 30 minutes late, or even more. Visitors greet each person in the group individually; a group greeting is inappropriate. Dinner guests often bring a small gift, such as flowers, candy, or pastries, to their hosts. Guests do not take a seat until the host directs them to do so. Compliments about the home, meal, or hosts' family are appreciated. When leaving, a guest again addresses every person present, using such common parting phrases as *¡Chau!* or *Hasta luego*. The host usually opens the door for guests when they leave.

Eating. Argentines typically eat three meals each day. The main meal traditionally is served at midday. However, due to work schedules, urban families may only be able to gather together for supper, which often is served after 9 p.m.

Argentines eat in the continental style, with the fork in the left hand and the knife remaining in the right. It is considered polite to keep hands (but not elbows) above the table, not in the lap. Using a toothpick in public is considered bad manners, as is blowing one's nose, talking with the mouth full, or clearing one's throat at the table. Eating in the street or on public transportation is inappropriate.

One summons a restaurant waiter by raising the hand with the index finger extended. Tipping is not required but is becoming customary in many restaurants.

LIFESTYLE

Family. Urban families tend to be rather small, averaging two children, but rural families are larger. The responsibility of raising children and managing household finances falls heavily on the mother, who, in turn, exerts great influence on family decisions. More women are working outside the home, but they presently comprise less than 30 percent of the workforce. Men tend to be occupied with their work, often not coming home before 9 p.m. Children are central to the family and receive a great deal of attention. Families will sacrifice much to give their children a good education. Until 1987, divorce was illegal in Argentina, but it is now increasing.

As in most Latin American countries, Argentines have two family names. The last name is the mother's family name. The second-to-last name is the father's family name and is also the surname. For example, Joaquín Martínez Goyena would go by Joaquín Martínez.

Dating and Marriage. Group activities between boys and girls begin at about age 15, when girls celebrate their most important birthday (*cumpleaños de quince*), which ends their childhood. A favorite activity of young couples is dancing. The youth also play sports, eat out, and go to movies. Serious relationships develop slowly over several years; most couples marry between 23 and 27 years of age. Weddings often are elaborate, containing three different events: the civil ceremony, the church wedding, and a large reception with dinner and dancing.

Diet. Argentines eat more beef per capita than any other people in the world. Because the country is a major beef producer, domestic prices are low enough for most people to eat beef every day. Road and construction companies are known to provide workers access to portable grills for use at lunchtime. A favorite way to entertain is the weekend *asado* (barbecue). Other foods include baked, stuffed beef and *empanadas* (meat or vegetable turnovers). A preferred winter stew is *locro* (made of meat, corn, and potatoes). Italian food, and especially pasta, is the primary cuisine of most Argentines. The average diet also includes chicken and a wide variety of fruits and vegetables. In the summer, particularly in the north, people drink *tereré*, a cold version of *mate* mixed with lemonade. French foods are widely available.

Recreation. Children and adults alike enjoy *fútbol* (soccer), the national sport. A typical weekend *asado* often includes a game of soccer. Other popular sports include basketball, volleyball, and rugby. Horse racing, field hockey, tennis, and polo are enjoyed by the upper class. In their leisure time, Argentines also enjoy watching television, reading, playing cards, relaxing with friends, and going to movies. Older men often play chess or *bochas* (lawn bowling) in public squares.

The Arts. European culture has strongly influenced Argentine art, particularly the fine arts such as symphonic music and operas. In contrast, Native American influence extends mainly to folk arts; a movement headed by the National Foundation for the Arts is striving to preserve these arts, including horn carving, silverwork, leatherwork, ceramics, and weaving.

Buenos Aires is home to a fine opera house (the *Colón*). The tango (the music and the dance) originated in Argentina. For years it has been more popular outside of Argentina than among Argentines, who prefer dancing and listening to U.S. American, Brazilian, or Central American music like salsa. However, the tango is enjoying a revival among some young adults. The guitar, the violin, and the *bandoneón* (similar to an accordion) accompany the dancers.

Representing bravery, freedom, and self-sufficiency, the *gaucho* is an important Argentine symbol and often frequents painting and literature. The national epic poem, "El gaucho Martín Fierro" (1872), describes *gaucho* life. Early 20th century composers also incorporated *gaucho* themes into classical music.

Holidays. Argentines celebrate religious holidays more festively than national ones, using the latter for leisure time or to do household repairs. On Christmas Eve, the extended family gathers at 9 p.m. for dinner, music, and often dancing. Sweetbreads and candies are served before midnight, when fireworks displays begin. The evening also includes opening

▼ **THE AMERICAS**

gifts from *Papa Noel* (Father Christmas). New Year's Day is marked with fireworks as well. Other holidays include Good Friday and Easter; Labor Day (1 May); Anniversary of the May Revolution (25 May); Malvinas Day (10 June); Flag Day (20 June); Independence Day (9 July); Death of General José de San Martín, who is known as the "Liberator" of Peru, Chile, and Argentina for his defeat of the Spanish in 1812 (17 Aug.); Student Day (21 September—first day of spring, marked by students gathering in parks for picnics and soccer); and Columbus Day (12 Oct.).

Commerce. In Buenos Aires, stores generally open at 9 a.m. and close at 8 p.m. In other cities, they open weekdays at 8 a.m., close for lunch between noon and 3 or 4 p.m., and remain open until 8 p.m. On Saturday, stores close around 1 p.m. Offices typically are open between 9 a.m. and 6 p.m. Banks generally open from 10 a.m. to 3 p.m. Restaurants open their doors for dinner around 9 p.m. Workers in Argentina enjoy an *aguinaldo* (13th-month bonus) equal to one month's pay, often paid in two semiannual installments.

Supermarkets and malls are becoming more common in urban areas. However, most Argentines still buy many basic items at neighborhood shops (*almacenes* or smaller *kioskos*).

SOCIETY

Government. The Argentine Republic has 23 provinces and 1 federal district (Buenos Aires). The executive branch consists of a president, vice president, and cabinet. The president is both chief of state and head of government. The National Congress has two houses: a 72-seat Senate and a 257-seat Chamber of Deputies. Members of the independent Supreme Court are appointed by the president. The voting age is 18.

Economy. Agriculture, which employs about 10 percent of the people, has always been the mainstay of the Argentine economy, although industry is also vital. Argentina is famous for its livestock and is the world's fifth largest exporter of beef, hides, and wool. The country also exports large amounts of wheat, corn, and flaxseed, as well as soybean and cotton. Important industries include food processing, meat packing, motor vehicles, consumer goods, textiles, chemicals, printing, and metallurgy.

Menem's reforms stimulated strong economic growth throughout the 1990s. Inflation decreased from 3,000 percent to less than 1 percent and foreign investment increased substantially. Growth rose to nearly 9 percent in 1997 but fell to 4 percent following the global emerging market crisis in the second half of 1998. Conditions worsened as Brazil, Argentina's largest trading partner, devalued its currency by more than 40 percent in January 1999. The loss of exports and foreign capital plunged the economy into a recession. The economy shrank by 3 percent in 1999 and grew less than 1 percent in 2000. However, economists predict growth of more than 2 percent in 2001. Unemployment is about 15 percent.

Argentina's overall economic progress in the 1990s has benefited many, but gaps between rich and poor and between

DEVELOPMENT DATA

Human Dev. Index* rank	35 of 174 countries
Adjusted for women	35 of 143 countries
Real GDP per capita	$12,013
Adult literacy rate	97 percent
Infant mortality rate	18 per 1,000 births
Life expectancy	70 (male); 77 (female)

different regions persist. People generally have access to health care, education, and a standard of living that enables them to make choices in their lives; however, women have fewer economic opportunities than do men. The currency is the *peso*.

Transportation and Communications. Transportation and communications systems are well developed. While Argentines have access to private cars, taxis, subways, and trains, buses generally are the favored form of intra-city transportation. A few people ride motorcycles, but bicycles are reserved for recreation. Airlines link major cities in Argentina and neighboring countries. Buenos Aires is the most important seaport. Televisions and telephones are increasingly common and service is improving. Postal service is extensive but not always reliable. Newspapers are widely available and often represent a defined ideological perspective. Internet use is growing rapidly; a large percentage of households have Internet access.

Education. School is compulsory and free from ages six through fourteen. Secondary and higher education are also free but require an entrance examination. Nearly three-fourths of all eligible students are enrolled in secondary schools. Argentines may seek higher education at 26 national and 24 private universities, as well as at teacher-training colleges, vocational schools, and other institutions. Argentina's adult literacy rate is one of the highest in Latin America. Most middle-class Argentines are educated in state-subsidized parochial schools.

Health. Argentines enjoy relatively good health and have access to both public and private health-care facilities. Public hospitals provide care for citizens free of charge. The most modern facilities are found in Buenos Aires. Care is less reliable and less available in rural areas. Trade unions often provide health services for their members. Access to safe water and sanitation is still lacking in some rural areas and in suburban shantytowns.

CONTACT INFORMATION

Argentina Tourist Information Office, 12 West 56th Street, Fifth Floor, New York, NY 10019; phone (212) 603-0443. Embassy of Argentina, 1600 New Hampshire Avenue NW, Washington, DC 20009; phone (202) 939-6400; Web site www.embassyofargentina-usa.org.

CultureGrams™
People. The World. You.

1305 North Research Way, Bldg. K
Orem, Utah 84097-6200 USA
1.800.528.6279; 801.705.4250
fax 801.705.4350
www.culturegrams.com

Republic of
Austria

Boundary representations are not necessarily authoritative.

BACKGROUND

Land and Climate. A landlocked country in central Europe, Austria covers 32,375 square miles (83,850 square kilometers) and is slightly smaller than Maine. Spectacular mountains, clear lakes, beautiful scenery, and green valleys all comprise Austria's grandeur. The famous Alps cover much of the west and south, while flatlands dominate in the east and northeast. The country generally enjoys a mild climate. Spring and summer are temperate. However, winters in some mountain areas can be very cold. In Vienna, the average temperature in winter is 32°F (0°C) and in summer is 67°F (20°C).

History. Austria has had a significant impact on European history and world culture. Present-day Austria was once part of both the Roman and Carolingian Empires. Otto I, who later became emperor of the Holy Roman Empire, began his rule in 955. He often is considered the real founder of Austria because of the borders he established. *Austria* is the Latin equivalent of the German *Österreich* (realm of the east).

In 1156, with Vienna as its capital, Austria became an autonomous duchy under the Babenbergs. The Hapsburg Dynasty came to power in 1273. For six hundred years, the Hapsburgs gradually spread their empire over central Europe through marriages and other strategies. They helped push the Ottoman Turks out of Europe after the 18th century. Their power was greatest in the early 19th century, after they helped defeat Napoleon. Wars and nationalist disputes soon led the government to establish a dual monarchy with Hungary in 1867 through the *Ausgleich* (Compromise).

By 1914, the Austro-Hungarian Empire covered present-day Austria, Hungary, the Czech Republic, Slovakia, Slovenia, Croatia, Bosnia-Herzegovina, and parts of Poland, Italy, and Romania. Still, it was in decline due to growing nationalism among its various peoples. In 1914, when the Archduke Franz Ferdinand, heir to the Hapsburg throne, was assassinated in Sarajevo, what should have been a local civil conflict quickly mushroomed into World War I, as most European nations became involved. The Great War, as it was called, led to the empire's destruction. Yugoslavia and Czechoslovakia were created from parts of the old empire; both countries have since divided.

The first Austrian republic (1918–38) struggled to survive and was swallowed up by Hitler's Germany before the start of World War II. After 1945, Austria was divided into four zones, each governed by one of the four Allied powers (Great Britain, France, the United States, and the Soviet Union). With the advantage of its central government in Vienna still in operation, Austria reestablished its territorial sovereignty and proclaimed its permanent neutrality in 1955, only 10 years later. With strong ties to Western Europe, the republic has since been a model of political, economic, and social stability.

Because of Austria's political neutrality, Vienna has become a key United Nations (UN) city where nations meet to discuss problems or negotiate treaties. Desires to open up to the West prompted the Hungarian government to tear down the barbed-wire fence along the Austrian-Hungarian border in 1989. This action is recognized as a significant event that encouraged the 1990 political reforms in Eastern Europe.

Austria joined the European Union (EU) in January 1995. While many remain skeptical about the introduction of the euro, the new European currency, the majority favors it. Membership in the North Atlantic Treaty Organization (NATO) was rejected in March 1998 by Chancellor Viktor Klima's government, which preferred to maintain Austria's traditional neutral stance. Following October 1999 general elections, the People's Party (ÖVP) entered into a partnership with the right-wing Freedom Party (FPÖ). Wolfgang Schüssel became the new chancellor. The coalition sparked international outrage because the FPÖ and its leader, Joerg Haider, are perceived as being antidemocratic and xenophobic. To protest Austria's new government, demonstrations were organized and sanctions were imposed against Austria by other EU member states. Although these protests failed to remove the FPÖ from power, the party's popularity has diminished somewhat and its future remains uncertain. As in other European countries, Austrians are concerned about food safety with the spread of mad cow disease.

THE PEOPLE

Population. Austria's population of about 8.13 million currently is not growing. At least 98 percent of the people are Germanic, while minorities include Croatians, Slovenes, and various other groups. Approximately 200,000 foreign workers—mainly from Turkey and the former Yugoslavia—live and work in Austria. About 58 percent of the people live in urban areas. Vienna (or Wien), the capital, has a population of more than 1.6 million. Graz (239,000), Linz (203,000), and Salzburg (145,000) are the next largest cities. Most people have excellent access to education, economic prosperity, health care, and other resources needed for personal advancement.

Language. The official language is German, but each area has its own dialect. Dialects are more pronounced in rural areas. A minority in southern Austria speaks Slovene. Hungarian and Croatian also are spoken by minorities and taught in some schools. English is a required language in high schools and is spoken by many people.

Religion. About 78 percent of all Austrians are Roman Catholic, while 5 percent are Protestant. Although a small number of other Christian and non-Christian religions are also present, many people do not belong to any denomination. Younger people generally are less devout than the older generation; many have withdrawn their membership from the Catholic Church. The Jewish community has approximately 10,000 members, down from 200,000 before World War II.

Although not as religious as other Europeans, Austrians still believe in traditional ways of living. Catholic traditions, shrines, and churches are highly treasured. Many people use churches for baptisms, weddings, and funerals. Churches also serve a social function, particularly in rural areas.

General Attitudes. Austrians are known for their *Gemütlichkeit*, a relaxed and happy approach to life. A good-natured sense of frustration and a bittersweet attitude toward reality are considered unique national traits. Although a relaxed people, Austrians are hardworking. They value cleanliness, neatness, and order. Litter is rare. People love to learn and engage in conversation. Austrians have a deep regard for the environment and take pride in their country's beautiful landscape.

Austrian society values its professionals, academics, and artists. Cultural arts are important to all segments of society, as Austrians are extremely proud of their culture's contributions to Western civilization.

Austrians are not Germans and should not be referred to as such; some Austrians may consider it an insult. While the two peoples speak the same basic language (with important differences in dialect), Austrians and Germans have a different historical and political heritage; they also differ in some customs, values, and attitudes.

Personal Appearance. Austrians generally wear European clothing fashions, but they often add a distinctive Austrian touch to their wardrobes. They take pride in dressing well, even if they are only going grocery shopping. Dressing properly for all events is also important. While older people might mix traditional Austrian clothing with conservative European fashions, young people prefer modern European attire.

Folk costumes (*Trachten*) are often worn on formal occasions and for celebrations. Each area has its own particular costume. Men's traditional clothing includes *Lederhosen* (leather knee-pants) and *Trachtenjacken* (woolen jackets) or a *Trachtenanzug* (suit). Women may wear a *Dirndl* (dress with an apron) or a *Trachtenkostüm* (suit). Traditional clothing articles often have intricate designs and usually are prized items in a person's wardrobe.

CUSTOMS AND COURTESIES

Greetings. Shaking hands when greeting and parting is an important social courtesy. Even children shake hands with adults when greeting. Common greetings include *Grüß Gott* (May God greet you), *Guten Morgen* (Good morning), *Guten Tag* (Good day), and *Guten Abend* (Good evening). Popular casual greetings include *Servus* (used as "Hi") and *Grüß Dich!* (Greetings to you!). Austrians do not ask "How are you?" (*Wie geht es Ihnen?*) unless they wish to hear a detailed account.

Professional titles are important among the adult population and are used whenever known. Otherwise, people combine titles such as *Herr* (Mr.) and *Frau* (Mrs. or Ms.) with family names when addressing acquaintances and strangers. Close friends and the youth use first names.

Gestures. Hand gestures are used conservatively in polite company, as verbal communication is preferred. It is impolite for adults to chew gum in public. Motioning with the entire hand is more polite than using the index finger. Twisting the index finger at the temple or side of one's forehead is an insult. People are generally polite and courteous in public. Men often open doors for women and usually help them with their coats.

Visiting. Austrians enjoy entertaining in their homes and having guests. Dropping by unannounced is impolite. It is better to make arrangements in advance or telephone ahead of an impromptu visit. Invited guests should arrive on time. Punctuality is important to Austrians. Customarily, guests remove their shoes when entering a home, although this practice is not always followed. Guests remain standing until invited to sit down and instructed where to do so. Hosts customarily offer the best seats to their guests. If the host must leave the room for a moment, the guest is offered something to read or occupy the time until the host returns. Men stand when a woman enters the room or when talking to a woman who is standing.

While guests usually are offered a drink (tea, coffee, mineral water, juice, or soda), further refreshments depend on the hosts. Invited guests bring flowers, candy, or a small gift (such as a handcrafted item or something appropriate for the occasion). Even married children often bring such a gift when visiting their parents. Gifts are given to the wife, or perhaps the children, but not the husband—even if the gift is for the family. People only give flowers in odd numbers (even numbers are bad luck). Flowers are unwrapped before the hostess appears. Red roses signify romantic love. Giving purchased flowers is more polite than flowers from one's own garden.

To show courtesy to the hosts, guests do not ask to use the telephone unless the need to call is urgent. In addition, guests do not offer to help make any preparations if they are not well acquainted with the hosts or if the hostess does not seem to have everything under control.

Austrians also enjoy socializing in restaurants and other public places. For example, following Sunday church services, many men, particularly those in small villages, customarily go to a *Gasthaus* (pub) to do business, exchange ideas, and drink. Such socializing is less about drinking and much more about networking and socializing with male friends.

Eating. Although the tradition of having the main meal at midday is still strong, eating habits are changing. Working people and students now eat the main meal in the evening. Other traditions remain, such as keeping hands above the table during the meal, not gesturing with utensils, and not placing elbows on the table while eating. It is impolite to begin eating until all persons at the table are served. Austrians eat in the continental style, with the fork in the left hand and the knife remaining in the right. When guests are present, the hostess nearly always will offer second helpings but will gracefully accept a polite *Danke, nein* (Thank you, no).

Restaurants serve mineral water rather than tap water. (Generally, tap water is drunk only in the home.) The bill, which usually includes a service charge, is paid at the table to the server. Most people round the bill up to the nearest five or ten *schillings* as a tip.

LIFESTYLE

Family. Austrian families usually are small, with one or two children. However, rural families are often a bit larger. Most Austrians expect to marry and have a family. Both parents generally work outside the home, with women comprising nearly 40 percent of the labor force. Duties related to the household and children are not necessarily shared, except among younger couples. Some homes, especially in rural areas, maintain a strict patriarchal family structure. The government has many programs to support families: family allowances for each child, maternity leave (eight weeks before and after child birth), and nursing allowances for care of the elderly. Children who are not in school and whose parents both work are cared for privately or in day-care centers. Most urban Austrians live in apartments; sometimes extended families will share one large house that contains several apartments. About one-fifth of all housing is publicly owned. Rural families generally live in single-family homes.

Dating and Marriage. Austrian youth begin associating in groups, but when they start getting together as couples, they usually date only one person at a time and the relationship generally is considered serious. Actual dates are rather casual affairs, as people often just agree to meet somewhere. Boys and girls pay their own expenses, with one or the other offering to pay for both only on special occasions. Eating out, going to movies, and dancing are favorite activities.

Couples often decide to live together before or instead of marrying. The typical age for marriage is between 25 and 28 years. A civil ceremony must be performed for the marriage to be legal; church weddings are optional.

Diet. Austrians love good food and have a rich and varied cuisine. Specialties drawn from cultures of the former Austro-Hungarian Empire include such favorites as *Wiener Schnitzel* (breaded veal cutlets) from Italy, *Kolatsche* (a pastry made out of yeast dough) from Bohemia, and goulash from Hungary. Goulash is served at most restaurants. *Backhendl* (fried, breaded chicken) and *Knödel* (moist dumplings) are also common. Popular soups include *Griessnockerlsuppe* (small semolina dumplings), *Frittatensuppe* (shredded crêpes), or *Leberknödelsuppe* (liver dumplings). Vienna is famous for its cakes and pastries, including apple strudel, *Sachertorte* (a rich chocolate cake with apricot jam and chocolate icing), and *Krapfen* (a kind of doughnut). Coffee is also a favored tradition; Austrians love to drink coffee and go to coffee houses.

A typical day begins early with a light breakfast of coffee or hot chocolate, rolls, bread, and jam or marmalade. Later in the morning, some eat a second, heartier breakfast, including goulash or hot sausages. The main meal may include soup, meat (often beef or pork) with potatoes or pasta, vegetables, a salad, and often dessert (such as a homemade pastry). *Jause* (afternoon coffee) may include sandwiches, pastries, and coffee. If the main meal is eaten at midday, families have *Abendessen* (evening meal) in the evening. *Abendessen* generally includes cold cuts, eggs, cheese, rye and other breads, and a salad. After a visit to the theater or other evening activity, a light supper might end the day.

Recreation. Austrians love the outdoors. Taking a walk (*ein Spaziergang*) is a national pastime. Hiking, skiing, cycling, tennis, boating, and swimming are all popular activities. Soccer is a favorite sport, but Austrians are better known for their excellence in winter sports. They are consistent medalists in Winter Olympic events. Gardening is popular, even when space is limited. Window boxes full of flowers are favorites throughout the country.

The Arts. Cultural arts play a key role in Austrian society. Both modern and traditional forms of arts and music are popular. Even large numbers of the youth attend opera performances and orchestral concerts. The names Haydn, Mozart, Schubert, Strauss, Beethoven, and Brahms (who all worked in Vienna), as well as Wolf, Mahler, Bruckner, and others, attest to Austria's musical heritage. The Vienna State Opera, the Vienna Philharmonic, the Vienna Boys Choir, and the Salzburg Festival are four of many music institutions that enjoy worldwide fame. Austria also is noted for its writers (Franz Kafka, Hugo von Hofmannsthal, Karl Kraus). Painters and architects have flourished in the 20th century, especially since World War II. Most Austrians approve of the

▼ EUROPE

government's strong role in the development and performance of cultural arts.

Folk music is also important in Austria. Common folk instruments include the *hackbrett* (hammered dulcimer) and zither (a stringed instrument). Guitars and harps are also prevalent in folk music. In addition, nearly every village has a band (usually brass), and any town of size has a professional orchestra. There are many local theaters.

Holidays. Austrians celebrate New Year's Day, *Heilige Drei Könige* (Three Kings, 6 January), Easter (Saturday–Monday), Labor Day (1 May), National Holiday (26 Oct.), All Saints' Day (1 Nov.), St. Nikolaus Day (5 Dec.), and Christmas (25–26 Dec.), as well as various religious holidays throughout the year. Numerous balls, including the famous Opera Ball in Vienna, are held on the last Thursday of *Fasching* (Carnival), which occurs in January and February. Christmas Eve (*Heiliger Abend* or Holy Evening) is the most important part of Christmas. Families gather to share a meal and sing Christmas carols. Children receive their presents, which are customarily put under the tree by the Christ child when they are out of the room. Christmas Day is reserved for visiting family.

Commerce. Large stores are open from 8 a.m. until 7 p.m. on weekdays and from 7:30 a.m. until 5 p.m. on Saturdays. Large chain stores remain open on Saturday until evening. Small open-air markets often open at 6 a.m. Some small, private shops still close for the traditional *Mittagspause* (midday break), which was once universal as the two- or three-hour break for the main meal. Only restaurants, gas stations, and tourist shops remain open on Sunday. Most families vacation in August. Small, family-owned shops might be closed the entire month while the family is away.

SOCIETY

Government. The Republic of Austria has nine states. The government's executive branch consists of a federal president, a federal chancellor, and the chancellor's cabinet. The president appoints the chancellor, approves all members of government, and represents Austria internationally. The chancellor conducts all other affairs. President Thomas Klestil was elected to a second six-year term in April 1998. The *Bundesversammlung* (Parliament) has a 64-member upper house, called a Federal Council (*Bundesrat*), and a 183-seat lower house, called a National Council (*Nationalrat*). Austria's various political parties have a tradition of cooperation, which has promoted political stability. The strongest parties include the Social Democratic Party of Austria (SPÖ), the ÖVP, and the FPÖ. The voting age is 18. Three types of high courts have jurisdiction over either justice, administration, or the constitution.

Economy. Austria is an industrialized nation with a mixed free-market/social-welfare economy. Social-welfare programs are fairly extensive and provide support for the unemployed. Agriculture plays only a minor role in the economy, although the country is mostly self-sufficient in food. Important resources include iron ore, timber, tungsten, coal, and

DEVELOPMENT DATA

Human Dev. Index* rank	16 of 174 countries
Adjusted for women	16 of 143 countries
Real GDP per capita	$23,166
Adult literacy rate	99 percent
Infant mortality rate	5 per 1,000 births
Life expectancy	74 (male); 80 (female)

other minerals. Austria exports machinery, lumber, textiles, iron, steel, chemicals, and paper products. Tourism is also an important industry.

The economy is generally strong and stable, a result of a unique system of social partnerships in which unions and owners or employers cooperate to exercise restraint on prices and wages. They also try to reach a consensus on managing the national economy. Unemployment is relatively low, and the inflation rate is one of Europe's lowest. Austria's economy is growing about 3 percent annually. Key economic goals include reducing government spending and encouraging privatization. The currency is the Austrian *schilling* (AS).

Transportation and Communications. Most families own at least one car, and private cars are important for daily transportation. The public system of trains, buses, and streetcars also is used heavily, especially in large urban areas. Buses reach even the remotest areas, and a good system of trains crisscrosses the country. On the expressway, there is a speed limit of 130 km/h (81 mph); seat belt laws are strictly enforced. Children younger than 12 must ride in the back seat. The communications system is efficient and extensive. Most homes have televisions and phones. Many Austrians have cell phones. Daily newspapers are available throughout the country.

Education. Each state is responsible for public schooling, which is free and compulsory for children ages six to fifteen. Most Austrians complete this amount of schooling and also gain other training or higher education. Education traditionally has been important in Austria, which is home to many Nobel Prize winners and noted scholars such as Sigmund Freud. Austrian universities offer a high-quality education; they attract many students from abroad.

Health. Health care is provided for everyone. Health insurance is required and provided by employers for even part-time workers. Private insurance may be used as a supplement or alternative. Austrians enjoy good health and have access to adequate care.

CONTACT INFORMATION

Embassy of Austria, 3524 International Court NW, Washington DC 20008-3035; phone (202) 895-6767; www.austria.org/index.html. Austrian National Tourist Office, PO Box 1142, Times Square, New York, NY 10108-1142; phone (212) 944-6880; Web site www.anto.com.

1305 North Research Way, Bldg. K
Orem, Utah 84097-6200 USA
1.800.528.6279; 801.705.4250
fax 801.705.4350
www.culturegrams.com

Barbados

Boundary representations are not necessarily authoritative.

BACKGROUND

Land and Climate. Barbados is the easternmost island in the Caribbean archipelago. The island is 166 square miles (430 square kilometers) in size—just smaller than 2.5 times the size of Washington, D.C. It has a gradually sloping landscape with some hilly areas. The tropical climate provides an average high temperature of 85°F (29°C). The rainy season is from June to October. Barbados has no rivers; instead, rainwater percolates through the soil to form underground channels that run to the ocean. A thin layer of topsoil covers the thick layer of coral that forms most of the island. Barbados soil is very fertile, making the island lush with flowering trees, shrubs, and tropical flowers. Three-fourths of the island is suitable for cultivation. Natural resources include crude oil, fish, and natural gas.

History. The original inhabitants of Barbados were Arawak Indians. They disappeared before settlers arrived (maybe even by 1536), but the reason is uncertain. Portuguese explorers found an abundance of bearded fig trees when they arrived on the island; hence, the name *Barbados* originated from the Portuguese term *os barbudos* (bearded ones). The British came to the island in 1625, when Captain John Powell claimed it in the name of King James I. In 1627, Powell brought the first colonists and settled Holetown. As the population grew, sugarcane was introduced, and slave labor was brought in from Africa. Independence-minded colonists were forced to surrender to England's forces in 1652 by signing the Articles of Capitulation, which became the Charter of Barbados.

Barbados later moved toward independence by emancipating its slaves between 1834 and 1838, enfranchising women in 1944, and providing universal suffrage in 1951. A leader of the independence movement, Sir Grantley Adams, became the first premier under home rule in 1954. Barbados became part of the West Indies Federation in 1958, but the federation dissolved in 1962. Barbados thereafter sought full independence from Great Britain, which was granted on 30 November 1966. The first prime minister of an independent Barbados was Errol Barrow. The country remains a member of the Commonwealth of Nations. Since independence, Barbados has enjoyed a high degree of political stability. The island capitalized on its natural strengths, and by the 1980s had developed a successful tourist industry. With economic and political stability, the nation was able to provide a high standard of living for its inhabitants.

During the global recession of the early 1990s, the economy suffered various setbacks. After his election in 1991, Prime Minister Erskine Lloyd Sandiford (of the Democratic Labour Party) introduced an austerity package to improve economic conditions. Reforms stabilized the economy but were unpopular among voters. Leaders in Parliament also became disillusioned with Sandiford's leadership, forcing him to call for early elections in 1994. A strong voter turnout brought economist Owen Arthur, leader of the Barbados Labour Party, to power as prime minister. Boosted by a strong economy and considerably lower unemployment, Arthur's Barbados Labour Party was reelected in January 1999, winning 26 of 28 seats. During his second term, Arthur seeks to eradicate unemployment and increase prosperity and economic growth.

Barbados

THE PEOPLE

Population. The population of Barbados is approximately 259,000 and is growing only slightly. The birthrate is actually higher than that, but emigration holds net growth to less than 1 percent. The island has a high population density: 1,600 persons per square mile (620 per square kilometer). About 60 percent of the population lives in urban centers stretching along the western side of the island, which is more sheltered from storms. The capital city of Bridgetown is the largest urban area. Actually, the island is almost a city-country, with Bridgetown serving as "downtown" for the whole island. Urban, commercial areas are referred to as *town* areas rather than cities. An estimated 7 percent of the population is white, 20 percent is of mixed heritage, and 70 percent is black, mostly of African origin. East Indian and Middle Eastern groups comprise the remaining 3 percent. The people of Barbados are called Barbadians, but they are often referred to as *Bajans*.

Language. The official language is English. Bajans also speak a dialect that descends from the English spoken by early colonists, indentured servants, and slaves. Referred to as *speaking Bajan* or *broken English*, the dialect is an easy, natural way of communicating informally with family and friends. In speaking Bajan, "What are you all doing tonight" becomes "Whuh wunna doin' tonight?" Numerous proverbs are also expressed in the dialect, including *Day does run 'til night catch it* (Whatever you do will catch up with you in the end).

Religion. The majority (67 percent) of Barbadians are Protestant Christians, with about 40 percent belonging to the Anglican Church and 7 percent to the Methodist Church. The Roman Catholic Church also has a strong presence. Nearly 30 percent of all people belong to smaller Christian and non-Christian organizations, or to no church at all. There are small Hindu, Muslim, and Jewish communities. A Jewish synagogue was first built on the island in 1654.

For many Bajans, religion plays an important role in daily life. The school day begins with an assembly that includes a Bible reading, hymn, and prayer. Many families pray before meals, and most official public functions open with prayer. Regardless of one's religious affiliation, funeral attendance is considered important. Bajans make a special effort to attend services of even distant relatives and acquaintances. The number of attendees at a funeral is often a gauge of the individual's standing in the community.

General Attitudes. Bajans are warm, happy, friendly, and generous. However, they may act reserved around strangers and are considered to be somewhat more restrained than their Caribbean neighbors. Bajan hospitality is evident in the country's successful tourist industry. A generally peaceful atmosphere in the country allows the police to patrol unarmed. Social unity is important to Barbadians. Their view of life is evident in their carefully kept, pastel-colored homes and in lively festivals that represent past and present culture. Such festivals often celebrate Bajan pride in their dual African/British heritage.

Bajans find arrogant, aggressive, and ostentatious behavior distasteful. Their independence—their ability as a nation to dictate their own affairs—is important to them. They take great pride in their country's educational, political, and economic successes. The accomplishments of Bajan athletes in cricket, track-and-field, and other sports are also a great source of pride. The people value honesty, humor, and education. Parents generally stress a good education as a means to a better future for their children. A car and a plot of land are other desired possessions.

Personal Appearance. North American fashions are popular in Barbados, and many Barbadians shop overseas for clothing. Women usually wear tailored dresses or blouses and skirts to work, but they get very dressed up for parties and other social events. They wear their finest dresses and hats to church meetings. For casual events, women usually dress in colorful, long skirts with sandals. Sometimes they wear their hair in small braids with colorful beads at the ends. Jeans and T-shirts are popular casual wear for both sexes.

Many (particularly older) men wear lightweight pants with a casual shirt of white, pastel, or flowered fabric. This *shirt-jac* suit generally is accepted everywhere (parties, offices, and churches), but a more formal suit is required for certain events. Younger men may wear tailored pants and a dress shirt in the workplace. Swimwear is limited to the beach and is not worn in the city or other public places.

CUSTOMS AND COURTESIES

Greetings. Bajans generally greet each other with a handshake and a smile. Friends often embrace upon meeting, sometimes followed by kissing on the cheek. Similar gestures are exchanged when parting. Young men may greet by bumping the top of the other's extended fist with a fist. A common greeting is *Hello! How are you?* An answer such as *Not bad* is a friendly, not a negative, response. Less formal greetings used by younger people include *Yo, what's up?*, *Wuh you sayin'?* (How are things?), and *How ya gine?* (How are you doing?). It is considered polite to greet strangers in passing with a *Hello* or a nod, particularly in rural areas. An evening telephone call begins with *Hello, good night*. . . .

Coworkers typically address one another by first name, while a superior generally is addressed by title (*Mr.*, *Mrs.*, *Ms.*, *Miss*) and surname. Friends and relatives may call one another by nickname. Children respectfully address older family friends as *aunt(ie)* or *uncle*.

Gestures. Barbadians often use their hands when conversing to emphasize or communicate a point. However, personal space is respected. They call taxis and buses by waving the hand. They often express disgust by clenching the teeth and sucking in air (sounding something like CHUPSE); the level of annoyance or contempt can be measured by the loudness of the *chupse*. People may show defiance, anger, or frustration by standing *akimbo* (placing their hands on their hips) while arguing a point. Bajans frequently will fold their arms as a sign that they are paying attention, but such a gesture can also signal defiance. An arm raised above the head with the palm facing out and waving side to side can signal good-bye. A similar gesture, with the palm at eye level and a quicker side to side motion, can indicate disapproval.

It is considered polite to forfeit seats to pregnant women or the elderly on public buses. Seated bus passengers may show courtesy by holding a standing passenger's parcel or child. If one must pass between conversing individuals, it is polite to wait for a break in the conversation to ask for permission to pass (*Excuse me please?*). Occasional (not constant) eye contact during conversation is appropriate. Pointing at people with the index finger is considered rude.

Visiting. Friends and relatives may visit at home unannounced, usually on weekends. A favorite time for men to get together is Sunday morning, when topics of conversation range from politics to cricket. Visits may take place on the patio. Otherwise, the visitor is invited in and offered a drink (juice, soda, beer, or rum).

Visiting also occurs at cricket and other sporting events when old friends see each other. Shops in the country districts and barber salons in the town are important places for lively discussion, especially around election time.

Eating. Bajans eat three meals a day. Families usually try to gather for breakfast and dinner, although this is subject to varying schedules. Sunday lunch is a traditional family meal. For most people, the traditional *teatime* has been replaced with midmorning and midafternoon snacks, which may include tea, coffee, juice, fruit (mangoes, cherries, tamarinds, bananas, or oranges), cheese, chocolate, peanuts, or sweetbread (usually made with coconut). Barbadians eat in the continental style, with the fork in the left hand and the knife remaining in the right. They keep the elbows off the table.

LIFESTYLE

Family. The extended family is important in Barbados, and parents, children, grandparents, and cousins enjoy substantial interaction. This pattern is changing somewhat with modernization, but it is still important. Extended families may live together or near one another. A high percentage of children are born out of wedlock. Teenage pregnancies continue to be a problem. Divorce is increasing. Single-parent families (usually with only the mother) are common. In homes where the father is present, he is the leader. Economic circumstances have caused many women to seek employment outside the home, leaving the care of children to grandparents. Nearly half of the workforce is female. People who have emigrated to the United States, the United Kingdom, or Canada for work still maintain extended family ties through monetary support and visits.

Many families live in traditional *chattel houses*. These look like mobile wooden homes, set on coral stone 3 or 4 feet above ground for better air circulation. They are designed for easy assembly and disassembly, as plantation workers in the past often were required to move from one working area to another. They are so well built that they may be passed from one generation to the next. Other, permanent homes are made of brick or concrete, and many are painted with pastel colors. Families commonly paint their homes before Christmas in preparation for holiday visitors.

Dating and Marriage. Dating usually begins in the early teens. Young Bajans socialize at school, church, parties, the beach, the cinema, sporting events, and each other's homes. Public displays of affection between couples (beyond holding hands) are uncommon. Many people do not marry. Even in two-parent homes, some couples are not married. Couples who have lived together for years are protected by common-law legislation. Many young people wait to marry until after

they have established themselves financially or have begun their careers. Weddings traditionally are held in a church, followed by a gala reception in a local hall, hotel, or restaurant. The reception typically features an elaborate wedding cake and music by a Bajan steel band.

Diet. Bajan food is a unique combination of African and English traditions. Staples include rice, *peas* (legumes), potatoes, chicken, and fish. The national dish is flying fish and *cou cou* (made of okra and cornmeal). Also popular are lobster, shrimp, *dorado*, red snapper, turtle, tuna, and kingfish. Sea urchin eggs are a delicacy. Black-belly sheep and goats provide meat. The tropical soil yields mangoes, papayas, bananas, cucumbers, tomatoes, guavas, avocados, coconuts, squash, eggplant, breadfruit, and numerous other vegetables. Popular local dishes include *jug-jug* (sorghum and green pigeon peas), *pepperpot* (a spicy stew), *macaroni pie* (made with cheese or mincemeat), and *conkies* (cornmeal, coconut, pumpkin, raisins, sweet potatoes, and spices steamed in a banana leaf). Favorite pastries include *jam puffs* (jam-filled sourdough pastry) and turnovers (filled with coconut and sugar). Fast foods such as pizza are becoming popular.

Both cow and goat milk are popular. *Tea* is the term used for any breakfast drink (tea, Milo, Ovaltine). Barbados is well-known for its rum.

Recreation. Cricket is the national sport. Bajans also enjoy soccer, cycling, basketball, rugby, and volleyball. With excellent wind and water conditions, surfing and windsurfing are favorites. Scuba and skin diving are popular due to extensive coral reefs, clear water, and interesting dive sites, some of which feature the wrecks of sunken ships. People enjoy swimming, particularly on the more sheltered south and west coasts. Other sporting activities include horse racing, squash, tennis, and table tennis. Favorite games include bridge, chess, dominoes, and *draughts* (checkers), the national game. Sunday and holiday picnics at the beach are popular. Vacationing Barbadians may visit another English-speaking island or relatives in the United States, Canada, or England.

The Arts. Music and dance are intrinsic parts of Bajan culture. Calypso, reggae, and *dancehall* (of Jamaican origin), *soca* (a mixture of U.S. American soul and calypso), and North American "pop" styles are favored. Musicians compete in annual competitions. *Wukking up* is a uniquely Bajan dance style, usually performed to calypso, that features rhythmic waist-winding movements. Popular folk songs may date back to songs brought by West African slaves in the 1600s.

Barbados's arts are intertwined with the island's natural surroundings, especially the ocean, flora, and fauna. Weavers incorporate plants and natural materials into baskets and mats. Jewelry made from shells, feathers, and wood set in copper or silver is common. Potters make use of red clay, which is an abundant resource, creating an array of pots, tiles, and domestic items. Many painters and sculptors have found success in Barbados's prosperous art market, and several galleries and museums display artists' work.

Holidays. Four annual festivals celebrate important events in Barbados. The Holetown Festival (three days in February) celebrates the arrival of the first settlers; the Oistins Fish Festival, held on Easter weekend, is a tribute to the fishing industry; the Crop Over Festival (June–early August) celebrates the end of

▼ **THE AMERICAS**

the sugarcane harvest; and the National Independence Festival of the Creative Arts (Nov.) allows people to display talents in various fields. Other holidays include New Year's Day, Errol Barrow Day (21 Jan.), Easter (Friday–Monday), May Day (1 May), Whitmonday, Kadooment Day (first Monday in August), Emancipation Day (3 Aug.), United Nations Day (first Monday in October), Independence Day (30 Nov.), Christmas, and Boxing Day (26 Dec.). Kadooment Day is the culmination of the Crop Over Festival, when *bands* (groups of people in brightly colored costumes) parade and dance through the streets, followed by trucks broadcasting calypso and other music. The festivities include costume and music contests, street vendors, and craft displays.

Commerce. Most businesses are open on weekdays from 8 a.m. to 4:30 p.m. and until noon on Saturday. Grocery and convenience stores are open somewhat later. Banking hours are generally shorter. Most businesses close on Sunday, although large stores remain open when cruise ships are in port. Standard government office hours are 8:30 a.m. to 4:30 p.m. Supermarkets are becoming more prevalent in Barbados. People also buy basic goods at small neighborhood shops. Outdoor markets feature fresh fruits, vegetables, spices, and fish.

SOCIETY

Government. Barbados is a parliamentary democracy. The country is divided into 11 parishes and the city of Bridgetown. As a sovereign member of the Commonwealth of Nations, Barbados recognizes Queen Elizabeth II as head of state. She is represented in-country by a governor-general (Clifford Husbands). Constitutional reforms are being considered that would change the form of government to a republic with a local head of state.

The prime minister is leader of the majority party in the House of Assembly, which has 28 seats. The current prime minister, Owen Arthur, also serves as minister of finance. Parliament also has a Senate, whose 21 members are appointed. National elections are held at least every five years. Political parties include the Barbados Labour Party and the Democratic Labour Party (the opposition). All citizens may vote at age 18.

Economy. Barbados has one of the highest standards of living in the Caribbean. Tourism, light manufacturing, and the sugar industry are primary sources of foreign exchange. Tourism has expanded in importance in recent years, and it provides much of the country's employment. Arthur's government has attempted to liberalize the economy by removing some price controls and privatizing some industries. It also has laid the foundation for the development of an offshore financial sector. Barbados exports sugar, rum, electrical equipment, and textiles. It trades with the United States, other Caribbean nations, the United Kingdom, and Canada. Barbados is an active member of the Caribbean Community and Common Market (CARICOM). A value-added tax of 15 percent implemented in 1997 has generated some public criticism, particularly among lower-income Barbadians. The currency is the

DEVELOPMENT DATA
Human Dev. Index* rank .... 30 of 174 countries
    Adjusted for women .... NA
Real GDP per capita $12,001
Adult literacy rate .... 98 percent
Infant mortality rate .... 12 per 1,000 births
Life expectancy .... 72 (male); 78 (female)

Barbadian dollar (Bds$), which is pegged to the U.S. dollar at a fixed two to one ratio.

Strong economic growth during the past five years has strengthened the economy. Unemployment fell from 22 percent in 1993 to 11 percent in 1999. It was 9.3 percent at the end of 2000. Nearly 85 percent of the people can meet basic needs and enjoy economic opportunities. Inflation is low. Women earn a comparable share of the nation's income.

Transportation and Communications. The majority of Barbadian households have at least one car. However, most people make use of the island's efficient network of public buses, minibuses, and taxis. The island has a central paved highway and an adequate network of roads. Following the British tradition, cars travel on the left side of the road. Barbados has one international airport.

One government-owned television station and a satellite subscription television service serve the island; there are many radio stations. In addition to two daily newspapers, foreign-language papers are available. Telecommunications links to other nations are well established, and Internet use is growing.

Education. Barbados boasts one of the finest public education systems in the Caribbean. More than 85 percent of all pupils complete primary schooling and attend secondary school. Attendance is compulsory to age 16. Private schools have less than 5 percent of the total enrollment. The government sponsors qualified students to study at the University of the West Indies, which has campuses in Barbados, Trinidad, and Jamaica. Technical-training schools, as well as schools for physically and mentally handicapped children, are also available. Primary and secondary schools generally require uniforms.

Health. The government-operated National Health Service includes the Queen Elizabeth Hospital and a network of *polyclinics*, which provides free medical and dental care to all Barbadians. A private hospital also offers services. Barbadian water is some of the purest in the world. Tap water is safe to drink and most homes have running water.

CONTACT INFORMATION

Barbados Tourism Authority, 3440 Wilshire Boulevard, Suite 1215, Los Angeles, CA 90010; phone (800) 221-9831; Web site www.barbados.org. Embassy of Barbados, 2144 Wyoming Avenue NW, Washington, DC 20008; phone (202) 939-9200.

1305 North Research Way, Bldg. K
Orem, Utah 84097-6200 USA
1.800.528.6279; 801.705.4250
fax 801.705.4350
www.culturegrams.com

Kingdom of
Belgium

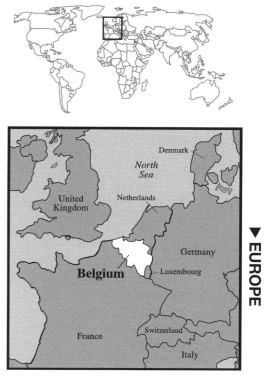

▼ EUROPE

Boundary representations are not necessarily authoritative.

BACKGROUND

Land and Climate. With an area of 11,780 square miles (30,510 square kilometers), Belgium is slightly larger than Maryland. It is generally flat, with increasingly hilly terrain near the southeast Ardennes forests. The highest elevation is only 2,275 feet (693 meters). Belgium has a system of dikes and seawalls along the coast to prevent tidal flooding. The climate is mild, damp, and temperate. Summer temperatures range from 54°F to 72°F (12–22°C); winter temperatures generally do not go below 32°F (0°C). Belgium's maritime climate is heavily influenced by the sea. Hence, fog and rain are common and there is little snow in winter. June through September are the most pleasant months.

History. Belgium has known heavy conflict as well as great achievement in art and commerce. Before the area was known as Belgium, the Belgians were a Celtic tribe in the area whose courage Julius Caesar thought had no equal in Gaul. In the fifth century, Germanic Franks took control and established the Merovingian Dynasty, later followed by Charlemagne, but fragmentation after his death eventually led to dukes and counts ruling four basic regions. As the 15th century approached, the French dukes of Burgundy began to consolidate territory and eventually gained all of what is now Belgium, reigning over several decades of prosperity and progress.

From the 1600s to 1830, the Belgium area was a battleground for France, the Netherlands, Austria, Germany, Spain, the Protestant-Catholic wars, and Napoleon (Waterloo is just south of Brussels). The territories of Belgium gained independence from the Netherlands in 1830 and united in a constitutional monarchy. However, divisions continued based on language: French speakers lived in the south while Dutch (Flemish) speakers settled in the north. The two groups developed separate cultural and linguistic traditions but remained together politically.

Because of Belgium's location and topography, it was often subject to battle, as is evident in the period preceding independence and again in the 20th century. Despite its claims to neutrality during both world wars, Belgium was overrun by conquering German armies in 1914 and again in 1940. Some of World War I's fiercest battles were fought in Flanders (northern Belgium). In World War II, the famous Battle of the Bulge was fought in Bastogne and central Belgium, where American divisions held off massive assaults by German troops attempting to reach the Allied port at Antwerpen. This pivotal battle helped secure an Allied victory in the war.

As a consequence of its vulnerability and size, Belgium has favored European cooperation and integration since the 1940s. It was a founding member of the North Atlantic Treaty Organization (NATO) and serves as that alliance's headquarters. Brussels is home to the European Union (EU) headquarters as well, making it an important city for business and diplomacy. Belgium also has devoted attention to internal cultural conflicts, creating a system to meet the needs of both major linguistic groups and various minorities. In 1960, Belgium granted independence to its African colony called the Belgian Congo.

Belgium remained a constitutional monarchy after World War II. From 1951 to 1993, King Baudouin I ruled as head of state; he was succeeded by King Albert II. In 1995, Jean-Luc Dehaene, a Christian Democrat from Flanders, was reelected as prime minister.

Widespread anger and frustration erupted in October 1996 in response to the government's handling of several child murder cases. More than 250,000 Belgians marched through Brussels demanding a more honest government, better law enforcement, and drastic changes to the judicial system. Another crisis erupted just before June 1999 elections, when high levels of cancer-causing dioxins were found to have entered foods via contaminated animal feed—information the government purportedly knew but did not reveal for a month. This led to worldwide restrictions on Belgian eggs, meats, and dairy products and cost about $1.5 billion in economic damages. Voters forced Christian Democrats out—the first time in more than 40 years. A coalition of both Flemish and French parties of Liberals, Socialists, and Greens is being led by Liberal Guy Verhofstadt as prime minister. Verhofstadt's coalition promises to reform civil service and lower taxes. Concerns about food safety have continued in Belgium with fears surrounding the spread of mad cow disease among Europe's livestock.

THE PEOPLE

Population. The population of Belgium is almost 10.2 million and is growing at 0.2 percent. Nearly 97 percent of the people live in cities or towns. The Walloons occupy the south (Wallonia) and comprise 31 percent of Belgium's population. The Flemish (58 percent) live in the northern half (Flanders), and the remaining 11 percent is of various mixed groups. The German-speaking minority (1 percent) lives east of Wallonia. Many Italians, Spaniards, and North Africans (mainly Moroccans) work in Belgian industry. Brussels (about 1,000,000), Antwerpen (500,000), and Gent (250,000) are the largest cities. Due to Brussels's international importance, nearly 25 percent of its inhabitants are foreigners. In all, almost 10 percent of the country's population is non-Belgian.

Language. French and Dutch (Flemish) are the primary official languages of Belgium. French dominates in southern areas and the capital, and Dutch is more prominent in the north. Dutch and Flemish have the same grammar and are written the same but are pronounced differently. Ten percent speaks German (also an official language). Many Belgians also speak English. Eleven percent of the Belgian population is officially bilingual. Although Brussels is in Flanders, 85 percent of its people speak French. Some towns in Wallonia have retained Latin dialects for festivals and folklore.

Because of the two distinct languages, French and Dutch names for the same city are often quite different. For example, the Wallonian city of Mons is referred to in Flanders as Bergen (both names mean "mountains"). Generally, road signs are not bilingual; they are written in the principal language of the region in which they stand.

Religion. Although Belgium is primarily a secular society, 75 percent of the population is considered to be Catholic. In fact, most cultural festivals have their origin in, or have been strongly influenced by, Catholicism. While only a fraction goes to church regularly, religion plays a role in people's personal lives, mostly in connection with such major events as birth, marriage, and death.

The Walloons have a history of being less devoted to the Catholic faith than the Flemish. Most other major world religions can also be found in Belgium. All Catholic, Protestant, Jewish, and Islamic clergy have official recognition from the government and receive their salaries from the state. Private religious schools also are subsidized with government funding.

General Attitudes. Differences in language and culture make Belgium appear like two separate countries. However, the Flemish and the Walloons have shown a remarkable ability to live together through the art of discussion and compromise. Conflicts tend be political and economic, but the groups are not antagonistic on an individual level.

A strong work ethic and an appreciation of culture are important to Belgians. The people tend to have tight regional and family ties, holding to the traditions of both. Nevertheless, Belgium's geographical position in Europe also makes the people cosmopolitan and open to outside interaction. Both the Walloons and the Flemish have a love for life and live it to the fullest, working and playing hard. A mixture of material wealth, good living, and family values is the lifestyle most Belgians hope for. Individuals generally like being regarded for their social achievements, having good housing, and enjoying pleasant living conditions.

Like those in other European countries, Belgians are struggling with their feelings toward immigrants. Most people accept them and would like to see their living conditions improved. Yet very little is done to integrate some immigrant groups into mainstream society. This tends to alienate immigrants, especially their children born in Belgium. Therefore, violence sometimes erupts in immigrant sections of large cities.

Personal Appearance. Belgians follow European fashions and tend to dress well in public. Extremely casual attire is reserved for the privacy of the home. Men who wear hats remove them in buildings. Suits and dresses are standard in offices.

CUSTOMS AND COURTESIES

Greetings. Belgians greet each other with a handshake, which is often quick with light pressure; people in some areas give firmer handshakes. The phrases used for greeting depend on the region. The normal greeting in Dutch is *Goeiedag* (Good day); the French equivalent is *Bonjour*. Informally, and if familiarity permits, one would say *Hallo* (Hello) in Dutch and *Salut* in French. English and German greetings would not be out of place in Brussels and some other cities. Between men and women and between women, close friends (even younger people) greet each other with three light kisses on the cheek. This gesture is actually more like "kissing the air" while touching cheeks. Belgians greet only friends and relatives by first name; otherwise, they address people by last name. However, in professional circles, there is a growing tendency to call each other by first name once a working relationship has been established. When leaving a group, Belgians usually shake hands with and bid farewell to each person in the group.

Gestures. Hand gestures are not used much during conversation. It is rude to talk with one's hands in one's pockets. Like most Europeans, Belgians do not talk with something in their mouths (gum, a toothpick, or food). Good posture is important, and people do not put their feet on tables or chairs. They avoid pointing with the index finger. Handkerchiefs are used discreetly.

Visiting. The importance of personal privacy extends to the home. Belgians enjoy inviting relatives and close friends to their homes, but other socializing usually is done in public places such as cafés, bistros, and restaurants. It is rare for Belgians to visit one another without prior arrangement or at least calling ahead. Once a visit has been arranged, punctuality is important; arriving more than 30 minutes late is considered rude. A Belgian host or hostess appreciates a small gift or some flowers from an invited visitor. Chrysanthemums are associated with funerals. In rural communities, it may be appropriate to remove one's shoes before entering the home. Guests usually are offered refreshments (or appetizers if invited for a meal).

Eating. Most Belgians eat three meals a day, with the main meal served around 6 or 7 p.m. The family usually gathers for this meal, which consists of a main dish and dessert. However, many adults and schoolchildren now have a hot meal at noon at their workplace and eat a lighter meal or snack in place of the traditional evening meal. A parent normally serves individual plates for each family member. Hosts also prepare individual plates for their guests. Meals are a social and cultural event in Belgium, and they are not to be finished quickly. The continental style of eating, with the knife in the right hand and the fork in the left, is most common. Belgians are thrifty and do not like waste; finishing one's food is expected. It is not impolite for guests to decline second helpings. In restaurants, one pays at the table and the tip is included in the bill. Still, one also may leave extra change if desired.

LIFESTYLE

Family. Even though the youth are becoming more independent, the family is still a strong and vital part of Belgian society. The average family has one or two children. Both parents often work outside the home. Women generally are responsible for most household duties and child care. Married children in Flanders seldom live with their parents, except in rural areas where families share farmland. Families often take excursions on holidays and Sundays. In the past, Wallonian extended families shared a large single house, but today they live separately. Still, they often remain in the same town or city as the rest of their family. In fact, throughout Belgium mobility tends to be low and people settle in or near the towns in which they were raised. Family and community roots are important to

Belgians. The elderly are generally well respected, but it has become customary and socially acceptable for parents to spend their declining years in a home for the elderly, where they are visited by children and grandchildren.

Dating and Marriage. Group dating usually begins by age 16, but dating behavior may vary according to regional traditions. The youth use public transportation and bikes at first, but when they reach driving age (18), they prefer private cars for dating. Young people go to movies, dances, and cafés. Long engagements are common. Many people live together before or instead of marrying. Only civil marriages are accepted by the government, but most couples also will have a Catholic religious ceremony attended by relatives and friends. However, the civil ceremony must precede the religious; it is usually attended by only a few relatives.

Diet. Belgians eat a rich variety of foods, including pork, game birds, fish, cheeses, fruits, vegetables, breads, and soups. Wine, beer, or mineral water often is served with meals. Belgium is famous for mussels, chocolates, three hundred varieties of beer, waffles, and french fries—which Belgians claim to have invented. French fries are served with mayonnaise rather than ketchup. Breakfast consists of a hot drink along with rolls or bread with jam or jelly. A snack at 4 p.m. is not unusual. Belgians take great pride in the quality of their food and the variety of cuisine—from domestically developed dishes to those adapted from other cultures. Restaurants offer a wide variety of international dishes.

Recreation. Participation in sporting activities is nearly universal; cycling and soccer are most prominent. The beach is a popular attraction, as are the beautiful forests in the south. Hunting, fishing, and pigeon racing have large followings in some rural areas. In pigeon racing, male pigeons are released far away from the females, and owners bet on which will be the quickest to fly back to its mate. Families enjoy picnics, the theater, and movies. Festivals, local and national, such as *Carnaval*, are popular. Most families take a one-month vacation each year; however, many families are now taking shorter vacations during the year when their children are out of school. Most schoolchildren have a week off in November, two weeks at Christmas, one week in February, and two weeks at Easter.

The Arts. Belgians are intensely proud of their rich cultural heritage, especially in art and architecture. Both ancient and modern art are admired. Belgium is known for such art masters as Brueghel, Van Eyck, and Rubens. Castle ruins and other historic buildings are seen as national treasures. Numerous theaters, festivals, and museums receive high patronage. Belgium sponsors national ballet, orchestral, and opera companies.

Mysteries are the most popular genre for plays and novels. Belgian cartoonists are among the most famous in the world. They have created such comic characters as Tintin and the Smurfs.

Holidays. Fairs, festivals, parades, and religious holidays are an integral part of the Belgian way of life. Legal holidays include New Year's Day, Easter Monday, Labor Day (1 May),

▼ **EUROPE**

Ascension Day, Whitmonday, Independence Day (21 July), Assumption (15 Aug.), All Saints' Day (1 Nov.), Veterans' Day (11 Nov.), and Christmas. *Carnaval* is celebrated in February or March, depending on the city. This festival is characterized by parades, parties, and colorful costumes. Local spring and fall cultural and folklore festivals, such as the Holy Blood Procession in Brugge, take place throughout the country.

Commerce. Because it is still customary to shop daily for fresh food, many open-air markets do business in the larger cities. Butcher shops are plentiful and well maintained. Supermarkets are available, although Belgium still has many small specialty shops. Businesses are open from 9 a.m. to 6 p.m., with a one- or two-hour break for lunch. Once a week (usually Friday), they remain open until 9 p.m. The average workweek is 35.8 hours.

SOCIETY

Government. Belgium is a constitutional monarchy under King Albert II, who holds executive power with the prime minister. Day-to-day affairs are handled by the prime minister and his cabinet. All governments have been coalitions, meaning no single political party has ever had a majority in Parliament. Parliament has two chambers: a 71-seat Senate and the more powerful 150-seat Chamber of Representatives. The cabinet contains an equal number of French- and Flemish-speaking ministers. Parliamentary elections are held at least every five years. The voting age is 18. The major political parties are split along linguistic lines. Belgium is divided into 10 provinces or *provincien*.

Constitutional reforms in 1981, 1988, and 1993 led to the organization of Belgium as a federal state. This move greatly reduced tensions related to linguistic divisions, as newly created government bodies have given greater decision-making authority to regions and communities (i.e., linguistic areas) in matters such as education, investment, welfare, and public works. The German-speaking minority also is protected.

Economy. Belgium's economy is diversified and highly industrialized; its labor force is highly skilled. Less than 3 percent of the labor force is involved in agriculture. Belgium is one of the world's major exporters of wool, beer, and meats, and a key producer of automobiles for major foreign companies. Belgian steel, the principal export, is world famous. However, due to steel- and textile-market fluctuations in the 1980s, that sector has declined and other industries—such as engineering, chemicals, food processing, and biotechnology—have grown. Exports now include items from each of these industries. Diamonds, crystal, and glass are well-established industries. Belgium is strong in foreign trade, partly because the third largest seaport in the world is located at Antwerpen and because of its central location among EU countries. Most Belgian trade (74 percent) is conducted with EU members, especially Germany.

Economic prosperity is available to most Belgians and wealth is well distributed. Although the dioxin crisis in 1999

© 2001 CultureGrams, a division of Millennial Star Network and Brigham Young University. It is against the law to copy, reprint, store, or transmit any part of this publication in any form by any means without written permission from CultureGrams. This document contains native commentary and original analysis, as well as estimated statistics. The content should not be considered strictly factual, and it may not apply to all groups in a nation. *UN Development Programme, Human Development Report 2000 (New York: Oxford University Press, 2000).

DEVELOPMENT DATA

Human Dev. Index* rank	7 of 174 countries
Adjusted for women	7 of 143 countries
Real GDP per capita	$23,223
Adult literacy rate	99 percent
Infant mortality rate	5 per 1,000 births
Life expectancy	74 (male); 81 (female)

limited economic growth, the economy is now recovering and inflation is low. Unemployment was above 8 percent for 2000. Leaders are making rapid progress in reducing the country's debt ratio. In 1999, Belgium, together with many other EU states, adopted the euro as its currency. It will replace the Belgian *franc* (BF) in 2002.

Transportation and Communications. Belgium claims the most complete transportation system in the world, with the fourth most train tracks per mile and the fifth most roads per mile (all freeways are lit at night). Trains are the fastest and most practical form of public transportation between cities. Buses and streetcars are widely available, but most people also own cars. Bicycles are popular for personal transportation. The efficiency of Belgium's postal system is recognized worldwide. There are both public and private television and radio stations. Cable television is available in all parts of the country and offers some 30 different channels. An increasing number of people use the Internet as a resource.

Education. Public education is free and compulsory between ages six and eighteen. Classes often are very demanding. Many Flemish families send their children to schools operated by the Catholic Church and subsidized by the state. A large portion of the federal budget is allotted to education, and 20 percent of the population is enrolled in school at any given time. All students learn at least two foreign languages. Beginning at age 14, students have opportunities to choose between different career and educational paths; comprehensive examinations determine one's entrance to higher education. Those who do not go on to a university receive training in their chosen careers at vocational and technical schools. Schools for the arts are also popular.

Health. Socialized medicine provides for the health care of all citizens. Doctors and clinics are private but are paid out of public funds. Health concerns are similar to those in the United States, as is the quality of care. Although the water is generally safe, Belgians drink bottled water rather than tap water.

CONTACT INFORMATION

The Belgian embassy, 3330 Garfield Street NW, Washington, DC 20008; phone (202) 333-6900; www.diplobel .org/usa/default_en.asp. Belgian Tourist Office, 780 Third Avenue, Suite 1501, New York, NY 10017; phone (212) 758-8130; Web site www.visitbelgium.com.

CultureGrams™
People. The World. You.

1305 North Research Way, Bldg. K
Orem, Utah 84097-6200 USA
1.800.528.6279; 801.705.4250
fax 801.705.4350
www.culturegrams.com

Belize

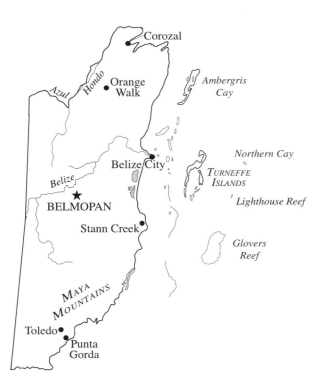

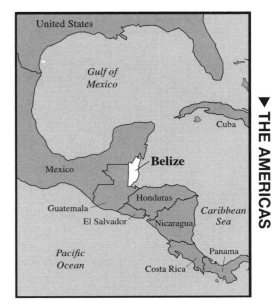

Boundary representations are not necessarily authoritative.

▼ THE AMERICAS

BACKGROUND

Land and Climate. Covering 8,866 square miles (22,963 square kilometers), Belize is about the size of Massachusetts. Located in Central America, it is bordered by Mexico, Guatemala, and the Caribbean Sea. The landscape is diverse for such a small area. The northern half of Belize is flat with marshes and lagoons, while coastal areas are covered by mangrove swamps. The land rises to the south and west, reaching an elevation of 3,688 feet (915 meters) in the Maya Mountains. More than 60 percent of the country is forested. Belize has the world's second largest barrier reef with hundreds of small islands called *cayes* (pronounced KEYS). Beautiful rivers, forests, reefs, and *cayes* are home to thousands of plant and animal species, from giant *guanacasta* trees to crocodiles and manatees.

Belize has two seasons: wet (August–January) and dry (February–July). Humidity is high year-round. The south receives the most rain. Temperatures average between 80°F and 85°F (27–29°C), although they are cooler in the mountains. In Belmopan, the capital, days are hot and nights are cool. Belize is subject to coastal flooding and hurricanes between June and October. In October of 2000, Hurricane Keith caused several deaths and millions of dollars in damage.

History. The Maya thrived in the area between the third and ninth centuries A.D. as part of a civilization that covered Guatemala, Honduras, Mexico, and El Salvador. Numerous city-states existed throughout Mayan lands, and these were often at odds with each other. Mayan ruins are still evident all over Belize. Little is known of the period after the decline of the Mayan people until the arrival of the first Europeans in the 16th century. The Spanish came in search of gold and found none. British pirates arrived during the 17th century and took advantage of the islands and reefs to lure ships onto the rocks for looting. British woodcutters soon followed and brought slaves to help in logging the huge forests. The pirates also turned to woodcutting. The logwood and later mahogany trade became very lucrative for these British, who were known as the Baymen.

The Spanish tried to claim the region, but at the decisive Battle of St. George's Caye in 1798, the Baymen and their slaves fought back Spanish invaders. With the Spanish Empire all around them, the Baymen asked Britain for protection. Spain and Britain signed a treaty to allow Belize to become a crown colony in 1862. England had promised to build a road between Belize City and Guatemala City as part of that treaty. The fact that it never happened led to a long-term dispute between the two neighbors. Guatemala claimed the area as its own territory because of the treaty's failure.

Belize was called British Honduras until 1973. The British granted internal self-rule in 1964. In 1981, with support from the United Nations and a strong independence movement, Belize became a sovereign country within the

Belize

Commonwealth of Nations. British troops remained to protect the borders, but after a 1991 agreement in which Guatemala relinquished its claim to Belize, Britain decided (in 1993) to withdraw most of its troops. Guatemala made a formal claim to the area in October of 1999. Negotiations between the two countries have been interrupted throughout 2000 and 2001 by border incidents, but an authoritative solution should be reached by August of 2001.

Said Musa of the social-democratic People's United Party (PUP) became the prime minister in 1998. He hopes to promote economic growth and develop the social sector. The PUP holds 26 of the 29 legislative seats. The United Democratic Party forms the opposition.

THE PEOPLE

Population. The population of Belize is about 249,183 and is growing at 2.75 percent. About one-fourth of the population lives in Belize City. Orange Walk is the next-largest city, with 12,000 people. Each of the country's six districts has a main town where the bulk of that district's population lives. Many Belizeans live and work abroad, especially in the United States.

Belize has a diverse blend of peoples. Creoles account for about 30 percent of the total population, and mestizos 44 percent. Mestizos are descendants of 19th-century immigrants from Mexico, as well as immigrants from other Latin American countries. Creoles, who dominate in Belize City, are persons with some degree of African ancestry. Many are descendants of early European (mostly English or Scottish) settlers and African slaves. Creoles were once the largest group but are now the group with the largest percentage of emigrants. Refugees from neighboring countries (mainly El Salvador and Guatemala) have added significantly to the mestizo population.

Most rural villages are comprised of mestizos, Mayas (Kek'chi, Mopan, and Yucatan), or *Garinagu* (mixed Caribbean and African). Mayas comprise 11 percent of the population; the Garinagu, who live in largest numbers in the south, comprise 7 percent. East Indians (3.5 percent) have been in Belize for generations and are joined by other minorities, including Mennonites (3 percent), Chinese, Arabs, and North Americans.

Language. English is the country's official language and, with the exception of people in remote areas, everyone speaks it. Most people also speak Creole, and everyday speech is often a combination of Creole and English. Creole is a melodic English-based language with roots in the days of slavery. Although it is traditionally an oral language, efforts are underway to establish grammar and spelling standards for a written form. Spanish is spoken by mestizos throughout the country (especially in the Cayo, Corozal, and Orange Walk districts) but not necessarily by all mestizos. Still, it has overtaken English as the first language of many Belizeans. While school instruction must be in English, Creole or Spanish may be used in the first few years to clarify instruction for children who do not speak English. Mayan groups speak their native languages. The Garinagu speak Garífuna and usually also English.

Religion. Freedom of religion is valued and respected in Belize. Most major Western Christian denominations are represented, but the Roman Catholic (60 percent) and Anglican (7 percent) Churches dominate. Most mestizos and Maya are Catholic. Creoles generally belong to Protestant churches, but many are Catholic. A number of other Christian faiths are practiced. Schools generally are run by churches, so most people are affiliated with a religion. Some indigenous religious practices are found among the Maya and Garinagu.

General Attitudes. Belizean society is nonconfrontational. People appreciate diplomatic honesty and value a sense of humor. Belizeans are fun loving, happy, and generally laidback. The pace of life is not regulated by the clock so much as by events or people. Punctuality may be admired but generally is not practiced. Men commonly practice *machismo*, demonstrating their manhood through macho acts or sexually oriented language. Women usually ignore such behavior and accept it as part of life.

Belizeans take pride in their diverse ancestries and linguistic abilities. But for a small nation of so many ethnic groups and cultures, Belize is relatively free of racial tension. Equality and coexistence are important concepts. Prejudices exist but not on the level of hatred. A neighborhood in Belize City might consist of every possible ethnic group and have few racial problems. One reason is that the people do not mix; they coexist. But another, more powerful reason is that most ethnic groups subscribe in some degree to Creole cultural practices, and Belizean Creoles have adopted aspects of the cultures around them. Most people can speak Belizean Creole, which further enhances harmony.

Although Belize is located in Central America, its history, culture, and government structure are closely linked to the Caribbean, which gives Belizeans great pride.

Personal Appearance. In Belize, the way a person is dressed is considered a mark of taste and status. Even those who cannot afford new or expensive fashions take pride in wearing clean, pressed clothing, particularly in the workplace. Office, bank, hotel, and school employees commonly wear uniforms. Many men, especially professionals, wear *guayaberas*, untucked cotton shirts that are sometimes embroidered. While women traditionally wear dresses or skirts at work, pants are becoming more common. Agricultural workers generally wear older clothing, with rubber boots or flip-flops.

U.S. fashions are popular in Belize City and other cities. Casual wear, including *short pants*, is the norm for leisure activities, while evening and religious events generally call for best dress. In rural areas, clothing tends to be casual.

The Maya often wear traditional clothing. This might include long, heavy brightly colored skirts with white embroidered blouses for women, and work clothes and straw hats for men. Garinagu women also commonly wear traditional clothing, which might include a simple, colorful blouse, a matching knee-length skirt, and a head scarf. The Mennonites, a group originally from Germany, maintain conservative, simple clothing and do not follow modern fashions.

CUSTOMS AND COURTESIES

Greetings. Belizeans are informal and friendly in *hailing* (greeting) one another. It is rude not to *hail* even a slight acquaintance or not to return a *hail*. *Hailing* strangers is not uncommon in Belize City or in the districts. When entering a place of business, one also *hails* the clerk or receptionist. When strangers pass on the street, a simple nod or wave is acceptable; acquaintances might add *Hey, how?* or *Y'aright?*

When greetings precede conversation, a handshake is common. Friends (particularly men) might shake by clasping the palms and locking thumbs or all fingers, or by exchanging a *knock-it* (lightly touching closed fists). Men often pat each other on the back when they shake hands. Women generally reserve hugs for close friends and relatives. Mestizos greet by saying *¡Buenos días!* (Good morning), *¡Buenas tardes!* (Good afternoon), *¡Buenas noches!* (Good evening), or just *¡Buenas!* any time of day. In Creole, one might use *Wa di gwan?* (What's happening?) or a number of other phrases.

In formal settings, people address others by title. Children usually address their elders by adding *Miss* or *Mister* before the name, and they often answer questions by saying *Yes, ma'am* or *No, sir*.

Gestures. Creoles and Garinagu are especially animated. Mestizos are very reserved unless they know others well. Nonverbal communication is prevalent; hand and facial gestures can be varied and complicated. Belizeans might indicate direction with the head or lips. Staring or pointing at someone is rude. Sucking air through the teeth can mean "Give me a break." People might hiss to get one's attention, but this is offensive to many (especially women). To hail a taxi or bus, people move the hand up and down before the vehicle passes.

Visiting. Belizeans are very hospitable. Unannounced visitors are welcomed and made to feel at home. Arranged visits most often occur on weekends. Before television was introduced in 1980, visiting was an integral part of everyday life. It has since diminished in cities but is still important in villages. When one visits a home, it is polite to *hail* the occupants from the gate or street until they come out. A lengthy conversation might take place over the fence before one is invited into the yard or home. Offering a guest refreshments, usually at least a drink, is considered good manners. In areas without refrigeration, people might offer fresh coconut. Though not expected, it is also polite for the guest to bring the host a small gift, such as sweets.

Eating. Families generally spend mealtime together, although in some Mayan and mestizo families, women eat after or separate from the men. Conversation is usually limited and mainly carried out between adults. For most, the main meal of the day is *dinner*, eaten at midday. Schools and businesses close so people can eat at home. In cities, people also frequent restaurants. The evening meal, called *supper* or *tea*, is lighter than dinner. For some groups (such as the Kek'chi Maya), the main meal is in the evening.

Meals in rural areas usually are less varied than in cities; rice, beans, tortillas, fresh fruit, and chicken often are the only available foods. Urban people might eat these foods in addition to burgers, *tamales*, fish, and a variety of other dishes.

LIFESTYLE

Family. Families tend to be large and often include the extended family. It is common for grandparents to raise grandchildren after their own children have left Belize for economic or other reasons. Leaving children behind has created problems in Belize, as minors now form a majority of the population in Belize City. Adult children usually remain at home until they marry or have a child. Single-parent families are abundant among the Creole population, and women have become the leading family figure in that group. In a Creole village, it is common for households to have a female head and several generations living together without any adult men.

In most other homes, the father takes the leading role. Younger mothers are more inclined to work outside the home than older women, but women are generally expected to take care of the home and family.

Apartment living is not popular. Most families own or rent homes. Rural homes may be simple thatched huts. In coastal towns and villages, houses are built of wood or cement and rest on stilts because of the threat of hurricane flooding. As elevation increases, stilts become less common. Because of the small population, the government can allot land to Belizeans who apply for it, making land and home ownership feasible.

Dating and Marriage. Urban dating (*courting*) tends to follow the same basic pattern as in North America. Schools may prohibit their students from going to popular dating destinations, such as discos, so private parties and school dances are the primary way for young people to meet. Village dating revolves around church activities or dances. Among the Maya and some mestizos, boys may only be allowed to meet with a girl in her home.

Many Belizean young women become single mothers early and never marry. Likewise, many young men father a number of children by several women and never formally marry. Or they may enter into common-law marriage relationships. For those who do marry formally, a church ceremony is usually followed by a lively reception that includes food, music, and dancing.

Diet. The most common staple is white rice and kidney beans. That dish may be accompanied by stewed chicken, beef, or fish. A staple among the Maya is corn, which is usually present in some form (such as tortillas) at every meal. Fish and seafood are common on the coast. Other popular foods include *tamales* (cornmeal dough stuffed with filling and steamed in banana leaves), *panades* (fried corn shells with beans or fish), meat pies, *escabeche* (onion soup), *chirmole* (soup), and *garnaches* (fried tortillas with beans, cheese, and sauce). Fruits (such as bananas, oranges, mangoes, papayas, and limes) are abundant and part of the daily diet. Vegetables are more limited and often imported.

Recreation. The most popular sports are *football* (soccer) and basketball. Organized leagues receive great local support. Softball is popular with men and women. National championships are held for both men's and women's teams. Volleyball, track-and-field, cricket, and boxing are enjoyed in many areas. Cycling is popular; the largest athletic event is the annual cross-country race held Easter weekend. It is a source of pride and a national tradition that attracts an international group of cyclists. Urban people like to go to the *cayes* for recreation. Belizeans also enjoy attending concerts and school fairs or watching the latest movies at home on cable and video.

The Arts. Native arts include a wide variety of wood and stone carving, textiles, baskets, and pottery. These are produced for tourists, used in many homes, and given as gifts.

Belizeans appreciate reggae, calypso, *soca* (a mixture of American soul and calypso), and various types of U.S. American music. A local favorite is *punta-rock*, which has its roots in the Garífuna culture. The *punta-rock* dance style is among the most popular forms and is thought of as a Belizean creation. Traditional drums made of hollow tree trunks are often used in performances.

▼ THE AMERICAS

Holidays. The largest and most celebrated national holidays occur in September. A street parade/party takes place on St. George's Caye Day (10 Sept.) and on Independence Day (21 Sept.). Various "September Celebrations" are held between these two holidays. Baron Bliss Day (9 Mar.) honors a Portuguese noble who left his wealth to the country and its people. Garífuna Settlement Day (19 Nov.) marks the arrival of the Garinagu to Belize. They originally came from Saint Vincent and settled in Honduras before migrating to Belize.

Belizeans celebrate Christmas with religious parades and services as well as with feasts, visits to friends and relatives, and lively parties. Easter weekend is popular for vacations; religious ceremonies are limited. Belize also celebrates Labor Day (1 May) and a number of other holidays.

Commerce. Weekday business hours are 8 a.m. to 5 p.m. Stores generally open again in the evening for two hours. Most businesses close for lunch. Bank hours vary. Most close at 1 or 2:30 p.m., Monday through Thursday, with longer hours on Friday. Larger grocery stores are open all day Saturday and on Sunday morning. Small shops have varying hours and usually are operated out of private homes.

SOCIETY

Government. Belize is a two-party democracy with a bicameral legislature. The legislature has 29 members and the Senate has 9 members. The two parties are the People's United Party and the United Democratic Party (UDP). Britain's Queen Elizabeth II is head of state but is represented in Belize by a governor-general, currently Sir Colville Young. Head of government is the prime minister, who is the leader of the National Assembly's dominant party. General elections are held at least every five years. The voting age is 18.

Economy. Belize's economy has been expanding since independence. Large amounts of foreign aid have contributed greatly to the economy's success. Belize is a member of the Caribbean Community and Common Market (CARICOM), a regional economic association. About half of the labor force is employed in agricultural production. The country's main exports are sugar, citrus fruits, molasses, bananas, wood and wood products, and clothing. Sugar traditionally has been the primary cash crop, but citrus fruits are now nearly as strong. Tourism is the fastest-growing source of income; ecotourism and adventure tours are very popular. Construction is also becoming increasingly important to the economy. Like many other Caribbean countries, Belize has established an offshore financial sector.

An economic citizenship program, begun in 1985, has further diversified the country's population and economic base. The program, aimed at attracting investment and skilled labor, grants foreigners the right to work, do business, and/or settle in Belize for the payment of a substantial fee.

Inflation is low, but unemployment averages around 13 percent and is even higher among the youth. Although the country has experienced economic progress, that progress has not yet benefited the majority of the population. Poverty affects about one-third of the total population and two-thirds of all rural people. The currency is the Belizean dollar (Bz$), which is pegged 2:1 to the U.S. dollar.

DEVELOPMENT DATA

Human Dev. Index* rank	58 of 174 countries
Adjusted for women	60 of 143 countries
Real GDP per capita	$4,566
Adult literacy rate	75 percent
Infant mortality rate	26 per 1,000 births
Life expectancy	69 (male); 73 (female)

Transportation and Communications. The Northern, Western, and Hummingbird highways are paved and link most cities. Roads leading to remote areas are rough. The national network of private bus systems is inexpensive and widely used. In cities and towns, most people get around by walking or riding bikes. The number of private cars is growing. Several small, private domestic airlines provide commuter and tourist travel.

In major towns, most people have telephones; villages usually have at least one phone. Radio and television broadcasts together reach nearly all Belizeans, who remain well-informed on local, regional, and international news.

Education. The majority of primary and secondary schools are church operated but receive large government subsidies. Students pay fees, buy their own books and supplies, and usually must wear uniforms. A few government schools exist for children of families that cannot afford these costs, but generally there are not enough spaces to accommodate all. Children are required to attend school until standard six (equivalent to the eighth grade in the United States), but secondary schooling is not required. Many students are unable to complete their primary education due to cost, family obligation, or other factors.

Space in secondary schools is limited, and acceptance depends on one's passing the Belize National Selection Exam. Those who complete a secondary education can attend junior college, teacher's college, or the University College of Belize. The government is focusing reform efforts on standardizing curriculum in all schools and providing more vocational education in each district.

Health. Health care is accessible to many citizens, particularly those in the towns and in Belize City. Each district has a small hospital and there is a large hospital in Belize City. A health worker is assigned to each village but might not always be present. Clinics and private doctors serve those who can afford to pay. Preventable diseases still afflict the country. Many Belizeans seek treatment from local "bush" doctors knowledgeable about natural and herbal remedies. Rainwater tanks and municipal water systems are used widely, although some concern for water safety exists.

CONTACT INFORMATION

Belize Tourist Board, PO Box 325, Central Bank Building, Level 2, Eaboral Lane, Belize City, Belize; phone (800) 624-0686; Web site www.travelbelize.org. Embassy of Belize, 2535 Massachusetts Avenue NW, Washington, DC 20008; phone (202) 332-9636; e-mail belize@oas.org.

CultureGrams™
People. The World. You.

1305 North Research Way, Bldg. K
Orem, Utah 84097-6200 USA
1.800.528.6279; 801.705.4250
fax 801.705.4350
www.culturegrams.com

Republic of
Bolivia

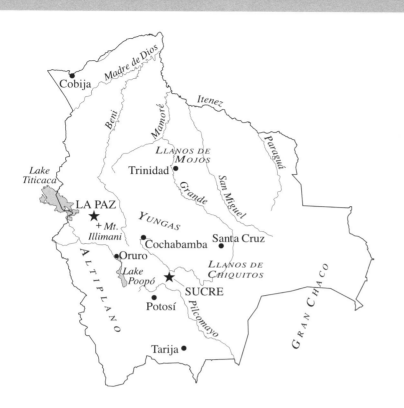

▶ **THE AMERICAS**

Boundary representations are not necessarily authoritative.

BACKGROUND

Land and Climate. Located in the heart of South America, Bolivia is a landlocked country of 424,165 square miles (1,098,582 square kilometers); it is almost three times the size of Montana. There are five distinct geographical areas: the high, cold, and dry mountain-rimmed Altiplano to the west; the medium-elevation *yungas* (valleys) northeast of La Paz and Cochabamba; the agricultural highland valleys in the departments of Cochabamba and Sucre; the Gran Chaco, a vast subtropical plain shared with Paraguay and Argentina; and the *llanos* or *el trópico*—wet, hot, forested lowlands in the east and northeast. Grasslands are common on these lands, which makes the area good for cattle ranching. Forests cover about half of Bolivia. The famous Lake Titicaca, the highest navigable body of water in the world (12,500 feet or 3,810 meters), lies on the north end of the Altiplano. It is shared equally by Bolivia and Peru.

Surrounding the Altiplano are the mineral-rich Andes Mountains, which climb to over 21,000 feet (6,401 meters) and are permanently covered with snow above 16,000 feet (4,800 meters). These mountains are known for their beauty, especially Mount Illimani near La Paz. The eastern foothills are home to a diverse variety of plants and animals; scientists have found more than seven hundred bird species there. Although Bolivia experiences four seasons, they are not all perceptible in some areas because elevation plays a more important role in climate than do seasons. Summer (November–April) is the rainy season. Winter is from June to September. In La Paz, the average annual temperature is 65°F (18°C).

History. The Tiahuanaco civilization inhabited the area near Lake Titicaca between 1500 B.C. to A.D. 1200. Aymara and other groups were conquered in the 1400s by Incan armies, bringing the area into the Inca Empire. The Incas introduced the Quechua language and a new social system. The Spanish began their conquest in 1532, and by 1538, all of present-day Bolivia was under Spanish control. Countless indigenous people died in forced labor in mines. Known as Upper Peru during Spanish rule, Bolivia was one of the first colonies to rebel. Political uprisings occurred frequently in the 1700s, but they always were crushed. It was not until the independence movement of 1809 that Upper Peru began to see success. After the 16-year War of Independence, the area gained independence on 6 August 1825 and was named after its liberator, Simón Bolívar.

Bolivia's first president was overthrown in 1828, and the country experienced decades of factional strife, revolutions, and military dictatorships. Much of its original territory was lost between 1879 and 1935 in wars with Chile, Brazil, and Paraguay. The War of the Pacific (1879–84) was most significant because Bolivia lost its access to the sea. This event basically doomed the economy, and Bolivians regularly appealed (and still appeal) to Chile for the return of the territory. In 1992, Peru granted Bolivia access to the sea via the Ilo port in southern Peru. With this access, Bolivia hopes to increase foreign trade.

The government attempted to improve conditions and stabilize the country during the 1950s, but a military coup ended the reforms in 1964. A series of coups brought various dictatorships to power, each of them oppressive to the indigenous majority's population. From 1971 to 1978, Hugo Banzer Suárez led an authoritarian military regime that helped create economic growth but was criticized for human-rights abuses. Economic conditions worsened through the 1980s, characterized by spiraling inflation that peaked at 11,700 percent. The economic downslide made it clear that military governments could not effectively lead the country.

A representative democracy finally was established in August 1985 with the election of President Víctor Paz Estenssoro. He reduced inflation to less than 20 percent and stabilized the economy. His term ended peacefully in 1989, when Jaime Paz Zamora was elected.

Gonzalo Sánchez de Lozada was voted president in 1993. Significantly, his vice president, Victor Hugo Cárdenas, was Aymara—the first indigenous person to rise to such a high office in Latin America. Sánchez implemented educational reforms and worked to integrate indigenous groups into society, but his privatization measures drew public protests.

Former military dictator Hugo Banzer Suárez won presidential elections in June 1997 with only 22 percent of the vote. Banzer's center-right National Action Party (ADN) formed unusual alliances with leftist and populist parties to ensure his confirmation as president by Congress. The top priorities of Banzer's government are to reduce poverty, eliminate drug trafficking, and end government and judicial corruption. Continuing to privatize public industries and lift restrictions on foreign companies and investments has stimulated economic growth.

THE PEOPLE

Population. Bolivia's population of almost eight million is growing at 1.8 percent annually. About half of all people live in urban areas. La Paz has more than one million and Santa Cruz, the fastest-growing city, has about the same number. Nearly 70 percent of the total population is composed of Native Americans, including Quechua (30 percent), Aymara (25 percent), Guaraní, Mojeño, Chimane, and smaller groups. Some 25 percent of the people are *criollo* (or mestizo), who are of mixed indigenous and European heritage. Another 5 percent are of European descent. Quechua Indians are prevalent throughout the country, but especially near Cochabamba and Sucre; the Aymara are concentrated in the Altiplano.

Language. *Castellano* (Spanish), Quechua, and Aymara are all official languages. Spanish is used in government, schooling, and business and is the native tongue of about 40 percent of the population. Most people speak some Quechua. Indigenous groups speak their own languages, especially in rural areas. However, Quechua and Aymara are often liberally peppered with Spanish words. Many indigenous immigrants to cities speak Spanish with their families to avoid stigma. Many young indigenous language speakers also speak Spanish.

Religion. Approximately 95 percent of the people are Roman Catholic. Some indigenous systems and an active Protestant minority (*evangélicos*) are present also. Bolivians of the Altiplano mix Aymaran and Quechuan traditions with their Catholic beliefs. For instance, *Pachamama,* or goddess Mother Earth, is popular. People toast to her or bless things in her name. A *ch'alla* is the blessing of any material possession or event by offering symbolic articles and alcohol to *Pachamama* and *Achachila,* god of the mountains. Homes are typically *ch'alla*-ed every year at *Carnaval.*

General Attitudes. Time is viewed differently in Bolivia than in North America. People enjoy getting as much pleasure out of an experience as possible, with less regard to how much time they spend. Scheduled events begin late, as all understand arriving on time is not expected. The Aymara view the past as something they can see in front of them but the future as unseen and therefore behind them.

Bolivians admire honesty and frown upon those who are too proud and who flaunt or talk about their wealth. They do not like confrontation and avoid disagreement. Kindness, gentleness, and concern for another's welfare are key to friendship in Bolivia. People like to remind others that they are also "Americans" because they live in South America. They call U.S. Americans *norteamericanos*.

Divisions exist in society between the ruling class—Europeans and mestizos—and indigenous groups, who have often been barred from participating in society because of their race. Those who have wanted to assimilate into society have had to speak Spanish and change their way of dress. Many also adopt Spanish names. The indigenous movement would like to extend all the benefits of a democratic society to all peoples in the country without forcing them to abandon their traditions. The ruling class believes other groups should assimilate into society by leaving tradition behind and adopting a more Westernized culture.

Personal Appearance. Bolivians wear different clothing depending on where they live and their social class. Generally, urban residents wear Western-style clothing. Children dress neatly for school. Having clean shoes is very important. Many women wear a *pollera* (a full, colorful skirt). Rural women (often called *cholitas*) wear a *pollera* with a *manta* (shawl). They often wear their hair in braids and may wear bowler derby hats, bonnets, or stovepipe hats, depending on where they are from.

Some indigenous people make their clothing out of wool. Common colors include red, black, and off-white. Native men might wear shin-length pants, a shirt, and a thick leather belt. They often wear a *poncho* and a hat. Women wear a long, dark-colored dress tied at the waist with a colorful belt. They also may wear a small shoulder cape and oval hat. Women carry babies on their backs in an *aguayo* (a woven square cloth).

CUSTOMS AND COURTESIES

Greetings. Spanish-speaking Bolivians greet friends and acquaintances with a cheerful *¡Buenos días!* (Good morning), *¡Buenas tardes!* (Good afternoon), or *¡Buenas noches!* (Good evening). *Hola* (Hi) and *¿Cómo estás?* (How are you?) are also common. One adds the title *Señor* (Mr.), *Señora* (Mrs.), or *Señorita* (Miss) for first-time introductions or when greeting strangers (such as a store owner). *Señorita* is used for any woman, unless she is older or the speaker knows she is married. Bolivians show respect for others by addressing them as *Don* (for men) or *Doña* (for women) before their first name. Rural people (*campesinos*) even use these titles with close friends. Strangers do not call each other by first name.

Greetings are accompanied by a handshake. However, if a person's hand is wet or dirty, he or she may offer an arm or elbow. It's important to greet everyone in a home. In cities, greetings for both men and women are always accompanied by a kiss on or near the cheek. Bolivians maintain little personal space and stand close during conversation. Close friends and relatives frequently greet with an *abrazo*. It consists of a hug, a handshake, two or three pats on the shoulder, and another handshake. Female friends often embrace and kiss each other on the cheek. They commonly walk arm in arm. Common Spanish farewells are *Hasta luego* (Until later) or *Hasta mañana* (Until tomorrow). Friends use the casual *Chau* or *Chau, chau. Adiós* implies good-bye for a long time. In southern areas, *Adiós* also is used as a quick greeting when people pass on the street.

Gestures. Bolivians often use hands, eyes, and facial expressions to communicate. To beckon children, one waves the fingers with the palm down. Patting someone on the shoulder is a sign of friendship. A raised hand, palm outward and fingers extended, twisting quickly from side to side, is a way of saying "there isn't any" or "no"—a gesture often used by taxi and bus drivers when their vehicles are full. Waving the index finger indicates a strong "no." One covers the mouth when yawning or coughing. Eye contact in conversation is essential. Avoiding another's eyes shows suspicion, lack of trust, or shyness.

Visiting. Bolivians enjoy visiting one another. Both arranged and unannounced visits are common. Urban visitors generally give flowers or small gifts to the host upon arrival. Hosts also might present visitors with gifts. They are not opened in front of the giver. Hosts make their guests as comfortable as possible. Compliments given during the meal instead of after will bring a second helping. Guests respectfully address hosts by first name, preceded by *Don* or *Doña*, to show familiarity.

Upon arrival, visitors are invited inside and offered a drink or light refreshments; refusing them is impolite. It is also impolite to start a conversation on the doorstep. Visitors staying a few days are welcomed with a hug and kiss on the cheek. Hosts provide special meals as a welcoming gesture, and if possible, all family members are present to greet the guest. Guests are not asked how long they will stay, as this is interpreted as a desire to have them leave soon.

Eating. Bolivian families eat most meals together. They typically have one large and two small meals per day. Rural families might eat four meals. Upon entering a room where people are eating, Bolivians often say *Buen provecho* (similar to *Bon appétit*). Everyone (including guests) is expected to eat everything on the plate. People eat meat with utensils, not hands. Generally, one is not excused from the table until all are finished eating. It is polite to say *Gracias* (Thank you) to all at the table when one finishes eating, and to wish them *Buen provecho* upon leaving. Eating out is most common at lunch. In restaurants, the host usually pays for the meal. A tip is usually left when in large groups or in a nice restaurant in the city. *Chicharias*, bars indicated by a white flag hanging outside, serve *chicha*, a home-brewed alcoholic drink made from corn. *Chicharias* are an important meeting place, especially in the Altiplano.

LIFESTYLE

Family. The family is central to Bolivian society. Middle- and upper-class families have one or two children. Poorer families traditionally are much larger, but children often die in infancy. While many rural couples live together in common-law arrangements, formal marriages are more common in cities. Children almost always live with their parents until they are married, and sometimes even after marriage.

Most women work in the home. Without modern conveniences, their work is difficult and requires more time. This can prevent women from pursuing work in the labor force. But they often run small businesses (sewing, cutting hair, selling soda and gum, etc.) from their homes. Upper- and middle-class families often have maids. While the father makes most family decisions, the mother exerts much influence on household affairs. Although children are taught the importance of education, illiteracy is high among the poor. Children generally are well disciplined and share in family responsibilities. The elderly live with their children's families.

Dating and Marriage. Chaperoned dating begins at about age 15. Dating is preceded by flirting. In many towns on Sunday (and other) evenings, young men and young women like to *dar vueltas* (take walks), where they walk in groups around the central plaza to make eye contact and flirt. The process of getting acquainted, dating seriously, and being engaged can take as many as three years. Men marry between the ages of 20 and 25, while women marry between ages 19 and 23. People usually do not marry until they have some financial security or property. For a marriage to be legal, a civil ceremony must be performed. However, most couples also have a religious ceremony, followed by a dance and reception. In rural areas, this can last up to a week. Because weddings are expensive, many rural people choose common-law marriages instead. Bolivians wear their wedding rings on the right hand.

Diet. Potatoes, rice, soups (which often include *quinoa*, a protein-rich grain), milk products, and fruits are common staples in the Bolivian diet. Starches vary by region: yucca is eaten in the lowlands; corn is plentiful in the valleys; and potatoes are eaten daily in the Altiplano. Bolivia has hundreds of potato varieties prepared in different ways. *Chuños* are freeze-dried potatoes used in soups or side dishes when rehydrated. Most foods are fried and seasoned with *llajua* (a spicy salsa). Peanuts may be used in soups (*sopa de Maní*) and sauces. Chicken is the most common meat. Southern Bolivians eat a lot of beef and enjoy barbecues. Breakfast usually consists of tea or coffee, bread, and perhaps cheese. In rural areas, it might be a hot drink made of corn spiced with sugar and cinnamon called *api*. Lunch, the main meal, consists of soup and a main dish. In cities, people enjoy *salteñas* (meat or chicken pies with potatoes, olives, and raisins) as a midmorning snack.

Recreation. *Fútbol* (soccer) is the national sport. Other popular sports vary by region. Leisure activities include watching television (in urban areas), visiting with friends, and attending festivals. In the Chaco region, people get together to drink several rounds of *yerba mate*, an herbal tea. Dancing and singing are popular at various events.

The Arts. Many of Bolivia's cultural traditions have their roots in pre-Inca civilizations. Textiles have changed little from those roots, often incorporating the same dyes and patterns that have been used for hundreds of years. Since colonial times, Bolivians have ornamented architecture, jewelry, and other objects with gold and silver. Basket weaving and wood carving are common crafts in the Guaraní region.

Music is an integral part of Bolivian culture. Played and promoted throughout the world, it can be divided into three types: fast, happy rhythms from the east and northeast; slow, romantic, and melancholic rhythms from the Andes Mountains; and happy, romantic rhythms from the central valleys. Much of the music is characterized by distinctive instruments: panpipes (*zampoña*), vertical flutes, various percussion instruments, and the *charango*, a 12-string, guitar-like instrument made from an armadillo shell. The *cueca*, *tinku*, and *saya* are traditional dances.

Holidays. Holidays include New Year's Day, *Carnaval* (Saturday before Ash Wednesday), *Día del Mar* or Sea Day (23 Mar.), Holy Week before Easter, Father's Day (19 Mar.), Labor Day (1 May), Mother's Day (27 May), Independence Day (6 Aug.), All Saints' Day (1 November, a day for the family to clean and decorate ancestral graves and enjoy a picnic), and Christmas. On Christmas Eve, some children place their old shoes in a window for *Papa Noel* (Santa Claus) to take them in exchange for new gifts. Children also receive gifts on Three Kings' Day (6 Jan.).

Dancing, wearing costumes, and pouring water on people are common during *Carnaval*. Oruro's celebration is one of the world's biggest. Each city and province has its own festival or saint's day. These local events are noted for their music and colorful costumes. Almost every *pueblo* (village) has its unique *fiestas* in honor of its patron saint or the Virgin Mary.

Commerce. Business generally is conducted weekdays from 9 a.m. to noon and 2 to 6 p.m. The midday break or *descanso* allows people to have lunch and relax. Government offices often close without warning. Strikes, or *paros cívicos*, occasionally interfere with business hours.

SOCIETY

Government. The president is both chief of state and head of government. A president, vice president, and cabinet form the executive branch. The Supreme Court sits at Sucre, the legal capital. *El Congreso Nacional* (National Congress), based in La Paz, consists of a 27-seat Chamber of Senators and a 130 seat Chamber of Deputies. The ruling alliance includes Banzer's center-right National Action Party, the Revolutionary Movement of the Left (MIR), and the populist Civic Solidarity Union. Constitutional reforms in 1997 extended presidential, vice presidential, and congressional terms to five years. Voting is mandatory beginning at age 18 for married individuals and 21 for singles.

Economy. With natural resources such as tin, natural gas, crude oil, zinc, silver, gold, lead, and tungsten, mining is Bolivia's major industry. Others include coffee and food production, textiles, and timber. Half of the labor force is engaged in agriculture. Coca (used in making cocaine) has been the largest (illicit) cash crop; however, exports are down from previous years. Government efforts to stop coca trafficking are complicated by its lucrative profits and because the coca leaf has been a traditional crop for centuries. It has many legitimate uses in society, including medicinal and dietary, and is a fundamental part of the culture.

Bolivia is one of the poorest and least developed Latin American countries. Limited access to adequate health care, education, and economic opportunities affects the quality of life for most Bolivians, particularly those in rural areas. About two-thirds of the population lives in poverty. Efforts to improve conditions for Bolivia's poor and indigenous populations remain a long-term goal. Underemployment affects more than 40 percent of the economically active population.

Bolivia's fight against poverty was boosted in October

DEVELOPMENT DATA

Human Dev. Index* rank	114 of 174 countries
Adjusted for women	96 of 143 countries
Real GDP per capita	$2,269
Adult literacy rate	84 percent
Infant mortality rate	60 per 1,000 births
Life expectancy	59 (male); 65 (female)

1998 as rich creditor nations forgave more than 80 percent of Bolivia's $1.1 billion external debt. Economic growth averages more than 4 percent. Inflation is decreasing as the government continues to cut expenditures. The currency is the *boliviano* ($B).

Transportation and Communications. Throughout its modern history, Bolivia has been handicapped by its landlocked location and lack of internal transportation and communications. Only a few major highways are paved. Airlines connect major cities and allow travelers to avoid rugged terrain. But buses, taxis, and trains are the most common forms of transportation. Buses are often crowded. More expensive minivans are faster and less crowded. Taxis often stop to pick up other passengers going the same way. Several radio and television stations are in operation.

Education. Schooling is free and compulsory for ages six to fourteen. School conditions are poor. Those with money send their children to parochial or private schools. Though illiteracy is declining, problems still exist. Less than half of all children complete their primary education, and only about one-third go on to secondary school. Strikes, long distances to schools, and family labor needs contribute to this. In the past, indigenous children could not receive instruction in their own language because Spanish was the language used in all schools. Recent reforms require bilingual education. Since 1985, six universities have been built, bringing the total to fifteen. One must pass two entrance exams to be admitted to a university.

Health. Sanitation facilities are poor. Contaminated water is the most serious health threat. Tap water must be boiled, but wood is hard to find and gas is expensive. Many rural areas lack running water and electricity. Local nurses and doctors have been training *responsables populares de salud* (community health-care workers) in basic skills. These trainees help serve the needs of the rural population. The infant mortality rate is high due to disease and widespread poverty.

Traditional medicine is used in many rural areas. Only about half the population has adequate access to medical care. Many illnesses affect the populace, including hepatitis, cholera, and *chagas*, a parasitic disease that causes intestinal problems and early death by heart attacks in about one-fifth of the population. The AIDS threat is growing.

CONTACT INFORMATION

Embassy of the Republic of Bolivia, 3014 Massachusetts Avenue NW, Washington, DC 20008-3603; phone (202) 483-4410.

1305 North Research Way, Bldg. K
Orem, Utah 84097-6200 USA
1.800.528.6279; 801.705.4250
fax 801.705.4350
www.culturegrams.com

Bosnia and Herzegovina

Boundary representations are not necessarily authoritative.

BACKGROUND

Land and Climate.   Bosnia and Herzegovina, covering 19,775 square miles (51,233 square kilometers) of the Balkan Peninsula, is slightly smaller than West Virginia. It is divided into two entities: the Federation of Bosnia and Herzegovina (51 percent of the territory) and the *Republika Srpska* (Serb Republic, 49 percent). Sarajevo is the national and Federation capital. Banja Luka is the Serb Republic (RS) capital. *Herzegovina* (Duchy) is the historical name for an arid southwestern region contiguous to Croatia and settled mostly by Croats.

Bosnia's center and south are dominated by the dense forests of the dramatic Dinaric Alps, whose highest peak is Mount Maglic at 7,828 feet. Fertile plains lie in the north along the Sava River, and a short coastline opens to the Adriatic. The Drina River forms part of the eastern border. Other major rivers include the Una, Vrbas, Neretva, and Bosna. The continental climate features long, hot summers and cold winters. Areas of high elevation have short, cool summers and long winters. Coastal winters are mild and rainy.

History.   Illyrians and Celts may have been the earliest inhabitants of Bosnia, followed by Romans and Greeks in the second century B.C., Goths in the third century A.D., and Slavs (including the Croat and Serb tribes) in the sixth century. The Bosnian state was first mentioned in Byzantine sources in the 10th century. An independent Kingdom of Bosnia emerged around 1200 and endured for more than 260 years in a tolerant religious environment that included three Christian churches: Roman Catholic, Eastern Orthodox, and Bosnian Bogomil. In 1463, Bosnia fell to the Ottoman Turks, who introduced Islam and ruled for four centuries.

Jewish merchants fleeing the Spanish inquisition settled in Sarajevo in the 16th century. They soon built their own quarter in this central trading city. Discrimination against Jews in the Ottoman Empire was less common than in neighboring Christian countries.

After the Ottoman demise, the Berlin Congress of 1878 gave Austria-Hungary a mandate to occupy Bosnia. Annexation followed in 1908. In 1914, a young Serb nationalist from *Mlada Bosna* (Young Bosnia) killed the heir to the Austro-Hungarian throne, who was visiting Sarajevo. *Mlada Bosna*, a multiethnic group, envisioned joining occupied Slavic lands to independent Serbia. The assassination was the spark necessary to ignite World War I between nations already engaged in an arms race. When the war ended in 1918, Bosnia and Herzegovina was included in the newly created Kingdom of Serbs, Croats, and Slovenes—later named the Kingdom of *Yugoslavia* (Southern Slavs). During this period, Bosnia's Muslim population was pressured to register as either Serb or Croat, and their political strength was undermined by nationalist leaders.

World War II brought disintegration to the Kingdom of Yugoslavia in 1941, leaving Bosnia under Croatian authority until 1945. Some of the bloodiest battles against Axis troops took place in the mountains of central Bosnia. During the war against the German and Italian occupiers, various nationalist movements also battled one another. Bosnia became a killing ground as Serbian *Chetniks* (royalists), Croatian *Ustashe* (fascists), local militia, German and Italian troops, and (to a lesser extent) the multiethnic communist Partisans all terrorized various segments of the civilian population.

The Partisans prevailed, and the new Socialist Republic of Bosnia and Herzegovina became one of eight federal units in communist Yugoslavia. Partisan leader Josip Broz Tito ruled Yugoslavia until he died 35 years later. Under Tito, Bosnian Muslims were recognized as having a separate identity in 1974. Overt manifestations of nationalism were forbidden, however, and religious devotion was discouraged as part of official political ideology. In essence, Tito tried to unite people under communism by suppressing those elements of culture that historically divided them.

When Tito died in 1980, Yugoslavia's federal system unraveled. Dormant nationalist feelings surged as communism crumbled. After multiparty elections in 1990 and a referendum in 1992, Bosnia and Herzegovina declared independence within its historical borders. The United Nations Security Council recognized the nation's sovereignty in May 1992.

The new republic was immediately threatened by its neighbors, whose ambitions were to create a Greater Serbia and a Greater Croatia. During the ensuing war from 1992 to 1995, brutal ethnic cleansing and fighting left more than 250,000 Bosnians dead and 1.8 million people displaced. Muslims and Croats were targeted mostly by Serbians, but all sides had responsibility for some bloodshed.

The 1995 Dayton Peace Accords negotiated in the United States and signed in Paris stopped the fighting by dividing the country into a Muslim/Croat entity and a Serb entity, loosely joined by a central government. A strong North Atlantic Treaty Organization (NATO) military presence ensures a secure environment, while an international High Representative coordinates Dayton's civil implementation. Although democratic transformation is underway, most refugees and displaced persons have not yet returned to their original homes. In the 1998 national election, voters chose Bosnian Croat, Bosnian Serb, and Bosnian Muslim (Bosniac) members of parliament. A rotating presidency was created to allow all three groups to share in national leadership. In March of 2001, Ante Jelavic, the Croat member of the Bosnian presidency, was dismissed after he threatened to form his own government. War crimes trials are underway for atrocities committed during the 1992 to 1995 war. Ethnic tensions in the region remain high.

THE PEOPLE

Population. Any data for Bosnia is subject to error because of the civil war. A 2000 U.S. estimate puts the population at about 3.8 million, with a growth rate of 3.1 percent. In 1991, Bosnia had about 4.3 million people and very few ethnically homogenous areas. Today, the RS is populated mostly by Bosnian Serbs (40 percent of the total population). Bosniacs (38 percent) and Bosnian Croats (22 percent) dominate in the Federation. During the war many Bosniacs came to Bosnia from Serbia and Croatia, while some Bosnian Serbs, Bosnian Croats, and Bosniacs fled to other nations. Returning people as much as possible to their homes is a major objective of the Dayton Accords. Small numbers of Albanians, *Roma* (Gypsies), and others also live in the country.

Language. Bosnians speak a Slavic language that linguists classify as Serbo-Croatian. Some ultranationalists are attempting to accentuate or even create differences among the Serbian, Croatian, and Bosnian variants of this language. It has 30 phonemes, each with its own letter. Schoolchildren learn the Latin and Cyrillic scripts, which are used in the Federation and Serb Republic, respectively. Gypsies speak Romany, and smaller groups speak Hungarian, Albanian, and Slovene.

Religion. Medieval Bosnia was entirely Christian, but Islam was attractive to many Bosnians in the 15th century, and the Ottomans offered better benefits to Muslims. These factors, coupled with weak organization in the Christian churches, prompted many people to adopt Islam as their new faith. In the 20th century, despite historical mixing of peoples, Bosnians whose ancestors were Catholic came to be identified as Bosnian Croats, while those of Eastern Orthodox background are considered Bosnian Serbs. Muslims are called Bosniacs because an archaic term *Bosnjak* (an old surname meaning Bosnian) was revived as a nonreligious term for them. Animosity between the three major groups remains a divisive factor. A small number of people are Protestant and Jewish.

During the communist period, most Bosnians became secularized, and as many as one-third of all urban marriages were between partners from different religious backgrounds. Many even assumed the ethnic identity of "Yugoslavs" to indicate membership in a broader national group (like "Americans"). Since 1990, religious activity has grown and several mosques and churches have been built or repaired.

General Attitudes. Bosnians are friendly, warm, and outgoing people who enjoy *merak* (a relaxed pace of life) but value hard work. Each major group is known for certain characteristics. For example, Bosnian Serbs consider themselves heroic and proud, Bosnian Croats emphasize their good behavior and historical ties to western Europe, and Bosniacs consider themselves warm in personal relationships. In general, people appreciate close relations with neighbors (*komsija*) and friends. Even during the war, Bosnians kept their extraordinary sense of humor that allows them to laugh at their own faults. *Ceif* (to act spontaneously for enjoyment and without regard for consequences like cost and time) is a common attitude.

With the war still present in the minds of many, and ethnic differences sharply emphasized by vocal nationalists, reconciliation is hard to achieve. The atrocities of the war committed by all sides in one region or another make those areas difficult to reintegrate, due in part to shame, fear, or anger. Still, some reconciliation is occurring, especially in rural areas, among people who just want to go home, and among those who do not understand how they could have listened to the nationalist politicians who led them into war. Bringing such war criminals to justice is an ongoing and necessary process.

Personal Appearance. Most people wear Western-style clothing. Urban residents pay particular attention to their appearance and brand names. The youth enjoy modern fashions and casual clothing. Natural fibers (cotton and wool) generally are preferred over synthetics. Wealthier families have silk clothing and furs from eastern countries. Women often dye their hair; gray hair seldom is seen. Young women like red and auburn shades.

Some rural people may wear elements of traditional clothing with Western attire. For example, one might wear *dimije* (long, wide Turkish pants ideal for working in the fields) with a T-shirt. Many Bosniac men wear traditional berets and women wear head scarves. Some people wear rubber *opanke* (shoes with upturned toes). A Bosnian Serb woman might wear her *nosnja* (long white skirt and cotton blouse) for a special occasion, as might a Bosnian Croat woman wear her white skirt, embroidered white blouse, and apron. Religious Bosniac women wear long skirts under long coats and full head scarves.

CUSTOMS AND COURTESIES

Greetings. When people meet, they usually shake hands. Under Islam's recent influence, covered Bosniac women are not to be addressed or offered a handshake. Younger people greet older people first, and women offer the hand first to men. The usual greeting is *Dobro jutro* (Good morning), *Dobar dan* (Good day), or *Dobro vecer* (Good evening). *Zdravo* (Hi) is an informal greeting usually followed by *Sta ima?* (What's up?). Friends add a kiss—once to each cheek for Bosnian Croats and Bosniacs, and three times total for Bosnian Serbs. When parting, Bosnians might say *Do vidjenja* (Good-bye), *Zbogom* (Farewell), or the more informal *Vidimo se* (See you) or even *Ciao*.

Gospodin (Mr.) has replaced *Drug* (Comrade), and *Gospodja/Gospodijica* (Mrs./Miss) has replaced *Drugarice* (Comrade) as common titles. Bosnians tend to use the informal *ti* (you) in conversation with peers. Friends and family call each other by first name, as do older people talking to those younger. In written form, a person's surname usually precedes the given name.

Gestures. Friends may wave to one another on the street. It is impolite to beckon with the index finger or shout in public. However, many such rules of etiquette are routinely ignored. Bosnians customarily offer older persons a seat on the bus. Eye contact is expected when people raise their glasses prior to a toast.

Visiting. Family and friends visit each other often, and weekends are the most popular time to get together. It is common to sit for hours over cigarettes and a cup of coffee or some *rakija* (brandy), reflecting the leisurely pace of life most Bosnians prefer. Such visits are informal; people simply drop by without prior arrangement. Invited guests often bring gifts such as flowers, coffee, wine, or a box of chocolates; a gift is nearly obligatory from first-time guests. Flowers are given in odd numbers, as even numbers are reserved for funerals. The exception is roses, which are given singly or in even numbers.

Bosnians generally remove their shoes when entering a home, replacing them with slippers. Hosts serve coffee at the beginning and end of a visit. For arranged visits, they offer *meze*: a spread of various fried pies, dried meats, cheese, and salads. Visiting is expected for events like weddings or funerals; guests do not need to call ahead, nor do they receive invitations. Bosniacs typically stay for a brief time to offer condolences or congratulations. Bosnian Serbs and Bosnian Croats tend to stay longer and have something to eat.

Eating. A day usually begins with coffee (black and strong), followed by breakfast at midmorning. Lunch in midafternoon is the main meal and consists of soup, meat with a vegetable, salad, bread, and dessert. Supper is served around 8 p.m. Bosnians eat with the fork in the left hand and knife in the right. One's hands remain above the table with elbows off the table. Rural Bosnians eat some foods like pies with their hands. It is impolite to speak with a full mouth, but it is not too impolite for friends to share food from the same plate.

When entertaining, hosts offer more food than can be eaten; this is a sign of hospitality and wealth. Indeed, hosts consistently urge guests to eat more during the meal and guests customarily decline several times before accepting. Still, it is impolite for a guest to eat too much. At restaurants, usually one person pays the entire bill. Tipping is not necessary but increasingly expected and appreciated. One does not tip the restaurant owner even if he or she served the meal.

LIFESTYLE

Family. Rural households include grandparents, parents, and two or more children. The male (father or grandfather) has a dominant role. Urban families have one or two children and the grandparents are less involved. Both husband and wife work for a wage and share in decision making. Children may go to day-care centers or be cared for by babysitters or family members. Parents often feel obligated to give grown or married children money or housing. In turn, children are expected to care for their elderly parents. Adult children often live with their parents until they marry. A typical urban high-rise apartment has one or two bedrooms. Rural houses are bigger but often close together; houses in mountain villages are necessarily more scattered. Except in some areas, rural gardens and yards tend to be small.

Dating and Marriage. Young dating couples enjoy going to cafés, fairs, cinemas, dance and disco clubs, or visiting each other at home. Rural youth gather in city squares. People usually marry after they finish their schooling. The bride and groom must have a civil ceremony for the marriage to be legal; many then also have a religious wedding. Rural celebrations are more elaborate than urban ones; they include big tents for guests and several days of festivities. Urban wedding parties usually are held at home or a restaurant.

Diet. Pies dominate the Bosniac menu: *burek* (meat pie), *sirnica* (cheese pie), *zeljanica* (spinach and cheese pie), cabbage pie, and many more. Breakfast pies are served with bread, cheese or cream, and smoked meat like *sudzuka* (a sausage). For lunch, people also eat a hearty soup, meats, and vegetables. Other favorite dishes include chicken and stuffed onions, peppers, or cabbage. Devout Muslims do not eat pork. Other Bosnians enjoy pork in various forms; it is customary for a family to slaughter a pig or two in November. Part of the meat is prepared for Christmas and the rest is dried.

Bosniac cooking is influenced partly by Turkish and Greek cuisine, as evidenced by its grilled meat, stews like *bosanski lonac* (with cabbage and meat), and sweets like *baklava* (a Turkish layered pastry with nuts). Bosniacs prepare desserts like *tufahija* (boiled apple stuffed with nuts and sweet cream) or *sevdidzan* (soft cake). Bosnian Serb and Bosnian Croat cooking is known for chocolate cakes, strudels, and pancakes. Bosniacs drink less wine than other groups in Bosnia, but *rakija* is found everywhere.

Recreation. Bosnians enjoy cultural, historical, or sporting events, as well as visiting in the home. Urban dwellers take evening strolls or meet at busy cafés and restaurants. Favorite sports include soccer, basketball, tennis, swimming, and handball. Older men gather in social halls to play checkers or chess. People watch television in the evening and on weekends. On May Day (1 May), families customarily enjoy games and roast lamb at a picnic. Grilling is common throughout the summer. The Adriatic coast is a popular destination for family summer vacations. People tend to gather at the same vacation sites year after year.

The Arts. Epic poetry is sung and accompanied by the *gusle* (single-string instrument). *Sevdalinka* songs, or love songs, are well known. Folk dance varies within cultures and regions. The *kolo* is a dance not accompanied by music. Architecture, weaving, silk embroidery, and calligraphy are other important arts.

EUROPE

Bosnia and Herzegovina

Bosnia and Herzegovina has a long and rich cultural tradition in award-winning film, literature, and art, but because of damage caused by war, the people are currently struggling to rebuild their artistic traditions. Bombing demolished many important monuments, and the National and University Library was ruined.

Holidays. Official public holidays include New Year's (1–2 Jan.), Day of the Republic (9 January in the RS and 1 March in the Federation), Labor Day (1–2 May), St. Vitus Day (28 June in the RS), and Statehood Day (25 Nov.). Catholics and Protestants celebrate Christmas on 25 December, while the Orthodox celebrate on 7 January. Muslims celebrate *Ramasan Bairam* (feast at the end of the holy month of *Ramadan*) and *Kurban Bairam* (Feast of the Sacrifice). Christians celebrate Easter, Ascension (15 Aug.), and All Saints' Day (1 Nov.). Jews can take a holiday on *Yom Kippur* and *Rosh Hashanah*. Women's Day is 8 March.

Commerce. Weekday business hours are from 8 a.m. to 4 p.m., while stores remain open until 8 p.m. Many shops are open Saturday until at least 5 p.m. and some even until 10 p.m. Grocery stores are open all week. Urban centers contain modern stores and small, neighborhood shops. Fresh food is available in daily urban markets and at weekly rural markets. In rural areas, and even on some small urban plots, families often grow their own vegetables and raise small livestock.

SOCIETY

Government. Bosnia and Herzegovina's status as a parliamentary democracy relies on ongoing political transformation at home and in Serbia and Croatia. The Dayton Accords endorsed a multiethnic society but complicated matters by creating the Federation and the Serb Republic. Brčko is a separate district under national jurisdiction. Positions in the weak central government are divided among the three main ethnic groups. Chief of state and chairman of the three-member rotating presidency is now Živko Radišić of the Socialist Party of Republika Sprska (SP RS). Prime Minister Bozidar Matic, a Croat, is head of state. The Parliamentary Assembly (*Skupstina*) consists of the National House of Representatives (42 seats) and the House of Peoples (15 seats). The voting age is 18 (16, if employed).

Economy. Bosnia and Herzegovina was one of the poorest republics of the former Yugoslavia. The war only made things worse. Production fell 90 percent between 1990 and 1996. Socialist military industries lay idle; other state plants are overstaffed, closed, or barely functioning. Much infrastructure and private enterprise remain devastated. Nearly 60 percent of all houses were destroyed in the war and a million people remain displaced. Resettlement is an enormous economic challenge; efforts are underway to enact new property laws and rebuild infrastructure. Limited foreign investment, corruption, and government bureaucracy hinders economic recovery.

Despite all these problems, some benefits of international business loans, reconstruction, and investment are being realized. Incomes are rising, though unemployment still reaches 50 percent in some areas. Exports are resuming and will eventually include such natural resources as coal, iron, manganese, copper, lead, zinc, and timber. However, Bosnia's greatest asset is a skilled and educated workforce. The currency is the convertible *marka* (KM), which is tied to the German *Mark*.

Transportation and Communications. A public trolley line serves most of Sarajevo, while public buses provide transportation between major cities. Private and public buses connect rural areas to cities. Passenger train travel is limited because of war damage. Rural people continue to rely on horse-drawn carts and bicycles. Cars do not normally allow pedestrians to cross the street, so one must watch out for traffic. Roads and bridges need repair. Bosnia has four international airports.

The free press is growing. Dozens of television and scores of radio stations exist, but most tend to promote the interests of a specific ethnic group. The Open Broadcast Network and the Free Election Radio Network are genuine multiethnic stations. The state-run telephone system still is being repaired and upgraded, while a private cellular network is growing.

Education. Children begin primary school at age seven and must attend for at least eight years. Secondary schooling lasts four years but is not mandatory. Thereafter, students may attend *gymnasium* (university-prep high school) or a vocational school to learn a trade or craft. After eighth grade, students must pass a matriculation exam to get a *workbook*. Without it, one cannot get a job. Sarajevo, Tuzla, Banja Luka, and Mostar have universities. Education is free to citizens at all levels. Students who can pay university tuition are allowed to enroll above the normal entrance quotas. Education is very important to Bosnians. A unified curriculum is being developed for the entire country that will allow students to receive a balanced view of history and culture.

Health. Primary health care is free to all citizens, but some treatments and medicines must be paid for by patients. Many rural clinics destroyed in the war remain to be rebuilt. Hospitals are found in regional centers. Private clinics have multiplied since the war, but most people cannot afford their fees. Hospitals face supply and equipment shortages. Despite a 1998 law that prohibits smoking in public places, public smoking is common throughout Bosnia. The greatest health challenges include lack of proper hygiene, tuberculosis, cancer, and kidney ailments due to poor water.

CONTACT INFORMATION

Embassy of Bosnia and Herzegovina, 2109 E Street NW, Washington, DC 20037; phone (202) 337-1500; Web site www.bosnianembassy.org.

DEVELOPMENT DATA

Human Dev. Index* rank	NA
Adjusted for women	NA
Real GDP per capita	$1,690 (est.)
Adult literacy rate	98 percent
Infant mortality rate	25 per 1,000 births
Life expectancy	69 (male); 74 (female)

1305 North Research Way, Bldg. K
Orem, Utah 84097-6200 USA
1.800.528.6279; 801.705.4250
fax 801.705.4350
www.culturegrams.com

Federative Republic of
Brazil

Boundary representations are not necessarily authoritative.

▼ THE AMERICAS

BACKGROUND

Land and Climate. Brazil is the fifth largest country in the world and the sixth most populous. At 3,286,488 square miles (8,511,965 square kilometers), it is larger than the continental United States and comprises half of South America. Forests cover 65 percent of Brazil's territory and include the world's largest tropical rain forest in the Amazon River Basin. Concerns over the destruction of the rain forests have prompted a global conservation effort. However, illegal logging and slash-and-burn clearing continue and may increase due to widescale government plans to develop the area.

Brazil has five distinct regions: north, northeast, southeast, south, and central west. The *Amazonas* (the Amazon), the world's largest river, traverses through lush rain forests in the north. Tropical grasslands and savannas extend across the sparsely populated central west region. The northeast's vast stretches of land are commonly subject to droughts. The southeast, which is the most populated and industrialized region, is rich in minerals and natural resources. Agriculture and manufacturing are common in the south, which boasts the world's largest hydroelectric dam near Iguaçu Falls.

Less than 5 percent of Brazil lies above 3,000 feet (914 meters). The country is south of the equator and has a mostly tropical climate. Humidity is high in coastal and forest regions, but the highlands (such as those around São Paulo) have a more moderate climate. The south is more temperate than the north. The warmest month is January; the coolest is July. Freezing temperatures are possible in the southernmost areas.

History. Brazil does not have a written history prior to the arrival of Europeans, but various groups inhabited the area when Pedro Álvarez Cabral arrived in 1500 and claimed the region for Portugal. The Portuguese colonized Brazil; the French and Dutch both attempted to establish colonies but eventually were driven out. After Spain conquered Portugal, it controlled Brazil from 1580 to 1640. Colonization took several decades and expansion did not really begin until after 1650.

When Napoleon captured Lisbon, Portugal, in 1808, the royal family fled to Brazil and established Rio de Janeiro as seat of the Portuguese Empire. Brazil then ceased to be a colony and became part of the Portuguese kingdom. The royal family returned to Portugal in 1821, leaving Dom Pedro I to govern. He declared Brazil's independence in 1822 after people in Portugal demanded that Brazil be returned to colonial status. His son, Dom Pedro II, was deposed by an 1889 military coup.

Since then, the military has seized control five times, although with relatively little violence. The dictator Getúlio Vargas ruled from 1930 to 1945, followed by elected presidents. A 1964 coup gave the military control until a return to civilian rule in 1985. A new constitution was ratified in 1988.

Elections in 1989 brought conservative Fernando Collor de Mello to office as the first directly elected president in 29 years. Collor's economic austerity campaign crippled the economy, and many measures only covered his corrupt activities. Collor resigned in December 1992 before impeachment proceedings could be carried out. The entire process was a historic test of democracy, since it marked the first time a leader was removed from office by legal, constitutional means.

Vice President Itamar Franco assumed the presidency until elections in October 1994. Franco's finance minister, Fernando Cardoso, introduced an anti-inflation plan so successful, the economy began to boom in 1994. Cardoso, who had spent years in exile (1964–85), eventually upset the front-running presidential candidate. Since taking office in 1995, Cardoso has pursued further economic reforms and solutions to social problems such as poverty, human-rights abuses, and clashes between wealthy landowners and landless peasants. Cardoso also has been faced with increasing crime and over-crowded prisons. Poor conditions precipitated coordinated riots in prisons throughout the country in which dozens of hostages and prisoners were killed.

THE PEOPLE

Population.   The population of Brazil is approximately 172.8 million and is growing annually at a rate of 0.94 percent. More than 80 percent of the people live in cities. The two largest cities of the southeast, São Paulo and Rio de Janeiro, together hold some 20 million people. Brasília, the capital, is a planned city that was completed in 1960; its population now numbers more than two million.

Nearly 50 percent of the population is younger than age 20. Brazilians of European (mostly Portuguese) descent make up 55 percent of the population, while 38 percent are of mixed heritage and 6 percent are Black African descendants. There are only about 200,000 indigenous peoples in Brazil, many of whom inhabit the Amazon region (including some who have never been contacted by modern society). Many of the mixed peoples have some indigenous blood through inter-marriage. Groups of German, Italian, Lebanese, and Japanese immigrants settled in the south and still maintain ethnic communities. In fact, Brazil is home to the largest cohesive community of Japanese outside of Japan. The black population descended from African slaves brought to Brazil before the 1880s; they live mostly in northeastern states like Bahia.

Language.   Portuguese is Brazil's official language. It differs slightly in pronunciation from the Portuguese spoken in Portugal. English and French are popular second languages. Spanish is becoming more popular in some circles as Brazil establishes stronger trade ties with its neighbors. (Although Portuguese speakers generally understand Spanish, some Brazilians are offended when deliberately spoken to in Spanish.) In southern cities, some descendants of European immigrants also speak German or Italian. Indigenous peoples speak a variety of more than one hundred languages.

Religion.   Brazil traditionally has been a strong Roman Catholic country. At one time, nearly 95 percent of the population claimed membership in the Catholic Church. However, membership has dropped to less than 70 percent, while membership in other Christian churches and Protestant groups is growing rapidly. Since the founding of the republic in 1889, there has been a separation of church and state, and religious freedom is guaranteed. Although Brazilians consider themselves quite religious, most attend church only on special occasions. Some in the northeast and in urban areas country-wide practice Afro-Brazilian religions that combine various indigenous African beliefs with Catholicism. These are known by different names, such as Candomblé, Macumba, and Xangô, but most have other differences as well.

General Attitudes.   Brazilians are warm, fun loving, and free spirited. They are also outgoing and enjoy being around others. At the same time, they are hard working. Brazilians are proud of the Portuguese heritage that sets them apart from other Latin American peoples. One point of pride is the "Brazilian way"—their ability to find creative ways around seemingly insurmountable problems. Brazilians often are opinionated and will argue for their conviction with a vigor that may seem like anger but is not. In spite of recent economic crises, most Brazilians are hopeful about their country's future as a stable democracy with a strong, growing economy.

Social status commonly is measured by one's power to acquire possessions. People (except those in São Paulo) tend to view time more as a sequence of events than as a matter of hours and minutes. Therefore, people in most regions appear to have an extremely casual attitude about time. Brazilians in the north and northeast regions and small inland towns are traditionally more conservative. Folklore is stronger in these areas; traditional religious and military celebrations are also more common.

Personal Appearance.   In general, Brazilians are fashionable and like to dress according to the latest styles. People in urban areas like to wear European fashions, particularly Italian. People in warmer and humid regions dress more casually and colors are lighter and brighter year-round. In São Paulo and parts of the southern region, people often dress in black, white, and other neutral colors. Stylish suits or a dress with a jacket is common business attire.

Both men and women pay careful attention to their appearance. Shoes are well kept and polished. Manicures and pedicures are popular. People like to dress up for special occasions and parties. In rural regions, more traditional clothing is common, especially among the native peoples.

CUSTOMS AND COURTESIES

Greetings.   In formal situations, Brazilians greet each other with a handshake. Female or male and female friends commonly embrace and kiss each other on alternating cheeks, although they may only touch cheeks and "kiss the air." In some regions, three "kisses" are exchanged. Common verbal greetings include *Olá. Tudo bem?* (Hello. Is everything fine?) and *Como vai?* (How are you?). Young friends greet each other with a simple *Oi* (Hi). When one joins or leaves a small group, it is polite to shake hands with all who are present. Common parting terms include *Tcháu* (Good-bye) and *Até logo* (See you soon).

Superiors and authorities often are addressed formally with the titles *Senhor* (Mr.) or *Senhora* (Mrs.) followed by their surname. In less formal situations, first names are commonly used, sometimes preceded by *Seu* (for men) or *Sua/Dona* (for women).

Gestures.   Brazilians often use gestures to communicate and express feelings. Gestures often accompany greetings. One beckons by waving all fingers of the hand with the palm facing either up or down. Pulling one eyelid down signifies disbelief or caution. One may tap the fingers horizontally under the chin to indicate that another person does not know what he or she is talking about. The U.S. American "OK" sign, with the thumb and index finger forming a circle, is an offensive gesture.

Brazilians tend to stand close and touch each other often during conversation. Eye contact is important. Passing between conversing individuals is rude. Brazilians are polite in crowds. Men tend to stare at and make comments about women passing by. This is not considered rude and generally is ignored by the women.

Visiting. Brazilians enjoy visiting. The tropical climate allows for much time outdoors, including chatting outside late into the evening. If a meal or snack is in progress, it is considered impolite not to ask visitors to join in eating. Most people will politely decline the invitation *Está servido?* (Will you join me?) with *Bom apetite* (Enjoy). Hosts generally also offer coffee or other refreshment toward the end of a visit. In rural areas, not accepting refreshments may be considered rude. If invited to dinner, one might take candy, wine, or a small gift to the hosts. Invited guests commonly arrive up to a half hour late, except perhaps in São Paulo. One generally is expected to stay at least two hours. While Brazilians enjoy conversation, they avoid controversial subjects (like politics and religion) at social gatherings. Asking personal questions about one's age, salary, etc., is considered rude.

Eating. Brazilians value mealtime with family and friends. Extended family members often gather together for lunch on Sundays. Brazilians eat in the continental style, with the knife in the right hand and the fork in the left. One wipes the mouth frequently throughout a meal before drinking. After-meal conversation often takes place over a cup of strong *cafézinho* (black coffee). In restaurants, diners call the waiter by holding up the index finger or by saying softly *Garçon*. While the bill usually includes the tip, one may leave extra change. If the tip is not included, leaving 10 to 15 percent is customary.

LIFESTYLE

Family. Families traditionally are large and may include the extended family. However, smaller nuclear families, with one to three children, are becoming more common. The family is led by the father, but the mother influences decisions, especially those affecting the home. Women, even those who work outside the home, are responsible for household duties. Middle- and higher-income families often hire domestic help. Children rarely leave home before they marry. Unmarried men may leave early for employment reasons, but they usually live at home until they are 30. The elderly who cannot care for themselves live with their children because it is considered improper to send them to a nursing home.

Family ties are strong, and members rely on each other for assistance and enjoy being together. Among the urban youth, however, some of these values are becoming less important. While middle-income families live in modest homes or apartments, the poor commonly lack the basic necessities of life, including food, sanitation, and shelter. Women and youth often work to help support their families.

Dating and Marriage. Group dating for youth starts around age 14; couples gradually emerge from the group. Traditional families expect the young man to ask the girl's father for permission to be her boyfriend. Serious dating and engagements may last two or three years. Brazilians tend to marry young. Weddings often include two ceremonies: a civil and a religious ceremony. Wedding parties are lavish and elegant, with much food, drink, and music.

Diet. Staple foods in the Brazilian diet include meat, bread, rice, beans, cheese, and eggs. Breakfast usually consists of *café com leite* (coffee with milk), fruit, and bread with marmalade. Lunch is the main meal and often includes beans, rice, meat, salad, potatoes, bread, and fruit. Dinner is lighter and may include a bowl of soup with bread, followed by coffee or milk with a piece of cake. Pastries are typical snacks. Favorite foods vary by region. In Bahia and other states, foods may be spiced with *dendê* (palm) oil. In Rio de Janeiro, the favorite is *feijoada* (black beans with beef, pork, sausage, and sometimes a pig's ears, feet, and tail). *Churrasco*, which originated in the south, is a barbecue with a variety of meats. *Bife à cavalo com fritas* (meat with egg and french fries) is popular in many areas. Common drinks include lemonade, milk, fruit juices and shakes, soft drinks, coffee, and *mate* (MAH-tay), an herbal tea enjoyed in southern states.

Recreation. The national sport and passion is *futebol* (soccer). Businesses and schools may even close during the World Cup or important national competitions. Basketball and volleyball are also popular. People enjoy visiting the country's many fine beaches, boating, fishing, and swimming. Brazilians are avid fans of auto racing. During leisure hours, people commonly visit friends or watch television, particularly *telenovelas* (nighttime soap operas). Traditional dances and festivals are popular and vary by region. Brazilians will celebrate any occasion, and get-togethers often include singing and samba dancing. Weekend and holiday barbecues are common.

The Arts. All cultures within Brazil have influenced its music, dance, and festivals. Samba, the most popular music and dance, is an example of blending musical styles, using African rhythms and European-style singing. Pottery, often made by hand and painted with religious or domestic scenes, is popular. Weaving is also a common art.

European movements have influenced Brazilian art and literature, and artists and writers often combine traditional and modern styles in their work. Brazilian folklore features different mythical characters, such as *Cobra-Grande*, a huge snake living in the Amazon that frightens people by changing shape.

Holidays. *Carnaval*, a five-day festival preceding Ash Wednesday, is the most famous holiday in Brazil. It is marked by street parades, samba and *bloco* (group) dancing, parties, drinking, costumes, conga drums, and music. Some people spend months preparing costumes and saving for *Carnaval*. During this week, crime and car accident rates are unusually high.

Tiradentes Day (21 Apr.) celebrates the death of Joaquim José da Silva Xavier (known as Tiradentes), a dentist and nationalist who died in the struggle for independence. The *Festas Juninas* (June Festivals) coincide with the feasts of St. John and St. Peter and are celebrated with local fair-type activities. Other holidays include Easter, Labor Day (1 May), Independence Day (7 Sept.), Memorial Day (2 Nov.), and Republic Day (15 Nov.).

On Christmas Eve, people eat a big meal (turkey or ham) and exchange gifts. Only those gifts from *Papai Noel* (Father Noel) arrive on Christmas Day; all other gifts are exchanged the day before. New Year's Eve is a time for large parties. In some areas, Candomblé believers dress in white and blue to honor the sea goddess Iemanjá and gain energy for the new

▼ **THE AMERICAS**

year. People place flowers and candles on beaches as part of the celebration.

Commerce. *Padarias* (neighborhood shops that sell bread and basic food items) open as early as 5 a.m. Most other stores are open weekdays from 8 a.m. to 6 p.m. and until noon on Saturday. Local business associations regulate business hours; in some areas, shops have longer weekend hours. Supermarkets are open every day of the week. Some offices and stores close from noon to 2 p.m. for the afternoon meal. Bank hours vary by state. Events are scheduled according to the 24-hour clock; for example, 3 p.m. is referred to as 15:00.

SOCIETY

Government. Brazil is a federative republic consisting of 26 states and one federal district (Brasília). Technically, each state is autonomous with a legislative body and elected governor, but all rights not delegated to the state are reserved by the federal government. The president is head of state and government. Cardoso is the first Brazilian president to be elected to a consecutive term. The National Congress has an 81-seat Federal Senate and a 517-seat Chamber of Deputies. Voting is universal and compulsory for ages 18 to 70. It is optional for 16- and 17-year-olds and those older than 70. A 1997 constitutional amendment allows presidents, governors, and mayors to run for two consecutive terms. Major political parties include Cardoso's Brazilian Social Democratic Party, the Brazilian Democratic Movement Party, Liberal Front Party, and Workers' Party. Many other parties also hold seats in Congress.

Economy. Brazil has the largest economy in South America and the ninth largest in the world. However, income distribution is highly unequal and poverty affects more than one-third of the total population. Unequal land distribution is a contributing factor: nearly half of all private lands are owned by only 1 percent of the people. Many of the landless live in *favelas* (shantytowns) on the outskirts of urban centers.

Hyperinflation and low growth marked the 1980s and early 1990s. In 1994, Cardoso introduced a new currency, the *real* (R$), as part of a program that dramatically cut inflation. Inflation was about 6 percent in 2000, and the government hopes to cut it to 4 percent in 2001.

The government's failure to cut spending following the Asian financial crisis in 1997 weakened investor confidence in the Brazilian currency. In January 1999, the government was forced to devalue its currency by more than 40 percent, plunging the country into crisis. Government spending cuts, tax increases, high interest rates, and other emergency measures were implemented to strengthen the *real* and stop the flight of foreign capital. However, despite predictions, the economy grew by almost 1 percent in 1999; growth in 2000 reached about 4 percent, and similar rates are expected for 2001. Unemployment is 7.1 percent overall and close to 20 percent in São Paulo.

Brazil is largely self-sufficient in food and consumer goods. Agriculture employs about 30 percent of the population. Brazil is the world's largest producer of coffee, oranges, and bananas. It also is a major producer of soybeans, corn, cocoa, beef, pork, and rice. Much of Brazil's sugarcane is

DEVELOPMENT DATA

Human Dev. Index* rank	74 of 174 countries
Adjusted for women	66 of 143 countries
Real GDP per capita	$6,625
Adult literacy rate	84 percent
Infant mortality rate	38 per 1,000 births
Life expectancy	59 (male); 68 (female)

used to produce ethyl alcohol, a fuel used in more than 1.5 million Brazilian cars. The industrial sector exports automobiles and parts, textiles, minerals, iron ore, steel, and metals; other industries include cement and chemicals. Natural resources include gold, nickel, tin, timber, and oil. A series of oil spills in 2001 affected not only the economy but also the environment. Most electric power is generated by hydroelectric dams. Brazil is a member of Mercosur, a regional free-trade pact that includes Argentina, Paraguay, and Uruguay.

Transportation and Communications. Domestic air travel is well developed between hundreds of local airports. Travel by intercity bus is more common, although buses tend to be crowded. São Paulo and Rio de Janeiro have rapid transit systems. City buses do not stop automatically; people must hail them with the wave of a hand. Readily available in large cities, taxis with red license plates have fixed meter rates. Brazil's media are highly developed, with one of the world's largest television networks. Televisions are found in even the poorest areas. The country also enjoys a large film and music industry. Urban telephone service is good. Pay phones are operated by tokens or phone cards, not coins.

Education. Education consists of eight years of compulsory elementary education (to age 14) and three years of secondary education. About 40 percent of those who enter school proceed to the secondary level. Entrance to Brazil's top universities is difficult and is preceded by a special college-preparation course and entrance exams. About half of secondary school graduates go on to trade schools. Brazil has many fine libraries and research centers. There are hundreds of higher education institutions. A national adult literacy program has raised the literacy rate substantially.

Health. Brazil's national health-care system provides universal coverage. However, rural areas rarely have adequate facilities. Excellent private care is available in large cities to those who can afford it. Water often is not potable. Sanitation in some areas is insufficient. Yellow fever and malaria are found in some rural areas. A grassroots effort is dispatching mobile health-care workers to rural areas to fight infant mortality through education and basic care. AIDS is a growing problem.

CONTACT INFORMATION

Brazilian American Cultural Center, 16 West 46th Street, Second Floor, New York, NY 10036; phone (212) 730-0515. Embassy of Brazil, Consular Section, 3009 Whitehaven Street NW, Washington, DC 20008-3613; phone (202) 238-2828; Web site www.brasilemb.org.

CultureGrams™
People. The World. You.

1305 North Research Way, Bldg. K
Orem, Utah 84097-6200 USA
1.800.528.6279; 801.705.4250
fax 801.705.4350
www.culturegrams.com

Republic of
Bulgaria

Boundary representations are not necessarily authoritative.

▼ EUROPE

BACKGROUND

Land and Climate.   Slightly larger than Tennessee, Bulgaria covers 42,823 square miles (110,910 square kilometers). Much of the terrain is mountainous; the Rila Mountains in the south are the highest on the Balkan Peninsula. The northern and central regions are dominated by plains. To the east lies the Black Sea. The northern border is the Danube River, which separates Bulgaria from Romania. The climate is similar to that of the U.S. corn belt, with cold, damp winters and hot, dry summers. Northern regions tend to be colder than southern ones.

History.   Thracians are the oldest known inhabitants of the area now called Bulgaria. They founded the Odrisaw Kingdom in the fifth century B.C. Slavic tribes began migrating to the area several hundred years later. In the seventh century A.D., Bulgars (a Central Asian people) migrated to the area and mixed with the Slavs and Thracians. A Bulgarian state was recognized by the Byzantine Empire in 681. Two Bulgarian kingdoms existed before Bulgaria was conquered by the Ottoman Turks in 1396. The period that followed is known in Bulgaria as the "Turkish yoke." The struggle for political and religious independence gave rise to a cultural renaissance at the end of the 18th century. The Ottomans ruled until 1878, when Bulgaria became independent as a result of the Russian-Turkish War. It was briefly divided into the Kingdom of Bulgaria (to the north) and Eastern Romelia (to the south). Eastern Romelia remained part of the Ottoman Empire until it was reunited with Bulgaria in 1885. Until 1944, this was the period of the Third Bulgarian Kingdom.

Allied with Germany in World Wars I and II, Bulgaria was twice defeated. Communists seized control in 1944 and con-

solidated power when Soviet troops marched into the country later that year. The monarchy was abolished by referendum in 1946. The prominent Bulgarian Communist leader, Georgi Dimitrov, who had been a national hero against the Nazis in World War II, died in 1949. The 1947 constitution was named after him.

In 1956, Todor Zhivkov came to power, first as Communist Party chief and later as prime minister. His authority remained unquestioned until a 1989 palace coup removed him as reforms swept through Eastern Europe. The Communists (renamed the Socialists) won free elections in 1990 but had trouble forming a stable government. A new constitution was approved in 1991, and subsequent elections established a multiparty parliament. Zhelyu Zhelev, a popular former dissident, was reelected president in 1992. The government worked to privatize industry, liquidate collective farms, and return property confiscated in 1948 to its owners or heirs. Petar Stoyanov of the Union of Democratic Forces (UDF) was elected president in November 1996.

In 1996, mass protests against the government's failed economic policies forced Socialist prime minister Zhan Videnov to resign more than a year early. UDF leader Ivan Kostov became prime minister in 1997, ending years of Socialist rule. Kostov enjoys broad support in spite of harsh economic conditions brought on by efforts to stabilize the currency. Chief government goals include economic growth, prevention of widespread organized crime and corruption, and membership in the North Atlantic Treaty Organization (NATO). In 1999, Bulgaria settled a long dispute with Macedonia over official recognition of Macedonian as a distinct language. The settlement has opened up the way for economic, political, and military cooperation.

Bulgaria was invited to start European Union (EU) accession talks in 2000 but must undertake substantial economic and political reform before membership will be granted. The government continues to work toward reducing corruption and increasing privatization.

THE PEOPLE

Population. Bulgaria's population of 7.8 million is shrinking by 1.2 percent per year. Most (83 percent) are ethnic Bulgarians. Of the rest of the population, 8.5 percent are Turks, 2.6 percent are Romany (Gypsies), and 2.5 percent are Macedonians. Armenians, Jews, Russians, and other groups also inhabit Bulgaria in small numbers. Sofia, the capital, has more than one million residents and is the largest city. Most people (69 percent) live in urban areas. In general, Bulgarians have only limited access to economic prosperity and opportunities for personal advancement.

Language. The official language is Bulgarian, and nearly all inhabitants speak it. About half of the Turkish population speaks Turkish as its native tongue, but most also speak Bulgarian. Bulgarian is a Slavic language that uses an alphabet first developed in the ninth century by Cyril and Methodius. The Cyrillic alphabet preceded, and is similar to, the Russian alphabet. Russian was previously a required subject in school, so many people can speak it, but Bulgarian is the language of instruction. English, German, and French are the most popular languages to study.

Religion. The Bulgarian Orthodox Church claims a membership of more than 83 percent of all Bulgarians. Muslims make up about 13 percent of the population. Orthodox monasteries are held in high regard for their religious and artistic significance. Many monasteries and churches contain frescoes and icons of significant historical value.

While religious worship was discouraged during the Communist era, it is relatively unrestricted today. Religious holidays are now openly celebrated throughout the country. Rural people and the older generation are more devout in attending services, but the urban youth also are showing an interest in religion. Traditional religious organizations registered with the government enjoy broad freedoms. Animosity toward outside groups has led to some restrictions on the existence and activities of foreign sects.

General Attitudes. Bulgarians generally respect those who are open, strong, capable, gregarious, good-humored, loyal to family and friends, and forthright. Group concerns and families are very important and play a role in individual decisions. Education is also highly valued.

Bulgarians take considerable pride in their heritage and culture, which have been preserved despite centuries of foreign domination. They are particularly sensitive about Ottoman rule. Democracy has always been important to Bulgarians. In fact, the 1879 constitution was one of the most progressive in Europe at the time. People are interested in politics, both domestic and international, and try to be well-informed. Political discussions are popular. Art and science are appreciated.

Bulgarians face many challenges during the transition to democracy. Most people are cautious about the future due to current economic hardships. The youth view the United States as a wealthy and fortunate country, and they also look to Western Europe as a model for their own development. At the same time, many older adults are wary of "foreign" influences in Bulgaria and oppose "non-Bulgarian" ideas or items. An entrepreneurial spirit is emerging, but businesspeople are not admired on a personal level. In the past, wealthy people could only be so through corruption and organized crime, so negative attitudes toward them still exist. Honest, private businesspeople have to work hard to gain respect and be regarded in a positive light. Bulgarians also are strengthening a work ethic that was weakened during the Communist years of guaranteed employment. Careers and professional skills are becoming more important.

Personal Appearance. European and U.S. American fashions are popular, but clothing is expensive. Many women knit sweaters for themselves and their families, and most people include sweaters in their wardrobe. Women are more concerned with their appearance than men, always making an effort to be well dressed and well-groomed in public. They may wear something more casual at home to keep nicer clothing in good condition. Professional women usually wear a skirt, a blouse or sweater, and high heels to work. Clothing is neatly pressed; wrinkled items rarely are seen in public. Sneakers may be worn with jogging suits or other outfits. Young women wear blue jeans and either a sweater or a shirt with buttons. Older rural women often wear a house dress, sweater, and scarf with conservative shoes.

Professional men wear suits and ties to work, although older men prefer trousers and sweaters. Young men wear jeans, denim or sport jackets, flannel shirts, and sneakers or loafers. Young children are considered the best-dressed people in the country, wearing imported clothing and newly hand-knit items. Hats, boots, scarves, gloves, and winter jackets or fur coats are worn during the cold winters.

CUSTOMS AND COURTESIES

Greetings. When meeting, Bulgarians usually shake hands. The handshake might be accompanied in formal situations by *Kak ste?* (How are you?) or *Zdraveite* (Hello). Friends, relatives, and colleagues use the informal terms for these greetings: *Kak si?* and *Zdrasti* or *Zdrave*. Close female friends might kiss on the cheek. People do not shake hands when saying *Dobro utro* (Good morning), *Dober den* (Good day), *Dober vetcher* (Good evening), or *Leka nosht* (Good night). They use first names in informal settings but otherwise address others by title and family name. *Gospodin* (Mr.), *Gospozha* (Mrs.), or *Gospozhitsa* (Miss) are common titles, but professional titles are used also. When one joins a small gathering, it is polite to greet each person individually, beginning with the women or the elderly.

Dovishdane (Till I see you again) is a common parting phrase. Friends might also say *Vsichko hubavo* (All the best) or *Ciao* (Good-bye). Urban people do not usually greet strangers passing on the street, but this is considered polite in rural areas.

Gestures. "Yes" is indicated by shaking the head from side to side, and "no" is expressed with one or two nods. One might shake the index finger back and forth to emphasize the "no" and even add a "tsk" sound to express displeasure. In conversation, people generally do not use hand gestures, but they often touch each other. Female friends might walk arm in arm down the street. Pointing with the index finger is rude. It is impolite for men to cross an ankle over the knee or for anyone to put feet on furniture. One should ask permission of other passengers before lowering a bus or train window.

Visiting. Visiting (*na gosti*) is an important part of Bulgarian life. Friends and neighbors commonly drop by for a short visit without prior arrangement, but more typically, an invitation is extended. Hosting friends for afternoon coffee and cake is popular, as is inviting them over for dinner. People often socialize at a café. Outdoor cafés provide opportunities to spend warm summer evenings visiting.

Women guests usually enter the home before men. Many Bulgarians remove their shoes upon entering, unless the hosts object. Slippers might be offered, or guests wear their stockings. Hosts usually offer refreshments and a drink; alcohol is rarely served without food. Invited guests often bring flowers (odd numbers only; even numbers are for funerals) for the hostess, a bottle of alcohol for the host, or chocolates. When visiting a newborn baby, people bring only odd numbers of gifts (even numbers bring bad luck), but they do not visit without an invitation.

Evening visits usually start after 8 p.m. and may last until after midnight (until 3 a.m. for special occasions). Bulgarians enjoy showing hospitality to guests and having long conversations, so leaving early is rude.

Eating. In addition to three meals a day, Bulgarians might have a midmorning snack and afternoon coffee. Breakfast is usually light, consisting of coffee and a cheese-filled pastry or some other bread product (sweet roll, toast, etc.). *Boza* (a malt-based drink) is a typical breakfast beverage. Traditionally, the main meal is eaten at midday. It consists of soup and/or salad, a main course, and dessert. When family schedules conflict with the traditional mealtime, people eat a lighter lunch—at a fast-food establishment, kiosk, or café, if not at home—and eat their main family meal after 7 p.m. If dinner is not the main meal, it is light and consists of some of the same foods as lunch, but not soup or dessert. Salads are eaten from a common platter with individual forks.

The continental style of eating is most common, with the fork in the left hand and the knife in the right. It is polite for guests to accept second helpings. An empty plate and glass will usually be refilled. A small amount of food left on the plate (usually after second helpings) indicates one is full. Conversation is expected, and everyone waits for all to finish before leaving the table. Meals for special occasions can include several courses and last many hours. Toasting (*Nazdravey*) is done at the beginning and throughout a meal; people maintain eye contact when clinking glasses during a toast.

Bulgarians generally eat at home, but some new restaurants have opened. Bills are paid at the table. *Mehana*, a traditional Bulgarian eating establishment, is still common throughout the country; it features traditional food, folk music, and dancing. Fast-food establishments are uncommon in Bulgaria except in major cities.

LIFESTYLE

Family. The family unit is strong and supportive of its members. Women usually work and take care of household responsibilities. Adult children often care for the elderly. Unmarried adults live with their parents until they marry. Young couples often live with one set of parents until they are able to get

housing for themselves. Most urban families live in apartments, which now are more plentiful, but expensive. Rural families usually have their own homes. Many village homes are owned by urban families, who use them for summer retreats, for retired parents, and for keeping family gardens or farms. Bulgarians still feel tied to their agricultural heritage.

Most families do not have more than two children. Some women may receive three years of maternity leave, two of which are paid. Because urban women usually work outside the home, grandmothers play an important role in child care. Men traditionally do not help with household duties, but the younger generation is assuming greater responsibilities.

Dating and Marriage. The youth associate in groups at first, but they may also date one-on-one while teenagers. Favorite activities involve getting together at a café to drink and talk, going to a movie, dancing at a disco, or relaxing in the park. Most Bulgarians expect to marry and have children. The average age for women to marry is between 18 and 25. Rural men marry in their mid- or late twenties and urban men in their thirties.

Weddings involve big celebrations and can be very expensive, which is one reason many wait so long to get married. A legal civil ceremony often is followed by a church wedding. A big reception is held in the evening. Folk music, dancing, and eating are common at the reception. Many traditions are kept by families, including filling the empty shoe of the bride with money to "steal" or "buy" her and having the bride and groom pull on opposite ends of a loaf of bread (whoever gets the largest piece will be the boss of the family). Newlyweds only now are beginning to go on honeymoons.

Diet. Bulgarians eat pork, chicken, fish, or lamb with most main dishes. Dairy products such as yogurt and cheese are common ingredients in many dishes. Popular main meals include *moussaka* (a casserole with pork or lamb, potatoes, tomatoes, and yogurt) and *nadenitsa* (stuffed pork sausage). *Kufteta* is a fried meat patty mixed with bread crumbs. *Sarmi* is a pepper or cabbage stuffed with pork and rice. Grilled meat (*skara*), such as *shishcheta* (a pork shish kebab), is popular, especially in restaurants. *Shopska salata* is a salad made with *cirene* (Bulgarian feta cheese), cucumbers, and tomatoes. A favorite cold soup is *tarator*, which includes cucumbers, yogurt, garlic, dill, walnuts, and oil. Cheese *banitsa* (a layered pastry) is eaten as a snack or for breakfast, while pumpkin *banitsa* is a popular dessert. Various cakes and *baklava* (a thin, leafy pastry with syrup and a nut filling) are also enjoyed for dessert. Coffee is usually either espresso or Turkish style. Meals usually are accompanied by a soft drink, alcohol, or coffee.

Recreation. People generally enjoy being out in nature, hiking, walking, or touring in the countryside. Soccer and basketball are popular sports. Volleyball is played by men and women at parks, clubs, and gyms. Skiing is a popular luxury in Sofia. August is the favorite time to go to the beach on the Black Sea. Summer vacations also typically include a trip to the mountains. Many professional organizations, schools, and local governments own lodges in the mountains where their members can stay for minimal cost. Urban youth have access to recreation centers. U.S. American movies are quite popular.

The Arts. Bulgarians enjoy folk music. Traditional instruments include the *kaval* (a type of flute) and the *gaida* (a bagpipe).

▼ **EUROPE**

Bulgaria

The *chalga*, a mix of Turkish, Romany, and Serbian music, is becoming more popular and is sung in Bulgarian. Festivals held throughout the year highlight various aspects of traditional Bulgarian culture. Urban dwellers enjoy the performing arts, and even small towns have a local theater.

Pottery, woodworking, and leatherworking are prominent. Government and educational institutions encourage both fine and applied arts.

Holidays. Public holidays include New Year's Day, National Day of Freedom and Independence (3 Mar.), Easter, the Day of Bulgarian Culture and Science (24 May), and Christmas Day (25 Dec.). On 24 May, Saints Cyril and Methodius are honored for developing the Cyrillic alphabet, but the country's accomplishments in science and culture are celebrated also. Name days (*immen den*) are celebrated with a family meal.

A popular Easter tradition is to go to the church at midnight, light candles, and walk around the church three times. Also, family and friends decorate eggs and knock them against each other to see whose egg will break last.

The most celebrated season stretches from Christmas Eve to New Year's Day. On Christmas Eve, products of the soil (no meat) are eaten to represent a successful past harvest and wish for a good future harvest. On New Year's Day, people eat a large meal and exchange presents. They often decorate a tree. Children go door-to-door wishing good fortune to friends and relatives, carrying with them a small decorated stick (*survachka*), with which they tap people they visit on the back in exchange for candy and money.

On 1 March, Bulgarians celebrate spring with *Martenitza*. People exchange red-and-white yarn designs to symbolize health. They wear the yarn designs on their clothing until they see a stork or a blossoming tree. They then either put the *martenitza* on a tree branch to bring on spring or hide it under a rock to represent the wish that the evil spirits in nature (and humankind) will go to sleep.

Commerce. Offices are open from 9 a.m. to 6 p.m. in most cases, but private shops often have additional hours. Some businesses close for the midday meal. Many close by noon on Saturday, and most are closed on Sunday. A strong capitalist spirit exists, and entrepreneurs are turning their garages or vacant buildings into shops or other small enterprises. Bulgarians shop daily for bread and other fresh foods. They purchase dairy, meat, and shelf products from small stores and fresh produce at open-air markets. Selection is best on a designated weekly market day.

SOCIETY

Government. Bulgaria is a multiparty democracy. The president, currently Petur Stoyanov, is head of state. The prime minister is head of government. Members of the 240-seat National Assembly (*Narodno Sobranyie*) are elected directly by the people. The UDF has control of the National Assembly; the Socialist Party is in opposition. All citizens are eligible to vote at age 18.

Economy. Bulgaria's transition to a market economy has been difficult. A severe devaluation of Bulgaria's currency, the

DEVELOPMENT DATA

Human Dev. Index* rank .... 60 of 174 countries
   Adjusted for women .... 53 of 143 countries
Real GDP per capita $4,809
Adult literacy rate .... 98 percent
Infant mortality rate .... 15 per 1,000 births
Life expectancy .... 68 (male); 75 (female)

lev (Lv), and hyperinflation (300 percent) led the economy to the brink of collapse in early 1997. With the support of international lenders, the government undertook a strict monetary policy to curb inflation and stabilize its currency. This system has succeeded better than expected in reducing inflation. However, additional reforms are needed to revive the devastated economy. Large public debts, a lack of foreign investment, and a small private sector remain challenges. Most people struggle to meet their basic needs. Unemployment remains high.

Bulgaria exports agricultural products (grains, tobacco, wine, dairy foods) and some machinery. It imports consumer goods, food, and heavy machinery. War in Yugoslavia has severely hindered trade on the Danube River and soured prospects for foreign investors. Finding new markets for Bulgarian goods is essential to progress. Tourism is an important source of foreign capital but is still underdeveloped.

Transportation and Communications. Many people use the reliable public transportation system, which consists of buses, trams, trolleys, and trains. Most families own one car. Taxis are plentiful in urban areas.

Two national political newspapers and several private papers are increasing their circulation. Television broadcasts are changing rapidly, as U.S. American and European programming is becoming more popular. Telephone service is expensive and not fully developed.

Education. Education, compulsory to age 15, was once free at all levels. Extreme financial pressures have even led primary schools to charge some fees. Science and technical training are stressed in school, but the lack of modern equipment hampers advanced training. Entrance to secondary schools is determined by competitive exam, and urban students often can choose from five types of schools, each offering a different focus (such as math and science or foreign languages). A number of universities and three-year training institutions offer higher education.

Health. A national health-care system provides free medical care to all citizens, but facilities often are not well equipped. Also, drugs and medical testing are expensive. Private doctors offer better care to those who can pay for it.

CONTACT INFORMATION

Embassy of Bulgaria, 1621 22d Street NW, Washington, DC 20008; phone (202) 387-0174; Web site www.bulgaria-embassy.org. Balkan Tourist USA, 20 East 46th Street, Suite 1003, New York, NY 10017; phone (800) 822-1106.

CultureGrams™
People. The World. You.

1305 North Research Way, Bldg. K
Orem, Utah 84097-6200 USA
1.800.528.6279; 801.705.4250
fax 801.705.4350
www.culturegrams.com

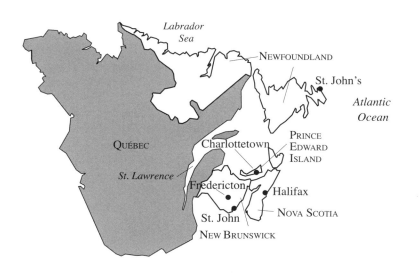

Boundary representations are not necessarily authoritative.

▼ **THE AMERICAS**

BACKGROUND

Land and Climate. Canada is the second largest country in the world, after Russia. It covers 3,851,788 square miles (9,976,085 square kilometers). The combined area of the Atlantic Provinces is a bit smaller than Texas and covers only 5 percent of Canada's total land area. Although Canada's four easternmost provinces are referred to as Atlantic Canada, three of them—New Brunswick, Prince Edward Island, and Nova Scotia—are also called the Maritime Provinces. Newfoundland, the fourth province, includes the mainland area of Labrador.

The region offers plateaus, valleys, and rocky coasts. The Maritimes terrain is fairly low and flat, although the Appalachian Mountains extend into northern New Brunswick (elevations up to 2,500 feet or 762 meters). The Cape Breton Highlands in Nova Scotia reach 1,700 feet (518 meters). Newfoundland has many low hills; the Long Range Mountains in the west reach 2,500 feet (762 meters). Prince Edward Island, also known as the Garden of the Gulf, has excellent soil, as do lowland pockets in Nova Scotia and the Upper Saint John Valley in New Brunswick. Eighty-five percent of New Brunswick is covered by forest. There is little farmland in Newfoundland and none in Labrador.

The area is generally subject to a humid continental climate, although the coast of Newfoundland experiences a subarctic effect from the Labrador Current. Winters are cold; summers are warm and humid. Coastal fog is common in spring and summer. During January, daily high temperatures average 0°F to 20°F (-18 to -7°C) in Labrador and 20°F to 40°F (-7 to 4°C) in the south. In July, daily highs average 50°F to 70°F (10–21°C) in Labrador and 65°F to

80°F (18–27°C) in the south. Labrador has a much more severe climate than the rest of Atlantic Canada and consequently is only sparsely settled.

History. Early native peoples included the Inuit and Inn (in Labrador), Beothuk (Newfoundland), Micmac or *Mi'kmaq* (the Maritimes and Newfoundland), and Malecite (New Brunswick) groups. The first Europeans were likely Vikings from Greenland who settled briefly in Newfoundland. Basque, Breton, and English fishers came to fish cod in the 1500s. In 1605, the French established a fur-trading post in Nova Scotia and began to settle the Maritimes region, which they called *L'Acadie* (Acadia).

The British began to gain control of the region in the 1700s, acquiring mainland Nova Scotia in 1710 and the rest of the Maritimes in 1758. Because the Acadians were not trusted by the English, many were forced to leave the region in the 1750s for other parts of North America. Acadians were among the first people to settle in Louisiana, and the term *Cajun* is derived from the word *Acadian*. Acadians were allowed to return (and did so) after 1764; however, many of their original lands had been settled by the New England Planters and other British settlers. At about the same time, British Loyalists who left the 13 colonies after the American Revolution had also begun settling in the area.

Most of the Maritimes remained a part of the colony of Nova Scotia until the 1780s. The Loyalist province of New Brunswick became a separate colony in 1784. Throughout the 1800s, all four provinces were engaged in trade with the West Indies, sending salted or smoked fish and receiving sugar and rum. Most of the British Empire's wooden ships were built in this region. The coal field area of Nova Scotia boomed in the late 1800s and early 1900s.

In 1867, the British North America Act created the Dominion of Canada out of Nova Scotia, New Brunswick, and a colony called Canada (present-day Québec and Ontario). Prince Edward Island did not join until 1873, and Newfoundland remained a separate colony until 1949. Canada has retained both formal and informal ties with Britain since becoming a Confederation. Although Queen Elizabeth II is the official head of state, Britain has had no control over Canada since constitutional changes made in 1982. A Charter of Rights and Freedoms also was established in 1982 guaranteeing fundamental human rights to all Canadians.

Regional fishing economies were dealt a serious blow in 1992 when, due to dwindling resources, the federal government banned cod fishing—the traditional occupation of Newfoundland and Cape Breton Island (Nova Scotia). The moratorium and other factors have led to forced closures of fishing ports, emigration, and high regional unemployment rates. In early 1998, Newfoundland's unemployment rate exceeded 17 percent. Relations between the provincial and federal governments have not always been smooth. Residents of the Atlantic region have felt in the past that the federal government has not done enough to stimulate economic development in their area; many young people leave the area to find jobs.

THE PEOPLE

Population. Canada's population is 31.28 million. The combined population of the four provinces of Atlantic Canada comprises almost 8 percent of that total, or 2.38 million, and is growing slowly. Emigration is a problem in some areas. The population density is moderately high in the Maritimes, low in Newfoundland, and very low in Labrador. Atlantic Canada's largest cities include Halifax, NS (356,000); Saint John's, NF (175,100); and Saint John, NB (127,700).

The ethnic origins of the people are basically French and British, with the latter having come mostly from New England and the mid-Atlantic States (the Planters and Loyalists) or from Scotland and Ireland. The French are concentrated in New Brunswick, while more than 95 percent of the people of Newfoundland are of British descent. The Micmac are the region's largest native or "First-nation" group. They number about 15,000; most live on reserves in the Maritimes. The region is also home to African-Canadian descendants of black slaves who fled the United States.

Language. English and French are official languages in Canada. French is a key language in New Brunswick and is spoken as a first language by about 32 percent its citizens (33 percent of the province is bilingual). Most others in Atlantic Canada speak English as their first language—even those of non-British descent. State-funded schools are mostly English, although French school boards are present in Acadian areas. Canadian spelling of English words follows U.S. standards in some cases (e.g., *organize* rather than *organise*) but British standards in others (*centre*, not *center*), and Canadians call the last letter of the alphabet *zed*, not *zee*.

Religion. Religious beliefs in Canada follow traditional lines. Those of French, Irish, and highland Scottish descent are mostly Roman Catholic (as are native peoples). Most others are Protestant, belonging primarily to the United Church, Baptist, and Anglican churches. Traditional religions remain strong in rural areas, with most people attending church regularly. Evangelical churches are growing at the expense of other churches.

General Attitudes. Most Canadians are proud of their cultural heritage, which includes French, British, and other European influences. Atlantic Canadians are considered conservative and traditional, due in part to their rural heritage. They see themselves as hardworking, unpretentious people who value nature, community involvement, and education. They believe their unique sense of humor and rural values set them apart. Due to economic difficulties in the region, they approach their future with cautious optimism and a will to preserve their way of life.

Regional and provincial allegiances are strong among Atlantic Canadians and often are placed before national allegiance. Newfoundlanders, in particular, see themselves (and are viewed) as different from other Canadians. Shared adversity and isolation have helped people maintain a strong sense of community and regional identity. This can also mean that strangers are not easily accepted. In larger cities, particularly Halifax, people are more cosmopolitan.

Personal Appearance. Although their dress habits are very similar to those of U.S. Americans, Atlantic Canadians are somewhat more conservative and less casual in their attire. For example, people may wear jogging suits for recreational purposes but not for shopping or visiting. It is polite to remove sunglasses when speaking to someone and to remove hats in buildings.

CUSTOMS AND COURTESIES

Greetings. Because the people of the Atlantic Provinces have various cultural backgrounds, greetings vary from place to place. A firm handshake is the most common greeting. Nodding the head may replace handshaking in informal situations. French-speaking people often are more outgoing and open than those of British descent. They might greet friends and relatives with a light kiss on the cheek. Common French greetings include *Bonjour* (Good day), *Ça va?* (How's it going?), and *Tu vas bien?* (How are you doing?). Common for English speakers are *Hi*, *Good morning*, *How are you?*, and *How's she going?* (Newfoundland).

When one passes a stranger on the street, a smile and a nod are appropriate. Rural people also often greet the person verbally, but this is less common in large cities. People use first names when addressing others in informal situations or when the more senior person requests it. Titles are used with new acquaintances and on formal occasions.

Gestures. Most gestures, positive and negative, are the same in Canada as in the United States. However, some gestures common in the United States might be offensive to a specific cultural group or in a particular area. Pointing at someone with the index finger is rude; using the entire hand to motion to someone is more polite. Eye contact is important when talking to another person. French speakers use hand gestures somewhat more often than do others during conversation. Atlantic Canadians usually stand farther apart than U.S. Americans when speaking to each other.

Visiting. Atlantic Canadians enjoy visiting with one another. Close friends might drop by unannounced, but most visits are arranged in advance, especially in urban areas. Dropping by during regular mealtimes is impolite. Hosts generally offer guests refreshments, including at least a drink and often a small snack. Not offering something would be rude. Refreshments are considered an unspoken invitation to stay a while. Dinner guests may be offered appetizers and a drink before the meal. It is appropriate for them to bring a gift, such as wine or chocolate and sometimes flowers, to the hosts. This is especially true if the guests are not related to the hosts. It is best to offer to remove street shoes upon entering a home. House parties, with alcoholic drinks and impromptu music (known as *ceilidh* in Scottish areas), are popular in both rural and urban areas.

Eating. The standard three meals per day are often complemented by afternoon tea and coffee breaks or snacks at work. Tea is popular among those of English heritage. It is important for the family to eat the evening meal (*supper*) together when possible. In some rural areas, the main family meal is at midday. People avoid talking with food in their mouth or placing their elbows or arms on the table. Leaving food on the plate is impolite; taking second helpings is a way to compliment the hosts on the food. Tipping is generally 10 to 15 percent.

LIFESTYLE

Family. Family lifestyles are similar to those elsewhere in North America. While the family unit is the center of society, both parents commonly work outside the home. Traditional norms are still valued, particularly in rural areas, but nontraditional households have increased considerably over the last 30 years. A high proportion of children are now born out of wedlock and there are many single-parent families. The average family size is comparable to that in the United States, but the divorce rate is lower. Children often live with their parents until they marry.

Dating and Marriage. Dating and marriage customs are similar to those in the United States. Dating usually begins around age 13. The youth enjoy going to movies, eating out, going to the beach, and attending sporting events such as hockey games. People generally marry in their twenties. Wedding traditions depend on a couple's religious affiliation.

Diet. Fish and seafood are important to the diet. The most commonly eaten seafoods include haddock, mackerel, mussels, and clams. Lobster is a favorite but is expensive and reserved for special occasions. Cod was a traditional staple in Newfoundland but now is rarely eaten. A main meal might consist of meat (chicken, beef, or pork) or fish, a vegetable, potatoes, dessert, and a drink. Despite a short growing season, fresh fruits are common, including apples and a variety of berries. Fruit pies are popular in season. Prince Edward Island is famous for growing 70 different types of potatoes. Dairy products are consumed in fairly large quantities. *Donair*, popular throughout the region, is pita bread stuffed with meat and sauce.

Acadian cuisine is somewhat different. A favorite Acadian dish is *rappée* pie (made with grated potato and ground meat). Newfoundland's dishes are also distinctive (e.g., cod-tongues, cod-cheeks, and boiled dinners).

Recreation. People enjoy participating in fishing, hunting, golf, soccer, ice and street hockey, baseball, and candlepin bowling. Popular spectator sports include ice hockey, college football and basketball, and *curling*. Since the Atlantic Ocean surrounds many of these provinces, lobster cookouts

and beach parties are common social events. In their leisure time, people enjoy gardening, hiking, fishing, and other outdoor activities. Spending weekends at summer cottages is popular. People also like to visit, shop, watch television, and read.

The Arts. Art galleries and museums are numerous, as are local art groups. Galleries display the works of local fine artists and artisans. Popular crafts include pottery and quilting. Many old churches are popular centers of attraction, as they symbolize the people's heritage. Contemporary architecture follows modern trends.

The ocean greatly influences Atlantic Canadian songs, art, poetry, and prose as well as folk festivals and other community events. Dance and music festivals with a Scottish flavor are common in *Nova Scotia* (New Scotland); other areas hold Irish and Acadian events. Prince Edward Island, birthplace of Lucy Maud Montgomery (author of *Anne of Green Gables*), is a popular destination for those interested in seeing sites associated with her books.

Holidays. Official Canadian holidays include New Year's Day, Easter, Victoria Day (third Monday in May), Canada Day (1 July), Labour Day (first Monday in September), Thanksgiving Day (second Monday in October), Remembrance Day (11 Nov.), Christmas, and Boxing Day (26 Dec.). Boxing Day is a day to visit friends and relatives. It comes from the old British tradition of presenting small boxed gifts to service employees. In addition to public holidays, annual local festivals are held throughout the region to commemorate everything from the shrimp harvest to military battles to cultural heritage. Most cities and towns also have a civic holiday, usually in August.

Commerce. Business hours are similar to those in the United States. Offices generally are open weekdays between 9 a.m. and 5 p.m. Stores usually open at 9:30 a.m. and close at either 6 or 9 p.m. Most retail shopping occurs in supermarkets and suburban shopping malls; retailing in some downtown areas remains vital. Most stores close on Sunday, except for convenience stores or shops in tourist areas.

SOCIETY

Government. Canada is a confederation with a parliamentary democracy; its government is patterned partly after Great Britain's but also has a federal system like that of the United States. The federal government is responsible for national defense and external relations, the banking system, the criminal code, and the aboriginal populations. The provinces are responsible for education, health care, the creation and regulation of municipalities, and for the social welfare system. The greater resources of the federal government have led to its involvement in matters originally provincial (e.g., employment, insurance, medicare, and in some provinces, policing). Each province has a one-chamber legislature; the leader of the dominant political party is the province's premier.

Canada's federal Parliament comprises an appointed Senate (as many as 104 senators), which only rarely exercises its full powers, and an elected House of Commons (301 members), which is the real legislative power. The prime minister, who heads the government and requires the support of the House of Commons to remain in office, is the de facto chief executive. Ceremonial duties of the head of state are performed by the governor-general, currently Adrienne Clarkson, who represents Queen Elizabeth II. The Liberals maintained power in the November 2000 elections, retaining Jean Chrétien as Canada's prime minister for a third term. Parliamentary elections are held at least every five years but may be called at any time. The voting age is 18.

The two major parties in the Atlantic provinces are the Progressive Conservatives (Tories) and the Liberals. Traditionally, they have alternated in power. The Liberal vote is strongest in Acadian and urban areas; the Tories are strongest in rural anglophone areas. The socialist New Democratic Party has strong support in some urban areas.

Economy. Overall, Canada has one of the strongest economies in the world. It is a world leader in the production of gold, uranium, silver, copper, oil, natural gas, agriculture, and in the supply of wood pulp and timber-related products. In 1993, Canada signed the North American Free Trade Agreement (NAFTA) with Mexico and the United States. NAFTA provides for freer movement of capital and goods, more cross-national investment, and a large market for many goods from each country. The Canadian economy grew by 3 percent in 2000; inflation remains low. National unemployment is almost 7 percent, but in the Atlantic Provinces it is much higher, ranging from about 16 percent in Newfoundland to around 9 percent in Nova Scotia.

Although most Canadians benefit from the country's general economic prosperity, about 12 percent of the population lives in human poverty.* This reflects a lack of access to health care, education, and economic prosperity needed to make choices in their lives. The currency is the Canadian dollar (Can$). Canadians refer to it as the *loonie*, after the image of the waterbird (the loon) minted on the gold-colored coin.

The four Atlantic provinces have suffered economically for most of the 20th century. Their economies traditionally have relied upon the region's resource-oriented export industries: fishing, forestry and forest products (e.g., pulp and paper), mining, and agriculture. Federal cod fishing limits (begun in 1992) continue to adversely affect Atlantic Canada's economies; cod fishing is permitted for personal consumption but not for commercial purposes. Nova Scotia's coal mining industry has declined significantly in the past few decades; non-coal mines have closed in New Brunswick. Employment in agriculture is decreasing throughout the Maritimes.

Current efforts to tap offshore petroleum resources are expected to increase revenue in the region. Tourism has become increasingly important, particularly in the Halifax region, Cape Breton Island, and PEI. Large hydroelectric power stations are located in Labrador and Newfoundland. Most people work in the service sector. Manufacturing, food processing, and construction also are important. Halifax is the regional financial center.

Transportation and Communications. Ferries are commonly used in the Atlantic Provinces; scheduled ferries link islands with the mainland. Major cities have bus systems. Private cars are an important mode of transportation. Air

DEVELOPMENT DATA

Human Dev. Index* rank	1 of 174 countries
Adjusted for women	1 of 143 countries
Real GDP per capita	$23,582
Adult literacy rate	99 percent
Infant mortality rate	5 per 1,000 births
Life expectancy	76 (male); 82 (female)

transport is increasingly important: Halifax is the regional hub. Communications systems are well developed; the vast majority of Canadians have telephones and televisions. Numerous cable-television systems provide service to all segments of the population. The Canadian Broadcasting Corporation (CBC) produces radio and TV programming at various centers in the region, particularly Halifax and St. John's. The major cities all have daily newspapers.

Education. Each province is responsible for its own educational system. Education begins at age 5 or 6 and is compulsory to age 16. Primary and secondary education is free. Newfoundland voters rejected their public-denominational system (in which schools are operated by different religious groups) in favor of nondenominational school boards, as used in the Maritimes. Separate French- and English-language school boards operate in parts of Nova Scotia and New Brunswick.

All four provinces have publicly supported universities, the largest being Memorial University of Newfoundland, the University of New Brunswick, and Dalhousie University in Nova Scotia. There are about 10 smaller universities (often with religious affiliations), including two French-language universities. About 30 percent of college-age people earn university degrees. Each province also operates one or more community colleges. Functional adult literacy is about 90 percent.

Health. Although Canadians generally enjoy very good health, Atlantic Canadians are somewhat less healthy. For example, about 30 percent of the people smoke, and almost half are overweight. Hospitals and quality of care are excellent. Canada has a compulsory national health insurance that covers doctors' fees and most hospital costs for all Canadians. Health insurance is funded by taxes and premiums collected by the federal and provincial governments but is administered by the provinces. Many people have supplementary private health insurance.

CONTACT INFORMATION

Canada's Atlantic Coast, 2695 Dutch Village Road, Suite 501, Halifax, NS B3L 4V2; phone (800) 565-2627; Web site www.canadacoast.com. Canadian Consulate General, 1251 Avenue of the Americas, New York, NY 10020; phone (212) 596-1628; Web site www.canada-ny.org. Embassy of Canada, 501 Pennsylvania Avenue NW, Washington, DC 20001; phone (202) 682-1740; Web site www.canadianembassy.org/splash.

CultureGrams™
People. The World. You.

1305 North Research Way, Bldg. K
Orem, Utah 84097-6200 USA
1.800.528.6279; 801.705.4250
fax 801.705.4350
www.culturegrams.com

Boundary representations are not necessarily authoritative.

▼ THE AMERICAS

BACKGROUND

Land and Climate.   Canada is the second largest country in the world, after Russia, covering 3,851,788 square miles (9,976,085 square kilometers). Much of the north (including parts of the Yukon, Nunavut, and Northwest Territories) is uninhabited due to the arctic climate and permanently frozen ground. Most of the population lives within 100 miles (161 kilometers) of the U.S. border. Although the Great Lakes moderate the climate of southern Ontario, freezing temperatures and snow are common in the winter; summers can be hot and humid. Northern Ontario, like the Prairie Provinces, has shorter and drier summers and very cold winters. The southern prairies of Manitoba, Saskatchewan, and Alberta are flat and vast; the northern portions of these provinces are characterized by forests and eventually tundra. British Columbia varies from the wet, mild climate of the southern coast to the near-desert conditions of the interior of the province. Beautiful scenery can be found in every region: from lakes and Niagara Falls in Ontario, to national parks and the towering Rocky Mountains in western Alberta, to British Columbia's mountains and coastline.

History.   The earliest European settlers in today's Canada were French colonists in the 1600s who established settlements along the Saint Lawrence River in the territory they called New France. Britain fought with France throughout the 1600s for the territory, and in 1763, the Treaty of Paris gave Britain control over New France, which it renamed Québec. In 1791, Québec was divided into two provinces, Ontario and Québec, and in 1867—along with the provinces of New Brunswick and Nova Scotia—they established the confederation that was named the Dominion of Canada. In 1876,

Canada purchased the vast northwestern area called Rupert's Land from the Hudson's Bay Company (a British trading company). This land became part of Canada and was divided into the provinces of Manitoba, Saskatchewan, Alberta, and the northern territories, now known as the Yukon, the Northwest Territories, and Nunavut. British Columbia joined as a province in 1871.

The Prairie Provinces (Manitoba, Saskatchewan, and Alberta) are known for the 1920s cooperative movement that significantly influenced the way communities organized financial, agricultural, insurance, and food distribution industries—a system that remains largely intact today. Saskatchewan was the birthplace of Canadian agrarian socialism, and it and Manitoba have long histories of electing democratic-socialist governments provincially.

Canada has retained both formal and informal ties with Britain since becoming a Confederation. Queen Elizabeth II is the official head of state; Britain has had no control over Canada since constitutional changes made in 1982. A Charter of Rights and Freedoms was also established in 1982 guaranteeing fundamental human rights to all.

The Western provinces traditionally have been at odds with the political establishment centered in Ontario and Québec. Ontario has generally supported more liberal political parties on the federal level—one reason why Pierre Trudeau, who died in September 2000, was prime minister for 15 years. The Prairie Provinces and British Columbia traditionally have been more conservative in federal elections, supporting governments such as the one led by Brian Mulroney's Progressive Conservative Party from 1988 to

1993. Elections in 1993 brought the Liberal Party to power. Jean Chrétien called elections one and a half years early and was elected to a third term as prime minister in November 2000. Improving health care remains his top priority.

In the west, self-government for First Nations (aboriginal peoples) and native land claims are important political issues. In the Northwest Territories, a vast but sparsely inhabited territory with a primarily native Inuit population has been created with a significant measure of self-government. First approved by Northwest Territory voters in 1992, *Nunavut* (which means "our land" in the Inuit language) became Canada's third territory in April 1999. Nunavut covers about two-thirds of the original Northwest Territories; the remaining one-third has retained its name and territorial status.

THE PEOPLE

Population. The total population of Canada is 31.28 million. Approximately 38 percent (11.7 million) of the people reside in Ontario, Canada's most heavily populated province. Nearly 30 percent (9.3 million) live in the combined region of the Prairie Provinces, British Columbia, and the Yukon, Nunavut, and Northwest Territories. Canada has one of the world's highest immigration rates and is one of the most culturally diverse countries. Ontario is populated not only by those of British and French descent but also by sizable Chinese, Italian, German, Portuguese, and Polish communities. Toronto has nearly 4.8 million residents. Large immigrant populations from Asia, the Caribbean, and Europe have added considerable diversity to the metropolis.

British Columbia was settled primarily by British and other European and U.S. American immigrants. The Prairies attracted many European nationalities in the 1800s. Only since the reform of Canada's immigration laws in the 1960s have immigrants from Asia and South Asia become a significant part of the Canadian population. Chinese now comprise 14 percent of the Vancouver region's two million people. Nearly three-fourths of immigrants to Canada settle in Toronto and Vancouver, two of the most culturally diverse cities in the world. Although there are native communities throughout Canada, about 80 percent are located in Ontario and Western Canada.

Language. Both English and French are official languages in Canada. French is the first language of 5 percent of the people in Ontario and Manitoba, but English dominates in these and all western provinces. In fact, in western provinces, less than 3 percent of the people are fluent in French, and many speak a language other than English or French as their native tongue (nearly one in five in the overall population). Among native groups, more than 50 languages are spoken.

Canadian spelling of English words follows U.S. standards in some cases (e.g., *organize* rather than *organise*) but British standards in others (*centre*, not *center*). Canadians call the last letter of the alphabet *zed*, not *zee*. In addition, Canadians have some unique phrases and idioms. For instance, *Eh* (pronounced *AE*) is used much like "Ya know" or "Isn't it?" is used in the United States.

Religion. Most Canadians are Christians, but the beliefs and doctrines of the different Christian churches are diverse, and society is highly secularized. The United Church (a union of Methodist, Congregationalist, and Presbyterian churches) has the largest membership in western provinces, followed by the Catholic, Anglican, Lutheran, and Presbyterian faiths. In Ontario, 29 percent of the people belong to the United Church, 25 percent are Roman Catholic, and 21 percent are Anglican. A number of other Christian churches are present, as well as various non-Christian denominations. A significant number of Muslim, Buddhist, Hindu, and Sikh religious groups are present in British Columbia. Vancouver has the largest Sikh community outside of the Punjab province of India.

General Attitudes. The people of Ontario are fairly reserved and formal, while those in the Prairie Provinces and British Columbia are more open and friendly. As Ontario contains large urban areas, life there is faster paced—similar to New York City—whereas the pace of life in the west is more relaxed. People take great pride in their individual provinces and heritage, as well as in being Canadian. Despite close ties and many similarities between their nation and the United States, Canadians emphasize they are not U.S.-type people just living in Canada. They consider themselves North Americans—not Americans. Canadians often see U.S. Americans as more aggressive and materialistic than themselves. They also feel they are more tolerant and community oriented than U.S. Americans, as well as more polite. For example, Canadians respond to *Thank you* with *You're welcome*, rather than with silence or some other phrase. Preserving Canadian culture against influence from the United States is important.

Canadians are known to be self-deprecating and have a sardonic sense of humor. They admire people who are well educated, skilled, modest, and polite. In relation to the rest of the world, Canadians see themselves as associated with fairness and humanitarianism. They consider themselves to be honest brokers in negotiations. Indeed, Canada frequently contributes troops to UN peacekeeping missions and relief operations. Canadians point proudly to the efforts of a former prime minister, Lester B. Pearson, who won the Nobel Peace Prize for advocating the use of peacekeeping forces in international conflicts.

Personal Appearance. Although dress habits are similar to those in the United States, the people are generally more conservative and somewhat more formal in their dress, especially when at work or in public. Men who wear hats remove them in buildings.

CUSTOMS AND COURTESIES

Greetings. A firm handshake and a sincere *Hello, how are you?* are the most common greetings when one meets new people. Otherwise, a wave of the hand or nod of the head are acceptable gestures when saying *Hello*. The majority of people in Ontario, the Prairie Provinces, British Columbia, and the Yukon and Northwest Territories speak English. In cities, it is not unusual to find people conversing in languages other than English. French greetings are common in cities near Québec with large French communities; Chinese greetings may be used in Vancouver among the ethnic Chinese minority. Still, in public situations people are expected to be able to converse in one of the two official languages (in most cases English).

Gestures. Most gestures, positive and negative, are the same in Canada as in the United States, but they do vary between ethnic groups. People often use hand gestures in conversation, but not excessively. Eye contact is important during conversation and smiles are always welcome. However, Canadian reserve dictates that a generous amount of personal space be protected when conversing with others. Also, casual conversations with clerks, servers, and other workers are kept to a minimum.

Visiting. Although Canadians get together often, unannounced visits are not common; it is considered polite to visit only when invited. In most areas, guests customarily remove their shoes when entering a home to avoid tracking in dirt. Guests follow the cue of the host or hostess. That is, if the host is fairly relaxed, guests are the same. Hosts usually offer refreshments, but refusing them is not necessarily impolite. Guests arriving in the morning may be offered coffee or tea and fruit or light pastries. The same foods, except for a heavier selection of sweets, may be offered to afternoon visitors. Evening visitors typically receive a drink (often wine) and light foods. Guests invited for a casual dinner commonly offer to help with preparations and/or bring part of the meal. It is polite to compliment the hostess on the meal. Reaching for items on the table is impolite. Houseguests staying for more than one day usually write a thank-you letter and either send or leave a thank-you gift. Promptness in showing gratitude is important.

Eating. Canadian eating habits tend to be a bit more formal than U.S. habits. Many people eat in the continental style, with the fork in the left hand and the knife remaining in the right. Canadians eat breakfast soon after they wake up each morning, lunch sometime between noon and 2 p.m., and dinner around 6 p.m. Mealtimes are later on weekends and holidays. Families eat their main meal together on most nights, although busy schedules sometimes prevent this. The main meal usually consists of an entrée, salad, and sometimes dessert. Children are taught not to place elbows on the table, to sit still while eating, and to say *Please* and *Thank you*. Food usually is placed on the table in serving dishes so family members can choose their own portions. Guests often are seated at the right of the host and are served first. They may decline second helpings without offending the cook. One places the utensils together on the plate after finishing a meal. Canadians tend to dress up when dining out (except at fast-food restaurants). Tipping about 15 percent is expected.

LIFESTYLE

Family. While the family unit is the center of society, both parents often work outside the home. Licensed day- and home-care facilities are widely available to assist working parents. Traditional norms have changed somewhat during the last decade; however, the father in a family usually takes the lead, while the mother exercises influence on all decisions. The mother also retains primary responsibility for household chores. The average family size is comparable to that in the United States. Families are close, although economic conditions (the need for employment) are causing relatives to move farther away from each other. This trend decreases daily contact between extended family members but encourages efforts such as family reunions to renew and preserve family ties. The number of single-parent homes is on the rise, creating a strain on social services. Outside large cities, most people (64 percent) own their home. Houses are of wood-frame construction, as in the United States.

Dating and Marriage. Dating usually begins between the ages of 14 and 16. Favorite activities include dancing and going to the movies. While most couples have a formal wedding, more than 10 percent (and growing) prefer living together in common-law arrangements. Another trend is that fewer young people expect to marry at all, and if they do, they expect to marry at a later age (at 30 or so). Weddings are celebrated with family and friends, but elaborate events are somewhat less common than in the United States.

Diet. The variety of foods and dietary habits found in Canada, especially in Ontario's two largest cities, Toronto and Ottawa, stem from the country's multicultural heritage. Throughout the prairies, one can find wild rice, smoked fish, beef, ethnic dishes, Pacific salmon, and a variety of foods similar to those in the United States. A particular region's diet is a reflection of location and the largest ethnic group of the area. For example, grains are more common inland because they are grown there, seafood is most popular on the coast, and various immigrant groups eat foods common to their countries of origin.

Recreation. Ice hockey is the most popular sport, but Canadians also enjoy boating, fishing, swimming, baseball, football, basketball, skiing, hunting, horseback riding, lacrosse, soccer, rugby, and *curling*. In *curling*, two four-person teams slide a large "stone" with a gooseneck handle over ice toward a target. Movies, local festivals and fairs, parks, and museums also offer recreational opportunities. Popular celebrations vary from the Calgary Stampede to the Yukon Quest dog races to Vancouver's Dragon Boat Festivals to Toronto's Caribana parade and summer festival.

The Arts. After World War I, artists began to develop uniquely Canadian art by focusing on the landscape of Ontario or other subjects relating to Canada. Many cultural organizations are stationed in Ontario (mainly Toronto), including the Toronto Symphony, the National Ballet of Canada, and the Canadian Stage Company. The Shaw and Stratford Festivals also are based in Ontario. The Canadian Opera Company produces new Canadian and traditional operas. Canadian writers such as Margaret Atwood, Robertson Davies, and Alice Munro have gained worldwide recognition for their works.

Immigrants living in Ontario have diversified the arts. Native Americans have traditions that began before European settlers arrived. These include clothing decorated with paint, beads, and porcupine quills; jewelry; tepees; and feather work. Some tribes are now reviving traditional arts.

Holidays. Official holidays include New Year's Day, Easter, Victoria Day (third Monday in May), Canada Day (1 July), Labour Day (first Monday in September), Thanksgiving Day (second Monday in October), Remembrance Day (11 Nov.), Christmas, and Boxing Day (26 Dec.). Boxing Day is a day to visit friends and relatives. It comes from the old British tradition of giving small boxed gifts to service employees or the poor. In addition to official holidays, local festivals are held throughout the region to commemorate various events. Each province also has its own official holidays, such as Alberta's Family Day (third Monday in February).

Commerce. A normal business day is from 8 a.m. to 5 p.m., Monday through Friday. Canadians usually begin full-time work between the ages of 16 and 25. Business habits are similar to those in the United States. Stores are open until at least

6 p.m., and many remain open until 9 p.m. on some week-nights. Some businesses also operate on Saturday and Sunday.

SOCIETY

Government.   Canada is a confederation with parliamentary democracy: its government is patterned partly after Great Britain's but also includes a federal system like that of the United States. The federal government is responsible for national defense and external relations, the banking system, the criminal code, and the aboriginal populations. The provinces are responsible for education, health care, the creation and regulation of municipalities, and the social welfare system. The greater resources of the federal government have led to its involvement in matters originally provincial (e.g., employment, insurance, medicare, and in some provinces, policing). The provinces each have a single-chamber legislature, and the leader of the dominant political party is the province's premier.

Canada's federal Parliament comprises an appointed Senate (of up to 104 senators), which only rarely exercises its full powers, and an elected House of Commons (301 members), which is the real legislative power. The prime minister, who heads the government, is the de facto chief executive. Ceremonial duties of the head of state are performed by the governor-general, currently Adrienne Clarkson, who represents Queen Elizabeth II. Parliamentary elections may be called at any time but must be held at least every five years. The voting age is 18. Five parties are currently represented in Canada's Parliament: the *Bloc Québécois* (from Québec) and the Liberal, Progressive Conservative (from the Maritimes), Reform (dominant in Alberta and British Columbia and strong in the west), and New Democratic Parties. In November 2000, Chrétien's Liberals won 173 seats in the House of Commons.

Economy.   Canada has one of the strongest economies in the world. Canada ranks second in the world in gold and uranium production, third in silver, and fourth in copper. It is a world leader in the supply of wood pulp and other timber-related products, the most important of which is newsprint. Ontario, the industrial heart of the nation, leads Canada's economy. As the financial and political center of Canada, it plays a role much like New York and California in the United States. Copper, nickel, and other minerals are mined in Ontario's Sudbury Basin. The western provinces produce vital raw materials, agricultural goods, and other products for export and manufacturing. The prairies are the breadbasket of the nation and also have important potash, oil, and natural gas reserves. Major products of British Columbia include timber, coal, oil, and minerals. British Columbia also serves as Canada's gateway to Pacific Rim markets. The north is rich in minerals and other natural resources. Economies in many provinces have expanded in recent years to include manufacturing, chemicals, and food processing.

In 1988, Canada signed a free-trade agreement with the United States, which led to the 1993 North American Free Trade Agreement (NAFTA) with Mexico and the United States. NAFTA provides for freer movement of capital and goods and a large market for many goods from each country.

DEVELOPMENT DATA

Human Dev. Index* rank	1 of 174 countries
Adjusted for women	1 of 143 countries
Real GDP per capita	$23,582
Adult literacy rate	99 percent
Infant mortality rate	5 per 1,000 births
Life expectancy	76 (male); 82 (female)

The national economy grew by 3 percent in 2000; unemployment averaged 6.9 percent for 2000. Although most Canadians benefit from the country's general economic prosperity, about one-tenth of the population lives in poverty. The currency is the Canadian dollar (Can$). Canadians refer to it as the *loonie*, after the image of the waterbird (the loon) minted on the gold-colored coin.

Transportation and Communications.   There are more cars per capita in the west than elsewhere in Canada because public transportation systems cannot serve the wide expanses of the prairies and north. Domestic air transportation provides an important link to isolated regions in the north. The national railway ships freight from the west to the east and vice versa. Communications systems are highly developed, including satellite systems, fiber optics, cable television, and excellent broadcast networks. Television often is dominated by U.S. American–made programs, but the federal government actively supports the development of Canadian films and television shows. Use of the Internet is common.

Education.   Each province is responsible for its educational system. In all provinces, education is compulsory and free for at least eight years, beginning at age six or seven. Each province also administers its own colleges and universities. While colleges are subsidized by the federal and provincial governments, students must pay tuition. Many students choose to complete a two-year technical training program and enter the workforce; about 40 percent enter a university. While only about 10 percent have college degrees, an additional 20 percent have completed at least some postsecondary training.

Health.   Canadians enjoy very good health in general. Hospitals and quality of care are excellent. Facilities and personnel are less available in rural and isolated regions. Canada has a compulsory national health insurance that covers doctors' fees and most hospital costs for all Canadians. It is funded by taxes and premiums collected by the federal and provincial governments. Private care is also available. Some Canadians also have supplemental medical insurance.

CONTACT INFORMATION

Canadian Consulate General, 1251 Avenue of the Americas, New York, NY 10020; phone (212) 596-1628; Web site www.canada-ny.org. Embassy of Canada, 501 Pennsylvania Avenue NW, Washington, DC 20001; phone (202) 682-1740; Web site www.canadianembassy.org/splash.

1305 North Research Way, Bldg. K
Orem, Utah 84097-6200 USA
1.800.528.6279; 801.705.4250
fax 801.705.4350
www.culturegrams.com

Québec Province of
Canada

Boundary representations are not necessarily authoritative.

▼ THE AMERICAS

BACKGROUND

Land and Climate. Canada, covering 3,851,788 square miles (9,976,085 square kilometers), is the second largest country in the world, after Russia. Much of the north is uninhabited due to the arctic climate and permanently frozen ground. Québec is Canada's largest province and is one-sixth the size of the United States. The Canadian Shield—a vast, U-shaped, rocky expanse surrounding the Hudson Bay—covers most of the province and includes 470,000 square miles (1,217,294 square kilometers) of rocky, coniferous forest. The bulk of the population lives in the Saint Lawrence Valley to the south. Summers are humid and warm; winters are very cold and snowy.

History. In 1534, Jacques Cartier landed in Gaspé and claimed French sovereignty over the territory. The following year, he traveled up the Saint Lawrence River to the present sites of Québec and Montréal, but real colonization did not begin until the 1600s. Québec City was founded in 1608. More towns eventually were established, and the number of French settlers gradually increased. By 1663, the area was under the firm control of Paris and was called New France. But the British also had settlements, and the two European powers fought for control of the land. In 1713, a war ended with France ceding most of its Atlantic coast holdings.

War again ensued from 1744 to 1748, but major fighting and conquest did not take place until the 1750s. In 1756,

France and England declared what became the Seven Years' War (French and Indian War). In 1759, the British conquered Québec City and, in the following year, Montréal. Peace was declared in 1763 with the signing of the Treaty of Paris, through which Britain gained control of all of New France. The area was then renamed Québec. At the time of the British takeover, the 70,000 French-speaking people in Québec outnumbered English speakers. The French culture remained firmly established during British rule and has continued to dominate the region.

In 1791, Québec was divided into Upper and Lower Canada, but the two were rejoined in 1840 as the province of Canada. In 1867, Canada was divided into Québec and Ontario, as the British North America Act created the Dominion of Canada. The new federal union included Québec, Ontario, Nova Scotia, and New Brunswick. Much of western Canada (then known as Rupert's Land) was added a few years later; British Columbia joined the Dominion in 1871. Canada eventually gained self-governing status within the Commonwealth.

Throughout Québec's history as part of Canada, its inhabitants have debated their status within the federation. Various independence and "special status" drives were launched in the 20th century. The movement gained momentum after the 1960s and seemed to peak by the 1980s under the political leadership of the Parti Québécois (or Bloc Québécois). A public vote defeated a 1980 referendum for independence. Québec opposed a new Canadian constitution in 1982, but a compromise was sought in the 1987 Meech Lake Agreement. The agreement would have recognized Québec as a distinct society within Canada and accorded it rights that other provinces would not have. However, the agreement failed in 1990 when several provinces balked at signing the agreement and Québec threatened to secede.

Demands in 1991 for secession led the federal government to seek a compromise. By early 1992, many Canadians had determined secession would harm the economy, so an increasing number came to favor recognizing Québec's distinct status. However, a referendum on the issue failed to pass that year. Québec opted to remain in the union and take advantage of other proposed constitutional changes and Canada's strong economy.

A referendum vote on Québec's independence came before the province again in October 1995. Separation was rejected by a surprisingly narrow 50.6 percent of the votes. In January 1996, Lucien Bouchard (Bloc Québécois), who was instrumental in leading the independence campaign to near victory, became premier of Québec.

Momentum has shifted away from holding another referendum in the near future, following provincial elections held November 1998. Voters narrowly returned Bouchard and the Bloc Québécois to power but without a clear mandate to seek independence. Bernard Landry, formerly Québec's finance minister, became premier after Bouchard resigned in January 2001. Landry hopes to revive the lagging separatist movement. The government continues to focus on the province's economic health.

THE PEOPLE

Population. Québec's 7.37 million people account for one-quarter of Canada's total population (31.28 million). Québec's largest cities are Montréal (3.48 million) and Québec City (689,700). Its urbanization rate (79 percent) is comparable to that of British Columbia and Ontario. About 83 percent of the people are of French origin, while 10 percent have a British heritage. This latter group generally is called Anglophones (as opposed to the French-origin Francophones). Anglophones tend to emigrate from Québec more than Francophones, as young English speakers seek jobs in other parts of Canada.

Native peoples in Québec include the Montagnais, Mohawk, Atikamekw, Cree, Malacite, and Inuit. The Inuit are an Eskimo people who live in the north. Other ethnic groups (principally from Europe or French-speaking Caribbean islands) are represented in the larger cities.

Language. Both French and English are official languages in Canada. However, in Québec, French is the first language of nearly 80 percent of the people and is used almost exclusively in some areas. According to provincial law, bilingual (French and English) signs are allowed inside buildings, but all street signs and external signs must be in French. Various groups have challenged this law; revisions may eventually allow bilingual signs on storefronts, and perhaps in other cases.

Fewer than one million people in Québec claim English as their first or primary language. Of these, about 60 percent also speak French. Many people, especially in large urban areas, mix French and English during conversation.

The Inuit speak Inuktitut, a complex and ancient language. Recent immigrants speak their native tongues at home but must learn French or English for public interaction.

Religion. Religious beliefs in Canada follow traditional lines. The French are generally Roman Catholic; those of British descent are mostly Protestant. Of course, other Christian and non-Christian groups are active in Québec, but the majority of people are Catholic. In fact, before Québec was controlled by Great Britain, it was ruled largely by the Catholic Church and French civil law. Although church and state are officially separate in Canada, religion is publicly recognized and private religious schools are often subsidized by the state. Religious organizations have played a greater role in Canadian politics than is typical in the United States.

General Attitudes. Both francophone and anglophone *Québécois* or *Québeckers* (Québec Canadians) are friendly and hospitable. Etiquette and politeness are important. People value a good education and comfortable lifestyle. French and English speakers generally have integrated well, but Anglophones sometimes express frustration over being a minority within a minority. In general, however, both Francophones and Anglophones view their bilingual society as a benefit rather than a drawback.

The French Québécois are particularly proud of their language and French heritage, insisting they are different from the rest of Canada and should protect their unique cultural institutions. A strong sense of nationalism motivates them to preserve French culture but does not necessarily require them to be independent. The majority still sees Québec as a vital part of Canada, despite voter support for separatist leaders. Threats of secession have caused tensions not only within Québec but throughout other provinces as well.

Personal Appearance. European and North American fashions are popular, with clothing trends very similar to those in the United States. Jeans, T-shirts, and tennis shoes are popular casual items. For formal events, Canadians tend to dress up slightly more than U.S. Americans.

CUSTOMS AND COURTESIES

Greetings. Due to past cultural and linguistic ties to France, Switzerland, and Normandy, Québec has experienced the most European influence of any Canadian region. Therefore, traditional European greetings are used in Québec, which include a firm handshake in most cases. *Bonjour* (Good day) is the common French greeting, although friends and young people often prefer *Salut* (Hey). Women who are close friends may embrace, and both men and women often exchange kisses on both cheeks as a greeting. Of course, not all of Québec is French, and greetings in predominantly English areas are similar to those in other parts of Canada (e.g., *Hello, how are you?*). Throughout Québec, first names and informal language forms are used by friends, relatives, or people of equal age or status. Conversation is direct and polite. The French term for *Good-bye* is *Au revoir*.

Gestures. Many gestures are the same in Québec as throughout the rest of Canada, but there are some differences. For instance, even if one excuses oneself, burping in public is offensive. The U.S. "thumbs down" gesture (meaning "no" or that something is bad) is offensive in Québec. Québécois tend to use their hands during conversation more than other Canadians to express themselves or emphasize a point.

Visiting. Québécois enjoy visiting with one another in a relaxed, informal atmosphere. A quick call in advance is all that is needed before one drops by a friend's or relative's home. In other cases, visits are arranged in advance—usually upon the hosts' invitation. Visitors nearly always remove their shoes at the door, as well as hats and coats. Hosts offer guests food or drink, even during short visits.

Etiquette is important in Québec and is adhered to on formal occasions. Guests invited to a home often bring the hosts a small gift of flowers, candy, or wine. Houseguests who stay overnight leave a thank-you letter and either leave or promptly send a thank-you gift to their host family.

Eating. In French-speaking areas, one keeps both hands above the table during a meal. Women rest their wrists on the table, men their forearms. Elbows may be placed on the table after the meal is finished. Supper time generally is at 6 p.m. This time is so important to families that a telephone call between 6 and 7:30 p.m. is considered impolite. Québec City and Montréal are well-known for their fine French cuisine. Tipping rates are the same as in the United States (10–15 percent). Eating on the streets is improper unless one is sitting at an outdoor café or standing at a food stand. During a meal, it is polite to wipe one's mouth before drinking from a glass.

LIFESTYLE

Family. While the family is the center of society, the extended unit is loosely knit. In the nuclear unit, both parents often work outside the home. Although traditional norms have changed somewhat over the last decade, the father is usually head of the family, but the mother exercises influence on all decisions. The average family has one or two children. To encourage growth, the government gives parents approximately US$500 at the birth of a child and adds a small monthly stipend. This amount increases over time and with the addition of each child. In urban areas, nearly half of the people live in rented apartments; outside large cities, 64 percent own homes.

Dating and Marriage. Dating and marriage customs are similar to those in the United States. Dating usually begins before age 16. Favorite activities include dancing and going to the movies. Many couples enjoy sporting activities together. Going out to eat is one of the most common dates in Québec. In the summer, picnics and outdoor dance festivals are popular. In Québec, it is now common for couples to live together for years before officially marrying. After two years, even without an official ceremony, the government recognizes the union as a common-law marriage. About half of all marriages end in divorce.

Diet. Québec regional cuisine displays a definite French influence and includes such foods as pea soup, French pastries and breads, crêpes, special cheeses, lamb, and veal.

Tourtière, a regional pie dish of the Saguenay–Lac-Saint-Jean area, is served in various forms throughout Canada. Potatoes and red meats are common with evening suppers. A favorite fast food is *poutine*, fries covered with spicy gravy and cheese curds. Maple syrup is produced in Québec and is a favorite in desserts. Food connoisseurs consider Québec's cuisine to be among the best in North America.

Recreation. Hockey is the most popular spectator and participant sport. Young people learn to play at a fairly early age on the province's numerous ice rinks. National Hockey League teams enjoy a wide following. Other favored sports include swimming, biking, baseball, curling, rugby, skiing, tennis, golf, and lacrosse (Canada's official national sport). Québec offers a variety of outdoor recreational opportunities, such as fishing, hunting, and hiking.

The Arts. Québec's rich cultural heritage is supported and funded by the provincial government, and Québécois regularly participate in the cultural arts. Montréal's annual film and jazz festivals are popular attractions; the filmmaking industry is known for its innovation. Internationally recognized Québec writers include Gabrielle Roy and Mordecai Richler.

The *Festival de théâtre des Amériques* and the *Carrefour international de théâtre de Québec* are well-attended events displaying foreign and Québecois plays. Québécois also enjoy popular, folk, and classical music. The *Orchestre symphonique de Montréal* is recognized worldwide. Contemporary as well as more traditional ballet companies enjoy wide audiences and critical acclaim.

Holidays. Holidays unique to Québec include the *Carnaval de Québec*, a two-week period in February filled with activities (although normal working hours prevail), and St. Jean-Baptiste Day (24 June), which is celebrated as Québec's national holiday (distinct from Canada Day). Canadian holidays include New Year's Day, Easter, Victoria Day (for the English) or *Dollard Des Ormeaux* (for the French) held the third Monday in May, Canada Day (1 July), Labour Day (first Monday in September), Thanksgiving Day (second Monday in October), All Saints' Day (1 Nov.), Remembrance Day (11 Nov.), Christmas, and Boxing Day (26 Dec.). Boxing Day comes from the British tradition of presenting small boxed gifts to service workers, tradesmen, and in the past, servants. It is now primarily a day for visiting family and friends or shopping. Almost every town has a winter carnival with parades and sports. During two or three weeks of spring, people often host "sugaring off" parties centered on maple syrup–making. Dancing at these celebrations is similar to square dancing.

Commerce. A normal business day is from 8 a.m. to 5 p.m., Monday through Friday. Most stores open from 9 a.m. to 9 p.m., Monday through Friday; some stores close at 6 p.m., Monday through Wednesday. Shops that open on weekends normally open from 9 a.m. to 5 p.m. on Saturday, and noon to 5 p.m. on Sunday. Banks open at 10 a.m. and close at 4 p.m.

SOCIETY

Government. Canada is a confederation with a parliamentary democracy: its government is patterned partly after Great

Britain's but also includes a federal system like that of the United States. The federal government holds considerable power in areas of national concern, such as health insurance, trade, the military, and development. Provincial governments have authority over education, property laws, and medical facilities. Québec's one-chamber legislature has 125 seats. The leader of its dominant party (currently the Bloc Québécois) serves as premier. The Liberal Party, led by Jean Charest, is the main opposition.

Canada's federal Parliament includes a body of as many as 104 appointed senators and an elected body of 301 members of the House of Commons. The prime minister, currently Jean Chrétien, is the leader of the dominant political party in the House. Britain's Queen Elizabeth II is represented by a governor-general, currently Adrienne Clarkson. Parliamentary elections may be called at any time but must be held at least every five years. The Bloc Québécois lost several seats in the House after elections in November 2000. Canada's strongest parties are the Liberal Party, the Reform Party, and the Bloc Québécois. The voting age is 18.

Economy. Canada has one of the strongest economies in the world. Its real gross domestic product per capita reflects the country's general economic prosperity. The economy grew by 3 percent in 2000. In 1993, Canada signed the North American Free Trade Agreement (NAFTA) with Mexico and the United States. NAFTA provides for freer movement of capital and goods, more cross-national investment, and a large market for many goods in each country. The Canadian dollar (Can$) is usually somewhat weaker than the U.S. dollar and can be affected by variations in the U.S. dollar's value.

Compared to most other provinces, Québec has a high rate of unemployment (more than 9 percent in 1999) and lower economic growth. It also has the largest tax burden and the highest poverty rate. The St. Lawrence Seaway makes Montréal Canada's most important port city. The James Bay project and other hydroelectric power plants provide nearly 90 percent of the province's electricity.

Mining is a major primary industry in Québec. Overall, Canada ranks second in the world in gold and uranium production, third in silver, and fourth in copper. Forestry is also important in the province. Canada is a world leader in producing wood pulp and other timber-related products; many U.S. newspapers are printed on Canadian paper. Manufacturing and technology industries are also important. Tourism has become an increasing source of revenue in the past several years.

Transportation and Communications. Transportation systems are excellent, especially in Montréal and Québec City, where bus systems are well developed. Montréal has one of the best subways in the world. In other areas, people travel in private cars. The national railroad network carries passengers and freight, and airlines provide an increasingly popular way to travel. Most people have telephones and televisions, and

DEVELOPMENT DATA

Human Dev. Index* rank .... 1 of 174 countries
   Adjusted for women .... 1 of 143 countries
Real GDP per capita $23,582
Adult literacy rate .... 99 percent
Infant mortality rate .... 5 per 1,000 births
Life expectancy .... 76 (male); 82 (female)

communications systems are highly developed. Radio networks and newspapers service the entire populace. All systems are highly modern, and Canada has several satellites in orbit to aid communications. Internet use is common.

Education. Like all provinces, Québec is responsible for its educational system. School is free and compulsory for children ages six to sixteen. Local Catholic and Protestant school boards are supported by the government to direct school curricula. The education system allows the children of English-speaking parents to be educated in English, usually at Protestant schools. These English students can take French courses offered in their schools. Immigrants who were educated in English schools in Québec can also send their children to an English school. However, new immigrants have to enroll their children in French schools.

While students may get permission to leave school at 16, high school continues another two years, and the government actively encourages students to finish. After graduation, students may enter a two-year technical training program (similar to a trade school or community college in the United States) or attend a two-year college preparatory program (similar to filling general education requirements in the United States). Those who opt for technical training then enter the labor force, while the others attend a three-year university. Although the provincial government subsidizes university education, students pay tuition costs. About 30 percent of college-age people earn university degrees.

Health. Canadians enjoy very good health in general. Hospitals and an advanced level of care are available to all citizens. Canada has a universal, compulsory national health insurance that covers doctors' fees and most hospital costs. It is funded by fairly high taxes and premiums collected by the federal and provincial governments. While patients must sometimes wait months for elective surgery and certain expensive procedures, all citizens have access to basic health care at public clinics.

CONTACT INFORMATION

Tourism Québec, PO Box 979, Montréal, Canada H3C 2W3; phone (800) 363-7777; Web site www.tourisme .gouv.qc.ca. Embassy of Canada, 501 Pennsylvania Avenue NW, Washington, DC 20001; phone (202) 682-1740; Web site canadianembassy.org/splash.

1305 North Research Way, Bldg. K
Orem, Utah 84097-6200 USA
1.800.528.6279; 801.705.4250
fax 801.705.4350
www.culturegrams.com

Republic of
Chile

▼ THE AMERICAS

Boundary representations are not necessarily authoritative.

BACKGROUND

Land and Climate. While slightly larger than Texas, Chile stretches along 2,672 miles (4,300 kilometers) of South America's western coast. Its average width is just more than 112 miles (180 kilometers), but total square miles are 292,260 (756,950 square kilometers). Chile's territory includes *Isla de Pascua* (Easter Island), *Isla Sala y Gómez*, and *Islas Juan Fernández*, among others; the first two islands lie almost 2,000 miles (3,219 kilometers) to the west. Chile also lays claim to a 480,000-square-mile (1.24 million-square-kilometer) disputed section of Antarctica, claimed by Britain as well.

Because of its north-to-south length, Chile has many different climates and landscapes. The climate ranges from arid desert in the north to temperate in the central region and sub-arctic in the south. One can find deserts, swamps, forests, the Andes Mountains, beautiful lakes, rich agricultural regions, volcanoes, and a wide variety of plants and animals. Chile has been called the "Switzerland of South America" for its natural beauty. The country is subject to relatively frequent earthquakes and resulting tidal waves. Because Chile lies in the Southern Hemisphere, its seasons are opposite those in North America: summer is between December and March.

History. The Incas from Peru were the first "explorers" of Chile, arriving in the north by the mid-15th century. They encountered the native Atacameño, Diaguita, Araucanian, and Mapuche cultures. The Portuguese sailor Ferdinand Magellan became the first European to sight Chilean shores in 1520, after successfully navigating around the southern tip of the American continent. Diego de Almagro claimed Chile as part of the Spanish Empire for Francisco Pizarro in 1536, and in 1541 Pedro de Valdivia commenced the Spanish conquest despite strong resistance by Araucanians. Chileans now revere many early indigenous warriors, like Caupolicán and Lautaro, as national heroes.

Chile began fighting for independence from Spain in 1810. Although initial revolts were suppressed, Chilean patriots eventually joined with the armies of José de San Martín in Argentina. In 1817, San Martín's forces invaded Chile by crossing the Andes Mountains. The Spanish were quickly defeated, and one of the revolution's heroes, Bernardo O'Higgins, became supreme dictator of the new republic. Opposed in land reform and other reform efforts, O'Higgins left the country in 1823 and Chilean politics remained unstable for several years. After 1830, however, stability and periodic reform allowed Chile to make progress. From 1879 to 1884, Chile fought the War of the Pacific against Peru and Bolivia. Victorious, Chile annexed the provinces of Tarapaca and Antofagasta in the north.

A civil war in 1891 was followed by less stable governments and military interventions. Chile returned to constitutional rule in 1932 with the reelection of President Arturo Alessandri. During most of the 20th century, Chile concentrated on promoting economic growth and addressing social problems. By 1970, many people had become convinced that socialism could solve some of those problems without hindering growth. That conviction allowed Salvador Allende to become the first freely elected Marxist president in South America. But the country soon faced economic disaster, and in 1973 General Augusto Pinochet Ugarte led a military coup that ended Allende's government.

Pinochet determined that authoritarianism was better than liberal democracy and, backed by the military, ruled by decree. In 1988, Pinochet subjected himself to a plebiscite to determine if he should continue in power. Upon losing, he called for elections in December 1989. Pinochet's choice for president was defeated by the centrist-left candidate, Patricio Aylwin Azocar. Aylwin took office in 1990 as the first elected president since 1970. Despite his reputation for years of human-rights abuses and a dictatorial style, Pinochet is credited for building a successful and productive economy. Aylwin built on that foundation, facilitating Chile's development as one of the most prosperous Latin American countries. He is credited with implementing successful antipoverty programs and maintaining a delicate balance between opposing political forces.

Aylwin did not run for reelection in 1993 but supported Eduardo Frei Ruiz-Tagle, who took office in March 1994. The son of a former president, Frei emphasized even more social spending for education and antipoverty measures. He pursued closer economic ties with North and South America and constitutional reforms to reduce the military's political power. Under these reforms, Chilean presidents are not permitted to serve two consecutive terms. Socialist Ricardo Lagos, of the Christian Democrat–Socialist coalition, succeeded Frei as president in March 2000.

Following Pinochet's October 1998 arrest in Britain, British authorities decided that the elderly former dictator was too ill to be extradited to Spain on charges of human-rights abuses committed against Spaniards during his regime. In March 2000, he was returned to Chile. Despite claims that Pinochet is too sick to stand trial, an appeals court ruled that he may indeed be tried, although on lesser charges than kidnapping and murder. After being released from house arrest, Pinochet is appealing the decision to the Supreme Court.

THE PEOPLE

Population. Chile's population of almost 15.2 million is growing annually at 1.17 percent, one of the lowest growth rates among South American countries. Only about 15 percent of the population lives in rural areas. More than five million people live in the Santiago metropolitan region. About 95 percent of the people have either a European heritage or are of mixed European-indigenous descent. Only 3 percent are purely indigenous (mostly Mapuche), and 2 percent have other ethnic origins. Those of European heritage may have ancestry from Spain, France, Germany, Switzerland, Croatia, Russia, Syria, or Lebanon, among other countries.

Language. Spanish, called *Castellano*, is the official language. But as in all South American countries, some terms common to Chile will not have the same meaning elsewhere. Chileans commonly add a suffix (*-ito*) to words and names to form diminutives. For example, *Chaoito* is a "small good-bye," while *Carlitos* means "little Carlos." English is taught in the schools and is understood by many with more formal education. Small minority groups also speak German (in southern Chile) and Mapuche.

Religion. Most Chileans profess a Christian faith. It is estimated that more than 80 percent of the population belongs to the Roman Catholic Church. Most other people belong to various Protestant groups or other Christian churches. There is a small Jewish minority, and many indigenous peoples follow traditional beliefs. There is a separation of church and state, and religious freedom is guaranteed.

General Attitudes. Although naturally friendly and warm, Chileans may be shy and reserved when first meeting someone. They are known for their sharp, witty, and somewhat cynical sense of humor. This and their cultural and educational refinements have earned them the distinction of being called the "British of South America." Chileans are very patriotic and take pride in their nation's cultural, educational, and economic achievements. When asked how they view Chile and its future, people commonly express confidence and optimism. However, their cynicism might express itself in a slight reservation or a biting remark about the country or its inhabitants. There is a large middle class in Chile, and education enables many poorer people to excel and build a better life. Chileans are a pragmatic people who believe in progress. Years of human-rights abuses under dictatorships have created in people a strong sense of and desire for social justice. At the same time, Chile has a relatively rigid class structure in which those of European descent are granted higher social status than those of indigenous heritage.

Personal Appearance. Fashions follow European styles and are quite sophisticated in urban areas. U.S. American casual fashions are also popular, particularly among the youth. Many commercial entities (banks, department stores) require their employees to wear uniforms, usually a stylish suit or dress. Individuals take considerable pride in their appearance. Even in rural areas, where people are not as wealthy, it is important to be bathed and neatly dressed. Although lower-income people may wear secondhand clothing from the United States, sloppy or tattered clothing is considered to be in poor taste.

CUSTOMS AND COURTESIES

Greetings. Greetings in Chile are important because they stress that one is welcome and recognized. The *abrazo* is the most common greeting among friends and relatives. It consists of a handshake and hug, supplemented with a kiss to the right cheek for women and family members. A handshake is appropriate when meeting someone for the first time. Eye contact is considered essential when greeting. Traditional verbal greetings include *¿Qué tal?* (What's going on?), *¿Cómo estai?* (informal "How are you?"), *¡Gusto de verte!* (Nice to see you), and *¿Qui'ubo?* (What's up?). Chileans show significant outward affection to friends and relatives. The *abrazo* is repeated with each individual when one leaves a small social gathering of friends or family. *Chao* is a common parting phrase.

Chileans customarily use titles when addressing people. *Señor* (Mr.), *Señora* (Mrs.), and *Señorita* (Miss) are common for strangers and acquaintances, as are professional titles, such as *Doctor(a)*, *Director(a)*, *Professor(a)*. When speaking with elderly men and women and other respected individuals, one uses *Don* and *Doña* with their first name to show special respect and familiarity. Chileans, more than other Latin Americans, address others with the formal *Usted* (you) more often than with the familiar *tú*.

Gestures.   Respect and courtesy are important to Chileans. Eye contact and correct posture are important during conversation, while excessive hand gestures are avoided. Yawns are suppressed or politely concealed with the hand. Items, including money, are handed, not tossed, to other people. Chileans point with puckered lips rather than with the index finger. An upturned palm with the index finger or all fingers motioning toward oneself (the U.S. American gesture for beckoning) is the gesture to pick a fight.

Visiting.   In general, people are considered more important than schedules in Chile, and punctuality is not stressed. People may arrive 30 minutes or more late to a dinner appointment or scheduled visit. Punctuality is more closely observed in the workplace. It is not uncommon for a business dinner to take place in an associate's home rather than a restaurant. Casual conversation usually precedes any business discussion.

Guests wait outside the door of a home until invited inside. Hosts usually offer something to eat or drink. Dinner guests may bring a gift of flowers, chocolates, good wine, or (in lower-income areas) bread for the host family. Guests invited to lunch might offer to bring a dessert, like cookies or ice cream. Chileans appreciate guests who show genuine interest in their family, especially their children.

Eating.   Chileans eat the main meal at midday and a lighter meal between 8 and 10 p.m. Afternoon teatime (*onces*) is customary. At teatime, a beverage, small sandwiches, and cookies or cakes are served. Chileans converse freely at the table. The hostess often is complimented on the meal. People eat in the continental style, with the fork in the left hand and the knife remaining in the right. They keep both hands above the table at all times. It is impolite to leave directly after eating; instead, guests stay for conversation.

In a restaurant, a waiter can be summoned with a raised finger; meal checks are not brought to the table until requested. It is traditionally considered bad manners to eat food, except for ice cream, while walking in public. However, as fast food increases in popularity, this habit is changing.

LIFESTYLE

Family.   The family unit in Chile encompasses the extended family. While men have tended to dominate private and public life in the past, recent years have seen a change in the attitudes about women in the home and professional world. Nearly 30 percent of the labor force is female. Many women hold key political and business positions. And while the father takes the lead in the family, the mother has considerable influence on decisions. Reciprocity characterizes the relationship between the husband and wife, with the man performing courtesies for the woman and vice versa.

It is customary for a person to bear two family names; the last name is the mother's family name and the second-to-last name is the father's family name. People either use their full name or go by their father's family name, which is the official surname. Therefore, a person named José Felipe Correa Péres

could use his full name or be addressed as *Señor Correa*. As in other Latin American countries, women retain their father's family name rather than use that of their husband's.

Dating and Marriage.   Young people begin dating by the time they are 16. Group dating is emphasized early on. Men marry at about age 22 and women marry between ages 18 and 23. Couples often date from one to three years before getting engaged. Many consider it important to finish one's education before marrying. A civil wedding ceremony often is followed by a traditional Christian ceremony. Receptions commonly are held at the home of the bride. Divorce is not legal in Chile, nor is it recognized by the Catholic Church. Legal means of annulling a marriage are available but expensive.

Diet.   Many national dishes are prepared with fish, seafood, chicken, beef, beans, eggs, and corn. Different regions feature different foods and dishes, but some favorites include *empanadas de horno* (meat turnovers with beef, hard-boiled eggs, onions, olives, and raisins), *pastel de choclo* (a baked meal of beef, chicken, onions, corn, eggs, and spices), *cazuela de ave* (chicken soup), *ensalada chilena* (cold tomato-and-onion salad), and seafood casseroles and stews. On rainy days, children enjoy eating *sopaipillas*, which are made from a deep-fried pumpkin dough sprinkled with sugar. *Manjar*, made by boiling an unopened can of sweetened condensed milk for hours, is a favorite bread spread and baking ingredient. Beverages usually are served at room temperature. Chile is well-known for its wines; *pisco* (grape brandy) is the national drink.

Recreation.   Popular activities include sports, theater, and music. *Fútbol* (soccer) is the most popular sport, and basketball is gaining in popularity. Chileans also enjoy swimming, going to parks, and watching videos at home. During the summer, vacations to the coast or the countryside are common. Taking advantage of the country's long coastline, Chileans enjoy fishing as well. Weekend or holiday barbecues are frequent social gatherings. Rodeo is popular in many areas. Cowboys (*huasos*) wear handwoven capes and straw hats. The main event consists of a pair of *huasos* skillfully guiding their horses to trap a steer against a padded arena wall. Points are earned for the portion of the steer that is pinned.

The Arts.   Of its cultural arts, Chile is best known for poetry. Two poets received the Nobel Prize for literature, Gabriela Mistral (1945) and Pablo Neruda (1971). Contemporary Chilean authors are known internationally.

European music and art are popular. Performing groups, museums, and galleries enjoy patronage in larger cities. Traditional arts are a source of inspiration to contemporary artists and musicians. Textile and pottery designs of indigenous peoples frequently are integrated into modern designs. Chilean music and dance reflect both Spanish and native heritage. The *cueca*, a rhythmic dance of courtship, is the national favorite. Chilean folk music (*tonadas*) has been influential in political and social reform. European and native instruments are used to create a unique sound.

Holidays.   Chile's important holidays include New Year's Day, Easter, Labor Day (1 May), Naval Battle of Iquique (21 May), National Day (11 Sept.), Independence Day (18 Sept.), Armed Forces Day (19 Sept.), Columbus Day (12 Oct.), All Saints' Day (1 Nov.), and Christmas. People celebrate Independence Day at parks, where they eat *empanadas*, drink *chicha* (a sweet drink made with fermented grapes), and dance the

▼ **THE AMERICAS**

cueca to guitar music. Christmas is celebrated in much the same way it is in North America, but some activities are different because Christmas takes place during summer. Families may hold an outdoor barbecue on Christmas Eve and open their gifts at midnight.

Commerce. In the capital of Santiago and other large cities, people usually work from 9 a.m. to 6 p.m., five or six days a week. In smaller cities and rural areas, midday meal breaks (*siestas*) are still observed, and shops and offices may close for up to two hours. Standard banking hours are from 9 a.m. to 2 p.m. Large supermarkets are found in major cities. Traveling markets (*ferias*) provide fresh fruits, vegetables, meat, fish, and flowers to smaller cities and towns. Chile has an active and modern business climate; its exports and investments link it to world markets.

SOCIETY

Government. The Republic of Chile is a multiparty democracy. The country is divided into 13 numbered regions, Region I being the most northern. President Lagos is chief of state and head of government. The National Congress has two houses: the Senate (48 members) and the Chamber of Deputies (120 members). Several political parties are officially represented in the government. However, a governing coalition of four main parties (Coalition of Parties for Democracy) currently dominates the legislature: the Christian Democratic Party, Socialist Party, Party for Democracy, and Radical Social Democratic Party. The main opposition is provided by the Union for the Progress of Chile coalition. The legislature sits at Valparaíso. The voting age is 18. All eligible citizens are required by law to vote.

Economy. Chile's economy is growing. Annual growth has averaged approximately 6.5 percent since 1984. Chilean foreign debt has decreased steadily, and the country enjoys considerable foreign investment. Chileans enjoy fairly good access to the health care, education, and the economic resources necessary for a decent standard of living; however, women's wages are substantially lower. The country's innovative pension system has generated substantial savings, with workers placing more than 10 percent of their earnings into their choice of mutual fund accounts. Inflation in 1999 was 2.6 percent; however, persistent drought and low copper prices in 1999 caused unemployment to rise to 10 percent (currently 8.4 percent) and the economy to contract by 1.1 percent. Growth in 2000 has rebounded to 5.4 percent, and a similar rate is expected in 2001.

Under President Aylwin, a program was instituted to help the poor by extending special small business loans and other credits, investing in the poorest schools, building permanent homes for low-income families, and sponsoring work-study programs for the youth. The income of the poorest Chileans has subsequently risen by 20 percent and the population living below the poverty line has fallen to 22 percent (1998) from 39 percent (1990). While much progress in income equality can still be made, the program's success has encouraged greater productivity and prosperity.

Chile is one of the world's largest producers of copper,

DEVELOPMENT DATA

Human Dev. Index* rank	38 of 174 countries
Adjusted for women	39 of 143 countries
Real GDP per capita	$8,787
Adult literacy rate	95 percent
Infant mortality rate	10 per 1,000 births
Life expectancy	72 (male); 79 (female)

which accounts for about 40 percent of all exports. Fresh fruit has become another chief export, with more than 40 countries importing its grapes, apples, nectarines, peaches, and other fruits. Agriculture, fish products, wood products, metals, light manufacturing, and the mining of minerals are all important to the diverse economy. Chile has actively sought to expand its export market through international free-trade agreements. The currency is the Chilean *peso* (Ch$).

Transportation and Communications. Public transportation in Chile is fairly efficient, although many roads remain unpaved. Traffic in Santiago is heavy and can be somewhat hazardous. Santiago has a subway, and elsewhere, private bus systems provide inexpensive and efficient travel in and between cities. Private cars are becoming more common. Trucks, motorcycles, and bicycles are used in rural areas to travel longer distances. Several airports serve domestic and international travelers. A satellite communications system, cable television, and other technological advances have helped Chile increase telephone access, establish global communications links, and improve radio and television service throughout the country.

Education. Chile has one of the best-educated populations in Latin America. Schooling is free and compulsory between ages five and seventeen. In addition to public schools, there are many private, commercial, and industrial educational institutions. Chileans value education, viewing it as the way to a better life. There are eight universities in Santiago alone; other universities and technical institutes are located throughout the country.

Health. Currently, health care is nationalized. However, the system is undergoing decentralization and private insurance institutions are taking over a portion of care payment. Citizens have a choice as to whether they use the private or public health-care system. Chileans have enjoyed increasingly good health over the past few years, with infant mortality rates dropping substantially. Water is potable in most areas. Typhoid fever and air pollution, particularly in Santiago, remain public health threats.

CONTACT INFORMATION

Lan Chile Airlines, Tour Information Department, 9700 South Dixie Highway, Suite Penthouse, Miami, FL 33156; phone (800) 995-4888. Embassy of Chile, 1732 Massachusetts Avenue NW, Washington, DC 20036; phone (202) 785-1746; Web site www.chile-usa.org.

CultureGrams™
People. The World. You.

1305 North Research Way, Bldg. K
Orem, Utah 84097-6200 USA
1.800.528.6279; 801.705.4250
fax 801.705.4350
www.culturegrams.com

▼ THE AMERICAS

Boundary representations are not necessarily authoritative.

BACKGROUND

Land and Climate. With 439,736 square miles (1,138,910 square kilometers), Colombia is about the size of California and Texas combined. It is located at the juncture between Central and South America and features an extremely diverse landscape. Divided by three branches of the Andes Mountains, Colombia has low coastal plains on the Caribbean Sea and the Pacific Ocean; cool mountain plateaus, valleys, and active volcanoes in the central Región Andina; and an eastern region with plains in the north and tropical jungle in the south. The country also includes several islands. While minor earthquakes are fairly common in Colombia, periodic, more serious tremors also have taken their toll.

There are no distinct seasons in Colombia, but differing elevations experience a variety of temperatures. Medellín at 5,000 feet (1,524 meters) above sea level averages 70°F (21°C), while Bogotá, the capital, at 8,000 feet (2,438 meters) averages 55°F (13°C). The coast is hot and humid. With such diversity in temperature, altitude, and rainfall, Colombia produces an incredible variety and abundance of vegetation and animal life. Middle Eastern coffee seeds, brought to Colombia by Spanish missionaries, found a perfect climate in Colombia. Coffee is now the country's most important export crop.

History. The history of Colombia before the arrival of Europeans is uncertain, but many groups thrived in the area, producing sophisticated art, stone, and gold work. Chibcha, Carib, Arawak, Tairona, and Muisca peoples were present when the Spanish began settling the region in the 1500s. The area was soon part of New Granada, which also encompassed present-day Venezuela, Ecuador, and Panama. Resentment against Spanish rule grew in the late 1700s until 1810, when nationalists claimed independence. However, independence was not really achieved until Simón Bolívar assembled an army to defeat Spanish troops at the Battle of Boyacá in 1819. He established the new *Gran Colombia* republic, from which Venezuela and Ecuador withdrew in 1830. With U.S. support, Panama declared itself independent in 1903 to make way for construction of the Panama Canal.

Colombia's name, originally the State of New Granada, changed several times before it became the Republic of Colombia. Civil war (*La Violencia*) between conservatives and liberals from 1948 to 1957 led to a constitutional amendment requiring the presidency to alternate between the Liberal and Conservative Parties until 1974. Fully competitive elections have been held since that time.

The Medellín and Cali drug cartels and various guerrilla movements, such as M-19, Revolutionary Armed Forces of Colombia (FARC), and National Liberation Army (ELN), caused unrest and violence in the 1980s. Some guerrilla factions eventually joined the democratic process in the 1990 presidential elections. Although drug traffickers (*narcoterroristas*) killed several presidential candidates and committed violent acts to dissuade Colombians from voting, elections were held and César Gaviria Trujillo was elected president.

Gaviria took a stand against drug trafficking and violence. However, to encourage peace, he allowed guerrilla groups to participate in a constitutional convention if they would disarm and renounce violence. Most groups accepted the offer and began participating in the political process. Gaviria also offered drug traffickers leniency if they would confess and renounce their crimes. Not all guerrillas and drug traffickers cooperated with the government, but the violence did diminish for a short time.

In 1990, a national assembly—including guerrilla organizations, indigenous groups, and nontraditional political parties—was formed to rewrite the 1886 constitution. The new constitution took effect 4 July 1991 and encourages political pluralism, the rule of law, and special rights for the long-ignored indigenous and black populations.

Elections in 1994 awarded Ernesto Samper Pizano of the Liberal Party a four-year presidential term. However, calls for impeachment came after Samper was accused of receiving campaign funds from the Cali drug cartel. Congress absolved Samper of wrongdoing in June 1996, but speculation about his guilt persisted. The scandal damaged the government's credibility, contributing to an economic downturn and escalated violence among guerrillas, drug cartels, paramilitary antiguerrilla groups, and the military. About 35,000 people—many of them civilians—have died by violence from these groups in the last 10 years. Much of the killing, kidnapping, and extortion involves drug-related lands and moneys. In 2000, the military began razing drug crops and laboratories in hopes of eliminating these groups' funding.

Andrés Pastrana, the son of a former president and an independent candidate backed by the Conservative Party, won the 1998 presidential election. He has pledged to end the country's internal conflict, rejuvenate the economy, and promote social justice. In November 1998, Pastrana withdrew thousands of troops and police from the southeast, a FARC stronghold, to meet FARC's precondition for peace talks. Negotiations have continued sporadically throughout 2001, but little progress has been made. Fighting is being taken more into the cities, and innocent civilians often are caught in the cross fire between right-wing paramilitaries and left-wing guerrillas.

THE PEOPLE

Population. Colombia's population of about 39.7 million is growing at 1.7 percent annually. The majority of Colombians live in the west; much of the southeast is covered by jungle. People of mixed Spanish, indigenous, and sometimes black origins compose 58 percent of the population. Caucasians account for 20 percent. Others include black-Caucasian mix (14 percent), black (4), indigenous-black mix (3), and indigenous (1). Blacks are descendants of African slaves imported during the Spanish colonial era. Many mixed with other peoples, especially after slavery was abolished in 1851. Blacks generally live along the coasts, comprising the majority of some large cities, including Quibdó (300,000). The largest metropolitan areas are Bogotá (seven million), Medellín (three million), and Cali (two million). Approximately 70 percent of the population lives in urban areas, and more than 40 percent is younger than age 20.

Language. The majority of Colombians speak Spanish, the country's official language. Most indigenous ethnic groups have their own languages. Among 80 groups, 40 languages are spoken. Dialects spoken by some blacks reflect their African roots. Natives of the San Andrés and Providencia Islands in the Caribbean speak Creole. Ethnic languages and dialects share official status with Spanish in certain areas, where formal education must be bilingual.

Religion. While Colombia's constitution guarantees freedom of religion, nearly 95 percent of the people belong to the Roman Catholic Church. Protestant and other Christian organizations have small growing memberships. Many indigenous and black peoples retain beliefs from non-Christian, traditional worship systems. Although society is becoming more secularized, Catholicism remains an important cultural influence. For example, Catholic religious instruction, though no longer mandatory, still takes place in most public schools. Colombians commonly express their faith with phrases like *Si Dios quiere* (God willing) and *Que sea lo que Dios quiera* (Whatever God wills).

General Attitudes. Colombians take pride in their rich and diverse culture. The country's various geographic regions, climates, and subcultures enrich its food, music, dance, and art. Colombians are also proud of their *rumbero* spirit—their ability to both work and play hard. The family is a great source of pride, and family solidarity and mutual support are important. The individual is also important and takes precedence over timetables and punctuality. Colombians value honesty, loyalty, a good sense of humor, and education. They find selfishness, arrogance, and dishonesty distasteful.

Colombians may seem somewhat cynical and suspicious of outsiders. However, an initial lack of trust is more a survival skill than a lack of courtesy. Gaining someone's trust often requires guarantees and manifestations of good faith. Colombians are proud of their history of democracy and independence. They may be critical of their own social problems but do not appreciate outside interference or criticism. While minorities traditionally have been marginalized, the new constitution embodies people's hopes for equal treatment and opportunity for all. Colombians are forward-looking and confident they can overcome their challenges. They take pride in the fact that, despite violence and political turmoil, Colombia's human and natural resources have allowed the country to reach high levels of economic development.

Personal Appearance. In Colombia, clothing is conservative, clean, and well kept. Appropriate attire for each occasion is essential. In urban areas, men wear suits, white shirts, and ties. In cities nearer the coast, suits generally are lighter in color. Women wear comfortable dresses, and urban youth dress casually. Dress in rural areas is less fashionable, but the people wear neat, clean clothing. Indigenous peoples often wear traditional clothing, which can include wraparound dresses, bowler hats, and *ponchos*.

CUSTOMS AND COURTESIES

Greetings. Men commonly shake hands (not too vigorously) with everyone when entering a home, greeting a group, or leaving. Women kiss each other on the cheek if they are acquainted but offer a verbal greeting or handshake otherwise. Close friends or relatives may greet each other with an *abrazo* (hug), sometimes accompanied by a kiss on the cheek. Youth of the opposite sex and young girls will also kiss each other on the cheek. It is customary to address people by a title (*Señor, Señora, Doctor*, etc.), rather than their first name, when being introduced. Common greetings include *¡Buenos* *días!* (Good morning), *¡Buenas tardes!* (Good afternoon), *¡Buenas noches!* (Good evening), and *¿Cómo está?* (How are you?). *¡Hasta luego!* and, less formally, *¡Chao!* and *¡Nos vemos!* are popular parting phrases. People answer the phone with *A la orden?* (May I help you?). Colombians commonly have two family names: the last name is the mother's family name and the second-to-last name is the father's family name. The father's family name is the official surname. Therefore, a person named José Muñoz Gómez would be called *Señor Muñoz*.

Gestures. During conversation, Colombians tend to be expressive with their hands and face, particularly if the discussion becomes animated or heated. Maintaining eye contact and standing close are important; interrupting or backing away from the other person is considered rude. People beckon others with the palm down, waving the fingers or the whole hand. Smiling is an important gesture of goodwill. Colombian males may show deference and respect to women and the elderly by forfeiting seats, opening doors, or offering other assistance.

Visiting. While visiting is an important part of Colombian culture, customs vary with ethnic group and region. For example, in smaller towns with warm climates, people often sit on their porches and converse with passersby. Friends and relatives may visit unannounced, especially in rural areas where telephones are not widely available, but otherwise it is polite to make arrangements in advance. Colombian hosts are gracious and attempt to make guests feel comfortable, usually offering refreshments such as coffee, fruit juice, or soft drinks. Dinner guests generally arrive at least a few, and often 30 or more, minutes late. They may bring a small gift to the hosts, but this is not expected. Hosts commonly offer dinner guests an alcoholic beverage (rum, beer, etc.) before and after dinner. Politeness and etiquette are emphasized in Colombia. During formal visits, guests wait to sit until the hosts direct them to a seat. It is improper to put one's feet on furniture when visiting. Hosts often accompany departing guests out the door and even down the street.

Eating. Good manners and courtesy when eating are important to Colombians. Pleasant conversation is welcome at the table, as it stimulates a feeling of goodwill. Overeating is impolite; a host may offer more helpings, but these should be politely refused. Many consider it important to keep hands above the table. In a group, it is impolite to take anything to eat without first offering it to others. Eating on the street is improper. Toothpicks, if used at all, are used discreetly. In restaurants, leaving a 10 percent tip is customary.

LIFESTYLE

Family. Family unity and support are important to Colombians, and family members share their good fortunes with one another. Traditional values still strongly influence family relations. Divorce is relatively uncommon, due largely to the influence of the Catholic Church. The typical family unit consists of a mother, father, and two to four children. The father feels an obligation to provide for his family, and the mother is responsible for most domestic duties. However, an increasing number of women also work outside the home; more than one-third of the labor force is female. Children traditionally live with their parents until they marry, but more university students and young businesspeople are leaving home earlier. Adult children often care for a widowed parent. Upper-class families enjoy many modern conveniences, but most Colombians lead simpler lives. About one-third live in absolute poverty. As Colombia becomes more urbanized, apartments are becoming more popular than single-family dwellings.

Dating and Marriage. Depending on family custom, dating begins around age 14 or 15. Urban youth may begin dating at a younger age. Popular activities include going to parties, restaurants, movies, and discos; shopping at the mall; and participating in sports. On the night before a wedding, the groom may hire a small band to serenade the bride. Marriage ceremonies generally follow Catholic traditions, including a mass. A reception, with music and dancing, follows at a club, restaurant, or home. Common-law marriages are gaining acceptance in Colombia.

Diet. Breakfast foods vary by region, including juice, coffee, hot chocolate, fruit, eggs, bread, or *changua* (potato-and-egg soup). A small, midmorning *merienda* (snack) may consist of *empanadas* (meat turnovers) or bread and a drink. Lunch, usually between noon and 2 p.m., is the main meal of the day. In smaller cities and towns, the family may gather (many businesses close) for the meal. Eating the main meal in the evenings is a trend in urban areas. Supper is usually at 7 or 8 p.m. Staple foods include soup, rice, meat, potatoes, salad, and beans. *Arroz con pollo* (chicken with rice), *frijoles con chicarrón* (pork and beans), and *sancocho* (stew with fish or meat and vegetables) are popular national dishes. *Arepa* is a cornmeal pancake. Coffee is the favorite drink of many. Sugar and milk are primary ingredients in popular sweets and desserts like *arequipe* (caramel sauce) and *arroz de coco* (rice pudding with coconut and rum). Ice cream is a common Sunday treat.

Recreation. *Fútbol* (soccer) is the most popular sport in Colombia, particularly among men. Other favorite sports include cycle racing, swimming, track-and-field, volleyball, basketball, and baseball. Attending bullfights is also popular. Colombians enjoy participating in the country's many festivals and joining with friends and family there to talk, dance, and laugh. Visiting is another favorite pastime. People socialize in their homes, in restaurants, or while strolling down city streets.

The Arts. Music and dance are central to Colombian culture. Much music is influenced by African or indigenous styles. Tropical rhythms are popular, including salsa, *merengue*, and *vallenato*. The *cumbia* is a favorite style, and the *bambuco*, from the Andes, is the national song and dance. Classical music is appreciated as well, and many people frequent the orchestras scattered throughout the country. Literature is important to Colombians, and many people take great pride in Gabriel García Márquez, who won the Nobel Prize in literature in 1982.

Elaborate gold work is a legacy of the early indigenous peoples. Today's Colombian artists weave hammocks, sashes, bags, and blue and red *ruanas* (wool shawls). They also produce ceramics and decorative trim for clothing or furniture, called *passementerie*.

Holidays. Holidays in Colombia include New Year's Day; Epiphany (6 Jan.); St. Joseph's Day (19 Mar.); Easter; Labor

▼ THE AMERICAS

Day (1 May); Feast of St. Peter and St. Paul (29 June); Independence Day (20 July); Battle of Boyacá (7 Aug.); Assumption Day (15 Aug.); *Día de la Raza* (12 Oct.), which celebrates the discovery of the Americas and the resulting mix of ethnicities; All Saints' Day (1 Nov.); Independence of Cartagena (11 Nov.); and Christmas. Cities and towns also sponsor annual local festivals.

The nine days before Christmas (*la novena*) are marked by religious observances and parties. On Christmas Eve, families eat a large dinner, pray around *el pesebre* (the nativity), sing Christmas carols, and exchange gifts. Children receive gifts from the baby Jesus on Christmas Day.

Commerce. The Colombian workweek is basically 8 a.m. to 6 p.m., Monday through Friday. Shops open from 9 a.m. to 6:30 p.m., Monday through Saturday, with some closing early on Saturday. Shops in larger cities may stay open later. Many urbanites buy basic goods at supermarkets. Open-air and farmers' markets sell fresh produce at cheaper prices. Banks generally close at 4 p.m., but some offer extended service.

SOCIETY

Government. The Republic of Colombia has a bicameral Congress, with a 102-seat Senate and 161-seat Chamber of Representatives. Senators are elected in a national vote, while representatives are elected regionally. The president is chief of state and head of government. The president and cabinet form the executive branch. The judicial branch is independent. All citizens may vote at age 18. The major political parties are still the Liberal Party and the Conservative Party, which forms the main opposition in Congress. Colombia has 32 states (*departamentos*).

Economy. Agriculture plays a key role in Colombia's economy. Coffee accounts for 30 percent of all export earnings; freshly cut flowers and bananas are also important exports. Other agricultural products include sugarcane, cotton, rice, tobacco, and corn. Oil is surpassing coffee as the country's main legal export. Natural gas, coal, iron ore, nickel, gold, copper, textiles, and chemicals all contribute to the economy. More than 90 percent of the world's emeralds are mined in Colombia. With half of the country covered by forests and woodlands, the timber industry is becoming important. Colombia produces two-thirds of the world's cocaine and much of its heroin, but drug earnings remain in the hands of relatively few. The currency is the Colombian *peso* (Col$).

Free-market policies during the past decades have led to high rates of foreign investment and solid growth for Colombia. Its people are proud of the fact that they are current on all foreign debt payments and have never defaulted. While the country has had a reputation for sound economic management, it is challenged by decaying infrastructure, illegal drug trade, and violence. Unemployment has grown to about 20 percent, and the economy shrank by nearly 5 percent in 1999—the worst recession in nearly 70 years. However, in 2000, the economy rebounded and grew by 3 percent. Inflation is about 9 percent, the lowest rate in more than 30 years. Rural poverty and an unequal distribution of income

DEVELOPMENT DATA

Human Dev. Index* rank	68 of 174 countries
Adjusted for women	58 of 143 countries
Real GDP per capita	$6,006
Adult literacy rate	91 percent
Infant mortality rate	25 per 1,000 births
Life expectancy	66 (male); 74 (female)

remain serious problems. Economic opportunities are more accessible to the ruling class. About 10 percent of the population lacks access to health care, education, and economic prosperity needed to rise above human poverty.*

Transportation and Communications. People in urban areas generally use public transportation, including buses, minibuses (*colectivos*), and taxis. A minority of people own cars; some use bicycles and motorcycles. Bus service is the most common link between cities, but air-passenger travel is on the rise. While road construction has increased, only about 10 percent of roads are paved and many are in poor condition; irregular terrain makes construction and maintenance costly. Coasts on two oceans provide shipping access to world markets. Colombia's television and radio infrastructure is government-owned, but stations are privately operated. The country's free press has played a role in investigating and protesting corruption and terrorist violence.

Education. Primary education is compulsory and is free in public schools; many schools are private. Colombia's literacy rate has risen substantially due to an increased number of rural schools; unfortunately, it remains only 40 percent among the indigenous and black populations. Slightly less than 60 percent of all students complete primary education (five years) and continue to the secondary level (six years). Secondary schools are found in most municipalities and offer either technical or academic tracks; many are private. Vocational schools and universities are located in major cities. Bogotá has 15 major universities. Scholarly achievement has been important throughout Colombia's history.

Health. Colombia's health-care system is changing from a public to a mixed (public and private) system. Individuals who can afford it usually seek private care. Private clinics and public or charity hospitals are available in cities but are lacking in rural areas. Urban facilities are better equipped. As many tropical diseases have been eradicated, life expectancy has risen; however, malaria and yellow fever still affect rural and tropical regions, and tap water often is not safe for drinking. Sanitation remains a problem in rural areas. Infant mortality is significantly higher and life expectancy is lower among black and indigenous peoples. Violence remains the leading cause of death in Colombia.

CONTACT INFORMATION

Embassy of Colombia, Consular Section, 2118 Leroy Place NW, Washington, DC 20008; phone (202) 387-8338; Web site www.colombiaemb.org.

1305 North Research Way, Bldg. K
Orem, Utah 84097-6200 USA
1.800.528.6279; 801.705.4250
fax 801.705.4350
www.culturegrams.com

Republic of
Costa Rica

Boundary representations are not necessarily authoritative.

▶ THE AMERICAS

BACKGROUND

Land and Climate. Costa Rica covers 19,730 square miles (51,100 square kilometers) and is just smaller than West Virginia. About 60 percent of Costa Rica is covered by different types of forests. More than 11 percent of the total territory is reserved as national parks. This small nation has a diverse landscape of tropical rain forest, mountain cloud forest, volcanoes, green countryside, and beautiful rivers. Although the country lies entirely in the tropical climate zone, elevation changes allow for cooler temperatures in the central highlands. The coastal lowlands are hot and humid with temperatures averaging 81°F (27°C) throughout the year. Most people live at elevations where the climate is generally mild. In San José and other parts of the central valley highlands, temperatures average 67°F (19°C) year-round. Rainfall varies between the dry season (December–April) and wet season (May–November). The land is subject to frequent earthquakes, hurricanes, and occasional volcanic eruptions.

History. A variety of native peoples lived in present-day Costa Rica before Columbus arrived in 1502. In the north, the indigenous cultures were influenced by Mayan civilization. Southern groups were more closely related to the indigenous peoples of South America. Spain eventually colonized the Costa Rican area along with most of Central America. Because minerals were scarce, the area was ignored by the Spanish crown and remained isolated. In 1821, Costa Rica joined other Central American nations in declaring independence from Spain during a nonviolent revolution. In 1824, it became a state of the Federal Republic of Central

America. After the republic collapsed in 1838, Costa Rica became a sovereign nation.

Costa Rica has a long tradition of changes in government via democratic means. This tradition has been interrupted by military coups only three times in 150 years. Consequently, Costa Rica has one of the most stable democratic governments in Central America. Civil war erupted for six weeks in 1948 after a dispute over elections. José Figueres Ferrer led an interim government until 1949 when the election dispute was settled. Figueres (who was elected president in 1953 and again in 1970) abolished the army in 1948, and a new constitution was introduced in 1949. Costa Rica has enjoyed peace and democracy ever since.

The nation practices a philosophy of nonintervention in the affairs of foreign governments. Former president Oscar Arias Sánchez (who left office in 1990) was an avid supporter of the Central American Peace Plan. Arias won the Nobel Peace Prize for his efforts to bring peace to the region. The award is a great source of pride for all Costa Ricans, as they believe it emphasizes their distinct heritage.

Weary of rising prices and falling incomes, voters elected businessman Miguel Ángel Rodríguez as president in February 1998. Promising to revitalize the country's economy, Rodríguez took office in May 1998, replacing José Maria Figueres Olsen. The election marked Costa Rica's 12th peaceful transfer of power since 1948. Government plans to privatize some state-owned industries led to the country's worst strikes, demonstrations, and unrest in many years. However, a court ruled the proposals unconstitutional in April 2000. The government now is pursuing other avenues to modernize the industries.

THE PEOPLE

Population. The population of Costa Rica is 3.7 million and is growing at 1.7 percent a year. About half a million Nicaraguans are illegal immigrants; Costa Rica deports thousands yearly. The population is relatively young, with more than 45 percent younger than age 20. Most people live in the central valley highlands. The majority of people (87 percent) have a European heritage. About 7 percent are of mixed heritage (European and Indian), although many of these are immigrants from other Latin American countries. Three percent of the population is black and lives mostly on the Atlantic Coast. These people are descendants of laborers brought from the Caribbean to build a railroad. They later worked on banana plantations and developed a distinct culture in the region around Puerto Limón. One percent of Costa Ricans are Native Americans, some of whom still live in the Talamanca mountain region. Another 1 percent are ethnic Chinese.

Language. Spanish is the official language of Costa Rica. English is understood widely. Patua (creole English) is spoken by the black population. Bribri, spoken by the Bribri people, is the most common native language. Ten other native groups speak Spanish or a native tongue.

Costa Ricans are known as *ticos* within their own country and throughout Central America. The nickname comes from their habit of ending words or phrases with the suffix *-tico* (instead of the more common Spanish diminutive *-tito*). So instead of saying *chico* (small) or *chiquitito* (very small), Costa Ricans say *chiquitico*. Individually, men are called *ticos* and women *ticas*, but the mixed company reference is *ticos*.

Religion. The Roman Catholic Church claims membership of about 95 percent of the population. Until the mid-1980s, the Catholic Church was the nation's official church, but it lost that status when the government decreed that a democratic nation should support no particular religion. Although the Catholic Church continues to be very influential, the constitution guarantees religious freedom to the people. As is the trend elsewhere, secularization in Costa Rica is leading some people away from organized religion. At the same time, a growing number of religious people are joining other Christian churches—and religion still plays an important role in society.

General Attitudes. Costa Rica is a land of courtesy, domestic enterprise, hospitality, and gentleness. Militarism is despised by nearly all. Children are taught in school that armies are created to oppress rather than protect people. Aggressiveness, brusqueness, and violence also are shunned. *Ticos* say they are lovers of peace and conciliation. They avoid confrontation when possible. People value privacy and quiet behavior but vigorously defend personal honor. A strong work ethic is prevalent among most segments of society, and rural people especially accept hard labor as a necessary part of life.

Individuality is an important characteristic, expressed in Costa Rica's relations with other nations, and to a lesser extent, on a personal level. This is due partly to Costa Rican isolation during the colonial period; because they had little contact with colonial rulers, *ticos* developed greater independence. Still, group conformity in values, interests, and thought is important in society. Individuals are recognized as such, and all people are given respect, regardless of their social class. There is little resentment among the classes due to this traditional respect and a belief that some things are determined by God. The belief that Deity controls some aspects of life, such as one's health or success at a given venture, is evident in daily speech. People often attribute their achievements to and place hope in God. This tradition is changing with greater education and people's desire for material progress.

Personal Appearance. Western dress is common throughout the country. Women generally pay more attention to their appearance than do men and always try to be fashionably dressed. Still, all *ticos* consider it necessary to be well-groomed in public. Clothing is neat, clean, and generally modest. People bathe every day and place great emphasis on personal cleanliness.

CUSTOMS AND COURTESIES

Greetings. Polite and respectful greetings are a social norm. Female friends or relatives greet each other with a light kiss on the cheek. If women are not yet acquainted, they may pat each other on the arm. Men shake hands. It is an insult not to shake every man's hand in a small group. Common terms for greeting include *¡Buenos días!* (Good day), *¡Buenas tardes!* (Good afternoon), and *¡Buenas noches!* (Good evening). *Ticos* often respond to the greeting *¿Cómo está?* (How are you?) with the expression *Pura vida* (Pure life). Also used as a way to say "OK," *Pura vida* has endless uses. *¡Hola!* (Hi) is a casual greeting popular among the youth; older people consider it disrespectful if used to greet them. In rural areas, people greet each other when passing on the street, regardless of whether or not they are acquainted. One might simply say *¡Adiós!* or *¡Buenas!* or more formally *¡Adiós, Señora!* or *¡Buenos días!* This tradition is less common in urban areas. Rural people often bow their heads slightly and touch their hats in greeting. Greetings between strangers or acquaintances are brief, but people who know each other usually take a few minutes to talk about family, work, or health.

One addresses others by professional title either with or without a surname, depending on the situation. *Señor* (Mr.) and *Señora* (Mrs.) also are used, especially for people with whom one is not well acquainted. *Ticos* address friends, children, coworkers, and subordinates by first name. They use the title *Don* or *Doña* with the first name of an older man or woman, respectively, to show special respect for and familiarity with the person. For example, a child might call the mother of his best friend *Doña Maria*.

Gestures. Hand gestures are common and important to everyday conversation. In fact, Costa Ricans often use their hands to express an idea, either with or without verbal communication. To indicate "no," one vigorously waves the index finger (palm out, finger up). When expressing shock or when faced with a serious situation, *ticos* will shake the hand vigorously enough to snap (slap) the fingers together three or four times. There are many different hand greetings in addition to the handshake or wave. For instance, young people slap hands together in a greeting similar to a "high five." Eye contact is important, especially when one is discussing a serious issue or talking to a superior. It traditionally is understood that the lack of eye contact means one cannot be trusted.

Chewing gum while speaking is impolite.

Visiting. Costa Ricans enjoy socializing but do not visit as often as people in other Latin American or Caribbean countries. Urban Costa Ricans generally prefer that visits be arranged in advance. Only close friends or relatives drop by unannounced, and then mostly in the afternoon after household chores have been done. Otherwise, uninvited visitors may not be asked into the home. In rural areas, people visit unannounced more often and rarely are turned away. Hosts usually offer visitors something to drink (like coffee) and refreshments (pastries, bread, or crackers). Invited guests generally are expected to arrive a few minutes late (later in rural areas). Punctuality is not customary, but being very late is also not appreciated.

Dinner guests usually bring a small gift to their hosts, such as flowers, wine, a plant, or something to share or mark the occasion. Close friends often bring more personal gifts. Gifts also are exchanged on special occasions. Hosts usually serve dinner guests refreshments and drinks while they socialize for an hour or so before the meal is served. After dinner, coffee and dessert accompany more conversation. Guests generally leave shortly thereafter.

If a Costa Rican invites someone to dinner or to spend a few days at his or her home, the potential guest must determine whether the invitation is sincere or whether the host is just trying to be polite. Polite invitations often are extended as a gesture of goodwill rather than as an expectation that guests will come.

Eating. Most people eat three meals a day, with midmorning and afternoon coffee breaks or snacks. Breakfast and dinner are the most important meals, as lunch is becoming more rushed and is more often eaten away from home. Business professionals make lunch dates, but dinner is otherwise the meal for entertaining guests. Mealtime is to be enjoyed and is extended by conversation. Costa Ricans enjoy conversation on a variety of subjects.

Table manners vary from family to family, but as a general rule, one keeps both hands above the table rather than in the lap. In restaurants, the bill customarily includes a tip of 10 percent. Further tipping is not expected.

LIFESTYLE

Family. Costa Ricans value family tradition and heritage. The immediate family has an average of three to five children. Rural families are usually larger. Rural extended families often either share a dwelling or live as neighbors. While the husband makes most final decisions in the home, he shares many responsibilities with his wife. Most women do not work outside the home, but a growing number are entering the labor force. Nearly 30 percent of the workforce is female. Women retain their maiden names when they marry. Children carry the surnames of both parents. The second-to-last name in a full name is the family surname. Many families, even many of the poor, own their own homes, which are either wood-frame or cement-block structures (or a combination, with block halfway up the wall and wood to the roof).

Dating and Marriage. Girls generally are more restricted in dating than boys. They seldom can have visitors past 10 p.m., unless courtship is close to marriage. A boy usually asks a girl's parents for permission to date her, but this custom is disappearing slowly, especially in urban areas. When a young couple is dating, the boy commonly is allowed a certain schedule for sitting with the girl on the porch or taking short neighborhood walks. This may be for two hours during a few evenings each week. Dating at an early age usually is done in groups, except in rural areas where there are fewer people. Movies, dances, picnics, the December bullfights, and a yearly civic carnival are favorite dating activities.

Marriage is a valued institution; Costa Rica has one of the highest marriage rates in Latin America. Families visit each other to show formal agreement on their children's marriage. Women generally marry in their early twenties, men somewhat later. Unmarried adults usually live with their parents, especially in rural areas. Typically, only university students live on their own if not married.

Diet. Costa Ricans eat rice and beans in various combinations for nearly every meal. Typical at breakfast is *gallo pinto* (mixture of rice and black beans). *Casado* (rice, beans, salad or eggs, meat, and plantains) is a common lunchtime meal. Favorite dishes include *olla de carne*, a beef stew with potatoes, onions, and many vegetables. *Tamales* (meat, vegetables, and cornmeal wrapped in plantain leaves and boiled) are served for Easter and Christmas. Also common are *lengua en salsa* (tongue in sauce), *mondongo* (intestine soup), *empanadas* (turnovers), *arroz con pollo* (rice with chicken), and *gallos* (tortillas with meat and vegetable fillings). Bread, tortillas, and fruits are also staple items. *Ticos* of all ages enjoy coffee. Adults may take two or three coffee breaks each day.

Recreation. *Fútbol* (soccer) is the most popular spectator and participant sport. Basketball, baseball, volleyball, surfing, auto racing, swimming, cycling, running, and tennis are also popular. Fishing is good in many parts of the country. The wealthy enjoy golf and polo. Beaches are crowded between January and April. Local carnivals, festivals, and bullfights are popular attractions at various times throughout the year. Media broadcasts from the United States are popular and have a significant impact on urban trends.

The Arts. Dancing is a favorite activity among *ticos* of all ages. Typical Latin dances such as salsa, *merengue*, and *cumbia* as well as the Costa Rican swing are popular. Folk dances include the national dance, the *Punto Guanacaste*, the *cambute*, and maypole dances. Typical musical instruments include the *chirimia* (oboe), guitar, xylophone, accordion, and the *quijongo* (a stringed instrument). People enjoy calypso, *soca* (a mixture of American soul and calypso), reggae, and music popular throughout the Caribbean and Central and North America.

Museums offer a glimpse of pre-Columbian life. Brightly painted *carretas* (oxcarts) are well-known throughout the world. Other arts include pottery, *molas* (appliqué for clothing or textiles), and carved wooden masks.

Holidays. Costa Rican holidays include New Year's Day; Feast of St. Joseph (19 Mar.); Anniversary of the Battle of Rivas against Walker (11 Apr.), in which the national hero, Juan Santa María, the drummer boy, lost his life; *Semana Santa* (Holy Week) and Easter; Labor Day (1 May); Annexation of Guanacaste to Costa Rica (25 July); Feast of St. Peter and St. Paul (29 June); Feast of Our Lady of the Angels (2 Aug.); Central American Independence Day (15 Sept.); *Día de la Raza,* recognizing the indigenous roots of Latin America

THE AMERICAS

(12 Oct.); Feast of Immaculate Conception (8 Dec.); and Christmas. Christmas is celebrated with family, but New Year's is a time for friends, parties, drinking, and dancing. However, many people interrupt festivities before midnight on New Year's Eve to go home and eat a small, quiet meal with the family before returning to their party after midnight.

Commerce. Most businesses are open on weekdays from 8 a.m. to noon and 2 to 6 p.m., although some shops do not close for the midday break. Many shops are open on Saturday, but most are closed on Sunday. Government offices close weekdays at 4 p.m. Few business meetings are strictly formal, and socializing is an important part of a business relationship.

SOCIETY

Government. Costa Rica is a democratic republic. The country has an elected president and two vice presidents in its executive branch. There is a unicameral Legislative Assembly, whose 57 legislators are elected to four-year terms. The judicial branch is separate. Costa Rica has seven provinces. All citizens age 18 and older are required to vote in national elections. Election day is always a national holiday; people travel to their town of birth to vote and enjoy grand celebrations. Voter turnout traditionally has been high but dropped significantly in the last election. Most Costa Ricans are affiliated with one of two major parties: the ruling Social Christian Unity Party (PUSC), and the National Liberation Party (PLN).

Economy. Despite a relative lack of minerals and other traditional natural resources, Costa Rica has a fairly prosperous economy. Real gross domestic product per capita has more than doubled in the last generation. This is due in part to Costa Rica's stability; successful tourism, timber, and agricultural industries; and a generally egalitarian society. The country experienced steady growth in the early 1990s. In the mid-1990s the economy slowed due to low world prices for agricultural products, adverse weather conditions, and government measures to control inflation. Growth recovered in 1998 and 1999, reaching levels of 6 and 8 percent, respectively. Inflation continues to hover around 10 percent. Unemployment is low, but underemployment remains a problem. Poverty affects about one-fifth of the population; however, only 4 percent (one of the lowest levels in Latin America) lacks access to adequate health care, education, and economic opportunities necessary to rise above human poverty.*

Exports include coffee, bananas, beef, sugar, cocoa, and fertilizer. Damage from El Niño caused coffee exports to drop in 1997 and 1998. Costa Rica is one of the largest banana producers in the world. Ornamental flowers are becoming an increasingly important export. Cattle raising is concentrated in the Guanacaste province but is expanding to other areas. Manufacturing and tourism now contribute more to the economy than agriculture. In 1998, Intel opened a factory near San José. Other industries include food processing, textiles, and construction materials. Costa Rica has excellent potential for hydroelectric power: nearly all of its electricity comes from hydroelectric power plants. Tourism facilities are well developed, so the industry is prosperous and important to the economy. Tourists are particularly drawn to Costa Rica's protected

DEVELOPMENT DATA

Human Dev. Index* rank	48 of 174 countries
Adjusted for women	46 of 143 countries
Real GDP per capita	$5,987
Adult literacy rate	95 percent
Infant mortality rate	11 per 1,000 births
Life expectancy	73 (male); 78 (female)

areas, and ecotourism has grown in popularity in recent years. Costa Rica has been a major recipient of foreign aid, and foreign investment in the country is increasing. The monetary unit is the Costa Rican *colón* (C) or plural, *colones*.

Transportation and Communications. Although cars are available, the most common form of transportation within and between cities is the bus. Fares are inexpensive and the system is efficient. Almost every town and tourist destination can be reached by paved roads. Taxis are commonly available; legal taxis are red. The domestic telephone system was expanded between 1989 and 1994; telephones are located throughout the country, although remote areas still lack service. Rural homes usually do not have phones, but each town has at least one public phone. Satellite systems are used for international communications. Radio stations transmit throughout the country. There are also a number of television stations in Costa Rica. Several national newspapers have wide circulation. The postal system is efficient. Mobile phone and Internet use are increasing.

Education. Costa Rica has one of the finest urban public education systems in the Americas. Nearly half of federal government spending goes toward education and health care. Primary education is compulsory and free for six years, beginning at age seven. Where facilities exist, children also attend kindergarten at age five and a preparatory year at age six. Enrollment in secondary schools is not mandatory, but more than 40 percent of all pupils advance to that level. Secondary schooling is also free. Both public and private universities serve the population. Evening schools educate the older generation as well as young people who cannot attend secondary school during the day. Gaining a high school diploma is considered very important. Costa Rica is home to four international education centers.

Health. A national health-care system serves all citizens, and medical care is considered very good. Life expectancy has risen in recent years. Infant malnutrition and inadequate prenatal care remain problems in rural areas. Malaria is common along the Nicaraguan border and at lower elevations, and dengue fever (also spread by mosquitoes) has been reported on both coasts since 1993.

CONTACT INFORMATION

Embassy of Costa Rica, Consular Section, 2114 S Street NW, Washington, DC 20008; phone (202) 328-6628; Web site costarica-embassy.org. Costa Rica Tourist Board, ICT PO Box 777-1000, San José, Costa Rica; phone (800) 343-6332; Web site www.tourism-costarica.com.

1305 North Research Way, Bldg. K
Orem, Utah 84097-6200 USA
1.800.528.6279; 801.705.4250
fax 801.705.4350
www.culturegrams.com

Republic of
Croatia

ZAGREB

PANNONIAN VALLEY

Drava

EASTERN
SLAVONIA

Rijeka

Sisak

Sava

Osijek

Danube

Slavonski Brod

KRAJINA
REGION

VELEBIT MTNS.

Knin

Zadar

DINARA MTNS.

Split

Ploče

Dubrovnik

Germany

Slovakia

Austria

Hungary

Slovenia

Croatia

Italy

Bosnia-
Herzegovina

Adriatic
Sea

Yugoslavia

Albania

▼ EUROPE

Boundary representations are not necessarily authoritative.

BACKGROUND

Land and Climate. Croatia is situated along the eastern coast of the Adriatic Sea. Its hinterland stretches close to the slopes of the Julian Alps in Slovenia and into the Pannonian Valley to the banks of the Drava and Danube Rivers. Covering 21,829 square miles (56,538 square kilometers), Croatia is about the size of West Virginia. Along the Adriatic are hundreds of islands that hug the highly indented coastline. The coast enjoys a Mediterranean climate with hot, sunny summers and pleasant winters. Many famous cities, including the medieval port of Dubrovnik, lie along the long coast. In mountainous regions, winters are cold and snowy, while summers are mild. In the Pannonian area, winters are cold and dry; summers are hot. The capital, Zagreb, lies on the Sava River.

History. Slavic peoples began settling the Balkan Peninsula in the seventh century A.D. Croatians were united first into a single state by King Tomislav in 925. Following Catholicism's Great Schism in 1054, Croats accepted Roman Catholicism and became associated with the West. In 1102, the Croatian and Hungarian monarchies came together in a personal union. In the 1500s, Croatia and Hungary became part of the Austro-Hungarian (Hapsburg) Empire, where they remained until the 20th century.

After two destabilizing Balkan wars in 1912 and 1913, the entire region was embroiled in World War I—sparked by the assassination (in 1914) of Austria's crown prince in Sarajevo (Bosnia). Upon Austria's and Germany's defeat, the Austro-Hungarian Empire collapsed. Several new states were created from it in 1918, with Slavs uniting together in the Kingdom of Serbs, Croats, and Slovenes. Relations between ethnic groups were hostile and not conducive to a peaceful union. By 1929, Serbia had increased its domination of the country and declared it the Kingdom of Yugoslavia (meaning "kingdom of southern Slavs"). Croats suffered repression under Serbian rule. So when Germany and Italy invaded in 1941, Croat fascists declared an independent Croat state under their leadership (called *Ustashe*) and allied with the Nazis. While Croats welcomed independence, they did not fully realize that the Ustashe regime was a puppet of the Nazis. At the hands of Croat fascists, many thousands of civilian Jews, Serbs, and Gypsies died in concentration camps or in massacres. The actual record of events from that era is hotly disputed even today, but the memory of Croat brutality (perceived and real) was one catalyst to Serbian atrocities committed in the 1990s.

During World War II, a great many Croats joined other Slavs in the antifascist movement that waged a civil war for control of Yugoslavia. Communist forces (antifascist partisans) emerged victorious over the *Chetniks* (royalists) as Germany was falling to Allied advances. Croatia subsequently became part of the Socialist Republic of Yugoslavia created under partisan leader Josip Broz Tito. The Yugoslav federation was quickly consolidated and Tito became its president in 1953. To keep opposing groups together, Tito's Communist Party carefully controlled nationalist sentiments among all ethnic groups and promoted the federalism concept. Attempts to revive Croat nationalism and culture were suppressed. When Tito died in 1980, his authority was transferred to a collective state presidency, which had a rotating chairman. That body was not able to rule effectively for long before simmering ethnic tensions erupted. By the end of the 1980s, the federation was on the verge of collapse.

With the fall of communism elsewhere in Europe, Croatia held elections in 1990. The newly elected leadership under President Franjo Tudjman declared independence in 1991. Croatia was recognized by the international community in January 1992, but it faced heavy military intervention from the Yugoslav army and Serbian government, which strongly opposed independence. Entire cities were nearly destroyed in fierce fighting between these forces, as well as between local Serbs and Croats.

The United Nations helped broker a cease-fire in 1992. Many people had been killed; thousands had been forced to leave their homes, creating a serious refugee problem; and historically rooted ethnic hatred boiled over on Croatian soil. Local Serbs had gained control of Krajina, or roughly one-quarter of Croatia's territory. They declared a Republic of Serb Krajina, but this was never recognized outside of Serbia. Rebel Serbs, supported by Serbia's government, launched rocket attacks on Zagreb civilians and threatened other violence if their independence were not recognized.

After negotiators and the United Nations failed to solve the crisis peacefully, Croatia forcefully recaptured Krajina in August 1995. Thousands of Serbs fled to neighboring Serb-held regions; by 1996, nearly 200,000 Serbs had left Krajina. Eastern Slavonia (near the border with Serbia), also held by rebel Serbs opposed to Croatian independence, was returned to Croatian control without violence. Croatia agreed to a two-year transition period (ending in January 1998) to avert another mass Serbian exodus. On the heels of his victory in securing Croatia's borders, President Tudjman called for early parliamentary elections near the end of 1995. His Croatian Democratic Union Party (HDZ) won 60 percent of the seats. Tudjman was reelected again in June 1997.

Croatian support for Croats and Muslims fighting Serbs in Bosnia added to tension and violence in the region during the 1990s. Under pressure from Western allies, Croatia eventually supported the Dayton Peace Agreement in 1996 and pledged to support a resolution of the Bosnian civil war. After two years under UN administration, Eastern Slavonia was transferred to Croatia's control in January 1998. In spite of UN efforts to gradually integrate ethnic Serbs and Croats together in Eastern Slavonia, more than half of ethnic Serbs in the enclave have left. The resettlement of ethnic Serbs who once lived in Croatia remains a contentious issue.

Following Tudjman's death in December 1999, a coalition led by the Social Democratic Party won a majority in the 2000 election and ended a decade in power for Tudjman's nationalist HDZ. Economic woes, international isolation, and corruption scandals contributed to the HDZ's defeat. Ivica Racan is the prime minister. Racan has pledged to push for Croatian membership in the European Union (EU) and the North Atlantic Treaty Organization (NATO), curb presidential powers, reduce unemployment, and stamp out corruption. Racan's government is also cooperating with the war crimes tribunal in The Hague to prosecute those guilty of atrocities during the Bosnian war.

THE PEOPLE

Population. Croatia has about 4.3 million residents and is growing at a rate of just less than 1 percent. The actual number is difficult to determine because of the refugee situation: Croat refugees left in 1992, Bosnian Croats came throughout the war, and Croatian Serbs left in 1995 and 1996. Croats form about 78 percent of the population. Serbs accounted for 12 percent before 1995 but account for less than 5 percent today. About 2 percent of the people claim to be Yugoslavs, although such an ethnic group does not really exist. It was promoted under Communist rule to suppress nationalism and provide an optional ethnic distinction for children of mixed marriages. Muslims of Slavic origin comprise 1 percent of the population, and another 0.5 percent is Hungarian. Slovenes and other small groups make up the rest of the population. More than 300,000 Croatians live abroad; most are in Bosnia, but some work in other European countries as guest workers. These Croatians have representation in the Sabor, Croatia's Parliament. Due to improving conditions, a modest number of people have access to opportunities for personal advancement.

Language. Croatian is the country's official language. It is a Slavic language that originated in the 11th century and adopted a Latin alphabet in the 14th century. Croatian law allows Serb, Italian, Hungarian, Czech, Slovak, and Ukrainian ethnic groups to use their language in education, and to some extent, in local official communication. Serbs and Ukrainians are permitted to use the Cyrillic alphabet. Slovene, Albanian, and Romany are spoken by their respective groups. Students may study English, French, German, and Italian in school beginning at age 10 or earlier.

Religion. Religion traditionally has been important to Croats. With the demise of communism and Yugoslav socialism, religion is once again playing an important role in Croatian society. It was a primary dividing feature between Croats and other Slavs because most Croats are Roman Catholic; some are Protestant or Jewish. Serbs are mostly Orthodox Christian. There are also many Muslims. Freedom of worship is guaranteed. The Catholic Church plays an active role in political and social affairs.

General Attitudes. The people of Croatia are sociable, optimistic, proud of their heritage, and hospitable to strangers. They value their families, education, and good careers. For centuries, Croats did not have their own independent state, and for decades, Croatia was part of Yugoslavia. Croats now have an internationally recognized sovereign country. They are extremely proud of their nation and are anxious for other countries to accept them and learn of Croatian history and culture. Their historical ties to western Europe also bring Croatians much pride, and they have worked to again integrate with European organizations. Most Croatians hope for the establishment of democratic principles and rights for all citizens. It is a difficult goal, since mutual tolerance and respect must precede any lasting peace.

Personal Appearance. It is important for clothing to be neat and clean. Adults do not wear shorts in public, except for recreation or on the coast. Women wear skirts and dresses as well as pants and follow current European fashion trends. In the workplace, women customarily wear dresses. Urban men wear suits and ties for special occasions and in some business or professional circles. The European tradition of wearing a tie (*kravata*) comes from the 18th century Croatian soldier's uniform. For informal situations, men prefer more practical daily clothing, such as jeans, knit shirts or sweatshirts, and casual shoes or sneakers. Natural fiber fabrics (cotton and wool) are generally preferred over synthetics. Older rural women often wear scarves on the head and aprons tied around the waist.

CUSTOMS AND COURTESIES

Greetings. A handshake is the most common greeting in Croatia, along with a phrase such as *Dobro jutro* (Good morning), *Dobra dan* (Good day), or *Dobra večer* (Good evening). The most common phrases for saying hello are *Zdravo* (Be healthy) and *Bok* (derived from *Zbogom*, it means "Hi"). Good-bye can be either *Zbogom* (With God) or *Do vidjenja* (Until we meet again). When friends and relatives greet, they may embrace and appear to kiss cheeks. Croats kiss once or twice—once to each cheek—while Serbs generally add a third kiss. Actually, most people brush cheeks and "kiss the air." In formal situations, a man waits for a woman to extend her hand. In formal greetings, the family name is preceded by *Gospodine* (Mr.), *Gospodjo* (Mrs.), *Gospodjice* (Miss), or a professional title. The younger person greets first. Close friends and relatives use first names. Kinship is important and terms used when addressing family depend on that relationship. For example, the word for "aunt" can be either *tetka* (mother's or father's sister) or *ujna* (mother's brother's wife) or *strina* (father's brother's wife).

Gestures. Hand movement is common during conversation and includes gestures popular throughout Europe. One indicates "money" by rubbing the thumb and index finger of the right hand. People beckon with the index finger or by waving all fingers inward with the palm up. Yawning in public is impolite. On public transportation, it is polite to offer one's seat to pregnant women or the elderly. While public approval is displayed by applause, whistling or shouting "ouuuu" shows disapproval.

Visiting. Croats enjoy visiting one another to socialize. Most visits are arranged in advance, but unexpected guests also are welcomed. When invited to a home, guests bring a gift to the hosts. It is usually a bottle of wine, sweets, or an odd number of flowers. Gifts are unwrapped in the presence of the giver, whom the hosts thank. Flowers are given to the hostess, other types of gifts to the host. Flowers, if wrapped, are unwrapped before the hosts open the door. The hostess puts them in a vase and places them in the room where the guests are seated. The host offers something to drink or a snack, and the hostess makes coffee (usually Turkish) and offers biscuits or cookies. It is impolite not to accept refreshments. At small gatherings, newly arrived guests greet each person separately. Evening visits usually end before 11 p.m., except on special occasions. Hosts who live in an apartment accompany departing guests out the door; those who live in a house sometimes accompany them a little way down the street.

Eating. Breakfast is light and usually accompanied by black coffee. Lunch is the main meal of the day and consists of soup, meat, salad, bread or potatoes, and a dessert. In urban areas, dinner usually consists of cold cuts, bread, cheeses, and eggs. Rural people might have this or a cooked meal. People eat in the continental style, with the fork in the left hand and the knife remaining in the right. They keep hands above the table. Conversation at the table is often lively. Regional cuisine varies, with northern food being somewhat heavier and spicier than southern food. In coastal areas, people might break at midmorning for *marenda*, a light meal of fish, cheese, and bread. A midday snack is common in some areas.

In restaurants, one pays the bill at the table. A 5 to 10 percent tip is customary; it is given to the waiter with the bill and not left on the table. Among friends or colleagues, one person often pays for the entire meal. Over time, these people will take turns paying the bill.

LIFESTYLE

Family. Rural families traditionally include grandparents, parents, and two or more children. The father or grandfather has a dominant role in the family. Urban families usually have two children. Both husband and wife work and share in decision-making. Grandparents may also be included but less often than in rural areas. Children of working mothers may go to day-care centers or be cared for by family members (usually grandparents). Parents often feel obligated, especially in rural areas, to support grown or married children by giving them money or housing. In turn, children are expected to care for their elderly parents. Adult children often live with their parents until they marry or are able to be on their own.

Dating and Marriage. The youth begin dating around age 15, beginning with small groups. They like to gather downtown in cities or at the town square in rural areas. Small cafés and disco clubs are popular dating destinations. Rural people marry in their early twenties and urban dwellers in their late twenties to early thirties. To be legally married, one must have a civil ceremony. Having a church wedding before or after the civil one has become popular since 1991. After the ceremony, the wedding party usually is held at a restaurant or home. Weddings in rural areas are a particular cause for celebration; festivities may last more than a day.

Diet. The Croatian diet is influenced by its varied climate, landscape, and neighboring cultures. Seafood and vegetables are most popular in coastal areas. Dishes made from chicken, beef, fish, pork, and lamb are common throughout Croatia. An inland specialty is *štrukli* (a salt or sweet-cheese strudel, boiled or in a casserole). Meals in the countryside are large and made with seasonal ingredients. The main meal of the day usually consists of some sort of meat or fish, potatoes, and rice or corn. Urban families have less time to cook than their rural counterparts and therefore eat foods more convenient to prepare. Wine is the most popular drink with a meal. Also popular are beer, mineral water, and fruit drinks.

Recreation. People are sociable and enjoy getting together on family occasions or for historical, religious, cultural, and sporting events. The most popular sport is soccer, followed by basketball, handball, water polo, and sailing. Croatia's national soccer team advanced to third place during its first World Cup competition in 1998. Other favorite sports include tennis, chess, volleyball, riflery, hockey, boxing, skiing, swimming, bowling, rowing, fishing, and hunting.

People enjoy going on walks and having picnics. Families usually have summer vacations of one to four weeks. Urban

▼ EUROPE

people enjoy outings in the countryside, vacationing on the Adriatic Coast, and traveling abroad. Television is watched in the evening and on weekends.

The Arts. The arts are well developed and enjoyed. Theaters, opera houses, movie theaters, and museums are popular. Croatian films have a growing international reputation, particularly animated films. In fact, the Zagreb animated film, *The Substitute*, was the first non-American film to win an Oscar. Traditionally, the country's literature often has focused on themes of nationalism and individual struggle. Miroslav Krleza, Marin Drzic, and Tin Ujevic are some of the best-known contemporary writers. Croatian sculptor Ivan Mestrovic has achieved international as well as national acclaim.

The folk dance, *kolo*, performed to the accompaniment of a traditional instrument, the *tamburitza*, is common at Croatian gatherings. Naive art, which is created by artists who lack formal artistic training, is widely appreciated. Croatian naive art tends to celebrate nature and the timeless cycles of life.

Holidays. Official public holidays include the New Year (1–2 Jan.), Magi (6 Jan.), Easter Monday (the second day of Easter), May Day (1 May), Day of Croatian Statehood (30 May), Day of the Antifascist Struggle (22 June), Day of Patriotic Thanksgiving (5 Aug.), Ascension (15 Aug.), All Saints' Day (1 Nov.), and Christmas (25–26 Dec.). Orthodox Christians celebrate Christmas on 7 January and receive a paid holiday for it. Muslims may take paid leave to celebrate *Ramasan Bairam* (the feast at the end of the month of fasting) and *Kurban Bairam* (Feast of the Sacrifice). Jews also may have paid leave for *Yom Kippur* and *Rosh Hashanah*.

Commerce. During the week, business and work hours begin at 8 a.m. and end at 4 p.m. Stores are open until 8 p.m. On Saturday, stores close at 1 p.m., except in tourist areas, where they stay open later. Socializing, especially after meetings, is important among business associates.

SOCIETY

Government. The Republic of Croatia has 21 counties. The president (currently Stipe Mesic) appoints the prime minister as head of government. Parliament (*Sabor*) consists of a 151-seat House of Representatives and a 68-seat Chamber of Counties. The constitution enacted in December 1990 is called the Christmas Constitution. Croatia's voting age is 18. Dominant political parties include the Social Democratic Party (SDP), the Liberal Social Party (HSLS), and the HDZ. A number of smaller parties also have legislative representation.

Economy. Central planning and state domination were ineffective in developing Croatia's economy when it was part of Yugoslavia, even though it was among the most prosperous of the federation's republics. In 1991, the Croatian government began to institute market-oriented reforms by encouraging privatization and entrepreneurship. Progress was interrupted by the war and refugee situation, but by 1995, inflation had been reduced to less than 4 percent. However, inflation has now started to rise again. The government continues to seek ways to attract more foreign investment and build a stronger economy. But economic growth is slow and the country faces

DEVELOPMENT DATA

Human Dev. Index* rank	49 of 174 countries
Adjusted for women	45 of 143 countries
Real GDP per capita	$6,749
Adult literacy rate	98 percent
Infant mortality rate	7 per 1,000 births
Life expectancy	69 (male); 77 (female)

a recession. Unemployment is high, at more than 20 percent. The government faces billions of dollars in foreign debt remaining from the Tudjman era. Regional instability caused by Serbian aggression and NATO intervention in Yugoslavia has significantly hurt tourism in Croatia.

Croatia has a developed industrial sector and exports ships, equipment, chemicals, textiles, and furniture. Many factories and workers, idled by the region's conflicts, have the potential to be highly productive. Tourism is a vital source of revenue and jobs, but its sharp decline has cost Croatia much needed revenue. Remittances from expatriate workers living in other European countries continue to be an important source of income for the country. The currency is the Croatian *kuna* (HRK).

Transportation and Communications. Although many own private cars, people often use public streetcars and buses for urban transportation because they are inexpensive and convenient. In small cities and rural areas, bicycles are popular for getting around. Air and waterway links connect Croatian cities together and with other countries. Plans are being made to build a highway linking Zagreb to Dubrovnik via Sisak. The communications system functions well but lags behind western European standards. The government is updating and improving it. The number of private newspapers is increasing, but the government has been criticized for its tight control of the media, particularly television, which is the main news source for most Croatians.

Education. Eight years of basic education are required, beginning at age seven. There are a number of secondary schools and four universities. Secondary schooling lasts four years but is not mandatory. Education is free to citizens at all levels. Those who gain entrance to a university may attend at no cost. Those who can or will pay tuition are allowed to enroll above the normal entrance quotas. Ethnic minorities may run their own schools.

Health. Health care is provided by the government, paid for by income taxes. Care is available to all and is of good quality. Facilities are most modern in large cities. People can pay to see private doctors.

CONTACT INFORMATION

Croatian embassy, 2343 Massachusetts Avenue NW, Washington, DC 20008; phone (202) 588-5899 ext. 28; Web site www.croatiaemb.org. Croatian National Tourist Office, 350 Fifth Avenue, Suite 4003, New York, NY 10118; phone (800) 829-4416.

1305 North Research Way, Bldg. K
Orem, Utah 84097-6200 USA
1.800.528.6279; 801.705.4250
fax 801.705.4350
www.culturegrams.com

Republic of
Cuba

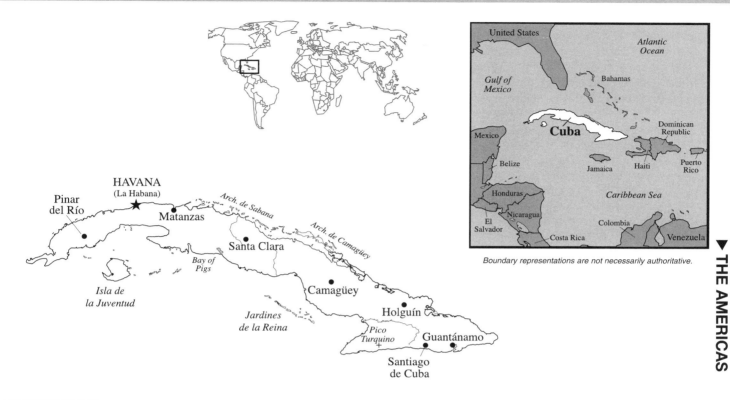

Boundary representations are not necessarily authoritative.

◄ THE AMERICAS

BACKGROUND

Land and Climate. Cuba is an archipelago of two main islands, Cuba and *Isla de la Juventud* (Isle of Youth), and about 1,600 keys and islets. The total area of 42,803 square miles (110,860 square kilometers) is nearly as large as Pennsylvania. Cuba lies approximately 90 miles (145 kilometers) south of the United States. Low hills and fertile valleys cover more than half the country. Mountain ranges divide the country into three regions: west, center, and east. The highest peak, Pico Turquino, rises to 8,320 feet (1,974 meters) in the east. Tropical forests in the east contrast with central prairies and western hills and valleys, where the royal palm is the dominant tree.

Cuba's subtropical climate is warm and humid. The average annual temperature is 75°F (24°C). Cuba experiences a dry season from November to April and a hotter wet season from May to October. About two-thirds of all precipitation falls in this latter season, when hurricanes are also frequent.

History. Prior to the 1492 arrival of Christopher Columbus, Cuba was inhabited by three indigenous groups, the largest and most advanced being the Taino. In 1511, a Spanish colony was firmly established; by 1535, the enslaved native population had been wiped out. Havana, founded in the early 1500s, became the capital and a gathering point for Spanish treasure fleets. In 1762, Havana fell into British hands for a short period until it was returned to Spain in exchange for Florida the following year. Beginning in the 18th century, African slaves were brought to Cuba to work on plantations. In the 19th century, sugar production became the basis of the economy. Despite numerous rebellions, and unlike much of Latin America, Cuba remained in Spanish hands. The various

uprisings culminated in the Ten Years' War (1868–78), which ended in failure after the loss of 200,000 lives.

José Martí, Cuba's national hero, led another revolt in 1895 but died early in the struggle. International protests over Spain's treatment of Cuba led to U.S. involvement and the Spanish-American War of 1898. Cuba gained independence, but it was not official until the end of the U.S. occupation in 1902. Other occupations (1906–9, 1912) were based on the Platt Amendment to Cuba's constitution, which allowed U.S. intervention to maintain stability. In 1934, the United States canceled the amendment, receiving a 99-year lease on Guantánamo Bay—territory still held by the U.S. military.

U.S. investment was crucial to the Cuban economy through the 1950s, and sugar remained the chief export. In 1952, Fulgencio Batista's military coup established a dictatorship that increased corruption and turmoil. Popular opposition was organized into a rebel movement under the leadership of Fidel Castro. After a two-year guerrilla war, Castro overthrew Batista, who left the country in 1959.

Extensive economic and social change took place after the revolution. Agrarian reform, nationalization of industry and banking, creation of rural cooperatives, and other reforms were part of Castro's socialist-oriented path of development. These measures clashed with U.S. interests, and Washington responded by breaking off relations and imposing a trade embargo that is still in effect.

Cuba enjoyed support in the communist world through the 1970s and 1980s. Economic growth was steady, and important advancements were made in education, public health, and social security. The dissolution of the socialist bloc in the early 1990s seriously harmed Cuba's economy and standard of living. The government responded by liberalizing some economic policies and welcoming more international investment. Hopes for better relations with the United States were dashed in 1996 when Cuban jets shot down two U.S. civilian planes near or over Cuban territorial waters. The United States tightened its embargo and isolation of Cuba.

Antagonism between the two neighbors softened slightly in 1998 after Pope John Paul II visited Cuba. However, friction returned in 1999 when child refugee Elián González was held in Miami by Cuban American relatives. Though the U.S. government intervened and returned him to the custody of his father, Elián remained in the United States seven months. In October 2000, the United States passed a bill allowing food and medicine sales to Cuba. Restrictions within the bill will prevent these items from reaching most Cubans, and Castro continues to demand that all trade sanctions be lifted.

THE PEOPLE

Population. Cuba's population of almost 11.14 million is growing annually at 0.4 percent. Three-fourths of the people live in urban areas; Havana has 2.2 million residents. Cubans of Spanish descent make up about 66 percent of the population, while 12 percent have Black African ancestry. Another 21.9 percent are of mixed heritage. The remaining 0.1 percent are of Asian origin. The Cuban culture is highly integrated because each ethnic group influences society in a variety of ways. More than half of all Cubans are younger than age 30. The Cuban American community in Florida has some one million members.

Language. Spanish is Cuba's official language. Slight accent and pronunciation differences exist among Cuba's three main regions. Many words, expressions, and idioms are unique to Cuban society and not used in other Spanish-speaking countries. Some examples are *pelotear* (to pass the buck), *plan jaba* (a special shopping plan for working women), *amarillo* (traffic official), and *rebambaramba* (a free-for-all). English is a required course in secondary schools and is popular among a growing number of people interested in the tourist industry.

Religion. Historically, Cuba has been among the least religious of all Latin American countries. Society is highly secularized, and most people show no preference for organized religion. However, recent years have seen growth in most congregations and a strong revival of religious devotion. This is due partly to a 1991 change in a policy that had excluded persons with religious beliefs from the Communist Party. Economic struggles have also led some people to seek comfort in churches. The Pope's 1998 visit encouraged many young people to explore religious issues.

Catholicism is the most prevalent faith, although many people combine it with ideas of African origin to form beliefs known as *Santería*. A number of Protestant churches also function in Cuba, including Baptist, Methodist, and Presbyterian. Spiritualism, emphasizing communication with the dead, and *brujería* (witchcraft) are practiced by small groups. To operate in Cuba, churches must register with the government and satisfy rules of association. Religion is not discussed in school, but it can be taught in any of Cuba's 1,800 churches and chapels.

General Attitudes. Cubans are friendly, warm, communica-tive, enthusiastic, and hospitable. It is uncommon to meet a Cuban who is not outgoing and fond of festivals, music, and dancing. Cubans' sense of humor allows them to joke about almost anything, even hardships. This does not mean Cubans are shallow or cavalier, but they generally face difficulties with a positive attitude. In hard times, they look to friends and family for support. Current economic hardships have complicated feelings for many who are disappointed with Cuba's relative poverty. Young people are increasingly confused by what they are taught about their society, which may contradict with their daily experiences.

Despite troubles, Cubans are patriotic and value their national dignity. They honor the memories of those who died fighting for their country. Cubans are often impassioned in their opinions and will argue their convictions with energy. Men especially like to debate the economy, international politics, and baseball. Cubans have a casual view of time. Punctuality and schedules are not stressed. The joy of an event is more important than how long it should last.

Personal Appearance. Most people prefer lightweight, casual clothing. Cleanliness is important, even in the current period of austerity. Women of all ages wear slacks, jeans, short skirts, blouses, and canvas shoes or sandals. Dresses are worn at more formal events. Men wear long pants, jeans, and shirts or T-shirts in everyday situations. More formally, they may wear a *guayabera*, a traditional square-cut shirt. Shorts are popular in urban areas and at the beach, especially among the youth. Primary and secondary school students wear uniforms, as do students in medical colleges.

CUSTOMS AND COURTESIES

Greetings. Men greet with a handshake and *¿Qué tal?* (How are you?). They often shake hands with everyone when entering a home or greeting a group. Most women kiss each other once on the cheek and offer a verbal greeting. Kissing on the cheek is also common between friends of the opposite sex, especially among younger people. Greetings between strangers are brief; friends spend a short time talking about their families or health. Common verbal greetings include *¡Buenos días!* (Good morning), *¡Buenas tardes!* (Good afternoon), and *¡Buenas noches!* (Good evening). *¡Adiós!* (Good-bye) is also a typical greeting when people pass on the street. When parting, people may say *¡Hasta luego!* (So long).

People usually address others by first name, or they may use a professional title without a surname. Strangers frequently use *Compañero/Compañera* (Comrade), *Señor* (Mr.), and *Señora* (Mrs.). Nicknames are common among friends, acquaintances, and coworkers.

Gestures. Cubans use hand gestures while talking to reinforce ideas and emotions, which makes conversation rather lively. It is not considered rude to interrupt a friend or acquaintance during conversation. Maintaining eye contact while talking is important, especially in a formal situation. Lack of eye contact may be considered a sign of insincerity or spite. People stand close when talking, often touching or tapping each other when making a point. One beckons by waving fingers inward with the palm down. Beckoning people with the palm up is a hostile gesture.

Visiting. Cubans are extremely social, and visiting in the home is common. Friends also socialize on the street, while waiting in lines, and at gatherings in neighborhoods and work centers. Daytime visits are often unannounced but welcome. They may be long or short, without too much concern for schedules. Weekends and holidays are the most popular times to visit. Hosts usually offer guests something to drink, such as black coffee, wine, or a soft drink. Declining such offers is not impolite. If visitors arrive at mealtime, hosts politely offer to share the meal, but guests respectfully decline and leave. When rural people visit urban friends, they may take a gift of food; urbanites visiting in rural areas may offer money to help pay expenses related to their stay.

While Cubans enjoy inviting friends over for an evening meal or party, the practice has become less common due to shortages and evening energy blackouts. Such socializing is casual, and guests often bring small gifts of rum, wine, or food to be consumed during the evening.

Eating. A light *desayuno* (breakfast) usually includes a cup of black coffee. Most workers and students eat *almuerzo* (lunch) at work or school. The family gets together for *comida* (dinner), the most important meal. Table manners vary from home to home. Generally, however, diners keep hands above the table, and pleasant conversation accompanies meals. Hosts expect to offer guests second helpings, but guests may decline. Except for expensive home restaurants, all restaurants are state owned. Ordinary citizens rarely eat in these establishments because of their price. People do enjoy snacks sold by street vendors.

LIFESTYLE

Family. Cubans maintain strong family ties. The nuclear family is standard, but many households include grandparents as well. Extended family members often build homes near one another to remain close. When adult children marry, they usually live with a parent until they can obtain housing, which is in short supply. The average family owns a small house or apartment with all major utilities available.

Women account for 37 percent of the labor force and 55 percent of the country's specialists. They hold 28 percent of leading government and administrative posts. However, traditional values maintain a strong influence on family relations, so women are also responsible for most household chores and child care. This situation is changing among younger couples.

As in most Latin American countries, a person bears two family names. The last name is the mother's family name; the second-to-last name is the father's family name and the person's surname.

Dating and Marriage. Young people have many opportunities to socialize. Couples usually meet at school, youth parties, dances, music festivals, beach outings, movies, and through conversations on park benches. Most people marry in their twenties. A civil ceremony is held in an urban "wedding palace," followed by a small family party. An increasing number of couples also are having church ceremonies. Common-law marriages are becoming more prevalent, due to changes in social conventions and the high cost of weddings.

Diet. At present, the Cuban diet is based on foods grown locally. *Arroz y frijoles* (rice and beans) is the traditional staple meal. Indeed, rice is served at most meals, along with a dish such as potatoes, *boniatos* (sweet potatoes), *yuca* (cas-

sava), *plátanos* (plantains), or tomatoes. Eggs are eaten boiled, fried, or as an omelette (called a *tortilla*). Corn is the basis of many foods, including the popular *harina de maíz* (cornmeal).

Roast pork, currently a luxury, is the favorite meat and is eaten on special occasions. Seafood is eaten in coastal areas. Tilapia, a freshwater fish found in Cuba's numerous reservoirs, is also popular. Favorite tropical fruits—mangoes, avocados, guavas, oranges, lemons, pineapples, and papayas—are eaten in season. Sweets (often homemade) usually are eaten as desserts or snacks; ice cream is popular but is in short supply. Coffee generally is served sweet and strong.

Recreation. Sports are highly developed in Cuba, which ranked eighth in the 2000 Olympic Games in terms of medals won. The most popular sport is baseball. Boys begin playing in leagues by age seven. Adult, college, and professional competition is well organized. Boxing, basketball, swimming, volleyball, and cycling are widely enjoyed. Girls enjoy sports in school, but women usually do not play sports. Dominoes is a national pastime, played by males of all ages (especially the retired) in front of homes and practically everywhere else. Cubans dance at discos, go to music festivals or movies, watch videos or television, and converse with each other.

The Arts. Cubans cannot be separated from their love of music and dance. The people's Spanish and African heritage joined to create uniquely Cuban rhythms and sounds. Maracas, guitars, bongos, the *tres* (a small three-paired stringed instrument), and trumpets combine to create the *son*, a genre of music that gave birth to the mambo. Cuban jazz and salsa have spread throughout the world. The cha-cha, which originated in Cuba, and *bolero* are also popular dances.

In the past, art and literature were outlets for political commentary. Late 19th century writer and revolutionary José Martí promoted independence from Spain in his works. Now, the arts are controlled to prevent antigovernment sentiment.

Holidays. Liberation Day (1 Jan.) commemorates the revolution of 1958 and 1959; it is preceded by New Year's Eve (31 Dec.) festivities. Other holidays are Labor Day (1 May), Anniversary of the Attack on the Moncada Garrison in Santiago de Cuba in 1953 (26 July), and Beginning of the War of Independence from Spain (10 Oct.). Mother's Day (second Sunday in May) is also popular.

Religious holidays are not officially recognized but may be celebrated with feasts and religious services. In 1997, Christmas Day was declared a holiday in advance of the Pope's visit. Christians attend special services during the Christmas season, Holy Week, and Easter. Often, a particular holiday honors a deity from Catholicism and Santería as one-in-the-same. For instance, St. Lazarus's Day (17 Dec.) honors both that Catholic saint and the African god Babalú Ayé. A chapel near Havana dedicated to St. Lazarus/Babalú Ayé draws tens of thousands of pilgrims annually. St. Barbara's Day (4 Dec.) represents both a Catholic martyr and the African goddess Changó. And Virgen de la Caridad del Cobre (8 Sept.) honors the patron saint of Cuba and the African goddess Ochún.

Commerce. Most establishments are open from 9 a.m. until 5 p.m. Many stores close on Sunday. Basic foods are rationed and sold in state-owned *bodegas* (neighborhood grocery stores). A much wider variety of items is available in stores that only accept foreign currency, primarily U.S. dollars. Cubans with access to dollars are far more able to provide for their families than those without. Various markets sell artisans' goods, prepared foods, and private agricultural produce. Bargaining is common in these private markets. Street vendors sell anything from rice to candles to flowers.

SOCIETY

Government.   Cuba is a socialist state, and its constitution regards the Communist Party as the leading force of society. The country has 14 provinces and 1 special municipality (Isle of Youth). Legislative authority is vested in the National Assembly of People's Power, with 601 deputies elected to serve five-year terms. Special commissions nominate approved candidates to run for seats in the assembly. Opposition parties are illegal. The National Assembly elects from its membership the Council of State as the sitting legislature. Its president is both chief of state and head of government. President Fidel Castro Ruiz has governed since 1959. The next elections are in 2003. The voting age is 16. Executive authority is vested in the Council of Ministers, appointed by the National Assembly upon the proposal of the head of state. Municipal and provincial assemblies deal with local affairs.

Economy.   After trade links with the Soviet bloc dissolved in the early 1990s, declining living standards and a large wave of attempted emigration led the government to liberalize some economic policies. It opened free markets for crafts and produce; granted 2.6 million hectares of state land to farming cooperatives; increased soybean production to boost protein consumption; promoted certain types of self-employment; reorganized some state enterprises; and established joint ventures with foreign firms in tourism, mining, communications, and construction. The economy experienced modest growth after 1994 but slowed to 1 percent in 1998. The economy recovered, averaging about 6 percent growth in 1999 and 4 percent in 2000. Mexico and Canada are Cuba's most important trading partners.

Agriculture employs about 20 percent of the labor force. The main crops are sugarcane, tobacco, citrus fruit, coffee, rice, grains, and vegetables. Sugar is the most important export, but others include nickel, tobacco, cement, and fruit. Tourism is eclipsing sugar production as the largest source of revenue and informal employment. The labor force is mostly skilled: three-fourths of all workers have a secondary or higher education. However, people lack opportunities and resources to fully achieve personal goals. Cubans cannot employ other Cubans in private businesses. The official currency is the Cuban *peso* (Cu$), but the U.S. dollar is legal and the preferred currency for most Cubans. The United States prohibits sending dollars to Cuba except in certain circumstances. Cuban Americans send money and gifts to their families in Cuba. These remittances allow about half of all Cubans to access goods not otherwise available.

Transportation and Communications.   In cities, people travel by bicycle or on crowded buses. Taxis are scarce. In the

DEVELOPMENT DATA

Human Dev. Index* rank	56 of 174 countries
Adjusted for women	NA
Real GDP per capita	$3,967
Adult literacy rate	96 percent
Infant mortality rate	8 per 1,000 births
Life expectancy	73 (male); 78 (female)

countryside, horse-drawn carts are widely used. Trains and buses travel between cities; an extensive highway system connects all parts of the country. Many roads are in disrepair. Motorcycles are more common than cars, and fuel is rationed. Strict laws prohibit moving from one province to another.

The telephone system is undergoing modernization; few homes outside Havana have phones. Media operations, including a well-developed film industry, are owned and controlled by the state. Most homes have televisions. There are more than 50 radio stations and 2 television stations. Several weekly newspapers are published, but a paper shortage restricts circulation. Postal and telegraph services cover the entire country.

Education.   Education is a priority in Cuban society, and the state provides free primary, secondary, technical, and higher education to all citizens. Education is mandatory between ages five and twelve (kindergarten through the primary level). More than 90 percent of all children continue with secondary education. Most teenagers attend boarding schools in rural areas; exemptions are made for those accepted to art school. Secondary graduates may take college entrance exams or go to a technical training institute. Cuba has an average of one teacher for every 45 inhabitants. Preschool is available in urban areas. Special schools educate the mentally or physically challenged, and there are schools for students gifted in sports and the arts. Cuba has 46 centers of higher education. Despite a shortage of basic supplies like textbooks and paper, no child is without schooling.

Health.   Cuba's health-care system is a government priority; Cuba has some 267 hospitals. More than 420 clinics provide various services, including maternal and infant care. Family doctors are assigned to serve each community, large and small, and there is one doctor for every 260 Cubans. Despite a shortage of medicines and other supplies, Cuba's average life expectancy and infant mortality rates are the best in Latin America. Many childhood diseases have been eradicated through massive vaccination campaigns. More than 20 medical schools and other institutions train health-care workers.

CONTACT INFORMATION

Cuban Interests Section of the Embassy of Switzerland, 2630 16th Street NW, Washington, DC 20009; phone (202) 797-8518; Web site www.swissemb.org. Office of Foreign Assets Control, U.S. Department of Treasury, 1500 Pennsylvania Avenue NW, Washington, DC 20220; phone (202) 622-2480; Web site www.treas.gov/ofac.

CultureGrams™
People. The World. You.

1305 North Research Way, Bldg. K
Orem, Utah 84097-6200 USA
1.800.528.6279; 801.705.4250
fax 801.705.4350
www.culturegrams.com

Czech Republic

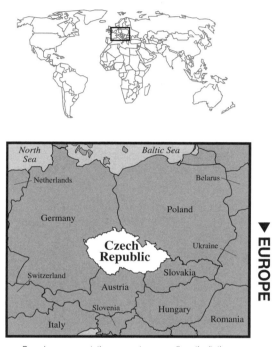

Boundary representations are not necessarily authoritative.

BACKGROUND

Land and Climate. Covering 30,387 square miles (78,703 square kilometers), the Czech Republic is just smaller than South Carolina. There are three principal geographic regions: Bohemia, Moravia, and Silesia. Bohemia comprises roughly the western two-thirds of the country. Moravia occupies nearly one-third of the eastern portion. Silesia is a relatively small area in the northeast near the Polish border. It is dominated by coal fields and steel mills centered around the city of Ostrava.

Mountain ranges form the northern and western boundaries with Germany and Poland. The interior of Bohemia is relatively flat, while Moravia has gently rolling hills. Bohemia's rivers flow north to the *Labe* (Elbe) River, and Moravia's rivers flow south to the Danube. Bohemia is dominated by industry, particularly in the northern and western portions. Moravia is largely agricultural. Serious flooding during the summer of 1997 caused extensive damage across Moravia.

A continental climate prevails. Summers are moderate. High temperatures are rare but may occur in July. Winters often are cold with snow, particularly in the mountains; temperatures are usually below freezing.

History. In the fifth century, Slavic tribes began settling the area, and by the middle of the ninth century they lived in a loose confederation known as the Great Moravian Empire. Its brief history ended in 907 with the invasion by the nomadic Magyars (ancestors of today's Hungarians). The Slovak region became subject to Hungarian rule, while Czechs developed the Bohemian Empire, centered in Prague. In the 14th century, under the leadership of Charles IV, Prague

became a cultural and political capital that rivaled Paris. In the 15th century, Bohemia was a center of the Protestant Reformation led by Jan Hus, who became a martyr and national hero when he was burned at the stake as a heretic in 1415. Civil war in Bohemia and events elsewhere in Europe led the Czechs (as well as people in Hungary and Slovakia) to become part of the Hapsburg (Austro-Hungarian) Empire in 1526.

When the Hapsburg Empire collapsed upon defeat in World War I (1918), Czech and Slovak lands were united to form a new Czecho-Slovak state (the hyphen was dropped in 1920). Tomas Masaryk became the first president. Democracy flourished and affluence began to spread, but the country was not able to withstand German aggression. Hitler first annexed the Sudetenland, a region of German-speaking people, in 1938. By 1939, all Czech lands had fallen into German possession. The Czechoslovak people then suffered through World War II, in which more than 350,000 citizens (250,000 Jews) lost their lives. After the war, three million Germans were forced out of the country.

Liberated in 1945 by Allied forces, Czechoslovakia held elections in 1946 under Soviet auspices. Left-wing parties performed well, and by 1948 the Communists had seized control of the government. The Soviet-style state promoted rapid industrialization in the 1950s. Social and economic policies liberalized in the 1960s in response to a deteriorating quality of life. This led to discussions about easing political restrictions. In 1968, reform-minded Alexander Dubček, a Slovak, assumed leadership and put into motion a series of reforms known as "socialism with a human face."

But the Soviet Union–led Warsaw Pact crushed the movement. The Communist Party was purged of liberals, and reforms were abolished.

In the 1970s, many dissident groups organized against the regime. Members of these groups joined with workers, university students, and others in peaceful demonstrations in 1989 in what was called the Velvet Revolution. A crackdown on a student protest in November 1989 prompted a general strike that led General Secretary Miloš Jakeš to resign. Dubček returned to prominence and was elected leader of Parliament. Václav Havel, dissident playwright and leader of Civic Forum party, became president in 1990.

Full multiparty elections under a new constitution were held in 1992. Differences between Slovak and Czech leaders on such issues as resource distribution, infrastructure investment, and the course of economic reform led the two governments to peacefully split into two sovereign states on 1 January 1993. Havel was reelected president of the Czech Republic; Václav Klaus continued as prime minister. With widespread support, Klaus launched an impressive program of economic reform.

Political infighting and economic stagnation increased following the 1996 elections. A financial scandal forced Klaus to resign in November 1997. Josef Tosovsky (not affiliated with any party) served as caretaker of the government until elections in June 1998. Short of a majority, the Social Democrats made a deal with the Civic Democratic Party a month later. The Czech Republic became a member of the North Atlantic Treaty Organization (NATO) in March 1999. The current prime minister is Social Democrat Milos Zeman. His government's priorities are bringing the economy out of recession, reducing government corruption, and preparing the country to join the European Union (EU).

THE PEOPLE

Population. The Czech Republic's population of 10.27 million is decreasing slightly. About 81 percent are Bohemian and 13 percent are Moravian. Ethnic Slovaks (3 percent) also live in the republic. The rest (2.5 percent) of the population is comprised of several groups: Poles and Silesians in the north, Germans in the west, and Romanians, Bulgarians, Ukrainians, Russians, and Greeks in the south and east. The Romany ethnic group (Gypsies) is nomadic and is difficult to count but officially forms 0.3 percent of the total population. The Romany are subject to discrimination throughout Europe and have not integrated into mainstream society. EU criticism of the country over its policies toward the Romany is one of the barriers to EU membership

Language. Czech is a Slavic language; it is similar to Slovak but also related to others (such as Polish, Croatian, and Russian). Czech uses a Latin alphabet with several distinct accent marks and letters. The marks ˇ, ´, and ˚ appear over consonants or vowels to soften or lengthen the sound. Minority groups speak their own tongues. Czechs also often speak German, Russian, or English, depending on their generation.

Religion. Although 80 percent of Czechs consider themselves Christians, many were influenced by 40 years of official (Communist) atheism. Therefore, their link to religion may involve more of the country's historical heritage than belief. In addition, Czechs tend to think of worship as a private mat-

ter. While they believe in a Universal Being, they may not necessarily be devoted to a religious institution. Still, around 39 percent belong to the Catholic Church, and many are Protestant. The Czech Brethren (a Lutheran/Calvinist group) claims 2 percent of the population as members. Many younger people are joining churches, some of which have been imported or established since 1990.

General Attitudes. Czechs value education, cleverness, social standing, modesty, and humor. Czech humor is dry and ironic rather than slapstick, and jokes and rustic parables are used commonly in conversation. Moravians and Slovaks are known to be more lighthearted and jovial than Bohemians. Irony also colors Czech realism, making it seem more like pessimism. While Czechs are individualistic to the degree that they may be stubborn in stating opinions or wishes, society's emphasis is on conformity and cooperation. For instance, community leaders (those who organize others) are held in high esteem. Young people are encouraged to belong to organizations such as the Boy Scouts or sports teams. Professionals (doctors, engineers, etc.) are admired, but so are skilled manual workers.

Personal Appearance. European fashions commonly are worn, and the youth wear the latest styles. Jeans and T-shirts are popular. Work attire for men generally is more casual than in some western European nations (e.g., sport jackets instead of suits, or blue overalls or jogging suits instead of shirts and ties). Older women generally do not wear slacks like the younger generation, and they wear hats more often. Adults wear shorts in parks or for recreation but not on city streets. Czechs dress up to attend cultural events; not being properly dressed is frowned upon. People in Moravia still wear traditional national costumes on festival days or for weddings and other special events.

CUSTOMS AND COURTESIES

Greetings. When strangers meet or when a young person greets an older person, they shake hands firmly and say their last names, followed by a verbal greeting, such as *Těší mne* (Pleased to meet you) or *Dobrý den* (Good day). A man usually waits for a woman to extend her hand before shaking. To show respect, one addresses both men and women by their professional titles (engineer, doctor, professor) and last names. It is common to preface the title with *Pán* (sir) or *Paní* (madam) when greeting the person: *Dobrý den, Paní Doktorká Čekanová*. One also uses *Pán* and *Paní* for persons without professional titles. People do not use first names until they are well acquainted, but relatives generally hug upon meeting and address each other by first names, as do young people of the same age.

To say good-bye, one uses the formal *Na schledanou* or the informal *Čau* (Ciao). *Ahoj* is an informal "Hi" and "Bye." One responds to *Děkuji* (Thank you) with *Prosím* (Please), meaning "You're welcome."

Gestures. People maintain eye contact while conversing. Czechs may often look at or even stare at other people in public, but usually with no ill intentions. People often gesture with their hands to emphasize conversation. They beckon and point with their index finger. When one counts on the fingers, the thumb (not index finger) is number one. Speaking loudly is impolite.

Visiting. Czechs consider the home to be private. They do not often visit one another unannounced; even spontaneous visitors (only relatives and very close friends) call ahead when possible. Others are not invited to a Czech's home for more than a drink or coffee. Most guests invited to dinner are taken to a restaurant; it is an honor to be invited to a home for a meal. Friends often socialize in pubs, coffeehouses, and wine bars.

Czechs remove their shoes when entering a home and leave them in the entryway. Visiting etiquette is fairly formal, but the atmosphere is warm. Guests are offered something to drink, or prior to a meal, hors d'oeuvres. Women guests may offer to help prepare the meal in the kitchen or to clear dishes, but the offer will be politely declined. Invited guests usually bring an odd number of flowers to the hostess. Any type of flower is acceptable, except chrysanthemums (used mostly in funeral arrangements). Small gifts for the children are appreciated. Guests might also bring wine or chocolates for the hosts. Flowers are given to students at graduation.

Eating. Czechs eat three meals a day and often a midmorning snack. For most families, lunch is the main meal. Dinner and breakfast are light. Women prepare meals, and men might help with cleanup. Few Czech men cook. Plates usually are prepared in the kitchen and carried to the table. The head of the household is served first, unless guests are present. People eat in the continental style, with the fork in the left hand and the knife remaining in the right. Hands, but not elbows, are kept above the table. Depending on the family, there is little dinner conversation unless the head of the household speaks first or special guests are present. The hostess generally offers seconds to guests, but it is not impolite to decline them after commenting on how good the food is.

Most Czechs do not eat out often. In restaurants, mineral water and bread and butter can be ordered, but they do not come with the meal. In pubs, there may be two waiters, one for the drinks and the other for the food. The headwaiter adds up the bill at the table. Drinking and toasting are common for formal and informal events. An empty glass is always refilled. When drinking socially, people do not pour for themselves.

LIFESTYLE

Family. Czech families traditionally are close and tight-knit. Urban families usually are small, rarely with more than two children. Rural families tend to be larger. Both parents generally work outside the home, but women are also responsible for the household and children. Urban housing is in short supply, so many families live in large apartment complexes on the outskirts of the city. Mothers receive several months of paid maternity leave, a subsidy for each birth, and child-care services when they return to work. Grandparents often help with child care, especially when a young couple is just starting out. Parents feel responsible for their adult children until they are financially independent. At the same time, adult children expect to take care of aging parents. Parents and children tend to share more expensive things like cars or *chaty* (cottages) for many years. Pets, especially dogs, are cherished members of many families.

Dating and Marriage. Young people tend to date in groups; they enjoy going to movies or the theater, hiking or camping, attending music festivals, or dancing at discos. Most men are married by the age of 30; women marry a few years earlier. Young couples tend to live with their parents after marriage because of a housing shortage, but they strive to become independent as soon as possible. Most urban weddings are held at city hall, with only the immediate family and closest friends present. A family luncheon or dinner is held afterward at a nearby hotel. Suit jackets and short dresses have been the standard wedding attire, but more formal gowns and tuxedos are being worn today. A church wedding, now legally binding, is becoming increasingly common. Honeymoons are also gaining in popularity. Rural weddings tend to incorporate more people, such as village members. Traditional costumes might be worn, and celebrations can last all day.

Diet. Traditional Czech food is heavy and arduous to prepare. In the last decade, a healthier diet (fewer heavy sauces, leaner meat, more vegetables) that is easier to prepare has become more popular. Lunch usually begins with a hearty soup, followed by a main dish of meat and potatoes or bread dumplings. A common dish is *vepřo-knedlo-zelí* (pork roast, dumplings, and sauerkraut). Ham on bread and sausages in buns are popular snack foods that can be purchased from sidewalk vendors.

A wide variety of breads and bakery items are available. Breakfast usually consists of rolls, coffee cake, butter, jam, and coffee. Many desserts are made from fruit. Beer, soda, and juice are common drinks.

Recreation. Czechs are known for their love of nature; on weekends, forests, fields, mountains, and lakes often are filled with Czechs (especially urban residents). A surprising number of families own cottages. Urban families often tend garden plots of flowers, fruit trees, and vegetables that are either near their cottage or in communal garden areas on city outskirts. Camping, hiking, swimming in lakes, gathering mushrooms and berries, and snow skiing are all favorite outdoor activities.

Popular sports are soccer, tennis, and ice hockey. The Czech Republic's national hockey team won the Olympic gold medal in 1998 and the world title in 1999 and 2000. Leisure pursuits include watching television, going to movies or concerts, dancing, taking walks, or getting together with friends. Gardening and home-improvement projects are also widely enjoyed. In the evening, men often gather in pubs to drink beer and talk, while women visit close friends at home. In smaller towns, people socialize while doing errands.

Czechs enjoy touring in a car or taking bus tours. Forty years of travel restrictions led to a pent-up desire for travel outside of the republic. Czechs usually vacation for one to three weeks. The Mediterranean is a popular destination.

The Arts. Czechs pride themselves on their support of the arts. Theater performances, concerts, and exhibits are held throughout the year. In the summer, small towns often sponsor informal, outdoor "forest theaters." The Prague Spring Festival is an important musical event. The Czech Republic also has a rich tradition of composers, including Dvořák and Smetana. Many Czech composers have taken their inspiration from folk music. Polkas and waltzes are popular folk dances.

Czech artists also have attracted attention in the visual arts, such as painting, lithography, and film. Czech painting influenced the art nouveau movement. Folk art includes puppet making, costume making, ceramics, toys, and glass.

EUROPE

Bohemian crystal is especially renowned. The Czech Republic also is known for its baroque, art nouveau, and cubist architecture.

Holidays. Public holidays include New Year's Day, Easter Monday, End of World War II (8 May), Cyril and Methodius's Day (5 July), Jan Hus Day (6 July), Founding of the First Republic in 1918 (28 Oct.), and Christmas (24–26 Dec.). Cyril and Methodius are honored for introducing Christianity and creating the Cyrillic alphabet (used before the current Latin alphabet). Christmas Eve is the most important part of Christmas, and people eat carp for dinner in honor of their Catholic heritage. They also eat *vánočka*, a fruit bread, in the days leading to Christmas and during Lent. Small marzipan candies or paper cards in the shape of pigs are given in the new year for good luck.

All Saints' Day (1 Nov.), Velvet Revolution Day (17 Nov.), and St. Nicholas Day (6 Dec.) are celebrated but are not days off from work. Each village or town also celebrates a day for its patron saint with fairs, dancing, feasting, and mass.

Commerce. The workday usually begins between 7 and 8 a.m. and ends between 3 and 4 p.m. Businesses and offices often close for lunch. Women might shop for fresh foods during this time. Government offices usually are open until 6 p.m., but people often leave for home by 4 p.m. Since 1989, more stores in town centers stay open later in the evening. Czechs shop weekly for groceries and other items, but they rely on small shops and market stands for daily purchases of bread, fruit, and vegetables.

SOCIETY

Government. The Czech Republic is a parliamentary democracy divided into eight regions. The president is head of state. Although ailing, President Havel was reelected in January 1998. The prime minister is head of government and leads Parliament's majority party or coalition. Parliament (or National Council) is composed of a Senate (81 seats) and a Chamber of Deputies (200 seats). The voting age is 18. The Social Democratic Party and the Civic Democratic Party are the two largest parties. Other parties include the Christian Democrats, Republicans, and Communists.

Economy. The Czech Republic enjoyed marked success in its initial years of transition from a planned to a free-market economy. Rapid reforms have encouraged privatization in many sectors. The export of manufactured goods is boosted by low labor costs and high quality work. Strong fiscal policies have led to balanced budgets and increased the country's likelihood of joining the European Union. However, economic progress has slowed considerably. The country experienced a sharp devaluation of its currency, the Czech *koruna* (Kc), throughout 1997. Budget cuts, the currency crisis, and severe flooding led to a recession. But, the recession appears to have ended with modest economic growth in 2000. Unemployment is around 8 percent.

Agriculture is important to the domestic economy, and the country is nearly self-sufficient in food. Crops include wheat, hops, sugar beets, potatoes, barley, rye, onions, and fruit. Tourism is increasingly important.

DEVELOPMENT DATA

Human Dev. Index* rank	34 of 174 countries
Adjusted for women	33 of 143 countries
Real GDP per capita	$12,362
Adult literacy rate	99 percent
Infant mortality rate	6 per 1,000 births
Life expectancy	70 (male); 77 (female)

Czechs form a cohesive, well educated, and hardworking labor force. The country's privatization program, which has sold stock to Czechs rather than outside interests or large firms, has given everyone a stake in economic performance. In 2000, the government took needed steps toward privatizing the banking and finance industries.

Transportation and Communications. Public transportation is extensive and reliable in most urban areas and between towns and cities. The fleet of trams, buses, and trains is aging, and the industry is being pressed to privatize and modernize. This will increase prices and decrease service along unprofitable routes. More people are buying cars, and the Czech-manufactured *Škoda* is popular. NATO plans on improving the condition of the republic's airfields.

Daily newspapers are widely read, as is an abundance of other printed media. Many homes have cable television and access to international programming in addition to local broadcasts. People without phones in the home have access to public phones. Post offices sell transit tickets, accept utility payments, and provide many other services; postal delivery is efficient.

Education. Young children go to nursery school or kindergarten, but compulsory education begins at age six. Public education is free. In 1994, the primary education structure changed so grade school lasts five years. At age 11, children begin eight years of secondary school in one of three basic tracks: academic (leading to university studies), technical (for learning an occupation such as electrician, mason, etc.), or teaching. Two-year, postsecondary job training programs are increasingly popular. There are several institutions of higher learning, the oldest of which is Charles University, founded in 1348. University students do not pay for tuition, although legislation is pending.

Health. Health care is universal and the government covers most costs. People pay a minimal insurance premium and pay for some prescriptions. Employers assist in covering these costs. Pollution is the most serious threat to health.

CONTACT INFORMATION

Embassy of the Czech Republic, 3900 Spring of Freedom Street NW, Washington, DC 20008; phone (202) 274-9100; Web site www.czech.cz/washington. Czech Center, 1109 Madison Avenue, New York, NY 10028; phone (212) 288-0830; Web site www.czechcenter.com.

1305 North Research Way, Bldg. K
Orem, Utah 84097-6200 USA
1.800.528.6279; 801.705.4250
fax 801.705.4350
www.culturegrams.com

Kingdom of
Denmark

Skagen

Skagerrak
Bay

Ålborg

Læsø

Kattegat
Bay

Viborg

Randers

Jylland

Ringkøbing

Århus

Samsø

FAROE ISLANDS

Helsingør

Hillerød

Vejle

COPENHAGEN
(København)

Esbjerg

Roskilde

Odense

Sorø

Sjælland

Åbenrå

Fyn

Møn

Rønne

Langeland

Lolland

Nykøbing

Falster

Bornholm

Faroe
Islands

North
Sea

Norway

Sweden

Finland

Denmark

United
Kingdom

Baltic Sea

Netherlands

Germany

Poland

France

Belgium

Luxembourg

▼ EUROPE

Boundary representations are not necessarily authoritative.

BACKGROUND

Land and Climate. Located between the North and Baltic Seas, Denmark is a flat country with low to gently rolling plains. It consists of more than four hundred islands, of which only ninety are inhabited. Its total area is about twice the size of Massachusetts and covers 16,629 square miles (43,070 square kilometers). The largest landmasses include *Jylland* (Jutland), connected to the European continent, and the islands of *Sjælland* (Zealand), *Fyn* (Funen), *Lolland*, *Falster*, and *Bornholm*. Fertile agricultural land dominates the country's landscape of moors, lakes, and woodlands. Moderated by the warming influence of the Gulf Stream, Denmark's temperate maritime climate is usually cool, humid, and overcast. Winters are windy but mild compared to other Scandinavian countries. In January, high temperatures average about 34°F (2°C). Summers are cool, with July daily temperature highs averaging 72°F (22°C).

History. The Kingdom of Denmark (*Kongeriget Danmark*) has been a monarchy as long as it has existed. During the rule of the Vikings (c. 750–1035), Denmark was a great power, but it is not known exactly when and by whom it was controlled in the first decades of that time period. The first known king was Gorm the Old, who ruled in the early 900s. His son, Harald Bluetooth, united the country under Christianity and ruled in the latter half of the 900s. Gorm's grandson, Canute the Great, commanded a vast empire that included England until 1035. Queen Margrethe I united Denmark, Norway, and Sweden in the Union of Kalmar in 1397. Sweden left the union in 1523 and Norway in 1814. King Frederik VII signed a liberal constitution in 1849, making the country a constitutional monarchy rather than an autocracy. Some territory was lost to Prussia (Germany) in 1864, but the country remained stable.

Denmark was neutral during World War I, but Nazi Germany occupied it during World War II. Denmark joined the North Atlantic Treaty Organization (NATO) in 1949 and the European Community (now European Union, or EU) in 1973. During the 1970s and 1980s, Denmark concentrated on maintaining its social welfare system, broadening opportunities, and increasing the standard of living. During the mid-1980s, Denmark became interested in environmental protection and has since passed some of the world's toughest environmental legislation.

In 1992, Denmark rejected the Maastricht treaty that would have led to a common currency and stronger political ties within the EU. In the following year, voters accepted a modified version of the treaty granting Denmark exemption from the European single currency (euro), European citizenship, a unified European military, and the elimination of borders. Danes are somewhat skeptical and fearful that integration will cause small countries such as Denmark to be overpowered by larger EU nations. In a referendum on European Monetary Union (EMU) membership in September 2000, Danes rejected adoption of the euro as their national currency by 53 to 47 percent.

The Social Democrats (center-left) narrowly retained power following early elections called by Prime Minister Poul Nyrup Rasmussen in March 1998. The government's current priorities include balancing the national budget, reducing foreign debt, increasing employment, and protecting the environment. As in other European countries, the spread of mad cow and foot-and-mouth diseases has raised serious concerns about food safety and the economic impact of restrictions on the sale of EU animals and animal products.

THE PEOPLE

Population. Denmark's population of nearly 5.3 million is growing annually at 0.31 percent. A slight increase in births has occurred over the past few years. The majority of the population lives in urban areas. Most people in Denmark (99 percent) are Danish. Greenland and the Faroe Islands are part of the Danish Kingdom but are autonomous nations. These areas have small populations: 56,000 and 45,000, respectively. The Faroese belong to the old Nordic, and mostly Danish, ethnic background. The Greenlanders are Eskimos or are of mixed Eskimo and European origin. Because these groups are autonomous, with their own languages and cultural heritages, they are only mentioned here as part of Denmark's kingdom; their cultures are not discussed. Excellent access to health care, education, and economic prosperity affords Danish men and women many opportunities and choices in their lives.

Language. Danish is the official language. Because Danish is a Scandinavian language, Swedes and Norwegians can understand its written form. But spoken Danish is more difficult for other Scandinavians to understand because of differences in pronunciation and intonation. Vocabulary also varies slightly. Members of a very small German-speaking minority live along the border with Germany, but they also speak Danish. English is widely understood and spoken; in fact, it is part of the school curriculum after the fifth grade. German is a popular language to study in school.

Religion. The Evangelical Lutheran Church is Denmark's national church. Its members, who comprise 97 percent of the population, are automatically enrolled; they support it through taxation. Membership is expected and not considered a choice by Danes unless they belong to another religion.

The Lutheran Church and its value system permeate daily life in Denmark, although with little visibility. Danes generally do not attend church outside of Easter and Christmas, when attendance is very high. Although less than 5 percent attend Sunday meetings, most Danes still participate in religious ceremonies such as baptism and confirmation. Tolerance is extended to most other religious groups, such as Islam, whose numbers are increasing due to emigration. The Lutheran influence on Danish values, public school curricula, and everyday life has been partially credited to N. F. S. Grundtvig, a 19th-century Danish bishop and poet who revitalized the Danish church and founded the movement *Grundtvigianism* or "the happy Lutheranism."

General Attitudes. Denmark's high standard of living reflects a progressive attitude. For example, more than 80 percent of all Danish paper comes from recycled sources. Danes have a strong tendency to create equality by supporting weaker members of society. Because of their respect for every citizen's right to a good life, they are willing to share responsibility for their nation's social welfare through heavy taxes. This attitude also has encouraged their contributions to the development of Third World countries, especially in Africa. Danes see the government as the benevolent supporter of all of its members and know they can count on access to a high level of social services.

Danes are known for their tolerance of other people and diverse points of view. They admire individuals with a friendly attitude, a sense of humor, intelligence, sociability, personal stamina, integrity, and an open mind. They also appreciate those who do not take themselves too seriously. Their European neighbors perceive them as socially progressive, self-confident, relaxed, friendly, and liberal. Danes are considered to be less formal and introverted than those in other Scandinavian countries. Danes are also well educated and respected for their accomplishments in science, art, literature, and architecture.

Most matters of common wisdom directly relate to the Lutheran viewpoint. A love for understatement, rather than exaggeration, prevails. In Jylland, for example, rich people are known to remove the labels off their expensive cars and to dress down rather than dress up.

Personal Appearance. Clothing varies according to the season. However, the windy and rainy climate makes waterproof clothing (and sturdy shoes or boots) essential year-round. As the saying goes, "There is no such thing as bad weather. You just have to dress right." From late fall to early spring, wool coats and knitted sweaters are important to the Danish wardrobe. With the arrival of warmer temperatures and brighter days, Danes enjoy wearing lighter fabrics and jackets, particularly in pastel colors.

In general, Danes wear relaxed, casual clothes and avoid flashy dress. Even at the most elegant restaurants, men are not required to wear a jacket and tie, though most do. Danes follow general European fashion trends. Businessmen wear suits. Professional women are expected to dress fashionably; both skirts and jackets or dressy pants are acceptable. Dressing up for special occasions is expected.

CUSTOMS AND COURTESIES

Greetings. Although usually informal, Danes shake hands when introduced to strangers, at the end of business meetings, and on formal occasions. However, this gesture is not considered necessary when greeting friends. Young people and close acquaintants usually greet each other with a nod or a wave and say *Dav* (pronounced DOW), which is like saying "Hello." The youth also say *Hej* (pronounced HEY) or even *Hi* when greeting or parting. The term for "Good day" is *Goddag*. Using a person's first name is the most common way of addressing others. Only in rare formal situations do people use last names. Even managers and university professors usually are addressed by first name.

Gestures. Danes appreciate courtesy in all interactions. Eye contact is important during conversation. Danes generally do not use many hand gestures. The few gestures used include "thumbs up" to signal "well done" or a circle formed with the thumb and index finger to indicate appreciation. Yawning or coughing without covering the mouth is impolite. Keeping hands in one's pockets during conversation also is considered rude. Displaying affection in public is accepted to a certain point. It is considered polite to give one's seat to pregnant women or the elderly. Most women allow men to open doors for them. Busy stores often have an automatic queue or number system for customers standing in line.

Visiting. Proper etiquette is important when visiting. Except when calling on close friends, Danes always plan visits in advance; they never arrive unannounced. Most invitations are for dinner or for a cup of coffee, which includes some kind of cake or biscuit. Because of the weather and the dark winters, Danes take great pride in keeping a nice and cozy home. They enjoy having visitors in their homes and do their best to make guests feel welcome; however, one should not follow a host into other rooms unless invited. Guests should arrive on time and follow the host's suggestions of where to sit. It is considerate to bring a gift to the hostess, such as flowers, wine, chocolates, or to bring something inexpensive for children. Leaving directly after a meal is impolite, and conversing about one's personal life is avoided.

Although most Danes socialize in the home, young people enjoy socializing at cafés, which in urban areas are gaining popularity among people of all ages. Socializing is also common at local community clubs known as *foreninger*. These clubs are based on a wide range of interests such as hobbies, sports, political and professional organizations, etc.

Eating. For many busy families, dinner is the only occasion during the day to meet and discuss family matters. Most families make an effort to have dinner together every evening. Danes eat in the continental style, with the fork in the left hand and the knife remaining in the right. At family meals, the father and mother sit at opposite ends of the table. Everyone is seated and served before anyone begins to eat. A parent will often say *Vær så god* (Please, eat well) to begin the meal, especially if guests are present. When passing and receiving food, one might say *Vær så god* and *Tak* (Thank you).

Hosts customarily offer their guests second helpings, as it is their duty to see that the guests are satisfied. One does not leave the table until the hostess rises. Then, upon leaving, the guest thanks the hostess for the meal by saying *Tak for mad!* (Thanks for the meal!). In restaurants, a service charge is included in the bill, but some people also leave a small tip.

LIFESTYLE

Family. Danish families are generally small, close-knit, and stable. More than one-third of children are born out of wedlock, often to couples living together. With women making up 47 percent of the workforce, both father and mother usually work outside the home. Government-funded day-care centers are crucial to working mothers. Women in the workforce get a six-month paid maternity leave; men get an optional two weeks. As the mother also shares the burden of earning an income, the father is increasingly expected to share household duties. Parents usually are liberal and allow their children a large measure of freedom in making decisions for themselves. As an ethnically homogeneous people, 65 percent of Danes have surnames that end in -*sen* (Hansen, Christensen, Andersen, etc.).

Dating and Marriage. Dating begins by age 15. Youth enjoy dancing, sporting activities, and going to movies. Most young Danes live together before deciding to marry. Although a large number of couples have children outside of marriage, they generally decide to marry after a while. The average age

at marriage is 31 for men and 28 for women. Weddings are held in either a church or a town hall. Rice throwing and dancing the bridal waltz are important wedding traditions. About one in four marriages ends in divorce.

Diet. Breakfast consists of coffee or tea, pastries or rolls, cheese, eggs or cereal, and milk. For lunch, Danes enjoy traditional open-faced sandwiches known as *smørrebrød*. Pumpernickel bread, known as *rugbrød* or "rye bread" is the traditional bread used for sandwiches. *Smørrebrød* is often served with slices of salami, *frikadeller* (Danish meatballs), hard-boiled eggs, or liver paste and topped with cucumber slices, dill, or parsley. Staple foods include pork roast (a favorite), fish, beans, brussels sprouts, potatoes, various fresh vegetables, and breads.

For dinner, Danes enjoy dishes such as *frikadeller* or *hakkebøf* (Danish hamburger) served with gravy, white potatoes, pickled red beets, and a salad. Salads are becoming a more popular part of dinner. *Bøf* (hamburger steak with a brown sauce and fried onions) and *frokostbord* (a cold buffet of many different foods) are also favorites. Popular desserts include fruit, apple cobbler, ice cream, and sweet waffles or pancakes served with ice cream. For Christmas, Danes enjoy pork roast, which is broiled until its skin is crisp, or goose. At Easter, lamb roast is served. Favorite drinks include coffee, tea, milk, beer, soft drinks, and mineral water.

Recreation. Soccer is by far the most popular spectator sport in Denmark. Danes also enjoy handball, badminton, swimming, sailing, cycling, rowing, and jogging. Among women, gymnastics, handball, horseback riding, and badminton are popular. Watching television, going to the movies, and reading are popular leisure activities. Danes like to travel. During vacation, families enjoy traveling throughout Europe by car, camping along the way.

The Arts. Danes pride themselves on their attention to culture. Music, theater, ballet, and other cultural activities are popular. Well-known Danish writers include Hans Christian Andersen, author of "The Ugly Duckling," and Isak Dinesen (Karen Blixen), author of the novel *Out of Africa*. Music is diverse in Denmark, and includes jazz, classical, opera, rock, and electronic music. Copenhagen is home to a large number of jazz artists. Medieval ballads and other songs are important in folk music. Folk dances, such as the polka and the waltz, are accompanied by the accordion, violin, or native instruments like the *skalmeje* (folk clarinet) or *bytromme* (town drum).

Denmark is known for its architecture, such as castles, palaces, and cathedrals. Danish architects have designed several impressive buildings abroad, including the Sydney Opera House. Danish furniture, ceramics, and silver are renowned for their design.

Holidays. Danes enjoy great holiday traditions. For example, on New Year's Eve people attend parties, listen to the queen's and the prime minister's annual speeches, wait for Copenhagen's City Hall bells to mark midnight, and then light fireworks to welcome the new year.

Other traditions follow throughout the year. On 5 January, the eve of Twelfth Night, Danes light the Christmas tree for the last time. In February or March, Danes participate in Mardi Gras–type activities during *Fastelavn*. At Easter, people

▼ **EUROPE**

take a long Easter holiday (Thursday–Monday) to eat, drink a special potent Easter beer, and have family gatherings. Queen Margrethe's Birthday (16 Apr.) is a school holiday, and Constitution Day (5 June) is a half holiday. Although they celebrate Christmas over three days, Danes enjoy Christmas Eve the most. With the Christmas tree lit, they sing songs while dancing in a circle around the tree. They later exchange gifts and eat a special meal.

Commerce. The Danish workweek, one of the shortest in the EU, averages 32 hours. Businesses are usually open from 8 a.m. to 4 or 5 p.m., Monday through Friday. Stores and shops open at 9 or 10 a.m. and close around 6 p.m. or 8 p.m. On Saturdays, stores close at 2 p.m. or 4 p.m. Wages and working conditions are determined jointly by employer and employee organizations for two-year periods. Each worker receives five weeks' paid vacation each year.

SOCIETY

Government. Denmark is a constitutional monarchy. The 1849 constitution (revised in 1953) gave the monarchy and Parliament joint legislative authority. The monarch must sign all legislation passed by Parliament, but executive power rests with the prime minister. Queen Margrethe II presides over the Council of State and performs numerous other duties as well. She came to the throne in 1972 as the first female monarch to rule since Margrethe I. Between 1513 and 1972, all kings were named either Christian or Frederik. The crown prince's name is Frederik.

The *Folketing* (Parliament) seats 179 members, including two from Greenland and two from the Faroe Islands. The prime minister is head of government. The main parties are the Social Democratic Party, the Liberal Party, and the Conservative Party. The Faroe Islands is giving some consideration to asking for more autonomy or independence from Denmark. Elections are held at least every four years. Those older than age 18 may vote.

Economy. Denmark has a shortage of natural resources, but it has been able to rely on its high-quality agricultural produce for revenue. About 60 percent of the land is arable, employing 6 percent of the population in agricultural pursuits and producing 15 percent of the nation's exports. Meat, beer, dairy products, and fresh and processed fish also are shipped around the world. Economic diversification has allowed manufacturing to become the most important exporting sector. Small and medium-sized companies are most prominent, producing furniture, medical goods, and machinery.

Denmark has a high-tech, modern economy with extensive welfare services and dependence on foreign trade. Following five years of strong growth, the economy slowed somewhat in 1999 and 2000. Inflation and unemployment remain low. The currency is the Danish *krone* (DKr). Danes enjoy one of the highest standards of living in the world but also pay some of the highest taxes. For example, taxes and duties on a new car may cause its price to triple.

Transportation and Communications. Although personal automobiles are important, bicycles are also a primary source

DEVELOPMENT DATA

Human Dev. Index* rank	15 of 174 countries
Adjusted for women	14 of 143 countries
Real GDP per capita	$24,218
Adult literacy rate	99 percent
Infant mortality rate	5 per 1,000 births
Life expectancy	73 (male); 78 (female)

of transportation for many Danes. Bicycles have been a popular means of commuting to work and an integral part of city life for decades. Most major cities have special bicycle paths along the busiest streets and have traffic lights especially designed for bikers. Rail traffic, bus lines, and ferry services also continue to meet the transportation needs of the country. Copenhagen has a rapid-transit system for daily commuters. The Great Belt waterway, the bridge-tunnel system connecting the island of Sjælland to the Jylland peninsula, opened for motorists in June 1998. It is the site of Europe's largest suspension bridge. The Øresund Link, a combined motorway and railway link between Copenhagen and Malmö, Sweden, opened in July 2000.

All communications systems are modern and efficient. Denmark has 2 national and 64 local television stations. Most Danes access television stations in other countries through cable networks or their own satellite dishes. Denmark has 42 daily newspapers; the majority of households receive at least one.

Education. Primary education is free and compulsory for nine years at the *Folkeskole* (People's School). Students must study a foreign language, among other required courses. About two-thirds then choose practical training schools for job training, and the rest choose secondary schools to prepare for a college education. Entrance to universities is determined by a highly competitive examination, but the education is free. Denmark was a pioneer in the community college (*Folkeshøjskole*) concept. Today, resident students are instructed in such subjects as literature, history, sports, photography, and religion; the focus is on personal development without exams. Denmark ranks among the highest in the world in per capita expenditures on education.

Health. Health care is provided through a comprehensive socialized medicine system. Each citizen may choose a family doctor to coordinate services, nearly all of which are provided free of charge (paid for by taxes). Medicine is available at a low cost. A few can get medicine free of charge.

CONTACT INFORMATION

The Royal Danish Embassy, 3200 Whitehaven Street NW, Washington, DC 20008-3683; phone (202) 234-4300; Web site www.denmarkemb.org. Scandinavian Tourist Board, PO Box 4649, Grand Central Station, New York, NY 10163-4649; phone (212) 885-9700; Web site www.goscandinavia.com.

CultureGrams™
People. The World. You.

1305 North Research Way, Bldg. K
Orem, Utah 84097-6200 USA
1.800.528.6279; 801.705.4250
fax 801.705.4350
www.culturegrams.com

Dominican Republic

Boundary representations are not necessarily authoritative.

BACKGROUND

Land and Climate. The Dominican Republic occupies the eastern two-thirds of the island of Hispaniola, which it shares with Haiti. Covering 18,815 square miles (48,731 square kilometers), it is about twice the size of New Hampshire. The central mountain range, Cordillera Central, boasts the highest point in the Caribbean, Pico Duarte, at just over 10,000 feet (3,048 meters). The *Cibao Valley* lies in the heart of the country and is the major agricultural area.

This nation has a variety of landscapes, from deserts in the southwest to alpine forests in the central mountains. Sugarcane fields spread over plains in the north and east, and coconut plantations cover most of the peninsula of Samaná. Pebble beaches under rocky cliffs afford spectacular views on the southern coast. Elsewhere, white-sand beaches and warm waters attract tourists to resort areas.

Weather generally is tropical, warm, and humid, especially in summer months and along southern and eastern coasts. A dry, desert-like climate, due to deforestation and little rainfall, prevails in western and southwestern regions. Rainy seasons may vary in different parts of the country, but they generally are in the late spring and early fall.

History. In pre-Columbian times, Arawaks and Tainos occupied the island. The arrival of Christopher Columbus in 1492 brought Christianity, colonization, slavery, and disease, decimating the native population within decades. With the vanishing indigenous workforce came the increased importation of West Africans to provide cheap labor for mines, sugar plantations, and cattle farms.

The first permanent European settlement in the New World was established by Spain in 1496 as Santo Domingo.

Santo Domingo's Colonial Zone is one of the great treasures of Spanish America today, with many original buildings intact and restored.

In 1697, the western portion (now Haiti) of Hispaniola was given to France. In 1795, the entire island was ceded. Rebellious slaves seized Santo Domingo in 1801 and established Haiti as the first independent country in Latin America. The resulting Haitian domination of the Dominicans (1822–44) left a legacy of mistrust and strained relations that still endures. The Dominicans declared independence in 1844. Spain returned intermittently between local attempts at government. After an occupation by U.S. Marines (1918–24), a constitutional government was established.

The Trujillo era followed, bringing the country under a military dictatorship. Rafael Leonidas Trujillo gained the presidency in 1930 and ruled for three decades until he was assassinated in 1961. His merciless persecution of Haitians in the late 1930s added to the list of grievances between the two countries. His death brought a division of the army, civilian unrest, and political revolt. In 1965, U.S. Marines and an inter-American peacekeeping force stepped in. With stability restored, elections were held and in 1966 the constitutional government was reestablished. Continuing under this system, today's Dominican Republic is the largest and most populous democracy in the Caribbean region.

An ally of Trujillo, Joaquín Balaguer, was nominally appointed president in 1961 but did not take office until 1966. For the next three decades, power rested in either his hands or those of rival Juan Bosch (of the Dominican Liberation Party, PLD). As head of the Social Christian

Reformist Party (PRSC), Balaguer narrowly won the 1994 elections and began his seventh term in office. Constitutional reforms called for elections two years later but did not permit Balaguer to run for a successive eighth term.

In 1996, centrist PLD candidate Leonel Fernández won the presidential election against José Francisco Peña Gómez of the Revolutionary Party. Fernández began economic reforms and sought greater openness in government and in foreign policy. However, frequent power outages, high food prices, poverty, and high unemployment fueled public discontent in late 1997. Amid such troubles, legislative elections held in May 1998 (shortly after Gómez's death of cancer) gave Gómez's Revolutionary Party a large majority in Congress, further complicating Fernández's plans for reform. In September 1998, Hurricane Georges, one of the worst storms in the country's history, caused significant damage to infrastructure. Rebuilding efforts led to political wrangling and renewed public discontent.

Hipólito Mejía of the center-left Dominican Revolutionary Party (PRD) was elected president in May 2000 with the promise that he would increase social spending and purge the government of corruption. Power cuts from recently privatized electric companies are causing public unrest.

THE PEOPLE

Population. The Dominican Republic's population is nearly 8.4 million and growing at 1.6 percent. More than one million of these people live full- or part-time in New York City and are called *Dominican Yorks*. More than one-third of the population is younger than age 16. The rural population is steadily decreasing through migration to cities. Mixed-race people account for 73 percent of the total population; 16 percent is Caucasian and 11 percent is black. The mixed-race group is a combination of Spaniards and other Europeans, descendants of West African slaves, and descendants of natives. A Haitian minority is included in the black population.

Language. The official language is Spanish, but Caribbean phrases, accents, and regional expressions distinguish it. For example, when eating, people request *un chin* of something instead of the Spanish *un poquito* (a little bit) . Many people drop the *s* at the end of words, turning *dos* (two) into *do'*. Cibao Valley residents, or *Cibaeños* may pronounce *r, l,* and *i* differently. The formal Spanish form of address for "you" (*usted*) is used, but urban people prefer the more familiar *tú*. Some creole is spoken near the Haitian border and in the *bateys* (sugarcane villages), where many Haitian workers live.

Religion. Dominicans are 95 percent Catholic by record, but a much smaller number regularly attends church or strictly follows doctrine. Rural residents might combine Catholic traditions with local practices and beliefs. Although Dominicans are fairly secular, Catholic traditions are evident in daily life. Some children are taught to "ask blessings" of their parents and other relatives upon seeing them. They might say *Bendición, tía* (Bless me, aunt), and the response is *Dios te bendiga* (May God bless you). Evangelical Christian churches, the Seventh-day Adventist Church, The Church of Jesus Christ of Latter-day Saints, and other denominations are also present throughout the country.

General Attitudes. Dominicans are warm, friendly, outgoing, and gregarious. They are very curious about others and forthright in asking personal questions. Children are rarely shy. *Machismo* permeates society, especially among rural and low-income groups, with males enjoying privileges not accorded to females. A proud and aggressive attitude is admired in sports, games, and business. Many people have a sharp entrepreneurial sense, but this does not mean that business etiquette is aggressive.

The common expression *Si Dios quiere* (If God wishes) may make Dominicans appear fatalistic or indifferent. However, it more fully expresses the attitude that personal power is intertwined with one's place in the family, community, and grand design of Deity. Relationships are more important than schedules, so being late for appointments and spending time socializing instead of working are socially acceptable.

Confianza (trust) is highly valued and not quickly or easily gained by outsiders. Borrowing is common, and although an item may be forgotten and never returned, everyone is generous and helpful. Class divisions, most evident in larger cities, are economic, social, and political, favoring historically prominent families. Light skin and smooth hair are preferred over strong African features. In spite of recent government efforts to build ties with Haiti, tension between Dominicans and Haitians continues.

Personal Appearance. Dominicans are clean and well-groomed. They take pride in their personal appearance and in dressing well. Dominicans draw on New York fashions, wearing the latest in dresses, jeans, or athletic shoes. Clothes tend to be dressy, always clean and well pressed, with bright colors, shiny fabrics, and, for some people, a lot of jewelry. Jeans and short skirts are acceptable for women in urban areas, but dresses or skirts and blouses are more common in the countryside. A special event, such as a town meeting, always requires dressing up. Men wear long pants and stylish shirts, except at the beach or if doing manual labor. Professional men wear business suits or the traditional *chacabana*, a white shirt worn over dark trousers. Children are also dressed up, especially for church or visiting.

CUSTOMS AND COURTESIES

Greetings. Men shake hands firmly when they greet. One offers a wrist or elbow if one's hand is dirty. Friends also may embrace. Most women kiss each other on both cheeks. A man with the *confianza* of a woman will also kiss her. A handshake and *¿Cómo está usted?* (How are you?) is a common formal greeting. It is polite to ask about a person's family. *¡Hola!* is an informal "Hi," as is *¡Saludos!* Adults, particularly in the *campo* (countryside), often address each other as *compadre* (for men) or *comadre* (for women). One might not greet a stranger on the street, but one would never enter a room without greeting everyone present. Nor would a person leave without saying good-bye to everyone.

Formal introductions are rare, but professional titles are used to address respected persons. Older and more prominent people may be addressed as *Don* (for men) or *Doña* (for women), with or without their first names.

Gestures. Dominicans are animated in conversation and often make gestures. They point with puckered lips instead of a finger. Wrinkling the nose indicates one does not understand, rubbing fingers and the thumb together refers to money, and an upright wagging forefinger means "no." To express disapproval, one points (with lips) at the object and rolls the eyes. "Come here" is indicated with the palm down and fingers together waving inward. One also says "pssst" to get another's attention. To hail a taxi or bus, one wags a finger or fingers (depending on the number of passengers needing a ride) in the direction one is going. Numbers often are expressed with one's fingers instead of words.

Sitting with legs apart is unladylike, and most women ride "sidesaddle" on the backs of motorcycles. Personal space is limited; touching is normal and crowding is common.

Visiting. Visiting is an important form of social recreation, especially in rural areas and poor *barrios* (neighborhoods). Visits in the home are common, but much socializing also takes place in public (while shopping, washing, and so forth). Women often gather in the kitchen. A visit may be long or short and may occur at any time, usually without prior notice. Urbanites with telephones may call ahead, but whether expected or not, company is always genuinely welcomed. In rural areas doors are kept open; people consider it strange to close them and not accept visitors. To Dominicans, privacy is unimportant; they perceive the desire for solitude as sadness and equate being alone with being lonely. Sitting in *mesadoras* (rocking chairs) talking or just sharing time is common. Nearly all homes have *mesadoras*. Hosts offer visitors something to drink (coffee or juice) and invite them to eat if mealtime is near. Refusing such offers is not impolite.

If guests interrupt (or passersby happen upon) someone eating, the person will immediately and sincerely invite them to share what is left by saying *A buen tiempo* (You've come at a good time). Guests may decline by saying *Buen provecho* (Enjoy), or they may sit down and eat.

Eating. The main meal, *comida*, is served at midday and often lasts two hours. Families prefer eating at home. Urban workers unable to return home may eat at inexpensive cafés or buy from vendors. *Desayuno* (breakfast) usually is light: sweetened coffee and bread. People in urban areas often eat a bit more. *Cena* (the evening meal) is also light, often not more than a snack or leftovers from *comida*. Guests are served first, and sometimes separately and more elaborately. Table conversation is often lively. Dining out is only popular among those who can afford it. Service is included in the bill.

LIFESTYLE

Family. Family ties are important; extended families commonly live together. Many households are led by women—widows, women who are divorced, women whose husbands work elsewhere, or older women with adult children and grandchildren. Women, men, and often boys all work outside the home. The boys shine shoes or sell snacks on the streets. Large families are normal, and many rural villages are composed of interrelated families. Within the extended family, informal adoption is common: other family members take in and raise children whose parents need help. Siblings raised by one mother may have different fathers, but all children are cared for equally. Cousins are often as close as siblings. Some men have more than one wife and family. Smaller, nuclear families are more common among the educated urban population.

Most families live in small houses, either rented or self-built. They may be constructed of cement, wood, or palm bark. They are brightly painted, have cement or dirt floors, and are covered with zinc roofs. Electricity and running water are luxuries. Affluent urban houses are larger and often have walled and landscaped grounds. Urban apartments are becoming popular, as are newly constructed condominiums.

Dating and Marriage. Attending movies, discos, dances, baseball games, and sitting on park benches are social activities for couples. Dating is relatively open and increasingly free of parental control. Girls are more closely supervised than boys and often go out in groups. Rural couples might have a sibling tagging along as chaperone. Marriages are often common-law (*por la ventana*), but many couples also marry in a church or civil ceremony. Elaborate urban weddings are major social events.

Diet. If Dominicans do not eat rice and beans at midday, they feel they have not eaten. Most meals feature rice served in large quantities, along with such favorites as *habichuelas* (beans) and *yuca* (cassava). *Yuca* may be boiled, prepared as fritters, or baked into rounds of crisp cracker bread called *casabe*. *Plátanos* (plantains) and bananas are plentiful. Mangoes, papayas, pineapples, guavas, avocados, and other tropical fruits (passion fruit, coconuts, and star fruit) are grown locally and eaten in season. People may eat small quantities of chicken, beef, pork, or goat with a meal. *Bacalau* (dried fish, usually cod) is eaten in some areas; fresh fish is eaten along the coast. Food generally is not spicy.

The national dish is *sancocho*, a rich vegetable-and-meat stew served on special occasions. *Habichuelas con dulce* (a sweetened drink made from beans) is popular at Easter. Dominican coffee is served sweet and strong. National beers and rums are highly regarded and widely consumed, as are bottled soft drinks and sweetened fruit juices.

Recreation. The game of dominoes is a national pastime. Outdoor tables in front of homes, bars, and rural *colmados* (neighborhood markets) are surrounded by men who play for hours, especially on Sundays. Outdoor players are almost exclusively men, but everyone may play at home. Even young children become adept. Cockfighting is another national pastime. Cockfight gambling stakes can be high. The lottery has high participation.

Baseball is the most popular sport. Competition is keen, and many Dominicans have become famous major league players in the United States and Canada. Strolling in parks, visiting friends, and watching television are popular activities.

The Arts. Dominicans love music and dancing. *Merengue* is the national dance, and many people, including small children, know the steps. It is also a fast-paced, rhythmic music traditionally performed with three instruments: a *tambora* (small drum), *melodeon* (similar to an accordian), and *guayano* (scraping percussion instrument). *Bachata* is a popular folk dance accompanied by accordions, drums, horns, and *guayanos*. Salsa and other Latino styles are popular, as are North American pop and jazz. Discos are found even in rural communities.

Literature from the Dominican Republic is well established. Much writing focuses on nationalistic themes, social protest, history, and everyday life. Common crafts include masks for *Carnaval*, colorful paintings, faceless dolls, and jewelry made from amber or *larimar* (a blue stone unique to the Dominican Republic).

Holidays. National holidays include New Year's Day (1 Jan.), *Día de los Reyes* (Day of Kings, 6 January), *Nuestra Señora de la Alta Gracia* (Our Lady of High Gratitude, 21 January), Duarte's Day (26 Jan.), Independence Day (27 Feb.), Easter, Labor Day (1 May), Corpus Christi, Restoration of Independence (16 Aug.), *Nuestra Señora de las Mercedes* (Our Lady of Mercies, 24 September), Columbus Day (12 Oct.), and Christmas.

Urban families go to the beach or mountains during *Semana Santa* (Holy Week before Easter). *Carnaval* is celebrated for several weeks in the early spring with costume parades, complete with masked participants hitting spectators with pig bladders, and other festivities. Gifts are not exchanged at Christmas, but they may be given to children on 6 January. The government may call special holidays to celebrate an event or project completion.

Commerce. Business hours vary, but most establishments open around 8 or 9 a.m., close between noon and 2 p.m., and open again until 5 or 6 p.m. Banks close by 3 p.m. Telephone offices do not close at midday and remain open until 10 p.m. Most shops are closed on Sunday. Small *colmados* have their own hours. Street vendors are most busy at midday. Bargaining is common in open-air markets, in some owner-operated stores, and on the streets. Prices in supermarkets and elsewhere are fixed.

Family ties and social relationships are important in obtaining employment or doing business. Business arrangements are seldom made between strangers.

SOCIETY

Government. The Dominican Republic is divided into 29 provinces. The president and vice president are elected by the people. A bicameral Congress of 30 senators and 120 deputies is also directly elected, as are local officials. The Dominican Revolutionary Party (PRD) currently holds the most congressional seats. Other major parties include the PRSC and PLD. National and local elections are held simultaneously every four years. The voting age is 18. A nine-member Supreme Court is appointed by the Senate.

Economy. The economy is based on agriculture. Coffee, sugar, pineapple, cocoa, tobacco, and rice are key crops, for both export and domestic use. Fluctuating world prices impact earnings and make the domestic market somewhat volatile. Dominican Yorks often send earnings back to families in the Republic; the money constitutes an important source of revenue. Tourism is another vital source of income. Industrial activity includes sugar refining, cement, and pharmaceuticals. Assembly plants for various products are located in duty-free zones. The environment has suffered from the exploitation of mineral and natural resources, but efforts at conservation are being made.

The Dominican Republic has the fastest-growing economy in Latin America. Despite massive damage from Hurricane Georges in 1998, the economy grew by more than 7 percent in 1999 and more than 9 percent in 2000. However, even though real gross domestic product per capita has nearly tripled in the last generation, most people (particularly women) do not have access to economic prosperity. A wide gap exists between rich and poor; nearly 70 percent of Dominicans are affected by poverty. Unemployment is high, while underemployment is more than 20 percent. Inflation averaged 6.5 percent in 1999 and 7.7 percent in 2000. The currency is the Dominican *peso* (RD$).

Transportation and Communications. Main roads are

DEVELOPMENT DATA

Human Dev. Index* rank	87 of 174 countries
Adjusted for women	73 of 143 countries
Real GDP per capita	$4,598
Adult literacy rate	83 percent
Infant mortality rate	36 per 1,000 births
Life expectancy	69 (male); 73 (female)

paved and heavily traveled. Rural roads are often unpaved and may be impassable during rainy seasons. Hurricane damage to roads and bridges in some areas is severe. Public transportation varies between a ride on the back of a motorcycle, a local or long-distance trip in a *guagua* (economical van or bus), and a ride on a larger bus. Pickup trucks or small vans travel to and from rural villages carrying passengers, animals, and cargo together. Urban Dominicans travel locally by *carros públicos* (public cars), taxis that follow certain routes. Private cars are expensive but by no means rare. More people have motorcycles.

Telephone service is available throughout the country; middle- and upper-class families have phones. Daily newspapers are read widely. Postal service is slow and unreliable. Most businesses use private messenger services. Private radio and television stations broadcast regionally and nationally.

Education. Free public education is provided through the high school level. Attendance is mandatory to sixth grade, but many children, particularly girls and those in the *campo*, cannot attend or do not complete school for various reasons (work, lack of transport, home and family responsibilities, or lack of money to buy required uniforms). While three-fourths of Dominicans begin school, only one-third finish. Nearly 1,400 schools were destroyed by Hurricane Georges. Scarce funding prior to the hurricane resulted in limited resources and understaffed facilities. Parents and teachers must provide basic supplies like pencils and paper. Textbooks and other materials are scarce. Many urban families send their children to private schools called *colegios*. University education is available, and trade schools provide technical training. The adult literacy rate is lower in rural areas.

Health. Public hospitals and clinics provide free care, but private doctors are preferred when affordable. Public institutions tend to be poorly equipped and understaffed. Village health-care workers have enough training to administer basic services, but rural areas often have no doctors and people must travel elsewhere for care. Many people still consult *curanderos* (native healers). Lack of early treatment and preventive care are genuine concerns. Vaccination campaigns are helping fight disease, but maladies such as intestinal parasites and malaria pose serious challenges.

CONTACT INFORMATION

Dominican Republic Tourist Board, 136 East 57th Street, Suite 803, New York, NY 10022; phone (888) 374-6361. Embassy of the Dominican Republic, 1715 22d Street NW, Washington, DC 20008; phone (202) 332-6280; Web site www.domrep.org.

CultureGrams™
People. The World. You.

1305 North Research Way, Bldg. K
Orem, Utah 84097-6200 USA
1.800.528.6279; 801.705.4250
fax 801.705.4350
www.culturegrams.com

Republic of
Ecuador

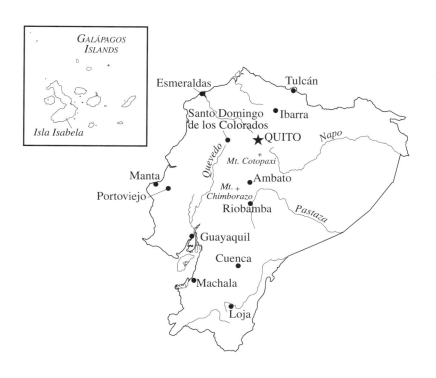

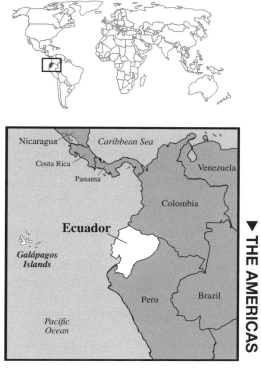

Boundary representations are not necessarily authoritative.

BACKGROUND

Land and Climate.   Ecuador is just smaller than Nevada, covering 109,483 square miles (283,560 square kilometers). The country is located on, and named after, the equator. Ecuador has four major geographic regions: *La Costa* (coastal lowlands), which contains rich agricultural land; *La Sierra* (Andean highlands), with snowcapped mountains; *El Oriente* (eastern lowlands), beginning at the eastern foothills of the Andes and containing mostly tropical rain forest; and the *Archipiélago de Colón* (or Galápagos Islands), a group of islands in the Pacific about 600 miles (966 kilometers) off the coast. Charles Darwin developed his theories of evolution based on his observations of Galápagos wildlife. In January 2001, an oil spill threatened the islands' unique ecosystem, but ocean currents prevented the oil from causing much damage. Ecuador is subject to earthquakes and volcanic eruptions. Ecuador has 31 active volcanoes; many of them are near Quito, which is surrounded by an Avenue of the Volcanoes. The two highest peaks are Chimborazo at 20,561 feet (6,267 meters) and Cotopaxi at 19,347 feet (5,897 meters).

The climate varies with elevation more than with season, but the rainy season is generally from November to May. The driest months are June to September. The coastal lowlands are hot and humid, while the highlands include everything from subtropical valleys to frigid mountains. Quito's temperature averages 71°F (22°C) year-round. The rain forest, which is part of the upper Amazon Basin, has a tropical climate. Temperatures in the Galápagos Islands average 76°F (24°C). Ecuador is located at the center of the El Niño weather phenomenon, which periodically causes destructive floods and mudslides.

History.   Various groups of indigenous peoples, whose ancestors first inhabited Ecuador, were conquered in the latter 1400s by Incas from the south. The Incan Empire ruled the area until, during an internal power struggle, the Spanish conquered it in 1534. The Spanish took ownership of vast tracts of land and large numbers of local people. In the early 1800s, Antonio José de Sucre, a compatriot of Simón Bolívar, led a successful military campaign against the Spaniards. Ecuador, along with Colombia and Venezuela, gained its independence in 1822 and became part of *Gran Colombia*, a federation led by Bolívar that was dissolved a few years later. Ecuador declared itself a republic in 1830.

In 1941, Peru and Ecuador battled over ownership of an area in the southern Amazon region then controlled by Ecuador. A 1942 treaty granted Peru most of the territory, but because the treaty referenced obscure landmarks and denied Ecuador access to vital mineral wealth and the Amazon River system, the country later rejected it. The two neighbors continued exchanging hostilities from time to time. A January 1995 clash lasted for several days before international observers helped negotiate a settlement. A final agreement was signed in October 1998 granting Ecuador a small portion of land as well as navigation rights on some rivers in Peru.

Between 1830 and 1948, Ecuador had 62 presidents, dictators, and military juntas. In 1948, Galo Plaza Lasso became the first freely elected president to serve a full term. Civilian governments alternated with military rule until 1979, when a new constitution allowed for a freely elected president.

The 1996 elections marked Ecuador's fifth consecutive peaceful transition of power. Abdalá Bucaram, nicknamed

El Loco (the Madman) for his flamboyant personality, won the presidency, promising to help Ecuador's poor. However, Bucaram's austerity measures prompted widespread strikes and protests. Congress responded by voting to remove Bucaram for "mental incapacity" and charging him with corruption. Bucaram stepped down when the military withdrew its support, and Congress voted its leader, Fabián Alarcón, interim president. Centrist candidate Jamil Mahuad, the mayor of Quito, won in 1998 presidential elections.

Strikes and protests against poverty and proposed price hikes led Mahuad's government to declare a state of emergency. In January 2000, massive demonstrations against the government by indigenous peoples led to a coup. The military ousted Mahuad and turned the government over to the vice president, Gustavo Noboa. President Noboa faces the difficult task of rebuilding a ruined economy and maintaining order in the face of widespread discontent. Indigenous groups again instigated protests over fuel prices throughout the summer, which escalated into riots in early 2001. After declaring a state of emergency, Noboa lowered the rates.

THE PEOPLE

Population.   Ecuador's population of nearly 12.92 million is growing at 2 percent annually. The majority (55 percent) is mestizo. Indigenous peoples comprise about 25 percent of the population. Another 10 percent is of Spanish descent, and 10 percent is black. Quito, the capital, is one of the oldest continuously inhabited cities in the Western Hemisphere and has 1.3 million people. The largest city is Guayaquil (1.8 million). Nearly 60 percent of all Ecuadorians live in urban areas.

Language.   Spanish is Ecuador's official language, although Quichua is spoken by Sierra highland Indian groups, including the Quichua, Saraguro, Otavalan, Cañari, and Chimborazo. Quichua is recognized by the constitution as an important part of Ecuadorian culture, but it is not an official language. Many Quichua words have been adopted into colloquial language to supplement the Spanish vocabulary. Indian groups (Shuar, Auca, Cofan, Cecoya, Cayapa, and Colorado) in other regions speak their own languages. Many Indians are bilingual in a native tongue and Spanish. Spanish tends to be spoken faster on the coast than in the Sierra highlands. Some consonants are pronounced differently between the two regions.

Religion.   While the constitution guarantees religious freedom, more than 80 percent of Ecuadorians belong to the Catholic Church. Many national and local holidays/festivals center on the Catholic faith. Rituals like baptism, first communion, and confirmation are celebrated in the community, as well as among family. Many other Christian churches are growing in popularity, and people generally are tolerant of other beliefs.

General Attitudes.   Ecuador encompasses a great diversity of cultures. Overlaying ethnic differences are regional differences that tend to influence politics and internal relations. *Serranos* (people from highland areas, including Quito) are considered more formal, conservative, and reserved than *Costeños* (coastal inhabitants). Costeños are considered cosmopolitan, open, and liberal; they generally are the businesspeople of Ecuador. Serranos are associated with government and banks. The two groups, political rivals, distrust each other in many respects but are united in others.

A common trait of all Ecuadorians is the value they place on familial relationships and responsibilities. People are warm and hospitable. Human relationships generally take precedence over schedules or timetables. A certain sentimentality is evident in popular songs and in the practice of exchanging or giving *recuerdos* (tokens of affection or remembrance). Oratory and leadership skills are admired, as are loyalty and honesty. Occupation, wealth, and family name are all indicators of social status.

Long marginalized by the effects of colonization, indigenous groups have begun to organize themselves to regain lost rights, press for environmental protection of their lands, and achieve recognition for their language and culture. Today, there is greater contact and cooperation between Indians and other Ecuadorians than in the past. Still, most indigenous peoples that remain in their home regions (and many who move to urban areas) retain strong, traditional cultural identities.

Personal Appearance.   In urban areas, many people wear standard Western-style clothing. Younger women often wear pants, while older women tend to prefer skirts. Every rural region has its own traditional clothing, colors, and fabrics. Generally, Costeños wear bright, clear colors (white, yellow, and red), while Serranos prefer blues, browns, and blacks. Rural women usually wear skirts and often wear hats—made of straw in coastal areas and wool or leather in the highlands. Special celebrations call for new clothing, either purchased at a store or, more often, made by local tailors.

CUSTOMS AND COURTESIES

Greetings.   People usually shake hands when first introduced. A handshake is then used in subsequent greetings, along with the exchange of good wishes. In rural areas particularly, one offers the wrist or arm rather than the hand when one's hands are soiled. Close friends greet with a kiss on the cheek. Actually, they "kiss the air" while brushing or touching cheeks. Men may embrace if well acquainted. It is customary to address people by a title (*Señor, Señora, Doctor, Doctora*, etc.) when being introduced. Among friends, the title *Don* or *Doña*, followed by the first name, is a common greeting indicating respect and friendship.

Typical greetings include ¡*Buenos días!* (Good day) and ¿*Cómo está?* (How are you?). It is courteous to greet people in small stores or restaurants, or when passing on rural roads. Friends commonly greet each other with ¡*Hola!* (Hello). After a long absence, one might greet another with ¿*Cómo has pasado? A los tiempos que nos vemos* (How have you been? It has been a long time).

Gestures.   Ecuadorians often use gestures to emphasize or replace verbal communication. During conversation, a person might touch another person of the same sex to show friendly concern. Drawing a circle or two in the air with the index finger means, "I'll be back." To indicate "Sorry, the bus is full" or "Sorry, we're out of tomatoes" or anything along that line, a person sticks out the hand, as if to shake hands, and twists it almost as if waving. Yawning in public, whistling or yelling to get someone's attention, and pointing with the index finger are considered impolite. Ecuadorians might point by puckering or pursing the lips. One can also indicate "up the road" by lifting the chin, and "down the road" by lowering the chin. *Dios le pague* (God will repay you) is a common expression of thanks for an invitation or a gift.

Visiting. Relatives and friends usually visit for a meal and conversation. Unannounced visits are also common and welcomed. If unexpected guests arrive during mealtime, they will be offered a full meal. Otherwise, they typically are offered something to drink. Refusing a meal, drink, or other refreshments generally is impolite. Hosts often give departing guests a small gift of fruit, candy, or something else on hand. When inviting a guest to visit, the host will state the starting time, but specifying an ending time is considered bad taste. Instead, an ending time is generally understood depending on the nature of the visit. Guests are not expected to arrive on time and can be anywhere from 10 minutes to an hour late, depending on the event. This tendency to arrive late is jokingly referred to as *la hora Ecuatoriana* (Ecuadorian time). Dinner guests stay for conversation rather than leave right after the meal.

Evening socials and parties might extend past midnight. They usually involve eating, dancing, and drinking. Furniture is placed near the wall so everyone, including children, can dance in the middle of the main room. The hosts serve refreshments on trays; guests do not serve themselves from a central location. A late meal usually is served, after which some guests may stay for more socializing.

At small gatherings, arriving guests greet each person individually. The host introduces the guests to people with whom they are not acquainted. Guests who fail to greet those they know are not placing enough value on their relationship. When leaving, one also says good-bye to each individual. Among the youth, less formal customs are becoming the norm. For instance, young people often extend group greetings rather than personal ones.

Eating. Food and eating habits play an important part in Ecuadorian culture. Each holiday is associated with a special kind of food and every town has a specialty dish. Mealtime is considered a good time for conversation—catching up, conducting business, or socializing. At family meals, the mother generally serves food to the father first, followed by male children and then female children (who help prepare and serve the meal). The mother will eat only after everyone else has been attended to. Guests usually are served first and receive the largest amount and choicest cuts of food. Taking leftovers home is acceptable; leaving food on the plate is not. It is customary to say *Buen provecho* (roughly *Bon appetit*) before beginning a meal and to thank the person who prepared the meal before excusing oneself from the table. A host who invites a guest to a restaurant is expected to pay for the meal. Youth often will split a bill.

LIFESTYLE

Family. Families generally are close-knit. The elderly are respected and treated well, and several generations may live under the same roof. While most families follow traditional roles, urban families are changing as more women work outside the home and more men share household duties. Still, mothers remain the emotional center of their families and are honored for their primary role of raising children. Many songs are devoted to mothers, and cities will typically have a park or monument dedicated to motherhood. Children used to live with their parents until they married. Now they commonly leave to get an education or to work. Urban families average two children, while rural families average three or four.

Dating and Marriage. Dating usually begins in groups, when the youth get together for dances or other activities. In couple dating, a girl must ask for her parents' approval when invited out. Girls often do not begin dating until after their *quinceañera* (coming-out party) at age 15. A Catholic ceremony officially presents the girl to society. If the family can afford it, a party with food, drinks, and dancing follows. Women usually marry by age 23 (younger in some rural areas) and men around age 25. Families often emphasize that young people should complete their education before marrying. Many urban couples do not live together before their church wedding, even if they have already been married by law. Common-law marriage (referred to as *estilo manabita*) is common and accepted as a legal marriage in rural, coastal areas. For most of these unions, the ceremony is only lacking because of the expense of a wedding.

Diet. The main meal is eaten at midday. Serranos favor corn and potatoes, while Costeños favor rice, beans, and bananas, of which there are several varieties. Fresh fruits abound. Chicken, meat, and fish (on the coast) are dietary staples. Soup is almost always served at both the midday and evening meals. Hot bread is a popular afternoon snack. Some favorite dishes include *arroz con pollo* (fried chicken with rice), *locro* (soup with potatoes, cheese, meat, and avocados), *llapingachos* (cheese and potato cakes), *ceviche* (raw or cooked seafood marinated in lime and served with onions, tomatoes, and spices), *fritada* (fried pork), *empanadas* (pastries filled with meat or cheese), *arroz con menestra* (rice with spicy beans, barbecued beef, and refried plantains), *caldo de bola* (plantain-based soup with meat and vegetables), and *cuy* (roast guinea pig).

Recreation. *Fútbol* (soccer) is the favorite sport, followed by volleyball and basketball. Others include tennis, track, and boxing. Ecuadorian volleyball (*Ecuavolley*) is played with a heavy ball by three players on each side. Visiting and sightseeing are common leisure activities. People in coastal areas take advantage of nearby beaches. Many Ecuadorians participate in community groups (women's, church, or sports clubs) and *mingas* (community improvement projects).

The Arts. Ecuador's music and dance reflect a mixing of cultures. String and wind instruments like bamboo flutes and *rondadors* (pan pipes) characterize indigenous music; "El Condor Pasa" is a traditional song from the highlands. Other folk music includes the *pasacalle*, *pasillo* (which has slow, waltz-like rhythms), and *yumbo*. The *bomba* is a rhythmic dance with African influences. Youth often gather at discos; salsa (the music and dance) is particularly popular.

Folk arts are diverse and vary by region. Many people weave items like carpets, bags, sashes, and Panama hats, which can take months to complete. Some make wood carvings of saints or Christ. Decorative crosses, musical instruments, jewelry, and leather work are other native arts.

Holidays. Ecuadorians mark the new year by burning effigies of the Old Year in the streets on New Year's Eve. They celebrate the *Carnaval* season (in February or March) by dousing each other with water; *Carnaval* culminates in a weekend festival of parades, dances, and parties. Easter, Labor Day (1 May), and the Battle of Pichincha (24 May), which marks Ecuador's liberation, are all national holidays. *Inti Raymi* (Festival of the Sun) occurs in June at the Incan ruins near

THE AMERICAS ▼

Cuenca. It features dancing and draws indigenous groups from Ecuador and other countries. Independence of Quito Day (10 Aug.) celebrates the country's first efforts (in 1809) to gain independence. Independence of Guayaquil is celebrated 9 October. On All Souls' Day (2 Nov.) people visit cemeteries, eat bread-dough dolls, and drink *colada morada* (thick drink made with berries, sweet spices, and purple flour). Communities celebrate Christmas and Easter with reenactments of religious events. Each city holds festivities marking the anniversary of its founding. The founding of Quito (6 Dec.) is celebrated with large festivals, bullfights, and sporting events.

Commerce. Stores generally are open weekdays between 8 a.m. and 6 p.m., with a lunch break from 12:30 to 2:30 p.m. Urban stores remain closed after 12:30 p.m. on Saturday and do not open on Sunday. Some rural stores may open on Sunday to accommodate farmers who cannot shop on other days. Banks close weekdays at 2 or 4 p.m.

Urban families often shop at supermarkets and department stores, but they also frequent open-air markets. Rural Ecuadorians usually shop at open-air markets and small local businesses. Open-air markets operate a few days a week and offer a variety of goods, including locally grown fruits and vegetables, food, clothing, household items, and crafts.

SOCIETY

Government. The Republic of Ecuador has a president and vice president in the executive branch. The unicameral legislature has 12 nationally elected members and 70 provincial representatives. Elections are held every four years for national offices and every two years for provincial representatives. All citizens 18 and older are required by law to vote. A number of political parties are active; the largest include the Popular Democratic, Roldosista, Democratic Left, and Social Christian Parties and the Christian Democrats.

Economy. Ecuador's economy is suffering from its worst economic crisis in decades. Damage from El Niño, low world oil and banana prices, and the country's banking crisis, budget deficit, and huge foreign debt ($16.4 billion) have plunged the country into a deep recession. Unemployment is 18 percent, and underemployment is extensive. Inflation reached 70 percent in 1999 and peaked in the high 90s in 2000, the highest in Latin America. The economy shrank by 7 percent in 1999 and doesn't show signs of recovering. Nearly half of the government's budget goes toward servicing debt. Opportunities for greater foreign investment and trade have been hindered by the uncertain political climate. Access to health care, education, and the resources needed for a decent standard of living has improved, but is still limited. Around half of the population lives in poverty.

One-third of the population is employed in agriculture, producing bananas, coffee, sugarcane, fruits, corn, potatoes, rice, and other foods. Ecuador is the world's biggest banana exporter. Petroleum accounts for 40 percent of the nation's exports, followed by coffee, bananas, cocoa, shrimp, and fish. Fluctuations in global market prices for these products have a major impact on Ecuador's economy. Food process-

DEVELOPMENT DATA

Human Dev. Index* rank	91 of 174 countries
Adjusted for women	78 of 143 countries
Real GDP per capita	$3,003
Adult literacy rate	91 percent
Infant mortality rate	35 per 1,000 births
Life expectancy	67 (male); 73 (female)

ing, textiles, chemicals, fishing, timber, and other industries employ one-fifth of the labor force. In March 2000, the U.S. dollar (US$) became Ecuador's new currency. The government transitioned completely from the *sucre* (S/) to the dollar in March 2001.

Transportation and Communications. In cities, transportation is provided by buses, taxis, and *colectivos* (minibuses that are more comfortable and faster than buses). In rural areas, *busetas* replace the *colectivos*. Roads connecting cities have been improved and about half are paved. Seaports provide shipping access to other nations. Air travel to and within Ecuador is increasing. Most urban homes and many rural homes contain a television and radio. Upper-class and urban homes are more likely to have private telephones. Cities and towns generally have a pay-phone center where people can make local or long-distance calls. Newspapers are readily available in towns and cities.

Education. Education is mandatory for six years, beginning at age six. Children attend school daily either from 7 a.m. to 12:30 p.m. or from 1 to 6 p.m. They usually wear uniforms. The government controls both public and private educational institutions. The school system is comprised of nursery schools, kindergartens, rural and urban primary schools, secondary and vocational schools, night schools, and special-education schools. There are 21 universities; the largest is in Quito and has 45,000 students. Illiteracy is decreasing slowly as more children enroll in the primary schools. Approximately 60 to 70 percent of school-aged children complete their primary education, but this percentage is lower in rural areas. Family economic need, as well as inadequate facilities and lack of personnel in rural areas, contribute to the dropout rate.

Health. The government provides medical care to all citizens at low (sometimes no) cost to the patient. However, healthcare professionals, facilities, and equipment are concentrated in urban areas. Those who can afford it might go to a private clinic or doctor. The country still battles diseases like typhoid, cholera, polio, malaria, and yellow fever. Dengue fever is carried by mosquitoes in some coastal areas. Only about half of the rural population has access to safe drinking water. With improved medical care, the infant mortality rate has been cut nearly in half over the last decade.

CONTACT INFORMATION

Embassy of the Republic of Ecuador, 2535 15th Street NW, Washington, DC 20009; phone (202) 234-7200; Web site www.ecuador.org.

1305 North Research Way, Bldg. K
Orem, Utah 84097-6200 USA
1.800.528.6279; 801.705.4250
fax 801.705.4350
www.culturegrams.com

CultureGrams™
standard edition 2002

Republic of
El Salvador

Boundary representations are not necessarily authoritative.

BACKGROUND

Land and Climate. With 8,124 square miles (21,041 square kilometers), El Salvador is just smaller than Massachusetts. A narrow band of coastal lowlands is divided from the mostly mountainous east and north by a central plateau. El Salvador is called Land of the Volcanoes for its more than two hundred extinct volcanoes that have enriched the country's soil. Lush cloud forests are found in the mountaintops. Some peaks rise to between 6,000 and 8,000 feet (1,829–2,438 meters). Although deforestation has taken a heavy toll on the country's forests, the government and private citizens now are working to protect endangered species of animals and plants.

The climate is tropical in the lowlands, with an average annual temperature around 85°F (29°C); semitropical on the plateau, with lower temperatures and less humidity; and temperate in the mountains. Temperatures rarely fluctuate more than 10 degrees year-round. El Salvador has only two seasons: the rainy *invierno* (winter), from May to October, and a dry *verano* (summer). Most of the rain falls in short evening storms. Hurricane Mitch caused extensive damage to crops and infrastructure in October 1998. San Salvador, the capital, lies on a plateau at the foot of the San Salvador Volcano. Small earthquakes are frequent in most areas; one region or another suffers a significant quake every 30 years or so. The series of earthquakes that struck in January and February 2001 killed more than 1,200 people, left about 1 million homeless, and caused more than 2 billion dollars in damage.

History. Various native civilizations (including Maya, Lenca, and Nahuat) inhabited the area long before the Spanish Conquest. Ruins of their cultures remain at Tazumal, Joya de Cerén, and Quelepa. The Pipil of Aztec origin were those encountered by the Spaniards. The natives called the region Cuscatlán. In 1524, Pedro de Alvarado conquered the area for Spain, which ruled for almost three hundred years. The native population nearly was wiped out under harsh colonial rule. For most of its early history, El Salvador was a minor province of Guatemala. Attempts by Father José Matías Delgado to gain independence from Spain in 1811 and 1814 were unsuccessful but earned Delgado a hero's recognition.

A wider regional attempt to gain independence was successful in 1821, but two years of instability followed, as Mexico's Emperor Agustín de Iturbide tried to annex Central America. When his empire collapsed, El Salvador and its neighbors formed the United Provinces of Central America, which disbanded in 1838. El Salvador claimed sovereignty in 1841 but intermittently was dominated by Guatemala through the end of the century.

The 1871 constitution marked the true birth of the nation. During the relatively stable period that followed (1871–1931), most present-day educational, artistic, and government institutions and large businesses were formed. A new wave of upwardly mobile European and Palestinian immigrants also arrived during this time; their descendants comprise the bulk of today's affluent urban class. Much of the prosperity was built on the coffee industry. However, coffee had become so successful that the government seized Pipil lands on which most of it was grown; small farmers were marginalized. When coffee prices collapsed during the depression, farmers rebelled in 1932. Many Pipil joined Augustín Farabundo Martí, a communist, in destroying property and killing scores of people. They were defeated quickly by government forces, who killed at least 10,000 natives. Native culture nearly died with the massacre as the indigenous people feared to be considered anything but Spanish.

For more than 50 years, El Salvador was plagued with internal strife and military dictatorships. Governments were hard on those who voiced dissent. A rebel movement born in the 1960s began to mature in the late 1970s. In 1979, a rival faction of the military overthrew the government. The next year, rebel groups formed the Farabundo Martí National Liberation Front (FMLN), named for the executed leader of the 1932 rebellion. The FMLN launched a civil war to force a change in leadership. In the midst of war, a new constitution was adopted (1983) and the Christian Democratic Party's candidate, José Napoleón Duarte, was elected president in 1984. His government was accused of serious human-rights violations, corruption, and other abuses of power.

Alfredo Cristiani of the National Republican Alliance (ARENA) became president following 1989 elections. Violence marred the elections, peace talks broke down, and the war intensified. Cristiani reopened discussions with FMLN leaders in 1990, and both sides accepted the United Nations as a mediator. Eventually, key concessions from both sides led to a 1992 UN-sponsored peace agreement between the leftist FMLN and the right-wing government. As many as 75,000 people had died during the years of violence.

Formal peace was declared in December 1992 amid huge celebrations. As part of the peace agreement, the FMLN became a legal political party, the size of the military was dramatically reduced, and a civilian national police force was established. The last three presidential elections have been won by ARENA party candidates, including Francisco Guillermo Flores Pérez, who was elected president in March 1999. The FMLN gained in March 2000 municipal and legislative elections; it is now the largest party in the legislature. The government has signed free-trade treaties with Chile and Mexico, developed better trade relations with its neighbors, and controlled inflation. President Flores now focuses on rebuilding the country after the earthquakes in early 2001.

THE PEOPLE

Population. El Salvador's population of 6.12 million is growing at 1.87 percent annually. About half of all people live in rural areas. Major cities include the greater San Salvador area (1.5 million residents), Santa Ana (250,000), and San Miguel (200,000). Near one million Salvadorans reside in the United States. The majority of people (94 percent) are mestizos, while about 5 percent are Native American, and roughly 1 percent are of European and Palestinian descent.

Language. Spanish (also called *Castellano*) is the official language of El Salvador. Only a few thousand people continue to speak the Native American language Nahua. School instruction is in Spanish, although English is emphasized strongly. Many Salvadorans with more formal education speak English in addition to Spanish.

Religion. El Salvador is a Christian nation, with about 70 percent of the people belonging to the Roman Catholic Church. Another 25 percent belong to a variety of other Christian faiths, including several Protestant movements whose memberships are growing. The state itself is secular; the only reference to religion in the constitution is a provision preventing clergy from holding public office. Still, priests usually pray or speak at school ceremonies and public meetings.

General Attitudes. Salvadorans are proud of their country and its accomplishments. Having endured 12 years of war, they now look forward to a future of peace and democracy. Past feelings of hatred and revenge gradually are being replaced with hope, optimism, and cooperation. It has been difficult for some people, given the suffering, to reach out to former enemies, but Salvadorans have done a remarkable job so far. Parents hope for a bright future for their children, even if they must continue to struggle with the devastation the war brought to the country.

On a personal level, some may be discouraged by the slow pace of reconstruction and reconciliation, but most are patient and willing to help rebuild the nation. Salvadorans have a strong work ethic. Honest work is considered to give an individual equal social standing with others. All family members contribute to the family's well-being. Social status is measured by occupation and land ownership. Salvadorans value personal relationships, friendships, and security. Devotion to the group is more important than individualism. Time is considered flexible: people are more important than schedules, and social events usually begin later than planned.

Some Salvadorans are offended when people from the United States introduce themselves as *Americans* because Salvadorans also consider themselves Americans—Central Americans. It is best to identify oneself as a U.S. citizen (*estadounidense*).

Personal Appearance. Because of the warm climate, summer clothing is suitable all year. Businesspeople often wear suits. Women wear dresses more often than slacks. During *verano* months, light jackets are sometimes necessary at night. Although the poor do not have extensive wardrobes, they keep their appearance neat and clean. Daily showers are considered a must. People without running water will go to considerable lengths to keep themselves, or at least their children, bathed as frequently as possible.

CUSTOMS AND COURTESIES

Greetings. In urban areas a brief, firm handshake is the customary formal greeting. People sometimes also slightly nod the head. Members of the opposite sex usually do not shake each other's hands. Weaker handshakes are common in rural areas. It is considered rude not to shake the hands of others in the vicinity. Children appreciate adults shaking their hands. In cities, friends and relatives of the opposite sex kiss lightly on one cheek. Friends or relatives who have not seen each other for a while exchange hugs. Placing an arm around the shoulders of another person shows friendship. Friends often stand very close when conversing.

The most common daily greetings include *¡Buenos días!* (Good morning), *¡Buenas tardes!* (Good afternoon), and *¡Buenas noches!* (Good evening). *Adiós* or *Hasta luego* are formal parting terms, while less formal good-byes are *Chao* or *Nos vemos*.

When addressing people older than themselves, Salvadorans show friendly respect by using the title *Don* (for men) or *Doña* (for women) with the first name (e.g., *Doña Mélida*). *Niña*, a less formal title, is also used for women. Among peers, professional and courtesy titles are used with the family name (e.g., *Señor Moreno*) or with full names

(*Doctora Isabel Pérez López*). Only close friends and relatives address each other by first name.

Gestures. In some circles, using excessive hand gestures is considered poor taste. But for many Salvadorans, hand gesturing is so important that people jest they could not talk at all if their hands were tied. Although pointing directly at people with the index finger is impolite, pointing at objects or animals is acceptable. One points at an angle to the street to hail a taxi or bus. To indicate "no," one can wag the vertical index finger from side to side. Touching the tip of the thumb and index finger together while facing the palm inward means "money," but facing the palm outward means "OK." A person can beckon to a friend with a hand wave, but strangers are summoned verbally.

Visiting. Friends and relatives visit one another frequently as a way to maintain strong relationships. Most people drop by without prior arrangement, although urban residents with phones try to call ahead when possible. Hosts usually serve guests refreshments or coffee. Visiting in the evening or on weekends is most popular. Visitors from out of town or who have not visited for a while commonly bring small gifts—fruit, pastries, and so on. Guests are expected to show dignity, courtesy, warmth, and friendship. It is appropriate to stand when a woman enters the room and when meeting other people. Polite hosts wait for their guests to decide when to leave. They walk their guests to the door and wait there while the guests walk or drive away.

Eating. Families usually eat at least the main meal together, whether it is at midday or in the evening. In urban homes, food usually is served on dishes from which diners choose their portions. In rural homes, plates are more often served prepared.

Guests compliment their hosts on the meal as a way of assuring the hosts they feel welcome. Hosts usually offer second helpings and feel complimented when they are accepted. However, one is careful in a poorer home not to eat too much since the family may not have much food. Hosts will continue to offer food until the guest says *No, gracias; estoy satisfecho* (No, thank you; I am satisfied). In many households, it is rude to say *Estoy lleno* (I am full). In rural areas, the wife will eat alone after the guests have been properly fed and attended to. Men commonly stand when a woman leaves the table. People leaving the table say *Buen provecho* (roughly "May you benefit from the meal").

LIFESTYLE

Family. The nuclear family is the basis of Salvadoran society. The father typically is head of the family, which has an average of five members. Single-parent families are also common, and a large number of babies are born to unwed mothers. Some men consider it a sign of virility to father children by more than one woman.

Families usually live close to each other. Most young adults remain at home until they marry. Excepting urban professionals, unmarried adults with children also usually live with their parents. Elderly parents often move in with their married children. Women care for the children and household, but a large number also are employed in the labor force. They may till the ground, clean homes, sew, run a small store (*tienda*) in the home, or work as skilled labor. Men help with farm work or water transportation. The majority of families belong to the peasant class (*campesinos*, who work on the land but do not own it) and the blue-collar working class. The gap between rich and poor is wide and expanding. Domestic violence is a serious problem.

Dating and Marriage. Dating for both genders begins after the 15th birthday, when many girls celebrate a *Quince Años* (Fifteen Years) party—the traditional entrance for young women into the social world. Urban youth often begin dating earlier. Traditionally, it has been improper for couples to date openly unless engaged, but for the most part, only rural couples maintain this tradition today. Asking a young woman's parents for her hand in marriage is more or less a polite formality and often an occasion for a festive dinner. In most cases, wedding ceremonies follow Catholic traditions, even among the secularized population. In some rural areas, family and friends of the bride may celebrate at the bride's home while the groom's family and friends may celebrate separately at his home. *Campesinos* often enter into common-law relationships because they cannot afford the expense of formal weddings.

Diet. Salvadoran food is much less spicy than that of many other Latin American countries. Most people eat red beans (*frijoles*) cooked in many ways, thick corn tortillas, rice, eggs, and fruit. One of the most common dishes is *pupusas* (thick tortillas stuffed with meat, beans, or cheese). People who can afford it consume beef, chicken, or fish regularly for lunch and/or dinner. Poorer rural families eat tortillas, whatever they can grow, and an occasional pig or chicken, a number of which are usually kept around the house as domestic livestock.

Recreation. The national sport in El Salvador is soccer (*fútbol*). Basketball (*baloncesto*) is also popular. Most towns have a gym and athletic field. Young women may play baseball or softball. In their leisure time, people like to visit, enjoy movies or music, or just relax. Many Salvadorans enjoy dancing at parties, discos (in larger cities), or dance halls (in smaller towns). Vacations are not common. Some people may take an excursion to the beach for the sunshine, fishing, and oysters.

The Arts. With the end of the civil war has come a return to traditional handicrafts and arts. Ilobasco, a little town in the center of the country, is known for its beautiful pottery, especially *sorpresas* (surprises)—small egg-shaped cases that display miniature scenes and figures of everyday life.

National issues and daily life have been subjects for Salvadoran writers for centuries. Religious subjects are popular for sculpture and painting. The sculpture of Christ in San Salvador's cathedral, called *Salvator mundi*, is one of the few major works left after natural disasters ruined older works. Colorfully painted scenes from Christ's life can be found as part of the works of Fernando Llort.

Holidays. The Salvadoran love for beauty and fun finds expression in the many colorful festivals held throughout the country during the year. National holidays include New Year's Day; Easter Week (*Semana Santa*); Labor Day (1 May); Mother's Day (10 May); Father's Day (17 June); August religious festivities (1–5 Aug.); Independence Day, which commemorates the day Father José Matías Delgado declared the country independent (15 Sept.); Columbus Day (12 Oct.); and Christmas. Each town has its holy day, which is celebrated over a long weekend or week. Holiday celebrations often include dances.

▶ **THE AMERICAS**

Commerce. Most businesses are open from 8 a.m. to noon and from 2 to 6 p.m., Monday through Friday. They close at noon on Saturday, except retail shops at large malls, which remain open through Sunday. Government offices open at 7:30 a.m. and close at 3:30 p.m. on weekdays. While fixed prices prevail in the stores, bargaining is common in open markets. People in small towns and rural areas purchase produce and meat at open markets but other groceries (bread, milk, soap, rice, etc.) at small, family-owned stores. In urban areas, this traditional retailing structure is being replaced quickly by *supermercado* (supermarket) shopping.

SOCIETY

Government. El Salvador is a democratic republic. The executive branch is led by a president and vice president. Both serve a five-year term and are ineligible for immediate reelection. The unicameral national Legislative Assembly has 84 members elected to three-year terms. The voting age is 18. Major political parties include ARENA, the FMLN, the Christian Democratic Party, and the National Conciliation Party. The country is divided into 14 departments and 262 municipalities. Although still weak, municipal power and autonomy, strengthened in the 1983 constitution, have been increasing steadily since 1990.

Economy. Mostly due to the effects of war, El Salvador has had one of the weakest economies in Latin America. Unfortunately, damage to crops and infrastructure caused by Hurricane Mitch and the earthquakes in 2001 has set economic progress back even further. Economic growth is low, but inflation remains under control.

Problems remain in areas such as income inequality, unemployment and underemployment (which affect more than half of the population), land reform, deforestation, and pollution. Opportunities for personal advancement are limited. Nearly 20 percent of the population is without access to the education, health care, and economic opportunities needed to rise above human poverty.* Training programs have been established to teach new skills, but a shortage of skilled labor remains a challenge. Salvadorans depend heavily on foreign aid and remittances from family members who have emigrated to the United States.

Coffee is the most important export, accounting for nearly half of all export earnings. It is grown on steep mountainsides: the higher the altitude, the higher the coffee bean quality. Children often help their parents pick coffee during school vacations. El Salvador also exports sugar, cotton, shrimp, and clothing. Important domestic industries include food processing, cement, textiles, and petroleum processing. While agriculture employs 40 percent of the workforce, the economy is becoming increasingly oriented toward manufacturing and services. In 2001, El Salvador adopted as its currency the U.S. dollar (US$), which will gradually replace the Salvadoran *colón* (¢).

Transportation and Communications. Because relatively few people own cars, most travel by bus. Rural people also travel on foot or by pickup truck. Taxis are available in larger cities. Roads in and around cities are mostly pavement or gravel. However, rural roads are rarely paved and can be impassable during the rainy season. Many roads have not been rebuilt since they fell into disrepair during the war. Hurricane Mitch has caused further damage to roads and bridges.

An effort is being made to improve communications, which are not well developed. Phones are concentrated in larger towns. Relatives who live apart and friends in rural areas often communicate through telegrams. The free press is growing, and there are two major daily newspapers in addition to a few smaller ones. Of the eleven television stations in El Salvador, nine are privately owned. There are also many private radio stations.

Education. Only about 35 percent of all rural adults are literate. The government is engaged in a vigorous campaign to increase that rate, building rural schools and encouraging enrollment. El Salvador, as a by-product of war and consequent poor quality of public schools, has hundreds of private schools and dozens of private universities. In all, there are 45 colleges or universities (public and private) in the country.

Elementary school (ages 7–12) is compulsory. It is followed by an optional three years of *Educación Básica* (Basic Education), after which students may choose between three years of technical school or three years of *Bachillerato*, the college track. The school year begins in mid-January and runs through October. Most children wear uniforms. Although public schooling is free, including at the university level, most people stop attending school at various ages to begin working and contributing to the family income.

Health. Medical care in El Salvador is free at all state health facilities, but many were damaged either during the war or by Hurricane Mitch. Rural areas often lack clinics, while urban clinics and hospitals are in poor condition. Patients often must provide their own sheets, syringes, and medicines. A large, higher-quality, private health-care system is available in cities to those who can afford it. The government is trying to improve health conditions through free immunizations, hygiene and sanitation education, water and sewage system development, and more modern hospital administration. Still, cholera, malaria, measles, intestinal disorders, dengue fever, and other diseases have increased recently, particularly in rural areas. Half of the country's school-age children suffer from malnutrition.

CONTACT INFORMATION

Consulate General of El Salvador, 1724 20th Street NW, Suite 200, Washington, DC 20009; phone (202) 331-4032. Embassy of El Salvador, 2308 California Street NW, Washington, DC 20008; phone (202) 265-9671.

DEVELOPMENT DATA	
Human Dev. Index* rank	104 of 174 countries
Adjusted for women	83 of 143 countries
Real GDP per capita	$4,036
Adult literacy rate	77 percent
Infant mortality rate	29 per 1,000 births
Life expectancy	67 (male); 73 (female)

1305 North Research Way, Bldg. K
Orem, Utah 84097-6200 USA
1.800.528.6279; 801.705.4250
fax 801.705.4350
www.culturegrams.com

England
(United Kingdom)

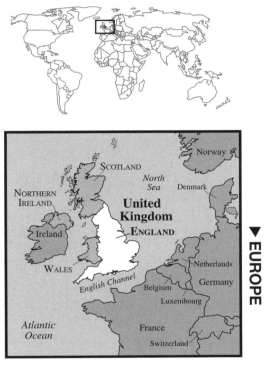

Boundary representations are not necessarily authoritative.

▼ EUROPE

BACKGROUND

Land and Climate. England is located in the British Isles, which include Great Britain, Ireland, the Isle of Man, and the Channel Islands (in the English Channel). England, Scotland, and Wales are located on the island of Great Britain. Politically, Great Britain and Northern Ireland comprise the country known as the United Kingdom (UK), which is about the size of Oregon. England itself covers 50,363 square miles (130,357 square kilometers) and is about the size of New York state.

Low mountains and rugged hills in the north contrast with flat countryside in the east and level and rolling plains in the southeast and southwest, the direction from which the prevailing wind blows. Nearly 30 percent of the land is cultivated. Almost half is meadow or pasture. The climate is temperate, but skies are overcast more often than not. Weather changes are frequent, but spring and fall weather is more predictable. The north and west are wetter and slightly cooler than the south and east. The east coast is very fog prone. Winter temperatures rarely drop below 25°F (-4°C); summer temperatures average 72°F (22°C). Humidity levels, ranging from medium to high, can make it seem colder or warmer than temperatures indicate.

History. The earliest signs of human presence in Britain date back to 5000 B.C.; the first remaining structures (stone circles, tombs, etc.) date back to 3000 B.C. Julius Caesar's expeditionary forces reached Britain in 55 B.C., but the Romans did not invade until A.D. 43 in the reign of Tiberius. They incorporated the area into the Roman Empire and stayed until 426, when Rome was in decline and raiding Angles and Saxons (two Germanic tribes) drove them out of Britain. They brought

organized government and many basic standards of living. Vikings began raiding the islands in the late eighth century. In 865, Danish-led forces invaded and ushered in two centuries of Viking domination. Other groups of Norsemen also invaded. The last invasion was in 1066, when William the Conqueror (or William of Normandy) won the Battle of Hastings. This Norman conquest ushered in a new period of great political and social change. The signing of the Magna Carta in 1215 was one such change; it established important principles of human rights and limits on the monarchy.

A long period of dynastic struggle ended in the 15th century after the War of the Roses, when power went to the House of York. Henry Tudor emerged with the crown. His son, King Henry VIII, created the Church of England with the Crown as its head. Henry VIII's daughter, Elizabeth I, reigned in an age when the empire began to span the globe, leading to the saying that "the sun never sets on the British Empire." Through acts of union, Wales (1535), Scotland (1707), and Ireland (1801) joined England. The empire was known as the United Kingdom of Great Britain and Ireland. When most of Ireland became independent in 1921, the name changed to the United Kingdom of Great Britain and Northern Ireland.

Britain established itself as a great naval power by defeating the mighty Spanish Armada in 1588. It became the world's most powerful economy during the Industrial Revolution. With these strengths and by acquiring colonies around the globe, Britain was firmly established as an international force and one of the Great Powers of Europe. Although its U.S. American colonies were lost in 1776 (Canada was a colony until 1867 and then became an autonomous part of the Commonwealth), Britain acquired new lands in the Mediterranean, the Caribbean, Africa, and Asia.

After World War I, expansion halted and the empire began to shrink (some colonies had already claimed independence well before the war). During World War II, under the leadership of Winston Churchill, the British withstood intense Nazi bombings, which nearly destroyed many areas. After the war, Britain granted most of its colonies (more than 50) independence and formed the Commonwealth. The majority remained voluntarily in the Commonwealth and some even retain Queen Elizabeth II as their nominal head of state. Britain was a founding member of the North Atlantic Treaty Organization (NATO) in 1949. It joined the European Union (EU) in 1973.

The UK established itself as a modern welfare state in 1945. Under the Conservative governments of Margaret Thatcher and John Major, the UK placed greater emphasis on the private sector. Elections in May 1997 brought Tony Blair's Labour Party to power, ending 18 years of Conservative rule.

Since taking office, Blair has initiated sweeping political changes. New legislative assemblies in Scotland and Wales were formed and granted limited powers. Blair is trying to resurrect the collapsed Northern Ireland peace agreement signed in April 1998 that established a Northern Ireland Assembly and stronger provincial links to the Republic of Ireland. He has also worked to implement welfare reforms and increase funding for health and education.

In February 2001, the highly contagious foot-and-mouth disease broke out among British livestock, prompting bans on British meat imports. Hundreds of thousands of cattle, pigs, and sheep were slaughtered in an effort to stop the disease. The disease has hurt England's economy, particularly the agriculture and tourism industries.

THE PEOPLE

Population. England is the largest nation of the UK, which has an overall population of more than 59.5 million and is growing at only 0.25 percent annually. The English comprise about 49.8 million of that total. The nation is highly urbanized, and nearly 90 percent of the people live in cities. London has close to 12 million people. Although most people living in England are Caucasian, Britain's colonial heritage has brought many cultures together. Ethnic groups from India, Africa, and Asia also reside in England (comprising about 2.8 percent of the population). South London is home to a large West Indian and African population; Leeds-Manchester has a large Asian population. However, as in other West European countries, the government recently has passed laws to limit immigration.

Language. English is the official language of the UK. Different dialects are spoken throughout England, as are the foreign languages of minority groups. What is known as BBC or Oxford English is now only spoken by a minority of British, principally those attending private schools.

Religion. During the reign of Henry VIII, England split from the Roman Catholic Church to form the Church of England (Anglican Church), which became the country's established religion. The Church of England exercised great influence over the country throughout history, but it no longer has political power. Still, the queen is head of the church. At least 27 million Anglicans reside in the UK. Large Catholic, Presbyterian, Methodist, and Jewish populations are found throughout the country. Other Christian and non-Christian religious organizations are also active. Hinduism, Sikhism, and Islam have significant followings.

Society is generally secular, despite the presence of an established church. Many congregations are diminishing as Sunday increasingly becomes a day to attend sports or go shopping. Only about one-tenth of all adults, mostly the elderly, regularly attend Sunday church services; of these, only about one-third attend the Church of England. Many English consider religion a private matter and feel it is impolite to ask about one's religious beliefs.

General Attitudes. Having a long and rich history, the English enjoy tradition and custom more so than do U.S. Americans. In general the English value moderate behavior and emotional reserve. Traditionally they are suspicious of extremes and may be embarrassed by displays of emotion or excessive enthusiasm. The great outpouring of emotion after the death of Princess Diana has challenged this tradition and revealed a deeper need for public compassion, particularly from the monarchy.

Politeness and humor are revered. Britons are known for a wry sense of humor and sarcasm that allows them to be self-critical. However, visitors are not given such freedom. Britons appreciate others who have some knowledge of their history and system. The dominance of England's traditional class system has begun to decline in the last generation. Apart from the upper class, which includes a handful of wealthy or titled families with royal connections, it is far less important in the lives of most people and is not discussed. Nevertheless, class distinctions still can be observed in people's accents, educational backgrounds, clothing, tastes in furnishings, and leisure activities. Social status generally is defined by one's home, car, and education.

Personal Appearance. The English dress much the same as people do in the United States, except that fashion trends are more closely tied to Europe. Casual dress is the norm. Dress for eating out is less formal than it is in the rest of Europe. Dress tends to be dark, reflecting the weather and mood of long winters. Older women tend to wear dresses more often than women in the United States. Business attire is conservative.

CUSTOMS AND COURTESIES

Greetings. A handshake is the most common form of greeting among the English, whether for formal occasions, visits, or introductions. Handshakes generally are firm but not aggressive. When people are already acquainted, they often use verbal greetings instead. Among friends, women often are kissed lightly (by men and women), usually on one cheek. When one passes a stranger on the street, it is appropriate to smile and say *Good morning, Hello, Good afternoon*, or *Good evening,* if one establishes eye contact with that person. Such exchanges occur less frequently in large cities. Most people call friends and young people by first name but use titles (*Mr., Mrs., Doctor,* etc.) in formal situations or to show respect.

Gestures. The English are in general a reserved people. They do not approve of loud or demonstrative behavior (except in very informal gatherings). People respect each other's personal space and feel uncomfortable when someone stands too close to them during conversation. Touching is generally avoided. Manners are important, although standards are not as high among the youth, who comprise nearly one-fifth of the population.

Visiting. Although it is a common courtesy to call ahead for local or spontaneous visits, people may or may not do so. Hosts are not expected to serve refreshments but may offer tea if they are not too busy to receive visitors. More formal visits are arranged in advance. Guests may bring gifts, such as a bottle of wine, chocolates, or flowers. Sending a thank-you note afterward is also appropriate. The English admire good manners and expect visitors to practice them. When one uses someone's phone, it is courteous to offer to pay, as even local calls are billed separately. However, hosts rarely accept the offer.

The English enjoy discussing a wide variety of topics during *tea*. This is a 4 p.m. snack of tea, *buns* (cupcakes), or *biscuits* (cookies). The food is often enough to constitute a meal. Due to work schedules, the English tradition of *tea* is no longer practiced widely, except when entertaining visitors.

Eating. The English eat in the continental style, with the fork in the left hand and the knife in the right. Proper table manners are a must; loud behavior is avoided. The English generally eat three meals a day. What each meal (except breakfast) is called depends on family background and local tradition. The majority call the noon meal *lunch* and the evening meal *dinner*. However, some call the noon meal *dinner* and the evening meal *tea*. Others call the evening meal *supper*, while still others use *supper* to refer to a snack before bedtime. Lunch is usually not heavy; most prefer to eat in the evening when the family is together. However, more and more families eat in front of the television. At a restaurant, diners summon a waiter by raising the hand. The waiter brings the bill on a plate, on which a 10 percent tip should be left. Tips usually reflect the quality of service given. *Pubs* provide the best value for eating out; fine restaurants are hard to find except in major cities.

LIFESTYLE

Family. English families are small and tight-knit. The traditional standard has been two children in a family. However, this pattern is changing. Fewer people are marrying and those that do, marry later. Women are having fewer children and having them later. More women work outside the home, and there are more single-parent families.

Most families enjoy a comfortable standard of living. The middle class represents Britain's majority. The English ideal is to have a house and garden. Two out of three families have their own homes. Apartment (*flat*) living is not popular and is only common in large cities. There is a trend away from urbanization. People are moving to the countryside to develop an attachment to the land and to avoid big-city problems.

Dating and Marriage. Dating activities in England are similar to those in the United States, but dating patterns are different. British youth generally have only one boyfriend or girlfriend at a time and do not date other people during that time. A person may legally marry at age 16, but most marry in their mid- to late twenties. Marriage customs are much the same as those in the United States.

Diet. A full traditional breakfast consists of bacon, sausages, grilled or fried tomatoes, mushrooms, eggs, and bread fried in fat or oil. Fewer people now eat this heavy meal on a regular basis, preferring to stick with various combinations of cereal, toast, juice or fruit, and tea or coffee. The British eat a wide variety of European and ethnic foods. Many traditional foods such as beef and potatoes have given way to poultry and pasta dishes. Fast food also has become more prevalent, and hamburger restaurants now rival the traditional *fish-and-chip*

(french fries) shops in popularity. Numerous Chinese and Indian restaurants and pizza houses provide *take-away* service, and many *pubs* (public houses) serve anything from snacks to full meals. Traditional English dishes include roast beef and *Yorkshire pudding* (a baked batter usually served in muffin form), and steak and kidney pie.

Recreation. A variety of activities are enjoyed in England, which developed many of the world's favorite sports. *Football* (soccer), which was first codified in England, is the most popular sport in the country. Rugby is also enjoyed. There are two types of rugby, Union and League, the latter of which is played in the north. Horse racing (over jumps in the winter and on a flat track in the summer) is also followed. The English enjoy cricket in the summer. Modern lawn tennis was first played in England, and modern boxing rules came from the country. Other favorite forms of recreation include badminton, sailing, swimming, *snooker* (a billiards game), darts, and squash.

The English like to walk and golf, and many participate in *angling* (fishing). Gardening represents a favorite way to relax and is a huge industry (gardening books can become bestsellers). Gardens of flowers, shrubs, and decorative plants are most common, but some people also plant vegetables. *Pubs* offer a place to meet, socialize, and relax with friends and neighbors. However, relaxing in the home is more popular. The English watch more television than any other people except U.S. Americans. They claim it is because of the quality of their programming. Movies and videos are also popular.

The Arts. The English have made significant and varied contributions in the arts. William Shakespeare is the most recognizable name from a long list of legendary English authors, including John Milton, Geoffrey Chaucer, and others. In the performing arts, England is widely recognized for its theater. London boasts some of the world's premier art galleries, theaters, and concert halls.

English music has crossed a variety of time periods, styles, and genres, with works by such artists as Henry Purcell, George Friedrich Handel, William Gilbert, Arthur Sullivan, and Gustav Holst. Since the Beatles in the 1960s, British rock music has maintained a worldwide influence. The English have made their mark in painting, architecture, and sculpture. Folk arts such as embroidery, tapestries, jewelry, furniture, and glass are appreciated by many today.

Holidays. The English have the fewest public holidays in Europe. They include New Year's Day, Good Friday and Easter Monday, May Day (1 May), spring and summer bank holidays, Christmas, and Boxing Day (26 Dec.). For New Year's Day and May Day, workers receive a day off on the following Monday if the holiday falls on Saturday or Sunday. Virtually everything closes for Christmas, including shops and restaurants. Many offices close between Christmas and New Year's due to slow business. Boxing Day is named for the tradition of giving small boxed gifts to servants and tradesmen. It is now a day for visiting friends and family.

Holidays that are celebrated but not treated as days off from work include the Queen's Birthday (second Saturday in June), Remembrance Day (closest Sunday to 11 November), and Guy Fawkes Day (5 Nov.). Guy Fawkes Day, or Bonfire Night, commemorates the capture of Guy Fawkes, who plotted to destroy the houses of Parliament in 1605. Huge bonfires are lit and firework displays are put on for the public. Most

▼ EUROPE

people receive four or five weeks of personal vacation from work. July and August are popular months for taking trips, and many people also vacation in the winter. Spain and Greece are favorite destinations, as are English resorts on the south coast.

Commerce. Businesses generally are open from 9 a.m. to 5 p.m., Monday through Friday. An increasing number of shops are lengthening business hours and staying open on weekends. Government offices and some rural shops close for lunch between 1 and 2 p.m. and stay open until 5:30 p.m. Most businesses are closed on Sunday, although some stores are open.

SOCIETY

Government. Britain has no written constitution. The constitutional arrangements are the result of acts of Parliament, common law, and precedent. The importance of a parliament was established following the 1649 civil war and execution of King Charles I. Upon the death of Oliver Cromwell, who had led the violent revolution, the monarchy was reestablished but parliamentary sovereignty remained prominent. The monarch, Queen Elizabeth II, is head of state, but elected officials govern through Parliament.

The House of Commons is the main legislative body. It has 659 members, 529 of whom are from England. The party with the most Members of Parliament (MPs) forms the government, and that party's leader becomes the prime minister (officially appointed by the queen). The prime minister and cabinet govern as the executive body. The voting age is 18. Elections are held at least every five years but can be called by the prime minister at any time. There are no limits to the number of terms the prime minister can serve.

Parliament's upper chamber is the House of Lords, which has 1,200 members. The chamber's chief legislative role is to veto legislation, which in practice simply delays it. In July 1999, Scotland held its own 129-member Parliament, with limited powers over taxation, health, and education. At the same time, Wales opened a 60-member Assembly with similar powers except for taxation.

Economy. With one of the largest economies in Europe, the UK remains a global economic power. Most people enjoy a good standard of living, although there is a fairly large gap between the upper and lower classes: the richest fifth of the population receives more than 50 percent of the nation's income. Economic growth was modest in 2000. Inflation and unemployment are low.

Britain does the bulk of its trading within the EU. Natural resources include oil, natural gas, iron ore, and salt. Important exports include crude oil (from the North Sea), manufactured goods, and consumer items. The service sector is more important than manufacturing, and London is one of the world's most important financial centers. The currency is the pound sterling (£); the English remain uncertain about the effects of adopting the EU's euro.

Transportation and Communications. Travel by road is the favored method of transportation for both people and freight. The British drive on the left side of the road, and a car's steering wheel is on the right side of the car. Taxis are common in the cities. Public transportation is well developed in most

DEVELOPMENT DATA

Human Dev. Index* rank	10 of 174 countries
Adjusted for women	10 of 143 countries
Real GDP per capita	$20,336
Adult literacy rate	99 percent
Infant mortality rate	6 per 1,000 births
Life expectancy	75 (male); 80 (female)

urban areas, with a subway in London called the *Tube* or the *Underground* and subways in such cities as Manchester and Newcastle. Buses and trains service major cities, but public transport in rural areas is not as extensive. Domestic and international air travel is well developed. London's Heathrow Airport is the busiest in the world.

The Channel Tunnel (or "Chunnel") connects England and France by rail under the English Channel. The tunnel offers a three-hour ride between London and Paris (about 35 minutes in the actual tunnel) for passengers, freight, and private cars.

Telecommunications are well advanced, with fiber optic cable links and satellite systems. Most British homes have telephones and televisions. Daily newspapers are available throughout the nation. Both tabloids and *broadsheets* (more serious newspapers) are popular. Internet use has grown rapidly as computer prices have dropped.

Education. A large portion of English tax revenues is spent on education needs. Schooling is free and compulsory between ages five and sixteen. Many students begin earlier with nursery school and some stay beyond age 16 to prepare for entrance to college. A grade is called a *form*. Public schools are called *state schools* and private ones are called *public schools*. At age 16, students take an exam to earn the General Certificate of Secondary Education. At 18, they may take the General Certificate of Education, which is used as an entrance exam by England's universities. In addition to more than 40 universities and various professional schools, England has an Open University, which offers correspondence and broadcast courses. England's quality of higher education is evident in many important scientific and technological contributions made by the British, as well as British achievement in the arts and other areas.

Health. Britain's National Health Service (NHS) provides, on the basis of taxation, free medical treatment and many other social services. Individuals only pay for prescriptions and some dental services. Quality of care and facilities are high, but the country struggles under the increasing cost of financing NHS. Private care is also available, and many people now have private insurance to avoid long waits for surgical treatment covered by the NHS.

CONTACT INFORMATION

The British Embassy, 3100 Massachusetts Avenue NW, Washington, DC 20008; phone (202) 462-1340; Web site www.britainusa.com/consular/embassy/embassy.asp. British Tourist Authority, 551 Fifth Avenue, Suite 701, New York, NY 10176; phone (800) 462-2748; Web site www.usagateway.visitbritain.com.

1305 North Research Way, Bldg. K
Orem, Utah 84097-6200 USA
1.800.528.6279; 801.705.4250
fax 801.705.4350
www.culturegrams.com

Republic of
Estonia

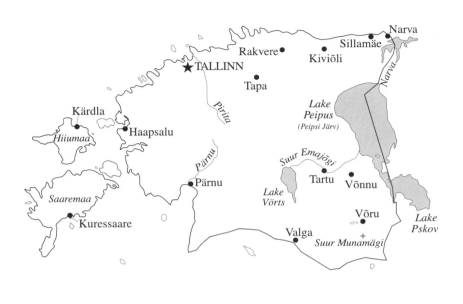

▶ EUROPE

Boundary representations are not necessarily authoritative.

BACKGROUND

Land and Climate. Estonia is a small European country, similar in size to Switzerland or the combined states of New Hampshire and Vermont. Water surrounds it on three sides: to the north and west is the Baltic sea, and to the east is Lake Peipus. It is one of the three countries known as the Baltic States (Estonia, Latvia, and Lithuania). More than 1,500 islands in the Baltic Sea make up nearly 10 percent of Estonia's total 17,462 square miles (45,226 square kilometers). The two largest islands are Saaremaa and Hiiumaa, each of which is populated.

Estonia is mostly flat, with hills in the south. The highest hill is Suur Munamägi (Great Egghill) at 1,043 feet (318 meters). Historically an agrarian country, Estonia also is endowed with oil shale deposits and phosphorite, particularly in the northeast. The country's major rivers include the Suur Emajõgi (Mother River), Pärnu, Narva, and Pirita. Lake Peipus dominates the eastern border. A number of smaller lakes and rivers, many rich in fish, dot Estonia's landscape. Forests, wetlands, and meadows harbor wildlife, berries, and mushrooms.

The climate is usually wet and often cloudy, with most cloudy days in October through March. Winters are cold and snowy, with temperatures often below freezing. Summers are cool; temperatures average around 65°F (18°C). Estonia is warmed by the Gulf Stream, which also brings rain at the end of summer.

History. The Estonian people belong to the ancient Finno-Ugric tribe that has inhabited the region for thousands of years. Before the 13th century, Estonians generally lived in free association, without an aristocracy of any kind. This

changed with the invasion and domination of German and Danish crusaders in the 1200s. Baltic Germans remained the ruling class into the 20th century. Estonia came under Swedish control in 1561 but became linked to Russia beginning in 1710.

Estonia took advantage of the chaotic conditions of Russia's Bolshevik Revolution in 1917 to declare its independence. The Red Army invaded but was defeated in the Battle of Võnnu. Estonia maintained its independence for 22 years. However, under the secret Molotov-Ribbentrop pact between Germany's Adolf Hitler and Russia's Josef Stalin, Estonia was invaded in 1940 by the Soviet Union (USSR). Germany occupied the territory from 1941 to 1944, when it was defeated in World War II. The Soviets then reestablished their power and incorporated Estonia into the USSR.

With the relaxed political climate under Soviet leader Mikhail Gorbachev, Estonia's quest for independence became visible outside the USSR. At large demonstrations and nighttime festivals, people sang outlawed nationalistic songs to show their determination. As the Soviet Union weakened and finally collapsed in 1991, Russian president Boris Yeltsin accepted Estonia's declaration of restored independence.

Despite periodic bouts of political instability, Estonia has moved steadily toward reestablishing its sovereign and democratic government since independence in 1991. Several reform-minded governments have come to power since democratic elections were held in 1992. The current center-right government, elected in March 1999, is a coalition of the Fatherland, Reform, and Moderate parties. Mart Laar is prime minister. His government seeks economic growth and closer ties with the West as Estonia works toward European Union (EU) and North Atlantic Treaty Organization (NATO) membership.

THE PEOPLE

Population. Estonia's population of about 1.4 million is currently decreasing by 0.6 percent annually. The majority is ethnic Estonian (65 percent), although Russians comprise 28 percent of the population. Other groups include Ukrainians (3 percent), Belarusians (2 percent), and Finns (1 percent). Most non-Estonians migrated to the area during the Soviet era. They are eligible for citizenship if they meet language, residency, and other requirements. Many ethnic Russians, heartened by Estonia's current economic and social development, are choosing to seek formal citizenship. Citizenship is vital for property ownership, social benefits, and other privileges of living in Estonia.

During World War II, thousands of Estonians fled their homeland and settled all over the world. The largest expatriate communities are located in Toronto, Canada, and New York City. Groups are found throughout the United States, Australia, and Sweden. These communities retain their roots through festivals, church worship, and newspapers.

Tallinn, the capital, is the largest city; it has about 408,000 inhabitants. Tartu (102,000) and Narva (73,000) are the next largest cities. Three-fourths of all people live in urban areas. Much of the Russian population has settled in industrial areas of the northeast; Narva's population is almost entirely Russian. People have moderate access to economic opportunities, education, and health care needed to make choices in their lives.

Language. Estonian belongs to the Finno-Ugric language group. It uses a Latin alphabet and is similar to Finnish. Many Estonians, especially around Tallinn, understand Finnish; some speak it. Estonian has 14 cases, which makes it difficult to learn. Vocabulary is limited, so many international words have been adopted: *finants* (finance), *televiisor* (television), etc. There is little profanity in Estonian. English is popular, particularly with the youth, and is taught in school. Russian may be the language of instruction in some Russian schools; however, students must also study Estonian and pass Estonian language tests prior to graduation.

During the Soviet era, Russian was imposed on the Estonian population. Although many Estonians can speak Russian, they prefer to speak Estonian. Young Estonians are less likely to have a good knowledge of Russian. Estonian became the official language after the country's independence in 1991. Passing an Estonian language test is now a specific requirement for citizenship, even though many ethnic Russians cannot yet speak Estonian. Ethnic Russians are proud of their language and feel it is unfair to have to learn Estonian in order to retain their homes and employment. The language requirement for citizenship remains a contentious issue between the Russian and Estonian populations.

Religion. Estonia was one of the last nations in Europe to convert to Christianity. Before the 13th century, Estonians followed a religion closely tied to nature that included the worship of a god called *Taara*. The adoption of Christianity came through foreign invasions and missionary work. Following the Reformation, the Lutheran Church became dominant in Estonia.

Because religious worship was suppressed during the Soviet era, the country today is quite secular. Less than one-fourth of the population is religious. Most of these people still attend the Lutheran Church, although other Christian denominations are active also. Religious freedom is guaranteed. Although the government is not tied to a particular religion, prayers are sometimes offered at official functions.

General Attitudes. Estonians view themselves as an industrious and efficient people who maintained these values even during the Soviet era. Because they are a reserved and shy people, they may be perceived at times as unfriendly and aloof. They are patriotic and proud of their ancient heritage. Although they are not part of Scandinavia, Estonians tend to identify with the Scandinavian value system and way of life. Estonians cherish freedom and their traditional culture. Despite occupation by other nations, particularly since 1940, Estonians are proud that they have retained their traditions and language. They look forward to closer ties with the West.

Estonians place a high value on family, education, and work. They value a good personal reputation for themselves and others. People desire future opportunities to travel and to obtain a higher standard of living.

Personal Appearance. Estonians tend to have fair-colored hair and blue eyes, so they appear to be Scandinavian or Nordic. They like to dress well in public and typically dress more formally when going out to eat, going to theater, or visiting friends. Women tend to wear dresses more than slacks, although the youth are adopting a more varied approach. Young people prefer European fashions. People dress warmly during the winter, preferring coats to jackets. Clothing styles in rural areas are more relaxed than in cities. Each county has its own traditional costume that is worn for song and dance festivals, some holidays, or weddings. Costumes are worn more often in rural areas than in the cities.

CUSTOMS AND COURTESIES

Greetings. Estonians usually greet with a simple *Tere* (Hello) and a handshake. The younger person initiates the greeting, and men greet women first. In a group, the elderly are first to be greeted. People often begin a conversation with *Kuidas läheb?* (How is it going?) or *Kuidas elate?* (How's life?). Other greetings include *Tere hommikust* (Good morning), *Tere päevast* (Good day), and *Tere Õhtust* (Good evening).

When one is approached, it is polite to stand and acknowledge the other person's presence, maintaining eye contact during the greeting. It is a courtesy to use the formal pronoun *Teie* (you) when meeting someone for the first time, with older people, and with those in authority. The informal *Sina* (you) is used with friends and relatives. Estonians seldom greet strangers when passing on the street or meeting in stores. Phrases such as "Hello, how are you today?" or "Have a nice day" are used when both individuals know each other.

Gestures. Chewing gum in public is impolite, especially when talking to someone. Estonians use the "thumbs up" gesture to indicate things are going well. Pointing with the index finger is impolite, as is talking with one's hands in the pockets. Hand gestures are kept to a minimum during conversation. Younger people often give their seats to the elderly on public transportation. It is polite for men to open doors for women, and many women expect it.

Visiting. An important aspect of social life is visiting or receiving friends. Punctuality is expected. Most visits are arranged in advance as a courtesy to the hosts. People customarily remove their shoes upon entering the home. When visiting friends or visiting someone for the first time, people commonly bring flowers. Flowers also are given to the hosts when celebrating their birthday and to students and teachers for graduation. Hosts usually offer their guests tea or coffee served with cookies or candies. People enjoy inviting friends over for dinner. Estonians appreciate conversation during the meal. Guests staying in the home generally give a gift to thank the hosts for their hospitality.

Eating. Dark rye bread, eggs, cheese, pastries, sandwiches, fried potatoes, and porridge are common breakfast foods, accompanied by milk or coffee. The main meal is at midday. It consists of three courses: soup, a main dish of meat, poultry, or fish, potatoes, and dessert. Common soups include bouillon, cabbage, or pea. Dessert is often cake, ice cream, fruit, or fruit preserves. Dinner is a lighter meal and is eaten after 6 p.m. It might include a sandwich and salad, potatoes, stew, pasta, or soup.

Estonians commonly wish one another *Head isu* (Good appetite) when beginning their meal; they wait for all to be served before eating. Hands generally are kept above the table. A knife and fork should be used whenever possible. In general, it is impolite to leave food on a plate. One thanks the cook upon finishing. One also waits for all to finish before leaving the table. Requesting second helpings pleases the cook.

LIFESTYLE

Family. Families tend to be small, commonly with one to three children. Ties with extended family members are important. Grandparents often care for their grandchildren while both parents work. In many cases, newlywed couples live with their parents until they are financially established. Parents try to assist their adult children financially when possible. Adult children take direct responsibility (financial and physical) for their aging parents. Nursing homes are used only for those who have no close relations. Although habits are changing with the younger generation, most men are not expected to share household responsibilities (prepare meals, clean the house, etc.).

Urban families tend to live in apartments or small, single-family homes with a fence and garden. Those living in apartments usually share a summer cottage in the countryside with a plot of land for growing fruits and vegetables. Most rural families live on farms and enjoy larger homes.

Dating and Marriage. Common dating activities include attending cultural events, going to the theater, dancing, participating in sporting events, and eating and drinking. Estonians usually marry after they have finished their education, which is usually in their early twenties. Some couples live together before or instead of marrying. Weddings are generally secular, but church weddings are becoming more popular. Parents from both sides help organize the celebration, to which plenty of friends and relatives are invited. Playing games, dancing, playing practical jokes, and seeking to "steal" the bride are common traditions. Estonians often have their first child early in their marriage.

Diet. Dark rye bread and fish (trout, salmon, cod, herring, sole, pike, perch, and whitefish) commonly are eaten. Fish may be smoked, grilled, baked, or pickled. Potatoes, cabbage, carrots, beets, and beans are the prevalent vegetables. The most common fruits are apples, cherries, pears, and a number of wild berries (raspberries, strawberries, cranberries, cloudberries, and blueberries). Fruits and vegetables usually are canned for winter. Pork, beef, lamb, veal, and chicken are common meats. Cheese and milk products are also staples of the diet. Most people drink tea and coffee each day. Vodka is also enjoyed. *Pirukas* (a pastry with meat and/or vegetables) is popular. A favorite Russian dish is *rosolje*, a pink potato salad made with beets and herring; another is *Seljanka*, a meat soup with pickles, onions, and olives. Sauerkraut soup is served with sour cream. At Christmas, people eat *verivõrst* (blood sausage), jellied meats, *sült* (head cheese), roast pork or goose, sauerkraut, potatoes, rye bread, and homemade ale.

Recreation. Estonians love sports. The country has produced a number of Olympic champions and has a strong national basketball team. Other recreational activities include volleyball, sailing, ice fishing, ice-skating, cross-country skiing, swimming, and cycling. In their leisure time, Estonians like to go to the beach, relax in saunas (often on a weekly basis), and work in their gardens. Even in urban areas, the people feel tied to the land and their agricultural heritage. A favorite summer pastime is picking wild berries and mushrooms in the forest. Backpacking is becoming more popular.

The Arts. Music is greatly appreciated, and attending concerts of all types is common. Nearly all age groups and professions have their own choirs. A national song festival has been held roughly every four years since 1869. A combined choir with as many as 30,000 voices sings a variety of traditional folk songs. Usually held the first weekend in July, the festival also includes parades, costumes, and dancing. Accordions, flutes, and simple percussion instruments are all found in traditional music. The *kannan* (a wooden stringed instrument similar to the zither) is considered the national instrument.

Between 1857 and 1861, Friedrich Reinhold Kreutzwald compiled and published the Estonian national epic, *Kalevipoeg* (Son of Kalev). Written in verse, the epic tells the story of Kalevipoeg, the mythical ancient ruler of Estonia. Local theaters or community playhouses are popular and crowded, especially during dark winter nights. Estonia has one of the oldest and richest knitting traditions in Europe.

Holidays. New Year's Day (1 Jan.) is followed by numerous holidays. For *Vastlapäev* (15 Feb.), people go sledding and eat special foods; a long sledding ride indicates good luck with the fall harvest. Independence Day (24 Feb.) celebrates freedom in 1918. Even though 20 August marks Estonia's reestablishment of freedom in 1991, the 24 February holiday remains the primary focus of independence celebrations. Easter is celebrated Friday through Sunday and includes the tradition of painting eggs and eating special foods. On Fool's Day (1 Apr.), people play tricks on each other. Two days in June commemorate historical events: 14 June honors those who were deported to Siberia by Stalin in 1949, and 23 June marks the Day of Victory at Võnnu.

Jaanipäev (Midsummer's Day) is 24 June. This marks the beginning of the summer's "white nights," during which the sun sets for only a few hours. People light huge bonfires or

EUROPE

place fires on small rafts. Parties, dances, and concerts are held. People traditionally search for a fern blossom on this night because it will bring happiness to them (but ferns do not have blossoms). Girls pick seven types of flowers to put under their pillows in hopes of dreaming about their future husband.

The Day of the Souls (2 Nov.) remembers the dead. *Kadri* Day (25 Oct.) and *Mardi* Day (10 Nov.) are days for children to paint their faces, dress up in old clothes, and go to their neighbors' houses. They knock, sing special national songs, and sometimes dance, asking to be let in out of the cold. They are given candy and fruit. Estonians celebrate Christmas over three days (24–26 Dec.). They decorate graves and eat a special meal on Christmas Eve.

Commerce. Estonian businesses usually are open between 8 or 9 a.m. and 5 p.m. Shops and restaurants do not close for lunch; most businesses do not close, either. Goods are sold in stores, open-air markets, and kiosks. Food stores usually are open until 9 p.m. on weekdays and are open on weekends. Other stores may be open on Saturday but close by noon and are closed on Sunday.

SOCIETY

Government. The Republic of Estonia has 15 counties. It is governed by a combined parliamentary and presidential system. President Lennart Meri is chief of state; he began a second term in September 1996. A prime minister is head of government. The 101 members of *Riigikogu* (Parliament) are elected by region. Several parties have legislative representation and most support Estonia's economic and democratic progress. The voting age is 18.

Economy. A free-market economy is being reestablished rapidly. Widespread support to reintegrate into Western Europe has enabled the government to implement ambitious programs of privatization and economic reform. Privatization of most state enterprises is nearly complete. Economic growth slowed to 0 percent in 1999 as a result of Russian and Asian financial crises but grew by about 6 percent in 2000. Inflation was close to 6 percent. However, unemployment more than doubled in 2000. Many Estonians now can take advantage of increasing economic opportunities and higher standards of living.

Estonia has a skilled, industrious workforce and an efficient agricultural sector. The main industries include timber (wood products), textiles, food processing (meat, milk), electronics, and chemicals. The country is generally self-sufficient in food production.

Foreign trade has shifted quickly from the East to the West, although Russia is still an important market for Estonian goods. Businesses are meeting the challenges of operating in a democratic, capitalist environment. The country is also one of the fastest-growing tourism markets in Europe. Estonia has been invited to participate in negotiations to enter the EU. The Estonian currency is the *kroon* (EEK); it has a fixed exchange rate tied to the German *mark* (1 DM=8 EEK).

Transportation and Communications. In cities, both public transportation (buses, streetcars) and private cars are used.

© 2001 CultureGrams, a division of Millennial Star Network and Brigham Young University. It is against the law to copy, reprint, store, or transmit any part of this publication in any form by any means without written permission from CultureGrams. This document contains native commentary and original analysis, as well as estimated statistics. The content should not be considered strictly factual, and it may not apply to all groups in a nation. *UN Development Programme, Human Development Report 2000 (New York: Oxford University Press, 2000).

DEVELOPMENT DATA

Human Dev. Index* rank	46 of 174 countries
Adjusted for women	43 of 143 countries
Real GDP per capita	$7,682
Adult literacy rate	99 percent
Infant mortality rate	13 per 1,000 births
Life expectancy	63 (male); 75 (female)

Many families own a car. Tallinn has both trams and trolleys. Electric trains are used in suburban areas. Trains and buses are used for transport between cities. Train and ferry services are also available to neighboring countries. Most Estonians have phones, even in remote areas. Mobile phone use is widespread. Estonia has the highest per capita number of Internet connections in Eastern Europe. Several commercial radio and television stations broadcast in Estonia. Broadcasts from other European countries also are received via satellite or by airwaves from Finland.

Education. Tallinn is home to several universities and technical colleges. Tartu University was built in 1632 by Swedish King Gustav Adolphus and is one of Europe's oldest academic institutions. Its library holds more than three million scientific dissertations.

Day-care centers and kindergartens provide preschool education before age six, when primary schooling begins. Students are required to attend school until age 14, when students can choose to attend technical school. However, most students go on to four years of high school. Many then continue on to a university or technical school. Public universities are free, but enrollment is limited. Entrance exams based on the desired course of study must be taken before admittance.

Estonia's education system is currently under reform, which involves the time-consuming process of rewriting textbooks and curricula to more accurately reflect Estonia's history, culture, and values.

Health. More than 93 percent of the population has access to health care through public and private facilities. Most hospitals are run by the government, and care is free. People must pay for visits to the dentist and care provided by private doctors. The health-care and pension systems are under reform; a new insurance system and updated equipment are needed. Physicians also are seeking to update their skills and procedures through contacts in the West. The leading causes of death in Estonia are cardiovascular disease, cancer, and accidents (mainly traffic).

CONTACT INFORMATION

Embassy of Estonia, 2131 Massachusetts Avenue NW, Washington, DC 20008; phone (202) 588-0101; Web site www.estemb.org. Consulate General of the Republic of Estonia, 600 Third Avenue, 26th Floor, New York, NY 10016; phone (212) 883-0636.

CultureGrams™
People. The World. You.

1305 North Research Way, Bldg. K
Orem, Utah 84097-6200 USA
1.800.528.6279; 801.705.4250
fax 801.705.4350
www.culturegrams.com

Republic of
Finland

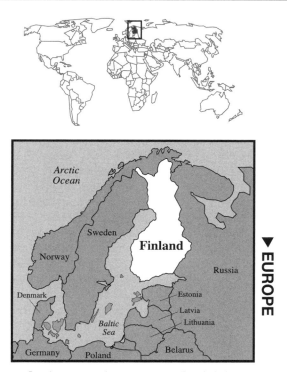

► EUROPE

Boundary representations are not necessarily authoritative.

BACKGROUND

Land and Climate. Finland is a Scandinavian or Nordic country that borders Russia. Just smaller than the state of Montana, Finland covers 130,127 square miles (337,030 square kilometers). Finland is known as a land of lakes and forests. More than 187,800 lakes and other bodies of water dominate the landscape. Forests cover three-quarters of the country's surface area. Only 8 percent of the land is arable. The terrain is low and flat in the south but gives way to rolling plains farther north and low hills in the far north. A few minor mountains are found in the far north of Lapland and in Saariselkä. Finland has implemented tough environmental standards and initiatives to protect its environment.

Although Finland is located at about the same latitude as Alaska, Siberia, and southern Greenland, the climate is not as harsh because of the warming North Atlantic current, the Baltic Sea, and Finland's lakes. Still, winters are long and cold, averaging temperatures below freezing. Summers are short and cool, averaging from 63°F to 68°F (17–20°C), but there are occasional warm spells. North of the arctic circle, the sun remains above the horizon day and night in the summer and below the horizon day and night in the winter. The aurora borealis lights up northern winter nights. South of the arctic circle, where most of the population lives, the summer day lasts 19 hours and the nights are never completely dark. By contrast, midwinter daylight lasts only six hours, with the sun low on the horizon.

History. Finnish people have lived in the area known as Finland since about 3000 B.C. Germanic peoples and other tribes, including the Tavasts, Lapps (Sami—pronounced SAW-me), and Karelians, also inhabited the area thousands of years ago. Eventually the Finno-Ugric tribe became dominant. In 1155, a crusade from Sweden to Finland brought Catholicism and Swedish rule to the region. Finland remained a part of the Swedish kingdom for the next several hundred years, although Protestantism replaced Catholicism during the Reformation. Upon losing a war to Russia in 1809, Sweden ceded Finland to Russia.

Under Sweden's rule, Finland existed as a group of provinces, not a unified entity. After his victory, the Russian czar Alexander I fulfilled his promise to grant Finland extensive autonomy; Finland soon became a grand duchy of the Russian Empire with Alexander as its grand duke. The years spent under Alexander's command are considered one of the best periods in Finnish history. A national movement led to the switch from Swedish to Finnish as the official language in 1863, and the Finns had a semiautonomous legislature to administer local affairs. Eventual resentment of this autonomy led to attempts to more fully integrate Finland into Russia in 1899. These Russification policies were resisted in Finland and eventually would have led to armed rebellion; however, the Bolshevik Revolution gripped Russia before that could happen. Finland declared its independence, which was recognized by the Bolsheviks, on 6 December 1917.

After a brief civil war, the Finns adopted a republican constitution in 1919. During World War II, Finland fought the Soviet Union twice: in the Winter War (1939–40) and then in the Continuation War until 1944. Finland was forced to cede one-tenth of its territory (roughly Karelia) to the Soviet Union but avoided Soviet occupation and preserved its independence.

In 1948, the Finns signed a friendship treaty with the Soviet Union, binding themselves to repel any attack on the Soviet Union that involved Finnish territory. The treaty still allowed trade and good relations with the West but created a situation where the Soviet Union could influence Finnish foreign policy. In 1989, Soviet President Mikhail Gorbachev officially recognized Finland's neutrality for the first time. In 1992, Russian President Boris Yeltsin and Finland's president signed a treaty voiding the 1948 agreement. The new treaty recognizes Russia's and Finland's equality, sovereignty, and positive economic relations. With the collapse of the Soviet Union, Finland moved towards integration with Europe. Voters supported European Union membership in a 1994 referendum; the country officially joined in 1995.

The 1991 elections brought Finland its first nonsocialist government in years, sending the once-ruling Social Democrats into the parliament's opposition. The new center-right coalition government took office during the global recession and suffered a loss of popularity when the economy weakened. Despite rebounding in 1994, the economy and other issues returned the Social Democratic Party to dominance in 1995. In April 1998, Parliament voted overwhelmingly in favor of joining Europe's single currency. March 1999 elections saw the Social Democrats retain the biggest share of seats in parliament. A coalition of five parties now governs, controlling 139 of the 200 seats. Prime Minister Paavo Lipponen hopes to reduce Finland's high unemployment. In 2000, Tarja Halonen, a Social Democrat, was elected as Finland's first woman president. As in other European countries, Finland is concerned about how the spread of the mad cow and foot-and-mouth diseases among European livestock will affect European economies as well as food safety.

THE PEOPLE

Population. The population of Finland is about 5.2 million, growing at a rate of 0.17 percent annually. The majority of the people are Finns, although there is a significant Swedish-speaking minority. Finland also has very small minorities of native Sami, Gypsies, Russians, and Somalis. The overall population density is only 6 persons per square mile, but most people live in southern Finland. More than 64 percent of Finns live in towns or cities. Urbanization is a relatively new trend, so most people still have roots in the countryside and their home villages. Excellent access to health care, education, and the resources needed for a decent standard of living affords men and women many choices and opportunities in their lives.

Language. More than 93 percent of the population speaks Finnish, a Finno-Ugric language belonging to a different language family than other Scandinavian languages. It is most closely related to Estonian. Swedish is also officially recognized and is spoken by about 6 percent of the people. While only the Sami minority speaks Sami, Finland recognizes it as a language (just not an official one). English is a popular second language, especially among the youth and the educated. Those who speak Finnish as a native language must study Swedish for three years in school. Likewise, Swedish speakers learn Finnish. Finnish words often include many vowels. Changing the length of a vowel or consonant sound can also change the meaning of a word. With 15 different cases, Finnish is often difficult for foreigners to learn.

Religion. Although about 89 percent of the population belongs to the Evangelical Lutheran Church of Finland, the government has an official policy of religious neutrality. In fact, freedom of religion has been guaranteed since 1923. The Evangelical Lutheran Church still performs important functions as a state church, however, including population registration and cemetery maintenance, and it is supported by state taxes. The Finnish Orthodox Church, also supported by the state, claims the next largest following in Finland (1 percent). Several other Christian groups and other religions are active. As in many European nations, growing secularization has caused a decline in church attendance and membership. Approximately 9 percent of Finns are not affiliated with any religion.

General Attitudes. Finns maintain high ideals of loyalty and reliability, taking promises and agreements seriously. People generally are reserved and appreciate etiquette and punctuality. They are proud of their Finnish heritage, especially since their language, culture, and national identity survived centuries of domination by other powers. Although Finland belongs to Europe, Europe is in some respects a place one goes *to* as much as it is a place one is a part *of*; cultural identity is strong. Finns are especially proud of their small nation's status in the world. Finland has been a leading nation in peace conferences and initiatives. Finns are proud to have one of the cleanest environments in the world, and they stress values that maintain this. Enjoying nature (through activities such as berry-picking in the forests) is an important part of their lives. Finland is also a leader in women's rights. Indeed, there is little talk of "feminism" because women expect to be involved in careers, politics, social issues, and motherhood, all as a matter of course.

Personal Appearance. Finnish dress is relatively casual. Young people follow trends, but Finns generally are not overly fashion-oriented on an individual level. Formal wear is popular on festive occasions. Hats are worn in winter when it is very cold. Colorful native Finnish costumes may be seen during festival times or weddings. They vary from region to region but usually involve a layered dress (including apron) and bonnet or cap for women, and trousers, shirt, and waist-length jacket or vest for men. Instead of caps, young women wear ribbons as headbands. Men also usually wear a peaked cap, woolen cap, or felt hat. These costumes have their origins in the 18th and 19th centuries. Stripes are popular for the dresses and jackets, but there are hundreds of variations.

CUSTOMS AND COURTESIES

Greetings. Men and women customarily shake hands and make eye contact when greeting. Embracing when greeting is rare in Finland. Often the form of greeting is a nod of acknowledgment and a *Hei*. During introductions, Finns often use only one name: the first name in informal situations or the last name in more formal settings. Titles are reserved for formal occasions. Using first names on first meeting is now quite common, especially among the youth. A general greeting is *Hyvää päivää* (Good morning/afternoon), or even just *Päivää*. Another expression for "Good morning" is *Hyvää huomenta*. In recent years, both young and old have begun using the more informal *Moi* (Hi) in greeting. Finns tend to carefully consider what they say and expect others to do so as well; the ability to "make small talk" generally is not valued.

Gestures. Finns use few gestures when speaking. However, talking with one's hands in one's pockets is considered impolite. Maintaining eye contact is important during conversation. When yawns cannot be suppressed, one covers the mouth.

Visiting. Finnish homes are private places. When one is invited to a home, one is in a sense invited into a friendship with that person. It is a meaningful gesture. Finns expect visitors to be punctual. Visitors usually take cut flowers, a bottle of wine, or chocolates as a gift to the hosts. Visits are nearly always an occasion for coffee and cakes or cookies. Guests wait until the host has taken a first sip before they drink. Most visits are more informal and involve relaxing and socializing. On special occasions, guests may be invited to sit in a sauna with the hosts. Spending time in the sauna is a national pastime.

Eating. When invited to dinner, visitors sit where the host asks them to, and they do not begin eating until the hostess or host begins. Table conversation is usually light but may span a variety of topics. Finns eat in the continental style, with the fork in the left hand and the knife remaining in the right. Dress is conservative in restaurants. The check is presented on request and is paid at the table. While some people leave small change on the table, a 15 percent tip usually is included in the bill and is therefore not otherwise expected. However, porters, doormen, and coat checkers receive tips.

LIFESTYLE

Family. The average Finnish family has one or two children. Population growth is so low that the Finnish government is trying to increase the birthrate because the number of working people is declining compared to the number of people receiving retirement benefits. Women are offered paid maternity leave of up to 11 months, and their husbands can share a portion of that leave. In addition, families receive a small monthly allowance for each child until the child is 17. Daycare facilities are provided by the government free of charge. Both parents usually work outside the home. In fact, half of all Finnish wage earners are women. Women hold more than one-third of Parliament's two hundred seats, and many women hold important government and business positions. The 18-member cabinet has eight women. An increasing number of men expect to share household responsibilities with their wives.

Young people tend to become independent fairly early in Finland, taking advantage of government assistance such as housing and education subsidies. Fifty percent of females have moved away from their parents' home by the age of twenty. Males usually leave a few years later because of military obligations.

Although many families own their own homes, many people also rent. Traditionally, houses were made of Finland's plentiful wood; many dwellings are now made of brick. Today, most Finns live in apartments and row houses. Taxes are high and housing is expensive. Most families have access to summer cottages for vacations.

Dating and Marriage. Dating begins at about age 15, first in groups, then in couples. Movies and dances are popular activities. Many young couples choose to live together before or instead of marrying. This is called an "open marriage." Couples may live for years this way, sometimes waiting until they have children to get married. The youth are moving away from many traditions and accepting more secular views of personal relationships. Finnish couples tend to marry in their late twenties. When two people marry, they both have the right to keep their original surname or to take that of their spouse. Their children may bear either surname.

Diet. Finnish cuisine has been influenced by many cultures, from French to Russian, but it includes a wide variety of Finnish specialties using fish and seafood, wild game, and vegetables. Reindeer steak is a traditional specialty, as is salmon. Wild berries (blueberries, cloudberries, strawberries, currants, and raspberries) are popular in desserts and liqueurs. Potatoes, cheeses, and a Finnish buffet (such as the *smörgåsbord*) are also popular. Rye bread is common, and open-faced sandwiches are eaten at breakfast and for snacks. Milk and coffee are the most common beverages for everyday drinking. Usually served with coffee is *pulla*, a sweetbread that comes in many forms, often flavored with cardamom. Finland has many pastries. *Makkara* (sausage) is roasted over a fire and eaten with *Sinappi* (mustard). Traditional Christmas foods include salmon, ham, herring, and various casseroles.

Recreation. Finns traditionally relate to the outdoors, and many of their favorite activities revolve around it, from picking wild berries and mushrooms to fishing, hiking, and boating. Favorite sports include skiing, track-and-field, basketball, *pesäpallo* (Finnish baseball), ice hockey, cycling, and boating. Golf is gaining popularity; some even play on the ice in the winter. The sauna is a traditional way for people of all ages to relax. During retreats to summer cottages, people like to run from their hot saunas for a swim in the cold, clear lakes nearby. Men and women go separately, but families with young children usually go together. Business meetings will sometimes end in the sauna. *Sauna* is a Finnish word that has been adopted by English and other languages. Finns love attending sporting events or watching them on television, especially formula or rally racing. Tinkering with computers is a popular hobby, especially with boys.

The Arts. The performing arts are widely appreciated. Because the government subsidizes theater, ticket prices are low, so many people can attend. Opera is popular, and many Finns also enjoy folk music. The national instrument of Finland is the *kantele*, a stringed instrument played with the fingers.

The *Kalevala*, Finland's national epic, is a compilation of folk songs and stories. Sculpture, often abstract, is a prominent art form. Finnish architecture is considered innovative. Finnish textiles, glass, and porcelain have also gained worldwide recognition.

Holidays. The most important holidays include New Year's Day (1 Jan.), Easter (two days), *Vappu* (1 May, May Day), Whitsunday (Pentecost), Midsummer (held on the Friday nearest 21 June, the summer solstice), Independence Day (6 Dec.), and Christmas (24–26 Dec.). The Finland Festivals (16 of them) are held around the country between June and September and include art, music, dance, opera, theater, and other festivities.

At Easter, families decorate Easter eggs and grow grass on plates in the home. On Palm Sunday (a week before Easter), children dress up as Easter witches and recite charms door to door; they receive sweets or money for their verses. Vappu is

▼ **EUROPE**

or not the weather is warm and spring-like, many students gather to party and picnic dressed in overalls and their matriculation caps. The overalls are colored according to the student's field of study.

Finns celebrate Midsummer with huge bonfires by the lake; people usually leave cities and towns to go to the countryside for this day. The blue and white Finnish flag is also prominent on this day. Christmas is a time of peace, family, and gifts. Families eat the main meal on Christmas Eve after visiting local cemeteries and placing candles on the graves of soldiers and family members. Later, Father Christmas (who looks like Santa Claus) arrives with gifts for the children. Rural families enjoy time in the sauna on Christmas Eve as well. Christmas Day and 26 December are days for visiting and relaxing.

Commerce. Stores are usually open from 9 a.m. to 8 p.m., Monday through Friday, and Saturdays from 9 a.m. to 6 p.m. Some shops and department stores are open until 9 p.m. on weekdays and 6 p.m. on Saturdays. Shops in Helsinki's subway stay open even later. Banks close at 4:15 p.m. on weekdays and do not open on weekends. The Finnish worker enjoys a workweek averaging 37.5 hours.

SOCIETY

Government. The republic's constitution provides for a directly elected president who serves as head of state for a six-year term. However, recently approved constitutional reforms limit presidential power in favor of a stronger parliament. Members of Parliament (*Eduskunta*) and the prime minister serve four-year terms. In addition to the Social Democratic Party, the Center Party and National Coalition Party are the largest political parties. Several smaller groups have representation in Parliament. Men serve from 8 to 11 months in the military but may choose to do civil service instead. The voting age is 18.

Economy. Finland has a large free-market economy that is highly industrialized. A skilled and well-educated workforce has contributed to Finland's global competitiveness, with the country's per capita output equaling that of large European economies. Natural resources include timber, silver, iron ore, and copper. Manufacturing and trade are essential, with exports representing 30 percent of the country's gross domestic product (GDP). Timber and timber-related products are the most important exports, followed by shipbuilding, chemicals, and textiles. The country relies heavily on imports for many raw materials, energy, and other important goods. It is self-sufficient in grains, dairy products, and some meats. High-technology industries such as communications are quickly becoming mainstays.

Finns enjoy a high standard of living. Most people have access to economic prosperity in spite of a high cost of living. The economy recovered from a severe recession in the early 1990s that was caused by depressed foreign markets and weakened trade with Russia. Finland's economy grew about 5.7 percent in 2000. Unemployment was at around 9.8 percent but has been declining. Inflation is low. Finland has joined Europe's Economic and Monetary Union. Integration and trade with Western Europe will continue to

DEVELOPMENT DATA

Human Dev. Index* rank	11 of 174 countries
Adjusted for women	12 of 143 countries
Real GDP per capita	$20,847
Adult literacy rate	99 percent
Infant mortality rate	4 per 1,000 births
Life expectancy	73 (male); 81 (female)

impact the economy's future. The currency is the *markka* or *Finmark* (FMk) until the euro becomes standard in 2002.

Transportation and Communications. Most Finnish families own at least one car. Overall, the roads in Finland are in good condition. Public transports such as railways, buses, a good domestic air service, taxis, and ferries (for lake, river, and ocean crossings) are excellent. Ferries cross regularly to Stockholm, Sweden, and other locations. Helsinki has a subway. Finland's modern communications network includes numerous television and radio stations, an efficient phone system, and more than 250 newspapers. Roughly half the population owns a mobile phone; users are asked to turn them off in places like cinemas and theaters. Most Finns are well acquainted with the Internet and e-mail; the country has a large number of Web servers.

Education. Education is a major priority for the Finnish government. Beginning at age seven, children are required to attend a free comprehensive school for at least nine years, after which they may attend a vocational school or complete three years of senior secondary school. Finland has a high rate of enrollment in secondary schools. Many students go on to further studies at one of Finland's several university-level institutions. The Åbo Academy in Turku was founded in 1640, but the University of Helsinki is the national university. Not only do university students not pay tuition, they receive a generous *opintotuki* (stipend) for up to four years and can qualify for further financial gifts for housing. Finns are well-read, and public libraries are well used.

Health. Finland takes great pride in its health programs. Health care is socialized, reliable, and modern. It is funded by national and local taxes. Citizens receive basic health care from municipal health centers for a minimal fee, but they can also pay to visit a private doctor if they choose. Public and private hospitals provide specialized care. Finland has one of the lowest infant mortality rates in the world. This is due in part to an extensive network of maternity clinics. Finland has high rates of alcoholism and suicide. Most festivities and celebrations are accompanied by liberal alcohol use.

CONTACT INFORMATION

Embassy of Finland, 3301 Massachusetts Avenue NW, Washington, DC 20008; phone (202) 298-5800; Web site www.finland.org. Scandinavian Tourist Board, PO Box 4649, Grand Central Station, New York, NY 10163-4649; phone (212) 885-9700; Web site www.goscandinavia.com.

CultureGrams™
People. The World. You.

1305 North Research Way, Bldg. K
Orem, Utah 84097-6200 USA
1.800.528.6279; 801.705.4250
fax 801.705.4350
www.culturegrams.com

France
(French Republic)

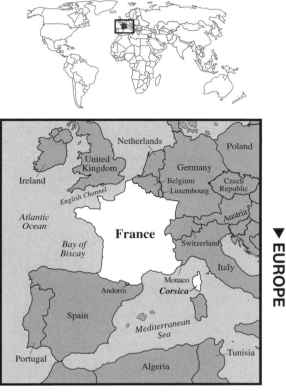

Boundary representations are not necessarily authoritative.

BACKGROUND

Land and Climate. Slightly smaller than Texas, France covers 211,208 square miles (547,030 square kilometers). The terrain is varied, from plains to mountains and forests to farmland. Mountains stretch along the borders with Spain, Italy, and Switzerland. France boasts Europe's highest peak, Mont Blanc (15,771 feet or 4,807 meters). The Rhine (*Rhin*) River forms part of the border with Germany; the northern border with Belgium is a flat plain with rolling hills.

The southern climate is Mediterranean, with warm, moist winters and hot, dry summers. The north is temperate and prone to rain. The west is also rainy and is influenced by the Atlantic, which moderates winter temperatures. The central, east, and upland areas have a continental climate, with fluctuating temperatures; in the mountains, thunderstorms are prevalent in summer. French sovereignty extends to the island of Corsica as well as 10 overseas *départements* and territories.

History. By 51 B.C., the Romans had conquered the area's Celtic inhabitants, the Gauls, who then adopted the Romans' customs, language, and laws. Clovis I, king of the Franks, defeated the last Roman governor in A.D. 486. In the late eighth century, France was just one part of the vast empire ruled by Charlemagne. In 987, France emerged as one of the empire's successor kingdoms. The following centuries brought intermittent conflict, particularly with the English, including the Hundred Years' War, from 1337 to 1453. In 1429, after 80 years of war, Joan of Arc led the French in victory over the English. Later burned by the English (1431), she remains a French heroine today.

By the late 1600s, France dominated Europe. Under Louis XIV (the Sun King), the movement toward centralized gov-

ernment reached its peak. His palace at Versailles was the envy of the continent. But by 1789, royal extravagance and defeats in foreign wars resulted in the French Revolution. The monarchy of Louis XVI was toppled and the country entered the "reign of terror." Despite the conflict, the French Revolution marks a milestone in world history: the general movement toward democratic government. After a decade of instability, Napoleon Bonaparte took power, declaring himself emperor in 1804. Napoleon conquered most of Europe before embarking on a disastrous campaign in Russia in 1812. In 1814, Austrian and Prussian forces seized Paris, and Napoleon was exiled. He returned in 1815 for the Hundred Days' War, which ended in his defeat to the English at Waterloo.

The monarchy was restored but was followed by the Second Republic (1848–52) and then the Second Empire (1852–70) under Napoleon III. Defeat at the hands of Germany led to the Third Republic in 1871. France was a major battleground during both world wars. It was occupied by the Germans between 1940 and 1944 and is famous for the D-Day invasion that turned the tide of World War II in favor of the Allies. In 1946, the Fourth Republic was declared, and after a referendum in 1958, a new constitution for a Fifth Republic was approved. Charles de Gaulle became president. France was a founding member of the European Community and is a central force in European Union (EU) politics today.

In 1968, students and workers protested over poor working conditions and a rigid educational system, resulting in lasting social change. The 1968 events were still fresh in the public's mind when students in the early 1990s took to the streets, protesting conditions in public schools and proposed changes in wage laws. The social unrest and economic difficulties led three successive prime ministers to resign before a Conservative was given the job in 1993. Hoping to increase support for continued austerity measures needed for European integration, Conservatives called for early elections in June 1997 and lost. Lionel Jospin's leftist Socialist government has enjoyed broad popular support, in part because of a strong economy and falling unemployment. France was part of the first wave of EU countries to join Europe's common currency, the euro, in 1999; full economic union will occur by the summer of 2002. The next legislative elections are not until 2002.

As in other European countries, there is growing concern in France about the spread of the mad cow and foot-and-mouth diseases because of the threat they pose to public safety and their economic impact. In order to deal with the crises, the government has increased the testing of livestock, ordered the destruction of infected animals, and limited imports and exports.

THE PEOPLE

Population.   France's population of close to 59 million is growing annually at 0.38 percent. Three-fourths of the population lives in urban areas. Greater Paris claims nearly 11 million inhabitants and Marseilles 1 million. Ethnically, the French have a Celtic heritage that has mixed with various other European groups (Latin, Nordic, Teutonic, Slavic, and others) over the centuries. Immigrants, including many from France's former colonial possessions, also inhabit France; they comprise about 7 percent of the population. The primary groups include Portuguese, Italians, Spaniards, North Africans (Algerians, Tunisians, and Moroccans), West Africans, Caribbean peoples, and Asians from the former Indochina region. Although they have integrated into French society, the various ethnic groups generally do not mix with one another. North Africans remain the most separate because of their religion, Islam.

Language.   French is an important international language. It is an official language of the United Nations and is second only to English in use between nations for communication, business, and diplomacy. The French government has stressed the language so much that almost everyone in France speaks French, despite the different nationalities represented. Even regional dialects have lost their importance in recent years.

Despite the prominence of French, France has recognized its citizens' need to learn other languages. In 1992, it announced that traditional language learning in school will start earlier (age nine) and that all students will be required to learn a second foreign language beginning at age thirteen. In addition, past emphasis on grammar and theory will be replaced by a focus on communication skills. English is the most common foreign language. Even before 1992, children were learning English outside of school. Despite this move toward other languages, the French government resists the inclusion of foreign words and phrases in the French language.

Religion.   Most French (nearly 90 percent) are Roman Catholic and practice their faith by celebrating the various religious holidays and attending mass once or twice a year. While regular attendance at mass is increasingly rare, many people visit places of special devotion, such as shrines, to worship. A small percentage of the people belong to other Christian churches (2 percent), the Jewish faith (1 percent),

and Islam (1 percent). About 6 percent claim no religion.

General Attitudes.   The French believe success is judged by educational level, family reputation, and financial status. They are extremely proud of their culture, heritage, and way of life. They are among the most patriotic people in the world, which is illustrated by their attempts to limit the influence of other cultures in France. This patriotism includes a general expectation that visitors have some knowledge of French and show appreciation for French culture. While French attitudes have traditionally been dominated by Paris, there seems to be a growing decentralization in administration as well as attitudes. The French are reserved and private, and people tend to be more hospitable outside Paris. Politeness is valued in human interaction, and *S'il vous plaît* (Please) is a valued phrase.

Political and social trends have caused the French to reexamine their national identity. Society seems divided over issues related to education, immigration, economics, language, and even the central government's structure. This introspection has led some to predict that French society will experience fundamental change during the next generation.

Personal Appearance.   In general, the French take great care to dress well and fashionably, whether they are wearing formal or casual attire, and they feel more at ease with visitors who show the same degree of attention to appearance. Paris is the home of many of the world's leading fashion designers. Professional attire, depending on the business and location, tends to be formal. Parisians dress more formally than people in other cities. In the southern sunbelt, dress is more casual but not less stylish.

CUSTOMS AND COURTESIES

Greetings.   Shaking hands upon greeting and parting is customary in France. An aggressive handshake is considered impolite. The French handshake is a light grip and a single, quick shake. Generally, a woman does not offer her hand to a man but waits for him to initiate the greeting. If their hands are dirty or wet, some French will offer their elbow or arm to shake. It is normal for women to be kissed on both cheeks by male and female friends. Actually, they touch cheeks and "kiss the air." The standard phrases for greeting include *Bonjour* (Good day) and *Comment allez-vous?* or the more informal *Ça va?* (both meaning "How are you?"). Greetings usually are combined with the person's name or a title and always precede any conversation or request. Good-bye is *Au revoir* (Until we meet again) or the less formal *A bientôt!* (See you soon!). A favorite among young people is *Salut!* for both greeting and parting. Friends and close colleagues use first names; otherwise, titles are important and customary. Besides professional titles, *Monsieur* (Mr.), *Madame* (Mrs.), or *Mademoiselle* (Miss) commonly are used.

Gestures.   The American "OK" sign (rounded index finger touching the tip of the thumb) means "zero" to the French. The French gesture for "OK" is the "thumbs up" sign. Slapping the open palm over a closed fist is vulgar and should be avoided. Sitting with legs spread apart is impolite; one should sit straight with knees together or with legs crossed at the knee. Feet are not placed on tables or chairs. The French are careful about their personal habits, being discreet when sneezing, blowing the nose, etc. They do not use personal items, such as combs and toothpicks, in public. It is improper to speak with hands in the pockets or to chew gum in public.

Visiting. The French are formal in their visiting customs, and people do not often visit unannounced. Guests usually arrive on time because punctuality is a sign of courtesy. However, for some social events it is also polite to arrive a few minutes late, allowing the hosts extra time for final preparations. Guests do not enter a home until invited inside. They generally sit where the host directs. It is a polite gesture to bring candy, wine, or flowers to the hostess, except red roses (which express love) and chrysanthemums (used in cemeteries). When ending a visit, a guest waits for a polite silence before rising. At the door, small talk, expressions of thanks, and repeated good-byes continue; it is impolite to be in a hurry to leave. Dinner guests often send a thank-you note the next day. At mealtime, pleasant conversation is appreciated as much as fine food. However, because the French are private people, it is best to avoid personal questions and sensitive topics such as politics and money. The hosts should be complimented on the meal; good cooking is a matter of pride in French homes.

Eating. Etiquette is important. Both hands remain above the table at all times. A man may rest his wrists, and a woman her forearms, on the table edge. One does not place the elbows on the table. Speaking with food in the mouth is impolite. It is improper to help oneself twice to cheese. The French eat in the continental style, with the fork in the left hand and the knife remaining in the right. Lettuce is folded into small pieces with the fork but never cut. Fruit is peeled with a knife and eaten with a fork. Bread is broken with the fingers and used to wipe the plate. One places the knife and fork parallel across the plate when finished. Formal lunches and dinners may last more than two hours, with as many as eight to twelve courses. Social meals begin with an appetizer in the living room, then hors d'oeuvres, followed by a course of fish or pasta or something cooked in a crust or sauce, the main course with vegetables, salad, cheese, and fruit, and then a dessert. Coffee finishes the evening. A typical family meal has two to four courses. When eating out, the person who invites or makes the suggestion is the one who pays.

Wine is consumed with most meals, except breakfast; countless varieties are available. The French are knowledgeable about wine. Unless certain of its high quality, foreign guests should not give wine as a gift.

LIFESTYLE

Family. While the nuclear family is still the most important unit of society, many people now are moving away from their extended families to work or study. Still, many children remain at home until they finish their education, and families enjoy getting together when possible. Most families enjoy a comfortable standard of living, although class distinctions are still fairly visible. In cities, most people live in apartments. The average family has one or two children. Pets outnumber children in France and receive special attention.

Dating and Marriage. The average youth starts dating around age 15. Favorite activities are going to dances and movies. The French cinema is well developed, and American films are also popular. Because French teenagers do not normally have jobs, their finances for social activities are limited. Social class, wealth, and level of education are important in the choice of a mate. Civil ceremonies are required by law. Religious ceremonies are optional but common. Many couples choose to live together before or instead of marrying. Many also choose not to have children.

Diet. The French consider cooking an art, and French cuisine is famous and popular around the world. French cookbooks date back to the Middle Ages, and French standards were the early gauge of fine cooking. Regional traditions are strong. There are several types of cooking, ranging from hearty, inexpensive fare to sophisticated dishes with costly ingredients and rich, complex sauces. *Nouvelle cuisine*, which emerged in the 1960s, was a reaction to this heavy style of cooking. While still made of expensive ingredients, it is much lighter, portions are smaller, and the presentation is more artistic.

Most French eat a light continental breakfast (croissants or bread, and coffee). Lunch was once the main meal of the day, but urban society has changed and many people now have a light lunch and eat their main meal in the evening. In Paris, lunch (*déjeuner*) usually is eaten around noon or 1 p.m. and dinner frequently is not before 9 p.m. In other parts of the country, particularly rural areas, people eat earlier.

Filled croissants and sandwiches in their traditional form can be purchased in vending machines, shops, and cafés. Cafés also offer toasted ham and cheese (*croque-monsieur*) and a plate of salad-type vegetables for a light meal. *Pâtisseries* sell cakes and some places sell crêpes. The French tend to resist foreign fast food because of health concerns about genetically engineered or modified foods and the threat of economic globalization, which is seen as a threat to France's small farmers. However, the resistance to fast food has not been entirely successful, as many hamburger restaurants operate across the country.

Recreation. The French are enthusiastic spectators, but fewer participate in team sports than might be expected. Soccer and rugby are popular spectator sports; France hosted and won the 1998 World Cup soccer competition. Participation is highest in individual sports: fishing, cycling, tennis, hiking, skiing, and sailing. Others enjoy hunting, riding horses, and golfing. People of all ages enjoy *pétanque*, a form of bowling that originated in southern France. Leisure activities include watching television, visiting museums, or attending plays and concerts. The annual *Tour de France* cycling race is a popular national event; U.S. American Lance Armstrong claimed the overall win in 1999. Most people take five weeks of vacation each year, four weeks in the summer and one week at Christmas. Camping is popular in the summer. During August, when many people travel, some shops and factories close. Summer music festivals occur throughout France.

The Arts. French literature, art, and architecture have greatly influenced the world. In the 20th century, French writers helped introduce movements such as surrealism, existentialism, and postmodernism. Impressionism began in France at the end of the 1800s. Impressionists were concerned with the reflection of light and subjective impressions. Famous examples of French architecture include the Eiffel Tower and Gothic cathedrals.

The first photograph was taken in France in 1827. Jacques Daguerre and other French artists helped make photography an art. The first motion picture was shown in 1895 in Paris. Later French contributions included the film projector and trick photography. France also is known for its fashion, cuisine, philosophy, ballet, and ceramics.

Holidays. The French celebrate several holidays each year. For New Year's (*Etrennes*), they often present flowers to older family members, and some exchange gifts. People celebrate

▼ **EUROPE**

New Year's Eve with parties and fireworks. In February, Mardi Gras (Shrove Tuesday) is celebrated with parades and parties. Easter Sunday and Monday are legal holidays. Labor Day (1 May) is marked by parades and celebrates the coming of spring. French Armistice Day (*Le Huit Mai*) is 8 May and Bastille Day (*La Fête Nationale*) is 14 July. Bastille Day commemorates the storming of the Bastille prison in Paris during the French Revolution. At Christmas (*Noël*), the tree is decorated on Christmas Eve, followed by a big meal and Midnight Mass. Shoes are left by the fireplace for *Père Noël* (Santa Claus) to fill. Other holidays include Ascension, Pentecost, Assumption (15 Aug.), All Saints' Day (1 Nov.), and World War I Armistice Day (11 Nov.).

Commerce. Businesses and nonfood shops open from 9 or 9:30 a.m. to 6 or 6:30 p.m., Monday through Saturday. Some large stores stay open until 9 p.m. one or two evenings a week. Small shops, especially in rural towns, may close for lunch and on Mondays. Many food shops open as early as 7 a.m. and on Sunday mornings. Banks close at 4:30 p.m. Many businesses close on holidays. The workweek currently averages 39 hours. However, in May 1998 the government passed a bill cutting the workweek to 35 hours by the year 2002.

SOCIETY

Government. The French Republic has 22 regions subdivided into 96 departments, not including overseas possessions. France's president serves as both head of state and executive head of government for a seven-year term. The president also appoints a prime minister from the majority party in the National Assembly and has the right to dissolve the Assembly to call for new elections. The president has no veto power but can rule by emergency decree in a crisis. Conservative Jacques Chirac (Rally for the Republic Party) became president in 1995, replacing retired President François Mitterrand (Socialist). The National Assembly's 577 members are elected for five-year terms. The Senate's 321 members serve nine-year terms and are elected every three years by about 130,000 local councillors. The voting age is 18.

Economy. France has the world's fourth largest industrial economy, enabling its people to enjoy the benefits of economic prosperity. Inflation is low, but unemployment and budget deficits are ongoing challenges.

As one of Europe's leading agricultural producers, France is self-sufficient in most foods. The agricultural sector employs about 7 percent of the workforce and is a world leader in wine, milk, butter, cheese, barley, and wheat production. Major industries include steel, motor vehicles, aircraft, textiles, chemicals, and food processing. Tourism is a backbone industry; France attracts more tourists than any other place in the world. Exports include machinery and transport equipment, steel products, and agricultural goods. The service sector employs two-thirds of the labor force. More than half of France's power is generated by nuclear power plants. The currency is the French *franc* (F); it will be phased out and replaced with the euro by 2002.

Transportation and Communications. The public transportation system is well developed. Buses serve most cities, and train service extends to even the smallest towns. Trains are

DEVELOPMENT DATA

Human Dev. Index* rank	12 of 174 countries
Adjusted for women	11 of 143 countries
Real GDP per capita	$21,175
Adult literacy rate	99 percent
Infant mortality rate	5 per 1,000 births
Life expectancy	75 (male); 83 (female)

best for long-distance travel. The TGV (*train à grande vitesse*) is one of the world's fastest passenger trains with a top speed of 300 mph (480 km/h). Most people own private cars, which are generally French brands, such as Renault or Peugeot. Taxis in urban areas are expensive. The subway in Paris is known as the *Metro*. The French domestic air system is efficient, and car ferries link France with Corsica and Great Britain. In 1994, a new rail link to England opened. A trip from Paris to London, crossing under the English Channel, takes three hours. The actual time in the tunnel is 35 minutes.

The communications system is modern. Pay phones generally use phone cards (*télécarte*) purchased at a post office. They are based on time used and can be used until the time paid for runs out. The post office is the center for various forms of communication and transactions.

Education. Schooling is free and compulsory from ages six to sixteen. Nearly 20 percent of all children attend Catholic schools that are partly subsidized by the state. Secondary education, lasting seven years, is offered by *lycées* and *collèges*. *Lycée* students gain the equivalent of a U.S. junior college education with an additional emphasis on philosophy. In early 2000, countrywide demonstrations by teachers and parents underscored funding, school violence, and job security concerns. After secondary education, students take an exam to determine if they may go on to higher education. Education is practically free at France's 60 universities, including the *Sorbonne* in Paris. However, the best students take further preparatory classes in order to attend the *Grandes Ecoles*, where they study for careers in government, the military, education, and industry (engineering, marketing, and management).

Health. The French enjoy good health. Medical care is generally good and is available to all citizens through a socialized system. Prices and fees are fixed by the government. Many French also carry private insurance to pay fees not covered by the government. In addition to public hospitals, private clinics are available.

CONTACT INFORMATION

Embassy of the French Republic, 4101 Reservoir Road NW, Washington, DC 20007-2185; phone (202) 944-6000; Web site www.info-france-usa.org. French Government Tourist Office, 444 Madison Avenue, 16th Floor, New York, NY 10022-6903; phone (410) 286-8310; Web site www.francetourism.com.

CultureGrams™
People. The World. You.

1305 North Research Way, Bldg. K
Orem, Utah 84097-6200 USA
1.800.528.6279; 801.705.4250
fax 801.705.4350
www.culturegrams.com

Georgia

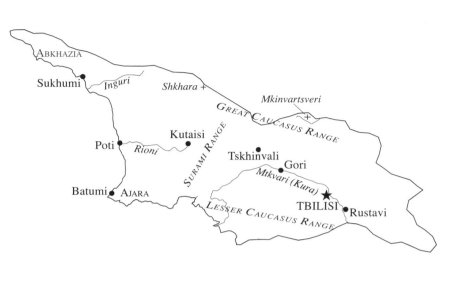

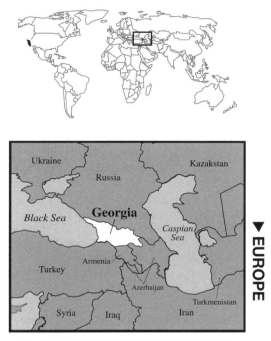

Boundary representations are not necessarily authoritative.

BACKGROUND

Land and Climate. Georgia covers 26,912 square miles (69,700 square kilometers) and is slightly larger than South Carolina. Most of the country is mountainous, including the highest peaks, Shkhara (17,656 feet) and Mkinvartsveri (16,677 feet) of the Great Caucasus Range. The Lesser Caucasus Range is in the south, and the Surami (*Likhi*) Range divides the country between east and west. Several rivers supply hydroelectric power, and natural and thermal springs are abundant.

Georgia's climate ranges from subtropical in coastal areas to a continental climate farther inland. The capital, Tbilisi, is located in a valley and along the slopes of high hills; its winter is windy and chilly with lows in the 30s and highs in the 40s (0–10°C). Snow falls mostly in mountainous areas. Spring begins late and summer is hot and dry, with temperatures reaching above 90°F (32°C). Rain is heaviest in coastal areas.

History. The native name for Georgia is *Sakartvelo*, or "the land of the Kartvels," as Georgians call themselves. *Georgia* is derived from the ancient Greek word for "farming," so named for the occupation of its early inhabitants. Historically, Kartvels were only one of several ethnic groups to settle Georgia, but their name was applied to the entire area. Western Georgia was known between the sixth century B.C. and third century A.D. as *Colchis* (the legendary land of the Golden Fleece). The east was part of Iberia. The wealth and power of Colchis was reflected in the ancient Greek myth about Jason and the Argonauts. The Egrisi (Lazica) Kingdom flourished in the third and fourth centuries. Situated on strategic territory, Georgia was either invaded or influenced by Romans, Arabs, Persians, and Turks prior to the 10th century.

Georgia's "Golden Age" occurred in the 11th and 12th centuries. King David the Builder (ruled 1089–1125) created a strong, ethnically mixed, and internationally active state. Under the rule of Queen Tamar (1184–1213), Georgia's territory and population (12 million) were at their largest. A 13th-century Mongol invasion ushered in a gradual decline.

Exhausted by repeated wars and famines, Georgia sought protection from the Russian Empire. A protectorate treaty signed in 1783 did not save the region from a Persian invasion in 1795. In 1801, the last Georgian king, Giorgi XII, urged Russia to honor its treaty commitments. Instead, Russia annexed eastern Georgia and, by 1864, the entire region.

Despite intense Russification, the 19th century was influenced by a Georgian cultural revival led by nobleman Ilia Chavchavadze. He was assassinated in 1907 by opponents of Georgian nationalism. The 1917 Russian revolution reopened the door to Georgian independence (1918). The door closed quickly in 1921 when the Soviet Red Army invaded.

Although Joseph Stalin was an ethnic Georgian (real last name: Jugashvili), Georgia suffered his repression, as did all Soviet republics. While resistance to Moscow's rule was not overtly apparent for many years, with the exception of a 1956 protest that was put down by tanks, Georgians never accepted Soviet ideology. On 9 April 1989, a group of protesters was killed by Soviet troops and Georgians pressed for independence—which they declared in 1991.

Although the Soviet Union soon disintegrated, peace did not come to Georgia. Georgia's first elected president, Zviad Gamsakhurdia, alienated ethnic minorities, and his policies combined with other factors to spark independence movements and insurgencies. The economy soon collapsed and 350,000 people became refugees. After Gamsakhurdia fled fighting in 1992 (he died in 1994), former Soviet Foreign Minister Eduard Shevardnadze assumed leadership. He began to implement democratic and market-oriented reforms, and Georgia joined the United Nations. Shevardnadze was elected president in 1995.

At the forefront of Georgia's troubles is Abkhazia. Around 270,000 ethnic Georgians were first driven from the region in 1992 and 1993 by Abkhazians demanding independence. A 1994 accord to end the struggle has never been implemented. Russia, which had been aiding Abkhaz rebels, cut off supplies in 1996, and rebel leaders agreed to new peace talks. Unfortunately, Russian peacekeepers sent to patrol a buffer zone did not prevent fighting from re-erupting in 1998. Another 30,000 or more Georgian refugees were driven from their homes in Abkhazia. A May 1998 cease-fire ended active fighting, and Abkhaz leader, Vladislav Ardzinba, said the newest refugees could return home. Since many homes had been burned down, it is doubtful they will return soon. The president has asked for UN action against Abkhazia, but so far none has been taken. In March of 2001, Georgia and Abkhazia signed a nonaggression pact and pledged to help facilitate the return of refugees.

Political instability, an energy shortage, crime, and other factors have worked against Georgia's efforts to improve living standards. The Russian financial crisis has led to a large drop in Georgian exports and industrial output. Georgia recently signed a five-year military cooperation deal with Turkey and joined the Council of Europe in 2000. Shevardnadze was reelected in 2000 despite the country's ongoing economic problems, regional conflicts, and rampant corruption.

THE PEOPLE

Population. Georgia's population of around five million is shrinking annually by 0.62 percent, mainly due to emigration. About 60 percent of the people live in urban areas. Ethnic Georgians comprise 70 percent of the population. Minorities include Armenians (8.1 percent), Russians (6.3 and declining), Azeris (5.7), Ossetians (3), Abkhazians (1.8), and several smaller groups (Kurds, Ukrainians, Germans, Greeks, and others). Exact tallies are impossible due to the refugee crisis.

Georgians are divided into a dozen distinct regional groups. Their differences are not unlike those among people in different U.S. states. For instance, eastern Kartlians and Kakhetians consider themselves more composed and even-tempered than Mingrelians, Gurians, Imeretians, and others. Mingrelians speak a unique ancient dialect.

Tbilisi, founded in A.D. 459, is home to 1.25 million people. The second largest city is Kutaisi, followed by Sukhumi (in Abkhazia) and Batumi. Large Georgian communities are found in France, Russia, Turkey, and Iran. Those in Iran are Muslim descendants of Georgians taken to Persia in the 17th century.

Language. The official language is Georgian. Most urban Georgians can also speak Russian. Minorities speak their native language in addition to either Russian or Georgian. Georgia's alphabet was created in the second century B.C. by King Parnavaz and is one of the world's 14 original alphabets. It has 33 letters and uses the original, but slightly modernized, script.

Abkhazian also ranks as an official language but is only used in Abkhazia. English is the most popular foreign language, followed by German, French, and Turkish.

Religion. Georgia adopted Christianity by A.D. 337. St. Nino is revered for doing much of the "enlightening" and is one of the most worshiped saints in Georgia. Despite long periods of non-Christian domination, Georgia remains a Christian nation. Even under Soviet rule, people considered religion crucial to cultural survival. The Georgian Church is autonomous but affiliated with the Greek Orthodox Church; its patriarch, Ilia II, is respected for preaching interreligious tolerance and nonviolence. Most people (65 percent) belong to the Georgian Church, but some are Russian Orthodox (10) or Armenian Gregorians (8).

The Ajara Autonomous Republic near the Black Sea in southwest Georgia is the only region to have a Muslim Georgian population, as the region spent considerable time under Turkic rule. Overall, 11 percent of Georgians are Muslim. Roman Catholics, Baptists, and Jews also live in Georgia. There are several functioning synagogues.

General Attitudes. Georgians are committed to their land of ancient history and tradition, even in difficult times such as those they are now experiencing. Centuries of multicultural interaction have made Georgians tolerant of other religions and cultures. For instance, Jews have lived in the land for at least 2,500 years without notable discrimination.

Despite a geographical link to Asia Minor, Georgians identify with the West and see their future as tied to Europe. Georgians are proud of their country and are pragmatic and positive about the future. Pessimism has increased in recent years because of the hardships, but Georgians try to remain cheerful and not too self-critical. They view themselves as a peaceful, beautiful, nonchalant, and romantic people with a difficult destiny—difficult because of their history of having to fight for a national identity and independence. Georgians have always valued friendship and time spent in pleasant company.

In Georgia, abstract norms and rules are generally less important as social regulators than are the mores and values formed between relatives, colleagues, and peer groups.

Personal Appearance. The standard dress is European. Traditional costumes are seen only at folk dance performances and during national holidays. Georgians pay attention to how they dress and choose quality clothing even if it is not affordable. Sloppy or careless dress is considered improper, even in casual situations. Jeans are popular among all segments of society. Adults and teenage girls do not wear shorts in public. Dress, hairstyles, and public behavior remain conservative. Eastern Georgians tend to have darker hair and eyes than western Georgians.

CUSTOMS AND COURTESIES

Greetings. When greeting, Georgians shake hands and say *Gamarjoba* (literally, "Let you win"), which means "Hello." Responses differ; the term is repeated for official greetings, or *Gagimarjos* serves as a responding "Hello" in informal cases. *Rogora khar?* (How are you?) is an informal way to begin a conversation. *Rogor brdzandebit?* is more formal. *Kargad ikavit* means "Bye, take care." *Mshvidobit* (Peace be with you) is used for a more substantial parting. In cities, it is uncommon for people to greet strangers on the street; in rural areas, however, people commonly greet, smile at, and sometimes speak to passing strangers.

Shaking hands is common, even at casual meetings. Embracing in a friendly manner or kissing on the cheek is also common, especially among young people and women. Small children might receive hugs and kisses. Adults are addressed by professional title and last name, or by first name following *Batono* (Sir) or *Kalbatono* (Madam). Using *Batono/Kalbatono* with just the last name is very formal, so first and last names are used in correspondence or in the media.

Gestures. Conversations can be animated, and Georgians often use their hands to express themselves. Eye contact is appreciated. People sometimes express appreciation for something by raising a "thumbs up." Pointing with the index finger is improper but practiced. Chewing gum in public, especially when talking, is impolite. Legs may be crossed at the knee, but feet never touch the furniture. Public displays of affection between young couples are inappropriate. People usually stand when an elderly person enters a room.

Visiting. Georgians are sociable and hospitable, known for friendly and generous treatment of even unexpected guests. A Georgian saying is "Any guest is God's messenger." Oral and phone invitations to the home are traditionally popular. The hardships of the 1990s have changed cultural habits; once-frequent visits to friends and relatives have declined. This is due not only to social unrest but also to the economic situation; hosts feel they cannot provide as adequately for guests as in the past. Still, hosts expect to offer at least a cup of coffee or cookies to guests. They offer full dinners to invited guests when possible. Guests bring gifts only on special occasions, but flowers are a polite and welcome gesture; something for the children is always appreciated.

In Tbilisi, people have long enjoyed strolling down Rustaveli Avenue in the evenings to meet friends, eat at sidewalk cafés, or attend theater or opera performances. During the civil unrest, they retreated to the safety of their homes. With life slowly stabilizing, these old pleasures are returning.

Eating. Family meals are shared together. Breakfast is light if eaten early and more substantial if eaten around 9 a.m. Lunch is called a "second breakfast" if eaten before noon and "dinner" if eaten after noon. The evening meal is called "dinner" if eaten around 5 p.m. and "supper" if eaten after that hour. Most people eat after 6 p.m. Georgians eat in the continental style, with the fork in the left hand and knife in the right. Some fish and meat dishes are eaten with the hands. Georgians would rather eat with a neighbor or someone else than eat alone.

Georgia is known for a traditional table ritual. Before a meal, a toastmaster (*Tamada*) proposes toasts to anything from national values to each person at the table, and drinks the entire glass after each toast. Women drink only symbolically, but men do as the *Tamada*. It is improper to serve alcohol without first proposing a toast. Traditionally, people drank Georgian wine from *Kantsi* (embroidered deer, bull, or goat horn) passed around the table. Today, a *Kantsi* is displayed in the home or sometimes used by the *Tamada*, but it is only passed around for special toasts.

When guests are present, the hostess prepares and serves the meal, although she eventually joins the group if other women are present. Hosts traditionally provided more than could be eaten, but hard times have changed that. Guests might not ask for seconds and can decline offers of such without insulting the hosts. However, they are expected to eat everything on their plates and compliment the hosts on the food.

LIFESTYLE

Family. Family attachment is highly valued in society. In most families, at least three generations have lived together for a considerable portion of their lives. The father is responsible for economic support, major financial transactions, and protecting the family's old and young. The mother is most influential in the decision-making process. Parents usually have two children. Most women care for the household and children, as well as hold jobs outside the home. Grandparents often provide day care in these cases.

Traditionally, a newlywed couple lives with the groom's parents until they can afford an apartment or home. This practice is changing now, and families try to accommodate couples who cannot rely on traditional arrangements. Also, more young adults are working to help support the household.

Urban families typically rent or own apartments, which until recently were government owned. The law now allows families to buy apartments, but many are waiting for society to stabilize before making the investment. A typical apartment has one or two bedrooms, a living room, a small kitchen, and a bathroom. Rural homes are more spacious, but constructing such houses is difficult due to the price of scarce building materials.

Dating and Marriage. When dating, couples might go to movies or concerts, visit each other's homes, listen to music, walk in city parks, or meet at cafés. Social unrest and economic hardship have made it unsafe and expensive to do some things, but greater stability is allowing for more recreational choices.

A person generally is free to choose a spouse, and families do not often interfere. A traditional wedding is rather flamboyant, with large feasts, folk dancing, and singing. Today's weddings are not as extravagant, and urban ceremonies are fairly quiet family events. Virginity on a woman's wedding day is a traditional value. Fidelity is extremely important in marriage, although men traditionally have taken some liberties that more wives now refuse to accept.

Diet. Georgians grow a variety of fresh fruits and vegetables, as well as wine grapes and tea. Variety and abundance in midautumn are celebrated by the rural harvest holiday *Rtveli*. Salads, vegetables, eggs, bread and butter, cheese, ham or sausage, and coffee or tea are eaten for breakfast. The "second breakfast" or "dinner" typically consists of soup and/or meat, potatoes, beans, vegetables, fruit, bread, and wine. Supper comprises the same basic foods as dinner; good wine is indispensable.

Dishes in the west tend to be lighter than in the east. Spices are popular everywhere. Walnuts are used extensively in Georgian cuisine. The most common meats include beef, pork, chicken, and lamb. Abundant vegetables include cucumbers, beans, eggplant, and cabbage. Popular fruits are apples, pears, peaches, and tomatoes. *Satsivi* (fried chicken or turkey soaked in walnut sauce with spices) and *mtsvadi* (marinated, skewered, grilled meat) are favorite dishes. Georgians eat *Khatchapuri* (various cheese-filled cookies) and on special occasions such as New Year's, *Gozinaki* (a honey-and-walnut confection).

Recreation. In their leisure time, people might watch television or videos, read, or go to theaters, movies, exhibitions, or

EUROPE ▼

concerts. Favorite sports include soccer, basketball, skiing, tennis, and chess. People also follow figure skating and hockey. Georgians enjoy weekend outings. Urban residents with summer cottages spend as much time there as possible, enjoying nature, gardening, or tending to greenhouses. Rural people generally are occupied by farming and have less time to relax.

The Arts.   Folk music and dance are prominent throughout the republic. Tempo and choreography of Georgian dance varies by region. Despite years of social evolution, Georgian folk music and dance have remained remarkably unchanged. Georgians also take pride in theatrical and performing artists. Their national ballet and several theater companies are well regarded internationally. Festivals supporting these and other arts are common.

Holidays.   The main official holidays include New Year's Day (1 Jan.), Orthodox Christmas (7 Jan.), Easter Sunday, and Independence Day (26 May). New Year's is celebrated mostly in families, but parties also are arranged. Special meals and champagne are common for New Year's Eve celebrations. People usually do not exchange gifts for Christmas, as this is primarily a religious holiday. Colored eggs and special cakes are prepared for Easter. Other prominent religious holidays include Epiphany (19 Jan.), Our Lady's Day (28 Aug.), and St. George's Day (23 Nov.).

Commerce.   Businesses usually are open from 10 a.m. to 7 p.m., with a break around midday. Prior to national holidays, offices close early but stores stay open longer. Bargaining occurs at farmers' markets or with spontaneous street traders, but state stores, private businesses, and kiosks have fixed prices.

Georgia's private industry is in its infancy, as are the standards of commerce. The most recent trend is the *trade fair*, where prices are lower than in stores, and bargaining for the wide variety of goods and foods is acceptable. Such fairs are held regularly in a growing number of cities.

SOCIETY

Government.   Georgia is a democratic republic. It is headed by a strong executive president, elected to a five-year term. The president is both chief of state and head of government. A new constitution was ratified in October 1995. Parliament has 235 seats. The largest party is Shevardnadze's Citizen's Union of Georgia, but various other parties also have representation. Georgia's Law of Citizenship allows every permanent resident to become a citizen, regardless of ethnic origin. It also sets generous guidelines for new settlers. In cooperation with President Shevardnadze, Parliament is strengthening democratic institutions and working to curb crime and corruption. The voting age is 18.

Economy.   Georgia traditionally has had a strong agricultural and industrialized economy, with exports of wine, tea, mineral water, brandy, fruit, vegetables, manganese, marble, and arsenic. In the post-Soviet era, when the system of supply and distribution had collapsed, many enterprises closed, and Georgia began importing basic necessities. Still, the country has the potential for food self-sufficiency. As the economy stabilizes, tourism, agriculture, and mineral sectors can

DEVELOPMENT DATA

Human Dev. Index* rank	70 of 174 countries
Adjusted for women	NA
Real GDP per capita	$3,353
Adult literacy rate	99 percent
Infant mortality rate	53 per 1,000 births
Life expectancy	61 (male); 68 (female)

expand. The 1998 Russian financial crisis severely hurt the Georgian economy, doing the most damage to the chemical, metallurgical, and machine-making industries. The conflict in nearby Chechnya has led to a drop in foreign investment. Unemployment is high and poverty affects most people. Georgia's national currency is the *lari* (GEL).

Transportation and Communications.   Georgia has a well-developed transportation system, with taxis, buses, trolleys, and streetcars serving urban areas. Tbilisi has a subway. The expense and scarcity of fuel have hampered transportation, but private enterprises and government efforts are filling gaps as the economy improves. Buses running between towns are crowded. Most roads are paved but are not in the best condition. Bicycles are not common, partly due to steep terrain in many areas. Airports operate in all major cities, and Tbilisi Airport receives daily international flights. Two large ports at Poti and Batumi are vital to shipping throughout the Transcaucasian region.

Most urban families and businesses have phones, and many in rural areas do as well. Media broadcasts reach most homes with independent television and radio programs. People read newspapers less regularly now, mostly due to declining living standards. The postal system, a remnant of the Soviet network, still depends on Moscow. It can take months for a letter from abroad to reach an addressee; those who can afford it use fax machines or e-mail to communicate internationally.

Education.   Children begin school at age six and graduate at seventeen, whereupon they receive a certificate of completion that entitles them to begin work or seek higher education. Major ethnic minorities have their own schools, some of which use their native language for instruction along with Georgian. Private and specialized schools are becoming more popular.

There are 21 state-run institutions of higher education and more than 100 private or cooperative ones. Obtaining a good education is a high priority.

Health.   Georgia's public health-care system is being transformed into a market-oriented, fee-for-service system. Many people are unable to afford such care, especially in rural areas. Georgian physicians are highly skilled, but hospitals lack supplies.

CONTACT INFORMATION

Embassy of Georgia, 1615 New Hampshire Avenue NW, Suite 300, Washington, DC 20009; phone (202) 387-2390; Web site www.georgiaemb.org.

1305 North Research Way, Bldg. K
Orem, Utah 84097-6200 USA
1.800.528.6279; 801.705.4250
fax 801.705.4350
www.culturegrams.com

Federal Republic of
Germany

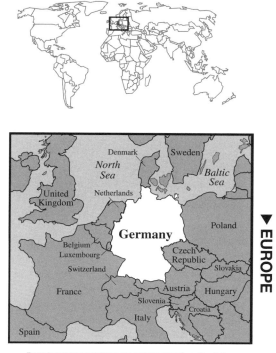

▶ EUROPE

Boundary representations are not necessarily authoritative.

BACKGROUND

Land and Climate. Covering 137,803 square miles (356,910 square kilometers), Germany is just smaller than Montana. There are four main geographic zones: the broad lowlands in the north; the central uplands, including various small mountain ranges; the wide valley and gorge of the Rhine River in the southwest; and the forested mountains and plateaus of the south. About 40 percent of Germany is forested. The Rhine, Danube, and Elbe Rivers flow through Germany. The climate is generally temperate and mild, with warm summers and wet winters.

History. Before becoming a nation-state in 1871, Germany was divided into a patchwork of small, separate principalities and was once part of the Holy Roman Empire. Through three wars (1864–70), Prussian leader Otto von Bismarck united Germany into a powerful, industrialized nation. In World War I (1914–8), Germany allied with Austria and Turkey. In 1917, the United States joined Britain, France, Russia, Italy, and Japan to defeat the German Empire. Germany was made to pay huge reparations, admit guilt for the war, and cede about one-tenth of its territory. A democratic government, known as the Weimar Republic, was established in 1918.

The country's humiliation was made worse by the economic depression of the 1920s and a lack of support for democratic ideals. Germany's distress gave rise to Austrian-born Adolf Hitler and his National Socialist (Nazi) Party. In 1933, President von Hindenburg named Hitler chancellor after the Nazis emerged as the dominant party in elections. In 1934, the day after von Hindenburg died, the posts of president and chancellor were combined, and Hitler declared himself *Führer* (leader) of the Third Reich. He soon embroiled

Germany and the world in World War II. Before being defeated by the Allied forces in 1945, the Nazis occupied much of the continent, killing many, including six million Jews.

Germany was split into occupation zones to facilitate disarmament and organize a democracy. When the Soviet Union did not comply with the agreement, the zones occupied by the Western Allies became the Federal Republic of Germany (FRG), a democratic nation. The Soviets in turn created out of the eastern zone the German Democratic Republic (GDR), which followed the Soviet model of development. When thousands of people fled the east, the GDR built the Berlin Wall (1961) to shut off access to West Berlin. The wall remained a symbol of the Cold War until late 1989 when it was opened to traffic on both sides. The wall was eventually torn down and the two nations became the reunified Federal Republic of Germany on 3 October 1990. Although Berlin regained its status as the country's capital, the actual transition from Bonn has lasted nearly a decade.

(Western) Germany was a founding member of the European Community, now known as the European Union (EU). It joined the North Atlantic Treaty Organization (NATO) in 1955, but German troops were restricted by constitution to German soil. In 1993, policy changes allowed troops to participate in UN relief operations in Somalia, Bosnia, and Yugoslavia.

Elected as chancellor in 1982, Helmut Kohl became a driving force behind German unification and Europe's plan for monetary union. Record-high unemployment and low economic growth led to Kohl's defeat at the polls in September 1998 against Gerhard Schröder. His government is challenged by a sluggish economy. Political scandal rocked the country in 1999 when former chancellor Kohl admitted to accepting more than one million dollars in secret payments to his Christian Democratic Union (CDU) party during the 1990s. The scandal severely damaged the reputation of Kohl and the CDU. Germany is preparing for Economic and Monetary Union (EMU) within the EU.

In 2001, Germany, like other European nations, was gripped by fears that foot-and-mouth disease would spread among Europe's livestock. In response to the crisis, the government ordered the killing of thousands of infected animals and limited the transport of livestock at risk from the disease. Germans are also concerned about preventing the spread of mad cow disease.

THE PEOPLE

Population.   Germany's population of more than 82 million is currently growing at about 0.29 percent. About 87 percent live in urban areas. The population is primarily ethnic German (92 percent). Noncitizen minorities from Turkey, the former Yugoslavia, Italy, Greece, and Poland live and work in Germany. Immigrants comprise up to 20 percent of some western metropolitan populations. In western states, numerous political refugees from the Middle East, India, Africa, and Asia receive room and board until their applications for asylum are processed. A small Slavic (Serbian) minority resides in the east, and a Danish population lives in the north. Many ethnic Germans have emigrated from eastern European nations to find work. The much-publicized violence against immigrant groups reflects the feelings of only a small minority; But such violence is on the rise, with a 40 percent increase in 2000. While most Germans do not support these actions, they do support stemming the flow of "economic" refugees. New laws restrict the definition of a valid asylum seeker and limit other forms of immigration.

Language.   German is the official language. However, the German taught in school and used in the media often differs from the German spoken daily. Dialects vary from area to area. In fact, a German from Bonn or Hannover may have trouble understanding a person from Munich (*München*), where Bavarian is spoken, or Halle (*Saxon*). While the dialects are mostly oral, they are part of folk literature and music and are also written. English, widely understood, is a required school subject. Many Germans in eastern states know Russian.

Religion.   Germany is essentially a Christian, but secular, society. About 34 percent of the population belongs to the Roman Catholic Church, 38 percent is Protestant (mostly Lutheran), and 2 percent is Muslim. A number of other Christian denominations are active throughout the country. About 26 percent of the people have no official religious affiliation. Historically, entire towns and regions belonged to one faith, according to the local ruler's choice. These lines are still visible today, as Catholics reside mostly in the south and west and Protestants in the north and east.

General Attitudes.   Germans are industrious, honest, thrifty, and orderly. They appreciate punctuality, privacy, intelligence, and skill. They have a strong sense of regional pride, a fact the federal system of government recognizes and accommodates. World War II broke down class distinctions, because most people lost their possessions and had to start over again. Germany emerged as a land of freedom and opportunity. Germans appreciate intelligent conversation but may be wary of unfamiliar or different ideas. Many are prone to skepticism. Most Germans have a strong classical education because of the nation's rich heritage in music, history, science, and art, and they expect others to appreciate that background. Former East Germans are also proud of how they have nurtured their cultural heritage through the performing arts and museums. After four decades of life under communism, however, it is not surprising that those in the east have somewhat different attitudes toward daily life and work.

Tensions exist between people in the west and east over matters relating to reunification. Easterners sometimes feel they are treated as second-class citizens, receiving lower salaries, getting blamed for tax hikes, and being ridiculed by their western counterparts. Westerners resent the economic burden of rebuilding the east; some still believe easterners are less capable and unrefined. Despite the emotional divisions, reconstruction and revitalization are adding to a united Germany.

Personal Appearance.   Germans follow European fashion trends and take care to be well dressed in public. Sloppy or overly casual attire is inappropriate. Shorts and sandals are common leisure wear in summer. Women wear cosmetics sparingly. Hints of traditional culture may be part of one's modern daily wardrobe. In southern Germany (mostly southern Bavaria), full traditional attire such as *Lederhosen* (leather pants, either short or knee-length), *Dirndlkleider* (dresses with gathered waists and full skirts, worn with an apron), Bavarian suits, and alpine hats usually are worn during festivals and celebrations.

CUSTOMS AND COURTESIES

Greetings.   A handshake is the most common form of greeting. A man waits for a woman to extend her hand before shaking it; in mixed company he shakes a woman's hand before a man's. In groups, several people do not shake hands at once; crossing someone else's handshake is inappropriate. Germans generally do not greet strangers on the street, although sincere smiles are appreciated. The most common verbal greeting is *Guten Tag!* (Good day). Some may use a simple *Hallo* (Hello). Many people in southern Germany use *Grüß Gott!* By tradition, only family members and close friends address each other by first name. Others use titles and surnames. However, this is changing among the youth. When addressing a stranger, acquaintance, or colleague, one combines *Herr* (Mr.), *Frau* (Mrs. or Miss), or other titles with the person's professional title and last name. The titles can also be used without the name. For example, a male professor is addressed as *Herr Professor*; a female head of a department in business or government could be addressed as *Frau Direktor*.

Gestures.   Chewing gum in public is inappropriate. Talking with one's hands in the pockets is disrespectful. People cross the legs with one knee over the other and do not place feet on furniture. Pointing the index finger to one's own head is an insult to another person. To wish luck, Germans "squeeze the thumb" instead of crossing fingers. That is, they fold the thumb in and close the fingers on it.

Visiting.   Germans appreciate punctuality, but hosts are not insulted if guests arrive a few minutes late. Dinner guests often bring an odd number of flowers, avoiding roses (symbols of love) or white flowers (for mourning). They unwrap flowers before giving them to the hostess. Guests usually stand when the host enters the room and remain standing until offered a seat again. It is also courteous to stand when a woman enters the room. Not everyone adheres to these rules of etiquette, but it is polite to do so. Hosts almost always serve refreshments to guests, even during short visits. Spontaneous visits, even between neighbors, are not very common, but this is changing among young people. Arrangements generally are made in advance. Germans enjoy gathering for conversation and social events. While dinner parties may last well into the night, daytime visits are usually short, except afternoon *Kaffee-trinken*, where tea or coffee and cakes or cookies are served.

Eating. Germans eat in the continental style, with the fork in the left hand and the knife remaining in the right. They keep hands above the table, with wrists resting on the edge. Potatoes and fish are not cut with a knife, because this indicates they are not fully cooked. Leaving food on the plate is considered wasteful. Most Germans prefer beer, wine, or mineral water with meals; they rarely drink tap water. Soft drinks and fruit juices are also popular. Germans prefer their drinks without ice. Germany does not have drinking fountains because of the tradition of bottled water. In restaurants, the bill usually includes a service charge and is paid at the table. Customers often round up the total to the next *Mark* or even five *Marks*, giving the waiter the difference as an extra tip (*Trinkgeld*).

LIFESTYLE

Family. Traditionally, the father is the head of the family. Both parents often work, more so in the east than in the west. Large families are not common, even in rural areas. The average family has only one or two children. While order, responsibility, and achievement are still traditional family values, people practice a greater variety of lifestyles today, especially those in the west. Most young adults prefer to live away from home once they become wage earners or go on to a university. Most families live in apartments. Single-family homes are by no means rare, just very expensive. Roughly 40 percent of all western homes (whether houses or apartments) are owned by the occupants. The rate is lower in the east. In urban areas, people often own or rent small garden plots (*Schrebergarten*) in or near the city.

Dating and Marriage. Dating is different in Germany than in the United States. The German language does not even have a word for dating. Young men and women socialize on a casual basis. If one wants to go out with another, either sex can suggest a *Verabredung* (appointment). They each pay for their own food and entertainment (unless one offers to pay for a special occasion). Young people usually marry in their twenties, but they often wait until they have some financial security. It is common for young people to live together before or instead of marrying. Legal marriages are performed at the city hall; religious ceremonies are optional.

Diet. While regional dishes vary among Germans, potatoes, noodles, dumplings, sauces, vegetables, cakes, and pastries are common. Pork is a popular meat, along with beef and chicken. Pork is prepared according to regional tradition; it may be boiled with cabbage in Frankfurt, roasted with

dumplings in München, or prepared as ham in Westphalia. Lamb is widely available in the north. Fish is popular in North Sea areas such as Hamburg but also in Bavaria, where trout is plentiful. Every region has its own type of *Wurst* (sausage).

Breakfast consists of rolls (preferably whole wheat or whole grain bread), jam, and coffee, tea, or milk. The main meal, traditionally served at midday, includes soup, a main dish, and dessert. For the lighter evening meal (*Abendbrot*), open-faced sandwiches (cheese, meats, and spreads) are common, unless people eat in a restaurant, where full meals are served. Two-income families rarely have a big midday meal; they eat the main meal in the evening. Germans buy groceries often and prefer fresh foods for cooking. Ethnic dishes (especially Italian, Greek, and Turkish) and fast foods are popular. Germans are known for their beer making and drinking. They also enjoy domestic and other wines. However, the youth consume less alcohol overall than the older generation.

Recreation. Germans enjoy hiking, skiing, swimming, cycling, touring in cars, and playing tennis, among other things. Garden plots with small gazebos offer relaxation on summer evenings. People also enjoy watching television or getting together with friends. Soccer (*Fußball*) is the most popular sport and millions belong to soccer clubs. Germany's team traditionally participates in World Cup competitions. Participation in organized sports is changing because of reunification; a uniform club system is being established. Germans in the west have long relished travel, something those in the east are also beginning to enjoy. *Carnival* (*Fasching*) is important in some regions, where dances, parades, and other celebrations take place before the Catholic Lent.

The Arts. Cultural arts, especially music and theater, are well supported in Germany. Festivals and performances draw large audiences throughout the country. Private support, as well as government subsidies, allow even the smallest cities to have professional orchestras and opera companies, as well as at least one museum. Expressionism continues to be a hallmark of German fine art. Local arts might include weaving, woodcarving, and woodblock printing. Numerous world-renowned composers, artists, philosophers, and writers were German.

Holidays. New Year's celebrations begin on *Sylvester* (31 Dec.) with midnight fireworks and parties, followed by a public holiday on 1 January. Easter is celebrated with Sunday worship services and Monday family gatherings. Labor union parades mark Labor Day (1 May). Various religious holidays (Catholic and Protestant) are celebrated, such as Pentecost, Ascension, and All Saints' Day (1 Nov.). The German Unification Day is celebrated on 3 October. At Christmas, people exchange gifts on Christmas Eve (*Heiliger Abend*); the family relaxes on Christmas day. Germans enjoy visiting on 26 December, also a legal holiday.

Commerce. Before reunification, shops in the east were open late to accommodate workers, while stores in the west closed by 6:30 p.m. to comply with labor laws. However, recent legislation allows stores to stay open until 8 p.m. on weekdays. On Saturday, shops may close at 4 p.m. rather than 2 p.m., and bakeries can open for three hours on Sundays. Business hours range from 8 a.m. to 5 p.m. on weekdays. Banks close

▼ **EUROPE**

at 4 p.m. but remain open a bit later on Thursdays. Some banks and small businesses in less metropolitan areas close for lunch. Many Germans shop daily for fresh produce (often at open-air markets) and bread (at bakeries).

SOCIETY

Government. Germany's president, currently Johannes Rau, is elected as head of state by members of the federal and state legislatures for up to two five-year terms; his duties are mostly ceremonial. The chancellor, Gerhard Schröder, is head of government. He governs in a center-left coalition of the Social Democratic Party (SPD) and Green Party. Germany's legislature has two houses, the Federal Council (*Bundesrat*) and the lower Federal Assembly (*Bundestag*). The country has 16 states (*Länder*), each of which has its own legislature and autonomy over schools and other matters. State governments elect the 68 members of the *Bundesrat*, while the 669 members of the *Bundestag* are elected by popular vote. In 1999, Germany began moving its seat of government from Bonn back to Berlin, the traditional capital. The voting age is 18.

Economy. Germany is one of the top five economic powers in the world and provides leadership and generous financial support to the European Union. It has a high gross domestic product per capita, although this is far lower in the east. East German prices typically are as high as those in the west, but salaries, rents, and overall living conditions remain lower. The east has made substantial progress in its shift toward a market economy; however, the region still relies heavily on subsidies (nearly $100 billion a year) from the economically powerful western states. The government has undertaken huge projects to retrain workers and rebuild roads, railways, public transportation, and communications facilities. With investment from the west, economic growth in the east averaged 8 percent in 1992 to 1995 but dropped to 2 percent in 1997 and has hovered at about that level since then. The German economy grew 3.1 percent in 2000, up from 1.4 percent in 1999, but there are indications that the economy will slow in 2001. Despite progress, more private investment is required to revitalize eastern industries and relieve the west of heavy tax burdens.

The unemployment rate is currently around 10 percent. Inflation is low. Generous social benefits, rigid work rules, and high labor costs—together with the 1998 and 1999 financial crises in Asia, Russia, and Latin America—have been obstacles to reviving the economy and regaining the country's global competitiveness. Germany is traditionally one of the world's largest exporters. Main exports include cars, steel, aluminum, televisions, and other manufactured goods. Construction, manufacturing, and service industries are strong components of the domestic economy. The German currency, the *Deutsche Mark* (DM), is one of the strongest in the world. In 2002 it will be replaced by the euro, the common currency of EU countries belonging to EMU.

Transportation and Communications. Most families own cars; the car is more important to Germans than to many other Europeans. They especially favor cars for touring or traveling long distances. Public transportation and bike riding are more

DEVELOPMENT DATA

Human Dev. Index* rank	14 of 174 countries
Adjusted for women	15 of 143 countries
Real GDP per capita	$22,169
Adult literacy rate	99 percent
Infant mortality rate	5 per 1,000 births
Life expectancy	74 (male); 80 (female)

efficient for daily travel in major cities because of heavy traffic and limited parking. Subways, buses, streetcars, and trains form the main transportation network. Trains travel to nearly every town and city. Drivers carefully obey traffic rules. One must attend expensive and rigorous driver-training classes to qualify for a driver's license. While there is no speed limit on sections of the *Autobahn* (freeway), there are strict limits on all other roads. The communications system is modern and fully developed. Telephone and postal services are centralized and efficient. Many Germans own computers and have access to the Internet. Most have access to cable or satellite television.

Education. Education is a source of pride, especially in the areas of technology and craftsmanship. The states administer public education. Preschool begins around age four. Full-time schooling is mandatory between the ages of six and fifteen, and part- or full-time schooling continues on a chosen track until age eighteen. Students may enter a job-training program, train for specific professional careers, or study to enter a university. Nearly every occupation, from mechanic to waiter to accountant, has a school or program designed specifically for it. For example, waiters and waitresses might attend school for up to three years before certifying as servers. Because of this training, their salaries are much higher than their U.S. American counterparts.

Education is free at all levels, but entrance to universities is difficult and can be gained only through success on the *Abitur* exam, taken at the end of *Gymnasium*. Adults can continue their education through evening classes.

Health. Medical care is provided free or at minimal cost to all citizens. Private doctors also practice, but most people have access to care in hospitals and clinics. The government controls fees, but some co-payments are required. In addition to government health insurance, private insurance is available. When workers become ill, they receive up to six weeks of full pay while they recover. People in eastern states suffer more often from pollution-related illnesses.

CONTACT INFORMATION

Embassy of the Federal Republic of Germany, 4645 Reservoir Road NW, Washington, DC 20007-1998; phone (202) 298-4000; Web site www.germany-info.org/f_index.html. German National Tourist Office, 122 East 42d Street, New York, NY 10168-0072; phone (212) 661-7200; Web site www.deutschland-tourismus.de/e/index.html.

1305 North Research Way, Bldg. K
Orem, Utah 84097-6200 USA
1.800.528.6279; 801.705.4250
fax 801.705.4350
www.culturegrams.com

► EUROPE

Boundary representations are not necessarily authoritative.

BACKGROUND

Land and Climate. Covering 50,942 square miles (131,940 square kilometers), Greece is just smaller than Alabama. Although it lies farther east than most of western Europe, Greece generally is considered part of the West because of its heritage and its membership in the North Atlantic Treaty Organization (NATO) and the European Union (EU). It is situated south of Albania, Bulgaria, and the former Yugoslav Republic of Macedonia. The latter nation has been independent from the Yugoslav federation since 1991, but its name is an issue of serious contention for Greece and other regional powers. Greece's northern province is called Macedonia, and Athens considers the neighboring country's use of the name a territorial threat.

Sparsely populated mountain areas cover much of Greece. Earthquakes are possible in these regions. The fertile valleys, plains, and coastal areas are more densely populated. Nearly 25 percent of the entire territory is arable. An archipelago of more than two thousand islands is part of the country, but only 166 islands are suitable for habitation. A warm, temperate Mediterranean climate prevails in the south, while the north is wet and cool. In general, winters are mild but wet; summers are hot and dry.

History. Although the history of ancient Greece stretches back to 3000 B.C., Athens had its beginnings in 1300 B.C., and city-states began forming around 1000 B.C. From this point, Greek culture began to thrive. The first Olympics were held in 776 B.C., and literature, philosophy, and art began to flourish. By 400 B.C., the glory of ancient Greek civilization

reached its peak. During that period, Athens was the center of a vast overseas empire. Many of the West's first studies of government, law, and the concepts of justice and liberty began in Greece. Its rich heritage of architecture, sculpture, science, drama, poetry, and government established a foundation for Western civilization.

Philip of Macedonia conquered Greece in 338 B.C., but he was assassinated. His son, Alexander the Great, led the Greeks to conquer an empire that covered much of what is now the Middle East. After Alexander's death in 323 B.C., the empire declined, and by 146 B.C. it had become part of the Roman Empire.

Centuries later, along with Constantinople (now Istanbul, Turkey), Greece was the center of the Byzantine Empire, which fell in A.D. 1453. In 1460, Greece became a Turkish province. After four centuries of Turkish rule (the Ottoman Empire), the Greeks began a war of independence, supported by Britain, France, and Russia. In 1832, Prince Otto of Bavaria was made king of Greece. In World War II, Greece was occupied by German and Italian forces and lost one-eighth of its population to fighting and starvation. After liberation in 1944, a civil war between the government and communist guerrillas cost another 120,000 lives. The government, with aid from the United States, was victorious in 1949.

In 1965, a political crisis developed between Prime Minister George Papandreou and King Constantine II, which resulted in Papandreou's dismissal. A group of army colonels staged a coup in 1967, and the royal family fled. From 1967 to 1974, the colonels ruled as a repressive dictatorship. Their eventual fall allowed for general elections, through which a republic was established when voters rejected a return to a monarchy. In 1981, Andreas Papandreou's Socialist Party won a majority in Parliament and he became prime minister. He was reelected in 1985 but lost the majority in 1989 in the face of various financial and political scandals.

Elections had to be held three times before Konstantinos Mitsotakis and his New Democracy Party received enough votes to form a government in 1990. Mitsotakis worked to privatize state enterprises, cut government spending, and prepare Greece for greater economic integration within the EU. Austerity measures that were necessary to accomplish those goals led to voter discontent. Hence, in the 1993 elections, the Socialist Party regained parliamentary leadership and Andreas Papandreou was returned to office as prime minister. He immediately began to reverse various privatization efforts and other economic policies.

After experiencing months of poor health, Papandreou resigned as prime minister in January 1996; he was replaced by Kostis Simitis. Simitis became party leader of the Panhellenic Socialist Movement (PASOK) after Papandreou's death in June 1996. Seeking a broad mandate for austerity measures needed to revive the country's ailing economy, Simitis called for legislative elections in September 1996, a year early. The governing Socialists enjoyed a strong victory, enabling Simitis to retain his position as prime minister.

The government's priorities include reducing inflation and unemployment, promoting private sector investment, curbing government spending, and improving Greece's infrastructure.

Greece seeks to develop closer ties with its Balkan neighbors, including its traditional foe Turkey. Signalling a thaw in relations, Greece announced its support of Turkey's application for EU membership in December 1999. However, disputes over control of the island of Cyprus and rights to resources in the Aegean Sea continue to strain relations with Turkey.

In January of 2001, Greece became the 12th country to join the euro, the European single currency.

THE PEOPLE

Population. The population is about 10.6 million and is growing annually at 0.21 percent. Nearly 98 percent is ethnic Greek, but there is a small Turkish minority. Much smaller minorities include Albanians, Pomachs, and Slavs. Almost 60 percent live in urban areas. Athens, the capital and the largest city, has a population of about 3.7 million. Most Greeks have good access to education, health care, and a decent standard of living.

Language. Greek is the official language of Greece. It has a long tradition, remaining relatively the same since the days of Homer (9th–8th century B.C.). About 1 percent of the population speaks Turkish. English and French are widely understood, and English is a popular subject in schools.

Religion. About 98 percent of the people belong to the Eastern (Greek) Orthodox Church, which is the official religion in Greece and is quite powerful. Although freedom of religion is guaranteed, the state supports the Eastern Orthodox Church through taxes, and other religions are not allowed to proselytize. The Orthodox Church is a Christian church directed by an archbishop (independent of the Roman Catholic Church) and the Holy Synod. Eastern Orthodox principles are taught in the schools. Religion is an inseparable part of the Greek way of life; however, Greeks generally are not religious. Older people, particularly women, attend church more frequently than young people. The Christian Orthodox patriarch based in Istanbul visited Athens in 1999 to improve ties with the Greek Orthodox faith.

More than 1 percent of the people (mostly of Turkish origin) are Muslim; there are also members of other Christian churches and some of the Jewish faith in Greece. Jewish communities are located in Thessaloníki and Athens.

General Attitudes. Greek society traditionally is dominated by males, although in the last generation women, particularly those in urban areas, have gained greater prominence and rights. Men consider it a matter of personal honor to fulfill obligations to their families and others. They may attribute their failures to external circumstances rather than to personal inadequacies. Also, a man may praise the food served in his home as especially good or be the hero of his own tales. Such self-praise is not considered bragging. While Greece's older generations value family, religion, tradition, and education, the younger generation tends to view status and friends as also very important. Greeks are very proud of their cultural heritage, which they view as being central to Western civilization. Greeks see themselves as individualistic, brave, and hardworking.

Personal Appearance. Greeks generally wear clothing influenced by European fashions. Fashionable clothing is popular among the youth and has become essential for working professionals. Rural and older people generally prefer to dress more conservatively. Greek women wear dresses more often than do North American women. Traditional costumes are worn at folk festivals and on special occasions.

CUSTOMS AND COURTESIES

Greetings. Greeks are often expressive in their greetings. Friends and relatives hug and kiss when they greet each other. Otherwise, people shake hands. Young men often slap each other's back or arm at shoulder level instead of shaking hands. There are many different verbal greetings; their usage depends on the situation. One term for "Good morning" is *Kaliméra sas*. "Good evening" is *Kalispéra sas*.

Close friends and family members call each other by first name, but most people address acquaintances and strangers by their title ("Doctor," "Professor," "Mrs.," etc.) and surname. In urban areas, people do not greet strangers while passing on the street. When getting on an elevator, one usually nods at the others present and might give a short, general greeting. Villagers briefly greet passing strangers in rural areas.

Gestures. Gestures frequently are used among people of a similar social status; using some gestures with superiors or elders may be improper. To indicate "no," one tilts the head either backward or side to side. To indicate "yes," one nods the head slightly forward. Pointing a finger at someone is impolite; it often indicates anger, a threat, or authority. A Greek may smile not only when happy but sometimes when angry or upset. A person may release a puff of breath through pursed lips to ward off the jealousy of the "evil eye" after he or she has given or received a compliment. People use the hands a great deal in conversation, both to accompany and replace verbal expressions.

Visiting. Ancient Greeks believed a stranger might be a god in disguise and were therefore kind to all strangers. This tradition of hospitality continues to the present. In small towns, friends and relatives commonly drop by unannounced. However, in urban areas it is polite to inform friends and family before visiting them. Greeks enjoy inviting friends to their homes for dinner or for special occasions—such as name days or New Year's Day. Christmas and Easter present opportunities for family gatherings.

Invited guests usually take a gift to the hosts, including flowers, a bottle of wine, or cookies. All guests, invited or unannounced, are offered refreshments. A cup of coffee is most common, but other drinks, a homemade fruit preserve, or cookies are also popular. If Greek hosts insist several times about anything (that a guest stay longer or eat more, for example), they usually mean it, and guests try to accommodate them so as not to hurt their feelings.

Eating. Traditionally, lunch was the main meal of the day and was served in the early afternoon (between noon and 2 p.m.). However, due to changing work schedules, this is no longer practical for many families. Dinner often is eaten as late as 8 or 9 p.m. Leaving the table before everyone has finished eating is impolite. Greeks are careful to finish everything on the plate so as not to insult the cook. Taking second helpings is the best way to show appreciation for the meal and to compliment the hostess.

At restaurants, a group often will order a number of different dishes that everyone shares. It is not unusual for guests to go into the restaurant kitchen and choose their dinner by looking into the different pots of food. People leave tips not only for the server but also for the busboy.

LIFESTYLE

Family. The family unit is strong in Greece. It is vital that no member bring shame or dishonor to the family. If the parents of a family die, the oldest child usually helps younger siblings finish their education and get out on their own. The elderly are respected, addressed by courteous titles, served first, and have much authority. Greeks care for their elderly parents at home when possible. If the parents must live in a home for the elderly, their children take care of all arrangements and make frequent visits. Parents traditionally treat their children with firm discipline; however, this practice is changing. Still, parents (even the poorest) usually spend a large portion of their income on clothing, feeding, and educating their children. In fact, parents believe it is their duty to provide for a good education. And they will always help their children, married or

not, if they can. Some newlywed couples live with their parents or in-laws until they can afford a home of their own.

Dating and Marriage. Traditionally, the man asks the woman's parents for permission to marry her. If the parents approve, the two date and become better acquainted during a formal engagement. Such formalities are now quite rare, except among rural people. Young people socialize as they do throughout Europe, and it is common for a couple to live together before or instead of marrying. On Sunday afternoon in rural areas, the youth often gather in the village square to socialize. The average age for women to marry is 25; men usually marry at age 30. Civil marriage and divorce were only legalized in 1982.

Diet. While tastes vary between urban and rural dwellers, certain foods are common to all Greeks. These include lamb, seafood, olives, and cheese. People also eat potatoes, rice, beans, breads, chicken, fruits, and vegetables. Olive oil is used in cooking. Garlic, onions, and spices are also popular. Salads often are eaten with the main meal. *Souvlaki* is a shish kebab with cubes of meat (pork or lamb), mushrooms, and vegetables. Eggplant, zucchini, stuffed tomatoes, and pasta are all favorites. Bean soup is popular in the winter. For Easter, Greeks enjoy roast lamb and *kokoretsi* (lamb liver, lungs, and spleen wrapped in intestines and roasted on a spit).

Recreation. Coffeehouses were once the focal point of leisure activity for men. Now rare in urban areas, they still provide a place for rural men to play cards and discuss politics. Rural women stay at home with other women to do crafts and enjoy conversation. Movies (both Greek and foreign) and the theater are also popular. People enjoy festivals throughout the year that highlight ancient Greek theater and literature. With an Olympic tradition, the Greeks love sports, especially soccer, basketball, swimming, windsurfing, and sailing. Skiing is also popular; Greece has more than 20 ski resorts. Athens is proud to be hosting the Olympic Games in 2004. On weekends, urban dwellers like to go to the beach or go skiing or fishing.

The Arts. Greek literature is centuries old but continues to be revered and studied around the world. Western literature, drama, and philosophical thought are based on Greek traditions. Greek plays still are produced on the ancient stages where they were once performed. Beginning in the latter half of the 20th century, Greek fiction writers, poets, and playwrights began to deal increasingly with contemporary problems and situations. Many people participate in societies devoted to archaeology, history, and folklore.

Modern Greek music combines Eastern and Western influences. *Rebétika*, a type of folk music with themes of poverty and suffering, is increasingly popular among the youth. Folk dancing is also common. Many traditional arts still are practiced, including embroidery, pottery, weaving, tapestry, and silver jewelry.

Holidays. Almost every city and village has a patron saint who is honored with a yearly festival. Easter is by far the most important holiday, celebrated with special feasts, processions, and gatherings. Greeks celebrate 1 January as St. Basil's Day and as a traditional day to give gifts, although many people

▼ **EUROPE**

now prefer to exchange gifts on Christmas (25 Dec.). For many holidays, a traditional greeting is *Chronia polla* (Many years). At midnight on New Year's Eve, a special cake (*vasilopitta*) with a coin in it is cut into various pieces. Whoever gets the coin is supposed to have good luck during the new year. Other holidays include Independence Day (25 Mar.), St. Constantine and Helen Celebration (21 May), Assumption (15 Aug.), and Ochi Day (28 Oct.). Ochi Day commemorates the day that Joannis Metaxas, then prime minister, said *Ochi* (No) to Hitler, and Greece entered into World War II on the side of the Allies. It is considered a heroic decision because of the size of the German and Italian armies.

Commerce. Work and business hours vary, depending on the season and type of business. Banks and government offices generally are open between 8 a.m. and 3 p.m. Shops may open and close when they want. During the hot summer months, many close between 2 and 5 p.m. In the past, most Greeks worked from 8 a.m. to 1:30 p.m. and from 5 to 8 p.m., Monday through Friday; however, this practice has nearly disappeared. Continuous shifts (9 a.m.–5 p.m.) are common in corporations and large department stores.

SOCIETY

Government. Greece is a presidential parliamentary republic. The president, currently Kostis Stephanopoulos, is head of state; his role is largely ceremonial. The prime minister, currently Kostis Simitis, is head of government. The unicameral Chamber of Deputies (*Vouli ton Ellinon*) has three hundred members. Informally, the body is called simply *Vouli*. Elections are held at least every four years. All citizens are eligible and required to vote at age 18. The two main political parties include PASOK and the conservative opposition, New Democracy. Smaller parties have legislative representation and sometimes can have a significant impact on political events.

Economy. Greece has traditionally been an agrarian nation. However, extensive socialist changes in the 1980s enlarged the public sector until it comprised nearly 70 percent of the country's gross domestic product. Agriculture currently employs 23 percent of the labor force, producing wine, wheat, wool, cotton, olives, raisins, and tobacco. The industrial sector has made important advances in recent years, and it accounts for 50 percent of export earnings. In addition to manufactured goods, exports include food, fuels, and raw materials. Greece's currency is the *drachma* (Dr).

The economy grew about 4 percent in 2000. Strict monetary policy has lowered inflation and reduced large budget deficits. Simitis faces strong opposition to further austerity measures and efforts to privatize the huge public sector. Tax evasion is widespread. Unemployment is high.

Transportation and Communications. Principal highways connect Athens with Thessaloníki and Pátrai. Roads may be poor in mountain areas, making travel to remote villages difficult. Buses and trains are the most common forms of public

DEVELOPMENT DATA

Human Dev. Index* rank	25 of 174 countries
Adjusted for women	25 of 143 countries
Real GDP per capita	$13,943
Adult literacy rate	97 percent
Infant mortality rate	7 per 1,000 births
Life expectancy	76 (male); 81 (female)

transportation. Greece has 37 commercial airports. In Athens, people commute by car and bus. Young people often drive motorbikes. Athens has one short subway line that cannot accommodate many travelers, so the government began building the Athens Metro subway in 1992. It is expected to be completed by 2002. Because traffic congestion is so bad in Athens, cars with license plates ending in an even number are allowed to drive in the center of town only on even days of the month (with odd numbers driving on odd-numbered days). There are more than one hundred daily newspapers in Greece and at least thirty are published in Athens. The government owns and administers the telephone, radio, and television systems.

Education. Education is free and mandatory. Although some start kindergarten earlier (age five), all children begin elementary school at age six. Students are required to complete six years of elementary school and three years of *gymnasia*. *Lyceums* are alternately available in three- or four-year courses that generally prepare a student for higher education. Universities, technical colleges, and schools of higher education are free to those who achieve enrollment through entrance exams. Student riots and demonstrations over educational reform that imposed more difficult school exams disrupted many schools in 1998 and 1999.

Health. All workers are required to have health insurance from either state-supported health-care systems, such as the Institute of Social Insurance (IKA), or through other agents. While the IKA provides all citizens with health benefits, it is not as efficient as people would like. Hospitals generally are understaffed and overcrowded. Doctors who work in public hospitals are not allowed to have private patients. A few private clinics do exist, but their services are not covered by state insurance. Many people feel they would obtain better care through a private system. Still, Greeks enjoy good health.

CONTACT INFORMATION

Embassy of Greece, 2221 Massachusetts Avenue NW, Washington, DC 20008; phone (202) 939-5800; Web site www.greekembassy.org. Greek National Tourist Organization, 645 Fifth Avenue, New York, NY 10022; phone (212) 421-5777; Web site www.gnto.gr.

1305 North Research Way, Bldg. K
Orem, Utah 84097-6200 USA
1.800.528.6279; 801.705.4250
fax 801.705.4350
www.culturegrams.com

Boundary representations are not necessarily authoritative.

▶ THE AMERICAS

BACKGROUND

Land and Climate. Grenada, Carriacou, and Petite Martinique occupy 131 square miles (339 square kilometers) of territory in the Caribbean. Grenada is some 100 miles (160 kilometers) north of Venezuela and about 20 miles (30 kilometers) from its sister islands. Marked by a central range of hills and mountains—the highest of which is Mount Saint Catherine (2,700 feet or 823 meters)—the island is lush, tropical, and humid. Coastal areas are prized for fine beaches and a warm surf. The rainy season runs from June to December, with November being the wettest month.

Carriacou and Petite Martinique are drier, more barren, and marked by cactus. These small islands do not get much rainfall, presenting a water supply problem for residents. Hurricane season is August to October. Average annual temperatures of 85°F (29°C) in the day and 74°F (23°C) in the evening vary only slightly, becoming hotter in July and August and cooler in January and February. The heat is moderated by a nearly constant breeze.

History. Grenada was originally inhabited by Arawak Indians, who were supplanted by the warlike Caribs. Christopher Columbus sighted the island (but did not land) in 1498 and named it Concepción. The origin of the name *Grenada* remains obscure. In 1650, the French government of Martinique purchased Grenada from a French company that had taken it from the Caribs. British forces captured the island in 1762. The Treaty of Paris (1763) formalized the acquisition and, except for a brief French occupation (1779–83), Grenada remained a British colony.

The French and then the British imported African slaves to work on plantations until slaves were emancipated in 1833. From 1855 to 1958, Grenada served as headquarters for the Government of the British Windward Islands. From 1958 to 1962, Grenada was a member of the West Indian Federation.

In 1967, it became a self-governing state in association with the United Kingdom. Eric Gairy, trade unionist turned politician, led Grenada to independence (7 February 1974). As prime minister, he governed with a strong hand until March 1979, when the left-wing New Jewel Movement under Maurice Bishop staged a coup d'état. Bishop formed the People's Revolutionary Government (PRG) and served as prime minister. He enjoyed popular support and still is regarded by many as a national hero. Most were drawn to Bishop's personality, if not his policies.

The PRG soon developed close ties with Cuba and the Soviet bloc, alienating neighboring states. Particularly alarming was the size of Grenada's People's Revolutionary Army (PRA). In October 1983, General Hudson Austin of the PRA and Bernard Coard, PRG finance minister, led an internal coup that resulted in the violent execution of Bishop and several key government officials. On 25 October 1983, U.S. Marines and a coalition of Caribbean peacekeeping forces invaded to safeguard foreigners and restore law and order. Democratic elections were held in 1984 and the peacekeepers left in 1985.

Subsequent elections in 1990 did not result in a clear mandate for any party. In June 1995 elections, the New National Party (NNP) received the most votes and Keith Mitchell became prime minister. Mitchell's administration has been marked by some controversy; he has sought stronger economic ties with Cuba and supported U.S. construction of a Grenada Coast Guard base on Petite Martinique for possible use in regional drug eradication efforts. Mitchell's government collapsed amidst charges of corruption and defection in December 1998. However, his New National Party returned to office, winning all 15 seats in elections held seven weeks later. Mitchell has promised more accountability and responsibility during his second term in office. Several strikes and trade disputes occupied the government in 2000.

THE PEOPLE

Population. Grenada's population of 89,018 is shrinking at 0.36 percent annually. The birthrate remains high, but emigration takes many from the island. Mitchell is encouraging educated young businesspeople to stay and work in Grenada. Most people (94 percent) live on Grenada, 5 percent live on Carriacou, and several hundred reside on Petite Martinique. Saint George's, the capital and largest city, is home to 7,500 people. Most people reside in small villages.

Most Grenadians (84 percent) are descendants of African slaves. Other groups include *mulattoes* (mix of African and European, 12 percent), East Indians (3), and whites of European origin (1). East Indians descend from laborers who came to work on plantations after the slaves were freed. Many also mixed with Africans to produce a group known locally as the *duglas.*

Language. English, the official language, is used in education, government, business, and the media. Grenadian English differs from U.S. English in idioms and some spellings. For instance, *now for now* means "urgent," and *one time* means "at the same time." One says *Happy* (not *Merry*) *Christmas* or *Happy returns* (on holidays or special events). A car accident is a *bounce.*

Informally, Grenadians speak a French-English-African patois, sometimes referred to as *creole* or *broken English.* The dialect has no past or future tense. Inflection and body gestures are primary tense indicators. Rastafarians (see Religion) have influenced Grenadian patois to a small degree, introducing such terms as *Irie* (Everything is cool) and the affirmative *Yes I.* Children are urged to use standard English in public, and Grenadians generally do not like outsiders to speak patois to them. But even spoken English contains patois elements, such as in the phrase "Don't *mamaguy* me" (Don't flatter me). Grenada's patois is noticeably different from that on Carriacou and Petite Martinique.

Religion. Roughly 60 percent of the population is Roman Catholic, while 35 percent belongs to various Protestant faiths (mostly Anglican). Most of the remaining 5 percent practice Islam or Rastafarianism. Christians generally worship Sunday morning, with prayer meetings throughout the week. Politicians freely invoke the powers of heaven, and schoolchildren pray at the beginning and end of the school day.

Rastafarianism is not practiced by many, but its stylistic influence (on fashion, vocabulary, etc.) is widespread. Practicing Rastas generally believe that Haile Selassie I (emperor of Ethiopia from 1930 to 1974) was "the living God," that marijuana is a sacred herb, that one's hair should be grown long in dreadlocks, and that all Afro-West Indians must eventually move to Ethiopia, the promised land.

General Attitudes. Grenadians are warm, friendly people who enjoy doing and returning favors. Their generous sense of humor helps them deal with difficult circumstances in a casual way. Disputes sometimes explode into angry shouting, but hard feelings seldom remain for long. Time schedules are not as important as people, and events usually start later than planned; it is customary to wait for everyone to arrive. Grenadians enjoy a strong sense of community. People often come together to finish a work project and share a meal or have a party. This cooperative effort is called a *maroon.*

How individuals feel about the 1983 U.S. military occupation is summed up by how they describe the event: "American Rescue Mission" (positive), "American Intervention" (neutral), or "American Invasion" (negative).

Personal Appearance. Grenadians, especially women, take great pride in their public attire. They make it a point to appear neat and well dressed, particularly for church and certain social functions. Sloppy or very casual clothing is frowned upon, as are tourists who are scantily clad away from the beach. Men wear trousers and either a button-down shirt or *shirt-jac* (square-cut, untucked shirt). Women typically wear a skirt and blouse or a dress. In rural areas, or around one's home, dress is more casual. Men may be bare-chested and people often go barefoot.

Youth fashions include blue jeans, T-shirts, and basketball shoes. Schoolchildren wear uniforms. Boys often untuck their shirts or unfasten their belts in the *ragamuffin* style, much to the chagrin of older Grenadians. Rastafarian colors (red, yellow, and green) are ubiquitous in Grenada, seen on everything from belts to shoes to caps. These colors are also on the Grenadian flag, but their use in fashion is tied to Rastafarianism and not patriotism.

CUSTOMS AND COURTESIES

Greetings. Grenadians greet one another with a handshake. Friends sometimes nod upwards or tap the faces of clenched fists instead. In a formal setting or among strangers, *Good morning*, *Good afternoon*, and *Good night* are typical greetings, followed by *Mr.*, *Miss*, *Mistress* (for married women), or *Madam* (for married women of higher social status) and then the person's last name, if known. If the speakers know each other, they might combine the title with a first name. Grenadians exchange verbal greetings before conducting business, beginning a conversation, or asking a question.

Rural acquaintances and friends casually greet each other with such patois phrases as *W'happen dey?* (What's happening?) or *Hows tings?* (How are things?). Typical responses include *Ah dey* (I'm all right) or *Just cool* (Everything is fine). Throughout Grenada, friends address each other by a *call name* (nickname). It is considered rude to *pass a friend straight* in the street without at least nodding or saying hello. Grenadians often call out a friend's or relative's name as they pass his or her house and may stop briefly to chat if time permits. When parting, friends often say *Later!* or *We go see* (See you later). Formally, people might say *Until we meet again.*

Gestures. Waving the hand at waist level, palm down, means "no." The "thumbs up" sign means "good." To beckon, people wave the fingers with the palm facing down. Men and women hiss to get a friend's attention, but when a man hisses at a passing woman, she ignores it as suggestive.

Visiting. Grenadians are considered to be among the friendliest people in the Caribbean; stopping to chat or socialize on the street or at a person's home is a favorite pastime. Such impromptu visits usually take place in the afternoon or early evening. Sitting on the porch, chatting at the roadside, or going to sporting events with friends is particularly popular after about 4:30 p.m. Visitors verbally announce their presence and wait to be invited in. Since most rural yards have watchdogs, this helps one avoid being mistaken for an intruder.

Grenadians nearly always offer guests refreshments, and it is impolite to refuse these entirely. If one cannot eat at a *fete* (party or gathering), it is polite to take something home for later. Funerals are social events. Men wear black suits and women wear hats with black or white dresses. People linger long at the graveside to talk. Men may go to a local *rum shop* to continue their conversations. In fact, rural men often socialize at *rum shops*—small bars where they can drink and play dominoes, cards, or *draughts* (like checkers).

Women socialize less in the evening, except in family situations, and more through church and neighborhood organizations. They may also visit friends during the day.

Family visiting reaches a peak during Christmas. Relatives and close friends expect a visit during this season, and people typically visit from house to house for days. With each visit, they are offered food and something to drink (beer, rum, whiskey, black wine, or *sorrel*—a red, clove-spiced drink made from the flower of a sorrel bush).

Eating. Grenadians usually eat breakfast early in the morning, a main meal around noon, and supper at dusk. Families try to eat the main meal together. Supper is light, often consisting of bread and cheese. Most people eat from a bowl with a spoon. Wealthier families may also use a fork and a knife. People drink coffee with breakfast and tea in the afternoon, but with lunch or supper they prefer soft drinks, fruit juice, or water. When eating at restaurants, Grenadians normally do not tip the server.

LIFESTYLE

Family. The extended family is central to Grenadian society, and one household often holds parents, children, grandparents, and cousins. Children might live at home well into adulthood. Family members look after one another and share resources and labor. Since most children are born out of wedlock and men typically do not consider it their role to raise them, they often are nurtured by the mother, aunts, grandparents, and cousins. Women run the household, and men generally provide income. However, women increasingly are working outside the home as well. Wealthier and urban households more often include a nuclear family with both a father and mother.

Homes are constructed of wood and/or cinder block. They usually have one to three rooms, electricity, and water (except on Carriacou and Petite Martinique, which lack public water systems). Wealthy urban families often have other modern conveniences. Some rural homes have detached kitchens for cooking on coal pots. All Grenadians take pride in the appearance and cleanliness of their homes and yards. They often paint their houses bright colors and give them names (Hideaway, De Fort, Fair Winds, etc.). Domestic livestock (sheep, goats, chickens) share the rural yard with the dog. Each

school day, children take sheep and goats to a grassy area for grazing and pick them up after school.

Dating and Marriage. Young people like to meet and date at dance halls or frequent street dances (*blockos*). Dancing (often called *wind and grind*) can be quite physical, and older Grenadians think it is lewd. Dating otherwise is inconspicuous, and public displays of affection generally are frowned upon. Couples often live together before or instead of marrying, but when weddings do occur, they are gala events. After a church ceremony, the entire village can enjoy plenty of food, music, and dancing.

Diet. Staple foods include plantains, corn, rice, breadfruit, and peas. Common produce includes onions, green peppers, *callaloo* (a green, leafy plant similar to spinach), tomatoes, and carrots. Chicken, fish, mutton, goat, pork, and beef are the most popular meats. Grenadians also like *manicou* (a type of opossum) and iguana. The variety of available seafood includes reef fish (barracuda and parrot fish), shark, snapper, sea turtle, tuna, lobster, and *lambi* (conch), as well as canned sardines and salmon. Many staple items are imported, including powdered milk, canned vegetables and meats, salt pork and salt fish, rice, cheese, coffee, and tea.

Local favorite fruits include bananas, mangoes, grapefruit, coconuts, and *paw paw* (papaya). Guavas are eaten fresh, stewed, as a jelly, or as *guava cheese* (a confection). A typical daily meal includes rice and *peas* (chickpeas or pigeon peas), a vegetable, and stewed meat. Soups, *souses* (boiled meat in a seasoned broth), fish broths, barbecues, and roasted foods are popular. Grenadians generously use hot pepper sauce, curries, and spices when cooking. The national dish is called the *oil down*, a stew of *callaloo*, breadfruit, meat or salt fish, and coconut oil. People also like *roti* (curried meat and vegetables wrapped in a flat bread) and *dahl* (curried chickpeas).

Recreation. Grenadians have a passion for cricket and closely follow the status of West Indian teams. Each town has cricket and *football* (soccer) teams, and boys begin playing at age 10. Basketball is becoming popular in urban areas. Girls play netball and watch other sports; both boys and girls participate in *athletics* (track-and-field). Men and boys like to fish, dive, or sail. Annual regattas draw fierce competition from around the region. Carriacou's Windward Village is widely known for its hand-built sailing vessels. Most people like to watch television, and urban residents can go to movie theaters.

The Arts. Music is extremely popular, calypso being the favorite. People of all ages also love *soca* (a mixture of U.S. American soul and calypso), reggae, *ragamuffin*, *dub*, and *pan* (or steel drum) music. Steel drums are used in many Grenadian music styles. U.S. American and British pop music, particularly slower, romantic *lovers' rock*, is also favored. Many Grenadians are competent on the guitar, violin, ukulele (often called *tenor banjo*), or drums. Jazz festivals are regular items on the yearly calendar, and a competition and parade of bands are held annually at *Carnival* celebrations. Potters, woodworkers, and silk screeners create and then market their crafts at the Grenada Craft Center, a government-sponsored institution.

Holidays. Grenadians celebrate Christmas, Good Friday, Easter (Saturday–Monday), Whitmonday, and Corpus Christi.

THE AMERICAS

Grenada

Secular holidays include New Year's Day, Independence Day (7 Feb.), Labor Day (1 May), Thanksgiving (25 Oct.), Emancipation Day (first Monday in August), and *Carnival*. Thanksgiving, related to the 1983 U.S. intervention, typically is marked only by official ceremonies.

Grenada's national *Carnival* is held in August in St. George's. Celebrations (Sunday–Tuesday) involve street dancing, concerts, and colorful parades. Carriacou celebrates *Carnival* three days before Catholic Lent. Each region, or *parish* (Saint George's, John's, Mark's, Andrew's, Patrick's, and David's), has a festival to honor the saint for which it was named. Villages and towns also hold local festivals, including Fisherman's Birthday (St. Peter's Day) in Gouyave and Windward, Grenville's August Rainbow Festival, and Carriacou's August Regatta and December Parang Festival (a competitive folk-music event).

Commerce. Businesses typically are open weekdays from 8 a.m. to 4:30 p.m., and Saturday from 8 a.m. to noon. Longer hours are common in urban areas. Shops close on Sunday. Banks open from 8 a.m. to 2 p.m. weekdays, except on Friday when they stay open until 5 p.m. Each large village or town has a Saturday open-air market for fresh fruits and vegetables. These markets are also a center for socializing. Street vendors are common and licensed.

Rural people buy staples from small family-owned *cum-rum* shops, fresh produce from the open-air market, and meat and fish from roadside butchers and vendors. Supermarkets are found in larger urban areas.

SOCIETY

Government. Grenada is a parliamentary democracy and a member of the Commonwealth. Hence, Britain's Queen Elizabeth II is the nominal head of state but is represented by a governor-general (Daniel Williams). The prime minister is head of government and is usually leader of the dominant party in the House of Representatives. Grenada's Parliament includes an elected 15-member House of Representatives and an appointed 13-member Senate. There is an independent judiciary. The Privy Council in the United Kingdom is the final court of appeal. The voting age is 18.

Economy. Grenada's developing economy centers on agricultural exports and tourism. Known as the Isle of Spice, Grenada is the world's second largest nutmeg producer and is well-known for cocoa, cinnamon, cloves, pepper, and ginger. Other exports include bananas, coconuts, and mangoes. Agriculture accounts for 40 percent of employment, most of it on small private plots. Tourism is important in and around St. George's. Remittances from Grenadians working abroad provide the country with needed income.

Most Grenadians are able to meet their basic needs. Poverty caused by a lack of economic diversification affects almost one-third of Grenada's population. Unemployment averages about 15 percent. However, Mitchell is credited with imrpoving the economy and providing more investment opportunities. The currency is the East Caribbean dollar (EC$).

DEVELOPMENT DATA

Human Dev. Index* rank	54 of 174 countries
Adjusted for women	NA
Real GDP per capita	$5,838
Adult literacy rate	96 percent
Infant mortality rate	15 per 1,000 births
Life expectancy	63 (male); 66 (female)

Transportation and Communications. Air service and regular, inexpensive boat service link the islands. Paved roads connect major towns and villages. While there is a public bus system, most people rely on private minibuses for local transportation. Minibuses wait in market areas until full and then depart for their destination, dropping and adding passengers along the way. Private taxis are available, and groups can charter a *board bus* (truck-turned-bus with a canvas top and wood sides) for special events. People commonly walk short distances, especially in more remote areas. The youth like to ride bicycles.

Grenada has six radio stations, and television provides a mixture of local news and overseas (usually U.S.) programming. Cable television is also available. Several weekly newspapers are published, but radio remains the primary source for news. Residential phone service is available, and most communities have public phones.

Education. Education is compulsory for ages five to sixteen. Churches own most schools, but the government sets the curriculum. Students may choose a school based on their religion, but the choice is most often based on a school's reputation, location, or other factors. About 88 percent of Grenadians finish primary school; students must then pass the Common Entrance exam to enter the secondary level. Of the roughly half that do advance, the vast majority graduate. Postsecondary education can be obtained at the University of the West Indies, which has a branch in St. George's, at various technical centers, or at a teacher-training college.

Health. Free health care is available to all Grenadians. Parishes and some towns have a clinic staffed with health assistants who perform preventive care and see minor cases. Government doctors make regular visits to the clinics. General Hospital in St. George's is somewhat crowded and underequipped. Two other hospitals (in St. Andrew's and Carriacou) provide basic services. High costs prohibit most Grenadians from visiting private doctors, whose level of care is generally better. Water is safe to drink on the main island but is untreated elsewhere.

CONTACT INFORMATION

Embassy of Grenada, 1701 New Hampshire Avenue NW, Washington, DC 20009; phone (202) 265-2561. Grenada Board of Tourism, 800 Second Avenue, Suite 400K, New York, NY 10017; phone (800) 927-9554; Web site www.grenada.org.

CultureGrams™
People. The World. You.
1305 North Research Way, Bldg. K
Orem, Utah 84097-6200 USA
1.800.528.6279; 801.705.4250
fax 801.705.4350
www.culturegrams.com

Boundary representations are not necessarily authoritative.

▼ THE AMERICAS

BACKGROUND

Land and Climate. Covering 42,043 square miles (108,891 square kilometers), Guatemala is just smaller than Tennessee. About two-thirds of the country is mountainous. There are 32 volcanoes, some of which are active: the Pacaya volcano near Guatemala City erupted in January 2000. Rich forests covering 40 percent of Guatemala, particularly in the northwest Petén region, are subject to rapid deforestation due to cutting. Deforestation has also put archaeological sites and wildlife at risk. Most people live on the slopes of the highlands or in the fertile, well-watered lowlands along the Pacific coast.

In the coastal lowlands, hot, humid weather prevails. In the highlands, days are warm and nights are usually cool. The eastern-central portion of the country is hot and dry. The people call Guatemala the Land of the Eternal Spring because 75°F (24°C) is the average annual temperature in the capital, which is on a plateau 4,800 feet (1,400 meters) above sea level. November to May is the dry season. Rain is abundant from May to October. The Caribbean coast is wet year-round.

History. The Mayan Empire flourished in what is now Guatemala for more than one thousand years until it began to decline in the 1100s. As one of the chief centers of the Mayan culture, Guatemala abounds in archaeological ruins, notably the majestic ceremonial city of Tikal in the Petén region. From 1524 to 1821, the Spanish ruled Central America. After winning its independence in 1821, Guatemala was briefly annexed by Mexico and then became a member of the Central American Federation until the federation dissolved in 1838.

Military dictatorships controlled Guatemala until a 1944

revolution. From 1945 to 1982, leaders tried to cure some of Guatemala's social ills, but full democracy proved elusive. Violence was common, and rebels began a civil war in 1954 after an elected president (Jacobo Arbenz Guzmán) was overthrown by a U.S.-backed military coup. Coups and civil war made political stability seem impossible until 1984, when an elected assembly wrote a new constitution.

In 1986, Guatemala returned to civilian rule under Marco Vinicio Cerezo Arévalo. Cerezo withstood two military coups, but the military had strong ties to the country's principal landowners and wielded more control over some regions than civilian authorities. Because the military was primarily responsible for human-rights abuses, such control presented enormous problems for political and economic progress.

Elections in 1990 brought the first transfer of power from one elected official to another. President Jorge Serrano Elías began peace talks with the rebels in 1991. However, in 1993, Serrano staged a "self-coup" backed by the army. He announced emergency rule, dissolving Congress and the Supreme Court and suspending the constitution. As public protests mounted, the military withdrew its support, forcing Serrano to flee to Panama. Military leaders recalled Congress, which chose its ombudsman for human rights, Ramiro de León Carpio, to finish Serrano's term.

New negotiations began when President Alvaro Arzú Irigoyen took office in 1996. In December 1996, the two sides signed a series of agreements culminating in a UN-brokered peace accord. The accord ended Latin America's longest civil war—one that lasted 36 years and claimed more than 150,000 lives. The agreements address military downsizing, the reintegration of soldiers and rebels into society, indigenous people's rights, and socioeconomic and agrarian reforms.

In December 1999, Alfonso Portillo of the rightist Guatemalan Republican Front (FRG) was elected president. He has promised social justice by ending class privilege and discrimination against Mayans. In May 2000, Guatemala made a free-trade agreement with Mexico, El Salvador, and Honduras in hopes of boosting the economy.

In October 1999, Guatemala formally claimed about half of Belize. Although Guatemala recognizes Belize's sovereignty, the border between the countries has been a source of contention for years. Officials hope to reach an authoritative solution to the claim sometime in 2001.

THE PEOPLE

Population. Guatemala's population of 12.6 million is growing at 2.6 percent annually. While 56 percent is *ladino* or mestizo, 44 percent is composed of some 28 indigenous groups descended from the Maya. Some of the largest are Quiché, Cakchiquel, Kekchí, Ixil, and Mam. They live throughout the country, but significant numbers reside in western highlands. Collectively, they refer to themselves as *indígenas* (indigenous) or Maya. *Ladinos* descend from the Spanish and Maya but relate more to their Spanish heritage. A small English-speaking black minority, the Garífuna, is concentrated on Guatemala's Caribbean coast. About 25,000 Guatemalan war refugees live in Mexico.

Language. Spanish is Guatemala's official language, but each indigenous group speaks its own language. While most male indigenous Guatemalans also speak some Spanish, indigenous women have fewer opportunities to attend school and have less contact with Spanish-speaking mestizos than do men; therefore, they often do not learn Spanish.

Religion. Roman Catholicism traditionally has dominated Guatemala, although many indigenous members combine it with Mayan beliefs. Some indigenous groups have not accepted Catholicism. Freedom of religion is guaranteed. While Catholicism influences most celebrations and habits, regardless of people's religious preference, devotion to the Catholic Church is declining. In the last 20 years, many have converted to Protestant and other Christian churches. About 45 percent of the people are now Protestants, known generally as *evangélicos* (Evangelicals). Increased religious devotion is credited with decreasing alcoholism and other social problems. However, tension between Catholics and *evangélicos* is rising.

General Attitudes. Guatemalans are generous, warm, polite, and humble. They value honesty, family unity, personal honor, work, and education. Optimism is less common than the acceptance of misfortune. People often believe they are unable to change their condition, either for lack of empowerment or because some things are God's will. Personal criticism is taken seriously and should be avoided. Punctuality is admired but not strictly observed because people are considered more important than schedules. Guatemalans are gracious and strive to make any social interaction comfortable. The phrase *No tenga pena* (Don't worry) is commonly used to set others at ease.

Family status and wealth are important to *ladinos*. The Maya, who have long been subjected to discrimination and human-rights abuses, desire to be treated as equals. *Ladinos*

consider the Maya to be inferior and uncivilized, and they avoid contact with those who do not adopt *ladino* ways. Maya who wear Western clothing and assimilate into *ladino* culture are treated somewhat better. Given that the peace accord addresses indigenous rights and that Quiché Maya activist Rigoberta Menchú won the 1992 Nobel Peace Prize, there is hope their circumstances may improve.

While the peoples of Guatemala are diverse, they have in common a desire for a tranquil life. Guatemalans are cautiously optimistic that the 1996 accord will bring a true and lasting peace.

Personal Appearance. People usually wear Western-style clothing in cities. Most rural Maya, particularly women, have retained traditional dress. Each group's clothing has unique qualities, but basic features include a *faja* (woven belt worn by both sexes), wraparound skirt (*corte*) for women, and knee- or calf-length trousers for men. Women may weave ribbons or fabric through their hair. Men generally wear hats made of straw or blocked felt. Clothing often is colorful. A woman treasures her *huipil* (blouse); its design identifies her social position and hometown.

CUSTOMS AND COURTESIES

Greetings. When meeting for the first time, people greet with a handshake and ¡*Mucho gusto!* (Pleased to meet you). Among acquaintances, the most common greetings are ¡*Buenos días*¡ (Good day), ¡*Buenas tardes!* (Good afternoon), and ¡*Buenas noches!* (Good evening). After an initial greeting, one might ask ¿*Cómo está?* (How are you?). Friends often greet with a casual ¡*Buenas!* or ¿*Qué tal?* (How's it going?). Shaking hands heartily is common in most areas. Among friends, men usually shake hands and sometimes embrace, and *ladino* women kiss each other on the cheek. A younger woman will kiss a male friend, but older women kiss only male relatives. Some older women greet by grasping the person just below each elbow.

In small groups, it is important to greet each individual. In larger groups, it is acceptable to offer a group greeting or simply greet as many persons as possible. When addressing others, using a title (*Señor, Señora, Señorita, Doctor*, etc.) shows respect. People show special respect for older individuals by using *Don* and *Doña* with the first name. Common parting phrases include *Que le vaya bien* (May you go well), *Nos vemos* (See you later), and *Mas tarde* (Later). Guatemalans generally begin all conversations, including business and telephone conversations, by exchanging pleasantries and asking about the health of family members.

Gestures. Guatemalans beckon by waving the hand downward and in. One hails a taxi or bus by raising the hand and pointing the fingers in the direction the vehicle is going. The bigger the hand motion, the farther one wishes to travel. A "tssst tssst" sound gets someone's attention. Pointing with the finger or hand can be misinterpreted because many finger and hand gestures are vulgar. To point, people often purse their lips in the direction of whatever they are indicating. To add emphasis, express surprise, or indicate "hurry," one shakes the hand quickly so that the index and middle fingers slap together and make a snapping sound. "No" can be indicated by wagging the index finger from side to side.

Urban couples tend to be more affectionate in public than rural ones. Rural people may hold hands but rarely show other affection. Personal space during conversation is relatively close, although touching is not common.

Visiting.   Visiting friends and relatives is important to building strong relationships. One's frequent visits reflect the value of a relationship. People who live close, especially in rural areas, drop by unannounced (or send a child to announce the adults are coming later); nearly any time of day is acceptable. Socializing also takes place at the market, community meetings, church, or the water well. Still, it is proper to visit the home to show that a person's hospitality is valued. Any guest, expected or unexpected, generally is welcomed, ushered in, and served refreshments: coffee, tea, water, or another drink and sweet bread or other snack. Refusing is impolite.

Frequent visitors usually do not bring gifts to the hosts, but anyone staying more than one day will give flowers, chocolates, or something for the home. The longer the stay, the nicer the gift. Hosts often send dinner guests home with food or something from the garden. When leaving a home, guests graciously thank the hosts and often invite them to visit.

Eating.   Most people eat three meals a day; poorer families might eat only one meal and then snack on tortillas the rest of the day. A rural breakfast may consist of tortillas and leftover beans. The main meal is eaten at midday; anyone in the family not working eats this meal. A light dinner usually is eaten after 7 p.m. The entire family gathers for the main meal on weekends. In some cases, women serve the meal and eat later. Many people have coffee and sweet breads around 4 p.m., and men working in the fields might have a snack at mid-morning. Schoolchildren are served hot cereal at 10 a.m.

Guatemalans generally use utensils but may eat some foods with the hands or use tortillas as a scoop. They keep hands above the table. Upon finishing the meal, each person (even the cook) thanks all others at the table with *Muchas gracias,* to which all reply *Buen provecho* (Good appetite).

Guests finish everything on their plates and wait for the host to offer more food. Asking for more might embarrass a host who is out of food, but eating more compliments the cook. When offered additional food, one first politely declines but then always accepts and eats it completely.

LIFESTYLE

Family.   The extended family forms the basis of society and exerts significant influence on an individual's life and decisions. The father is the head of the family, but the wife controls the household; she is considered the heart of the family. Rural extended families often share a single home or live next to each other in a family compound. This includes parents, married sons and their families, unmarried children, and often grandparents. Urban families generally live in nuclear family settings, although grandparents are often present. Unmarried adults live with their parents unless they must go elsewhere for work. Family members are expected to share responsibilities and be devoted to the unit. Adult children are responsible for the care of their elderly parents.

Ladino women often work as secretaries, teachers, nurses, or in other professions. One-fourth of the labor force is female. Mayan women also work, but less often in the formal workplace. They may sell produce at markets, embroider or weave products for sale, or work in community groups. Within the home, women are responsible for the food, household, children, education, and religion. Men work professionally or do field work and other physically demanding labor.

Ladino families generally live in urban areas or towns in small, single-family homes. Housing for indigenous groups follows their various traditions, such as a modest adobe or bamboo dwelling with a thatched or tin roof. Poverty is a serious problem for many in Guatemala, and land ownership is unavailable to most. In poorer families, children must work as soon as they can help support the family. Many rural families have no running water or electricity, although the cities are well equipped with these.

Dating and Marriage.   Urban youth begin socializing in groups around age 15. They enjoy going to movies, eating out, or just being together. Rural youth take walks, meet after school, visit at church or community events, or meet in town (at the market or water well). A girl's honor is important; a proper couple is "chaperoned" by younger siblings or cousins.

Among *ladinos*, social status is important in choosing a spouse. Traditionally the man's parents asked for the woman's hand in marriage; now the man asks the woman's father. Women often marry by age 20 (earlier in rural areas) and men by 24. Common-law marriages are accepted and often necessary, especially if the groom cannot afford his responsibility to pay for the wedding, new clothes for the bride, and any celebrations. An indigenous couple's relationship is cemented through a series of formal meetings between the families. At the final meeting, the woman's parents ceremonially "give" her to her new parents-in-law.

Diet.   Corn tortillas, or in many regions, *tamalitos* (cornmeal dough wrapped in corn husks and steamed) are eaten with every meal. Other foods include black beans, rice, tamales, greens, and fried *plátanos* (bananas) with honey, cream, or black beans. Meats (beef, pork, and chicken) usually are stewed, and sauces are important. Often a particular dish is unique to a certain village since key ingredients (such as spices) are found only in that village. Papaya, breadfruit, and other fruits are popular. Coffee often is served with a great deal of milk and sugar. The poorest rural families eat only tortillas (or *tamalitos*) and whatever food they can grow or gather in the forest.

Recreation.   The most popular sports are soccer, basketball, and volleyball. Family outings to a beach or lake are common holiday and festival activities. *Cofradías* (religious fraternities dedicated to a particular saint) offer a variety of recreational and leisure activities. Urban people enjoy watching television, but visiting is the most common leisure activity for all Guatemalans.

The Arts.   Music permeates society. The *marimba*, which is similar to the xylophone, dominates most of Guatemalan music and can be played by up to six people at a time. Its keys are made of rosewood, most of which comes from Guatemala. The *marimba* often is accompanied by flutes, guitars, and various percussion instruments. Some youth are turning more to North American and Mexican music.

Many ancient arts have survived in Guatemala, namely ceramics; silver-, gold-, and ironwork; and wood carving, especially wooden masks. Rock sculptures and carvings are another ancient Mayan art form and stand in front of temples. Guatemala's textiles are famous for their vibrant colors and intricate patterns. The designs may reveal information about the wearer, such as marital status or place of birth. Black and green jade carvings and jewelry are popular and can be purchased at local markets.

▼ THE AMERICAS

Guatemala

Guatemala claims several internationally known writers, among them a Nobel Prize winner. One literary work, the *Popol Vuh*, dates back to the mid-1500s and describes the Mayan creation story.

Holidays. A popular Guatemalan saying claims there are more celebrations than days in the year. Major celebrations are divided into two periods: Christmas and Easter. The Christmas season begins 7 December, when people clean house and burn their garbage to ceremonially cleanse their homes of evil in preparation to receive Christ. On Christmas Eve (*Noche Buena*), families set off firecrackers at midnight and then eat a large meal of tamales and hot chocolate. Firecrackers accompany most celebrations, especially New Year's. Easter is celebrated with Holy Week, during which numerous large processions fill the streets. In these, figures representing Christ are carried on special platforms by men wearing purple robes (black robes on Good Friday). On Saturday, effigies of Judas Iscariot are burned.

National holidays include Labor Day (1 May), Army Day (30 June), Independence Day (15 Sept.), *Día de la Raza* (Day of the [mestizo] Race, or Columbus Day, 12 October), Revolution Day (20 Oct.), and All Saints' Day (1 Nov.). The most important holiday in rural towns is often the annual *feria* (fair) honoring the local patron saint.

Commerce. Business hours vary from town to town but generally range from 8 a.m. to 6 p.m. in the cities, with a one- or two-hour break around noon. Work hours also vary because so many are involved in agriculture. Urban residents purchase food and other basics from small shops and large supermarkets. Fresh produce is available at open-air markets. In rural areas, farmers produce some of their food and buy basics and other produce at open-air markets or small shops. Villages might have a market just twice a week, with one day offering only basic goods. All neighborhood stores operated out of homes stock about the same items, so one buys from family and friends first.

SOCIETY

Government. Guatemala's president is head of state and head of government. The Congress of the Republic has 80 seats; legislators are popularly elected to four-year terms. The Supreme Court and judicial branch of government exist but do not really work; the system has not yet recovered from years of war and dictatorship. The voting age is 18. The two largest political parties are the Guatemalan Republican Front (FRG) and the Party of National Advancement (PAN). PAN is the opposition party in Congress. A few minority parties also have representation in Congress.

Economy. Guatemala is a relatively poor country. Three-fourths of the population lives in poverty. Wealth is concentrated among the upper class. Progress has been hindered by decades of civil war, the existence of large commercial farms that produce for export but keep rural farmers landless and poor, and the lack of a diverse manufacturing sector. About 60 percent of the people are employed in agriculture. Coffee accounts for 25 percent of all export earnings. Other leading products include cotton, cacao, corn, beans, sugarcane, bananas, broccoli, and livestock. Nickel, oil, fish, rubber, and

DEVELOPMENT DATA

Human Dev. Index* rank	120 of 174 countries
Adjusted for women	100 of 143 countries
Real GDP per capita	$3,505
Adult literacy rate	67 percent
Infant mortality rate	47 per 1,000 births
Life expectancy	62 (male); 68 (female)

chicle (used in chewing gum) are important natural resources. Tourism and manufacturing are also vital to the economy. The currency is the *quetzal* (Q).

Women earn roughly one-fifth of the nation's income, the lowest proportion among Latin American countries. More than 29 percent of the people lack access to the education, health care, and economic opportunities necessary to rise above human poverty.*

Transportation and Communications. Buses (many of them colorfully painted old school buses) provide the main form of long-distance travel. Paved roads connect the capital to major cities and neighboring countries, but most other roads are unimproved. Some villages are inaccessible by vehicle. For short distances, most people will walk, ride a bicycle or motorcycle, or take the bus. The wealthy have private cars. Commuter airlines fly domestically.

Telephones are widely used in cities but not in rural areas. Urban newspapers are available, but rural people rely on radio for news and entertainment. Television is popular where electricity is available.

Education. Although there are several thousand primary schools, more than half of primary-age children do not attend. Literacy is higher for males and for urban dwellers. However, girls now tend to stay in school longer than boys. Children often leave school because of family needs or inadequacies in the system. In rural areas, many children do not speak Spanish, the language of instruction. Facilities often are crowded, books in short supply, and teachers underpaid. After primary and middle school, students may attend three years of secondary schooling (vocational training). Those desiring to enter one of Guatemala's five universities must attend college preparation, which usually is available only to the wealthy.

Health. Guatemala faces serious health problems, including malnutrition, lack of potable water in many areas, and disease. Medical resources are concentrated in urban areas, although a national system is structured to provide health posts to outlying areas. However, most rural posts are not properly supplied. Care generally is free or costs a small fee, but medicines must be purchased. Many deaths are caused by preventable gastrointestinal and respiratory diseases.

CONTACT INFORMATION

Embassy of Guatemala, 2220 R Street NW, Washington, DC 20008; phone (202) 745-4952/3/4; Web site www.guatemala-embassy.org.

1305 North Research Way, Bldg. K
Orem, Utah 84097-6200 USA
1.800.528.6279; 801.705.4250
fax 801.705.4350
www.culturegrams.com

Cooperative Republic of
Guyana

Boundary representations are not necessarily authoritative.

BACKGROUND

Land and Climate. Covering 83,000 square miles (214,970 square kilometers), Guyana lies just north of the equator and has a tropical climate. Trade winds moderate coastal humidity. Rain falls primarily between April and August and from November to January. Guyana is interlaced with rivers. In fact, its name is an Amerindian term for "Land of Many Waters." The major rivers flow north to the Atlantic. The coastal plain, which supports agriculture, lies slightly below sea level but is protected by drainage canals, dams, and walls. South of the coastal plain are white sand hills. Although unfit for agriculture, these hills support rain forests rich in hardwood trees and are home to a varied and abundant animal population. The interior is characterized by plateaus, flat-topped mountains, and savannas.

History. Little is known about the area's early inhabitants, but historians speculate they gradually migrated from central South America as early as A.D. 1000. These Amerindians were divided into at least nine tribes, including the Warrau, Wapisiana, Machushi, Patamona, Arawak, and Carib. The Amerindians were nearly decimated by Spanish conquistadors.

The Dutch established the first European trading post in 1580 but soon were joined by the English, French, and Spanish. In 1621, the Netherlands established the Dutch West India Company and gave it control of their colony, known as Essequibo. Dutch colonies were later established on the Berbice River (1627) and Demerara River (1741), despite Spanish claims to the entire region. The colonies changed hands between the British, French, and Dutch with confusing frequency until the British purchased and united them and, in 1831, renamed the area British Guiana.

African slaves were brought to the area in the mid-1700s to meet labor needs. By 1807, when the slave trade was abolished, about 100,000 Africans lived on plantations. After full emancipation in 1838, many freed slaves formed their own villages. Eventually, planters brought indentured workers from India. By 1917, when Indian immigration ended, 341,000 Indians had settled permanently in British Guiana.

After World War II, the British gradually prepared for the colony's independence. Political parties formed to participate in elections; 1953 was the first year of universal suffrage. The most dynamic new party was the People's Progressive Party (PPP), established by Cheddi Jagan. The son of Indian immigrants, Jagan embraced Marxism while studying dentistry in the United States. The PPP splintered in the late 1950s after the British tried to halt its rise to power. A new party, the People's National Congress (PNC), was led by leftist Linden Burnham. His support came from Afro-Guianese, while Jagan's came from the Indo-Guianese community.

After Britain granted internal self-rule (1961), an anti-communist party formed to challenge the PPP, which had gained a majority in 1961 elections. The party became the United Force (UF) and joined with the PNC and other groups to oppose the government. Violence and turbulence characterized the next few years. When the three parties failed to negotiate a solution, Britain stepped in to revise electoral law to include proportional representation.

In 1964 elections, the PPP did not gain enough of the vote to form a government, so the PNC and UF formed a coalition under Burnham's leadership. Independence was granted in

1966, and British Guiana became Guyana. The PNC consolidated power in 1968 elections, and Burnham used that power to commit Guyana to socialism. In 1970, he renamed the country the Cooperative Republic of Guyana; by 1974, it was essentially a one-party state.

For the next decade, the country was wracked by political and economic turmoil. After Burnham's sudden death in 1985, his successor, Vice President Desmond Hoyte, introduced political and economic reforms. Nevertheless, the standard of living remained low and Hoyte was urged to hold free and fair elections. Elections in 1992 brought the PPP back to power. Jagan continued to reform the political, social, and economic systems that had been corrupted by Burnham, but he died in March 1997 before he could complete his term.

Jagan's U.S.-born widow, Janet, ran for president in the December 1997 elections and claimed victory against Hoyte and the PNC. The PNC refused to recognize the PPP government. After weeks of unrest, the Caribbean Community and Common Market (CARICOM) brokered an interim peace agreement between the PNC and the PPP in January 1998. Politically motivated violence erupted again in June after an independent audit declared the December election fair. In July, Jagan and Hoyte signed a second agreement ending the PNC's boycott of parliament and calling for major constitutional reform.

Jagan's poor health led her to step down in 2000, leaving the presidency to Finance Minister Bharrat Jagdeo. Protests and violence surrounded March 2001 elections because of voting fraud allegations. Bharrat Jagdeo was sworn in as president after a court determined that his election was legal.

In May 2000, a territorial dispute with neighboring Suriname over potential undersea oil fields heightened tensions between the two nations. Negotiations were held throughout 2000 and 2001, but little progress has been made. As a result of perceived agression from Suriname, Guyana is strengthening its navy.

THE PEOPLE

Population. The population of Guyana is estimated to be 697,286 and shrinking by 0.1 percent annually because of emigration. More than 30 percent of Guyanese live in three urban areas: Georgetown, Linden, and New Amsterdam. The villages and fertile acres of the coastal lowlands are home to another 65 percent of the population. The remaining 5 percent, mostly Amerindians, are scattered throughout the interior.

Guyana is ethnically diverse. The Indo-Guyanese are the largest group, with nearly 50 percent of the population. Next are the Afro-Guyanese (36 percent), *mixed* (7 percent), and Amerindians (6 percent). Small groups of ethnic Chinese, English, and Portuguese comprise 1 percent. The *mixed* people are, for the most part, descendants of Afro- and Indo-Guyanese but may also descend from other groups.

Warrau and Arawak Catholics fled to British Guiana from Venezuela in the 19th century to escape religious persecution. Their settlements, such as Santa Rosa, are protected reservations. Today's Amerindians are seeking title to the lands they occupy, as they feel increasingly threatened by local and international companies looking for mineral and timber wealth. At the same time, many Amerindians are taking jobs with these companies in hopes of overcoming poverty on the reservations.

Language. English is the official language and is used by the media, for education and commerce, and in government. However, the spoken English that many people use on a daily basis is a dialect known as Creolese. Unlike the French-based creoles of the Caribbean, this oral (unwritten) dialect is based on English. Creolese adds flavor to the country's cultural life and is especially popular for songs and colloquialisms like *Awe a go a Georgetown fore day morning* (We're going to Georgetown before sunrise). Older Amerindians speak their native languages in addition to English.

Religion. Christianity came to Guyana with the colonists. Other religions came with later immigrants. The Guyanese are a religious people. Even such socialists as Burnham professed some religious beliefs. Under the British, the Anglican Church had official status, but today all major religious groups have equal recognition under the law.

More than half of the Guyanese (57 percent) are Christians. The major congregations (Roman Catholic, Anglican, and Protestant) are joined by various other Christian churches. Hinduism is practiced by 33 percent of the population; its adherents are almost exclusively Indo-Guyanese. About 9 percent of the people are Muslim. Islam also came to Guyana with the East Indians, but in Guyana, there is no friction between Hindus and Muslims. Traces of African folk practices and traditional Amerindian religious beliefs still are found.

General Attitudes. The Guyanese are warm, outgoing, friendly, and fun loving. They are also resilient, as evidenced by how they survived terrible hardships associated with plantation life in colonial times. Personal goals center on providing a better life and an education for their children. For example, rural men and women may work to purchase and develop a plot of land, acquire a milk cow and a good fishing net, and perhaps open a small shop—all while working several odd jobs if necessary. However, the sharp decline in the standard of living after independence has led thousands to seek a seemingly better life abroad. For most families today, the thing most desired is a visa to the United States or Canada.

Personal Appearance. The Guyanese generally follow North American and European fashion trends. At the same time, they value modesty, and skimpy clothing is frowned upon. Burnham had at one time decreed all men would wear trousers and *shirtjacs* (open-necked shirts with side pockets worn over the trousers). Although the *shirtjac* is still popular, suits are now also common. Women generally wear dresses or suits (with a skirt, not pants) in the workplace. Informal dress includes slacks or shorts and T-shirts for both men and women. Special occasions call for women to wear dresses and considerable jewelry, often crafted from Guyanese gold. Schoolchildren wear uniforms, but after school they prefer T-shirts with slacks, jeans, or shorts.

CUSTOMS AND COURTESIES

Greetings. Relatives and friends may greet each other with a hug, and between women, a brief kiss on each cheek. A handshake is the norm between business and professional associates. Young people say *Hi* or *Hi, man, how you doin'?* They may add backslapping or a "high five." They also might ask *Wha' it saying?* to which the response is either a "thumbs up" signal (for good) or an open palm turned down (for bad).

Amerindian greetings vary according to the language. The Wapisiani use *Kaimen Pugar* (roughly, "Peace be with you"). The Machushi say *Morogeh koman honah* (I'm glad to see you) and respond with *Enah* (Yes, meaning "Hello").

The youth address most adults who are not members of their families as *auntie* or *uncle*. If the adults are gray haired, they are *grannie* or *grandpa*. Teachers and school personnel are addressed as *Miss* or *Sir*. Adults do not address each other by given name until they become close friends. Using the titles *Mr.*, *Mrs.*, *Miss*, *Professor*, *Doctor*, etc., with the family name is appropriate.

Gestures. The Guyanese talk with their hands, especially when angry or excited. They point their fingers in one another's faces to stress a point and shake the forefinger to alert one to their displeasure. Most Guyanese do not wear shoes inside their homes. Guests entering someone's house for an informal gathering leave their shoes at the door as well.

Visiting. Unannounced visiting is an accepted practice. If the weather is nice, the host and caller may visit outside; otherwise, the visitor is invited in. Once the guest is seated, the host offers a cold drink and a snack. Such visits usually occur in the late afternoon or on weekends. Gifts are not expected at informal parties and family dinners, but guests may bring the hostess something from the garden or another small token.

An invitation to someone's home for a special event is an invitation to a feast. On arrival, one is offered a cold drink; dinner is served after most guests have arrived (which may be long after the appointed hour). If the event is a wedding or birthday, guests bring gifts that are opened after the party.

Eating. Guyanese usually eat breakfast at home. Those working outside the home either carry their midday meal or eat it in a small restaurant or at a *snackette* stand. Schoolchildren go home to eat, bring their lunch, or buy it from vendors who operate stands outside the schools. The family usually gathers for dinner, the main meal of the day. In addition to regular meals, Guyanese enjoy snacks. *Snackettes* sell finger food and drinks; vendors offer highly seasoned barbecued meat, and ice cream is popular anytime.

LIFESTYLE

Family. Urban couples customarily have three to five children; rural families may have five or more. Both urban spouses usually work outside the home; the husband is head of the household and primary breadwinner, and the wife is the homemaker. Men generally do not help with household chores. It is not uncommon for grandmothers to care for young children while mothers are at work. Indeed, extended family members may live together to share living costs and child-care responsibilities. People living in cities may help raise a sibling's children who are originally from rural areas to afford them better opportunities. Although rural people generally marry within their respective ethnic groups, mixed marriages are common in cities.

Indian indentured laborers came and worked as families. Today, Indo-Guyanese parents carefully monitor unmarried daughters. Should a young woman become pregnant before marriage, the entire family is disgraced. Slavery, on the other hand, did not encourage marriage and reserved child care for older women. Its impact on the Afro-Guyanese, especially among lower-income families, is clear: when an unmarried girl bears a baby, she commonly brings it to her mother to raise. Grandmothers may rear the children of more than one daughter, and as a rule, both the mother and grandmother work to provide for the family. Such single-parent and multigenerational families are increasingly common among other ethnic groups as well.

Dating and Marriage. Young people socialize in groups until they finish their formal schooling. Couples go to the cinema, public celebrations, church functions, and other activities they enjoy in groups. Weddings are important events and are celebrated according to traditional religious rites. A Christian marriage takes place in a church, followed by a reception that includes food, drink, dancing, and speeches honoring the couple and their parents. After a Hindu wedding, guests are served a traditional supper of seven vegetarian curries on a water lily pad. They return the next day for a Western-style reception. Muslim festivities can last three days.

Diet. Guyanese cuisine is as diverse as the population, with each ethnic group contributing favorite foods. Rice, eaten at both lunch and dinner, is grown locally. Beef, pork, mutton, chicken, and both freshwater and saltwater fish are abundant. Many Guyanese, especially Hindus, are vegetarians.

Breakfast might include coffee and toast with perhaps a piece of fruit. Heartier eaters may add eggs, salt fish, or boiled *ground provisions* (plantains, cassava, yams). Meat pies, cheese rolls, *roti* (unleavened bread wrapped around chicken or beef and potatoes), and rice with bits of vegetables or meat are popular lunch items. *Spicy curry* is a favorite dinner. Another, *cook-up rice*, is made with coconut milk, rice, meat or fish, and—as the name implies—almost anything the cook has on hand. *Metemgee* is like *cook-up rice*, but with a *ground provision* instead of rice.

Adults drink soda, fruit juices, or beer with lunch and dinner. Coffee and milk are for breakfast; tea can be served at breakfast or between meals. Men drink substantial amounts of rum when they socialize.

Christmas calls for special treats: garlic pork, *pepper pot*, *black cake*, and ginger beer. No Christmas breakfast is complete without garlic pork. *Pepper pot*, served throughout the season, is a meat stew flavored with *casareep*, a cassava extract. Dried local fruits, soaked in rum and caramelized sugar, give *black cake* its unique color and distinct, sweet taste.

Recreation. Cricket is an obsession, while *football* (soccer) comes in a distant second. Both men and women play field hockey, tennis, and golf. Large crowds attend regular car races near the Timehri International Airport. Boxing is popular among Afro-Guyanese men. Dominoes is a favorite table game at schools and in offices during the lunch hour.

The Guyanese like action movies made in India or the United States. Bars, discos, and karaoke clubs are places to relax with friends and enjoy the latest Caribbean music. Church and school fundraising fairs draw crowds on weekends and provide an inexpensive and pleasant way for families to spend an afternoon.

The Arts. Guyana has produced several internationally respected painters and sculptors. Fine arts are supported through museums and galleries. Authors such as E. R. Braithwaite, who wrote *To Sir, with Love*, also are known internationally. Amerindians are known for woven goods. Straw, grass, and thin strips of wood are woven into baskets, mats, and other household items. Other prominent crafts include wood carving and pottery.

Holidays. Nearly all Guyanese celebrate the Christmas season with gift giving and feasting. Boxing Day (26 Dec.) is a day to relax after Christmas. New Year's Day is also quiet, as revelers recuperate from the parties of Old Year's Night.

▼ THE AMERICAS

Republic Day (23 Feb.) marks the date Guyana became the Cooperative Republic of Guyana. The holiday is known as *Mashramani*, an Amerindian word for the celebration at the end of a cooperative project. Fireworks and a presidential address are traditional on Independence Day (26 May). On CARICOM Day (first Monday in July), the Guyanese celebrate their relationship with Caribbean nations. Freedom Day (first Monday in August) marks emancipation.

Easter (Friday–Monday) is popular and features kite flying along the seawall as a rite of spring. *Devali*, the fall Hindu Festival of Lights, features a light parade. *Phagwah* welcomes spring, and the Indo-Guyanese greet each other with a sprinkling of water, powder, and *abeer* (a red liquid). Official Muslim holidays are *Id ul Fitr*, the feast at the end of *Ramadan*, and *Id ul Azha*, the Feast of the Sacrifice. For the latter, people distribute food and clothing to the poor. Muslims also commemorate *Yaum an Nibi* (Muhammad's birthday), but it is not a public holiday.

Commerce. Major markets in Georgetown are open around the clock year-round. Other businesses and urban markets are open from 8 a.m. until 4:30 p.m.; markets close at noon on Wednesday and Saturday. Except for food vendors (open 10 a.m. to 2 p.m.), urban markets are closed on Sunday. Village markets are open one or two days a week. Unlicensed street vendors flourish despite efforts to curb their activities. As part of the black market before 1992, they were essential to the local economy. Today, they mainly undermine established retailers.

SOCIETY

Government. Guyana is a democracy divided into 10 regions. The president serves as chief of state, and the prime minister, appointed by the president, is head of government. All but 10 of the 65-seat National Assembly members are directly elected; the 10 are indirectly elected through regional Democratic Councils. The voting age is 18.

Economy. Guyana's economy is showing signs of growth after years of decline; it grew by 3 percent in 2000. Sugar continues to be the chief export, but rice also is benefiting from high world prices. Gold and diamond mining have potential, but the nation's substantial bauxite reserves are less profitable to extract. Possible off-coast oil fields could present enormous revenue possibilities for the country. Economic growth is hampered by poor roads, insufficient energy, lack of skilled labor, and a large national debt. In addition to expanding fish processing, Guyana is experimenting with shrimp farming. Although the country is rich in timber, an inadequate infrastructure and environmental concerns have so far spared Guyana's forests.

About half the population lives in poverty, providing for their basic needs but little else. Due to the years of turmoil, most Guyanese still lack access to resources that would allow for personal advancement. Women earn about one-fourth of the nation's income. Expatriates often send money back to relatives in Guyana. The currency is the Guyanese dollar (G$).

Transportation and Communications. Guyana's infrastructure is poorly developed. Bikes, scooters, cars, horse- or donkey-drawn carts, and pedestrians compete with minibuses, *lorries* (small trucks), and *bush trucks* (four-wheel-drive trucks) for space on Guyana's roads. Minibuses have designated routes and fares but no schedules. Drivers wait at a *car park* until their bus is full (and crowded) before they set out. Outside the coastal plain, the only roads lead to the airport and to Linden. Access to the rest of the country is by air or water. Guyana Airways serves the interior, but seats are limited. Speedboats provide passenger and cargo service along the rivers. In many locations, the family boat is essential to get to the market, school, church, and nearest village.

Dependable phone service is available in most coastal areas. Efforts are underway to expand service. Communication with remote areas is possible via radiophone. A free press circulates several daily and weekly newspapers. Two radio stations broadcast nationwide, and Georgetown has a choice of television channels.

Education. Education is free and compulsory, but the cost of uniforms and books keeps some children from attending or advancing. Others cannot attend because their families need their labor. Children attend nursery school at age three, primary school by age six, and the first *form* (year) of secondary school by age ten. After the fourth *form*, a student may enter the job market, seek additional training, or prepare for a university. Education standards declined sharply after 1976, when the government took over private schools. Teachers are poorly paid and schools are not well supplied. Parents who can afford to do so send their children to after-school lessons for tutoring, and private schools are beginning to reopen.

Students pay tuition to attend the University of Guyana. Higher education also is offered through a teachers' college, several technical institutions, and three schools of nursing.

Health. Guyanese receive free medical and dental care at public clinics and hospitals, but these are not always well equipped or supplied. A national health insurance plan reimburses income lost to illness, maternity leave, or disability. Most clinics operate with a *medex* (an individual trained in primary health care), a nurse, or an untrained village matron. Community health workers provide basic care to interior villages. Six private (expensive) hospitals operate in Georgetown.

CONTACT INFORMATION

Embassy of the Cooperative Republic of Guyana, 2490 Tracy Place NW, Washington, DC 20008; phone (202) 265-6900.

DEVELOPMENT DATA

Human Dev. Index* rank	96 of 174 countries
Adjusted for women	80 of 143 countries
Real GDP per capita	$3,403
Adult literacy rate	98 percent (est.)
Infant mortality rate	39 per 1,000 births
Life expectancy	61 (male); 67 (female)

1305 North Research Way, Bldg. K
Orem, Utah 84097-6200 USA
1.800.528.6279; 801.705.4250
fax 801.705.4350
www.culturegrams.com

Republic of
Haiti

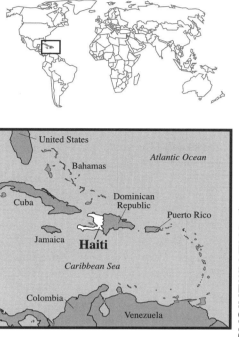

Boundary representations are not necessarily authoritative.

▼ THE AMERICAS

BACKGROUND

Land and Climate. Haiti covers 10,714 square miles (27,750 square kilometers) of the island of Hispaniola, which it shares with the Dominican Republic. Just smaller than Maryland, Haiti is comprised of two peninsulas split by the Gulf of Gonâve. The mountainous, nearly barren island of Gonâve rests in the center of the gulf.

Haiti's portion of the island is by far the most mountainous, with successive mountain chains running east to west on both peninsulas. A new arrival to Haiti can be overwhelmed by the massive mountains that seem to rise from the sea. The northern Massif du Nord is part of the island's backbone that is called the Cordillera Central in the Dominican Republic. The southern peninsula boasts the Massif de la Hotte and Massif de la Selle, the highest peak of which rises to 8,793 feet (2,680 meters). Hills and valleys punctuate the mountains, and it is here where most people live and work. Four main plains include the Central, Northern, Artibonite, and Plaine du Cul-de-Sac (where the capital, Port-au-Prince, is located). Haiti is crossed by several large rivers, the longest of which is the Artibonite.

Haiti's climate is warm and only mildly humid. Frost, snow, and ice do not form anywhere—even at the highest elevations. The average temperature in the mountains is 66°F (19°C), while at Port-au-Prince it is 81°F (27°C). Spring and autumn are rainy, whereas December to February and June to August are dry. July is the driest summer month. The hurricane season lasts from June to October.

History. The island of Hispaniola was originally inhabited by Taino and Arawak Indians. After Christopher Columbus arrived in 1492, opening Spanish colonization, the indigenous peoples were enslaved. Within a few decades, a million of them died from starvation, hard labor in Spanish gold mines, and European diseases like smallpox and measles. In a belated effort to save the remaining Indians and to prosper their sugar plantations, the Spanish settlers began importing African slaves by 1517. By 1560, few Indians remained. The 2,000 Spanish settlers controlled the island and some 30,000 African slaves.

In 1697, Spain ceded the western third of Hispaniola to France, which soon enjoyed the coffee, sugar, and cotton riches of its new colony, Saint Domingue. France obtained the entire island by 1795.

The slaves had begun revolting in 1791, but their efforts were futile until Toussaint L'Ouverture (a freed slave) led a revolt in 1798. He was eventually captured, and he died in a French prison. However, Jean-Jacques Dessalines became the slave leader and gained victory over the French in 1803. Haiti declared its independence on 1 January 1804. French settlers who were not killed left the island. Dessalines became emperor.

When Dessalines was killed in 1806, political chaos and rivalries led to General Henry Christophe gaining the throne, but not the south, in 1811. He ruled the north as King Henry I until he committed suicide in 1820. North and south were reunited under President Jean-Pierre Boyer, who also gained domination over the Dominican Republic in 1822. Tensions remain between the two neighbors over this era that ended in 1844, which is when Boyer was overthrown. Power changed hands a few times until the 20th century, which found Haiti near anarchy. Under the United States's Monroe Doctrine, which essentially sought to maintain U.S. American dominance in the Western Hemisphere, U.S. troops invaded and occupied Haiti from 1915 to 1934.

The following years seemed no more stable for Haiti, as people revolted against the government and elites who controlled it. In 1957, François Duvalier won presidential elections, despite charges of fraud. He killed his opponents and ruled with impunity, terrorizing the populace with his *Tontons macoutes*, the secret police. Before he died in 1971, "Papa Doc" Duvalier designated his son, Jean-Claude Duvalier, "Baby Doc," as his successor. Riots in 1985 forced Duvalier to flee Haiti in 1986.

A succession of military-led governments ruled Haiti until 1990, when Jean-Bertrand Aristide became the nation's first democratically elected president. Glee over his election was followed by impatience for reform and violence between Aristide's supporters and opponents. After just eight months in office, the military overthrew Aristide. General Raoul Cédras took power. Aristide made his way to the United States and set up a government in exile. His supporters in Haiti either went into hiding or were killed. The military dictatorship became increasingly brutal, and the international community decided to intervene with an embargo.

The embargo, ineffective at first, isolated Haiti in 1994 after the United States threatened further action. In September 1994, 20,000 U.S. soldiers landed in Haiti to overthrow the military. Two weeks later, Aristide returned from exile and served out his term, which ended in 1996. In 1995, a UN peacekeeping force replaced the U.S. mission and began to train Haiti's new police force.

René Préval, who had served as Aristide's prime minister, became president in 1996. A power struggle soon developed between Préval and opposition lawmakers, who controlled parliament. Premier Rosny Smarth resigned to protest irregularities in the 1997 legislative elections. Préval named a new premier, let parliament's term expire, and ruled by decree. The UN Security Council urged Préval to hold early elections to solve the crisis. Violence preceded the elections, which were postponed until May 2000. The election results were disputed widely and denounced internationally, causing the opposition to boycott presidential elections in November 2000. Former President Aristide was elected, but the opposition refused to recognize his legitimacy and announced its own president. The international community has withheld much-needed aid until Aristide can peacefully resolve the situation.

THE PEOPLE

Population. Haiti's population of 6.87 million is growing annually at 1.4 percent. The birthrate is much higher, but emigration keeps growth down. Most Haitians are descendants of Black African slaves who came to the island beginning in the 16th century. A small proportion (5 percent) are of mixed heritage. A large number of Haitians live in Florida and New York, although there are Haitian communities in other U.S. states as well.

Language. Haitian Creole is the language of daily conversation. French is used in government and business. Only educated adults or secondary school students speak French. Haitian Creole is a unique mixture of French and African languages, though it is similar to Creole spoken on some other Caribbean islands like Guadeloupe and Martinique. Haitian Creole is traditionally an oral language, though it had a written form even in the 19th century. Use of written Creole began to spread after the 1940s with the introduction of adult literacy programs. People are increasingly interested in English, which is heard on television broadcasts from the United States. Also, because most Haitian families have a relative in the United States, English is used more often than in the past.

Religion. The majority (80 percent) of Haitians are Catholic. Protestants claim 16 percent or more of the population, with Baptists, Pentecostals, and the Seventh-day Adventist Church being the largest denominations. Perhaps as important as organized religion is voodoo, which is practiced to some degree by a majority of Catholics. Though Catholic priests oppose voodoo, it has incorporated the worship of Catholic saints and the use of other Catholic rituals. Voodoo ceremonies and rituals, held in temples, usually are performed at night. Not all voodoo adherents practice the religion openly. Still, certain voodoo temples are the focus of annual pilgrimages. A variety of superstitions also are associated with voodoo.

General Attitudes. Haitians are warm, friendly, and generous. Their tradition for hospitality is clear in how they treat guests or go out of their way to help strangers find an address or something else they need. Haitians are proud of their culture and history. The stories of past Haitian heroes are not forgotten by today's youth. Some claim this is because the present offers no heroes, but others believe the past gives hope for the future.

Everyday life is hard for most Haitians, so parents strive to send their children to school, trusting that an education will give the next generation a better life. No matter society's conditions, Haitians celebrate life with joy, laughter, and dancing. *Carnaval* is an important expression of this joy. People prepare for it for weeks. Beginning just after New Year's, pre-*Carnaval* activities occur every Sunday.

Rural and urban people have different perspectives on life, as their cultural practices and attitudes vary significantly. Urban people consider themselves to be more European or cosmopolitan than people from the countryside. The rural dwellers value their traditions and slower pace of life.

Personal Appearance. Whenever possible, people pay great attention to their public appearance. Urban Haitians prefer to wear Western-style clothing. Women enjoy both pants and colorful dresses. Some wear a headdress that matches their outfit. Young people like to wear shorts; they also follow the latest North American fashion trends. Sandals are the most popular footwear. Government officials and businessmen wear suits and ties. Rural men wear T-shirts and shorts or pants when working. Rural women wear dresses and head scarves, but they rarely wear pants. All Haitian women enjoy jewelry and brightly colored clothing. Men also wear gold jewelry as a status symbol.

CUSTOMS AND COURTESIES

Greetings. Personal greetings are very important to Haitians. When entering a room or joining a group, a person is expected to physically greet each individual. Usually this involves shaking hands with new acquaintances. Everyone else, from relatives to friends and casual acquaintances, receives a kiss on each cheek. The most common verbal greeting is *Bonjou, kouman ou ye?* (Good day, how are you?). The response usually is *Byen mèsi, e ou?* (Well, thank you, and you?).

Haitians address superiors or persons of status by title and last name (*Monsieur, Madame, Doctor*, etc.). Friends use first names or nicknames. An older person might be called "aunt" or "uncle" even if not related to the speaker.

Gestures. Haitians are an animated people who enjoy impromptu gatherings wherever they may be—at the market, in the street, at movie theaters. At such gatherings, people enjoy loud conversation and laughing. Hand gestures usually accompany any discussion or storytelling. If one is too busy to talk, one will greet a passerby by nodding the head up. To get someone's attention, Haitians often say "pssst."

Visiting. Visiting is a national pastime. Friends, neighbors, and relatives are welcome in the home at any time of day until about 8 p.m. It is not necessary to call ahead. Visitors arriving during a meal may be asked to wait in another room until the family finishes eating. Close friends might be invited to share the meal. They may accept or decline. It is also acceptable for guests to decline refreshments. Hosts typically offer fruit juice or soda. In addition to impromptu visits, Haitians enjoy inviting friends over for an evening of socializing or for dinner. When a visit ends, hosts accompany guests to the door. Rather than leaving, however, Haitians frequently extend their visit for a while by standing and talking with their hosts.

Special occasions also call for visits. Guests take gifts to hosts celebrating a communion, baptism, graduation, or wedding. The events may prompt people to organize an elaborate party. Friends and relatives also expect to visit the bereaved after a funeral. On New Year's Day, Haitians traditionally visit their parents and friends to wish them well in the new year.

Eating. Haitians eat three meals a day if they can afford it. Peasants may eat *cassave* (bread made from manioc) and coffee for breakfast, and they may not eat again until evening. The family gathers at the table for the main meal, which is usually at midday in cities. Diners take their portions from serving dishes on the table. If guests are present, they are given first opportunity to serve themselves. Salad, meat, rice, and beans constitute a typical meal. A favorite daytime snack might be bread and butter or pastries. People eat at restaurants for special occasions. Sunday dinner traditionally is reserved as a family meal.

LIFESTYLE

Family. The basic unit of society is the extended family. Parents live with their married children and grandchildren. It is uncommon and generally unacceptable for the elderly to live alone or in a nursing facility. The father, if present in the home, is head of the household and responsible for earning an income. Single-mother households are very common, as men typically have children by more than one woman in their lifetime. Children stay with the mother in a divorce; the divorce rate is fairly high.

Urban families might have three or four children, while rural families have as many as ten or more. Most Haitians do not enjoy living in apartments, so houses are more common. Urban homes are built of cement block. The rural poor might use mud brick. Wherever possible, people have a garden next to their homes. Rural men work their fields, while women sell produce in the market. Rural and urban women care for the household and children. Urban families may have a servant to cook and do other chores.

Dating and Marriage. Although Haitian youth socialize in groups, they do not usually begin dating until their late teens, when they finish school. Young people are free to choose their spouse; families are not to get involved with the decision. When dating, the man will visit the woman at her home to become familiar with her parents and family members. Couples like movies, dancing, or other social events.

Urban couples typically have a church wedding followed by an evening reception. In rural areas, a couple will not officially marry until they can afford a big wedding. They live together and have children as if married until they save money for the wedding.

Diet. Haitians usually eat rice and beans every day, although a main meal can also include meat, salad, and a vegetable. Spicy foods are most popular. *Piman zwazo* (small hot pimentos) and garlic often are added to dishes. Meat is marinated in sauces such as sour orange. For breakfast, one might eat the traditional urban fare of coffee, herring with plantains and avocados, corn with codfish, or liver with plantains. A lighter breakfast consists of coffee with bread, butter, and jam.

Pork is the most popular meat, but Haitians also eat goat, chicken, guinea pig, seafood (shrimp, conch, crab, etc.), and fish. Meat-filled pastries are favorite snacks. Eggplant, yams, sweet potatoes, and a variety of fruits round out the diet. Haiti is especially known for its fresh-pressed juices made from passion fruit, oranges, *pamplemousse* (grapefruit), cherries, papayas, *kachiman, kaïmites, zikak*, and other fruits.

Recreation. All Haitians have access to radios, and people generally listen to music and news throughout the day. A growing number of urban families are able to afford a television in their homes. Few people own VCRs, but they can watch videos at TV stores. Haitian music videos are favored.

The most popular sport is soccer. Streets are empty if an important regional or world match is being televised. Children begin to play soccer at an early age; leagues are organized throughout the country. Unlike in some countries, girls play soccer, too. Adult soccer stars are extremely popular among people of all ages. Men enjoy cockfighting, usually on Sunday afternoon. They also spend hours playing dominoes and cards.

The Arts. Music and dancing are integral to everyday life. Disco, reggae, and *konpa* are also popular in cities. *Meringue*, a mixture of African rhythms and European music, is the national dance. Urban residents enjoy a variety of North American music.

Haitian artists and sculptors are known for their unique images and striking colors. One such art form is sculpture made from cut, pounded, and painted scrap metal. *Tap-taps*, also considered art, are public transportation painted with bright pictures. Many artists choose Haitian history or daily life for their subjects. Nature is also an important theme. Painted screens, papier-mâché, wood carving, basketry, pottery, and painted wooden boxes are prominent crafts.

Oral literature is abundant in Haiti and includes songs, proverbs, and riddles. Storytellers carefully craft their performance, acting out the story with their voice. Most written Haitian literature is in French, although Creole now commonly is used.

Holidays. Haiti's national holidays include New Year's (1 Jan.), which is also Independence Day; National Heroes Day (2 Jan.); Constitution Day (29 Mar.); Easter; Flag Day (18 May); *Fête Dieu* (Corpus Christi, first Thursday in June); and Christmas. Other dates mark freedom from the Duvalier dictatorship (7 Feb.) and the return of Jean-Bertrand Aristide (15 Oct.). Various Catholic feasts also are marked but are not necessarily public holidays. *Fèt Gede* (2 Nov.) honors the dead, who are highly venerated in Haitian culture. Each village or town has a holiday for the local patron saint, celebrated with a morning mass, daytime festival, and evening ball. Some of these festivals are very large, such as the *Fête de Notre Dame*. From mid-January to Easter, local bands known as *Rara* dance and perform in the streets; they have their own rituals that carry some religious overtones. *Rara* is a more traditional version of *Carnaval*, which is not really celebrated in the countryside.

Carnaval, held before the Catholic Lent, is a festive time for dancing and parades. While people await the main parade, they dance to music they play on their own portable stereos. The partying continues all night and into the early morning hours for two or three days. Stores are only open in the morning on these days.

Commerce. Most businesses are open from 9 a.m. to 5 p.m., but summer hours may be limited to 3 p.m. Open-air markets have varying hours, depending on their location. Most shops are closed on Sunday, except for urban supermarkets. The majority of people lack refrigeration and so shop daily for perishable foods. Rural people often grow their own food.

SOCIETY

Government. The Republic of Haiti is divided into nine departments (provinces), but the central government has most control over political affairs. The president is head of state and the prime minister is head of government. The constitution allows for a bicameral parliament, with a 27-seat Senate and an 83-seat Chamber of Deputies. The voting age is 18. The two most powerful political parties, *Fanmi Lavalas* (Lavalas Family Party) and the Struggling People's Organization, oppose each other in political conflicts. The Lavalas party is led by Jean-Bertrand Aristide.

Economy. Haiti's economy is based on agriculture, which employs more than two-thirds of the workforce. Large farms are rare, so production is in small quantities. Nearly three-fourths of all Haitians live in poverty. Real wages have not risen in a generation. The most important cash crops include coffee, cacao, and sugar. However, little is actually exported, and international aid is necessary to develop future agricultural potential. Industrial activity is minimal, geared mostly for domestic needs (cement, sugar refining, etc.). Light industries make toys and clothing for export. The economy grew little more than 1 percent in 2000. Corruption, high

DEVELOPMENT DATA

Human Dev. Index* rank	150 of 174 countries
Adjusted for women	123 of 143 countries
Real GDP per capita	$1,383
Adult literacy rate	45 percent
Infant mortality rate	97 per 1,000 births
Life expectancy	47 (male); 51 (female)

unemployment, political instability, and inefficient state enterprises are major stumbling blocks to additional development. The government is working to privatize some state companies, but the process is slow and unpopular with the public. Haiti's currency is the *gourde* (G).

Transportation and Communications. For short distances, most Haitians travel by foot. In cities, they also may ride buses, taxis, or a colorful *tap-tap*, which travels fixed routes but not on a fixed schedule. Intercity transportation is made by bus, boat, or plane. Few people own private cars.

Middle- and upper-income urban homes have phones. Otherwise, people go to a central telephone office. Phone booths are rare because of vandalism. The postal system is generally reliable but not protected against theft. A person can post a message on certain radio stations or send a written message via truck drivers. The drivers drop the messages at a store on their way and recipients can retrieve them. Haiti has two daily newspapers, nearly one hundred radio stations, and several television stations.

Education. Haiti's school system is patterned after the French model, with kindergarten, primary school (six years), and secondary school (seven years). Many urban dwellers send their children to private schools, even though tuition can be a burden. In fact, two-thirds of all schools are private. Regardless of where children attend, their daily schooling has been interrupted in the past few years by street demonstrations. Because these events can be very violent, parents tend to keep children home whenever a protest is announced or feared.

Students who complete secondary school may pursue higher education at a university or other private institutions. The country's main university is the State University of Haiti. Students who do not complete their education often work on family farms, especially in rural areas.

Health. Haiti's national health system is unable to meet the needs of most people due to the lack of funds, staff, and modern equipment. Malaria, hepatitis, HIV/AIDS, dengue fever, and other diseases combine with malnutrition to keep life expectancy rates low and infant mortality rates high. Most children do not receive proper vaccinations. Proper sanitation and clean water are also lacking.

CONTACT INFORMATION

Embassy of the Republic of Haiti, 2311 Massachusetts Avenue NW, Washington, DC 20008; phone (202) 332-4090.

1305 North Research Way, Bldg. K
Orem, Utah 84097-6200 USA
1.800.528.6279; 801.705.4250
fax 801.705.4350
www.culturegrams.com

Republic of
Honduras

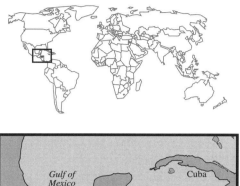

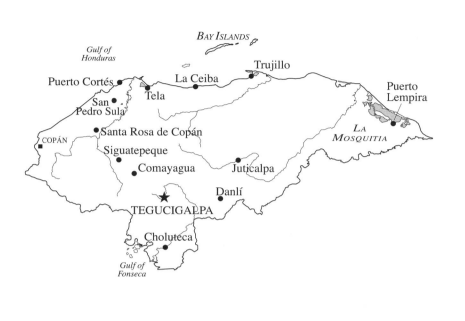

Boundary representations are not necessarily authoritative.

▶ THE AMERICAS

BACKGROUND

Land and Climate. Covering 43,278 square miles (112,090 square kilometers), Honduras is just larger than Tennessee. Located in Central America, Honduras borders both Pacific and Atlantic Ocean coasts. La Mosquitia, an area of wetlands, mountains, and tropical forests, covers the lower eastern coast. The largest pine forest in Latin America, the Olancho Forest Reserve, is about the size of Connecticut. The climate varies according to elevation: subtropical in the lowlands and temperate at higher levels. Tegucigalpa, the capital, enjoys a relatively mild climate year-round. The South is warmer than the rest of the country, excluding the north coast; it is also drier. The rainy season extends from May to November, although rains sometimes may not begin to fall until as late as October. March through May are the hottest months. Summer highs reach 95°F (35°C).

While Honduras is mountainous, it is the only Central American country without volcanoes, which is a factor in its low food production. Volcanic soils are usually good for agriculture. Due to the poor soil, many people have practiced migratory agriculture, moving every few years to clear new land and plant crops. This and timber operations have caused Honduras to lose 30 percent of its forest over the past 25 years. Wildlife has also been affected. Many efforts are now underway to reverse this trend and preserve the forests for indigenous peoples, wildlife, and the environment. Precious woods, gold, silver, copper, lead, zinc, and other minerals are found in Honduras.

Heavy rains and high winds from Hurricane Mitch pounded the country for a week in 1998, leading to more than nine thousand deaths and causing billions of dollars in damage.

Widespread devastation altered the nature, location, and course of many geographical features. New maps are being drawn to reflect changes to many of the country's rivers, towns, villages, roads, and railways.

History. The great Mayan Empire flourished in present-day Honduras until about A.D. 800, when the Mayan population began to decline. Smaller empires controlled various regions until the arrival of Spanish *conquistadores*. Columbus landed in 1502 and called the area *Honduras* (depths) because of the deep waters off the north coast. The Indians battled the Spanish until 1539, when the last of their chiefs (Lempira) was killed and the Spanish established a provincial capital at Comayagua. Honduras was incorporated into Spain's Captaincy General (colony) of Guatemala. Immigration increased when silver was discovered in the 1570s.

The Misquito Indians of the Mosquitia region requested and received a British invasion, but troops were only able to occupy that area of the country. The British withdrew in 1859. In September 1821, Honduras and four other provinces declared independence from Spain and briefly joined the Mexican Empire. Complete independence for Honduras came in 1838, when a republic was established. By the end of the 1800s, the government had become unstable and the country came under Nicaraguan influence. Instability continued until Tiburcio Carías Andino took power in 1932. His military rule ended in 1949, but military leaders continued to exercise control until 1981, when elections restored civilian rule.

Rafael Leonardo Callejas took office in 1990, but the military continued to exercise a great deal of power and influence. Constitutional term limits prohibited Callejas from seeking a second consecutive term. Carlos Roberto Reina Idiaquez was voted president in 1993 elections. Reina worked to reduce the military's role in politics. He also pursued economic reform, attacked corruption, and promoted human rights. Presidential elections in December 1997 brought newspaper owner Carlos Flores Facusse (Liberal Party) to office, marking the country's fifth democratic transfer of power since the end of military rule.

Reconstruction loans, debt forgiveness, and foreign aid have helped Honduras begin its recovery from Hurricane Mitch. Flores remains popular, but the task of rebuilding infrastructure, replanting lost agricultural land, and jump starting the economy is daunting. Rising crime also presents a problem. The next elections are in November 2001.

THE PEOPLE

Population.   More than 6.2 million people live in Honduras, a population that is growing annually at 2.5 percent. Ninety percent of the population is mestizo, while only 7 percent is native Indian. Two percent is black and 1 percent is of European descent. The Indians live mostly in isolated regions like La Mosquitia and Lencas. The principal Indian ethnic groups include Misquito, Payas, and Xicaques. The blacks are primarily Garinagu, commonly known as Garífuna. There is also a group known as the Sambos—a mixture of black and Indian inhabitants.

Language.   Spanish is the official and dominant language. However, some Garinagu speak Garífuna, and Indians speak a number of different indigenous languages. About 10,000 people, mostly on the Bay Islands, speak Creole English. English is a required course in secondary schools, but few people are fluent. Major hotels have bilingual employees.

Religion.   About 88 percent of the population is Roman Catholic, but various other Christian groups are active and freedom of religion is guaranteed by law. Protestantism is growing rapidly, with a variety of churches present in even the smallest towns. Most Protestants (or *evangélicos*) attend church regularly. Some follow specific rules affecting their lifestyle (no coffee, dancing, etc.). The Catholic Church maintains a strong influence on society through festivals, family celebrations, and politics. Many public holidays center on religious themes. Each town and city has a patron saint for whom it holds an annual festival.

General Attitudes.   In Honduras, as in much of Latin America, social philosophies like fatalism, *machismo*, and *hora latina* are evident. Fatalism exists partly due to the difficulties of life in poverty; people are aware of limited social mobility and try to accept their position in life as something they cannot control. This attitude often relieves frustration and allows people to focus on what is good in life rather than what is unpleasant. During conversation, people often add the phrase *Si Dios quiere* (God willing), particularly when making commitments. *Machismo* is indicative of a male-dominated society in which women are expected to remain submissive. Women comprise less than one-third of the formal labor force, and most rural women do not work outside the home. *Hora latina* refers to the concept of time and schedules. Since individuals' needs are more important than schedules, being late for appointments or social events is a way of life. For example, a person would not hesitate to stop and talk to a friend on the way to an appointment, even if it meant being late. This occurs even in urban settings, where punctuality is a bit more important, because personal contacts and relationships are often necessary to conduct business and work with the government.

Hondurans value their Christian beliefs, as well as their ties to the land and to agriculture. Environmental issues are important to Hondurans, but poverty causes money to take precedence in many cases.

Personal Appearance.   Hondurans normally wear Western-style clothing. Shorts rarely are worn in public except in the coastal areas, where it is hot and humid. Urban men often wear a *guayabera* (a decorative shirt of light fabric that hangs to just below the waist) instead of a more formal shirt and tie. Urban women are especially stylish with respect to clothing, hair, and makeup. In rural areas, where the majority is poor, many people wear secondhand clothing imported from the United States. Men wear rubber boots when working in the fields while women wear flip-flops. Baseball or wide-brim hats are common. T-shirts with English slogans are popular throughout Honduras, even though the wearer probably does not speak English. Dressing up for special occasions is important to Hondurans. People are careful to keep dress clothes separate from clothes worn at work and at home. The wealthy wear the latest Western fashions.

CUSTOMS AND COURTESIES

Greetings.   A handshake is an appropriate greeting for men and urban women. Middle- and upper-class women kiss male and female friends on the cheek. Rural women greet one another by placing one hand on the upper arm of the other woman. The *abrazo* is a warm embrace shared by close friends and relatives. When meeting someone for the first time, a person addresses the other by official title or *Señor*, *Señora*, or *Señorita* (Mr., Mrs., or Miss). The titles *Don* (for men) and *Doña* (for women) also are used before first names to show respect. *Usted* (the formal version of "you" in Spanish) is appropriate among acquaintances or those meeting for the first time.

One customarily gives a general greeting when entering a room. In small groups, people greet and say good-bye to each person individually. People commonly say *Que le vaya bien* (May it go well with you) when parting. While passing someone in the street, one says *Adiós*. Meaning "Good-bye," *Adiós* in this case is meant as a general greeting. One always says *Buen provecho* (Enjoy your meal) at the table before a meal. A person approaching or passing a table in a restaurant also says *Buen provecho* to the people at the table.

Gestures.   Hand and body language are important to communication. Waving the index finger is often used to say "no." Clasping both hands indicates strong approval. Touching the finger below the eye warns caution. And a hand placed under an elbow usually means someone is thought to be stingy. People commonly point with their lips or chin. To express enthusiasm, they place their middle finger and thumb together and shake their hand, producing a snapping noise. One beckons by waving the hand with the palm facing down. Beckoning with the index finger is rude. Poorer people tend to avoid eye contact when speaking.

Visiting.   Visiting is a common pastime on Saturday afternoons and Sundays, and people often visit unannounced.

People in rural areas also visit on days when they are not in the fields. Hondurans are courteous and generous to guests in their homes. Hosts almost always offer their guests refreshments, such as juice, soda, coffee, or sweets; refusing is impolite. Unexpected visitors arriving at mealtime often are extended an invitation to eat with the family. Even people of humble circumstance will share whatever they have to make a guest feel welcome. If a guest does not feel like eating, the host may wrap up a little food to send home with him or her. When leaving a home, guests are especially respectful to the head of the household.

Social events may have an indicated starting time, but hosts and guests understand this is very flexible; being several minutes or even an hour late is not uncommon.

Eating. Hondurans eat breakfast between 6 and 8:30 a.m., the main meal around noon, and a lighter evening meal sometime between 6 and 8 p.m. Coffee breaks are customary in the late morning and midafternoon. Meals are eaten in a leisurely manner. Diners keep both hands (but not elbows) above the table. People customarily hold the fork in the right hand and knife in the left; rural people might use pieces of corn tortillas instead of utensils. Families do not necessarily eat together, due to lack of plates or table space or simply as a matter of convenience. At finer restaurants, a 10 to 15 percent tip is appropriate; tips are not necessarily expected at less formal restaurants.

LIFESTYLE

Family. Family ties are strong in Honduras. Members of the extended family, including grandparents and other relatives, often occupy the same household. While the father is respected as the head of the household, the mother has the greatest responsibility and influence in everyday family life. Girls are expected at a young age to help with household chores and child care; boys do little until they are old enough to help in the fields. Hondurans carry both their paternal and maternal surnames. The father's surname is the individual's family name; the mother's surname appears at the end of the person's name. Both surnames follow one or two given names. When a woman marries, her name does not change.

Unfortunately, a large number of families live in poverty. Most Honduran homes do not enjoy modern conveniences. Small adobe houses with dirt floors are common in rural areas. Cities have both modern, luxurious housing and poor slums. People in remote areas lack electricity and other modern conveniences.

Dating and Marriage. Young women have their formal initiation (*La Fiesta Rosa*) into social life at age 15, when elaborate parties are held to recognize their coming of age. Youth begin dating in groups; a young woman usually is accompanied by one or more other young women. Later on, couples date without accompaniment. Activities are simple and usually just involve socializing. Couples often get together and establish themselves at dances.

In rural areas, most poor people will start their families without marrying, often as young as age 14. Common-law marriages generally are accepted, so many people never officially marry. Single mothers are common in all social classes, and many siblings in these families have only the one parent in common. Young single mothers often return to live with their parents until they are older or find another spouse.

Diet. Red beans, corn, tortillas, and rice are the staple foods. Bananas, pineapples, mangoes, citrus fruits, coconuts, melons, avocados, potatoes, and yams are the most common fruits and vegetables. Special dishes include *tapado* (a stew of beef, vegetables, and coconut milk), *mondongo* (tripe and beef knuckles), *nacatamales* (pork tamales), and *torrejas* (similar to French toast and served at Christmas). *Topogios* or *charamuscas* (frozen fruit juice in plastic bags) are popular during the summer months. People also enjoy soft drinks. Coffee with or without milk is traditional and usually is served with the main meal of the day. Some restaurants in major cities serve pizza, hamburgers, and other North American dishes.

Recreation. *Fútbol* (soccer) is the national sport. Young boys play the game almost anytime, anywhere, and professional competition is available as well. Although in recent years more girls have become involved in *fútbol*, they are still more likely to play basketball. Boys and men in rural areas enjoy playing card and dice games. In villages on the north coast, men like to play dominoes after they return home from a day's work of fishing. Wealthy Hondurans enjoy cycle races, baseball, golf, tennis, and swimming. Movies are popular in urban areas.

The Arts. Honduras is known for brightly painted ceramics, carved wooden trunks, handmade musical instruments, and other woodwork. Metalwork, embroidery, and weaving are other arts. Honduras is home to many Mayan ruins, including Copán, which is located near the Guatemalan border. Pottery and stone carvings have been discovered there.

Many people enjoy music and dance. A popular music is *la punta*, which originated with traditional Garífuna music and dance. It is traditionally played with instruments like drums, a conch shell, and maracas and has a complex rhythm. The *marimba* (similar to a xylophone) is a common instrument; other traditional instruments include flutes and trumpets. Other styles of music are *la varsoviana*, *el barreño*, and *el sueñito*.

Holidays. Public holidays include New Year's; Day of the Americas (14 Apr.); Labor Day (1 May); Independence Day (15 Sept.); Birth of Morazán, the national hero (3 Oct.); Columbus Day (12 Oct.); Armed Forces Day (21 Oct.); and Christmas. Independence Day is the most popular national holiday. Schoolchildren practice for months in preparation for parades and programs. Constructing nativity scenes is a popular Christmas tradition. Since money is scarce, the scenes are made from scratch each year with clay figures and other natural resources.

During Easter's Holy Week (*Semana Santa*), businesses close from Wednesday through the end of the week. Many people go to the beach, while others may swim in the rivers. The Day of the Child (10 Sept.) is not an official holiday but is still popular. Children receive sweets and gifts at school, and adults congratulate the children when passing them on the street. Private home celebrations also may take place among the wealthy. In addition to these holidays, Honduras has community celebrations honoring patron saints and regional *fiestas* such as *Carnaval* in La Ceiba.

Commerce. Government office hours are from 8 a.m. to 4 p.m. or 7:30 a.m. to 3:30 p.m., Monday through Friday. Private businesses operate from 8 a.m. to noon and 1 to 5 p.m., although some do not close at noon for the *siesta* (midday break). Banks usually close by 3 p.m., while post offices may remain open as late as 9 p.m., depending on the city. On Saturdays, most businesses close between noon and 2 p.m. In marketplaces and shops where prices are not posted, bartering is common; otherwise, prices are fixed. Small shops called *pulperias* are run out of people's homes in most communities. They sell food, medicine, and cleaning and school supplies and are open all day, everyday.

SOCIETY

Government. The Republic of Honduras is divided into 18 *departamentos* (provinces). Its president is chief of state and head of government. He governs with a cabinet and serves one four-year term. The judicial branch of government is independent. The unicameral *Congreso Nacional* (National Congress) has 134 seats. All citizens are required to vote beginning at age 18. Two parties dominate in Congress, although smaller parties have representation. President Flores is a member of the governing Liberal Party (PLH). The opposition National Party (PNH) has two factions (Monarca and Oswaldista), each devoted to an individual leader. Party affiliation is taken seriously.

Economy. Honduras is one of the poorest countries in the Western Hemisphere, and income and productivity rates are low. The economy is based largely on agriculture, which employs more than 60 percent of the population. The most profitable exports are bananas and coffee, followed by seafood, timber, cotton, sugar, and metals. Adverse weather conditions and fluctuating global prices for these raw materials can cripple the economy from one year to the next. Manufactured items slowly are becoming more important.

Economic reforms implemented in the early 1990s and scaled back by President Reina were beginning to improve some conditions prior to widespread devastation from Hurricane Mitch in late 1998. Damage to crops, farmland, and infrastructure from Mitch has been substantial. The economy shrank by 3 percent in 1999 and continues to struggle, although it is recovering somewhat. Obstacles to growth include an already weak infrastructure (services, roads, markets), large foreign debts, and a large, inefficient bureaucracy. Unemployment or underemployment affects approximately half of the population. The Honduran currency is the *lempira* (L), but it is sometimes referred to as a *peso*.

With nearly 80 percent of the population living in poverty, most people do not earn an income sufficient for their needs. Only the wealthiest Hondurans enjoy economic prosperity. About 23 percent lack the health care, education, and economic opportunities to rise above human poverty.*

Transportation and Communications. Hurricane Mitch caused extensive damage to roads and bridges throughout the country; rebuilding may take years. Periodic floods also take their toll on roads. Highways connect Tegucigalpa with some other principal cities, but roads generally are in poor condition, particularly in more remote areas. People rely on buses for public transport because few own cars. Rural areas are isolated from cities due to poor transportation and communications. In areas without buses, pickup truck owners may

DEVELOPMENT DATA

Human Dev. Index* rank	113 of 174 countries
Adjusted for women	94 of 143 countries
Real GDP per capita	$2,433
Adult literacy rate	71 percent
Infant mortality rate	31 per 1,000 births
Life expectancy	68 (male); 72 (female)

provide travel on specific routes. Tegucigalpa, San Pedro Sula, La Ceiba, the Bay Islands, Puerto Lempira, and some villages in La Mosquitia are accessible by airplane. Private telephones are found only in major cities. Most large towns have one public telephone and a telegraph service, usually used for urgent messages. Many people communicate by placing messages on the radio. Mail service is slow but fairly reliable.

Education. Schooling is required for six years beginning at age seven. However, while nearly all children begin their schooling, many drop out before the end—especially among the rural poor. Less than half of all children actually complete the full six years, and less than one-third advance to the secondary level. Children often are needed at home to help with farming or household chores, and having them gone all day at school can be too great a sacrifice for many families. In some areas, schoolchildren attend classes in tents because of damage to school buildings from Hurricane Mitch. The National University of Honduras and some trade schools provide higher education, but only 9 percent of the population advances to those levels of study. Honduras has some of Central America's best agricultural and forestry schools.

Health. Various health challenges face Hondurans. Malaria is prevalent below 3,000 feet (about 900 meters), and rabies, typhoid, hepatitis, parasites, dengue fever, and dysentery, as well as intestinal disease, present problems for the population. A serious cholera epidemic struck the country in 1991. Honduras also has the highest number of AIDS cases in Central America. Vaccinations are provided free of charge, and nearly all people have access to them. But while most Honduran children (83 percent) are immunized, up to half suffer from malnutrition.

Rural areas have health centers, but many villagers must walk hours to reach one. Facilities often are not equipped with medicine. Urban medical care is more adequate but still lacking by modern standards. Basic health care is subsidized throughout the country, but patients must pay small fees for each visit. Poorer citizens often cannot afford prescription medicine.

CONTACT INFORMATION

Honduras Institute of Tourism, 2100 Ponce de Leon Boulevard, Suite 1175, Coral Gables, FL 33134; phone (800) 410-9608. Embassy of the Republic of Honduras, 3007 Tilden Street NW, Suite 4M, Washington, DC 20008; phone (202) 966-7702; Web site www.hondurasemb.org.

1305 North Research Way, Bldg. K
Orem, Utah 84097-6200 USA
1.800.528.6279; 801.705.4250
fax 801.705.4350
www.culturegrams.com

Republic of
Hungary

▼ EUROPE

Boundary representations are not necessarily authoritative.

BACKGROUND

Land and Climate. Hungary is a landlocked nation in central Europe. Covering 35,919 square miles (93,030 square kilometers), it is slightly smaller than Indiana. Most of the east is flat, but the northwest has rolling hills and low mountains. Almost 55 percent of the land is suitable for cultivation, allowing Hungary to be nearly self-sufficient in food. The capital, Budapest, is actually the union of two cities (Buda and Pest) lying on opposite sides of the Danube River. They united in 1872 as Budapest, once called the Paris of the East. The climate is continental, with cold winters and warm, pleasant summers. The average temperature in winter is 32°F (0°C) and in summer is 70°F to 75°F (21–24°C).

History. Present-day Hungary became part of the Roman Empire in 14 B.C. as the province of Pannonia, but the east remained in the hands of Germanic and other tribes. In the fifth century, Magyars began migrating from the east. In A.D. 896 the Magyars invaded and conquered the resident Slavs and began permanent settlement. They were led by Árpád. Christianity was introduced by his grandson, Géza, in the late 10th century. Géza's son, István (Stephen), became Hungary's first Christian king in A.D. 1000, and István converted the people to Christianity. The dynasty lasted until the 14th century, after which time nonnative powers controlled the area. During the Renaissance of the 15th century, the country reached a high level of culture and political power, but large portions of the country were conquered by the Ottoman Turks. Later, Hungary was ruled over by the Austrian Hapsburgs during their rise to world prominence (16th–18th centuries). Hungarians rose in rebellion in 1848 but were defeated after two years of fighting.

In 1867, the Dual Monarchy, a sharing of power between Austrians and Hungarians in Central Europe, was established. The Austro-Hungarian Empire was later shattered by heightened national awareness and desire for self-rule among Slavic minorities. This division contributed to the beginning of World War I in 1914. In treaty settlements following the war, Hungary became an independent republic but lost two-thirds of its former territory and three-fifths of its people to new neighbor states. Hungary was a German ally through most of World War II, but Germany invaded in 1944 after Hungary began surrender negotiations with the Allies. Soviet troops liberated the country in 1945, and elections again established a republic. The Communist Party, under heavy influence from the Soviet Union, seized power within two years and by 1949 had declared Hungary a socialist state called the People's Republic of Hungary.

Communist reformer Imre Nagy tried to change the system that emerged. He even withdrew Hungary from the Warsaw Pact and declared the country neutral in 1956. In response, the Soviet Union attacked Hungary, repressed the movement, executed Nagy, and buried him in disgrace. Until 1988, when he was forced to resign under pressure for reform, János Kádár was the leader of the Communist government. By October 1989, Hungary had changed its name to the Republic of Hungary and abolished the Communist monopoly on power. Nagy was reburied as a national hero.

The country's first free elections were held in 1990. The Hungarian Democratic Forum swept the Communists from power and József Antall became prime minister. Antall died in 1993. Due to people's disillusionment with the course of economic reform, Antall's party was narrowly defeated in May 1994 elections by the Socialist Party (MSZP), which emerged from the Communist Party. Prime Minister Gyula Horn continued the process of economic reform but also sought to meet people's basic needs. Horn won praise from the West for his economic policies and the country's economic performance. However, in May 1998 runoff elections, Horn lost to Viktor Orbán, a young center-right leader of the Federation of Young Democrats–Hungarian Civic Party (FIDESZ). Orbán has promised voters better public safety, faster economic growth, and support for small businesses.

The status of ethnic Hungarians living in Slovakia and Romania continues to challenge Hungary's leaders. Hungarians have especially close ties to their past cultural center of Transylvania (in Romania since 1920), where Hungarian kings lived in exile during Turkic rule. Treaties promoting their rights were signed with Slovakia (1995) and Romania (1996) after years of tough negotiations. Treatment of Hungarians who reside in neighboring nations is an important component of foreign relations. Hungary, together with Poland and the Czech Republic, joined the North Atlantic Treaty Organization (NATO) in March 1999. However, popular support for use of Hungary as a departure point during NATO strikes on Yugoslavia waned during the conflict because 300,000 Hungarians reside in the adjacent Yugoslavian province of Vojvodina. Environmental pollution, corruption, organized crime, and discrimination against the Roma, or Gypsies, are some of the problems that Hungary is struggling with. Sustained economic development in preparation for European Union (EU) membership is the state's chief goal.

THE PEOPLE

Population.   Hungary's population of 10.1 million is decreasing by 0.33 percent annually. Magyars (Hungarians) form the largest ethnic group and 90 percent of the population. The Romany (Gypsies) comprise around 4 percent of the people. Germans (2.6 percent), Serbs (2), Slovaks (0.8), and Romanians (0.7) comprise significant minorities. Budapest, the largest city, has a population of about 1.8 million. Hungarians comprise 10.8 percent of Slovakia's population and 7 percent of Romania's. About 40 percent of the population lives in severely polluted areas.

Language.   The official language is Magyar, or Hungarian, as it is referred to in other countries. Ninety-eight percent of the population speaks it. Magyar is part of the Finno-Ugrian group of the Uralic language family, which includes Estonian and Finnish. It has a complex grammar, which includes restrictions on what sort of vowels may occur together within a word. In addition, the presence or absence of diacritical markings on words may change meaning. Most minority groups speak their own languages in addition to Hungarian. German and English are popular courses in school.

Religion.   Roughly two-thirds of the population is Roman Catholic. Various other Christian groups make up the other third, including Calvinists (20 percent) and Lutherans (5 percent). During Communist rule, religious groups were carefully regulated through a government agency. In 1990, religious freedom was granted to all. While religion does not affect their daily life much, many people consider themselves devout Christians.

General Attitudes.   As a nation that experienced a form of democracy before most other European nations, the new democratic Hungary is proud of its heritage. Even during the Communist regime, Hungary was considered one of the most prosperous and open countries in Eastern Europe. It was one of the first to announce sweeping reforms and was able to accomplish them without violence or serious upheaval. The people earnestly wish to become part of an integrated Europe. Hungarians also view their past achievements with pride.

However, accompanying pride is a historical tendency for pessimism. Individual Hungarians will express doubt about their own future or condition, even if their neighbors are worse off. Hungarian humor incorporates pessimism, which then becomes a whimsical, light-hearted cynicism. Some say pessimism is only natural for Hungarians, who as traditional farmers found it bad luck to predict good harvests. Individually, Hungarians value independence, a strong and stable family, education (including good performance in school and an advanced degree), security (be it a job, home, or social benefits), property (a home, garden, and car), access to or ownership of summer cottages, and travel outside of Hungary. People admire professionals but generally do not admire the wealthy, who are often associated with corruption.

Personal Appearance.   Clothing styles in urban areas generally follow those in Western Europe, with blue jeans being the most popular among the youth. Businessmen wear conservative suits, although formal dress for younger people tends to be more colorful than in the United States. Women pay particular attention to style and their appearance.

Traditional costumes are seen only in rural areas and during special celebrations. They may include intricately embroidered blouses and skirts for women, who also wear colorful hats or scarves. Each region has its specialty. The men often wear vests over loose-fitting shirts. Pants may be pleated, baggy, and less than full-length—or tight, black, and tucked inside boots. Men wear a variety of hats.

CUSTOMS AND COURTESIES

Greetings.   Adults greet each other with a firm handshake. A man usually waits for a woman to extend her hand first. If one's hand is dirty, one may offer a wrist or elbow. Except between men, many Hungarians also *puszi*, or hug and kiss each other lightly on each cheek. Polite verbal greetings include *Jó napot kívánok* (Good day), *Jó reggelt kívánok* (Good morning), and *Jó estét kívánok* (Good evening). *Kívánok* is often left off in more casual circumstances or is replaced by a person's name. Children greet older women with *Kezét csókolom* (I kiss your hand). Men might also use this with older women to show special respect.

Popular informal greetings include *Haló*, *Szervusz*, or *Szia*, which all mean "Hello." The latter two terms come from the Latin *servus*, which once meant "I am here to serve you." One might follow a greeting with *Hogy vagy?* (How are you?) or another question. When addressing someone, it is polite to use the person's professional title with his or her surname. People introduce themselves by surname, usually followed by the given name. Greetings on a first-name basis are limited to close friends and relatives. However, adults address the youth, and the youth address each other, by first name. Urban Hungarians do not usually greet strangers on the street, but rural people will. When parting, Hungarians say *Viszontlátásra* (See you again) or simply *Haló*, *Viszlát*, or *Szia*.

Gestures. Personal space in Hungary tends to be relatively small, and showing affection in public is accepted. Good friends, especially among the youth, will put their arms around each others' shoulders when they walk in public. Talking with one's hands in one's pockets is considered impolite by many. While blowing one's nose in public is acceptable, repeated sniffling is considered to be rude. It is polite to chew gum with the mouth closed. To wish a person happy birthday, some Hungarians will pull the person's earlobe slightly while saying "Happy Birthday."

Visiting. While close friends, relatives, and sometimes neighbors make short unannounced visits, urban or extended visits are arranged in advance when possible. Relatives visit often. Guests remove shoes upon entering a home; hosts may have a pair of guest slippers for them to wear. First-time guests do not stay long, leaving just after coffee is finished. When guests arrive, hosts often help them remove their coats. An informal atmosphere prevails. Hosts accompany departing guests outside.

Hungarians enjoy socializing in the home but also frequently meet at restaurants, coffeehouses, and tearooms. Guests in the home usually are offered such refreshments as coffee, tea, fruit juice, brandy, or one of many popular regional wines. When one is invited to dinner, it is polite to bring a small gift of flowers, boxed chocolates, or wine. Flowers are presented in odd numbers; they remain in cellophane wrapping until the hostess puts them in a vase. The hosts usually will display the flowers in a room where the guests will be after dinner, or sometimes on the table.

Eating. Breakfast may be a light meal with only rolls and a drink, or it may be heartier and include eggs, salami, cheese, yogurt, and even hot peppers. Lunch is often the main meal in rural areas, including soup, often salad, a main dish of meat and potatoes, and dessert with coffee. In urban areas, lunch is light and dinner is the main meal. Rural people eat a light dinner of cold cuts, fruit, bread or rolls, and a drink.

Before eating or when entering a room where someone is eating, Hungarians say *Jó étvágyat* (literally "good appetite"). They keep hands above the table but do not rest the elbows on it. Napkins are kept on the table throughout the meal. It is not usually necessary to ask that food be passed across the table. Reaching for what one wants is considered a sign that the guest is comfortable with the host. Leaving food on the plate is impolite. Although tap water is safe to drink, many people prefer mineral water or some other beverage. As throughout Europe, the continental style of eating is used, with the fork in the left hand and the knife remaining in the right. Tips are customary in restaurants at the same levels as the rest of Europe (10–15 percent).

LIFESTYLE

Family. The average Hungarian family has three people. Urban families tend to be smaller than rural families. The cost of living is high in cities and housing is often limited. The father maintains a dominant role in the family. Both parents usually work. In fact, nearly 80 percent of all women work. Men share some household responsibilities but traditionally take the "outside" chores (yard work, gardening, etc.). Adult children often live with their parents until married. Aging parents generally are cared for by their children, who may live in the same house or nearby. Urban families live in either small apartments or small single-family homes, while rural families have single-family homes.

Dating and Marriage. Young people like to go to movies, concerts, and theaters. They enjoy dancing, watching television, and just talking together on park benches. Many ski and hike together. Most Hungarians expect to marry and raise a family (in that order). Urban newlyweds tend to be older than rural couples. Most people wait until after they have finished schooling or are working before they marry. Traditional weddings were elaborate three-day affairs but are rare today. Still, the ceremony at city hall is often followed by a lavish dinner. With housing in short supply, young couples often must live with parents for their first few years of marriage.

Diet. Hungary's location in central Europe makes it a prime gathering point for many ethnic culinary specialties. One of the most famous Hungarian specialties is *gulyás* (goulash), a soup of meat, potatoes, onions, and paprika. Paprika is a familiar spice in many dishes. Pork is the most common meat in the Hungarian diet, but chicken is also popular. Side dishes include noodles, potatoes, and dumplings. A cabbage-and-vinegar salad is popular with main meals. Except for certain seasonal varieties, vegetables and fruits are in ample supply year-round. Bread and pastries are available in a wide variety. Fish soup (*halászlé*), stuffed paprika, stuffed chicken, and various kinds of strudel and pancakes are all part of the diet. Hungary is also proud of its many wines.

Recreation. Hungary's most popular sport is soccer. Other important sports include swimming, tennis, fencing, and sailing. Hunting and fishing are popular activities as well. In their leisure time, many Hungarians like to take walks, visit parks or local museums, attend concerts, watch television, or work outside in the garden. They meet in town for afternoon tea or an ice-cream treat or relax at the local thermal bath. For vacations, many like to go to resort spas. Longer vacations often are spent at Lake Balaton. Many also travel to neighboring countries.

Hungary was once known as a nation of horsemen, especially for the time when the *Hussars* (15th-century light cavalry) were famous for their horsemanship. Today, horses are used mostly in the tourist industry, but some Hungarians enjoy riding them for recreation.

The Arts. Hungarians consider their music and performing arts companies, art galleries, and other cultural institutions to be national treasures, and they attend whenever possible. Prominent Hungarian composers include Ferenc Erkel, Franz Liszt, Béla Bartók, and Zóltan Kodály. Bartók and Kodály both incorporated features of traditional Hungarian folk music into their works. Hungarian folk music and dancing are still popular. The youth also enjoy contemporary music. The national dance is the *csárdás*, a courting dance in two parts (slow, then fast), which is performed at weddings, festivals, and other special occasions.

Hungary has a strong folk tradition—embroidery, ceramics, ceiling and wall painting, and wood and bone carving—but commercialization threatens the existence of some of these art forms. Free-market policies introduced in the 1990s significantly reduced government support of the arts.

Holidays. Public holidays include New Year's Day, War of Freedom Day (15 March, a day marking the 1848 rebellion and war), Easter (Sunday and Monday), Labor Day (1 May), Pentecost, St. Stephen's Day (20 Aug.), National Holiday (23 October, in honor of the 1956 uprising), St. Nicholas Day

EUROPE ▼

(6 Dec.), and Christmas (25–26 Dec.). In addition, local festivals commemorate various folk or religious events throughout the year. At Easter, it is customary in some places for boys to "sprinkle" girls with water or cologne as a sign that the girl is a flower that should not wilt. Also popular at this time are elaborately painted Easter eggs. St. Stephen's Day celebrates the harvest and honors the first king of Hungary.

Commerce. Businesses open around 8 a.m. and remain open until 6 p.m. Some close for an hour at lunch. Many, but not all, businesses are open on Saturday until 2 p.m. Most close on Sunday. Produce stands often operate on sidewalks, and open-air markets are found in most towns. Produce, fresh bread, and other items are available at these markets. People shop often for fresh produce and dairy products, which are easily obtained at neighborhood stores. Supermarkets are located in large cities.

Formalities are important in business dealings. People tend to use formal names, discuss business politely, and treat people with respect. Refreshments are usually served. Important business discussions may be followed by an invitation to dinner, regardless of the progress made in the meeting.

SOCIETY

Government. Hungary is composed of 19 counties. An elected president (Árpád Göncz) is chief of state, and a prime minister is head of government. Parliament has one 386-seat house, called the *Országgyulés* (National Assembly). FIDESZ, the Hungarian Socialist Party, and the Independent Smallholders' Party hold the most seats in parliament. The voting age is 18.

Economy. Overall, Hungary is performing better than many former communist countries and has the potential for a bright future. Strong foreign investment, stable government institutions, a booming small business sector, and a hardworking labor force are key strengths. Having started its economic reforms prior to 1989, Hungary made good progress in its initial transition toward a free-market economy. Economic reforms slowed from 1993 to 1994 but resumed in 1995. Hungary intends to be among the first countries to join an expanded EU. The country still faces a large budget deficit despite recent austerity measures. Further budget reforms may require unpopular cuts in social benefits (some of the most generous in the region). The economy grew by more than 5.3 percent in 2000.

The transition has been difficult for many of Hungary's citizens who have endured higher prices, higher taxes, and a lower standard of living. Average inflation for 2000 was around 10 percent. Unemployment was about 6 percent. Many are able to afford the flood of consumer items now available on the market; however, others, especially in the east, are at or below the poverty line.

Industries account for 40 percent of the gross national product. Important natural resources include bauxite, coal, and natural gas. The government is selling all state-owned small businesses and pledges to accelerate privatization of larger industries. Hungary welcomes foreign investment and trade in order to build its economy and increase its hard currency reserves. The currency is the *forint* (Ft).

DEVELOPMENT DATA

Human Dev. Index* rank	43 of 174 countries
Adjusted for women	38 of 143 countries
Real GDP per capita	$10,232
Adult literacy rate	99 percent
Infant mortality rate	9 per 1,000 births
Life expectancy	67 (male); 76 (female)

Transportation and Communications. Public transportation in Hungary is well developed. Budapest has a subway. Taxis are also available. More and more people own private cars, but public transport is still the principal mode of travel. Bicycles are used for short distances. An extensive train network serves most of the country. Some transportation (mostly for tourists) is provided on the Danube River.

The communications system has improved since privatization, although many homes lack telephones. Most families have a television and radio. There are several local broadcast channels, and cable television is available but expensive. *Kossuth Radio Budapest* is popular. Four daily national newspapers and several regional papers service the country. Magazines and other publications abound. The free press is active and striving to be competitive with foreign media companies investing in Hungary.

Education. Schooling is free and compulsory for all children ages six to fourteen. Most then go on to secondary schools for technical training or preparation for higher education. Teachers are well trained and students receive a solid education. Beginning in elementary school, foreign language classes are offered. Those who successfully complete secondary school may go on to any of the five academic, four medical, and nine technical universities in Hungary, provided they pass tough entrance exams. Several other institutions of higher learning are also available. University education was free before 1994, but students must now pay tuition.

Health. Hungary's health-care system is well organized and modern. Standards in hospitals and clinics are generally high. However, the lack of adequate funding for the health system seriously threatens the quality of care. Health-care professionals are well trained but not necessarily well paid. All citizens receive free care in public institutions and most medicine is paid for. Patients must pay to see private doctors. Major health hazards include pollution, a traditionally high-fat diet, high alcohol intake, and widespread smoking. Hungary also has one of the highest suicide rates in the world. These factors combine to give Hungary one of Europe's lowest life expectancy rates.

CONTACT INFORMATION

Embassy of the Republic of Hungary, 3910 Shoemaker Street NW, Washington, DC 20008; phone (202) 362-6730; Web site www.hungaryemb.org. Hungarian National Tourist Office, 150 East 58th Street, 33d Floor, New York, NY 10155-3398; phone (212) 355-0240; Web site www.gotohungary.com/home.htm.

1305 North Research Way, Bldg. K
Orem, Utah 84097-6200 USA
1.800.528.6279; 801.705.4250
fax 801.705.4350
www.culturegrams.com

Republic of
Iceland

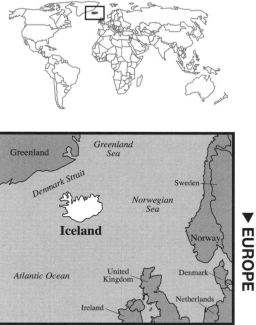

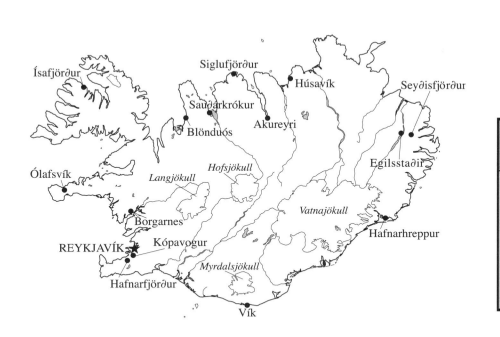

Boundary representations are not necessarily authoritative.

▼ EUROPE

BACKGROUND

Land and Climate. Slightly smaller in area than Kentucky, Iceland (39,768 square miles or 103,000 square kilometers) is the second largest island in Europe and is surrounded by many smaller islands. The land is rugged with varied scenery. About 80 percent uninhabited, this "land of fire and ice" is one of the most active volcanic countries in the world. It is, in fact, a volcanic island and averages one eruption every five years. In 1999, Mount Hekla, Iceland's most active volcano, erupted for the first time in almost 10 years. Earthquakes are also frequent, but they are rarely strong enough to cause damage. Iceland has more hot springs than any other country in the world; in fact, the English word *geyser* comes from Icelandic. The uninhabited interior is a popular place for many outdoor activities. It has many beautiful features, including mountains, lakes, volcanoes, and even deserts. More than 10 percent of the country is covered with glaciers, such as Vatnajökull and Langjökull.

Despite the country's northerly location, the climate is much milder than one would expect. The warm Gulf Stream nearly encircles the island. The average temperature in July is 51°F (11°C); the January average in Reykjavík is 30°F (-1°C). However, it does often become bitterly cold in both summer and winter when the polar winds blow. There are two or three months of continuous daylight in the summer, while during the winter (mid-November–January) there may only be four or five hours of daylight (10 a.m.–3 p.m.).

History. The first permanent settlers in Iceland were Norwegian and Celtic peoples. Iceland claims the Norwegian Ingólfur Arnarson as the first settler in 874; he founded Reykjavík, the current capital. In 930, Icelanders created the

Althingi, their national assembly, but they had no central government or monarchy. The *Althingi* established laws and also served as a court. Christianity was adopted by the *Althingi* in the year 1000, the same year that Leifur Eiríksson is said to have discovered America, landing at Newfoundland.

In 1262, Iceland became subject to the Norwegian crown, partly to end civil war between various local chieftains. Despite the new ruler, Iceland remained fairly autonomous. In 1380, both Iceland and Norway united with the Danish crown. Denmark introduced Lutheranism to Iceland in the 1530s but met with stiff opposition to the Reformation. The last Catholic bishop, Jón Arason, was beheaded in 1550 and the Lutheran Church was established. Even though today's Iceland is Lutheran, Arason is a national hero because he resisted the Danes.

By the 1600s, Denmark had established a trade monopoly with Iceland, and Iceland became little more than a Danish colony. Accordingly, the 17th and 18th centuries are now considered a dark period in Iceland's history, a time when it lost its self-government and free trade. This period had a profound influence on later political developments and is one reason why Icelanders are very nationalistic. It is also why Iceland is usually among the first nations to recognize new countries. Iceland was first to recognize the independence of Latvia, Lithuania, and Estonia in 1991.

The 18th century brought famine and economic troubles, but an independence movement did not really begin until the 1800s, when the people experienced a revival of national literature and history. When Denmark's monarchy became subject to a constitutional democracy, Iceland was given an opportunity to regain home rule. A constitution was granted in 1874, but Iceland remained accountable to Denmark.

It was not until 1918 that Iceland became an independent sovereign state under a common Danish king. During World War II, the United States and Great Britain helped defend Iceland, and Iceland's ties with Denmark essentially were broken. The Republic of Iceland was formally declared in June 1944 and a new constitution was adopted. Iceland developed a progressive economy and stable political system. Cooperation between political parties has always been high because nearly all governments have been coalitions, with no one party dominating the *Althingi*. The current government, led by Prime Minister David Oddsson, is a coalition of the conservative Independence and centrist Progressive parties; it retained a majority in May 1999 elections. Oddsson has been prime minister since 1991.

THE PEOPLE

Population. Iceland has a population of more than 276,000 people. The population is growing at nearly 0.6 percent a year. Prior to the 1990s, few people emigrated to other countries. About 109,000 people live in Reykjavík. Kópavogur (23,000) and Hafnarfjörður (19,000) are the next largest towns. The central part of the country is uninhabited. Icelanders are descendants of the Norwegian and Celtic peoples who settled in the ninth and tenth centuries. They are considered a homogeneous people. Small but increasing numbers of immigrants integrate well into the population. Excellent access to health care, education, and economic prosperity affords both men and women a high standard of living and freedom for individual choices.

Language. The official language is Icelandic. Icelanders are, as a minimum, taught Danish from age 10 to 16 and English from age 11 to 16. Those who continue with their education after age 16 receive further instruction in one or both languages. Nearly everyone can speak both of these languages. During the Viking era (8th–10th centuries), all Nordic peoples shared a common language. After that, separate tongues evolved in the areas of present-day Norway, Sweden, and Denmark. Iceland retained the old language, which remained essentially unchanged through the centuries. (In fact, modern Icelandic is more similar to ancient Norwegian than modern Norwegian is.) As a result, Icelanders can read medieval Icelandic *sagas* (stories) from the "Age of Sagas" (1200–1400) with relatively little difficulty. Because of this heritage, Icelanders enjoy tracing their ancestral roots. The *sagas* cover centuries of Scandinavian and British history. Through them, the lives and exploits of the Vikings and peoples that came after them are known to the world today.

Religion. The bulk of the population (more than 90 percent) belongs to the state church, the Evangelical Lutheran Church. Despite the existence of a state-sponsored church, religious freedom is fully guaranteed, and other Christian churches (Roman Catholic, Protestant, and others) have members in Iceland. Two percent of the population has no religious affiliation. Attendance at the state church is sporadic; people usually go to baptisms, confirmations, weddings, funerals, and Christmas mass. But while religion is not a public matter, Icelanders are privately very religious. They have a strong belief in spiritual and supernatural things, and people are quite devout.

General Attitudes. Icelanders are proud of their advanced society, which is egalitarian and highly literate. People's abilities are more important than their station in life. In general, the people are known to be individualistic, independent, and open-minded. They are friendly and genuine but tend to be reserved. There is little crime and very little pollution in the country. Cleanliness is highly valued. Most areas are heated almost entirely by geothermal energy produced naturally by hot springs. A source of pride for Icelanders, geothermal springs provide the country with renewable, clean energy. Icelanders also have a strong work ethic; the country's workweek is one of the longest in Europe. Self-respect and well-being are tied to productivity.

Icelanders have a great love of history, literature, and language. Per capita, Iceland publishes more books than any country in the world. Whereas many languages will adopt or adapt foreign words (often English) into their language to describe a new item or habit, Icelanders want to keep their language as pure as possible. In fact, an official committee exists for the sole purpose of creating new Icelandic words, for terms such as *telephone* or *computer*, when necessary. Doing well in school and finishing one's education is a widely held societal priority.

Personal Appearance. Icelanders dress well, especially when attending theaters and fine restaurants. Because the climate is generally cool, warm clothing is necessary during much of the year. Iceland is known for its woolens, especially sweaters. Dressing neatly in public is important, and most people spend a lot of money on clothing. U.S. American and especially European fashions are popular, particularly among young Icelanders, who like to wear trendy clothing.

CUSTOMS AND COURTESIES

Greetings. A handshake is the normal way to greet someone, along with saying *Sæll* (to a man) or *Sæl* (to a woman). The phrase roughly means "Happy" or "Glad." A more casual greeting for friends and relatives is *Halló* (Hello) or *Hæ* (Hi). One says *Góðan daginn* (Good day) when greeting a stranger. One says *Bless* (To be blessed) or *Bless Bless* to say goodbye. Strangers are often greeted, but not greeting a stranger is not considered impolite.

All Icelanders are properly and officially called by their first name (and sometimes nickname), even though they also have a last name. This is true even for doctors, teachers, politicians, etc. A first name is used after a person's title as well. A woman does not change her name with marriage. A woman's last name is formed by the possessive form of her father's first name, followed by *dóttir*, meaning daughter. A man's last name is the possessive of his father's first name, followed by *son*. Names in a phone book are alphabetized by the first given name, but it is necessary to know the last name as well.

Gestures. Body language traditionally has not been important to communication in Iceland. Consequently, few hand expressions are used during conversation. People don't normally eat on the street, with the exception of foods like ice cream and hot dogs. Smoking is prohibited in public buildings.

Visiting. Icelanders are usually casual about visiting; they commonly drop in on people unannounced or telephone just before visiting. Truly formal invitations are rare. Hosts are expected to invite a visitor in even if he or she has not been invited. Hosts may offer a cup of coffee. Because society is home centered, most social visiting occurs in homes. Due to the cold weather, Icelanders spend a lot of time indoors and devote plenty of time, effort, and money to making their homes pleasant. Indeed, beautification of the home is a lifetime pursuit, and creating a nice atmosphere brings much prestige. Icelandic homes are usually larger and better furnished than the average Scandinavian or European homes, and therefore are natural places for entertaining guests.

Although dinner guests are not expected to bring a gift to the hosts, flowers or candy may be appropriate. Icelanders do not typically introduce their guests to everyone. At the end of a meal, or even refreshments, guests are careful to express their appreciation to the hosts.

Eating. Breakfast is usually a light meal and includes cereal or toast with tea or coffee. Icelanders typically eat lunch around noon and dinner between 7 and 8 p.m. The continental style of eating is followed, with the fork in the left hand and the knife remaining in the right. Dinner is usually the only meal that is shared with the whole family. Icelanders do not eat out often, preferring to go on special occasions or make an evening of it by following food with a movie or play or other activity.

At restaurants, service charges and tax are included in the bill. Before the mid-1970s, going out to eat was not popular and being a waiter or waitress was a demeaning job. Offering a tip was an insult and emphasized the waiter's position as a servant. Consequently, there is no tradition of tipping in Iceland. Since the 1970s, restaurants have increased dramatically in number and waiting tables is fully respectable. Icelanders still do not tip, but the practice would no longer be considered an insult. The increase in restaurants has also led to a wider variety of foods available in the country. Coffeehouses and restaurants serving most European and Scandinavian dishes can be found in Reykjavík.

LIFESTYLE

Family. Family ties are strong and families tend to be larger than other Scandinavian families. Even though people are individualistic, family members rely heavily on each other. Because the country is small, personal ties are important and family relations play a key role. This is evidenced by the tradition of asking "Who are your people?" when meeting someone for the first time. This inquiry is an attempt to place a person in a family or professional level. The initial response is to name one's parents. If they are not known, the parents' professions might be named or the grandparents' names given. Today's youth do not practice this, but their parents' generation still does. Family history is a passion for many people, facilitated by the language having changed so little in the last one thousand years.

Children are expected to do well in school and find good hobbies, such as sports and music. They may live with their parents until they are about 20 to 25 years old. It is popular to send kids aged 8 to 16 to a farm owned by a relative (uncle, aunt, grandparent, etc.) during the summer months while school is out. Grandparents usually live on their own.

More than 80 percent of Icelandic families own their own homes. Family patterns are changing as more women are becoming part of the workforce; close to 90 percent of women have jobs outside the home. In 1983, an all-woman

political party won several seats in Parliament. They hold fewer seats today, but women's issues are addressed more readily than before. Both mothers and fathers share responsibility for household chores, from doing the dishes to painting the house.

Dating and Marriage. Dating begins around age 15 or 16. Going to parties, coffeehouses, and dance clubs are among the most popular activities. Schools and workplaces are also common places for people to find a spouse. The government recognizes common-law marriage, so many couples choose to live together without formal marriage. Some choose to marry at a later date, but they may have a few children by then. Weddings can be large affairs that include serving lunch or dinner. Guests stay at the wedding party for a long time, eating, talking, and perhaps dancing. The newlyweds usually go abroad for their honeymoon.

Diet. The basics of the Icelandic diet include fish, lamb, and dairy products. Fresh fish is plentiful and includes such varieties as cod, haddock, halibut, plaice (a type of flounder), herring, salmon, and trout. Popular dishes are *hangikjöt* (smoked mutton) and *skyr* (similar to yogurt). Potatoes (usually boiled) are served with most meals. *Hangikjöt* is the traditional meal on Christmas day. For many years, greenhouses heated with geothermal water have made it possible for Iceland to service its need for tomatoes, peppers, cucumbers, and other produce. Water is safe to drink and clean throughout the country.

Recreation. Traveling and camping are favorite pastimes in Iceland. Hiking, trout and salmon fishing, swimming in pools heated by natural hot springs, soccer, basketball, handball, skiing, and golf are other common forms of recreation. Snowmobiling and four wheeling are popular year-round. Many enjoy riding the small horses unique to Iceland. Chess is popular. Iceland is known as a bird-watcher's paradise. Merchants Holiday provides a three-day weekend that is popular for camping and travel. Cities practically empty as everyone heads to the countryside, especially the interior, to camp. People try to enjoy the summer as much as possible. There are many large, established campgrounds where people gather. Some also camp in more private areas. Others stay in summer cabins.

The Arts. Iceland's rich cultural life includes the National Theatre, the Iceland Symphony Orchestra, and the Icelandic Ballet Company. These groups often perform works by native composers, playwrights, and choreographers. Government support of cinematic arts has encouraged their success as well. Museums exhibit both modern and folk arts. Annual festivals call attention to traditional arts such as weaving, wood carving, and silversmithing.

Poetry, fiction, and playwriting are very popular. Nobel Prize recipient Halldór Laxness is one of the best-known Icelandic writers. Pop singer Björk, born in Reykjavík, has achieved international success.

Holidays. Public holidays include New Year's Day, Easter (Thursday–Monday), First Day of Summer (usually third Thursday in April), Labor Day (1 May), Ascension Day, Whitsunday and Whitmonday, *Sjómannadagurinn* (Fisherman's day, first Sunday in June), National Day (17 June), Merchants Holiday (first Monday in August), and Christmas (24–26 Dec.). Christmas Eve is the most sacred and important time of Christmas. It is the evening for exchanging gifts and

▼ **EUROPE**

celebrating the birth of Christ. The 25th is a day for the big family meal and visiting, while the 26th is spent relaxing with family and friends or enjoying some form of recreation.

New Year's Eve is extremely popular. Icelanders celebrate with many parties, fireworks, and bonfires. These light up the dark winter night and create excitement throughout the country, as well as attract tourists from around the world. *Bolludagurinn* (Cream Puffs Day, third Monday in February) and Ash Wednesday (third Wednesday in February) are not public holidays but are still important celebrations.

Commerce. Business hours are generally from 9 a.m. to 6 p.m., Monday through Friday; banks and post offices open at 9:15 a.m. and close at 4 and 4:30 p.m., respectively. Many government offices close at 3 p.m. Some businesses stay open until 7 p.m. on Fridays. Saturday's hours depend on the business and season. Stores usually close an hour earlier in the summer. Kiosks or small vending-type shops remain open until 11:30 p.m. Some prices are still regulated by the government. Workers take advantage of a mandatory four- to five-week vacation each year. Working overtime is not as common as it was a few years ago. This is partly due to the fact that Iceland has become a member of the European Economic Area and is subject to European regulation on working hours. July is the most popular month for vacationing because it is warm. Many people also vacation abroad; southern Europe is a favorite destination.

SOCIETY

Government. The Republic of Iceland is divided into 23 counties and 14 independent towns. A president, currently Ólafur Ragnar Grímsson, is head of state. In June 1980, Icelanders selected Vigdís Finnbogadóttir as president—the world's first freely elected female head of state. The prime minister is head of government. Iceland's legislative body, the *Althingi*, is one of the world's oldest parliaments. It has 63 seats, which are shared by five parties. Members are elected to four-year terms by proportional representation. The voting age is 18.

Economy. Fish, the country's most abundant natural resource, is the most important export industry. Even manufacturing efforts tend to focus on the fishing industry; Iceland produces and exports machinery used in fish processing. Almost 12 percent of the population is employed in fishing or fish processing, which accounts for about 75 percent of all export earnings. The government remains opposed to joining the European Union due to concerns about how it would affect fishing rights. Only 1 percent of the land is suitable for cultivation; agriculture (including raising livestock) employs 5 percent of the population. There are many pastures and meadows used for livestock grazing. Sheep and wool are important commodities.

Industrially, Iceland has great potential for geothermal and hydroelectric power and is developing ways to exploit these renewable resources. Aluminum and aluminum smelting have become profitable industries. Other industries include publishing, cement, and diatomite. Some factories are able to use geothermal energy for power. Iceland is one of the most

DEVELOPMENT DATA

Human Dev. Index* rank	5 of 174 countries
Adjusted for women	5 of 143 countries
Real GDP per capita	$25,110
Adult literacy rate	99 percent
Infant mortality rate	4 per 1,000 births
Life expectancy	77 (male); 81 (female)

affluent countries in the world, known for low unemployment rates and strong economic performance. The economy grew by nearly 3 percent in 2000. The majority of Icelanders earn a good income and have access to economic prosperity. The currency is the *króna* (IKr) or plural *krónur*.

Transportation and Communications. Most Icelandic families have at least one car. When teenagers turn 17 they get a driver's license and often purchase a car soon thereafter. In and around Reykjavík, the capital, there is also an excellent bus system. People having fun or drinking over the weekend usually use taxis. School buses operate in the capital and in rural areas, where they go from farm to farm. Iceland has no railroad. Some roads outside the capital are not paved, but most are passable year-round. One cannot travel inland or in certain remote areas in the winter. The communications system is modern and efficient. Iceland has the second highest per capita rate of mobile phone use in Europe. Many Icelanders are proficient with computers, the Internet, and e-mail.

Education. School attendance is compulsory for ages six to sixteen. Every child must know how to swim to graduate from elementary school. Education has always been important. Iceland has the highest percentage of children enrolled in school in the world. A large percentage of youth continue their education through specialized training schools or college preparation schools, which lead to a university education. The University of Iceland is the primary university, but several private universities are being opened. Many people go abroad for advanced degrees.

Health. Icelanders enjoy good health; they have one of the highest life expectancy rates in the world. All citizens have compulsory health coverage through a national system. Dental care is partially paid for by the government, although schoolchildren receive free care. There are no major health problems in the country. Iceland recently sold the medical and genealogical records of all of its citizens to a private medical company as part of a massive research project to find cures for various diseases.

CONTACT INFORMATION

Embassy of the Republic of Iceland, 1156 15th Street NW, Suite 1200, Washington, DC 20005; phone (202) 265-6653; Web site www.iceland.org. Scandinavian Tourist Board, PO Box 4649, Grand Central Station, New York, NY 10163-4649; phone (212) 885-9700; Web site www.goscandinavia.com/main.html.

CultureGrams™
People. The World. You.

1305 North Research Way, Bldg. K
Orem, Utah 84097-6200 USA
1.800.528.6279; 801.705.4250
fax 801.705.4350
www.culturegrams.com

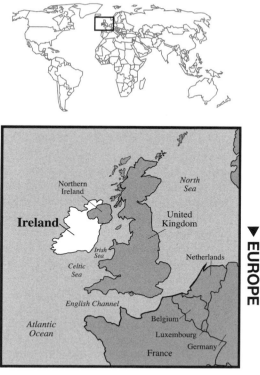

Boundary representations are not necessarily authoritative.

BACKGROUND

Land and Climate. Covering 27,135 square miles (70,280 square kilometers), the Republic of Ireland is somewhat larger than the state of West Virginia. The Republic of Ireland covers five-sixths of the island of Ireland, which is off the northwest coast of Europe. It shares the island with Northern Ireland, which is part of the United Kingdom (UK). Rugged coastal hills and low mountains surround the island's fertile, central plains and numerous lakes and bogs. Some say Ireland is like a badly baked pie—crusty around the edges and soggy in the middle. No part of the country is more than 70 miles (112 kilometers) from the coast. The Shannon is the longest river. Snow falls only on a few days in winter and quickly melts because of the moderating effect of the North Atlantic Current; winters are therefore wet and mild. The coldest temperatures average 30°F to 40°F (-1 to 4°C). Summers are cool; the warmest month of July has an average temperature below 65°F (18°C). Ireland's dampness, fog, and rain make the country lush and green.

History. Although the Irish can trace the history of their island back several thousand years, the period of the Celts offers the most famous historical record and marks the beginning of Ireland's modern history. The Celts conquered the island in the fourth century B.C. Legend has it that St. Patrick came to Ireland in A.D. 432, bringing Christianity and converting the people. Norse Vikings invaded in 795 and established seaports in Ireland. The Norse eventually were defeated in 1014, but then the English began invading in the 12th century. In 1171, King Henry II of England forced Irish nobles to recognize his supreme rule. Over time, though, the English invaders adopted local culture and allowed the Irish

some autonomy. In 1603, England established rule over all of Ireland after defeating the last major Gaelic leaders. Irish Anglicans, supported by England, excluded Catholics from controlling land and politics. In 1801, the United Kingdom of Great Britain and Ireland was established with the Act of Union, but it was not popular with Irish Catholics.

The country was devastated in the 1840s by the great potato famine; at least one million people died in five years and another two million emigrated to other countries, particularly the United States. Political conflict intensified after the famine, bringing rebellions and agitation for independence. The movement climaxed in 1921 with the signing of the Anglo-Irish Treaty. This treaty established the Irish Free State as a British dominion and allowed six northern counties (with a Protestant majority) to remain in the UK as Northern Ireland.

Under a new constitution in 1937, The Irish Free State changed its name to Ireland (*Éire*). The country began to decrease its association with the British Commonwealth. In 1949, Ireland formally withdrew from the Commonwealth and declared itself completely independent. The six northern counties remained part of the UK.

Many Irish have often sought the union of Northern Ireland and Ireland, but talks over the years have not been fruitful. The issue has been complicated by significant violence initiated by vocal and violent minorities who favor the use of violence to support or oppose unification. Militant forces include the Irish Republican Army (IRA), which favors unification, and loyalist Protestant paramilitary groups who oppose it. Nationalist and Unionist groups have opposing views, but as the vast majority they favor peaceful means of reaching agreement. Very few people actually support the agendas of the violent minorities.

Talks in the 1990s opened and repeatedly failed. When the IRA finally called a cease-fire in 1994, the gesture was soon returned by loyalist militias. Encouraged by this, Great Britain, Ireland, and some Northern Ireland leaders pressed forward with a peace plan. By 1995, all-party talks on the issue of power sharing between Northern Ireland political/religious groups were met with optimism on all sides. However, talks stalled, and in February 1996 the IRA broke its 17-month cease-fire.

In June 1996, former U.S. Senator George Mitchell led efforts to revive the talks, despite sporadic violence. In April 1998, eight political parties and the British and Irish governments were able to reach agreement on a historic peace accord. The Good Friday Agreement called for the creation of a Northern Ireland Assembly and cabinet-style administration, with power to govern local matters in Northern Ireland; a North-South Ministerial Council for joint policymaking between Belfast and Dublin; and a British-Irish Council for summit-level meetings. Ireland also agreed to give up constitutional claims to Northern Ireland. Seventy-one percent of voters in Northern Ireland and 94 percent in Ireland supported the accord in a June 1998 referenda.

Although sectarian violence in Northern Ireland complicated matters, many remained hopeful for peace. However, ongoing negotiations to form the new assembly's cabinet failed after a final 30 June 1999 deadline because of a dispute over IRA disarmament, which Unionists want started before Sinn Féin begins sharing executive power. A last-ditch attempt to devolve power led to a Unionist boycott of the Assembly session where leaders would have been nominated. Beginning in 1999, the Northern Ireland Assembly operated for 10 weeks in a joint sharing of power between Catholics and Protestants but was suspended because of conflict over disarming the IRA. The Assembly later resumed operation following a pledge from the IRA to put their weapons in arms dumps subject to verification by international inspectors. Continued violence, IRA and paramilitary disarmament, and other issues complicate chances for lasting peace. Despite the setbacks, negotiators continue their work in the hope that the Good Friday Agreement may yet be salvaged.

In March 2001, the first case of the highly contagious foot-and-mouth disease, which began in the UK, was discovered among Ireland's livestock. As in other European countries, Ireland is trying to stop the spread of the disease through testing, banning the transport of animals and animal products, and killing infected livestock.

THE PEOPLE

Population. Ireland's population is nearly 3.8 million and growing at 1.2 percent. Emigration tends to increase or decrease population growth more than the natural birthrate does. Many people are returning to Ireland from the United States or the UK to secure employment. Conversely, more than 20,000 people a year are emigrating from Ireland, principally to Britain, the United States, and Australia. Nearly one in four people lives in the metropolitan Dublin area. Overall, almost 60 percent of the population lives in urban areas. Ethnically, the people of Ireland are Celtic. There is also a strong Norman influence and a small English (Anglo-Irish)

minority. There is an increasing non-European minority.

Language. The Irish-Gaelic language (also known as Irish) is the first officially recognized language. Its usage is limited, but increasingly popular. It is spoken on a daily basis in Gaeltacht areas and in parts of Meath and Cork. English, recognized as Ireland's second language, is spoken by everyone. Government documents and road signs are in both languages, and Gaelic is required in schools. Ireland has an all-Irish programming television station. The government wants to increase fluency in the primary language.

Religion. About 92 percent of the population is Roman Catholic. Three percent belongs to the Anglican Church. The remaining 5 percent holds various other beliefs—both Christian and non-Christian—or has no religious affiliation. The Catholic Church has played an important role in Ireland's cultural and political history, and continues to shape the values of the people and laws of the land. For instance, the constitutional ban on abortion (and previously divorce, until 1995) remains in effect largely due to efforts of the Catholic Church. Despite Catholicism's dominance, freedom of religion is guaranteed.

General Attitudes. The Irish are easygoing, lighthearted, good-humored, polite, and cheerful. They are quick-witted and have the ability to laugh at themselves. A general attitude that things will work out in the end affects their daily lives. The pace of life is somewhat influenced by the old maxim "God gave us time and he gave us plenty." Traditions are important and material goods do not have the same priority as in the United States. Still, some groups are calling for social and political liberalization, including greater tolerance for nontraditional lifestyles.

Traditional Irish values include having a good education and a secure job, owning a home, and possessing a good sense of humor. Individualism is admired but aggressiveness, arrogance, and fanaticism are not. The Irish avoid personal confrontation; they rarely say "no" to a person's face but communicate it in a different way. Most Irish resent outside criticism of their society or politics, preferring to be the only ones openly critical of themselves. Ireland is politically neutral.

Some people wonder what differences exist between the people of Ireland and those in Northern Ireland. Because both nations share a common cultural heritage, much is similar. The differences that do exist have their roots in centuries-old conflicts over exploitation, political affiliation, and religion.

Personal Appearance. European fashions are most common, although traditional Irish styles influence those fashions. For example, earth tones and warm colors are more popular. Sweaters and other woolen items are common because of the cooler climate. Fine-quality tweeds and linens are produced in Ireland. Casual dress is acceptable in most situations, but attire worn in public is generally conservative. Light rainwear is necessary for anyone living or traveling in Ireland.

CUSTOMS AND COURTESIES

Greetings. The Irish may shake hands when being introduced. Greetings vary by locale and ancient tribal tradition. English phrases such as *Hello* and *How are you?* are used throughout the country. Depending on the situation, they may say *Good morning*, *Good evening*, *Hello*, and so on. The most typical Irish-language greeting is *Dia Dhuit* (God to you), to which the response is *Dia is Muire duit!* (God and Mary to you!). *Slan* (meaning "safe") is used for good-bye. The more formal phrase is *Slan agus Beannacht.*

When addressing friends, relatives, and acquaintances, the Irish generally use first names. However, titles (*Mr.*, *Mrs.*, *Ms.*, *Miss*, *Dr.*) and last names are used formally or with persons of higher status. Rural Irish greet each other when passing on the street, even if not acquainted, but urban residents reserve such greetings for neighbors and people they know.

Gestures. The Irish do not use hand gestures excessively during conversation, but they do not keep hands entirely still—some gesticulation is common.

The Irish value politeness and generally do not push (even if in a hurry), eat on the street (or on the run), comb hair in public, or otherwise offend those around them. If one breaches social norms, apologies are usually in order.

Visiting. The Irish are warm and hospitable. People often invite others, particularly families, to their home for dinner. *Calling by* (visiting) is a common custom. It stems from the tradition of gathering groups of people together by going from house-to-house. In rural areas, stays are usually longer and more informal. Guests are always offered tea or coffee. If it is *teatime* (dinnertime), visitors are invited to stay for dinner.

People like to get out and gather for conversation in *pubs* (public houses). Some say conversation is the national pastime. Many *pubs* feature folk music as entertainment. Visiting in the home takes place during holidays, especially between Christmas and New Year's Day. Parties are also popular during holidays. It is polite to take a gift to someone if overnight accommodations are provided.

Eating. The Irish eat three meals a day, with the main meal either at midday (if a family's schedule allows) or supper. When possible, families sit down together for their meals. Supper often is served later in the evening. The Irish eat in the continental style, with the fork in the left hand and the knife remaining in the right.

Traditional Irish dishes are hearty, simple, and delicious. In addition to Irish cuisine, European dishes are popular. Many types of restaurants, including U.S. fast food, are found in Ireland. "Farmhouse" restaurants feature traditional recipes. *Tea kitchens* serve hot drinks and homemade cakes and pastries in the afternoon. Tipping is not customary.

LIFESTYLE

Family. Family cohesiveness in Ireland is very important. Extended families often live near one another. When work or study takes members to distant parts of Ireland or to other countries, they make great efforts to return home for family celebrations—especially Christmas.

The average family has two or three children. Irish women stay at home to care for the children and household more often than do women in some other countries. Still, many younger women are becoming career oriented, and some 32 percent of the workforce is comprised of women. Competitive salaries and support services for women lag behind those for men. But Ireland's president presses her agenda for greater women's equality.

Although many young families rent an apartment (*flat*) or house, most eventually own a home. In fact, home ownership is high in Ireland. Houses usually are constructed of brick or concrete. Traditional thatched cottages can still be seen in some western areas, but these are no longer built today. Many families also have resort homes or chalets for summer vacations.

Dating and Marriage. While couples commonly married in their late twenties or later during the 1960s and 1970s, some are now marrying in their early twenties. This may be due to the fact that young people begin dating at an earlier age. Teenagers enjoy going to movies and dancing. The tradition of taking a special date to the graduation ball (similar to the prom in the United States) has developed in the last decade. *Debs* (graduation balls) call for formal suits and dresses, a large meal, and a dance at a local hotel. Going to *pubs* is a popular social activity for people of all ages. *Pubs*, which serve more than alcohol, are open to those under drinking age and are prized for their food and atmosphere.

Most weddings are performed in a church and are automatically accepted as legal, but some also are performed in a registry office. Until 1995, Ireland's constitution prohibited divorce. The Irish traditionally had supported the ban due to influence of the Catholic Church. Efforts to lift the ban arose in the 1980s but did not succeed, and controversial debate between liberals and conservatives continued in the 1990s. Government efforts led to a national referendum in November 1995, in which voters chose to legalize divorce by a margin of 1 percent. The current law permits Irish couples to divorce after four years of separation.

Diet. As an agricultural country, Ireland produces many fresh vegetables. Fresh dairy products, breads, and seafood are also widely available. Potatoes are a staple food. A wide variety of fruits have become available since Ireland joined the European Union (EU). Smoked salmon is considered an Irish specialty, as are Irish stew and Irish lamb. Other local delicacies include *crubeens* (pig feet) and *colcannon* (a cooked mixture of potatoes and cabbage). Tea is the most common drink. Breakfasts usually are large, including such foods as bacon and eggs. The main meats eaten for dinner include chicken, pork, beef, and lamb.

Recreation. The Irish are sports oriented, and most weekends include some sporting activities for the family or individual. Popular sports include the two national pastimes: *Gaelic football* and *hurling* (the women's version of hurling is called *camogie*). *Hurling* is played on a soccer-type field with wooden sticks and a small leather ball. *Gaelic football* is played with a round ball and seems like a cross between soccer and basketball. Players can touch the ball with their hands, but they cannot pick it up from the ground. The ball is punched, not thrown, and it can be kicked. Teams score for getting the ball into a soccer-type net but can also make points for putting it over the top of the goal. Soccer, rugby, sailing, cycling, golf, and horse racing are also favorite activities. Fishing is also a common recreational activity, featuring mainly trout and salmon fishing.

The Arts. Literature is a major part of Irish culture, and the country has produced many distinguished writers, such as Jonathan Swift, George Bernard Shaw, Oscar Wilde, and James Joyce. Irish literature is written in Irish and English. Much traditional folklore is in Irish and records genealogy or tells stories of patron saints, ghosts, and fairies.

Ireland's music tradition is thousands of years old. When the native language was outlawed, history was transmitted by song. Traditional music, often blended with contemporary forms, is popular around the world. Common instruments are bongos, lutes, flutes, bagpipes, fiddles, button accordions, concertinas, harps, bodhráns, and penny whistles.

▼ EUROPE

Many Irish people enjoy participating in events or clubs that focus on the arts. They also enjoy handicrafts such as knitting and embroidery.

Holidays. The main public holidays in Ireland are New Year's Day, St. Patrick's Day (17 Mar.), Easter (Friday–Monday), Labour Day (1 May), the bank holidays (the first Monday in both June and August, and the last Monday in October), Christmas, and St. Stephen's Day (26 Dec.). St. Patrick's Day features street parades in every city, but the largest is in Dublin. In honor of St. Patrick, Ireland's patron saint, the Irish wear a shamrock and have banquets. However, some U.S. Americans celebrate the day more fervently than the Irish. Christmas is the main family and social celebration. Families return home to share a traditional meal of turkey and ham. It is a popular time for the wealthy to take a "sun" holiday in a warmer climate.

Commerce. Generally, business and banking hours are from 9 a.m. to 5 p.m., with an hour break for lunch in all but the major cities. Shopping centers remain open until 9 p.m. on Thursday and Friday evenings. Most people buy basic goods from shopping centers, which have replaced the more traditional corner shops and open markets.

SOCIETY

Government. The Irish republic is headed by a popularly elected president who serves a seven-year term. The president, Mary McAleese, was elected in November 1997. She replaced Mary Robinson (now UN High Commissioner for Human Rights). The president has only a few executive powers but can exercise considerable influence on national politics. A prime minister serves as head of government. The cabinet is drawn from members of Parliament. The current prime minister, Bertie Ahern, took office after parliamentary elections in June 1997. Ahern leads a minority coalition government composed of his Fianna Fáil Party and the Progressive Democrats.

The bicameral legislature is structured to provide both vocational and proportional representation. All members of the 166-seat House of Representatives (*Dáil Éireann*) are directly elected. Of the Senate's 60 members, 49 are indirectly elected and the rest are appointed. All citizens may vote at age 18. Parliamentary elections are held at least every five years. Ireland has 26 counties. Many people in Ireland refer to Northern Ireland as the "six counties."

Economy. Ireland has a small, but rapidly growing, open economy. In recent years, the government has been able to drastically reduce inflation, encourage more exports, and attract foreign investment, especially from high-tech companies. The economy grew by 11 percent in 2000 and inflation was around 5 percent. Ireland relies heavily on trade, especially with nations of the EU. Unemployment is high. Most people enjoy good access to economic prosperity, education, and health care needed to make choices in their lives.

While agriculture was once the main sector of the economy, only 15 percent of the population is now employed in it. Instead, a diversified economy now relies more heavily on the technology sector, as well as industry, including textiles, chemicals, and machinery. In agriculture, animal husbandry

DEVELOPMENT DATA

Human Dev. Index* rank	18 of 174 countries
Adjusted for women	18 of 143 countries
Real GDP per capita	$21,482
Adult literacy rate	99 percent
Infant mortality rate	6 per 1,000 births
Life expectancy	74 (male); 79 (female)

and dairy farming are important. Key crops include potatoes, sugar beets, turnips, barley, and wheat. Ireland is generally self-sufficient in foodstuffs, although fruits and some other items must be imported. Tourism is a large and growing sector of the economy. The currency is the *punt* (IR£).

Transportation and Communications. Buses (single- and double-decker) are the most common form of public transportation. They are efficient within and between cities. Taxis are expensive and not regulated by the government. Irish rail systems provide links to major cities. Nearly all roads are paved and in good condition; however, the highway and commuter infrastructure is seriously inadequate. Most families have at least one car. Vehicles travel on the left side of the road. Although the communications system is small, it is modern and efficient. There are several radio and television stations in Ireland. A variety of daily newspapers are published throughout the country.

Education. The Irish constitution recognizes that parents have the freedom to provide for the education of their children, either in their own homes, in private schools, or in schools established by the state. Schooling is compulsory between ages four and fifteen, and about two-thirds of all children are still in school full-time at age sixteen. The government provides free education in primary and secondary schools and gives substantial aid to institutions of post-secondary education. University education is free.

Local boards composed of parent representatives, teaching staff, and relevant religious authorities manage primary schools. To be accepted as a pupil in secondary school, a child must be at least 12 years old and have completed primary education. Following secondary school, one may attend vocational or technical colleges, or a university if one passes proper examinations.

Health. Ireland's population is generally healthy. Well-equipped public medical clinics are located throughout Ireland. Care in public hospitals is provided at government cost. Many people choose to go to private doctors and facilities to avoid the waiting lists and other inconveniences of the public system. Long-term medical services are free to persons with infectious diseases and to children suffering from certain conditions.

CONTACT INFORMATION

Embassy of Ireland, 2234 Massachusetts Avenue NW, Washington, DC 20008; phone (202) 462-3939; Web site www.irelandemb.org. Irish Tourist Board, 345 Park Avenue, 17th Floor, New York, NY 10154-0004; phone (800) 223-6470; Web site www.ireland.travel.ie/home.

1305 North Research Way, Bldg. K
Orem, Utah 84097-6200 USA
1.800.528.6279; 801.705.4250
fax 801.705.4350
www.culturegrams.com

Boundary representations are not necessarily authoritative.

BACKGROUND

Land and Climate. Italy, including the islands of Sardinia and Sicily, covers 116,305 square miles (301,230 square kilometers) and is slightly larger than Arizona. It boasts a variety of natural landscapes: from the Alpine mountains in the north to the Mediterranean climate of coastal lowlands in the south. Shaped like a boot, the country is generally mountainous. The Italian Alps run along the northern border and the Apennines form a spine down the peninsula. Sicily and Sardinia are also rocky or mountainous. The "heel" and some coastal areas are flat. The Po River basin to the north holds some of Italy's richest farmland and most of its heavy industry. Southern agricultural areas are subject to droughts. The climate is temperate but varies by region. Winters are cold and rainy in the north, cool around Rome, and mild in the south. Summers are moderately hot but can be very hot in the south (up to 104°F or 40°C).

Italy surrounds two independent nations: San Marino and Vatican City (Holy See). San Marino has been independent since the fourth century. As part of the Papal States, Vatican City was protected by France in the 19th century. It was occupied by Italy in 1870 but recognized as the sovereign State of Vatican City in 1922.

History. Much of the West's civilization and culture comes from the Italian Peninsula. The area's history dates back several thousand years, but one of the first civilizations to flourish was that of the Etruscans between the eighth and second centuries B.C. They influenced mostly central Italy and later the Roman Empire. Before the Romans became prominent, Greek civilization dominated the south. Rome later adopted much of the Greek culture and became a major power

after 300 B.C. as it expanded throughout the Mediterranean region. By the fifth century A.D., the western Roman Empire had fallen to a number of invasions. The peninsula was then divided into several separate political regions. In addition to local rulers, French, Spanish, and Austrian leaders governed various parts of Italy. The Italian Peninsula was the center of many artistic, cultural, and architectural revolutions, including the great Renaissance of the 15th and 16th centuries.

Risorgimento, the Italian unification movement, began in the 1800s. National unification was declared in 1861 by the first Italian Parliament in Turin. Victor Emmanuel II was named king and the inclusion of Rome in 1870 completed unification.

Italy experienced a fascist dictatorship under Benito Mussolini from 1922 to 1943 and initially aided Germany's Hitler in World War II. In 1943, the fascists were overthrown and Italy supported the Allies. Italy established itself as a republic in the 1946 elections, officially abolishing the monarchy by national referendum. Political violence and terrorism marked the 1970s. Conflicts within the coalition governments led to frequent government collapses during the 1980s. Political changes in Eastern Europe led Italy's powerful Communist Party to change its name and structure to maintain voter loyalty.

Elections in April 1992 hurt the ruling coalition but failed to bring a strong government to power. The proportional system of voting, originally designed to prevent totalitarianism, was blamed for consistently bringing weak coalitions to power. On its 16th vote in May 1992, Parliament finally chose Oscar Luigi Scalfaro, a Christian Democrat, as president.

The country was soon rocked by dozens of political scandals. Numerous top officials resigned, including the prime minister, and charges of past corruption became even more widespread. By 1994, six thousand individuals were under investigation for corruption.

Political instability continued with successive governments. Silvio Berlusconi became prime minister in May, only to have his government fall in December 1994. Scalfaro named Treasury Minister Lamberto Dini, a member of no political party, prime minister in January 1995. Dini's caretaker government pressed ahead with fiscal and other reforms until it fell in December 1995.

Wanting a clean and workable government, voters in the April 1996 elections brought economist Romano Prodi of the Democrats of the Left (formerly the Italian Communist Party) to power as prime minister. Despite various setbacks, Prodi's Olive Tree coalition remained in office more than two years, making it Italy's second longest-lasting government since World War II. The government enjoyed broad support (70 percent) for joining the euro, Europe's single currency, and Prodi aggressively pursued economic reforms needed to qualify for the European Monetary Union. In October 1998, Prodi lost a no-confidence vote by one vote when the Communist Refoundation Party withdrew its support over the proposed 1999 budget. A new center-left coalition was formed with Massimo D'Alema as prime minister. However, D'Alema's coalition collapsed after 18 months because of his inability to push through political and constitutional reforms and his failure to get Italy's sluggish economy on track. President Carlo Azeglio Ciampi, who was elected in May 1999, appointed former treasury minister Giuliano Amato as prime minister. In May 2001, billionare Silvio Berlusconi became Italy's new prime minister after his center-right coalition won in general elections. His government is the 58th since World War II. Attempts to stabilize Italy's tricky coalition politics have been unsuccessful.

THE PEOPLE

Population. Italy's population is about 57.6 million and not growing. Most people are ethnic Italians, but there are small groups of ethnic Germans, French, and Slovenes, as well as Albanian-Italians and Greek-Italians. Although traditionally a country of emigrants, Italy has experienced a large influx of immigrants in the last two decades. Italians' access to health care, education, and economic prosperity affords them many choices.

Language. Italian is the official language, although dialects differ from city to city. The Florentine and Roman dialects had a major influence on modern Italian. Most youth also speak English, the most common second language, while older generations prefer to speak French. There are significant French-, German-, and Slovene-speaking minorities. An ethnic minority in southern Tyrol speaks Ladin.

Religion. Nearly all Italians are Roman Catholic, although many neglect religious devotion. Attendance at services is not high, and secularism is more appealing to many segments of society. At the same time, many Catholics are finding alternate ways to worship (through pilgrimages, informal gatherings, praying at shrines, and so forth). However, the Catholic Church does wield significant social and even political influence in Italy. Vatican City, home of the Roman Catholic pope and headquarters for the Roman Catholic Church, is located within Rome.

General Attitudes. Due to improved economic and social conditions in southern regions and the influence of the media, differences between northern and southern Italians are diminishing. However, Italians still refer to one another by their city of origin (Milanese, Roman, Florentine, etc.) and some regional attitudes remain. Adopting practices of their German and Austrian neighbors, people in the industrialized north traditionally value punctuality, reliability, organization, and economic success. They often feel more pressure and view time as a resource not to be wasted. They take pride in having a low tolerance for high levels of criminality and public corruption. Southerners are appreciated for their warm character and friendliness. They enjoy a leisurely life and take their time doing business. Family values prevail in the south and are often more appreciated than economic success.

Regional economic differences have led to tensions within the country. Many in the more prosperous north feel they are too heavily taxed to subsidize special projects in the south. Those in the south often resent the higher incomes and better employment rates of the north. Political movements calling for more regional autonomy in a federal system have gained some momentum, particularly in the north. However, most Italians still oppose a political separation.

Italians consider social life and interaction very important; they try not to miss social events such as parties and celebrations. People desire a good reputation in their social circle and seek approval from their peers. Often the ability to influence others is associated with how well one can accommodate different interests or points of view. Humor, agreeability, reliability, and success in business and social life are regarded more favorably than individual assertiveness. Italians value their health, family, serenity, and financial security.

Personal Appearance. Italians take care of their appearance and tend to dress up, even for an evening stroll. They seldom wear worn, dirty, or sloppy clothing. Although attitudes vary among the youth, many people base their opinions of others on how they dress. Italy is a major center of the European fashion industry. Youth throughout the country follow the latest fashion trends. Older women generally wear dresses.

CUSTOMS AND COURTESIES

Greetings. Men and women greet each other by shaking hands. In groups, Italians avoid crossing other people's handshakes. If a person's hand is dirty, he or she may offer a forearm, a finger, or a simple apology instead. When a man and a woman are introduced to each other, the man waits for the woman to extend her hand first. Close friends often greet each other with a hug or with a kiss on both cheeks. Actually, they touch cheeks and "kiss the air." Except in southern Italy, the kiss on both cheeks between men is reserved for family members. Friends and family members say *Ciao* (Hi or Good-bye) as an informal greeting. Other terms include *Buongiorno* (Good morning) and *Buonasera* (Good afternoon or Good evening). Persons of the same gender often walk arm in arm in public.

Gestures. Italians are known for their use of hand gestures during conversation, especially in the south. In fact, they often communicate with their hands instead of words. A common gesture is rubbing the thumb rapidly against the fingers to indicate "money." A finger placed under the eye and pushed down slightly on the skin says someone is smart or clever. In some areas of the south, a person might indicate "no" by nodding the head upward. Gestures are so numerous that there is actually a dictionary of Italian gestures. Men remove their hats when entering buildings. Removing one's shoes in the presence of others is impolite. One covers the mouth when yawning or sneezing.

Visiting.   As a people inclined to long friendships, Italians enjoy visiting one another, especially on holidays and Sundays. In urban areas, visits are usually planned due to busy schedules. In villages, people are used to unannounced visits by friends and neighbors. Hosts might offer their guests coffee, cake, ice cream, or drinks. Dinner guests often bring a bottle of good wine, a box of chocolates, or flowers (in odd numbers) as a gift for the hosts. In the south, guests often wait for the hosts to sit before they are seated and to begin eating before they eat. At the end of the meal, southern guests may leave some food on the plate if they have been served more generous portions. Guests wait for the host to offer second or third helpings.

If visiting before supper, guests generally are expected to stay for the meal. Not staying may be considered impolite, especially in the south. In the evening before supper or on holidays, Italians enjoy taking a walk in town.

Eating.   Italians eat in the continental style, with the fork in the left hand and the knife remaining in the right. Hands are kept above the table; placing them in the lap is improper. When finished eating, a person places the utensils parallel on the plate. One does not leave the table until everyone has finished.

Although Italian families traditionally eat lunch together, this custom is disappearing, especially in large cities. Most families at least try to get together for supper (often around 7–8 p.m. in the north or 8:30–9:30 p.m. in the south). When eating with guests, Italians usually do not hurry; a meal may last one to four hours. Regular family meals are much shorter. Dinner conversation often includes soccer, politics, family matters, business, and local events. Hosts appreciate compliments on the home and meal. Guests do not volunteer to help clean up. At restaurants, the bill often includes a service charge, but leaving a small tip for the waiter is also appropriate.

LIFESTYLE

Family.   Italians enjoy strong ties and, when being together or helping each other is possible, they honor their family obligations. Parents are willing to help their children, even as adults, when necessary. Many parents will help their children buy a home or pay for an apartment—even if it means significant financial sacrifice. Grandparents frequently help with child care. Single adult children tend to live with their parents, even into their thirties. Most families in the north live as nuclear units, and the average family has one or two children. Southern families are traditionally larger, and many generations often live in the same town or house. Extended families throughout the country get together often and frequently live near each other, although there is some indication that this is changing. Urban dwellers generally reside in apartments; houses are common in suburbs and rural areas. The divorce rate is growing and the marriage rate is slowing because more couples are living together instead of marrying (especially in northern Italy). In the more traditional South, single parents are no longer rare exceptions and are becoming more accepted.

Dating and Marriage.   As in other Western countries, Italians date either in groups or as couples. Dancing and going to movies are frequent activities. Women usually marry by age 26, while the average age for men is 29. A man will rarely marry before he has finished his education and found employment. Therefore, engagements can last several years. Some couples live together before marrying. Marriage ceremonies most often follow Catholic traditions. Divorce is granted only after three or more years of legal separation.

Diet.   An Italian breakfast traditionally is light, consisting of a cup of coffee or cappuccino (warm milk for children) and a *cornetto* (cream-filled croissant) or bread with jam or honey. However, with fewer people eating the main meal at midday, heavier breakfasts are becoming common. The main meal, whether lunch or dinner, traditionally includes three courses: pasta, fish or meat, and vegetables. In the north, pasta or rice is part of every main meal. Pasta is dominant in the south. A simple salad (lettuce and tomatoes) is served with the second course (meat dish). The standard salad dressing contains olive oil and vinegar, but not spices. Wine commonly accompanies meals and also is used widely in cooking. *Pomodoro* (tomato sauce) and *ragù* (sauce with meat) are popular with various types of pasta. Veal is a favorite meat. Italian pizza is not the same as U.S. American pizza and differs from region to region. Contrary to popular belief in North America, spaghetti and meatballs is not a typical Italian meal. While some pasta sauces have small amounts of meat in them, Italians usually eat the main meat dish after the pasta course. Italians enjoy literally hundreds of different cheeses, including mozzarella and Parmesan.

Recreation.   For recreation, Italians go to the beach, countryside, movies, dances, or sport events. Soccer is by far the most popular sport. Avid fans follow the World Cup competition, which Italy's national soccer team has won three times. Bicycling, horse racing, skiing, tennis, boxing, fencing, swimming, and track-and-field are also popular.

During the day, Italians often go to bars to socialize. Bars, which are more like coffee shops, have a light, open atmosphere and serve both coffee and drinks.

The Arts.   Italy has been a birthplace and center of the arts for centuries, shaping art movements throughout Europe and the world. The Renaissance began in Italy. Some of the greatest Western painters, architects, and sculptors are from Italy, including Giotto, Donatello, Michelangelo, Raphael, da Vinci, Titian, Bernini, Carravagio, and Modigliani. The Romans also played a key role in the development of Western architecture, using techniques such as the arch, dome, and vault to build larger, more structurally sound buildings. Museums in Italian cities such as Florence, Naples, Rome, and Venice house internationally renowned art collections.

In music, Italians invented opera, musical notation, and the piano. Well-known Italian composers include Vivaldi, Puccini, Rossini, and Verdi. Opera is highly regarded, and opera houses are found in many towns. Music festivals are popular as well.

Italy has also made significant contributions to world literature. Dante, Petrarch, and Boccaccio are three of the

▼ EUROPE

most influential. In film, Italian actors and directors have achieved international recognition.

Traditional folk arts also are practiced. The tarantella, a famous dance, is perfomed at many celebrations.

Holidays. Religious and national holidays include New Year's Day; Epiphany (6 Jan.); Easter (including Easter Monday); Liberation Day (25 Apr.), which commemorates Italy's liberation in World War II; Labor Day (1 May); the Anniversary of the Republic (2 June); the Assumption of the Virgin Mary (15 Aug.); All Saints' Day (1 Nov.); Immaculate Conception (8 Dec.); Christmas; and St. Stephen's Day (26 Dec.). Nearly every city and town honors the local patron saint with an annual celebration, and various other festivals also are held throughout the year.

Commerce. The work schedule is from 8 or 9 a.m. to 1 p.m. and from 3 to 6 or 7 p.m., Monday through Friday. Government offices close by 2 p.m. Many Italians work six days a week. Grocery stores close one afternoon of the week, and barber shops close on Mondays. However, new super-stores that sell everything from car stereos to fresh produce are open from 9 a.m. to 9 p.m. every day of the week. Many small stores are disappearing because of the competition. Businesses generally are closed on Sunday.

SOCIETY

Government. The Italian Republic is divided into 20 regions. Some regions favor a more federal system of government that would give them increased autonomy from the central government in Rome. Italy's president is chief of state, while the prime minister is head of government. The prime minister is usually the head of a majority party or a majority coalition of parties but can also be appointed from other parties. In all cases, a proposed prime minister must be approved by a parliamentary vote of confidence. Prime ministers can be removed from office at any time if Parliament passes a vote of no confidence.

Italy's upper legislative chamber is the 326-seat Senate. Eleven senators are appointed for life by the president and the others are elected to seven-year terms. The 630 members of Italy's Chamber of Deputies also hold office for seven years unless Parliament is dissolved early for new elections. Citizens may vote in senatorial elections at age 25. The voting age for all other elections is 18.

Because numerous parties often hold seats in Parliament, it is difficult for one party to gain a majority. Coalitions are usually necessary but often fall apart during disputes, power struggles, or scandals. Parties usually are grouped as rightists, centrists, and leftists when forming coalitions, although some coalitions have been between opposing forces.

Economy. Italy's economy is based on agriculture in the south and industry in the north. Small- and medium-sized businesses in the north are a strong driving force in the economy. Agriculture employs less than 10 percent of the labor force, but agricultural products are important and allow Italy to be nearly self-sufficient in food production. Italy is one of the world's largest wine producers and a major producer of

DEVELOPMENT DATA

Human Dev. Index* rank	19 of 174 countries
Adjusted for women	19 of 143 countries
Real GDP per capita	$20,585
Adult literacy rate	98 percent
Infant mortality rate	6 per 1,000 births
Life expectancy	76 (male); 82 (female)

cheese. Other important crops include wheat, potatoes, corn, rice, fruits, and olive oil. Italy is a major steel and iron producer; industry accounts for more than one-third of the gross national product. Tourism is also a vital source of revenue.

Having made considerable progress in reducing the government deficit, Italy was granted membership in the European Monetary Union in May 1999. However, continued fiscal discipline is needed to reduce Italy's public debt and overcome high unemployment (more than 11 percent nationwide but particularly high in the south). Strict budgets have slowed economic growth to almost 3 percent in 2000. Inflation is low. Most people enjoy a standard of living consistent with Italy's position as one of the world's seven major industrialized countries. The currency is the Italian *lira* (Lit).

Transportation and Communications. Buses and trains, the principal means of public transportation, are punctual and inexpensive but not always adequate to meet the needs of commuters. Subways operate in Milan, Naples, and Rome. Most households have at least one car. A domestic air system flies between major cities. People and goods are also transported on the seas surrounding Italy. The communications system is modern and extensive but not always well maintained. Mail delivery is also unreliable at times. Cellular phones are common; there are more cell phones in Italy than telephone lines. Numerous radio and television stations broadcast on a regional basis, and Italians have access to many daily newspapers.

Education. School attendance is compulsory from ages six to fourteen. Classes are held Monday through Saturday. Education is a serious matter, and most young people spend a great deal of time doing homework. The adult literacy rate is somewhat lower in the south. The oldest university in Europe was founded in Bologna in the 12th century. Italy has more than 50 universities and institutes of higher learning.

Health. Health-care services are coordinated through government agencies. Individuals can choose their family physician; the government pays for most services. Private care is also available, but the patient must pay for it. Smoking is common. Only about 10 percent of Italians wear seat belts when driving, although a 1998 law made it mandatory.

CONTACT INFORMATION

Embassy of the Italian Republic, 3000 Whitehaven Street NW, Washington, DC 20008; phone (202) 612-4400; Web site www.italyemb.org. Italian Tourist Board, 630 Fifth Avenue, Suite 1565, New York, NY 10111; phone (212) 245-5618.

1305 North Research Way, Bldg. K
Orem, Utah 84097-6200 USA
1.800.528.6279; 801.705.4250
fax 801.705.4350
www.culturegrams.com

Jamaica

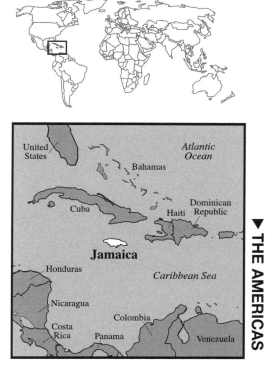

Boundary representations are not necessarily authoritative.

BACKGROUND

Land and Climate.   Jamaica is part of the Greater Antilles, a chain of islands that forms the northern boundary of the Caribbean Sea. Its nearest neighbor is Cuba (about 90 miles to the north). Only 51 miles across at its widest point, Jamaica covers 4,243 square miles (10,989 square kilometers) and is just smaller than Connecticut. Eighty percent of the island is mountainous. Less than 20 percent is suitable for continuous cultivation. Jamaica has a tropical maritime climate, but rainfall varies, depending on the region. The rainy seasons occur in May and October. Hurricanes are possible from June to November. The tropical island climate prevents extreme temperature variations; temperatures generally are 80°F to 90°F (26–32°C) on the northern coast. Jamaica's capital, Kingston, is a large port city.

History.   Jamaica's original inhabitants were the Arawak Indians, who called the island *Xaymaca*, meaning "land of wood and water." Columbus landed on the island in 1494. Because of the harsh life imposed on them by settlers, the Arawaks virtually were decimated within a few decades of Spanish colonization. The Spanish occupied the island until 1655, when it was captured and colonized by the English. By the late 17th century, the English had established sugarcane plantations and were importing large numbers of slaves from Africa. Slavery was abolished in 1838. Some Spaniards stayed in Jamaica, having fled to the hills to fight the British. Over time, the Spanish mixed with the African peoples. Today this small group is called the Maroons, a people that have some political autonomy.

In the 1860s, Jamaica's status was upgraded from colonial possession to British crown colony. During the 1930s, people began calling for self-determination. In 1938, serious social unrest was fomented by long-standing injustices and labor problems. Alexander Bustamante, aided by Norman Manley, championed labor's cause and sparked important social change. The two also formed today's major political parties. A new constitution in 1944 ended rule by the British crown colony government and granted adult suffrage. However, Jamaica remained under nominal British rule until it gained full independence in 1962.

Manley's son Michael headed a socialist government in the 1970s. Severe economic problems led to a 1980 victory for Edward Seaga and his conservative Jamaican Labour Party (JLP), which dominated government throughout the decade. In 1989 and 1993, the socialist People's National Party (PNP) again took control through national elections. Since the 1980 campaign, elections have been marked by fraud and violence, as political parties strive to maintain control over communities known as *garrison constituencies*. However, December 1997 elections largely were spared the level of fraud and violence that had characterized previous races. In those elections the PNP, led by P. J. Patterson, won an unprecedented third term.

In April 1999, violent protests led the government to rescind a proposed gasoline tax hike. The government continues to address the struggling economy and rising crime.

THE PEOPLE

Population.   Jamaica's population of 2.65 million is growing at 0.46 percent annually. The majority of people are Black African (76 percent). Afro-Europeans (15 percent) as well as Afro–East Indians and East Indians (3) comprise significant minorities. The population also includes whites of European descent (3 percent), some Chinese, and other groups. More than half of the population lives in urban areas. Kingston and Montego Bay are the largest and second largest cities, respectively. Because of heavy emigration, nearly as many Jamaicans live outside of Jamaica as on the island. Most expatriates live in England and the eastern United States.

Language. English is the official language of Jamaica. However, the ability to speak and understand Standard English may vary, depending on a person's level of education. *Patois*, an English-based creole with West African retentions, is commonly used in everyday conversation. Jamaican speech, in English or *patois*, has a distinctive rhythmic and melodic quality.

Religion. Most Jamaicans are Christians, and all major denominations are represented on the island. The Anglican Church is the official national church. Anglicans and other Protestants represent about 55 percent of the population. Five percent of the people are Roman Catholic. Jamaicans commonly use the term *Christian* to mean practicing members of a Protestant (often evangelical) church. Religion plays an important role in society through the spiritual values and social opportunities it provides. Church gatherings are particularly popular with rural women. Small groups practice ceremonies and rituals from India, China, and Africa, which have been Jamaicanized from their original roots.

The politico-religious Rastafarian movement originated in Jamaica. Although it is practiced in various forms, adherents generally regard Africa as the promised land and Ethiopia's late ruler Haile Selassie I as "the living God." Many also observe Old Testament laws, including dietary restrictions, and regard marijuana as a sacred herb. While only a small percentage of Jamaicans practice Rastafarianism, it has had a profound impact on Jamaican and Caribbean culture.

Jamaica is home to a long-standing Jewish community, whose first members arrived with Columbus as ship hands to escape the Spanish Inquisition. Jews usually attend services as families, but the vast majority of other churchgoers are women and children. Religious education commonly is included in school curricula. Ecumenism (unity among all churches) comes naturally to Jamaicans.

General Attitudes. Jamaicans like being with people and generally are outgoing. They enjoy lively conversation and often hold strong views. People are warm and hospitable but may be reserved with strangers. It is considered important to be thoughtful, neighborly, and charitable. Selfish or standoffish behavior is looked down upon. Jamaicans have a fairly flexible approach to life. A common, good-natured answer to life's challenges is *No problem, man*, even if there is no solution at hand. Flexibility is also evident in attitudes toward time and schedules. A common phrase is *Soon come*, which can mean anything from five minutes to next week. Events and meetings do not necessarily begin on time, although people are more punctual in urban areas.

Rural Jamaicans appreciate honesty and hard work. Urban Jamaicans are increasingly building a strong professional and cooperative atmosphere for business and work. Financial security, prestige, a home and property, and a motor vehicle are valued possessions.

Personal Appearance. While many Jamaicans reserve the right to dress according to their own tastes, women generally are mindful of "appropriate" dress for themselves and their children. They and their children wear their best clothes to church. Older women and women belonging to some religious sects generally wear skirts or dresses. Professional women wear attractive clothing, much of which is made by local seamstresses. Institutions (banks, insurance companies) may provide employees, particularly women, with uniforms.

Men wear casual Western-style clothing for most occasions. Youth fashions commonly follow U.S. American or music-industry trends and are often brightly colored. On weekends, many young people wear *dance hall* (a popular form of music) outfits, which reflect current trends.

Rastafarians do not cut their hair, wearing it in long dreadlocks. Clothing and accessories worn throughout the island often feature Rastafarian colors (green, red, and gold).

CUSTOMS AND COURTESIES

Greetings. Jamaicans consider it important to recognize and greet others, and to be recognized in return. Greetings range from a nod or bow, to a handshake or a slap on the back, to a kiss—depending on the persons involved and the occasion. People being introduced usually shake hands and say *Good morning*, *Good afternoon*, *Good evening*, or *Good night*. Professional or formal titles (*Mr.*, *Mrs.*, *Miss*) are used with the surname unless people are well acquainted. Children usually refer to adults who are not family members as *Sir*, *Mr.*, *Mrs.*, or *Miss*. Elderly people in rural areas may bow or curtsy when greeting. It is considered rude not to greet someone properly before beginning a conversation or asking a question. Greetings among friends are casual. Friends and acquaintances passing on the road often call out greetings. A common phrase is *Whaapun?* (What's happening?) or *Alright, alright* (as if to bypass asking and responding to "How are you?"). Common parting phrases include *Later*, *Tomorrow then*, *Next time*, and *Me we see you* (I'll see you later).

In casual situations, people often use nicknames. Jamaicans (particularly men) might have many nicknames given them by various friends or groups. The nickname usually refers to a physical trait or station in life. Examples include Fatty (for a fat person; it is a compliment because it indicates life is treating that person well), Whitey (white person; also not an insult, but references to the "blackness" of a Black Jamaican may be considered insulting), or Juicy (man who sells juice on the street). Family members more often call one another by pet name or yard name, which often is a shortened or slightly altered version of a person's given name (Nicky for Nicholas).

Gestures. Jamaicans can be very animated when speaking and tend to use hand gestures to help make a point (especially men who are talking about cricket or politics). People show respect for or approval of shared ideas by touching fists. They emphasize greetings by holding on to an initial handshake, or by touching the person's arm or shoulder. To hail a taxi, one keeps the hand down (rather than holding it above the head) and waves. To get someone's attention, one might say "pssst," clap hands, or tap on a grill or gate of a home. Sucking air through the teeth expresses exasperation or "give me a break."

Traditional social courtesies are common. Men offer seats on a bus to older women, women with young children, or pregnant women. Seated passengers commonly offer to hold packages or children for standing passengers. Men open doors for women in urban areas. Kissing, chewing gum, or combing one's hair are not common in public. Women rarely smoke in public.

Visiting. Informal visits take place at the house gate. Visitors simply knock, ring a buzzer, or otherwise call attention to themselves. Only close friends or relatives of the home's occupants will approach the door before being greeted and invited past the gate. Conversations held on the street are called *meet-and-greet* activities. Visitors inside homes usually are offered a drink and sometimes a meal. Guests often bring their hosts a small gift (fresh produce, garden flowers, a bottle of wine). Families and friends get together often and always enjoy a good laugh. Because telephones traditionally have been rare in Jamaica and many rural homes still lack them, visits commonly are unannounced. Surprise guests nearly always are welcome.

Eating. Rural families tend to eat dinner together each day after 4 p.m., while urban families may eat together only on weekends, due to work and school schedules. Many Jamaicans say grace before or after meals.

When guests are present, the meal is usually relaxed and sociable. Buffet meals are popular, as is eating outdoors—in gardens or on patios. Jamaicans eat in the continental style, with the fork in the left hand and the knife remaining in the right. While family meals may be casual, good table manners in public are considered an important social refinement.

Restaurant bills usually include a service charge, but if not, one leaves a 10 to 15 percent tip. Caterers, restaurants, and street vendors often sell *take-away* (take-out) meals served in boxes. Roadside stands or carts commonly feature pineapples, melons, and water coconuts sold as quick snacks or thirst quenchers. Because eating while walking is considered inappropriate, people often eat snacks on the spot.

LIFESTYLE

Family. The family structure varies in Jamaica according to several factors, including one's social standing. For example, families in lower socioeconomic groups usually are larger than those in the middle or upper classes. In addition, some women in lower-income groups have several children by different men, known as *baby fathers*. The men refer to these women as *baby mothers* (as opposed to "wives" or "girlfriends"). While some associate motherhood with femininity or blessings and fatherhood with virility, caring for children generally is seen as a serious responsibility and financial commitment. Women assume the primary responsibility for child care, but children often live with grandparents, relatives, or godparents when the mother works outside the home. Therefore, in these circles the extended family plays a crucial role. Most families live in houses or town houses, built of concrete or (in rural areas) wood. Apartments are not common.

Dating and Marriage. Young people socialize at dances, movies, parties, church functions, the market, and on the street. Wealthier Jamaicans often date in pairs and marry in their twenties, before children are born. Lower-income youth tend to socialize in groups. Marriage ceremonies often are prohibitively expensive, with a church ceremony (that includes decorations, formal clothing, and a motorcade) and a party (with much food, drink, and music). Therefore, lower-income couples may marry only after years together as a couple, usually after children are born. A formal marriage is commonly associated with becoming "Christian."

Diet. Jamaican food generally is spicy. Breakfast often includes *ackee* (a rich red fruit) and salt fish, the national dish. Fish may be eaten two or more times a week. Stews and curries (such as curried goat) are popular. *Jerk* (spicy barbecued pork or chicken, roasted in open pits or on makeshift grills) often is served with a bland, hard bread or with *Jamaican yams*. *Bammy* (cassava bread), a staple food, is still prepared in the style of the Arawak Indians. *Bammy* or *festival* (fried dough) with fish is a frequent combination. Many Jamaicans enjoy Indian and Chinese dishes. Rice and *peas* (red beans) is a common accompaniment to Sunday meals. *Box food* (food eaten out of a box when one is away from home) generally consists of fish, chicken, or goat served over rice and *peas*. Boiled green bananas or fried dumplings are popular side dishes. Fruits (mangoes, bananas, papaya, pineapple, oranges, grapefruit, tomatoes) are plentiful, and one or more types usually are in season. Vegetables also play an important role in the diet. A typical salad includes lettuce and tomatoes or cabbage and carrots. Coffee, herbal teas, fruit juices, drinks made from boiled roots, and a variety of alcoholic beverages are common. All hot drinks (coffee, cocoa, green tea, etc.) are called *tea*. Beer and white rum are especially popular. Women usually do not drink alcohol in public.

Recreation. Cricket and *football* (soccer) are the most popular sports in Jamaica. The 1998 Jamaican national soccer team became the first ever to qualify for the World Cup finals. Dominoes is the favorite indoor game. Many also enjoy table tennis, field hockey, tennis, and *athletics* (track-and-field). Girls play netball in school. People attend discos, community centers, and clubs. A frequent pastime is listening outside of *rum bars* to music from stereo systems. Other leisure activities include going to movies and enjoying spectator sports, such as boxing or team competitions. Various festivals, community events, and church activities provide entertainment and recreation. Jamaicans also take advantage of the outdoor activities their island offers.

The Arts. The most famous Jamaican musician, Bob Marley, used reggae music to advocate tolerance and justice. An annual festival commemorates his birthday. Reggae is still the most popular form of music, but Jamaicans are also fond of jazz, calypso, and gospel. Young Jamaicans enjoy *soca* (a mixture of American soul and calypso) and *dance hall* music. The latter incorporates elements of reggae, disco, and rap. *Soca* is popular during *Carnival*.

Theatrical comedies performed in *patois* are popular. Galleries throughout the island display local fine art, and folk art can be found at open-air markets. Folk arts are produced primarily for tourists and include basketry, pottery, and textiles.

Holidays. Official Jamaican holidays include New Year's Day, Ash Wednesday, Easter (Friday–Monday), Labor Day (23 May, a day for community improvement projects), Independence Day (first Monday in August), National Heroes Day (third Monday in October), Christmas, and Boxing Day

▼ **THE AMERICAS**

(26 Dec.). Boxing Day is a day to visit family and friends. Maroons celebrate 6 January as their independence day. *Carnival* is a springtime festival involving parades, costumes, and parties.

Commerce. Business hours generally extend from 9 a.m. to 5 p.m., Monday through Thursday, and until 4 p.m. on Friday. Banks close weekdays around 2 p.m.; on Friday they stay open for a few more hours. Grocery stores and other shops might open earlier and close later, depending on the town and type of shop. Street vendors sell goods and food from early in the morning until late at night. Open-air markets sell fresh produce. Those from lower-income households tend to shop often, as they have less access to refrigeration.

SOCIETY

Government. Jamaica's government is based on a Westminster (British) model parliamentary democracy. The PNP and JLP are the only parties represented in Parliament. A third party, the National Democratic Movement, was founded in 1995. Elections must be held at least every five years. The voting age is 18. Parliament consists of an elected House of Representatives with 60 members and an appointed Senate with 21 members. The prime minister appoints 13 and the opposition appoints 8. The cabinet, led by Prime Minister P. J. Patterson, holds executive power. Although Jamaica is independent, it is part of the Commonwealth of Nations and recognizes Queen Elizabeth II as head of state. She is represented in Jamaica by a governor-general (Howard Cooke).

Economy. Bauxite and tourism are key elements of Jamaica's economy. Bauxite, aluminum, sugar, bananas, rum, and coffee are important exports. Agriculture employs more than 20 percent of the population.

An austerity program lowered inflation (from 25 percent in 1995 to about 6 percent in 2000) but also resulted in a declining gross domestic product (GDP). For the first time in years, the economy is showing signs of growth. The government hopes to further spur the GDP by lowering interest rates, pursuing free-trade opportunities, and attracting foreign investment. It also is moving to reduce its foreign debt. Jamaica is part of the Caribbean Basin Initiative (CBI), a program designed to improve economic relations between Caribbean nations and the United States. It is also a member of the Caribbean Community and Common Market (CARICOM), a regional economic association. The currency is the Jamaican dollar (J$).

A growing portion of the population earns a decent income, but unemployment stands at 15 percent and is even higher for women. Slow economic growth inhibits greater prosperity, and both urban and rural poverty remain a challenge. More than one-fourth of the total population lives below the poverty line. About 13 percent of the population lacks access to health care, education, and economic opportunities needed to rise above human poverty.*

Transportation and Communications. Cars and buses are the most common form of transportation. Following the British tradition, traffic moves on the left side of the road. Most roads are paved. Buses serve all parts of the island and

DEVELOPMENT DATA

Human Dev. Index* rank .... 83 of 174 countries
    Adjusted for women .... 67 of 143 countries
Real GDP per capita $3,389
Adult literacy rate .... 86 percent
Infant mortality rate .... 15 per 1,000 births
Life expectancy .... 73 (male); 77 (female)

are often crowded; accurate schedules are not always available. *Route taxis* follow set local routes with set fares. Regular taxis, with negotiated fares, are plentiful. Jamaica's communications system is modern and adequate, although rural homes seldom have phones. Public phone booths, usually found near police stations and post offices, require phone cards, which are purchased at post offices and some stores. There are several radio and television stations and various daily newspapers.

Education. Children attend basic schools (ages 3–6) and primary schools (6–12). Secondary schools (ages 12–17) include technical, comprehensive, vocational, and high schools. Secondary enrollment is limited and admission is determined by competitive examinations. A lack of money for fees, uniforms, lunch, and transportation makes attendance difficult for some, although some government aid is available. Most children (93 percent) who enter school finish the primary level. About 60 percent of all eligible children are enrolled in secondary schools.

Most Jamaican adults have completed at least five years of education. Boys generally value education less than girls do. Young women increasingly recognize the economic benefits of an education in providing for a better future. More young women than young men attend secondary school, and the number of women in postsecondary institutions is approaching that of men. Higher education is provided at six teacher-training colleges; a college of art, science, and technology; a college of agriculture; schools of music, art, dance, and drama; and the University of the West Indies. The new Caribbean Institute of Technology aims to train Jamaicans in programming and software development.

Health. Most large towns or cities have a hospital. Medical clinics are community based and available across Jamaica. The public health-care system covers basic care for all citizens at no or low cost. Fees might be required in some cases, especially for more complicated care. Private facilities are available. Piped water is safe to drink. Life expectancy has risen in recent years.

CONTACT INFORMATION

Jamaica Tourist Board, 801 Second Avenue, 20th Floor, New York, NY 10017; phone (212) 856-9727; Web site www.jamaicatravel.com. Embassy of Jamaica, 1520 New Hampshire Avenue, Washington, DC 20036; phone (202) 452-0660; Web site www.emjam-usa.org.

1305 North Research Way, Bldg. K
Orem, Utah 84097-6200 USA
1.800.528.6279; 801.705.4250
fax 801.705.4350
www.culturegrams.com

CultureGrams™
standard edition 2002

Republic of
Latvia

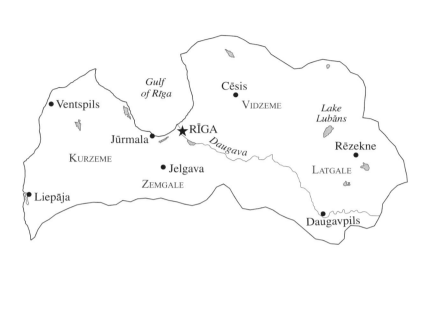

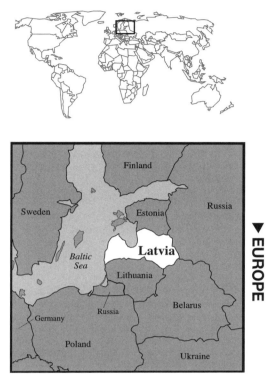

▼ EUROPE

Boundary representations are not necessarily authoritative.

BACKGROUND

Land and Climate. The Baltic state of Latvia covers 24,750 square miles (64,100 square kilometers) and is somewhat larger than West Virginia. Latvia is mostly low and flat, but it features numerous lakes, rivers, and dense forests of fir, pine, birch, and aspen trees. The Daugava River divides Latvia in half; south and farther west of it lie the grain-rich plains of the Kurzeme and Zemgale regions; to the east and north, plains give way to the hills and lakes of Vidzeme and Latgale. The Daugava was historically an amber trade route linked with Russia's Volga and Dnieper Rivers. Today, the Daugava is a major source of hydroelectric power. Latvia's capital, Rīga, was founded in 1201.

Due to its northern location, Latvia experiences broad seasonal variations in weather and sunlight. Midsummer days can last seventeen or more hours, while December days last no longer than six. The climate is moderated somewhat by a warm gulf stream, but in winter, snow is still common. Daytime temperatures average 24°F (-4°C) but can drop to -4°F (-20°C). Inland areas are colder. In summer, rain is common and the mild temperatures rarely climb above 86°F (30°C).

History. Records of settlements in the Baltics date back to at least 2000 B.C. Ethnic Balts eventually came to dominate the region and then to divide into various groups. Settlers in the area prospered between the second and fifth centuries A.D. by trading amber. People generally lived in free association for many years, but Teutonic knights in-vading from Germany in the 13th century established the Livonian Confederation in much of what is present-day Latvia and Estonia. They created German feudal estates and introduced Christianity to the inhabitants.

Ivan the Terrible's forces invaded from Russia in 1558, and Livonia was partitioned mostly between Sweden and the Polish-Lithuanian state. Kurzeme became the duchy of Courland, a semi-independent vassal state of Poland. It was strong enough to hold colonies in Africa and the Caribbean (Tobago). Russian expansion in the early 1700s eventually brought all of Latvia under Peter the Great's rule. Throughout this time, German barons owned the land and the local peoples worked as serfs on their estates.

In the 19th century, intellectuals and Latvian students abroad helped awaken a sense of Latvian nationality. Writers, teachers, and other leaders collected and published thousands of folk songs and poems and wrote about Latvian culture and language. Many groups formed, among them a group of socialists that eventually (in 1905) led a peasant revolt against German landowners and Russian oppression. Czarist troops crushed the rebellion and continued an ongoing policy of Russification.

When Germany occupied half of Latvia in World War I, Latvian volunteers formed the Latvian Riflemen to halt the German advance. In the wake of the Russian Revolution (1917), Latvia declared independence (18 November 1918) and set up a provisional government. The Riflemen supported Lenin, fought in the Red army, and returned as heroes at the end of World War I. Latvians were divided between support for Kàrlis Ulmanis's provisional government and the Bolsheviks. The Riflemen were also divided, and many eventually fought against fellow Latvians who remained loyal to the Soviet cause. At the same time, the soldiers fought against

German troops attempting to topple Ulmanis in favor of a pro-German government. The Germans were driven out in 1919, and Russia recognized Latvian independence in 1920.

With a newly elected parliament (*Saeima*) and constitution (*Satversme*), the country quickly flourished economically and culturally. Democracy was cut short in 1934 when President Ulmanis dissolved the Saeima, declared a state of emergency, and later established authoritarian rule. In 1939, the secret Molotov-Ribbentrop Treaty between Adolf Hitler and Josef Stalin consigned Latvia to the Soviet sphere of influence. The Red army occupied the country in June 1940. Within a year, the Soviets executed or deported thousands of people from Latvia, sending more than 20,000 to Siberia on one day alone (14 June 1941), including children and the elderly. The Nazis invaded the following month, but Russian troops returned in 1944. At least 130,000 Latvians fled with the retreating German army to escape the Soviets. Most of these people eventually settled in Europe, North America, and Australia.

The Soviets annexed Latvia and the other Baltic states, a move never recognized by Western nations. Thousands more people were deported, and ethnic Russians were encouraged to settle in the region. The Soviets collectivized all farmland and built many factories for newly arriving Russian workers.

In the late 1980s, Soviet leader Mikhail Gorbachev's policies of *glasnost* (openness) and *perestroika* (reform) allowed people to organize and show renewed support for greater independence. After the Latvian parliament passed a Declaration of Renewal of Independence in May 1990, Soviet troops intervened. However, with the Soviet Union's collapse in 1991, parliament reaffirmed the 1920 constitution and set up a provisional government.

Democratic elections in 1993 brought Guntis Ulmanis to power as president. In 1999, Vaira Vike-Freiberga became president, the first woman president in Eastern Europe. A center-right coalition was formed with Andris Shkele as prime minister. In April 2000, Shkele resigned in a privatization dispute. Andris Berzins is the current prime minister. Latvia's government hopes to gain membership in the North Atlantic Treaty Organization (NATO) and the European Union (EU) in the next several years.

THE PEOPLE

Population. Latvia's population of 2.4 million is shrinking at a rate of 0.84 percent a year due to a low birthrate and high emigration rate. Most people live in cities. Ethnic Latvians comprise at least 56 percent of the population, with Russians totaling 30 percent. Belorusians (4 percent), Ukrainians (3), Poles (3), and others also live in Latvia. Post–World War II Russian immigrants are concentrated in Rīga and Daugavpils. "Peter's Russians" live mostly in Rēzekne and Latgale. They settled in Latvia during the time of Peter the Great and are well integrated into Latvian society. They generally speak Latvian, participate in Latvian traditions, and have citizenship rights.

The government actively encourages non-Latvians to leave Latvia. Several thousand have left, but the majority remain. Citizenship is granted to ethnic Latvians, pre-1940 residents (and their descendants) of all nationalities, and anyone who has been educated in Latvian. Citizenship is necessary to vote, hold government jobs, and participate in the privatization program for businesses. A 10 November 1998 amendment to citizenship laws has made the naturalization process much easier. Officials estimate that 20,000 ethnic Russians will naturalize each year—a number greater than the total who have naturalized since independence. Tension between Latvians and ethnic Russians is still evident in this transitional period. This tension has led to strained relations between Latvia and Russia.

Language. Latvian is an Indo-European language related to Lithuanian. It uses the Latin alphabet with numerous diacritical marks. Although Latvian is now the official language, restoring it to dominant use will take time. Most Cyrillic street signs have been changed to Latvian. Russian was the official language before 1991 and many people speak it as their first language. Russian still is used in commerce and everyday life, but more people are learning Latvian. Many people speak English or German.

Religion. Most people in Latvia are Christian. Due to the oppression of Soviet rule, at least half of all people do not identify themselves with a church. Lutherans (12 percent) are found primarily in Kurzeme, Vidzeme, and Zemgale. Catholics (20 percent) dominate Latgale. The Russian Orthodox Church is the country's third largest (4 percent). With religious freedom restored, churches are being rebuilt or reopened, more people are expressing their beliefs, and newer congregations are being established. Some people continue to practice pre-Christian rites that focus on natural deities.

General Attitudes. In public and toward strangers, Latvians are reserved, professional, and formal. Among friends and family members, they are warm, inviting, and trusting. People often make new acquaintances through networking with mutual friends.

After decades of avoiding public debate, Latvians are enjoying a new era of expression. They have become comfortable with vocalizing personal convictions and ideals, and they engage in lively discussions about politics, culture, sports, and a number of other topics. Like others who suffered under Soviet occupation, Latvians are proud that their culture has persevered. They fondly recall the days when Rīga was called the Paris of the North (for its architecture and social life) and had an economy to rival those of Western Europe. Nostalgia for that era kindled hope in Latvian hearts throughout the Soviet years. Children were taught at home to have pride in Latvian culture. This patriotism and focus of purpose is helping Latvians rebuild their society today.

Personal Appearance. Latvians prefer European fashions and tend to dress well. Even young people favor dressier clothing over jeans for school and social gatherings. Men wear suits, pressed shirts, and ties to work. Women wear nice dresses. Informally, people wear clean and neat slacks, sweaters, shirts, skirts, and dress pants. People usually wear multiple layers of clothing in winter. In summer, men wear slacks and women wear shorter skirts. When gardening at summer cottages, Latvians prefer to wear swimsuits.

Women enjoy jewelry, especially traditional Latvian items made with silver and amber. Latvia's coast is known as the Amber Coast, and people sometimes still comb the beaches early in the morning for pieces of amber.

Traditional attire is an important part of any folk festival. For women, this includes wool skirts, white linen blouses, and wool vests decorated in ways that reflect a person's home region. Men wear wool slacks and long wool jackets.

CUSTOMS AND COURTESIES

Greetings. Latvians shake hands when they greet, being careful to make and hold eye contact. To show special respect or deep friendship, men and women might add a light kiss. It is considered impolite for people to shake hands across a doorway; instead, one is expected to step into the room with the other person before shaking hands. To introduce themselves, Latvians state their name and surname; Russians state their name and father's name. Titles such as Mr. (*kungs*), Mrs. (*kundze*), and Miss (*jaunkundze*) are added if a person is introducing someone else. In this case, the title follows the name, the ending of which also changes. So a Mr. Kalns would be introduced as *Kalna kungs* and a Miss Muceniece would be *Mucenieka jaunkundze*.

Friends address each other by first name, but different endings are used for different purposes. For example, to call to a friend named Jānis, one would say *Jāni!* To express affection or to talk to a child, Latvians add a diminutive ending (-īts or -iņš for males; -ina or -īte for females). So, Maija can be called *Maijina*, Jānis might be *Jānītis*, and Valdis could be called *Valdiņš*.

Gestures. Latvians freely use hand gestures to emphasize verbal expressions. They otherwise keep hands in reserve. People generally do not wave in greeting, as they only greet people they know, and then with a handshake. Direct eye contact connotes honesty and sincerity. Latvians rarely drink or eat on the street, except for ice cream.

Visiting. Latvians prefer to visit by invitation rather than spontaneously. Rural Latvians and older urban residents tend to entertain at home, while younger adults visit in bars, clubs, and cafés. Home gatherings are relatively small. Guests dress up and arrive promptly or just a few minutes late. Visitors remove their shoes at the door, sometimes replacing them with slippers the hosts offer. They then present the hosts with a gift. Latvians love flowers, which are given only in odd numbers (even numbers are reserved for funerals). A great variety of flowers are sold by street vendors and at markets. Guests also might give liquor, apples, small sandwiches (*maizītes*), meat-filled pastries (*pīrāgi*), or cakes (*kūkas*).

Hosts usually provide guests with plenty of food served in several courses. Presentation—how the food looks—is very important. Along with the soup, meats, desserts, coffee, and drinks that fill the evening, Latvians enjoy lively conversation. It is not uncommon for people to break into song during social gatherings. Latvia boasts more than 200,000 folk songs, and many people know many by heart. Guests usually say good-bye a few times in the process of getting ready to leave. Kisses and handshakes accompany a final good-bye.

Eating. Families try to eat meals together whenever possible. A typical breakfast includes one or more of the following: bread and butter; tomatoes; cold cuts; porridge; pancakes; bacon, ham, or sausages; and tea, milk, or coffee. Lunch is eaten from 1 to 3 p.m. and is, for many, the main meal of the day. It consists of three courses: soup (*zupa*), the main course with meat (*gaļa*) and potatoes (*kartupeļi*), and dessert (*saldais ēdiens*). Bread is served with every meal. Latvians eat a lighter dinner after 6 p.m.

Latvians eat with the fork in the left hand and the knife remaining in the right. They keep napkins on the table. Rīga's restaurants offer a wide variety of international cuisine. Traditional Latvian fare includes pork steak (*karbonāde*),

cabbage soup (*kāpostu zupa*), potatoes, and juice (*sula*) and coffee. Russians also favor beet soup (*borscht*) and Russian soup (*soljanka*). The check is paid at the table upon request. Tipping is not common in rural areas but is becoming standard in Rīga restaurants.

LIFESTYLE

Family. Families tend to have one or two children. Three generations often share a single household due to a housing shortage. The elderly live with family members whenever possible. Grandparents often care for grandchildren while both parents work. Extended family members try to help each other financially when necessary. Latvians take great care in tending grave sites, decorating them with fresh flowers or plants.

The average family apartment has one or two bedrooms. At night, the living room couch (*dīvāns*) folds out as a bed. All family members work to keep the living quarters neat and clean. Rural houses are larger. A person's identity is tied to the family's home region. It is uncommon for Latvians to choose to move away from the area where they were born. Even if young people seek jobs or education in Rīga, they return to their hometowns for holidays and summers.

Dating and Marriage. Young people begin dating in high school. They enjoy dancing at clubs or discos, getting together for coffee at cafés, or attending sporting events. Most people marry in their early twenties and begin a family shortly thereafter.

Although more wedding ceremonies are being held in churches, most are secular events attended by a few close friends and relatives. In rural districts wedding ceremonies tend to be big events. The groom wears a dark, formal suit, and the bride wears a white gown and holds a white bouquet.

A "matchmaking couple" (*vedejparis*) plays an integral role in the ceremony and the newlyweds' life. Traditionally, the *vedejparis* introduced the groom and bride. Today, this is an honorary position for admired friends. The *vedejparis* helps make wedding arrangements, serves as the ceremony's witnesses, and symbolically helps the new couple make the transition from single to married life. After the ceremony, the newlyweds leave in a car decorated with greenery, flowers, and a symbolic set of wedding rings. Newlyweds often move in with one set of parents to save money.

Diet. Staple foods in Latvia include soup, potatoes, red meat, poultry, and fish. Imported summer fruits (pineapples, bananas, and oranges) join locally grown produce (onions, potatoes, beets, cucumbers, apples, mushrooms, and berries) to give variety to the diet. Rye bread (*rupmaize*) and other whole-grain breads are preferred to white bread (*baltmaize*). Latvians drink beer and soft drinks at room temperature. Cold drinks are considered unhealthy. In addition to vodka, brandy, and wine, Latvians consume *balzāms*—a thick herbal/alcohol mixture that is either drunk alone or with coffee, or is poured over ice cream. It is said to have medicinal value.

Recreation. Favorite summer activities include berry and mushroom picking and relaxing at summer cottages. Most urban Latvians own simple cottages with nearby sauna huts. Family members of all ages may go in the sauna several times in the course of an evening. Extensive gardens around the cottages allow families to produce their own fruits and vegetables, which often are made into jams and preserves.

The most popular sports in Latvia include soccer, volleyball, basketball, hockey, biathlon (Nordic skiing and

EUROPE ▼

shooting), motocross racing, cycling, fishing, boating, hunting, hiking, and orienteering. For their vacations, people may work on household repair projects, visit friends and family, or travel to the countryside or abroad.

The Arts. In the fall, people go dancing or attend concerts and theater productions. In all seasons, singing is a national pastime. Folk festivals held throughout the year feature song, dance, and poetry that celebrate Latvian culture. Prominent art institutions include the Rīga Ballet, the National Symphony Orchestra, and the Rīga Dome Boys Choir.

Amber jewelry is a well-known art form. Others include weaving, metalwork, ceramics, leather work, wattle work, and wood carving. The arts suffered during Soviet rule because of government control, but since independence, artists have worked to create a distinct Latvian style.

Holidays. Officially, Latvians celebrate New Year's Day (1 Jan.), Easter (Friday–Monday), Labor Day (1 May), Mother's Day (second Sunday of May), Whitsunday, Līgo Day (23 June), *Jāņi* (Midsummer's Day), Independence Day (18 Nov.), Christmas (25–26 Dec.), and New Year's Eve (31 Dec.).

For Easter, people color eggs by boiling them along with onion skins and wildflowers. At the Sunday family meal, each person selects an egg and takes turns cracking it against others' eggs. Amid laughter and much strategy, the person with the last egg to crack is deemed the winner.

Jāņi is the year's most festive holiday. Held on the summer solstice, it marks the beginning of the summer's "white nights," when the sun sets for only a few hours. Food is prepared weeks in advance. Businesses close for two days. People light huge bonfires, and revelers attend parties, dances, and concerts. They sing songs and many stay up all night.

For public holidays, Latvians fly flags, attend speeches, and have parades. Flag masts carry black ribbons on commemorative days: 25 March (for victims of communism), 8 May (for victims of World War II), 14 June (for victims of 1941 deportations), 4 July (for victims of anti-Semitic genocide), and 11 November (Veterans' Day). In August, each village or congregation appoints a Sunday for visiting family graves. Latvians also celebrate birthdays and name days.

Commerce. Businesses open weekdays from 8 a.m. to 5 p.m.; some close for lunch. Rīga's restaurants stay open for lunch; rural ones close. People shop at open-air markets (*tirgi*) and supermarkets. *Tirgi* carry the widest variety of food and goods; prices often are negotiable.

SOCIETY

Government. Latvia is a parliamentary democracy. Delegates to the nation's 100-seat Saeima are elected to four-year terms, as is the president. All citizens may vote at age 18. The Saeima elects the president, who selects a prime minister. This person forms a government, the structure of which is ratified or rejected by the Saeima.

Economy. As part of its transition to a market economy, Latvia is returning collectivized land to previous owners or their descendants, privatizing state industries, encouraging joint ventures with Western businesses, and seeking foreign trade. Forest products account for the bulk of current

DEVELOPMENT DATA

Human Dev. Index* rank	63 of 174 countries
Adjusted for women	51 of 143 countries
Real GDP per capita	$5,728
Adult literacy rate	99 percent
Infant mortality rate	16 per 1,000 births
Life expectancy	62 (male); 75 (female)

exports, followed by textiles and foodstuffs.

As in other new democracies, the transition process is painful and many people have lost their jobs. Tax evasion is a serious problem. Since a banking crisis in 1995, many Latvians are wary of keeping their money in the bank. Latvia's gross domestic product grew by around 6 percent in 2000 and inflation was low. Unemployment remains high. Although Russia used to be Latvia's biggest trading partner, markets in Western Europe are more lucrative now. Despite economic difficulties, Latvia has an educated work force, a good industrial base, excellent ports, and other resources that eventually will allow people to achieve personal and societal goals. The national currency is the *Lat* (LVL).

Transportation and Communications. Most people use public transportation, but ownership of private cars is increasing. Latvia's extensive rail and bus systems connect most locations. Ferries, trolleys, trams, and taxis are also part of the transportation network.

Latvia has been improving its phone system since 1992. Most Rīga homes have phones, although smaller cities and rural areas often still lack private lines. Three television and numerous radio stations deliver news and entertainment throughout Latvia. Most people also read a newspaper.

Education. Children begin attending elementary school (grades 1–4) at age six. They are required to attend through primary school (grades 5–9). Three optional years of secondary school (grades 10–12) are available through trade schools, university-track high schools, or more general secondary schools. Several institutions of higher learning, including the University of Latvia, offer degree programs. Some higher education programs are free, but students must compete for positions by examination. Otherwise, students can pay tuition at private and some state-sponsored schools. Many people eventually complete postgraduate work.

Health. Latvia's public health-care system provides access to all residents but lacks funding and supplies. Rural hospitals and clinics suffer most from lack of equipment and supplies. It costs very little to visit a doctor, but prescribed medications may be too expensive for some people. Private medical and dental clinics offer more modern care at prices the average worker cannot afford. In Rīga, nonprofit organizations have begun donating equipment and have started educational programs for doctors.

CONTACT INFORMATION

Embassy of Latvia, 4325 17th Street NW, Washington, DC 20011; phone (202) 726-8213; Web site www.latvia-usa.org.

1305 North Research Way, Bldg. K
Orem, Utah 84097-6200 USA
1.800.528.6279; 801.705.4250
fax 801.705.4350
www.culturegrams.com

Principality of
Liechtenstein

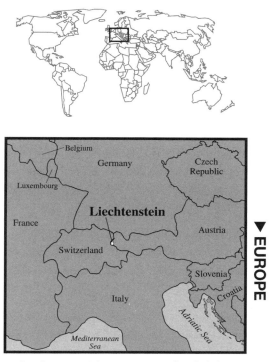

Boundary representations are not necessarily authoritative.

BACKGROUND

Land and Climate. Covering only 61.8 square miles (163 square kilometers), Liechtenstein is the fourth smallest state in Europe, situated between Austria and Switzerland. The principality enjoys a beautiful Alpine landscape that is dominated by the valley of the Rhine River and the Rhaetikon Massif. The highest point is Grauspitz at 8,525 feet (2,599 meters). Small vineyards are found in the foothills. The climate is temperate and strongly influenced by the *Föhn*, a warm southerly wind. The *Föhn* was one of the three "national plagues" that once endangered the country. It sometimes kindled extensive fires, jeopardizing the then mostly wooden houses. Today, building materials are mainly brick and concrete, and each village maintains a well-equipped voluntary fire brigade. Like the *Föhn*, the other two sources of natural disaster have also been brought under control. High embankments contain the formerly wild Rhine River; the last big flooding (*Rheinnot*) of the river took place in 1927. The debris slides (*Rüfen*) coming down from the mountains have been enclosed and rendered harmless. Avalanches, such as one in February 1999, which forced the closure of the Malbun valley, are another potential danger.

History. The area of Liechtenstein has been inhabited continuously since 3000 B.C. It was colonized by Celts and Rhaetians. In 15 B.C., the Romans conquered the territory. In the fifth century, the Alemanni settled it, and in the twelfth century, the German language established an exclusive foothold. Historically, Liechtenstein is composed of two areas, the Lordship of Schellenberg and the County of Vaduz.

The two domains had been owned by various dynasties of counts before Prince Johann Adam Andreas of Liechtenstein purchased them in 1699 and 1712, respectively. As territories under the direct suzerainty of the German Empire, they provided the prince with a seat in the Diet of the Princes.

In 1719, the two domains were united and elevated to the Imperial Principality of Liechtenstein. It is the only country that still carries the name of its dynasty. Napoleon made Liechtenstein and 15 other regions part of the Rhine Confederation in 1806, granting each independence in exchange for loyalty. At the Vienna Congress of 1815 (after Napoleon's defeat), Liechtenstein became part of the German Confederation. It remained a member until the Confederation was dissolved in 1866. Since then, Liechtenstein has remained fully sovereign. It has had no army since 1868 and is a neutral country. From 1852 to 1919, it formed a customs union with Austria-Hungary. Since 1924, Liechtenstein has benefited from a customs union with Switzerland and the use of the Swiss *franc* as its currency.

The constitution of 1921, which is still in force today, established "a constitutional hereditary monarchy upon a democratic and parliamentary basis." Prince Franz Josef II became the first prince to reside in Liechtenstein rather than in Vienna, Austria. He ruled from 1938 until his death in 1989. He was succeeded by his son, Prince Hans Adam II, who rules today. Liechtenstein joined the United Nations in 1990. It has always enjoyed political stability. A rare interruption was a vote of no confidence in 1993 for a newly appointed prime minister. The current government, led by Premier Mario Frick of the Fatherland Union, took office in April 1997.

In the past several years, the government has instituted banking and other reforms amid allegations that Liechtenstein has become an international center for money laundering. Also at issue is the role of the hereditary monarchy. Debate continues on constitutional reforms designed to clearly define the authority of the prince, government, and Parliament.

THE PEOPLE

Population. The population of Liechtenstein is more than 32,000 and is growing around 1 percent annually. It expanded rapidly after World War II due to an increased demand for imported labor. Approximately 38 percent of the inhabitants today do not possess Liechtenstein citizenship. The large number of foreign nationals, who come mainly from German-speaking countries, has led the government to pursue a restrictive immigration policy. As a result, the nation's growth has stabilized, but the numbers of daily commuters from the Swiss and Austrian border regions have increased. Only 40 percent of the workforce is native to Liechtenstein.

Language. The language spoken in Liechtenstein is German. High German is taught at school and is used as a written language, but people speak an Alemannic dialect. This dialect is similar to Swiss German (*Schwiizertütsch*) and is difficult for people from other German-speaking countries to understand. Its nuances vary from village to village. The mountain commune of Triesenberg was founded in the 13th century by people from southwestern Switzerland. Their descendants still speak a Walser dialect. The primary foreign languages taught at school are French and English.

Religion. The constitution guarantees religious freedom. The people of Liechtenstein are mostly Roman Catholics (80 percent). The Catholic Church is the state church. The priests are employed by the communes. Almost 20 percent of the people belong to a variety of other Christian churches or to no church at all. Religion still has some impact on daily life, but society has become more secularized in recent years.

General Attitudes. Liechtensteiners are proud of their high standard of living and modern achievements, but they cherish tradition as well. They value hard work and a good sense of humor. Conservative, deliberate, and pragmatic, they are also sincere and warmhearted. Many view Liechtenstein as one of the most beautiful spots on earth and consider it good luck that the country is so small and unimportant. Despite the lack of an army, for instance, it has escaped war since the end of the 18th century. People tend to know each other well. This creates a sense of personal responsibility but also encourages gossip and envy. The small society depends on the commitment of its citizens to participate, and civic duties are taken seriously. Liechtensteiners like to talk politics and many are involved in some way.

The national identity of Liechtensteiners is linked closely to their respective communes and to the princely house. The prince plays an important role in public life and enjoys far-reaching constitutional rights. In contrast to other European monarchs, his tasks are not just representational. Liechtensteiners have always held the princely house in high esteem.

It is only recently that attitudes toward the monarchy have become more critical. In addition to current debate on constitutional reform, Liechtenstein faces the challenge of defining its place in international society. A more active foreign policy recently has opened Liechtenstein to the outside world. This has heightened awareness of being a distinct nation but also of the limits of independence. Political efforts to participate in European integration are likely to have a profound impact on the way Liechtensteiners view themselves.

Personal Appearance. People in Liechtenstein generally dress well and neatly. They prefer modern European fashions that tend to be more colorful than those in the United States. Overly casual or sloppy attire in public is frowned upon. *Trachten* (traditional costumes) are worn only on special occasions, especially by women. The typical woman's *Tracht* consists of a dress with gathered waist and full skirt, an apron, and a headdress. A man's traditional attire includes knee breeches, a straight loden jacket, and a flat, black hat.

CUSTOMS AND COURTESIES

Greetings. A handshake is usually the appropriate form of greeting. To wave or nod to somebody across the street is acceptable. People also commonly greet one another verbally when passing on the street or entering a store. The traditional terms to address strangers are either the Swiss German *Grüezi!* or the *Grüss Gott!* used in Austria and southern Germany. Both terms mean "Greetings!" It is appropriate to add the other person's name, if known. Among friends, young and old greet each other with a short *Hoi!* Most people in Liechtenstein address each other with the familiar *du* form, and young people generally use first names. However, this is only common among locals and not toward foreigners. The prince is addressed as *Durchlaucht* (Your Serene Highness). Greetings in languages other than German are also acceptable; keeping silent might be considered impolite. English, French, and Italian are the foreign languages most likely to be understood.

Gestures. Liechtensteiners do not use the hands much during conversation, but they consider talking with hands in the pockets to be impolite. People remove gloves before shaking hands. Pointing the index finger to one's own head is an insult. Any acts of personal hygiene, such as cleaning one's fingernails, are not appropriate in public. If one cannot suppress a yawn, one covers the open mouth with a hand. Both men and women may sit with legs crossed, one knee over the other.

Toasting with alcoholic beverages is common. Whether in the home or at a restaurant, a toast usually precedes any drinking. It is extremely impolite to begin sipping or drinking from one's glass before the host proposes the first toast. The host will not do this until all persons have a full glass. Once the first toast is made, all guests are free to take a drink and propose additional toasts. In a group, pairs next to each other, not across from each other, lightly tap their glasses simultaneously while maintaining eye contact.

Visiting. For business meetings, punctuality is important. Dinner guests are expected to arrive no more than a quarter of an hour late. They often bring flowers, candy, or a bottle of wine. Flowers are unwrapped before being given to the hostess, but other small gifts are not. Red roses are reserved for romantic occasions. In formal situations, guests wait to sit down until they are invited to do so. Even during short visits, guests usually are offered refreshments such as coffee, beer, wine, or mineral water. It is appropriate to give notice of a visit in advance. Dropping by is only common between neighbors or close friends and relatives. While dinner invitations may last well into the night, daytime visits are usually short.

Eating. Lunch typically is eaten at noon, and dinner is eaten around 6 or 7 p.m. When going out for dinner, people meet around 8 p.m. Liechtensteiners eat in the continental style, with the fork in the left hand and the knife remaining in the right. They may rest their wrists on the table edge. Soft food such as potatoes, dumplings, and fish are cut with the fork. Fish also may be cut with a special knife. Lettuce and spaghetti are not cut at all. It is considered polite not to leave any food on the plate. Second helpings are a compliment to the cook. When finished, one places the utensils side by side on the plate.

In restaurants, diners do not take home leftovers. Most people drink bottled mineral water, wine, or beer with meals. Drinks are not served with ice. The bill is paid at the table. The waiter usually asks whether each person prefers to pay separately. Service charges are included, but customers usually round the total up to the next *franc* as *Trinkgeld* (an extra tip).

LIFESTYLE

Family. The nuclear family is the most important social unit in Liechtenstein's society. Family bonds play an important role. The father generally is the head of the household. Both men and women train for careers, and an increasing number of married women work outside the home. The size of the average family has decreased to about two children. While singles and couples often live in apartments, families tend to prefer houses. The majority live in single-family homes, but more and more young families are becoming tenants because real estate is expensive. Many people prefer to settle in the village where they grew up. Adult, unmarried children usually move out of their parents' homes by the time they finish their professional training.

Dating and Marriage. Young people socialize on a casual basis in school and in numerous recreation clubs. There are close to three hundred clubs and *Vereine* (associations). Dating practices differ from those in the United States, and there is no German word that precisely means "dating." Either sex can suggest an activity, and it is assumed that they each pay for their own entertainment.

People usually marry in their late twenties. It is considered important to first complete one's education and enjoy some financial security and independence. Some couples live together before or instead of marrying. Legal marriages are performed at the national registry office. Having a church wedding is optional but common. It usually takes place the day after the civil marriage. Some old wedding customs are still practiced, such as decorating the door frames of the couple's home with garlands or organizing a mock kidnapping of the bride.

Diet. *Zmorga* (breakfast) usually consists of coffee and bread with jam. There are many different kinds of bread. *Zmittag* (the main meal) is served at midday and includes a soup or salad, a main dish, and dessert. *Znacht* (dinner) is typically light and often consists of open-faced sandwiches with cheese and meat. Full meals are served for dinner invitations and in restaurants. The national dish, *Riebel*, is made of cornmeal stirred in a frying pan with milk, water, and salt. It is often eaten with elderberry purée. Other traditional dishes are *Käsknöpfle*, a sort of pasta with sharp cheese, and *Rösti*, grated and fried potatoes.

Recreation. People in Liechtenstein love nature and outdoor activities such as hiking, cycling, and skiing. They enjoy a diversity of leisure-time clubs. Among the most popular team activities are soccer, gymnastics, music bands, and choirs. Eighty percent of all youth are involved in sports; 75 percent belong to a club or youth group. Many clubs organize public festivals and other social events. People also enjoy traveling abroad.

The Arts. A great cultural attraction in Liechtenstein is the prince's art collection, which includes world-famous paintings. A small part of this extensive private collection is exhibited in connection with the State Art Collection in Vaduz. Museums of folk art, stamps, and history also are located in Vaduz. Private galleries display the works of local artists and craftspeople. Tourists are the target market for these artisans.

Musical training is pervasive. More than four hundred musical societies and organizations instruct and perform classical and modern music. Jazz, operettas, and classical music are popular. Styles ranging from rock to classical are hosted at musical festivals and concerts. Performances draw artists and audiences from all over Europe.

Holidays. Liechtenstein recognizes many Catholic holidays as public holidays: Epiphany (6 Jan.), Candlemas (2 Feb.), Feast of St. Joseph (19 Mar.), Easter (Good Friday–Easter Monday), Ascension, Whitmonday, Corpus Christi, Nativity of our Lady (8 Sept.), All Saints' Day (1 Nov.), Immaculate Conception (8 Dec.), and Christmas (24–26 Dec.). Christmas is the biggest celebration of the year. On Christmas Eve, the family gathers around the Christmas tree and exchanges gifts. Most people relax on Christmas Day and visit relatives and friends on the day after. In addition to these religious holidays, New Year's Day (1 Jan.) and Labor Day (1 May) are public holidays. The national holiday (15 Aug.) is celebrated with festivities, speeches, and fireworks. Mother's Day is celebrated the second Sunday in May. Many old customs, partly pagan in origin, are still continued as folklore, such as *Funkasunntig* (Bonfire Sunday) or *Fasnacht* (Carnival).

Commerce. Business hours may vary. In general, they are from 8 a.m. to noon, when everything closes for lunch, and from 1:30 to 6:30 p.m., Monday through Friday. On Saturdays, stores close at 4 p.m., and some shops are closed Monday morning. There are no supermarkets in Liechtenstein, so people buy food and other consumer goods in a variety of small shops.

SOCIETY

Government. Liechtenstein is divided into 11 communes that uphold their traditional autonomy. They enjoy extensive

▼ **EUROPE**

rights, are organized as cooperatives with a strong sense of community, and have their individual coats of arms. The communes form two regions that correspond to the two historical domains. They are called the *Oberland* (Upper Country) and the *Unterland* (Lower Country). The principality of Liechtenstein combines democracy and monarchy, as people and prince govern together. The *Fürst* (ruling prince) is head of state. He sanctions all laws and can issue pardons and emergency decrees.

Landtag (Parliament) has 25 members elected for four years. The *Regierungschef* (prime minister) serves as head of government. Liechtenstein's government traditionally has been a two-party coalition of the Fatherland Union and Progressive Citizens' Party, both conservative people's parties. In April 1997, however, Parliament approved a new government headed solely by the Fatherland Union, marking the first time since 1938 that the country was not led by a coalition. The courts are presided over by Liechtenstein judges as well as Swiss and Austrian judges; this is due to the country's size and the fact that its legal system is a combination of Austrian, Swiss, and Liechtenstein law. Citizens may vote at age 20. The right to vote was not extended to women until 1984. The people enjoy direct democratic rights, such as the rights of initiative and referendum.

Internationally, Liechtenstein continues to straddle issues arising from its ties to Switzerland and its membership in the European Economic Area (EEA). The EEA bridges the European Free Trade Association, of which Switzerland and Liechtenstein are members, and the European Union (EU). Liechtenstein joined the EEA in May 1995, but Switzerland did not. Liechtenstein has benefited from its membership in the EEA but needs to be able to impose a stricter border policy with EU countries in order to preserve its immigration laws and open border with Switzerland.

Economy. Despite a lack of natural resources, Liechtenstein has a strong, modern economy. It enjoys one of the highest standards of living in the world. There are no budget deficits. Unemployment and inflation are low.

After World War II, Liechtenstein experienced an economic boom as many companies invested heavily in the country. They took advantage of low taxes and other favorable conditions, rapidly transforming the agrarian economy into an industrial state. Today, less than 2 percent of the gainfully employed still work in agriculture. Textiles, ceramics, and chemicals/pharmaceuticals all have long traditions in Liechtenstein. While industry produces mainly for export, a large number of small enterprises produces goods for domestic consumption. Industry and trade are important employers, but the service sector has grown recently and today provides about 53 percent of all jobs.

Liechtenstein's high level of economic prosperity is due mainly to the economic and monetary union with Switzerland, the favorable tax situation, strict bank secrecy, and

DEVELOPMENT DATA

Human Dev. Index* rank .... 13 of 174 countries
    Adjusted for women .... 13 of 143 countries
Real GDP per capita $25,512
Adult literacy rate .... 99 percent
Infant mortality rate .... 5 per 1,000 births
Life expectancy .... 75 (male); 82 (female)

political stability. The currency is the Swiss *franc* (SFR).

Transportation and Communications. Liechtenstein's road network is well developed. Private cars are the most important means of transport. Public transportation is provided at low cost by postal buses. Only one railway line crosses the country; it is operated by the Austrian Federal Railways. Good international connections are available through the nearby Swiss train stations and *Autobahn* (expressway). The closest international airport is in Zürich, Switzerland.

Communications facilities are good. Since January 1999, the telephone and postal services have been managed by Liechtenstein rather than Switzerland. Liechtenstein issues its own postal stamps. They are renowned for their beautiful design and are collected throughout the world. With regard to media, Liechtenstein is rather underdeveloped. The first radio station began broadcasting in August 1995. Television broadcasts come from other countries. There are two daily newspapers, which function as the mouthpieces of the two main political parties.

Education. School education is free and mandatory between the ages of seven and sixteen. Pupils may thereafter continue to study in preparation for entering a university or vocational training. The system of apprenticeships is quite popular and successful. Up to the level of the university entrance qualification, the *Matura*, Liechtenstein has a well developed educational system. For further training, agreements with Switzerland and Austria ensure that Liechtensteiners have places in educational institutions abroad. There is virtually no illiteracy, and adult education is actively promoted.

Health. Medical care is provided by a relatively high density of private doctors. There is one small public hospital in Liechtenstein. In addition, the country has concluded agreements with its Swiss and Austrian neighboring regions that ensure the availability of beds in hospitals there. The government provides for age and disability insurance, unemployment benefits, and social welfare. It requires people to purchase private health insurance.

CONTACT INFORMATION

Embassy of Switzerland, 2900 Cathedral Avenue NW, Washington, DC 20008; phone (202) 745-7900; Web site www.swissemb.org. Switzerland Tourism, 608 Fifth Avenue, Swiss Center, New York, NY 10020; phone (212) 757-5944.

1305 North Research Way, Bldg. K
Orem, Utah 84097-6200 USA
1.800.528.6279; 801.705.4250
fax 801.705.4350
www.culturegrams.com

CultureGrams™
standard edition 2002

Republic of
Lithuania

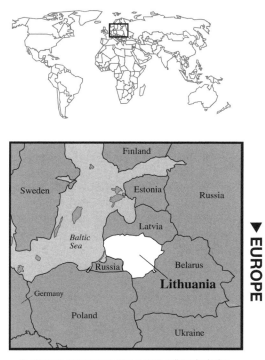

Boundary representations are not necessarily authoritative.

▼ EUROPE

BACKGROUND

Land and Climate. Lithuania is slightly larger than West Virginia (25,174 square miles or 65,200 square kilometers). It lies on the western fringe of the east European plain with a short coastline on the Baltic Sea. It is a green country with rolling hills and more than 750 rivers and more than 4,000 lakes. The two longest rivers are the Nemunas and the Neris. Summers are short and winters are cold and foggy. The general climate is comparable to that of southeastern Canada. Forests cover about 30 percent of the country and are rich in wild animals, mushrooms, and berries. Forests and the Čiuronian Lagoon, a large freshwater lagoon on the Baltic, are favorite destinations for recreation. Rain falls throughout the year but less so in the summer. A westerly breeze is common. Temperatures average 23°F (-5°C) in January and 63°F (17°C) in July.

Although the country technically is divided into 44 regions and 11 municipalities, Lithuanians tend to identify with one of five main regions: Dzūkija (around Vilnius), Aukštaitija (northeastern lakes), Suvalkija (far south), Žemaitija (center/northwest) and Mažoji Lietuva (Lithuania Minor, in the southwest).

History. Although Lithuanian people had lived in the area for centuries, it was not until 1236 that Duke Mindaugas united the lands they inhabited with those of the Yatwingians and Couronians to form the Grand Duchy of Lithuania. The new state grew in prominence, especially during the 14th century when it annexed neighboring lands and was ruled by strong monarchs. Vilnius became the capital in 1323. In 1386, reacting to a serious threat from Germanic invaders, the Grand Duke Jogaila married the Polish crown princess and became

king. This alliance brought Lithuania into a dynastic union with Poland, which eventually allowed the two nations to defeat the German (Teutonic) invaders in 1410. Because of the union, the Lithuanians adopted Roman Catholicism in 1387 and began to adopt Western culture. Poland and Lithuania tightened their association in 1569 when they united under the Lublin Union.

After the Polish-Lithuanian state was partitioned by its neighbors (in 1772, 1793, and 1795), the Grand Duchy of Lithuania was left largely a part of the Russian Empire. Many attempts were made to regain independence, but all were unsuccessful. In World War I, it was occupied by the Germans. After the Russian Revolution in 1917, the Germans permitted Lithuania to elect its own officials, who in turn declared Lithuania an independent state in February 1918. In December, however, Communists in Lithuania established a government and the Bolsheviks invaded from Russia.

Determined to regain sovereignty, people drove the Soviet army from most of Lithuania in 1919. During the same period, Poland sought to restore the territory it had claimed before 1795 and began fighting the Soviets. Poland soon gained control of Vilnius; Kaunas then became the temporary capital of Lithuania. In the interwar period (1920–40), Lithuania was independent and had a free-market economy, trading agricultural products with European and Scandinavian countries.

After a number of border disputes, Vilnius eventually was returned to Lithuanian sovereignty in World War II as compensation for the presence of Soviet military bases. Unfortunately, the Soviets soon dismissed the government and officially occupied the entire nation in 1940. Reneging on its 1939 Ribbentrop-Molotov agreement with Russia, Germany invaded and occupied Lithuania from 1941 to 1944. Gestapo forces killed thousands of Jews and brought suffering to the entire country. The Soviets returned in 1944, only to incorporate the country into the United Soviet Socialist Republic (USSR).

Thousands of armed partisan fighters, known as Forest Brothers, fought unsuccessfully for independence between 1940 and 1954. As a result of the resistance and Stalin's policies toward the Baltics, Lithuania suffered mass deportations and other difficulties. Relations were less confrontational after the 1950s, but Lithuanians never gave up their goal for independence. Their desires were realized in 1990 when the freely elected legislature of Lithuania restored independence (first declared in 1918). Weakened by various international and domestic factors, the Soviet government could not force Lithuania to cancel the declaration.

After the entire USSR collapsed in 1991, Russia recognized Lithuania's independence, already recognized by many countries. The government, led by independence hero Vytautas Landsbergis and members of the political movement *Sajūdis*, embarked on an aggressive campaign to reform the economy and other social structures. Hampered by a poor global economy, soaring energy prices, and other problems, progress was slow and painful. In 1992, voters rejected the *Sajūdis* leadership in favor of former Communists, who had formed a new political party. The new government slowed privatization and other reform measures to soften the impact of political and social change. More cooperative relations with Russia enabled a full withdrawal of Russian troops in late 1993. Still struggling with the effects of reform, the country faced a banking crisis at the end of 1995 that led to the dismissal of the prime minister.

Promising to revive the economy and fight corruption, Landsbergis's Homeland Union/Conservative Party returned to power after parliamentary elections in the fall of 1996. The economy's sharp downturn in the wake of the Russian financial crisis in 1998 hampered the government's economic and political reform. Economic woes also led to the defeat of the conservative Homeland Union in parliamentary elections of October 2000. Following the elections, President Adamkus appointed Rolandas Paksas of the Lithuanian Liberal Union as the new prime minister. North Atlantic Treaty Organization (NATO) and European Union (EU) membership remain top government priorities.

THE PEOPLE

Population. Lithuania's population of more than 3.6 million is shrinking slightly by 0.29 percent. Most people (80.6 percent) are ethnic Lithuanian, but the country is also home to Russians (8.7 percent), Poles (7), Belarusians (1.6), and Ukrainians (1.2). About 74 percent live in urban areas. The term *Lithuania* was first used by Tacitus in the first century A.D. in reference to one of many peoples emerging from the Balts, who inhabited the Baltic region between the first and fourth centuries. Lithuanians began to form their distinct society in the early second century. In Lithuania, all national minorities have full citizenship rights and are treated as equals. Except for Russians, minorities generally maintain their own customs and have not adopted Lithuanian culture. Most Russians have

integrated with mainstream society, combining their own customs with those of ethnic Lithuanians.

A modest number of people have access to resources that enable them to pursue personal goals, and women earn a significant share of the nation's income.

Language. Lithuanian is the country's official language. Its soft, gentle, and melodic sounds reflect the nature of the people. Strong and offensive words are uncommon. As one of the oldest Indo-European languages still in everyday use, Lithuanian belongs to the Baltic language group, along with Latvian, Yatvangian, and ethnic Old Prussian (now extinct). Grammatically, it is similar to Sanskrit and Homeric Greek. The formation of standard Lithuanian was not completed until the 19th century because Polish (and sometimes other languages) had been used as the state language after the 13th century. By the 17th century, Lithuanian survived only among rural peasants because urban dwellers spoke Polish. After 1795, when Lithuania and Poland ceased to exist as independent countries, Russian was introduced and encouraged among Lithuanians. When the Soviets took over in 1940, Russian was reintroduced; therefore, most Lithuanians today can speak Russian. English and German are other popular languages, particularly among the youth.

Religion. Most Lithuanians belong to the Roman Catholic Church. Under Soviet occupation, churches were closed, clergymen repressed, and teachers forbidden to teach religion. People practiced their faiths mainly at home. In 1990, the Act of Restitution of the Catholic Church restored it to its prominence and allowed religious freedom. Pope John Paul II visited in 1993 and brought the clergy up to date on the liturgy of the Church. The Hill of Crosses near Šiauliai, once a pagan worship site, became a place for erecting Christian crosses of thanksgiving and petition. Though the Soviets would bulldoze the crosses down, the people kept returning with more crosses and ultimately prevailed. Many different Christian churches also operate in the country. Muslims and Jews have active congregations.

General Attitudes. Lithuanians are generally reserved, even somber, although they are sincere and full of emotion. They simply mask their feelings to maintain privacy. They appreciate skill and intelligence. They are often critical of their own personal faults and are openly critical and distrustful of public institutions. They commonly describe their nation as melancholy (due to its past history). Individually, people are also nostalgic for such things as old friends, youth, and fond memories. Lithuanians are patient and industrious. They value moderate thrift but view "excessive" thrift as stinginess. They also value education, family, music, and loyalty to one's nationality.

Lithuanians are proud of their heritage but not of the Soviet period. For the future, they wish to be politically neutral and peaceful; however, they are willing to defend themselves to maintain Lithuania's independence. Many people are frustrated with the current period of transition and are uncertain of the future.

Personal Appearance. It is important to be cleanly dressed. Styles are mainly from Europe and increasingly from the United States. Lithuania's national dress is worn only on special occasions. Because clothing is expensive and the market does not always meet demand, people often wear handmade clothing, especially rural dwellers or persons wishing to create their own style. As Lithuania's economy continues to integrate with the world's, the use of handmade clothing is expected to decline. Older rural women wear scarves on their heads. *Fedoras* (fur caps worn by men) and European-style hats are common in winter. Men remove their hats in a building. Wool and fur commonly are used for clothing when the weather is cold. Older women wear cosmetics sparingly.

CUSTOMS AND COURTESIES

Greetings. Shaking hands with men, and less often women, is customary when greeting. A handshake nearly always is used in professional contacts. Men sometimes kiss the extended hand of women in greeting, and good friends may kiss cheeks. When introducing a man, one uses *ponas* (Mr.) before the last name; for a woman, the term is *ponia* (Mrs.) or *panele* (Miss). A person's professional title also is used before the last name when applicable. Doctors and teachers are respectfully addressed by title alone. Adults do not address each other by first name until invited to do so, but young people are called by their first names. Men raise their hats or nod to greet people at a distance. The most common terms for greeting are *Laba diena* (Good day), *Labas rytas* (Good morning), *Labas vakaras* (Good evening), *Su Diev* (Go with God), and *Viso gero* (Good-bye). Friends use the more informal *Labas* (Hello), *Viso* (Bye), and *Iki* (Later). *Sveikas* (for a man), *Sveika* (for a woman), and *Sveiki* (for a group or in a formal situation)—all roughly meaning "How are you?"—are friendly ways to say hello. Urban Lithuanians do not greet strangers passing on the street.

Gestures. It is impolite to talk with one's hands in one's pockets. Eye contact is vital during conversation. People sometimes extend the thumb upward to express approval, but verbal communication is preferred. Using the hands during or instead of conversation is not uncommon, only less formal. Avoid shaking hands through a doorway. Chewing gum in public is not appropriate for adults.

Visiting. Visiting in the home is popular because outside social opportunities are somewhat limited and expensive. Spontaneous visits, even between friends and neighbors, are not very common. It is polite to call before any visit, but unannounced guests will be welcome. Hosts expect punctuality of invited guests. It is customary to bring an odd number of fresh flowers for even a brief visit. An even number is for funerals. Dinner guests also may bring wine. Guests should unwrap flowers before giving them to the hostess. White flowers usually are reserved for brides, and carnations are for mourning or certain other occasions. In formal situations, guests wait to sit down until invited or until the host sits. For informal gatherings, guests may act more at home. Hosts always offer guests refreshments, which may include coffee or tea and cake or cookies. They offer an abundance of food to indicate their home's prosperity. Drinking vodka (usually only men) or other alcohol is typically part of most social visits. The length of an evening visit depends on the occasion. If the hour is late, a host may accompany departing guests outside.

Eating. Lithuanians eat in the continental style, with the fork in the left hand and the knife remaining in the right. They usually eat three meals each day. Breakfast is between 7 and 9 a.m., lunch 1 and 2 p.m., and supper 6 and 8 p.m. Rural inhabitants eat meals as much as two hours earlier. The midday meal is the main meal, and some businesses close for it.

People either go home or eat at work site canteens. Meals are taken leisurely and socially. Toasting is common for lunch and supper, whether guests are present or not. Leaving food on the plate is impolite, as it suggests to the hostess that the meal was not good. In a restaurant, one must request the bill from the waiter and pay at the table. Tipping is not customary but is becoming more common.

LIFESTYLE

Family. The average family has one or two children. The father is generally the head of the family, but both parents share in raising children and working outside the home. Women do household chores; men handle repairs. The elderly prefer to live alone, but many live with their adult children. In cities, most people live in apartments. Due to limited space, apartment furniture often serves several purposes. Single-family homes are more common in rural areas. As land confiscated by the Soviets is returned to people throughout the country, people are building more private homes. All families have gardens either near their rural home or on the outskirts of cities. Each family member helps tend the "kitchen garden," a source of fresh food, relaxation, and contact with the land.

Dating and Marriage. Young people enjoy dancing, going to clubs, and traveling together. They usually marry in their early twenties, but some wait until they are financially secure. Young couples often rely for a time on financial support and even housing from their parents. It is becoming more popular to live together before, or instead of, marrying. Legal marriages are performed at the city hall; many couples now also have a church ceremony.

Rural weddings can be lavish, and it is becoming popular to practice older traditions. For example, after the wedding ceremony, the wedding party's way home is blocked by "ropes" of branches and flowers. The groom's friends and the matchmaker have to "buy" their way out with candy and alcohol. Sweets also are given to children along the way. The last rope is usually stretched across the gate of the couple's home. Parents meet the newlyweds at the door with bread, salt, and wine glasses filled with water. Many customs surround the two-day wedding celebration, including the mock punishment (and eventual rescue) of the matchmaker for convincing the bride to marry the groom.

Diet. Lithuanian cuisine has adopted many dishes from neighboring cultures, including *blynai* (pancakes), *barščai* (beet soup), and *balendėlai* (stuffed cabbage leaves). Traditional specialties include smoked sausage, various cheeses, *cepelinai* (meat cooked inside a ball of potato dough, served with a special sauce), *vedarai* (cooked potatoes and sausage stuffed into pig intestines), and *kugelis* (potato pudding with a sour cream sauce). Potatoes are prepared in numerous ways. Soup commonly is served with lunch. Local fruits (apples, pears, plums, and strawberries) and vegetables (carrots, cabbage, peas, and beets) are also popular. People grow much of their own produce and preserve some for winter consumption. They regularly eat rye bread and dairy products. Tea, milk, and coffee are the most common drinks.

Recreation. Basketball is the favorite sport, followed by soccer, boating (rowing), volleyball, cycling, tennis, cross-country skiing, and others. Camping is popular for family outings, as is picking mushrooms or berries in the forest and going to the beach. Men also enjoy fishing. Watching

EUROPE ▼

television, knitting and sewing (for women), and visiting are common leisure activities. People also relax by visiting their garden plots or by playing chess or cards. Many enjoy caring for pets (mostly dogs), reading, and going to cultural events, especially those involving national dance and song.

The Arts. Folklore, riddles, and local myths are very popular, and their themes are incorporated into other forms of Lithuanian folk art. Traditional ballads deal with nature, love, and mythical creatures. Music frequently is accompanied by the accordion and a harp-like instrument similar to a dulcimer.

Folk arts include straw baskets, leather goods, wood carvings, clay or straw sculptures, and amber jewelry. A recent revival of folk arts has encouraged artistic production.

Holidays. Official public holidays include New Year's Day, Independence Day (16 Feb.), Mother's Day (first Sunday in May), Anniversary of the Coronation of Grand Duke Mindaugas of Lithuania (6 July), and National Day of Hope and Mourning (1 Nov.). Families traditionally have a 12-course, meatless meal on Christmas Eve (*Kučios*). The Day of Hope and Mourning, also known as All Souls' Day, is a day to remember the dead. For the pre-Lent *Užgavinès*, people dress in costumes and children go door-to-door asking for treats. Easter is celebrated with family. St. John's Day (24 June) marks the advent of summer. Various local festivals are held throughout the year. Birthdays are hosted by the birthday person, and jubilee years (every 10th year) are very special. Name days also may be important celebrations.

Commerce. Business generally is kept separate from socializing. Offices are open weekdays 9 a.m. to 6 p.m., with an hour break at 1 p.m. Food shops are open 8 a.m. to 7 p.m., Monday through Saturday, with a break at 2 p.m. Some shops are open 10 a.m. to 10 p.m., with a break around 2 p.m. Banks are open weekdays 9 a.m. to 6 p.m. Kiosks and small shops have more flexible hours. Most Lithuanians shop at open-air markets, which operate at least twice a week in every town. These feature a wide array of foods, clothing, and household items.

SOCIETY

Government. Lithuania's 1992 constitution provides for a president to serve a five-year term as head of state. Lithuanian-born Valdas Adamkus, who had spent 50 years in the United States after fleeing a Soviet coup in 1944, was elected president in January 1998 at age 71. The prime minister is head of government. The prime minister is chosen by the president with the approval of the 141-seat Parliament (*Seimas*), which is the highest body of state power. The governing four-party coalition includes the Lithuanian Liberal Union and the New Union. The voting age is 18.

Economy. Lithuania is an industrial state, producing precision machinery, processed foods, and light industrial products. The country has few natural resources, so it depends on imported raw materials. Main exports include machinery and parts, meat and dairy products, and consumer goods. Imports include oil and gas, chemicals, metals, and equipment. Production declined with independence, as traditional supply arrangements were interrupted, but ties are being established with Western Europe and neighboring countries to increase rev-

DEVELOPMENT DATA

Human Dev. Index* rank	52 of 174 countries
Adjusted for women	47 of 143 countries
Real GDP per capita	$6,436
Adult literacy rate	99 percent
Infant mortality rate	15 per 1,000 births
Life expectancy	63 (male); 75 (female)

enue, investment, and productivity. Privatization of key sectors, needed to increase foreign investment, is also underway.

The standard of living has fallen in the last few years due to difficulties associated with the transition to a market economy. Public reaction to high inflation, low wage growth, and poverty was strong in the mid-1990s. The Russian economic crisis in 1998 threw Lithuania's economy into a recession from which it is still recovering. The economy grew 2 percent in 2000. Unemployment averaged around 12 percent. The national currency is the *litas*.

Transportation and Communications. Public transportation is convenient and important because most families do not own private vehicles. Local buses and trolleys operate in cities; bus and train services operate within the country. Airlines, trains, and sea ferries connect Lithuania with various European destinations. Private newspapers and three state-owned government newspapers (one each written in Lithuanian, Russian, and Polish) are available. Several private television stations broadcast in addition to the state-run station. The telephone system is not extensive but is fairly efficient. Cellular phones are increasingly popular because the networks are cheaper to use than existing phone lines.

Education. Children attend elementary school for nine years, assigned in the second *form* (grade) to one of three levels ("A" being for advanced students). Students may then pursue three years of secondary school, go to a vocational school, or begin working. Education is provided free at all levels. General education schools offer an optional course in religion. Sunday schools are open for Jews, Karaites (a small group descended from the 14th-century Tatars), and other religious minorities. Ethnic minorities have the option of attending schools that teach in their language. Difficult entrance exams are required for the 16 institutions of higher education, including Vilnius University, the University of Vytautas Magnus, and Kaunas Technical University.

Health. Lithuania has a national health-care system, but some aspects are scheduled to be privatized; several private clinics already exist. The system provides for basic needs, although modern equipment and supplies are lacking. Home remedies and long recuperations are standard practices.

CONTACT INFORMATION

Embassy of the Republic of Lithuania, 2622 16th Street NW, Washington, DC 20009-4202; phone (202) 234-5860; Web site www.ltembassyus.org. American Travel Services, 9439 South Kedzie, Evergreen Park, IL 60805; phone (800) 422-3190.

1305 North Research Way, Bldg. K
Orem, Utah 84097-6200 USA
1.800.528.6279; 801.705.4250
fax 801.705.4350
www.culturegrams.com

Grand Duchy of
Luxembourg

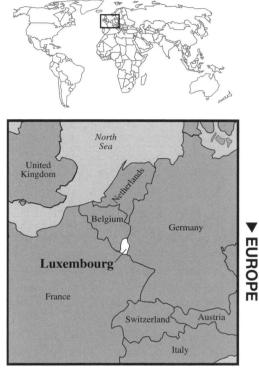

▼ EUROPE

Boundary representations are not necessarily authoritative.

BACKGROUND

Land and Climate.   Luxembourg is a small, landlocked country bordered by France to the south, Belgium to the north and west, and Germany to the east. Covering 998 square miles (2,586 square kilometers), it is about the same size as Rhode Island. Nearly 25 percent of the land is suitable for cultivation. Luxembourg has gently rolling hills with shallow valleys and many forests, including those in the Ardennes uplands of the north. The northern third of the country is called the Eisléck or Oesling. The central and southern region (the Good Land) is dominated by farmland and woods and comprises about 68 percent of the territory. The landscape is dotted with castles and the ruins of castles and fortresses. The Moselle River forms the southeastern border. The climate is mild. Winter temperatures are generally above freezing and summer temperatures average 75°F (24°C). The sunniest summer months are May and June.

History.   Luxembourg is one of Europe's oldest and smallest independent countries. But before it became independent, the area was ruled by many kingdoms and empires, including that of the Romans and, much later, Charlemagne's. In 963, Count Siegfried of the Ardennes built a castle in present-day Luxembourg and founded the Luxembourg Dynasty. Charles of Luxembourg became the king of Bohemia in the 14th century and strove to make Prague (now in the Czech Republic) as beautiful as Paris. Indeed, Luxembourg gave more than one monarch to other countries during the medieval period.

Luxembourg was ruled by the Austrian Hapsburgs in the 17th and 18th centuries and then by the Netherlands. In 1815, it became a Grand Duchy in the Dutch Kingdom. The Luxembourgers revolted in 1830 after the Belgians also rebelled against Dutch control. After the revolt, Luxembourg was divided between Belgium and the Netherlands. The Netherlands's portion is what eventually gained independence as today's Luxembourg. The 1867 Treaty of London declared Luxembourg an independent neutral state, although it remained closely tied to the Netherlands. Personal union between the monarchs of the Netherlands and Luxembourg ended in 1890 when both died without leaving heirs to their thrones. In Luxembourg, the crown passed to the House of Nassau, which holds it today.

Although neutral, Luxembourg was invaded by Germany in both world wars. After its liberation, Luxembourg ended its neutrality (1949) and joined the western European alliances, including the North Atlantic Treaty Organization. In 1964, the Grand Duchess Charlotte abdicated, allowing her son, Grand Duke Jean, to become ruler. In the first formal step towards passing the crown, Grand Duke Jean named his son Prince Henri, the heir apparent, as governor in March 1998.

Luxembourg has enjoyed peace, economic growth, and beneficial relations with other European nations for decades. Luxembourg is particularly well represented in the European Union (EU), of which it is the smallest member. The European Court of Justice, Investment Bank, Court of Auditors, Secretariat of the European Parliament, and services of the Commission of the EU, such as the Statistical Office (EUROSTAT), are based in Luxembourg.

In June 1999 elections, the Christian Democrat–Socialist ruling coalition resigned after the liberal Democratic Party eclipsed the Socialists. A new Christian Democratic–Liberal coalition was formed. Jean-Claude Juncker is prime minister. In October 2000, Crown Prince Henri became the new grand duke following the abdication of his father, Grand Duke Jean. Although the grand duke has limited political power, Henri hopes to play a more active role in state affairs.

THE PEOPLE

Population. After remaining steady for several years, Luxembourg's population of more than 437,000 currently is growing at 1.27 percent annually. Nearly one-quarter of the population lives in the city of Luxembourg. The Luxembourgers, who are an ethnic mixture of French and German origins, account for about 65 percent of the population. The rest consists of guest and worker residents from Portugal, Italy, France, and other European countries. The immigrant population is growing faster than the number of native Luxembourgers. Foreign residents make up more than 50 percent of Luxembourg City's population.

Language. *Lëtzebuergesch* (Luxembourgish) is the native tongue of Luxembourgers. It comes from a Franco-Moselle dialect, mixed with many German and French words. It was declared the national language in 1984, although it had always been used as the daily language of the people. Luxembourgish is used more as a spoken language than a written one. French and German also have official status. German often is used for newspapers, while French is the official language of the civil service, law, and parliament. Children begin learning German in school at the age of six and French at seven. English also is taught in the schools and is widely understood.

Religion. The Roman Catholic Church claims membership of more than 95 percent of the population. While most adhere to Catholic traditions, society is basically secular. Most of the rest of Luxembourg's residents either belong to various Protestant and other Christian churches or are Jewish. A small number claim no affiliation. Most Christians do not attend church services on a regular basis, but many show their devotion through actions or attitudes (such as tolerance, charity, etc.).

General Attitudes. Although the people of Luxembourg are descendants of different nationalities and speak several different languages, they maintain a strong feeling of national pride. Their independence and separate identity in Europe are important. This character is reflected in the national motto: *Mir wëlle bleiwe wat mer sin!* (We want to remain what we are!). By both conquest and peaceful exchange, Luxembourg has been influenced by the neighboring countries of Belgium, Germany, and France. Many traditions of each of these countries are evident in the customs of the Luxembourgers. There are differences, however. For example, the pace of everyday life in Luxembourg is not as hurried as in other European countries. Luxembourgers value education, privacy, friendship, and humor. They do not appreciate loud behavior in polite company or in public.

Personal Appearance. Luxembourgers follow European fashion trends, chiefly those from France, Germany, and Italy. Men wear suits to work. Many men wear hats. Women wear dresses somewhat more often than pants. The youth follow the latest fashion trends. Luxembourgers stress cleanliness and neatness in appearance. People are always well dressed in public; tattered clothing is inappropriate. Very casual clothing is reserved for the home or recreational activities.

CUSTOMS AND COURTESIES

Greetings. A gentle handshake is most common and most appropriate when greeting acquaintances or meeting someone for the first time. Close female friends may hug three times. Other close friends who have not seen each other for a long time may kiss each other's cheeks three times. Polite inquiries about a friend's health or colleague's work might accompany a greeting. The most common verbal greetings in Luxembourgish include *Moien* (Morning), *Gudden Owend* (Good evening), and *Wéi geet et?* (How are you?). Also common is *Bonjour*, French for "Good day." Upon parting, one might say *Äddi*, a casual "Good-bye," or the more formal *Au revoir*. Young people like *Salut* or *Ciao* for a quick good-bye. Friends and acquaintances also use longer phrases, such as *Bis eng aner Kéier* or *Bis härno*, both of which roughly mean "See you later." *Äddi, bis mar* (Until tomorrow) is also appropriate. Like most Europeans, Luxembourgers are reserved when first meeting strangers. However, they are friendly and remember those who befriend them. Friends and relatives address each other by given names or nicknames, while acquaintances use titles and surnames. High-ranking persons may be addressed by more than one title, such as *Här Minister* (Mr. Minister), with or without the surname.

Gestures. Although Luxembourgers might use hands to emphasize their speech during conversation, specific gestures rarely are used to complement or replace verbal communication. Proper behavior in public is expected; one refrains from yawning, shouting, or using offensive language. Handkerchiefs are used inconspicuously. Chewing gum while speaking is impolite.

Visiting. Luxembourgers enjoy visiting friends and relatives at home, but they rarely drop by unannounced. Most visits are prearranged, usually by invitation. Hosts take care to make guests feel welcome. They nearly always offer refreshments, usually in the form of something to drink. A cocktail is common before a meal. Good friends visiting a couple that has just moved into a new home bring bread, salt, and a bottle of wine to wish them well. Dinner guests normally bring flowers, chocolates, a small gift, or a bottle of wine to their hosts. Among younger people, the guests often bring dessert. Good friends and relatives might bring gifts on holidays or for special occasions (first communion, final exams at secondary school, obtaining a college degree, birthdays, and so forth).

When guests depart, they thank the hosts and are accompanied outside of the home. Guests are seldom invited to the home to discuss business. Such matters are taken care of in public places, such as restaurants, cafés, or offices.

Eating. Luxembourgers usually eat breakfast between 7 and

9 a.m., lunch at noon, and dinner around 7 p.m. Some people have coffee around 4 p.m. The main meal of the day was traditionally at midday, but this is not possible for people who work all day or are too far from home each day to eat at that time. For these families, lunch is light and dinner is the main meal. At the family meal, serving dishes are placed on the table for each person to choose his or her portion. When guests are present, each person's plate usually is prepared in advance. Hosts expect their guests to ask for second helpings. Some cooks will believe their food is not liked if guests do not eat seconds. People eat in the continental style, with the fork in the left hand and the knife remaining in the right. They keep both hands, but not the elbows, above the table at all times. It is not proper to have one's hands resting in the lap during a meal.

In a restaurant, the waiter usually is paid at the table. The bill often includes a service fee. If so, an extra tip is not necessary but is appreciated. If service is not included, one normally leaves a tip of 10 to 15 percent.

LIFESTYLE

Family. The importance of the family is well established in Luxembourg. Parents still exert influence on the social and professional choices of their children. Parents are required by law to pay for their children's education, and adult children are required to meet certain financial obligations of their parents if in need. Over the past decade, traditional family ties have been weakened somewhat as more young people travel abroad for study or employment. However, bonds still are maintained through family gatherings and celebrations. Families usually are small, having on average fewer than two children. Many women work outside the home; they comprise one-third of the labor force. If working parents have younger children, grandparents may be called upon to care for them during the day. Day-care facilities and other options are also available. More than 60 percent of all families own the homes or apartments in which they live.

Dating and Marriage. Dating usually begins at age 15, after compulsory education requirements have been met. Parental approval, although less important than in the past, is still a factor in a young person's dating choices. The youth enjoy going to movies and theaters, eating at cafés and restaurants, having parties or dinners, and dancing. Couples may postpone marriage until they are financially established or complete their educational goals. Some couples choose to live together before marriage, but this is not an official union, and most Luxembourgers expect to marry eventually.

Only civil marriages are recognized by law. To be married in a church, a couple must present a certificate showing that they have been legally married by a civil authority. A reception for acquaintances and friends may follow a civil wedding, while a dinner for close friends and relatives traditionally follows a church ceremony.

Diet. Food in Luxembourg is influenced by French and German traditions, but it has its own unique flavor. People appreciate fine foods and there are many national favorites. Popular dishes include *Judd mat Gaardebounen* (smoked collar of pork with broad beans), *Bouneschlupp* (bean soup), *Kachkéis* (a soft cheese known as *cançoillotte* in French), *Quetschentaart* (plum tart), *Fritten, Ham an Zalot* (french fries, ham, and salad), *Träipen* (black pudding commonly eaten on Christmas Eve), and freshwater fish (usually trout). Sausages, potatoes, and sauerkraut are common elements of the diet. Fresh fruits and vegetables are eaten in season. A variety of cheeses and other dairy products are important. Coffee, wine, juice, and beer are popular drinks. Luxembourg also exports some domestic wines and beer to other countries in Europe.

Recreation. Cycling and hiking are favorite activities in Luxembourg, mostly because of the beautiful scenery. People also enjoy soccer, jogging, and volleyball. There are facilities for golf, tennis, squash, and water sports. Hunting and fishing are popular seasonal activities. Numerous parks, theaters, movie theaters, and museums are available. Gardening and watching television are popular leisure activities.

The Arts. Cultural arts are important to Luxembourgers. A large art market in Luxembourg City helps satisfy the demand for traditional and contemporary art and sculpture. Important art and historical collections are housed in the Musée de l'Etat. To help sustain musical and theatrical arts in the country, the Grand Duchy has established cultural agreements with other European nations. Private banks are also important cultural patrons.

Luxembourgers enjoy attending the well-respected Grand Orchestra of Radiotelevision Luxembourg. During the summer, Wiltz and Echternach host festivals involving music, dance, and theater. In the capital, orchestras and folk bands give open-air concerts regularly. Besides going to performances or museums, Luxembourgers like to paint, play musical instruments, or perform in village playhouses.

Holidays. In addition to some national holidays, several religious holidays are celebrated in Luxembourg. The national holidays include New Year's Day, Labor Day (1 May), the Grand Duke's Birthday—also called National Day (23 June), and Fair Day (early September). Fair Day occurs during fair season in the capital city. An ancient shepherds' market serves as the fairgrounds and many traditions focus on sheepherding.

Religious holidays include Shrove Tuesday (Feb.), Easter (including Monday), Ascension, Whitmonday, Assumption (15 Aug.), All Saints' Day (1 Nov.), All Souls' Day (2 Nov.), and Christmas (24–26 Dec.). Christmas and Easter are the most important holidays.

At Easter, young children take part in a tradition called *klibbere goen.* According to legend, all church bells go to Rome three days before Easter for confessional. So the boys use rattles to announce church services, since the bells cannot ring. When the bells return on the Saturday before Easter, the children collect money and colorful Easter eggs from each home in the neighborhood as their reward. Every family colors Easter eggs during this season, and on Easter Sunday, children receive the eggs and other gifts hidden in the garden.

Christmas celebrations begin weeks before the actual holiday. Some time before 6 December, small children place a shoe outside their bedroom before bedtime and expect to receive a piece of chocolate from St. Nicholas (*Kleeschen*) if they have been good. Otherwise, they might receive a birch twig from his helper, *Housecker*. Then, on 6 December, *Kleeschen* visits good children and brings them gifts. Small parades often are held in various cities to celebrate the event. On Christmas Eve, families have a big meal and Catholics go to mass. Nearly all families have a tree in the home; many have a nativity scene. Christmas day is a family day.

Carnival is celebrated in the spring in many cities. There are also wine fairs, art festivals, and festivities to mark historical events.

Commerce. Business hours are generally from 8:30 a.m. to 5:30 p.m., Monday through Friday. Some shopping and recreational facilities are open longer. Some small shops may close for an hour at lunchtime. Most people shop in large supermarkets for their groceries, but a fresh produce open-air market operates on Wednesday and Saturday. Luxembourg has a favorable business climate and there are few labor disputes. All workers receive 25 vacation days each year. Women receive from four to six months' maternity leave.

SOCIETY

Government. The Grand Duchy of Luxembourg is a constitutional monarchy, led by the Grand Duke Henri. However, the constitution vests sovereignty in the people. The 60 members of Luxembourg's unicameral legislature (Chamber of Deputies) are directly elected. A prime minister is head of government. A Council of State advises the legislature. Most governments are coalitions. The major political parties include the Christian Social People's Party, the Democratic Party, and the Socialist Workers Party. Several smaller parties also hold legislative seats. All citizens older than age 18 are required to vote in national elections.

Economy. Luxembourg enjoys one of the highest standards of living in the world, which derives in part from the economy's constant stability. Despite its lack of natural resources and its policy to no longer exploit its iron ore reserves, Luxembourg has been able to develop, diversify, and keep its economy strong. Inflation and unemployment generally remain low. In 2000, the economy grew by around 8 percent. The agriculture sector is modern and employs less than 3 percent of the labor force. About one-third of all workers in Luxembourg are foreign laborers from Portugal, Italy, France, Belgium, and Germany. The service sector of the economy has grown substantially as the manufacturing sector, which is based on the steel industry, has become less important. Services (especially financial) now employ almost half of the workforce. Nevertheless, steel, chemicals, rubber, and other products are still important exports. The government currently is working to broaden the economic base of the country by promoting investment in communications and audiovisual companies.

Luxembourg has benefited from European economic integration and cooperates closely with Belgium and the

DEVELOPMENT DATA

Human Dev. Index* rank	17 of 174 countries
Adjusted for women	20 of 143 countries
Real GDP per capita	$33,505
Adult literacy rate	99 percent
Infant mortality rate	5 per 1,000 births
Life expectancy	74 (male); 81 (female)

Netherlands in the BENELUX economic union. Luxembourg has already met the Economic Monetary Union (EMU) criteria to join the single European currency; it will phase in the euro by the summer of 2002. The government actively encourages foreign investment. Both the Belgian *franc* (BF) and the Luxembourg *franc* (LuxF) are accepted as currencies of equal value.

Transportation and Communications. Luxembourg is a hub of travel in Europe. Trains connect to most major European cities and are well maintained. Roads and railways are in excellent condition. Most domestic consumer goods are transported in trucks. Most families own cars. Taxis are plentiful in the cities. The urban bus system is efficient. The communications system is modern and efficient. The government administers telephone, telegraph, and postal systems. Television, radio, and newspapers are privately owned.

Education. Luxembourg's education system is well developed. Children attend primary school for six years and secondary school for seven years. Upon successfully passing exams at the end of the secondary level, students may go on to university studies. This might include a two-year banking course at Luxembourg's university, Cours Universitaire; training for primary-level teachers at the Institut Supérieur d'Etudes et de Recherches Pédagogiques; or the first year of college studies at the Cours Universitaire. That first year in humanities, law, economics, secondary education, science, or medicine is recognized by many foreign universities to which Luxembourgers must transfer to complete their studies. Various technical and vocational schools exist to train those who seek careers outside of these professions.

Health. Public health standards are high, facilities are modern and advanced, and the cost to patients is low because of a compulsory social insurance system. People also may carry private insurance to cover certain expenses. Clinics serve local needs, and hospitals are located in large towns.

CONTACT INFORMATION

Embassy of the Grand Duchy of Luxembourg, 2200 Massachusetts Avenue NW, Washington, DC 20008; phone (202) 265-4171; Web site www.luxembourg-usa.org. Luxembourg National Tourist Office, 17 Beekman Place, New York, NY 10022; phone (212) 935-8888; Web site www.ont.lu.

CultureGrams™
People. The World. You.

1305 North Research Way, Bldg. K
Orem, Utah 84097-6200 USA
1.800.528.6279; 801.705.4250
fax 801.705.4350
www.culturegrams.com

Republic of
Malta

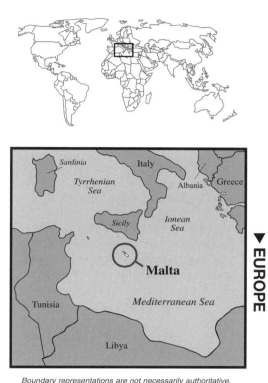

Boundary representations are not necessarily authoritative.

BACKGROUND

Land and Climate.   Malta is an archipelago of five islands situated in the center of the Mediterranean basin. Together the islands cover 122 square miles (316 square kilometers), with Malta and Gozo being the largest. Comino has a small tourist resort, and Cominotto and Filfla are uninhabited. The longest distance on Malta is 17 miles (27 kilometers) from southeast to northwest. The indented coastline has many natural harbors, bays, creeks, rocky coves, and some sandy beaches. Except for limestone, Malta has no natural resources. Malta's terrain slopes gently from west to east and features valleys, low-lying hills, and terraced fields. Valletta, the capital, hosts the main harbor. Gozo is more rural, with flat-topped hills dotting the landscape. Rugged coastal cliffs are penetrated by steep valleys and bays. Gozo is 9 miles long and 4 miles wide. Its main town is Rabat; the main port is Mgarr.

The Mediterranean climate is marked by hot summers and mild, rainy winters. Clear skies are common throughout the year. Winter temperatures average 57°F (14°C). Summer temperatures average nearly 90°F (32°C) but can exceed 100°F (40°C) from July to September. Summer heat is tempered by cool northwesterly sea breezes, but a hot and humid sirocco wind also occasionally reaches the islands. Colder Atlantic air sets off thunderstorms in September to mark the end of summer. Rain falls only for short periods of time (mostly from October to March), so 60 percent of Malta's water must be provided by reverse osmosis installations.

History.   Malta has a rich historical legacy. Its strategic position at the crossroads of the Mediterranean and its natural harbors have attracted various settlers and colonizers through the ages. The earliest inhabitants built impressive megalithic temple structures between 4000 and 2000 B.C. Beginning in 800 B.C., Phoenicians and later Carthaginians used Malta as a maritime outpost until the Romans annexed the islands in 218 B.C. Romans ruled until the fifth century A.D. and were followed by the Byzantines and then the Arabs (870–1090). The Arabs left notable imprints on the Maltese language and culture. Arab domination was ended by Count Roger the Norman. The fortunes of Malta then fell into the hands of various houses of Spain until 1530, when Spain's King Charles V granted the islands to the religious Order of the Knights of St. John of Jerusalem.

The rule of the different Grand Masters of the Order marked an important turning point in Malta's history. In 1565, they prevailed against invading Ottomans in the Great Siege of Malta. One year later, they began building the fortress city of Valletta. The Grand Masters administered the islands until 1798, when Napoleon Bonaparte occupied Malta in the name of the French Republic. The French surrendered after a two-year land and sea blockade by combined British and Maltese forces. In 1800, Malta became part of the British Empire. Malta played a pivotal role in World War II and was one of the staging areas for the Allied invasion of Sicily.

In 1964, Malta became an independent state recognizing Britain's queen of England as nominal head of state. In 1974, Malta became a republic with an elected president. British troops left in 1979. Malta remains a member of the Commonwealth.

Maltese politics were dominated by the Labour Party until the Nationalist Party came to power in 1987. Malta applied for membership in the European Union (EU) in 1990. When the Labour Party again gained control in 1996, it froze the application process. The Labour Party called for early elections but lost to the Nationalist Party in September 1998. Dr. Edward Fenech Adami is currently prime minister. Working toward EU membership and reducing the budget deficit remain at the top of the government's agenda.

THE PEOPLE

Population. Malta's population of 391,670 is growing annually at 0.74 percent. Most people live on Malta, while close to 8 percent live on Gozo. The Maltese are a homogeneous people. Less than 2 percent of permanent residents are non-Maltese (mostly British). Malta is primarily an urban island with a high population density. Overbuilding has made environmental issues a major concern. The highest concentrations of people are found in the Inner Harbor Region around Valletta, Senglea, Hamrun, and Sliema. Gozo is more rural and less populated.

Language. Maltese and English are both official languages. Maltese has a Semitic structure that initially developed from a medieval variation of Arabic. A large number of Romance and Anglo-Saxon words (mostly Italian and English) were later added, and the result is a very unique language. Maltese is written in a Latin script with some diacritical markings. It is used in daily interaction, business, and public instruction. Many people understand Italian, the official language until 1934. English is taught in school, and most people are bilingual. People often switch between Maltese and English in daily conversation. Many young people are learning German and French.

Religion. Roman Catholicism is Malta's official religion. Christianity was introduced when, as a prisoner, Paul the Apostle was shipwrecked on Malta on his way to Rome in A.D. 60. The Catholic Church is powerful enough to block legislation it opposes; it also sponsors a variety of volunteer organizations, a radio station, and a weekly newspaper.

Freedom of worship is guaranteed by the constitution, and Anglican, Methodist, Greek Orthodox, Islamic, and Jewish denominations have places of worship in Malta. Although Maltese society is becoming increasingly secularized, religious celebrations and extravagant family festivities mark the major stages of a person's life. Children generally receive Catholic catechism lessons both at school and in evening village centers. More than half of all Maltese regularly attend Sunday mass.

Each village and town has a patron saint to whom the parish church is dedicated. Between May and October, local people celebrate the *festa* (feast day) that honors their patron. Churches and streets are lavishly decorated, and marching bands and fireworks witness the people's devotion and zeal. At Easter, somber Good Friday processions are followed by merry Easter Sunday *Irxoxt* (Risen Christ) processions.

General Attitudes. The Maltese pride themselves on being open, generous, gregarious, and hospitable. They place great importance on the family and often stay in close contact with parents and grandparents. Weekly or daily visits are common. Given their traditional religious heritage, the Maltese do not easily tolerate alternative faiths and lifestyles. Most adults are frugal and astute in their use of resources, but the younger generation is more likely to take advantage of current economic and consumer options.

Because the islands are small, privacy is rather a luxury and anonymity is impossible. Networking plays an important part in regulating social interaction and access to resources. Malta's climate and sunny skies invite people to go out for a stroll or to meet friends in the *pjazza* (village square) and socialize. Although the Maltese tend to be courteous, strong intervillage rivalries can lead to antagonistic exchanges over such issues as politics, soccer, or village saints.

Personal Appearance. The Maltese enjoy being well dressed in European fashions. The style and quality of clothing are important indicators of social status. A great deal of attention is given to hairstyles, and people avoid appearing sloppy or dirty, even on informal occasions. Dress codes generally are formal in the service, business, and professional sectors. Employees at manufacturing and financial institutions sometimes wear uniforms.

Older people, especially in rural villages, tend to wear at least some traditional items. For instance, men might wear a *beritta* (cap), and women dress in somber-colored, long skirts. Black is worn for up to a year as a sign of mourning. Men and women, especially from blue-collar backgrounds, like to wear gold jewelry. Nearly all children wear uniforms to school, although they enjoy colorful fashions at home and on weekends. When visiting places of worship, men do not wear shorts; women wear trousers or knee-length dresses and something to cover their shoulders.

CUSTOMS AND COURTESIES

Greetings. Greetings depend on familiarity and on a person's age, gender, and social background. The Maltese have integrated both Mediterranean expressiveness and English reserve. More formal meetings begin and end with a handshake. Adults use applicable professional and religious titles to address one another. People from a rural or working-class background might pat each other on the back, shoulders, or arms to show friendship or closeness. In some villages, persons are identified more by their family nickname than by their surname.

The older generation tends to greet friends with a diminutive. For example, one might greet a man with *Hawn Ġuż, kif aħna?* (Hi Guz, how are we?). *Ġuż* is the nickname for Guzeppi. Other greetings include *Bonġu* (Good morning) and *Bonswa* (Good evening). On parting, one might say *Saħħa* (Health to you) or *Ciaw* (Bye). Younger people tend to use English greetings. Students address teachers as "Sir" or "Miss," followed by the surname.

Gestures. Like most Mediterranean people, the Maltese use a variety of gestures when speaking. Head, hand, and body language reflect and emphasize moods, feelings, and thoughts. Sometimes these gestures even replace language. Lifting one's chin up is a way of saying "no," while bending it forward means "yes." A quick left-right-left movement of the head means "no"; if this is accompanied by puckered lips, the person is showing displeasure, dismay, and even disgust. Clenched fists indicate anger, while surprise is shown by quickly placing the fingers of the right hand on the mouth. Tapping one's forehead with the index finger implies one finds a person stupid. A sudden lifting of the index and middle fingers and the thumb of the right hand in an outward curling direction means "How are you?"

Visiting. Friends generally prefer going out rather than spending time in each other's houses. It is considered polite to prearrange a home visit, particularly if the stay is to be lengthy. Many women clean the house daily and receive guests formally in the front sitting room reserved for visitors and major family occasions. Generally, hosts offer a drink and some sort of refreshment (biscuits, cakes, sandwiches). Visitors bring gifts (wine, flowers, chocolates) when invited to lunch or dinner. Often, foreign guests present the family with a souvenir from their country.

Eating. The Maltese eat in the continental style, with the fork in the left hand and the knife remaining in the right. They keep their hands above the table. When finished, a person places the utensils parallel on the plate and does not leave the table until everyone is finished. Families try to eat meals together, but this depends on work and school schedules. Breakfast and lunch are light meals, the latter consisting of a salad and sandwich. Dinner is eaten sometime between 6 and 8 p.m. Most people eat snacks at 10 a.m. and 4 p.m., usually some tea or coffee, a sandwich, or in the morning, *pastizzi* (cheesecake). Many workers and most students eat packed lunches from home. Weekend (especially Sunday) meals are eaten together. During the summer, many families have their evening meal near the sea as they enjoy a picnic or a barbecue after a swim. In small tea shops, cafés, and clubs, people enjoy eating Maltese sandwiches and *pastizzi*, and drinking local beer or soft drinks. U.S. American-style fast-food outlets are becoming popular with youths and young families.

LIFESTYLE

Family. The family is very important in Malta. Grandparents, uncles, aunts, cousins, nieces, and nephews meet regularly to celebrate events such as the village *festa*, important birthdays, and markers of life's passages (baptisms, communions, confirmations, betrothals, marriages, anniversaries, and funerals). While there are signs of strain on traditional family structures, with an increasing number of single-parent homes, there is little public enthusiasm to legalize divorce or abortion. As a rule, parents focus their energy and resources on acquiring a home and raising their children, who usually remain at home until they marry. Young people seldom live on their own, although this trend is growing. Many parents help their children buy a home or pay for an apartment, even if it means significant financial sacrifice.

Most families live in flat-roofed, terraced houses. The Maltese lavish a great deal of attention on their homes, as if to "carve out" a private space on the small, crowded island. The lack of land has lately forced the government to stop encouraging people to build homes; instead, it subsidizes rental housing.

Traditionally, the man is the head of the family, but the woman wields a lot of power in the private domain. Mothers are guardians of the Catholic faith, ensuring the family follows church precepts. They also nurture their children, supervise homework, and oversee other activities. Women often control the family budget.

While Malta has Europe's lowest rate (34 percent) of female participation in the formal labor market, more women are taking full-time or part-time jobs—especially after their children are older. Working parents may rely on grandparents and the extended family for child care, as there are few day-care facilities in Malta. In the past, it was common for the family to care for aging parents. However, with more women in the workforce and with the pace of life becoming faster,

this practice is changing. There is increasing pressure on the state and church to provide residential homes and other support to senior citizens.

Dating and Marriage. Young people usually start dating in groups around age 14 and as couples at age 16. The couple is said to be "going steady" when they are formally introduced to each other's families. Engagements are celebrated through the exchange and blessing of rings, as well as by a feast to which families and friends are invited. Engagements tend to last a long time, with marriages taking place when the couple is in their mid-twenties and has saved enough money for an apartment or house. Most young people do not live together before marriage. Weddings are grand affairs, with lavish feasts following a Solemn Mass. The bride's parents traditionally pay for most wedding expenses, which can exceed a year's salary. The reception, held at a hotel or garden, may include more than one thousand guests.

Diet. The Maltese diet includes Italian and British cuisine. The most common breakfast consists of cereal, tea, and toast with butter and jam or marmalade. Occasionally, one eats fried eggs, bacon, and beans. British dishes (turkey, baked potatoes, fruitcakes, puddings) are common at Christmas. However, most dishes are Mediterranean. Tomatoes are used with practically every dish, as are onions and garlic. Fresh bread accompanies all meals. A typical sandwich includes tomato paste, olives, and tuna. Pasta dishes are served almost daily, either as an appetizer or main course. Popular fish dishes include sea bass, *lampuka* (dorado), and swordfish. *Fenkata* (stewed rabbit) is a national dish, as is *timpana* (baked macaroni pastry). *Soppa ta' l-armla* (widow's broth), *minestra* (vegetable soup), and *aljotta* (fish chowder) are some of the more common soups. *Pastizzi* and *qassatat* (pastry filled with either cheese or peas, and occasionally anchovies or spinach) can be eaten at any time of day, often with tea. Many pastries reflect Malta's Arabic heritage. These include *imqaret* (filled with dates), *qubbajt* (filled with nougat), and a variety of almond sweets. In the summer, people enjoy ice cream or seasonal fruits such as watermelon.

Recreation. Soccer is the most popular sport, with fans avidly following the fortunes of their favorite local and, more commonly, foreign "football" teams. Italian and English teams are the most popular. Team and fan rivalries are intense; fans often crowd their homes or local bars to watch important games. Victory celebrations are noisy and very public. Other popular sports include netball (for girls), water-skiing, swimming, water polo, and windsurfing. *Bocci* is a traditional form of outdoor bowling. Since few schools are well equipped for sports, young people join private clubs to engage in various sports from tennis to fencing to scuba diving. Most young people enjoy dancing at discos.

The Maltese love to spend summer evenings at the beach; in winter they go for walks along the coast or in the countryside. At home in winter, they may watch television or videos and go out only on weekends. Men might enjoy bird hunting, trapping, and fishing. Many people have a summer residence near the sea. Families from the larger island may spend time on Gozo because it is considered quieter and more attractive. Women like jogging and aerobics. Working-class or rural men tend to spend evenings drinking, smoking, and playing cards in *każini* (pubs). Most village pubs are accessible only to men, while town bars are open to both sexes. Women and children participate in club activities sponsored by the church.

The Arts. The Maltese display an interest in literature, theater, painting, and ceramics. The National Library of Malta dates from the late 18th century. Malta's ancient Neolithic temples at Raal Gdid offer inspiration to contemporary artists and symbolize the rich history of the islands.

Maltese music mixes traditional and imported sounds. The islanders practice a form of singing known as *ghana* (pronounced ah-nah). *Ghana* incorporates both Arabic and Italian influences and is sung by *ghannejja* and accompanied by guitars. A popular pastime is a song duel between two *ghannejja*, in which each replies to the other in rhyming stanzas, with a guitar interlude between each stanza. The Malta Song Festival competition is held yearly. Jazz has become popular through the Malta Jazz Festival in July. The *Parata* (a sword dance) and *Il-Maltija* (the national dance) are important events at the *Carnival* in Valletta.

Holidays. Public holidays include New Year's Day (1 Jan.), St. Paul's Shipwreck (10 Feb.), Feast of St. Joseph (19 Mar.), Freedom Day (31 Mar.), Easter, Workers' Day (1 May), Sette Giugno (7 June, commemorating an uprising against the British), Imnarja (29 June, harvest feast dedicated to St. Peter and St. Paul), Assumption (15 Aug.), Victory Day (8 September, celebrating victory over the Turks in 1565 as well as the end of World War II), Independence Day (21 Sept.), Immaculate Conception (8 Dec.), Republic Day (13 Dec.), and Christmas. A *presepju* (nativity) is a traditional part of Christmas, as are processions with the statue of baby Jesus, Midnight Mass (which includes the traditional Boy's Sermon, or *Priedka tat-Tifel*), and Father Christmas. In addition, village *festas* on Sundays and *Carnival* (40 days before Easter) provide enjoyment at the local level.

Commerce. Businesses are open every day but Sunday from about 9 a.m. to 12:30 p.m. and 4 to 7 p.m. Banks close by noon on Saturdays. Traditional grocer's shops are being replaced by larger markets in more urban areas. Weekly open-air markets where vendors sell vegetables, bread, and fish are found in villages and towns.

SOCIETY

Government. Malta is a parliamentary democracy with a president (Dr. Guido de Marco) as head of state; this is a largely ceremonial role. The prime minister is head of government. Parliament consists of a 65-member House of Representatives. In 1993, Malta was divided into 67 regions to promote decentralization and give more power to local government. Each region has a locally elected council led by a mayor. The authority of these councils is currently limited, but powers are supposed to increase in the future.

Economy. Malta's economy is based on industry and tourism. German, Italian, and French firms have invested in manufacturing goods for export. Locally owned enterprises tend to be small. Expansion is inhibited by the lack of raw materials, a small local market, and increasingly high wage aspirations of Maltese workers. The service sector is promising, with tourism being particularly important. Other promising economic pursuits include transshipment services, off-

DEVELOPMENT DATA

Human Dev. Index* rank	27 of 174 countries
Adjusted for women	29 of 143 countries
Real GDP per capita	$16,447
Adult literacy rate	91 percent
Infant mortality rate	6 per 1,000 births
Life expectancy	75 (male); 81 (female)

shore banking, and insurance. Since the state provides most essential utilities and postal services, it employs at least one-third of the workforce. Malta's economy grew by around 4 percent in 2000. Unemployment dropped from 5 percent to 4 percent. In order to qualify for EU membership, Malta must reduce government spending and limit some of its protectionist trade policies. People sometimes supplement their modest incomes with part-time work or activities in the informal economy. The currency is the Maltese *lira* (LM).

Transportation and Communications. Most families own at least one car, but the public bus system can efficiently transport people to all parts of Malta. Roads are not always in good repair. Traffic moves on the left side of the road. Ferries connect Malta and Gozo. There is a new international airport. The Malta Freeport project is designed to make the island a major Mediterranean transshipment center. The communications and postal systems are efficient. The use of mobile phones and computers is increasing rapidly. Malta has four daily newspapers (two in English and two in Maltese). Six local television stations and several foreign ones reach Maltese homes via cable or satellite. Radio stations operate on a national and local basis.

Education. School is compulsory between the ages of five and sixteen. Nearly all three- and four-year-olds also attend kindergarten. Students may choose either public or private (usually Catholic) schools, between which a certain degree of rivalry exists. About 30 percent of students attend private schools. Others attend after-school private lessons to increase their chances of passing competitive exams. Students may enter the workforce at age 16, but 60 percent seek additional schooling. Some 15 percent of all pupils continue to the university level. The University of Malta traces its origins to 1592.

Health. Malta enjoys a high standard of medical care. Comprehensive health service for all Maltese residents is funded through general taxation. There are two general hospitals, one on Malta and one on Gozo. Government and private health clinics are plentiful. The main health problems include diabetes and heart disease.

CONTACT INFORMATION

Embassy of Malta, 2017 Connecticut Avenue NW, Washington, DC 20008; phone (202) 462-3611; Web site www.foreign.gov.mt/ORG/ministry/missions/washington2.htm. Malta Tourist Office, 300 Lanidex Plaza, Third Floor, Parsippany, NJ 07054; phone (877) 466-2582.

1305 North Research Way, Bldg. K
Orem, Utah 84097-6200 USA
1.800.528.6279; 801.705.4250
fax 801.705.4350
www.culturegrams.com

Boundary representations are not necessarily authoritative.

▼ THE AMERICAS

BACKGROUND

Land and Climate.   Covering 761,602 square miles (1,972,550 square kilometers), Mexico is about three times the size of Texas or one-fifth the size of the United States. It shares its northern border with the United States and its southern border with Guatemala and Belize. Mexico is rich in natural resources, including oil, natural gas, silver, iron ore, coal, copper, gold, lead, and zinc. Temperature and rainfall vary with elevation and region. Much of the north is dry and hot; humidity is higher in the south, where tropical jungles are found, and along coastal areas. The high and cooler central plateau, where Mexico City is located, is bounded by two mountain ranges: the Sierra Madre Oriental and Sierra Madre Occidental. Rain falls mainly in the summer (June–October) on the central plateau. Mountains, including many extinct volcanoes, cover two-thirds of the country. The Popocatepetl volcano, by Mexico City, erupted in December 2000; those living near the area were evacuated, but no one was injured from the blast.

History.   Mexico's history boasts a long line of advanced Indian civilizations whose accomplishments rival those of the Egyptians and early Europeans. They had accurate calendars, understood astronomy, were skilled artisans, and built huge empires. The Olmecs were among the first inhabitants of the area around 2000 B.C. The Mayan Empire built incredible cities throughout North and Central America but fell in the 12th century. The Aztecs were the last great empire, conquered by the Spanish in 1521. The Spanish assimilated some aspects of the Aztec culture while destroying others. They brought Christianity to the land and ruled until the 19th century.

Mexico was one of the first countries to revolt against Spain. The drive for independence began in September 1810,

led by priest Miguel Hidalgo, and ended in 1821. A constitution was adopted in 1824 and a republic was established. However, Antonio López de Santa Ana took power in 1833 and ruled as a dictator. During his regime, Mexico diminished in size: Texas seceded (1836) and came under U.S. control, and due to a war with the United States (1846–8), Mexico lost territory comprising much of the current western United States. Santa Ana resigned in 1855 and Benito Juárez became president. In 1861, French troops invaded Mexico City and named Austrian Archduke Maximilian the emperor of Mexico. Forces under Juárez overthrew Maximilian in 1867. Dictator Porfirio Díaz came to power in 1877 and was overthrown in 1910, when Mexico entered a period of internal political unrest and violence. That period, which ended in the 1920s and produced a new constitution, became known as Mexico's social revolution.

Political unrest continued in the 1930s, but the situation stabilized in the 1940s. The Institutional Revolutionary Party (PRI) emerged as the national leader in 1929; it ruled the country as a single party and restricted political dissent for many years. Many changes did take place, but none to challenge the PRI's position. Elected in 1988, President Carlos Salinas de Gortari signed the North American Free Trade Agreement (NAFTA), but after his term he fled the country because of allegations of corruption.

However, events in the mid-1990s helped weaken the party's power: The Zapatista National Liberation Army (EZLN) staged a 1994 rebellion in the state of Chiapas to protest government policy toward indigenous peoples. Charges of corruption against high-level government officials and the 1994 assassination of PRI presidential candidate Luis Donaldo Colosio shocked the ruling party. PRI replacement candidate Ernesto Zedillo Ponce de León took office in 1994 but immediately faced an economic and currency crisis. These challenges, combined with electoral reforms, led to historic results in 1997 midterm elections. Opposition parties won important posts throughout the country, and the PRI lost control of the lower house in Congress for the first time since its founding. In July 2000, Vicente Fox of the National Action Party (NAP) was elected president, ending more than 70 years of PRI control of the government. Since taking office, Fox has made substantial progress with the EZLN. In early 2001, Zapatista leaders, led by Subcomandante Marcos, marched to the capital to voice their demands. Fox pulled troops out of Chiapas and released political prisoners, and Congress is considering an amendment to the constitution giving indigenous peoples more rights.

THE PEOPLE

Population.　Mexico has more than 100 million people, a population that is growing at 1.53 percent annually. About 60 percent of the population is mixed Spanish and Indian. Thirty percent belongs to various Amerindian groups. Most of these are descendants of the Maya and Aztecs. About 9 percent is of European ancestry. Most Mexicans tend to identify with their Amerindian and Spanish heritage. Mexico City, the capital, is one of the largest cities in the world; its metropolitan area has a population of approximately 20 million. Guadalajara (2.2 million) and Monterrey (1.7 million) are also important financial and cultural centers.

Language.　Spanish is the official language. The Spanish spoken in Mexico is somewhat unique in pronunciation and the use of idioms. One characteristic is the common use of diminutives: *chico* (small) becomes *chiquito*; *abuelo* (grandfather) becomes *abuelito*, etc. As many as one hundred Amerindian languages are still spoken in parts of Mexico, including Tzotzil and Tzeltal (Mayan dialects), Maya, Nahuatl (Aztec), Otomi, Zapotec, and Mixtec. Most people who speak an Amerindian language also speak at least some Spanish.

Religion.　The majority of Mexicans (89 percent) are Roman Catholic, although many do not attend church services regularly. The Catholic Church has greatly influenced the culture, attitudes, and history of all Mexicans, and Catholic holidays are celebrated widely. The Virgin of Guadalupe is the patron saint of Mexico and a national symbol. According to legend, she appeared several times to the Indian Juan Diego in December 1531. Other Christian churches are also active in Mexico; some are growing quite rapidly.

The Mexican constitution was drafted during the revolution in an attempt to transfer power from the Catholic Church to the people. Although it guaranteed freedom of worship, it banned religious instruction in public schools and public displays of worship and did not allow churches to own property or exist as legal entities. In 1992, the law was changed, endowing churches with more legal rights. Although government officials often ignored the previous restrictions, the new law relieves tension between the state and various religions—without forcing the government to endorse a specific church.

General Attitudes.　Mexicans value friendship, humor, honesty, hard work, and personal honor. Power, wealth, family name, and education are all measures of social status. Mexicans also respect individuals who, regardless of level of education, use their ingenuity to solve daily problems. In rural areas, land is an important asset. *Machismo*, the ideal of a strong, forceful man, is still prevalent. The elderly are respected, particularly in Amerindian communities. Mexicans are patriotic and generally proud of their country, despite its challenges. They may call citizens of the United States *americanos* or *norteamericanos* but like to remind U.S. citizens that Mexico is also part of North America.

Mexicans traditionally have had a relaxed attitude toward time, although this is changing in urban areas. Generally, they believe individuals are more important than schedules; people will stop to talk to unexpected visitors, regardless of other commitments.

Personal Appearance.　Most Mexicans, especially in urban areas, wear clothing that is also common in the United States. Many indigenous groups wear traditional clothing—either daily or for festivals. In some areas, a man wears a wool poncho (*sarape*) over his shirt and pants when it is cold. He also may wear a wide-brimmed straw hat. Rural men and professional men in the north may wear cowboy hats, boots, and jeans. Rural women wear dresses or skirts, often covered by an apron. They may use a shawl (*rebozo*) to carry a child, cover the head or arms, or act as a coiled support for water buckets carried on the head. Fabric designs and colors can be characteristic of a specific region. Regardless of clothing style, color and beauty are features appreciated by all. People dress up for special occasions and parties.

CUSTOMS AND COURTESIES

Greetings.　Mexicans usually greet with a handshake or nod of the head, although friends commonly embrace. Women often greet with a kiss on the cheek, and men may greet close female friends in the same way. Common verbal greetings include *¡Buenos días!* (Good morning), *¡Buenas tardes!* (Good afternoon), *¡Buenas noches!* (Good evening/night), and *¿Cómo está?* (How are you?). A casual greeting is *¡Hola!* (Hello). Mexican males often make *piropos* (flattering personal comments) in passing to females, to which the females generally do not respond.

Mexicans commonly have more than one given name and two surnames (e.g., José Luis Martínez Salinas). The first surname comes from the father and the second from the mother. Coworkers address one another by professional title followed by the first surname (e.g., *Ingeniero Martínez*). Acquaintances or coworkers without a title are addressed as *Señor* (Mr.), *Señorita* (Miss), or *Señora* (Mrs.), followed by the first surname. Respected elders often are addressed as *Don* or *Doña*, followed by a given name.

Gestures.　Mexicans typically stand close to each other while talking, sometimes touching their friend's clothing. They often use hand and arm gestures in conversation. Amerindians generally are more reserved, conversing with little physical contact and touching their mouth or cheek when they speak. A person can indicate "no" by shaking the hand from side to side with the index finger extended and palm outward. The "thumbs up" gesture expresses approval, but the "thumbs down" gesture is considered vulgar. Tossing items is offensive; one hands items directly to another person. If someone sneezes, a person may say *¡Salud!* (Health). If passing between conversing individuals is unavoidable, one says *Con permiso* (Excuse me). It is considered important to say *Gracias* (Thank you) for any favor or commercial service rendered.

Visiting. Mexicans are very hospitable. Unexpected visitors usually are welcomed and served refreshments such as juice or a soft drink. Refusing refreshments may be considered impolite. Unannounced visits are fairly common, but as more people get telephones, more are calling ahead. Mexicans enjoy conversing and socializing with relatives or friends. At a dinner party, the meal might not be served until after 8 p.m. because people work late and enjoy socializing before eating. Guests are expected to relax and do not offer to help the host unless it is evident some help is needed. They stay for conversation rather than leave directly after the meal. On weekends, conversation may last until very late. On special occasions such as birthdays or Mother's Day, gifts are important and serenading is still popular (often in rural areas).

Eating. Although eating schedules vary, many Mexicans eat four daily meals: a light breakfast from 7 to 8 a.m., lunch between 10 to 11 a.m., and the main meal between 2 and 4 p.m.; the *cena* or *merienda* is a light snack at night. A main meal may consist of an entrée, soup or salad, main dish, and dessert (*postre*). Eating as a family is common. Urban professionals often eat meals at restaurants or street-side stands. Food purchased on the street usually is eaten at the stand. It is inappropriate for adults to eat while walking on the street. Spicy food is called *picante*, while hot (temperature) food is called *caliente*. *Picante* foods are often eaten with bland foods such as bread, tortillas, or rice to relieve the burning sensation. Many also use a pinch of salt for relief. When eating, Mexicans keep both hands above the table. Some foods are eaten with utensils, others with the hand. Meals usually are not rushed. One should always ask to be excused when leaving a table or room.

LIFESTYLE

Family. Except in urban areas, where the trend is to have smaller families, Mexican families generally have more than three children. Family unity and responsibilities are high priorities. Divorce is relatively low, due in part to the dominance of the Catholic faith. In traditional families the father is the family leader and provides economic support, while the mother is responsible for domestic and child-care duties. However, more women are entering the formal workplace. Rural men and women often work together in the fields. A household, especially in rural areas, may include members of the extended family. Children generally live with their parents until they marry and sometimes after they marry.

Dating and Marriage. When dating, a young man often meets the young woman at a prearranged place rather than picking her up at her home. However, parental approval of the activity and the boyfriend is important. In some rural areas, it is considered a mark of poor character for a young woman to go out alone after dark, so a young man may call on her at home. Many people marry first in a civil ceremony and then in a church, following Catholic traditions. Wedding celebrations include music, dancing, games, and food. Common-law marriage is also practiced and recognized.

Diet. Staple foods include corn, beans, rice, and chiles. These typically are combined with spices, vegetables, and meats or fish. Some foods and dishes are regional, but others are common throughout the nation. Cornmeal or flour tortillas are eaten everywhere. Other common foods include *tortas* (hollow rolls stuffed with meat, cheese, or beans), *quesadillas* (tortillas baked or fried with cheese), *mole* (spicy sauce

served with meat), and *tacos* (folded tortillas with meat or other filling). Popular soups include *pozole* (pork-and-hominy soup), *birria* (goat soup), and *menudo* (spicy tripe soup). *Enchiladas* are tortillas filled with meat and covered in a chile sauce. *Tamales* are cornmeal dough stuffed with meat, cheese, fruit, or other filling; they are wrapped in a corn husk or banana leaf and steamed. Popular "Mexican" foods and restaurants in the United States usually are very different from those found in Mexico.

Recreation. *Fútbol* (soccer) is the most popular sport in Mexico; the national team has competed in the last five World Cups. Bullfighting draws the next highest number of spectators. Professional wrestling (*la lucha*) has a large following. Popular participation sports include baseball, basketball, tennis, and volleyball. Mexicans enjoy their own form of rodeo called *charreada*, which often is accompanied by a fair-like atmosphere. Many recreational activities include music and dancing. Daylong *fiestas* and weeklong festivals nearly always include fireworks, feasts, or bullfights. Watching television is a favorite leisure activity, especially in urban areas. *Telenovelas* (soap operas) are especially popular.

The Arts. Song and dance are integral to Mexican society. Originating in Mexico, *mariachi* music has found many international audiences. *Mariachi* bands vary in size but generally consist of a singer, violins, trumpets, and various guitars such as the *vihuela*, a small five-string guitar, and the *guitarrón*, a six-string bass guitar. *Corridos*, songs that tell stories, and *ranchera* are other forms of traditional music. Mexico has become a major recording and distribution center for the Americas. Dancing, such as the *jarabe tapatio* (Mexican Hat Dance), often accompanies traditional music and *fiestas*.

Revolutionary themes dominated all types of art the first half of the century and remain important today. For example, brightly colored murals commissioned by the government in the 1920s and 1930s decorate many public buildings. Diego Rivera and other Mexican artists inspired muralist movements worldwide. Museums feature the art of ancient civilizations, such as ceramics and weavings, as well as fine art. Textiles, pottery, and silver work continue to be popular and can be seen in many markets.

Holidays. National public holidays include New Year's Day; Constitution Day (5 Feb.), which also marks the beginning of Carnaval, the week of parties and parades before Lent; Birthday of Benito Juárez (21 Mar.); Labor Day (1 May); *Cinco de Mayo* (5 May), which celebrates an 1862 victory over the French; Independence Day (16 Sept.), which is marked by a presidential address and *El grito* (the cry of freedom) on the evening of 15 September; Columbus Day (12 Oct.); Revolution Day (20 Nov.); and Christmas day. Many offices close for a half day on Mother's Day (10 May), when schools sponsor special festivities.

Major religious holidays include St. Anthony's Day (17 Jan.), when children take their pets to church to be blessed; *Semana Santa* (Palm Sunday–Easter Sunday); Corpus Christi (May or June); and Assumption (15 Aug.). During the period known as *Día de los Muertos,* or "Day of the Dead" (1–2 Nov.), families gather to celebrate life while they honor the dead, sweep graves, build special altars to honor the newly dead, and place items on graves to accompany spirits on their journey to heaven. Day of the Virgin Guadalupe (12 Dec.) and *Nochebuena* (Christmas Eve) are so popular

▼ **THE AMERICAS**

that most offices and businesses honor them as public holidays. Christmas celebrations begin 16 December with nightly parties (*posadas*) and end on Day of the Kings (6 Jan.), when most children in central and southern Mexico get their presents. Santa Claus is becoming more popular, especially in northern Mexico.

Commerce. Businesses generally are open from 9 a.m. to 6 or 7 p.m., although many shops in smaller towns close between 2 and 4 p.m. for the midday meal, particularly in hotter areas. Legislation passed in March 1999 prohibits government workers from taking the traditional afternoon *siesta* break by limiting their lunches to one hour and not allowing them to work after 6 p.m. Private companies may offer midday breaks at their own discretion. Business contacts often are made during lunch breaks. These are largely social meetings, with business conducted in the last few minutes. Urban residents buy basic goods in supermarkets and smaller neighborhood stores. Street vendors and open-air markets are common and often open to bargaining. In rural areas, weekly market days provide foods and other goods. Government offices usually close by 4 p.m. Standard banking hours are 9 a.m. to 5 p.m.

SOCIETY

Government. Mexico's federal republic of 31 states operates under a central government led by a directly elected president. While states technically are autonomous, the central government controls sectors such as education, security, and national industries. A president can serve only one six-year term, and a legislator cannot serve two consecutive terms. The legislature is composed of a 128-seat Senate and 500-seat Chamber of Deputies. Voting is compulsory (but not enforced) for adults 18 and older.

Economy. The two most important industries, mining and petroleum, employ less than 2 percent of the labor force. Pemex, the government-owned petroleum company, is the world's sixth-largest oil company. Tourism earns foreign exchange and provides employment for many. In addition to oil, Mexico exports coffee, agricultural products, and engines. Agricultural pursuits employ one-quarter of the labor force. Major crops include corn, cotton, wheat, coffee, sugarcane, sorghum, oilseed, and vegetables. Mexico is also a major supplier of marijuana; efforts to stem the drug trade have been significant but very costly.

At the end of 1994 Mexico's economy plunged into a deep financial crisis. Restructuring and a U.S. loan package helped Mexico regain its footing: inflation, interest, and unemployment rates declined steadily from their highs in 1995. The economy grew a strong 7 percent in 2000. Inflation reached almost 9 percent. Many are optimistic about full economic recovery. Export industries have enjoyed strong growth since 1993, when Mexico signed NAFTA with the United States and Canada. NAFTA lowered trade barriers and led to an increased number of *maquiladoras* (border industries), where U.S. investment employs Mexican labor. Mexico has made new free trade agreements with the European Union, much of Central America, and Israel.

Most Mexicans have access to basic resources and opportunities to make choices in their lives; however, access varies

DEVELOPMENT DATA

Human Dev. Index* rank	55 of 174 countries
Adjusted for women	50 of 143 countries
Real GDP per capita	$7,704
Adult literacy rate	90 percent
Infant mortality rate	26 per 1,000 births
Life expectancy	68 (male); 75 (female)

widely between regions and ethnic groups. Economic opportunities have not improved proportionally among the indigenous, rural, and southern populations. Many are poor, and about 10 percent of the population lacks access to the health care, education, and economic opportunities needed to rise above human poverty.* The currency is the Mexican *peso* (Mex$).

Transportation and Communications. Personal cars are common in urban areas, but the majority of Mexicans rely on public transportation. Buses and minibuses are plentiful and inexpensive. Mexico City has a fine subway system. Taxis are numerous, but many operate illegally. The highway system has grown steadily over the last decade, and Mexico has an extensive system of roads, although many remain unpaved or semi-paved. Most people use the sophisticated private bus system for intercity travel. There are several domestic airlines. Communications are well developed and modern, although many rural families do not have telephones in their homes. Numerous radio and television stations and several daily newspapers serve the public.

Education. Education is compulsory and free between ages six and fifteen. However, attendance is not enforced and schools may require that students pay some fees. After six years of primary education and three years of basic secondary education, students may enter one of two tracks: preuniversity education (three years) or a technical education program (two to three years). Obtaining a university degree takes from three to seven years. The essentially free National Autonomous University of Mexico (UNAM) is prestigious; only one-third of all applicants pass its entrance exams. Enrollment has increased rapidly in the last decade. Student protests over fees closed UNAM for most of the 1999 to 2000 school year. The literacy rate is much lower among indigenous and rural populations.

Health. By law, all citizens have access to medical services free of charge at government-operated facilities. Medical facilities are good in large cities but limited in rural areas. Sanitation and access to safe water are problems in some regions. Air pollution is a serious problem in big cities, and water pollution in many regions.

CONTACT INFORMATION

Mexican Government Tourist Office, phone (800) 44 MEXICO. Embassy of Mexico, 1911 Pennsylvania Avenue NW, Washington, DC 20006; phone (202) 728-1600; Web site www.embassyofmexico.org.

CultureGrams™
People. The World. You.

1305 North Research Way, Bldg. K
Orem, Utah 84097-6200 USA
1.800.528.6279; 801.705.4250
fax 801.705.4350
www.culturegrams.com

Republic of
Moldova

Boundary representations are not necessarily authoritative.

BACKGROUND

Land and Climate. Moldova, the second smallest former Soviet republic, covers 13,010 square miles (33,700 square kilometers) in southeastern Europe. The Prut River defines Moldova's border with Romania, and the Nistru (Dniester) River flows north to south in the east. Both rivers drain into the Black Sea. Moldova's hilly terrain, or rolling steppe, and rich black soil allow for 50 percent of the territory to support agriculture. There are few forests; ancient woodlands were plowed under for farming.

Moldova's climate is characterized by cold winters and warm summers. Average winter temperatures hover around freezing, while summers average between 70°F and 80°F (21–26°C). Humidity intensifies both cold and warm temperatures. The south is slightly warmer than the north. Rainfall is variable but can be heavy in the summer. Dry spells are not uncommon, and crop irrigation is necessary in some areas.

History. Known in centuries past as Basarabia, the main area now occupied by Moldova has had a long, troubled history of shifting borders and foreign domination. In 1359, it was incorporated into a principality called Moldavia. Basarabia became a tributary state to the Ottoman Empire in the 15th century. In 1792, Turkey ceded land on the Nistru River's east bank (now called Transniester) to Russia. Then, following the Russo-Turkish War (1806–12), Russia annexed Basarabia as well.

With the exception of small territorial shifts in 1859 and 1878, the region remained as is until Russia's Bolshevik Revolution in 1917. In March 1918, Basarabia's ethnic Romanian majority (between the Prut and Nistru Rivers) voted to unite with Romania, with which they shared cultural and historical (pre-Turkish) roots. The new Soviet government opposed such a union and established, in 1924, the Moldavian Autonomous Soviet Socialist Republic in Transniester.

Basarabia was annexed by the Soviet Union in 1940, reoccupied by Romania until 1944, and later fully incorporated into the Soviet Empire as the Moldavian Soviet Socialist Republic. Some districts were transferred to Ukraine.

Freedoms introduced by Soviet President Mikhail Gorbachev in the late 1980s allowed Moldavia to join other republics in a quest for independence. Elections in 1990 brought the Moldovan Popular Front to power, forcing out the Communists and leading to Moldavia's 1991 declaration of independence as the Republic of Moldova. The new country was immediately beset with ethnic divisions, economic chaos, and extremist political tendencies. The Popular Front, prior to independence, had severely alienated ethnic Russians in Transniester (and elsewhere) and ethnic Gagauzi in the south by introducing legislation to effectively marginalize minorities in the new state. The two minorities declared their independence. In Transniester (called *Dnestr* by ethnic Russians), where the elite Russian 14th army formerly under General Alexander Lebed had been and is still based, the situation erupted into open civil war in 1992. Russian troops participated and then helped establish a cease-fire. The Popular Front and political parties polarized and factionalized, leading to parliamentary gridlock. A 1993 vote disbanded Parliament.

In February 1994, a new, smaller Parliament was elected. Several parties posted candidates, but those (such as

Popular Front) strongly advocating unification with Romania or suppression of ethnic minorities were defeated in favor of more moderate groups (primarily the Agrarian and Socialist Parties). The new Parliament quickly ratified a new constitution that guarantees minorities their rights and worked to implement further political, constitutional, and economic reforms.

In 1994, the government signed an agreement with Russia over the eventual withdrawal of its troops from Transniester. Moldova's moderate leaders extended greater autonomy to both separatist regions while maintaining Moldovan sovereignty. A "republic within Moldova" status was accepted in 1996 by Transniester leaders and Russia. President Petru Lucinschi, who was elected in December 1996, continued efforts to normalize Moldovan relations with Transniester. A peace accord with Dniester separatists was signed in Moscow in May 1997.

In 2001, the Communists swept to power, winning 71 of 101 parliamentary seats. Vladimir Voronin, also a Communist, was elected as president. The shrinking economy is currently the country's most pressing concern. Dealing with the breakaway Transniester region is also a priority.

THE PEOPLE

Population. Moldova's population of 4.43 million is not growing. Roughly 64 percent of the people are ethnic Moldovans (of Romanian descent). Ukrainians (13.8 percent) and Russians (13) are the largest minorities. They tend to live in cities and in Transniester. The Gagauzi (3.5 percent), a Turkic people of Orthodox faith, live in southern Moldova. Moldova is also home to some ethnic Bulgarians (2 percent) and smaller groups. The capital of Chisinau is home to more than 750,000 people. Tiraspol (186,000 residents), Balti (164,000), and Tighina (141,000) are the next largest cities. Fifty-four percent of the population is urban and 46 percent is rural.

Language. During the Soviet era, Russian was the official state language, and Romanian, the language of ethnic Moldovans, had to be written in the Cyrillic alphabet. In 1990, Romanian was declared the sole official language, and efforts were implemented to help schools, businesses, and government shift to using Romanian and the Latin alphabet. The transition is necessarily slow and costly, and Russian is still heavily used in urban areas, especially among minorities.

By law, non-Romanian speakers have six years to learn Romanian as a condition of their continued employment. Flexibility exists if the six-year target is unreachable. Ethnic minorities may continue to speak their own languages. Bulgarians and Gagauzi also generally speak Russian.

Religion. Most people in Moldova are Eastern Orthodox Christians. There are small populations of Jews (1.5 percent), Evangelical Protestants, and Roman Catholics. The practice of religion was repressed during the Soviet era, but people are now rebuilding their churches, attending services, and celebrating religious holidays. Religious devotion is rising, and religion is expected to play a greater role in the society's future.

General Attitudes. Moldovans value strong personal relationships with friends and relatives. Educated persons are respected above others, including the wealthy, as education generally is not associated with wealth. Material possessions increasingly are desired, which has given rise to greater corruption but also has encouraged private enterprise. Moldovans appreciate their agricultural heritage and tend to be politically and socially conservative. They are cautious toward people they do not know but warm and trusting with good friends. Moldovans tend to be pessimistic about their individual circumstances; even if they are inwardly optimistic, they more readily express doubts before hopes.

As with many newly created countries, Moldova's hardships and social upheaval have confused people's attitudes toward society's goals. Those who initially favored unification with Romania were disappointed by the feeling in Romania that Moldovans had lost their "Romanian-ness" and that Russian influence remains strong. In 1992, however, the presidents of Moldova and Romania agreed to pursue a balanced policy between their countries. Many Moldovans have been disappointed by the economic hardships of transition. People's perceptions are strongly influenced by political and economic trends, both of which are changing rapidly.

Personal Appearance. Moldovans wear their best clothing in public. Women wear dresses or skirts and high heels. Young women prefer flashy outfits, jewelry, and considerable makeup. Urban youth favor jeans and T-shirts. Urban professional men wear suits with ties. Urban men otherwise wear sweat suits and tennis shoes; jewelry indicates their social status. Rural men often wear older suit coats with sweaters. Older rural women (*batrana*) wear scarves on their heads, a practice that originally denoted one's marital status (unmarried women did not wear scarves). Men often wear fur hats in colder weather.

CUSTOMS AND COURTESIES

Greetings. Urban Moldovans generally shake hands when they greet, although a man waits for a woman to extend her hand first. In mixed company, a man shakes a woman's hand before another man's. Good friends and relatives often hug as well. Rural Moldovan men, and increasingly urban ethnic Moldovan men, greet a woman by kissing her on the hand and saying *Sarut mâna* (I kiss your hand). Other verbal greetings include *Buna Ziua* (Good day), *Ce mai facetz* (How do you do?), *Noroc* (Cheers, meaning "Hi"), and the Russian *Privet* (Hi) or *Zdravstvuite* (Hello). "Good-bye" is *La revedere.*

When addressing others, young people generally use first names. Adults use titles (*Domnul* for "Mr.," *Doamna* for "Mrs.," *Dominsoara* for "Miss") with the family name for all but close friends and relatives. Some adults introduce themselves by first name and patronymic (e.g., Ion Petru), often preceded by the family name (e.g., Ciorbu Ion Petru). A patronymic is formed by the possessive of the father's first name. Use of this Russian custom is decreasing. Urban people do not greet people they do not know and rarely smile (as a greeting) at strangers on the street. Rural people are more likely to greet strangers. A young woman is called a "girl," since the term "woman" is considered an insult that implies the person is old or married.

Gestures. Moldovans generally do not point with the index finger; they prefer using the open hand. It is impolite to put feet on furniture, cross legs in front of elders, or chew gum while speaking. Eating while walking in public is rude, unless one is eating ice cream or *pirozhki* (a stuffed pastry). Society generally frowns on public displays of affection. Moldovan men usually remove their hats when entering a building or home. It is rude for men not to open doors for women or to neglect other such chivalrous acts.

Visiting. Most socializing takes place at home. Visitors remove their shoes at the door before entering. On special occasions, guests are treated to large meals. Otherwise, people sit in the kitchen or living room to chat for hours. Hosts generally provide guests with something to drink (coffee, tea, wine, cognac, etc.). Vodka is popular among ethnic Russians. Close friends and family feel comfortable visiting without prior arrangement, but a telephone call among those with phones usually is appreciated. If visitors plan to stay only a few minutes, they indicate this upon arrival so as not to make the hosts feel their quick departure indicates they did not like something.

Guests often take small gifts, such as flowers or wine. It is impolite not to take at least flowers to people on special occasions or holidays. Hosts, especially in rural areas, usually reciprocate with a small gift (cake "for the next morning" or wine). Foreign visitors, especially U.S. Americans, are considered honored guests and are treated to the family's best.

Eating. The urban breakfast is usually light, consisting of open sandwiches with sausage or cheese, coffee or tea, and fruit preserves. Rural people often eat more substantial meals of *kasha* (hot porridge), potatoes, bread, and sheep cheese. Indeed, breakfast can be the main meal, as the rest of the day is spent farming. Lunch and dinner are light. On weekends, however, lunch is the main meal. The urban lunch is generally the main meal, consisting of soup, salad, and an entrée. For dinner, people eat only an entrée, though it is not necessarily light. Children at elementary schools usually have an afternoon "tea" (juice and a sweet roll). Coffee and juice are common beverages among urban people, while rural people drink wine, tea, juice, milk, or stewed fruit. Ice is almost never served with drinks, as cold drinks are considered unhealthy.

Food is prepared by a woman; it is considered embarrassing for a man to admit he cooks. Serving dishes, from which each person takes his or her portion, are placed in the middle of the table. Urban Moldovans eat with the fork in the left hand and the knife in the right. They keep the hands and forearms above the table throughout the meal. Hosts offer guests additional helpings at least three or four times. Initially declined, the food should then be accepted. One is expected to eat everything on the plate; the presence of leftovers is considered a sign that guests did not like the food.

Moldovans rarely eat at restaurants, which are expensive, except during vacations and for business functions. Families go out for ice cream, coffee, or dessert. When one does eat out, the host pays the bill; tips are not given.

LIFESTYLE

Family. Moldovans value their families. They often marry early in life because of their rural lifestyle and because young people want to be treated as adults. Urban families usually have only one or two children, while rural families may have three or more. Children remain close to their parents throughout life. Young urban couples often have difficulty finding housing, so they usually move in with the bride's parents. Hence, many families have two or three

generations living in a small one- or two-bedroom apartment. Rural extended families share a larger home, but they often lack modern conveniences (such as running water). Gender roles are defined clearly, especially in the countryside. Men lead the family, work the fields and raise livestock, or have a wage-earning job. Women are responsible for all household chores and child care, as well as farm work, if applicable. A successful career is less important for a woman than being a good cook and housekeeper, but more women are also becoming merchants, selling at outdoor markets goods they produce or buy in Romania and other countries.

Dating and Marriage. Young people date with the goal of getting married. They go to movies or for walks in the park, watch videos, and dance at large holiday or birthday parties. Couples marry at a "wedding palace," the Soviet-era office where the only legal weddings could be held. Today, many get married in a church first and then go to the "wedding palace" for the civil ceremony. Fall is the most popular time for a wedding because it is the season of new wine. After the ceremony, the bride takes off her veil and puts on a scarf to indicate she is now a wife and a mature woman. The veil is given to the maid of honor, who is expected to marry next. Wedding guests usually stay through the morning and sometimes for an entire weekend. Divorce is common, but second marriages are not. Women with children find it hard to remarry.

Diet. Romanian, Russian, Ukrainian, and Bulgarian cuisine are all part of the Moldovan diet. The most common soup eaten at lunch is *borscht* (made of tomato juice and beets). Meat, bread, potatoes, and vegetables are staples for the main meal. Bread is served with most meals; wine is served with lunch and dinner. Traditional Moldovan dishes include *mamaliga* (cornmeal mush that resembles pudding) with *brânza* (sheep cheese), *mititei* (grilled meat sausages), fried onions with sour cream, and *placinte* (flaky stuffed pastry). Garlic, onions, and herbs are used in cooking many foods. Fruits (apples, grapes, plums, cherries, strawberries, watermelon, and tomatoes) are eaten in season. Typical vegetables are eggplant, peppers, cabbage, and potatoes. As fresh produce is expensive for urban dwellers, many families have gardens on the outskirts of town. All meats are popular but expensive; chicken and pork are most affordable.

Recreation. In their leisure time, Moldovans visit, go to movies, or read. Soccer is the most popular sport. Chess is also a favorite pastime. Some enjoy basketball. A small number of urban adults jog or exercise. Public exercise and swimming facilities are available but need repair.

The Arts. Moldovans love music and art. Folk music is popular at national festivals. Common instruments include the violin, flute, accordion, and *cembalo* (harpsichord). The *Miorita* is a well-known ballad. Moldova is home to several professional theaters, including the Licurici Republic Puppet Theater. Ceramics, carpet making, wood carving, basketwork, and weaving are common crafts.

During the Soviet period, the government controlled the arts. Artists were pressured to produce works that glorified communism. In more recent years, artists have had more freedom to express themselves and have been experimenting with new materials, techniques, and styles.

▼ **EUROPE**

Moldova

Holidays. New Year's Day is a favorite day for decorating trees and for children to go to parties with *Mos Craciun* (Santa Claus) and *Alba-ca-Zapada* (his granddaughter, Snow White). Adults enjoy New Year's Eve parties with family and friends. At the beginning of the new year, people greet each other with *La multi ani* (Happy New Year). Christmas (7 Jan.) is only now being revived after a ban under the Soviets. People are rediscovering a rich tradition of caroling, folklore, trees, ornaments, and gifts. Some of the nonreligious aspects of Christmas had been transferred to New Year's by the Soviets, and that date remains the biggest holiday of the year. For non-Orthodox Christians, Christmas is 25 December, and 7 January is St. John's Day. For all Christians, Christmas and Easter (Saturday–Monday) are the most important religious holidays. An all-night ceremony ends with a dawn feast on Easter morning, followed later by visits and other celebrations.

National holidays include International Women's Day (8 Mar.), Independence Day (27 Aug.), and Limba Noastra (31 August, to celebrate the proclamation of Romanian as the official language). For Hram, each village and city celebrates its birth or the birth of its patron saint. People visit from house to house and eat; community activities include wrestling, concerts, and dancing.

Commerce. Offices typically open at 8 or 9 a.m., close for a lunch hour around 1 p.m., and reopen until 5 or 6 p.m. Grocery stores have a longer lunch break and stay open until 8 p.m. Only grocery stores, restaurants, cafés, and farmers' markets are open on Sunday. Prices at most stores are set, as are open-market and street prices. Serious business cannot be conducted between strangers. Personal contacts are necessary, and major transactions are preceded by social interaction.

SOCIETY

Government. The Republic of Moldova has a president as head of state. The president is chosen by the members of the Parliament according to a constitutional amendment passed in July 2000. Prior to this amendment, the president was elected by popular vote. The prime minister serves as head of government. The 104-member Parliament is directly elected; the voting age is 18. Citizenship is granted to ethnic Moldovans and others who meet certain residency and ancestry requirements.

Economy. Moldova is one of the poorest countries in Europe. It is mostly an agrarian nation, with an economy based on its fertile land. Agriculture employs more than 33 percent of the workforce, while 22 percent are involved in food processing and related industries. Chief products include fruits and vegetables, wine, sugar beets, grains, sunflower seeds, tobacco, and dairy items. Most exports go to neighboring countries. Moldova also exports small appliances, textiles, leather goods, and tools. Fuel and energy are imported, as are some consumer items. The national currency is the *leu* (MLD). Russia, Ukraine, and Romania are Moldova's biggest trading partners.

Moldova is struggling to make the difficult transition toward a capitalist economic system. The government has sought to privatize firms, transfer ownership of state farms to

DEVELOPMENT DATA

Human Dev. Index* rank	102 of 174 countries
Adjusted for women	81 of 143 countries
Real GDP per capita	$1,947
Adult literacy rate	98 percent
Infant mortality rate	43 per 1,000 births
Life expectancy	60 (male); 69 (female)

peasant joint-stock associations, and reform investment and other market-related laws; however, actual implementation has been slow. The Moldovan economy shrank by 8.6 percent in 1998 in the wake of Russia's severe financial depression and has continued to fall since then, shrinking by 7 percent in 2000. Inflation is around 20 percent. The economy is at a level last seen in the 1960s. Black market activity is an ongoing problem. The lack of progress on budget and privatization legislation has led to a suspension of some IMF and World Bank funding. Life is difficult for many, and it will take time before the benefits of an open market reach the average person, especially in rural areas.

Transportation and Communications. Urban dwellers benefit from an extensive and inexpensive public transport system of buses, trolleys, and minivans. Taxis are uncommon, expensive, and unregulated. Commuter buses and trains travel between cities. In rural villages, people may use horse-drawn carts (*karutsa*). Some Moldovans own cars, but most cannot afford them. Fuel and spare parts are expensive for those who drive. Many people do not have phones, but post offices have public phones. An urban home is more likely to have a telephone than a rural home. Moldovans enjoy reading daily newspapers: there are 219 newspapers and 71 journals. The free press is growing and changing rapidly. Television and radio facilities are state owned.

Education. Moldova's basic education system consists of primary, secondary, and high schools. Children begin attending at age six or seven and finish high school 11 years later. An additional year of secondary school is optional at the high school level. Students who do not attend or complete high school may attend vocational school to learn a trade. Even in high school, students may learn one of several trades by going to a professional education center one day a week. Successful students receive a professional license in the given trade upon graduation from high school. Students often gain hands-on experience in their chosen trade during summer vacations. Moldovans value higher education, and many compete for the limited number of available university spots. An increasing number are studying abroad.

Health. Moldova's health-care system lacks modern facilities, skilled staff, and supplies. Preventive and maternal care are especially lacking. This contributes to high infant mortality and low life expectancy rates (see box above).

CONTACT INFORMATION

Embassy of Moldova, 2101 S Street NW, Washington, DC 20008; phone (202) 667-1131.

CultureGrams™
People. The World. You.

1305 North Research Way, Bldg. K
Orem, Utah 84097-6200 USA
1.800.528.6279; 801.705.4250
fax 801.705.4350
www.culturegrams.com

Montserrat

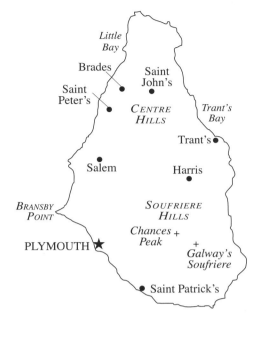

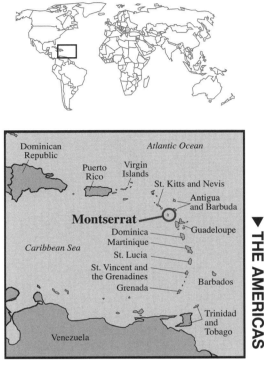

Boundary representations are not necessarily authoritative.

BACKGROUND

Land and Climate. Montserrat is located in the Caribbean Sea about 250 miles (400 kilometers) southeast of Puerto Rico. Part of the British West Indies, it is considered one of the Leeward Islands of the Lesser Antilles. Montserrat is known as the Emerald Isle, for both its early Irish settlers and its lush vegetation. The island is volcanic in origin and several fumaroles still emit sulfur fumes, steam, and boiling water. Chances Peak, the highest mountain, has been the site of recent volcanic activity, which has resulted in the growth of its dome from 3,002 feet (915 meters) to more than 3,220 feet (977 meters). Montserrat's land area had been only 39 square miles (101 square kilometers), roughly half the area of Washington, D.C. Recent pyroclastic flows have increased the land mass slightly to 40 square miles (103 square kilometers). Natural vegetation is confined mostly to the summits of the Centre Hills. Sheltered bays are few and all beaches but one have black volcanic sand.

The climate is tropical, with temperatures ranging from 76°F to 86°F (24–30°C) year-round. Rainfall is abundant and the sea breeze is constant. The wettest months are September through November, while the dry season lasts from March to June. The hurricane season usually occurs between June and November. In 1989, Hurricane Hugo devastated the island, but the international community helped rebuild it.

History. The pre-Columbian name of Montserrat was *Alliouagana* (land of the prickly bush); it was named by the Carib Indians who overtook the Arawak long before the coming of Europeans. Christopher Columbus sighted Montserrat in 1493, naming it after a monastery near Seville, Spain. However, the Spanish did not settle the island. In 1632,

Thomas Warner began settling Montserrat with English and Irish Catholics who were uncomfortable in nearby Protestant Saint Kitts. Overbearing rich planters emerged as Montserrat developed into a sugar and slave colony in the 17th century. Repression eventually ignited a slave uprising, which failed, on St. Patrick's Day in 1768.

In the 17th and 18th centuries, France and Britain fought for dominance over the sugar islands of the Caribbean, and Montserrat changed hands several times. It finally came into permanent English possession after British admiral Rodney's victory at Les Saintes, near the French island of Guadeloupe. The Treaty of Versailles in 1783 made Montserrat permanently British. It remains a dependent territory of the United Kingdom (UK).

In 1834, Britain's Parliament abolished slavery in the Caribbean. Sharecroppers (or black laborers) began cultivating many of the properties that had become burdened by debt and had been sold. Limes and cotton eventually replaced the sugar industry. Montserrat lime juice was in demand by the British navy for combating scurvy and is believed to be the source of the British nickname *Limey*.

After the decline of cotton and limes in the 20th century, many Montserratians emigrated to Panama (to work on the Panama Canal), Cuba, the Dominican Republic, the United States, or the UK. When remittances from Montserratians abroad declined, the island turned to real estate and construction, building luxury winter homes for North American and British citizens.

A long-dormant volcano on Chances Peak began rumbling and spewing ash in July 1995. When the capital of Plymouth was ordered evacuated, many residents relocated in the north, while others left the island. The volcano claimed its first fatalities in June 1997 when part of the dome collapsed, sending a pyroclastic flow toward the eastern end of the island. Nineteen people who had returned to the "unsafe zone" were killed and seven villages were destroyed. The largest dome collapse occurred in December 1997, claiming no fatalities but damaging several southern villages. The southern two-thirds of the island is now uninhabitable and 90 percent of the buildings are abandoned. A central buffer zone is open during daylight hours only, while the northern "safe zone" is considered unconditionally safe.

Aid from Britain has helped establish in the north housing, government offices, utilities, and other services and institutions previously centered in Plymouth. The British government also offered resettlement funds to those who wished to leave. In August 1997, Chief Minister Bertrand "Sonny" Osborne resigned amid public protests when Britain's aid package fell short of expectations. Upon taking office, new Chief Minister David Brandt openly criticized what he believed to be Britain's bias toward evacuation, rather than development, of the island. The Montserrat and British governments have since begun cooperating on the creation and implementation of a sustainable development plan.

The overall level of volcanic activity decreased during 1998 and 1999, and scientists believed the eruptions had ended. The British government began financing the return of evacuees from the Caribbean and the UK in May and June of 1999. However, in November 1999, the volcano began spewing rock, and in March 2000, it erupted again, crushing the hopes of many to return to the island or to their homes.

In April 2001 elections, voters handed the New People's Liberation Movement (NPLM) a landslide victory. John Osborne became the new chief minister. The new government hopes to rebuild the community, boost the economy, and build better relations with Britain.

THE PEOPLE

Population. Montserrat now has a population of approximately five thousand concentrated in the safe zone. That number fluctuates, depending on economic opportunities or hardships experienced abroad. In 1999, about 320 still lived in official shelters. Nearly 70 percent of the population (which numbered some 11,000 in early 1995) has emigrated to Antigua, other Caribbean islands, Britain, or North America. Even before the crisis, the population grew by only 0.3 percent each year, due to smaller family size and emigration. The majority of Montserratians are of African descent, with a relatively recent infusion of North American, European, and East Indian residents.

Language. The official language is English, but most people speak a West Indian dialect. The dialect, referred to as *speaking Montserratian* or *speaking dialect*, is a form of English mixed with elements of Irish brogue and various African tongues. In Montserratian, *me* indicates both first person singular and past tense; therefore, *Me no me know* means "I did not know." *Fe true* is a common phrase that adds emphasis. For example, *Me vex fe true* means "I was really angry." Some people consider using the dialect as improper, but most enjoy the way it makes speech more colorful and even poetic.

Religion. Montserratians are genuine about their religious devotion. This is manifest in the dignity and respect with which they treat each other and strangers. Anglican, Methodist, and Roman Catholic are the main Christian denominations. The Seventh-day Adventist Church, Pentecostal, and other Christian churches are assuming increasing importance. Religion affects many aspects of daily life. Public schools have daily prayer and gospel singing before classes begin. Most public functions are opened and sometimes closed with prayer.

General Attitudes. Montserratians take great pride in their country and (recently) in their African roots. Friendliness, forthrightness, and honesty are viewed as proud assets of the island. Interactions are easy and amiable and most people display politeness, courtesy, and respect to all. The general attitude is one of tolerance and "live and let live." People generally take the time to talk with each other and are considered more important than schedules. Therefore, being late is not a problem, and an event will sometimes go on much later than advertised. Montserratians are observant; very little goes unnoticed when they watch passersby, a group, a scene, or an activity.

While the volcano has introduced a stressful element of uncertainty, most Montserratians are facing the future with optimism, perseverance, and humor. Many emigrants would like to return when housing is available and/or volcanic activity subsides. The destruction caused by the volcano has drawn remaining islanders together as they join in community clean-up and improvement projects.

Personal Appearance. Montserratians wear their finest clothes for church or other important social functions. Women wear dresses or dressy skirts and blouses to work, along with sandals. Men wear sport shirts or a shirt jacket (square-cut cotton shirt), slacks, and shoes. Ties, jeans, and tight-fitting clothing seldom are worn due to the climate. Loose-fitting clothes made of lightweight fabric are most comfortable and popular. Older rural women rarely wear pants, but younger urban women do.

CUSTOMS AND COURTESIES

Greetings. Montserratian greetings include the more formal *Good morning, Good day, Good evening,* and *Good night* (after dark), as well as the casual *You alright?*, which means "How are you?" The response is *Okay.* When parting, people might say *Good-bye* or *All the best.*

People often shake hands or touch when greeting. Friends may remain holding hands for some minutes while they converse. The youth sometimes touch clenched fists after a traditional handshake to show solidarity. When passing friends or acquaintances, people may raise the index finger of one or both hands, with palms facing forward, as a silent acknowledgment. Drivers commonly honk horns or flash headlights (during the day) to greet friends who are walking or driving by.

When addressing friends and relatives, Montserratians use colorful nicknames that usually are acquired in childhood. Some nicknames also may be acquired in adulthood as a result of one's occupation, personality, body type, etc. Acquaintances might use one's nickname as well, but formal situations call for the use of given names and titles. An older person or superior at work might be called *Mas* (for men) or *Miss* (for women), but most people use *Mr., Mrs.,* or *Miss.*

Gestures. Montserratians are affectionate and loving. They

commonly touch each other's hands, arms, or shoulders while talking. Hand gestures might be used to emphasize verbal expressions, especially between friends. People often use a quick "pssst" or hissing sound to get one's attention while walking by or when in a crowd.

Visiting. Montserratians are friendly with their neighbors and often stop by to see how they are doing or to *talk up* the latest island news. Neighbors might bring homemade gifts like banana bread or guava juice. People often have house parties for birthdays, anniversaries, graduations, or other special occasions. When they get together, the atmosphere is amiable, courteous, and relaxed. Invited guests usually are offered at least something to drink (soft drinks, juice, etc.). Visitors rarely leave empty-handed. Hosts, even those now living in shelters, send guests away with a gift (garden produce, tea leaves, canned goods) or make profuse apologies if nothing is available.

Men commonly socialize and discuss politics at the local *rum shop* (neighborhood tavern), where they watch television, play dominoes, listen to music, and eat chicken or bread. Women more commonly socialize in the home or in connection with their children's activities.

Eating. Lunch and dinner are the main meals, as breakfast is usually light. Many Montserratians eat lunch at restaurants. They might have fried chicken and *chips* (french fries), a hamburger, or *pelau* (rice, beans, and chicken). Bread and cheese are eaten for a quick meal. Families usually eat dinner together at home. Barbecues are popular for community or family gatherings.

LIFESTYLE

Family. The extended family is the primary social unit in Montserrat. Grandparents often live with their children's families and help raise the grandchildren. Siblings usually have the same mother but may have different fathers. Women generally hold the family together, caring for the household and commonly working outside the home. Men support their families and help raise children with a firm but loving hand. Discipline is stressed and children are well behaved.

Volcanic activity has disrupted family life for many. Those from the south were forced to abandon their home, land, and livestock. School and business closures, concerns for safety, and inadequate housing have forced some families to splinter: women and children emigrate and men remain behind. Many who did not emigrate have had to live in crowded community shelters (converted schools and churches) or relatives' homes.

Dating and Marriage. Dating begins in secondary school and centers on social or school functions. Young couples traditionally enjoyed attending cricket matches, basketball games, or concerts, but volcanic activity has curtailed many of these activities (see Recreation). Nighttime drives are popular. At church *fetes* (fund-raising parties), young people gather to enjoy the games, music, food, and fun.

Couples marry in their twenties or thirties and begin to raise a family. Churches stress formal marriage, but common-law unions are not unusual. There are many single mothers, but they generally receive support from the fathers of their children. Weddings traditionally are held in a church, followed by a reception. At the reception, the bride, groom, and their parents give testimonials in tribute to each other's families while toasting with champagne. Musical entertainment

follows and guests enjoy plenty of food, including *goat water* (stewed mutton).

Diet. Due to the cost of imported goods, the island had attempted to become more self-sufficient in food production. However, volcanic activity has destroyed much of the agricultural land. Still, Montserratians—even those living abroad or in some shelters—take pride in their *kitchen gardens*. These small plots produce fruits (guavas, mangoes, papayas, etc.), *ground provisions* (root crops such as yams, sweet potatoes, dasheen, and *tannia*), and herbs for tea. They might also include a small patch of sugar cane. Green bananas and breadfruit are common crops—often boiled and served with steamed fish. While fish and meats are popular, chicken is the most consumed protein food. Rice, white potatoes, and bread are also important; several small bakeries operate on the island.

Goat water and *mountain chicken* (actually frog) are popular dishes. Saturday lunch often consists of a highly seasoned stew made from vegetables (peas, pumpkin, sweet and white potatoes, etc.), meat, and flour dumplings. *Souse* (pork pickled in brine and served with cucumber slices) is typical Saturday evening fare. Sunday breakfasts usually consist of *saltfish* (reconstituted dried cod stewed with tomatoes, onions, green peppers, and garlic) served with boiled eggplant and *bakes* (fried flour dumplings). Most older Montserratians drink *bush* (herbal) teas first thing in the morning and last thing at night. Soft drinks, homemade fruit juices, beer, coffee, lemonade, and iced tea are other popular drinks.

Recreation. Almost all sports facilities were made inaccessible by volcanic activity. Plans are underway to develop new facilities and reclaim those that were appropriated for other uses during the volcano crises. Cricket is the national sport. During a *test match*, schools and businesses would often close for a half day so people could watch Montserratian athletes compete. Basketball, netball (for girls), *football* (soccer), tennis, swimming, biking, boating, jogging, and hiking have gained in popularity. On weekends, friends enjoy music at *street blockoramas* (open-air parties). *Jumpups* (block parties that involve street dancing) are popular during the Christmas festival or on other special occasions.

The Arts. Cultural activities such as plays, school arts festivals, and folklore and gospel choir concerts enjoy community support. Churches and beaches now serve as performance sites. Calypso, *soca* (a mixture of U.S. American soul and calypso), reggae, gospel, folk, steel pan, and *dub* (disc jockeys rapping street poems) are favorite types of music.

Holidays. Christmas and Easter are the most important holidays. Traditional Christmas practices (giving gifts, singing carols, and attending church) combine with the Montserrat Festival, a Caribbean carnival featuring cultural shows, calypso competitions, dancing, and parades. Many Montserratians who live overseas return for the festival, which culminates in a New Year's Day parade. Easter is a time for family gatherings and church services.

St. Patrick's Day (17 Mar.) is celebrated as a national holiday in memory of the 1768 slave uprising. Festivities traditionally centered in the now-evacuated village of St. Patrick's. Other important holidays include Emancipation Day (first Monday in August), Whitmonday, Labor Day (first Monday in May), and Queen Elizabeth II's Birthday (second Saturday in June).

▶ **THE AMERICAS**

Commerce. Normal business hours are from 8 a.m. to 4 p.m., with an hour taken for lunch. Businesses close at noon on Wednesdays and Saturdays, and most are closed on Sunday. Many businesses have been forced to close permanently, relocate abroad, or relocate several times in the north.

SOCIETY

Government. As a territory of the UK, Montserrat recognizes Queen Elizabeth II as head of state. She is represented locally by a crown-appointed governor (Anthony John Abbott). The governor's Executive Council includes a chief minister (John Osborne) and five other members. Following legislative elections, the leader of the majority party generally becomes chief minister. Elections are held at least every five years. The Legislative Council has eleven members, nine of whom are elected. In the last elections, the NPLM won seven Legislative Council seats, and the National Progressive Party (NPP) took the other two. The legal system is based on English common law, and the highest judicial authority is the East Caribbean Supreme Court. Brades will be the new home to government offices in the safe zone. The voting age is 18.

Economy. Montserratians traditionally enjoyed a decent standard of living. The country had low unemployment and steady economic growth. However, volcanic activity has had a devastating effect on the economy, which has shrunk the last few years. Before 1995, tourism accounted for approximately 30 percent of the gross domestic product. The economy was also based on construction, real estate, agriculture, and some light industry (mostly assembly). But the island's hotels, as well as many other businesses, have closed, and the majority of agricultural land has been rendered useless. Exports have declined sharply. In 1995, unemployment jumped from 6 to 54 percent; since then it has dropped, largely due to emigration.

Many displaced families have had to rent new homes while paying mortgages on homes in which they can no longer live. The British government offers some housing and food subsidies, but rent and food costs have increased dramatically. The majority of insurers on the island canceled their property coverage in 1997.

The government is considering areas of potential economic development, including the small business sector, high-tech industries, and ecotourism. A number of offshore, government-regulated banks are in business. Montserrat is a member of the regional trade organization CARICOM (Caribbean Community and Common Market). The stable East Caribbean dollar (EC$) is the currency.

Transportation and Communications. Villages are linked to each other by paved roads on the western side of the island. Private cars and trucks account for a large portion of traffic. Buses run regularly between Saint John's and Salem; taxis are also available. Regular ferry and helicopter service between Montserrat and Antigua was established when the June 1997 eruption cut off access to Plymouth's port and airport. Plans are underway to establish a permanent port facility at Little Bay.

Most homes have telephones and televisions; even with the volcanic activity, telecommunications services have

© 2001 CultureGrams, a division of Millennial Star Network and Brigham Young University. It is against the law to copy, reprint, store, or transmit any part of this publication in any form by any means without written permission from CultureGrams. This document contains native commentary and original analysis, as well as estimated statistics. The content should not be considered strictly factual, and it may not apply to all groups in a nation. *UN Development Programme, Human Development Report 2000 (New York: Oxford University Press, 2000).

DEVELOPMENT DATA	
Human Dev. Index* rank	NA
Adjusted for women	NA
Real GDP per capita	$5,000 (est.)
Adult literacy rate	97 percent
Infant mortality rate	9 per 1,000 births
Life expectancy	74 (male); 77 (female)

proven reliable. Through satellite technology, Gem Radio Network links nodes on Montserrat and various Caribbean islands. It also facilitates service for local government-owned Radio Montserrat (ZJB). A weekly newspaper and newsletter are published and available electronically. A monthly newsletter also keeps residents up-to-date on volcanic activity. Many Montserratians, at home and abroad, stay in touch with each other and abreast of developments via the Internet.

Education. Given the reduction in students, staff, and facilities, only two nursery schools, two primary schools (one public, one private), and one secondary school now operate on the island. The final *form* (grade) in secondary school has been discontinued. Primary and secondary schooling are free. Pupils traditionally have attended school for 13 years, and most complete secondary school. The education system reflects a strong British influence. *School-leaving* (graduation) exams are set by the Caribbean Examinations Council and the London and Cambridge syndicates.

Montserrat's Technical College remains closed. The University of the West Indies continues to offer distance education programs. Some Montserratians seeking higher education are pursuing home-study programs or attending colleges overseas. The American University of the Caribbean, an off-shore medical school that caters to students from abroad, has relocated to Saint Maarten.

Health. Montserrat traditionally has been a healthy island with an abundance of clean drinking water. A plan is underway to develop water storage and pumping facilities in the safe zone. Volcanic dust and ash measurements are taken regularly due to the concern that long-term exposure could cause silicosis. Hospital facilities are being developed in St. John's. Free care is provided to children, pregnant women, and the elderly. Working adults have health insurance to cover their medical costs. Private doctors are in practice, and specialists from other countries visit periodically to provide care. Patients requiring special care are flown to other Caribbean islands.

CONTACT INFORMATION

Montserrat Tourist Board, PO Box 7, Plymouth, Montserrat, West Indies; phone (664) 491-2230; Web site www.visitmontserrat.com. Caribbean Tourism Organization, 80 Broad Street, 32d Floor, New York, NY 10004; phone (212) 635-9530; Web site www.doitcaribbean.com. U.S. Embassy in Barbados, PO Box 302, Bridgetown, Barbados; phone (246) 431-0225; Web site usembassy.state.gov/bridgetown.

CultureGrams™
People. The World. You.

1305 North Research Way, Bldg. K
Orem, Utah 84097-6200 USA
1.800.528.6279; 801.705.4250
fax 801.705.4350
www.culturegrams.com

Kingdom of the
Netherlands

▼ EUROPE

Boundary representations are not necessarily authoritative.

BACKGROUND

Land and Climate.   The Netherlands is roughly the size of Massachusetts and Connecticut combined. It covers 16,036 square miles (41,532 square kilometers). Western areas that have been reclaimed from the sea are called *polders*. In the past, windmills pumped water from the land, and dikes held back the ocean. Today, modern machines do the pumping, but about 930 windmills (out of an original 10,000) still dot the landscape. Close to 300 continue to function, mostly for tourists, but some mill grains or perform other work. However, because pumping has led to sinking land, water pollution, and problems with the water table, the government is buying large tracts of agricultural land in the reclaimed territory and returning it to nature. Some dikes are being destroyed, and marshes and wetlands gradually are being allowed to return to their original state. In the east, the land is above sea level and even has a few hills. Grasslands used for grazing are common in the north. The climate is temperate. Rain is common throughout the year. In 1995, the Rhine and other rivers flooded wide areas and prompted the largest peacetime evacuation in the country's history. Winters can be cold, but some are quite mild. Likewise, summers can be warm and sometimes cool; average temperatures range from 28°F (-2°C) in the winter to 72°F (22°C) in the summer.

History.   Although its official name is the Kingdom of the Netherlands, most U.S. Americans know the country as Holland. However, the use of Holland is not appreciated by the Dutch who do not live in either North or South Holland provinces. Until 10 B.C. there were Germanic tribes in the area who were ruled by the Romans. After the great European migrations at the time of the fall of Rome, the Franks,

Saxons, and Frisians settled there. They remained part of the Frankish Kingdom until A.D. 800. In medieval times, the entire area consisted of autonomous duchies and counties. In the 1500s, they, along with Belgium and Luxembourg, were known as the Low Countries. During this time, the countries were ruled by a Spanish monarch. In 1568, Prince William of Orange rebelled against the Spanish crown and began an 80 year war for independence. In 1648, with the Peace of Münster, the Netherlands became independent. In the years following, it built a vast overseas empire, becoming for a time the world's leading maritime and commercial power. In 1795, French forces made the Netherlands a vassal state, and Napoleon completely annexed the territory in 1810. The Congress of Vienna ended French occupation, and the United Kingdom of the Netherlands was created in 1815. It originally included Belgium, which seceded in 1830.

The Netherlands remained neutral during World War I but was invaded by Germany in World War II. After the war, the Netherlands played an important role in European economic development and granted most of its overseas holdings independence, including Indonesia and Suriname. In 1980, Queen Juliana abdicated in favor of her daughter, Queen Beatrix, who is head of state today. The heir to the throne is her son, Crown Prince Willem Alexander. If he ascends to the throne, he will be the first male monarch since 1890. The United States and the Netherlands have enjoyed unbroken diplomatic relations since 1782.

In 2000, the Netherlands became the first country in the world to legalize euthanasia according to strict criteria. As in other European countries, in 2001 there was growing concern in the Netherlands about the spread of foot-and-mouth disease. In order to deal with the crisis, the government has increased the testing of livestock, ordered the destruction of thousands of infected animals, and limited the transport of livestock. The next parliamentary elections will be held in 2002.

THE PEOPLE

Population. The Netherlands has a population of more than 15.9 million, which is growing annually at 0.57 percent. More than 40 percent of the population lives in the two western provinces of *Noord* (North) Holland and *Zuid* (South) Holland. These two provinces, from which the Netherlands received its nickname, "Holland," contain the three largest cities of the country: Amsterdam (population 725,000), Rotterdam (600,000), and The Hague (446,000). The population is 91 percent ethnic Dutch, although there are some Indonesians (50,000) and Surinamese (210,000). Turkish and Moroccan guest workers and their families or descendants number more than 250,000; most live in the two western provinces.

Also included in the Kingdom of the Netherlands are the Caribbean islands of Aruba (population 69,539) and the Netherlands Antilles (210,134). These islands have unique cultural aspects, and therefore are not discussed in this text. Excellent access to health care, education, and economic prosperity gives the Dutch many opportunities for personal advancement.

Language. The official language is Dutch, a Germanic language. Frisian is also spoken in the northeastern province of Friesland. English, German, and French are commonly understood and spoken and are taught in the secondary schools. Flemish, a form of Dutch, is spoken in a region of Belgium called Flanders.

Religion. About 34 percent of the people are Roman Catholic. Most Catholics live in the southern provinces of Brabant and Limburg. Another 25 percent are Protestant (mostly Dutch Reformed), 3 percent are Muslim, and 2 percent belong to other churches. The rest are not officially affiliated with any religion. The royal family belongs to the Dutch Reformed Church. The Netherlands, like many European countries, is a secular society, in which the role of religion has diminished steadily for some time. There is a strong tradition of maintaining the separation of church and state.

General Attitudes. There is a noticeable difference in attitudes among those who live north of the Rhine Delta, a traditionally Protestant (Calvinist) region, and those who live in the traditionally Catholic south. By reputation, people in the south are more gregarious. In general, the traits most admired by the Dutch are honesty, humor, modesty, and good education. Social status is measured mostly by occupation.

As a small, trade-dependent nation, the Netherlands has recognized throughout history the importance of being internationally minded. It has a strong tradition of involvement in international affairs, primarily European since World War II. It is active in the United Nations. Dutch attitudes about society helped them create one of the most extensive welfare systems in the world, which remains a high priority in the country despite the increasing difficulty of supporting it.

Dutch openness to the world has made the people no less proud of their own culture and heritage, whether it be in politics, the arts, technology, or a strong tradition of liberalism. Through hard work and engineering skill, the Dutch took much of their territory from the sea by pumping water from land that is below sea level and building dikes to keep the water back. Because of this feat and their pioneering spirit, the Dutch have a saying: "God made the earth, but the Dutch made Holland." Keeping their country clean is important to the Dutch. They separate organic waste from other garbage, which is collected in different containers, and they recycle paper and bottles.

Personal Appearance. European fashions are popular. The Dutch enjoy stylish casual attire, as long as it is neat and clean. Traditional attire is rarely worn. The Dutch are famous for their *klompen* (wooden shoes or clogs). Traditionally, different *klompen* were created for different purposes, such as working in the fields, spending leisure time, and even getting married. *Klompen* are no longer worn in everyday situations, except on the farm, where field workers might still wear them. Most *klompen* produced today are exported.

CUSTOMS AND COURTESIES

Greetings. A warm and hearty handshake is an appropriate greeting for both men and women. It is also popular among friends to kiss on alternating cheeks three times when greeting. A common phrase is *Hoe gaat het?* (How are you?) or *Alles goed?* (Is everything all right?) While people may wave if greeting from a distance, shouting is impolite. The use of given names generally is reserved for close friends and relatives, except among the youth. Otherwise, the Dutch address others by their titles and family names. When answering the telephone, both the caller and the receiver identify themselves before starting a conversation. It is rude not to do so.

Gestures. Eye contact and facial expressions are important, though one should not stand too close to another person when speaking. One covers the mouth when yawning. When someone sneezes, a person nearby will say *proost* or *gezondheid*, the equivalent of saying "Bless you." It is impolite to pass between conversing individuals or to chew gum while speaking. Pointing the index finger to the forehead to imply someone is crazy is an insult. Wagging the index finger emphasizes a point.

Visiting. The Dutch are hospitable and enjoy having visitors. Unannounced visits are not common, except between very close friends or relatives. It is important to be punctual. If no time is stated for an evening visit to new acquaintances, it is usual to arrive after 8:30 p.m. and to leave before midnight. Guests shake hands with everyone present, including children. Hosts nearly always offer refreshments and serve them to guests. On a first visit to someone's home, a guest does not expect a meal (unless specifically invited for it). Rather, coffee or tea is served with sweet biscuits, and then drinks are served later in the evening. Dinner guests usually give the host a bottle of wine and the hostess some flowers.

Social visiting is especially important on birthdays; one is normally invited. The visit usually goes from 8 p.m. to midnight and begins with coffee or tea accompanied by birthday cake. Afterwards one is served beer and wine or juice and lemonade (for the children). The table will be spread with cheese, chips, or nuts.

Eating. The Dutch generally eat three meals a day. Dinner (around 6 p.m.) is the main meal for most people, but some rural families and older people retain the tradition of eating the main meal at midday. For them, the evening meal is light and often consists of bread, cold cuts, cheese, and salad.

Washing hands before eating, being on time to the table, and starting to eat at the same moment is important. It is impolite to begin eating before others. A parent or host often indicates when to eat, usually by saying *Eet smakelijk* (pronounced ATE smahk-ay-lick), which literally means "Eat deliciously" but is used in the same way as *Bon appétit* (Enjoy the meal). It is proper to keep hands above the table (rather than in the lap) but not to rest elbows on the table. The Dutch use the continental style of eating, with the fork in the left hand and the knife remaining in the right. Forks are not used to eat dessert; small spoons are provided. One does not leave the table until all have finished eating.

LIFESTYLE

Family. The Dutch have strong families, which are moderate in size. Most have only one or two children, but southern (Catholic) families tend to be a bit larger. Single parents are common. Grandparents live on their own or in a nursing home. People generally live close to extended family. Many holidays emphasize family gatherings. As is the case throughout Europe, both parents often work outside the home. However, Dutch women are somewhat less likely to work outside the home than women in other European countries. Thirty-nine percent of the labor force is female. However, more and more younger women are entering the job market, partly due to better access to education. Young people often leave home at age 18 to continue their education or to work. Children are expected to behave at home and at school. Parents help children with their studies but also encourage them in sports, music, and other activities.

Dating and Marriage. Dating habits are similar to those throughout Europe. Teenagers begin with group activities. Dancing, watching movies, and going to cafés are popular. Many young people get to know each other at clubs (sports, dance, film, etc.). Couples often live together before or instead of marrying.

For weddings, a large party in a restaurant (200–400 persons) is popular. A live band will play and guests will sing or tell something funny about the couple. All guests give a present; it may be money, because bride and groom cover the expenses.

Diet. Bread or toast with jelly, Dutch cheese or meats, boiled eggs, and coffee or tea are the most common foods for a Dutch breakfast. The most popular breads include multigrain and dark-grain varieties. Most people eat something sweet on their bread for breakfast or lunch; *hagelslag* (chocolate sprinkles) or chocolate spread are most common. Children often eat hot cereal for breakfast. *Krentenbollen* (raisin rolls) are also a favorite. Open-faced sandwiches are common for lunch, as is *kroket* (a deep-fried sausage). A typical meal may be *groentesoep* (vegetable soup), *gekookte aardappelen* (boiled potatoes), *karbonade* (pork chop), *bloemkoel* (cauliflower), and *yoghurtvla* (yogurt pudding). Seafood is also an important part of the Dutch diet; herring and eel are particular favorites.

Dutch pastries are world famous. Favorite snacks include fries (eaten with mayonnaise, not ketchup), *stroopwafels* (syrup waffles), and many varieties of Dutch licorice. Restaurants in larger towns offer a wide variety of cuisine, and Indonesian food has become an established part of the Dutch diet. Eating out is not as common as it is in the United States. Families usually eat most meals in the home.

Recreation. The most popular sport is soccer. Tennis, field hockey, swimming, sailing, ice-skating, wind surfing, basketball, badminton, and other sports also are enjoyed. Many

Dutch participate in cycling; nearly every person old enough to ride a bicycle has one. *Fietspaden* (bike paths) run throughout the country. People participate in sports through clubs. Games are organized locally, regionally, or nationally depending on the level of the players. Each sport has a national association that oversees its organization. *Football* (soccer) clubs have a million members; tennis clubs have 800,000.

Some people enjoy *korfbal*, a sport played on a grass field (or indoors) that combines some principles of soccer and basketball. Some people in Friesland play *Kaatsen*, a team sport similar to baseball; players hit a small, soft ball with the hand. Poles were traditionally used for jumping over ditches, and pole vaulting (for distance, not height) is popular in the north. It is called *Fiereljeppen*. In years when the ice is hard enough, a day-long ice-skating race takes place on a route that encompasses Friesland's 11 main towns and parts of the sea. As many as 80,000 people participate.

The Dutch and tourists alike take advantage of sandy beaches on the North Sea, although it is windy and the water is often cold. Discos are popular gathering places for young people.

The Arts. There are more than six hundred museums in the Netherlands. Some of the world's most famous artists are Dutch, including Rembrandt, Vermeer, and Van Gogh. The Dutch school of painting was a major influence on the art world. Dutch artists now also explore such media as performance art and photography. The government provides significant support for the arts without limiting free expression.

The prestigious Amsterdam Concertgebouw Orchestra, the National Ballet at Amsterdam, and the Dutch National Opera Company are examples of the Netherlands's excellence in the performing arts. The Dutch also have a long tradition in literature, as well as folk art, music, and dance.

Holidays. Official public holidays include New Year's Day, Easter (Friday–Monday), Queen Beatrix's Birthday (30 Apr.), Ascension, Liberation Day (5 May), Whitmonday, and two days for Christmas (25–26 Dec.). Though not a holiday, the third Thursday of September is the queen's opening of a new year of parliament; she sits on a golden coach and rides through The Hague.

Christmas festivities begin well before Christmas day. The Dutch usually do not exchange gifts on Christmas day; it is a day for families and feasts. Some families exchange gifts on Christmas Eve, but gift giving traditionally is associated with St. Nicholas Day (6 Dec.). *Sinterklaas* (St. Nicholas) is dressed like a Catholic bishop, rides a white horse, and leaves gifts in shoes. Children place hay or a carrot in their shoes for the horse, and it is replaced with candy or a small present. *Sinterklaas* also rides in parades and visits children wherever they may be. His servant throws small pieces of *pepernoten* candy (gingerbread) for children to gather and eat. Family members and friends who exchange gifts at this time (evening of 5 December) must disguise or hide the presents. They are all anonymous (said to have come from *Sinterklaas*) and are accompanied by an amusing poem about the receiver. Good-natured teasing and embarrassing others accompanies this festivity.

Each region is known for local festivals held throughout the year, often in celebration of the harvest. *Vlaggetjesdag* (Little Flag Day) is celebrated in coastal areas. Held in May, it marks the beginning of the herring season. Ships leave the harbor decorated with little flags. In the south, *Carnival* celebrations are popular. They begin on the Sunday before Lent

EUROPE

and end at midnight Tuesday. Businesses may close or cut back hours, and many people enjoy festivities in Den Bosch, Breda, and Maastricht. The Dutch receive a month of paid vacation each year. Many people take a week at Christmas, a week at Easter, and two weeks in the summer.

Commerce. Business hours are generally between 8:30 or 9 a.m. and 5 or 5:30 p.m., Monday through Friday. Shops normally are open weekdays from 8:30 a.m. to 8 p.m. and Saturdays from 8:30 a.m. to 6 p.m. Shops often close one morning each week, usually on Monday. Some also close at lunch, although not in large urban areas. Except in large cities, all shops close by 6 p.m. Amsterdam's so-called "night stores" are open later but charge higher prices. Many small shops are having to close. No businesses are open on Sunday, and there is no Sunday newspaper.

SOCIETY

Government. The kingdom is a constitutional monarchy. The queen is head of state, but the prime minister is head of government. Labour leader Willem (Wim) Kok won a second term as prime minister in national elections held May 1998. A Council of State, of which the queen is president, serves as an advisory body that must be consulted before legislation is passed. Amsterdam is the capital, but the government is headquartered at The Hague.

Legislation can be introduced either by the crown or the lower house of parliament. The prime minister and other ministers are responsible to the bicameral parliament (States General). Members of parliament's 75-seat upper house (First Chamber) are elected by the nation's 12 provincial councils. Members of the 150-seat lower house (Second Chamber) are elected directly by the people. The voting age is 18.

Economy. The Netherlands has a strong economy. Based on private enterprise, it is highly industrialized and efficient. The distribution of income is among the most equitable in Europe. Inflation is low. The economy grew by about 4 percent in 2000. Recent government efforts have reduced the budget deficit and lowered unemployment. The country qualified for the first round of Europe's Economic and Monetary Union in 1999.

Although agriculture and horticulture employ less than 6 percent of the labor force, the Netherlands produces food for export, as well as large numbers of cut flowers and bulbs for Europe and other parts of the world. The Netherlands accounts for more than half of the world's flower exports. Animal husbandry is a chief agricultural activity, producing meats, cheeses, and other dairy items. Leading industries include petroleum refining, machinery, chemicals, and construction. The Netherlands also has developed a strong economic base in computing, telecommunications, and biotechnology. Trade accounts for half of the country's gross domestic product. Banking and tourism are also key sectors of the economy. The currency is the *guilder* (g) or plural *gulden*; it will become the euro in 2002.

Transportation and Communications. The public transportation system in the Netherlands is one of Europe's best. An efficient network of trains connects major and minor cities. Most people also own cars and prefer to use them for

DEVELOPMENT DATA

Human Dev. Index* rank	8 of 174 countries
Adjusted for women	8 of 143 countries
Real GDP per capita	$22,176
Adult literacy rate	99 percent
Infant mortality rate	4 per 1,000 births
Life expectancy	75 (male); 81 (female)

daily travel; however, the country's six million cars mean traffic is a serious problem. Buses and streetcars are common in urban areas; Amsterdam and Rotterdam have subways. The country is divided into zones for public transportation. A universal ticket called a *Strippenkaart* is purchased at stations or from drivers or machines. Rotterdam is one of Europe's most important ports, handling 30 percent of Europe's sea transit; it is the world's largest port.

The communications system is efficient and well maintained. Television and radio stations are privately owned and there are dozens of newspapers and periodicals. The national radio and television associations affiliated with each station have certain backgrounds, such as liberal, socialist, Protestant, Catholic, or neutral.

Education. Schooling is free and compulsory between the ages of five and sixteen. Children may be enrolled for an optional year at age four. Primary education ends at age twelve. Students may go to a Catholic, Protestant, Muslim, or "non-religious" school, but the basic curriculum is the same. Secondary school begins with two years of "basic education"; all students study the same 15 subjects that emphasize practical application of knowledge. After that, they can choose between different types of high schools, ranging from prevocational to preuniversity. The number of years varies with the program. Vocational schools train students in such professions as accounting, nursing, or teaching. Graduates of vocational and general high schools often enter apprenticeships. The government subsidizes higher education. There are 13 universities, the oldest of which, Leiden, was founded by William of Orange in 1575.

Health. Medical facilities are excellent and are subsidized by the government. For persons earning less than a specified amount, the government covers insurance and health care. Those making more than that amount must buy private insurance. The government also provides unemployment and disability benefits. The most important person in health care is the *huisarts* (family doctor); he or she decides if a specialist is necessary. For example, a woman cannot go to the gynecologist without the *huisarts'* permission. Cancer and heart disease are the two biggest health concerns.

CONTACT INFORMATION

Royal Netherlands Embassy, 4200 Linnean Avenue NW, Washington, DC 20008; phone (202) 244-5300; Web site www.netherlands-embassy.org/f_explorer.html. Netherlands Board of Tourism, 355 Lexington Avenue, New York, NY 10017-6603; phone (888) 464-6552; Web site www.visithol land.com.

CultureGrams™

People. The World. You.

1305 North Research Way, Bldg. K
Orem, Utah 84097-6200 USA
1.800.528.6279; 801.705.4250
fax 801.705.4350
www.culturegrams.com

Republic of
Nicaragua

Boundary representations are not necessarily authoritative.

▼ THE AMERICAS

BACKGROUND

Land and Climate.   Covering 49,998 square miles (129,494 square kilometers), Nicaragua is about the size of Iowa. Although it is the largest country in Central America, only about 9 percent of the land is suitable for cultivation. Lago de Nicaragua borders the Pacific Ocean and is the only freshwater lake in the world to have sharks and sawfish. Low central mountains and hills separate the populated west from the east. Forests cover about one-third of the country. Large pine forests are located in the northwest and mountain areas while tropical rain forests and coastal wetlands spread across the east. Natural resources include gold, silver, copper, lead, zinc, and timber. Nicaragua's climate is tropical, although the highlands are cooler. Humidity is generally high and temperatures average 80°F (27°C). The dry season starts around 15 November and ends around 15 May. Several volcanoes along the Pacific coast are active; eruptions and earthquakes are common. Occasional hurricanes and tidal waves can be very destructive. Hurricane Mitch caused widespread devastation in late 1998, destroying crops and villages and killing thousands.

History.   Columbus was the first European to visit Nicaragua (1502), which was later explored by Spanish *conquistadores*. Spanish settlements date from the 1520s. Indigenous groups resisted the Spanish until finally conquered in 1552. Britain established settlements along the Mosquito Coast (*Costa de Mosquitos*) in the 17th century and claimed sovereignty over the coast in 1740. However, Nicaragua essentially was ruled by Spain until it declared independence in 1821. With independence it became a member of the United Provinces of Central America but chose to be an independent republic in 1838. Political power alternated between liberals and conservatives over the next few decades. The competition sometimes led to violence.

Internal chaos and U.S. economic interests led to U.S. military intervention beginning in 1909. During the 1920s and 1930s, guerrillas led by Augusto Cesar Sandino fought the U.S. occupation. Sandino was assassinated in 1934. In 1936, General Anastasio Somoza García seized the presidency. He ruled as dictator until his assassination in 1956. The Somoza family continued to rule the country, beginning with Somoza's son Luis Somoza Debayle, who died in 1967. He was succeeded by his brother, General Anastasio Somoza Debayle.

In 1962, the *Sandinistas*, a revolutionary group named after the martyr Sandino, was formed with the goal of overthrowing the Somozas. For the next 15 years, Sandinistas carried out various unsuccessful terrorist attacks on Somoza's National Guard, which was armed by the United States. In 1978, after the assassination of Pedro Joaquín Chamorro, a prominent anti-Somoza newspaper editor, riots broke out, Sandinistas stormed the national palace in Managua, and civil war followed. Somoza was forced to flee the country in July 1979, when the Sandinistas took control. Fifty thousand people were killed in the civil war.

The new Marxist-oriented government seized the Somoza fortune, redistributed their lands to the peasants, suspended the constitution, and began tightening controls. Concerned that Sandinistas were aiding Marxist rebels in El Salvador, the U.S. government suspended economic aid to Nicaragua in 1981, beginning a decade of strained relations between the two nations. Throughout the 1980s, U.S. funds supported the

Contras's opposition to Sandinista rule. General elections brought Sandinista leader Daniel Ortega Saavedra to power in 1985. The United States responded by imposing a trade embargo that severely handicapped the country's economy.

Eventually, the Sandinista government agreed to ensure free elections if the Contras would disarm. In 1990, Ortega was defeated by Violeta Barrios de Chamorro, widow of the assassinated newspaper editor. The United States supported Chamorro's presidency, ended trade restrictions, and pledged aid to rebuild the economy. The Contras began to disband in 1990. Although sporadic violence erupted throughout the early 1990s, widespread fighting did not resume. Striving for national reconciliation and economic recovery, Chamorro's government made some progress. It lowered inflation, depoliticized the army and national police force, and initiated reparations for lands seized in the 1980s. However, Chamorro was unable to solve Nicaragua's severe economic problems. Constitutional reforms disqualified her from seeking a second term.

Ortega sought the presidency again in 1996 but was defeated by Liberal Constitutionalist Party (PLC) candidate José Arnoldo Alemán Lacayo, a lawyer and coffee grower. The elections marked the first time in a century that one democratically elected civilian president in Nicaragua transferred power to another. Ortega and his Sandinista National Liberation Front (FSLN) continue to demand a voice in government policy. The FSLN made a strong showing in municipal elections in November 2000, and Ortega won his party's primary and will run for president in 2001 elections. Alemán has promised to create private sector jobs and resolve land disputes; however, the government's top priorities are rebuilding from Hurricane Mitch, strengthening the economy, and addressing its large external debts. Providing that reforms take place within the next few years, Nicaragua qualified for a major debt relief package from the World Bank and International Monetary Fund.

THE PEOPLE

Population. Nicaragua's population of 4.8 million is growing at 2.2 percent annually. The majority (69 percent) is mestizo, 17 percent is of European descent, about 9 percent is black, and 5 percent is native Indian. Most people live on the western plains. The population of Managua, the capital, is more than one million. Granada has about 700,000 people. The Caribbean side is sparsely populated—mostly by smaller ethnic groups. Nicaragua's population is young; at least 45 percent is younger than age 15.

Language. Spanish is the official and predominant language. Along the Caribbean coast, small groups speak English or other ethnic languages. Garífuna is common among the black population, as are English and Spanish, while some Indian groups speak Miskito, Sumo, or Rama. Some residents of Managua and other large cities speak English.

Religion. Approximately 95 percent of the population is Roman Catholic. Protestant, Evangelical, and other Christian organizations are also present. Although relations between the Catholic Church and the government were strained during the Sandinista period, the church has maintained its strong influence. Weekly attendance of mass is the norm. Catholic traditions, such as baptisms, communions, and weddings, remain a significant part of family life. Some older women attend mass daily. Religious icons, particularly pictures of the Virgin Mary, decorate many homes and vehicles. When parting or making future plans, people often add *Si Dios quiere* (God willing) as a qualifier to their commitment. Freedom of religion is guaranteed.

General Attitudes. Nicaraguans enjoy being with others and are sociable. Politics is a favorite subject. They value honesty, friendliness, respect, and good humor. They are kind and thoughtful and willing, even if they have little, to give to those in need. Individuals are more important than schedules, so punctuality at meetings may be admired but not strictly observed. Nicaraguans defend honor vigorously, sometimes even physically. Those in power are esteemed for their opinions and generally are afforded wealth. Therefore, power is highly valued and often sought. Social status is measured by material possessions and land ownership, family name, and connections. Personal criticism is taken seriously and usually avoided. Getting a job, having a large family, and owning a home or plot of land are important long-term goals for Nicaraguans.

The Sandinista influence still pervades civilian life. Collectivism and helping others are common values in all social classes. Years of strife have caused many to become wary and distrustful. Some now look at the government as a source of problems.

Personal Appearance. Neatness and cleanliness in physical appearance are important to Nicaraguans. Even if they cannot afford expensive clothing, they will make special efforts to be neat and well-groomed. All clothing is bleached and ironed.

People throughout the country wear lightweight clothing. In rural areas, men wear cotton shirts (button-down and T-shirts) and khaki pants. Jeans are also common. Rural women usually wear light cotton dresses or skirts and blouses. When working on daily agricultural tasks, both men and women wear *chinellas* (flip-flops), reserving regular shoes for trips to town or special occasions. Farmers might wear boots, sombreros, and old army fatigues.

Urban men wear cotton slacks and shirts (often long-sleeved). Urban women wear light cotton dresses, although many also wear pants. Many businessmen will wear a *guayabera* (an embroidered dress shirt) as semiformal wear instead of a tie and suit jacket. Suit coats are not worn during the hottest months of the year.

CUSTOMS AND COURTESIES

Greetings. When meeting another person for the first time, Nicaraguans smile, shake hands, and say either *Mucho gusto de conocerle* (Glad to meet you) or *¿Cómo está usted?* (How are you?). Inquiring about the health of family members demonstrates friendliness between acquaintances. Complete attention is given to the person being greeted. Common terms for greeting include *¡Buenos días!* (Good morning), *¡Buenas tardes!* (Good afternoon), and *¡Buenas noches!* (Good evening). A casual greeting, especially among the youth, is *¡Hola!* (Hi) or *¿Como le va?* (How's it going?). Men greet each other with a hearty handshake, and close friends hug and pat each other on the back. Men and women usually greet female friends with a kiss on the cheek and a gentle hug; rural women pat each other on the upper arm rather than hug. Those of higher social standing are greeted with titles like *Señor*, *Señora*, or *Señorita* (Mr., Mrs., or Miss) to show respect. One uses the titles *Don* and *Doña* with first names to indicate special respect, familiarity, or affection. Professional titles also are used before surnames.

Gestures. Nicaraguans use many gestures when speaking. To beckon, one waves all fingers with the palm facing down. One points by puckering the lips or extending the chin in the intended direction. If a person wants to pay for something, he or she may rub one index finger repeatedly down the other, similar to the U.S. American gesture for shame. Many people snap the forefinger against the middle finger to emphasize that something is very rich, expensive, or difficult to accomplish. This is done by holding the thumb to the middle finger and quickly shaking the wrist.

Avoiding eye contact during conversation generally is not acceptable; however, some women may do so in deference to others. Offering a seat to pregnant women, the elderly, or women with children is common. Women may also offer to hold other people's children on their lap if the parents are standing. Upon entering a building, men remove their hats or caps. Raising one's voice and displaying affection in public generally are not acceptable.

Visiting. Nicaraguans are hospitable and enjoy visiting. In rural areas, people commonly (even daily) visit family and friends unannounced. Those in urban areas with access to telephones usually plan visits in advance. Relatives and friends who live in other areas often visit for weekends and holidays.

Due to the hot climate, hosts always offer their guests a cool drink. Water, juice, or natural beverages like the corn-based *pinol* are served most commonly. Refusing a drink is considered a serious discourtesy. When one enters a home, it is important to greet everyone and wait for an invitation to sit. When visiting for a special purpose, guests first inquire about the health of the family before they discuss other matters. Good-byes may be drawn out and full of well-wishing. Visitors who arrive during mealtime are invited to join their hosts.

Guests tend to express admiration for their hosts rather than for material objects in the home. Dinner guests may take small gifts, such as flowers or candy, to the hosts. People also give gifts on special occasions, such as anniversaries, birthdays, and Catholic ceremonies.

Eating. Breakfast usually is eaten at 6 or 7 a.m., although people in rural areas may eat earlier during busy agricultural seasons. Lunch, the main meal of the day, is eaten at midday and often is followed by a *siesta* (afternoon rest). In rural areas, the *siesta* is taken from noon to 2 p.m., the hottest time of day, when work is difficult. Most people in urban areas eat lunch between noon and 2 p.m., with the *siesta* reduced to an hour break. Dinner is usually between 7 and 9 p.m.

Rural families eat lunch together; however, due to work and school schedules, many urban families do not. Most families make special efforts to eat together on weekends and holidays. In rural areas, people eat with a spoon or scoop their food with a tortilla. Sometimes the spoons are made from sections of a dried gourd shell. In urban areas, people may eat with a tortilla or spoon, but they also use knives and forks. They hold the fork in the left hand and the knife in the right. Many fried foods are eaten with the hands. People keep both hands (not elbows) on or above the table. Hosts expect their guests to eat what is served. They may offer second helpings. Diners are expected to praise the quality of the meal.

LIFESTYLE

Family. The extended family is the basis of society and strongly influences an individual's life and decisions. Parents, children, aunts, uncles, and cousins commonly live together. The oldest male is the head of the family. Nearly all Nicaraguans aspire to have large families; both men and women gain social status by being a parent.

During the Sandinista period, women were given a greater role in society and the right to participate more actively in family matters. Military service was common for women under the Sandinista regime, and many became involved in civic affairs. About one-third of the labor force is female. Because a number of men died or were sent away during the civil war, many women became heads of families. While men are still seen as the authorities and women generally defer to them, women control most household affairs. Rural homes often are made of straw and wood. Many family members often share one bed or room. Urban homes and more expensive rural homes are made of concrete. Patios and open areas are common. The redistribution of land and homes seized by the Sandinista government remains a sensitive issue.

Nicaraguans have two family names. The last name is the mother's family name and the second-to-last name is the father's family name, which functions as the surname. Therefore, a person named José Muñoz Gómez would be called Señor Muñoz.

Dating and Marriage. A girl formally enters social life at age 15, and a large *fiesta* (party) is held in her honor. Thereafter, she is allowed to have a boyfriend and attend dances. Group dating is common among the youth.

Civil marriages are the most common, although those who can afford it also have a large church wedding. Most marry between the ages of 16 and 23. In small towns, the bride and groom walk a full circle around the town directly after their ceremony. *Machismo*, the male attitude of proving one's manliness or superiority, continues to be a strong cultural influence. Although marriage is a valued tradition, male infidelity, which is a part of *machismo*, is widely tolerated.

Diet. Most meals include beans and rice; obtaining a well-balanced meal is difficult for many people who cannot afford more. Among wealthier families, the main meal of the day generally consists of rice, beans, some kind of meat, and a salad or vegetable. This is served with tortillas and fruit juice. Corn is an important ingredient in many foods. Oil is used frequently in cooking. *Gallo pinto* (a dish of rice and beans fried together) is eaten in many households for breakfast and dinner. Other typical dishes include tortillas, enchiladas, *nacatamales* (meat and vegetables, with spices), *mondongo* (tripe and beef knuckles), *vigorón* (vegetables with pork skins), and *baho* (meat, vegetables, and plantains). Tropical fruits generally are plentiful. Fried plantains (*plátanos*) are popular.

Recreation. Baseball is the national sport. Soccer, boxing, softball, basketball, and volleyball are also popular. Kickball is extremely popular among women. Youth often socialize at night in the park after dark until about 9 p.m. Dances are held on Friday and Saturday nights in local schools or on basketball courts. Going to the beach and participating in club activities are also popular.

The Arts. Nicaraguans of all ages love to dance, so most parties or large events include dancing. The national instrument the *marimba* (which is similar to a xylophone) and usually is

THE AMERICAS ▼

accompanied by guitars, maracas, and traditional flutes (*zuls*). Salsa is the most popular music. Folk music is prevalent at festivals. African culture influences music on the Caribbean coast.

Handicrafts, such as ceramics, hammocks, wall hangings, hats woven of hemp, embroidered blouses, and wood carvings, are common. Rubén Darío made poetry a national pastime, and a literary movement called *La Vanguardia* (the Vanguard) seeks to restore Nicaragua's cultural identity. Colorful, revolutionary-style murals called *primitive paintings* are popular.

Holidays. Public holidays include New Year's Day, Easter (Thursday–Sunday), Labor Day (1 May), Battle of San Jacinto (14 Sept.), Independence Day (15 Sept.), Gritería Day (7 Dec.), Feast of the Immaculate Conception (8 Dec.), and Christmas. Workers also receive a half-day vacation on Christmas Eve. Numerous holidays honoring local patron saints are the main annual events in towns and regions; celebrations may last one to three days. Because Catholics do not eat red meat during Lent, Nicaraguans traditionally eat iguanas as a paste or in *garrobo* soup before and during Easter.

Commerce. Most merchants' shops are open from 8 a.m. to noon and 1 to 6 p.m., Monday through Friday, and on Saturdays from 8 a.m. to noon. Government offices generally are open from 7 a.m. to 5 p.m., Monday through Friday. While some businesses close for the *siesta*, many in urban areas do not. In rural areas, business hours vary depending on the crops cultivated. Most people purchase basic supplies at open-air markets, although supermarkets are available in large cities.

SOCIETY

Government. The Republic of Nicaragua consists of 15 *departamentos* (provinces) and 2 autonomous regions located on the Atlantic coast. The executive branch is composed of a president, vice president, and cabinet. Constitutional reforms in 1995 transferred many powers previously held by the executive branch to the legislative branch. The National Assembly has 93 members. Legislators are directly elected to serve six-year terms. While more than 20 political parties are active in Nicaragua, many are joined in coalitions. The Liberal Alliance, comprised of Alemán's PLC and several other parties and factions, holds the most legislative seats, followed closely by the FSLN. The next national elections are scheduled for 2001. The voting age is 16.

Economy. Devastated by a decade of central planning under the Sandinistas, a civil war, the U.S. trade embargo, and Hurricane Mitch, the economy remains the country's greatest challenge. Economic stabilization plans have dropped inflation from more than 750 percent in 1991 to less than 12 percent; however, expectations for change have greatly exceeded the government's ability to provide it. Unemployment and underemployment affect more than 50 percent of the population. Nicaragua's per capita foreign debt (totaling more than six billion dollars) remains one of the highest in the world. The economy relies on agricultural exports such as coffee, cotton, sugar, bananas, seafood, and meat. About 44 percent of the labor force is employed in agriculture.

DEVELOPMENT DATA

Human Dev. Index* rank	116 of 174 countries
Adjusted for women	97 of 143 countries
Real GDP per capita	$2,142
Adult literacy rate	63 percent
Infant mortality rate	35 per 1,000 births
Life expectancy	65 (male); 70 (female)

Nicaragua has the potential for a much stronger economy. Despite devastation from Hurricane Mitch in 1998, the economy registered 6 percent growth in 2000. Damage to the country's economy and infrastructure has set development back decades. Controversy surrounds property rights; settlement of land disputes is needed to increase foreign investment.

Real gross domestic product per capita continues to fall. More than half of the population lives in poverty. More than 24 percent of the population lacks access to adequate health care, education, and economic opportunities needed to rise above human poverty.* The currency is the gold *córdoba* (C$).

Transportation and Communications. Years of fighting, the poor economy, and Hurricane Mitch have damaged both the transportation and communications systems. Most roads are unpaved or are in disrepair; many areas cannot be reached by car. Oxcart trails provide access to some rural regions. Buses provide service in cities. Postal, telegraph, and telephone services are limited in rural areas. About 25 percent of the population has a phone. The press is free and publishes four newspapers.

Education. Schooling is mandatory between the ages of six and thirteen. Most children begin primary school, but only 36 percent complete it. Students have to pay for their own supplies, uniforms, tuition, and expenses, which often becomes too difficult for the poor. Those who complete primary training generally proceed to the secondary level. Nicaragua has five private and five state universities.

Health. Health care is limited, particularly outside of Managua. Community volunteers have become active in promoting prevention and early detection of diseases. However, many people, particularly those in rural areas, do not get adequate care. Patients who need to go to a hospital must provide their own dressings and medications; many cannot. Low wages led doctors to strike against the public health system in 1998. Still, more than three-fourths of all infants are immunized and about the same number of women receive some prenatal care. Access to safe water and sanitation is a problem in rural areas.

CONTACT INFORMATION

Embassy of the Republic of Nicaragua, 1627 New Hampshire Avenue NW, Washington, DC 20009; phone (202) 939-6570. Nicaraguan Institute of Tourism, Hotel Intercontinental Managua, 1 Cuadra al Sur, 1C Abajo, Managua, Nicaragua; Web site www.intur.gob.ni.

1305 North Research Way, Bldg. K
Orem, Utah 84097-6200 USA
1.800.528.6279; 801.705.4250
fax 801.705.4350
www.culturegrams.com

Northern Ireland
(United Kingdom)

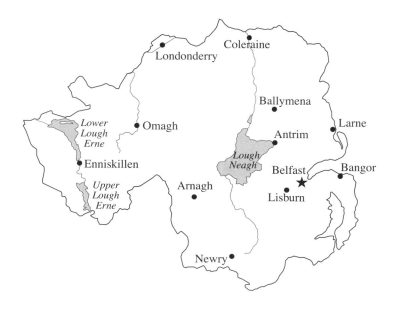

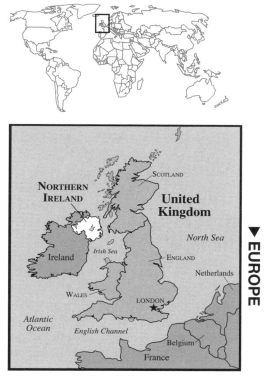

Boundary representations are not necessarily authoritative.

▼ EUROPE

BACKGROUND

Land and Climate. Northern Ireland is the smallest of the four nations that make up the United Kingdom (UK). Covering 5,482 square miles (14,199 square kilometers), it is about the same size as Connecticut. Summers are mild (average 55°F or 13°C) and wet; winters are cold (average 32°F or 0°C) and windy. The climate makes for a lush, green countryside.

Northern Ireland consists of the six northern counties on the island it shares with Ireland. The six counties, together with three in Ireland, make up what is called *Ulster*. Northern Ireland is often just referred to as Ulster. A large lake (Lough Neagh) dominates the terrain near Belfast. Rolling hills, a few low mountains, a rugged coastline, and forests are all part of Northern Ireland's landscape.

History. Celtic tribes invaded the island during the fourth century B.C. In the fifth century A.D., legend holds that St. Patrick converted the island to Christianity. The English began invading in the 12th century. In 1603, Irish revolts caused England's King James I to force Irish Roman Catholics in Northern Ireland to give up their land to English and Scottish Protestants. In 1801, the United Kingdom of Great Britain and Ireland was formed by the British Parliament.

In southern Ireland, the Easter Rebellion against British rule took place in 1916. This led to the formation of the Irish Free State, established in 1921 under British dominion. However, the south was largely Catholic. Meanwhile, the mainly Protestant northern counties of Ulster chose to remain in the UK as Northern Ireland. In 1949, the Irish Free State (not including Northern Ireland) became a republic, Ireland, and formally withdrew from the Commonwealth. The six northern counties remained part of the UK.

Seeking to unite all of Ireland, the Irish Republican Army (IRA), which is made up primarily of Catholics, began a campaign of assassinations and bombings against the Northern Ireland Protestants and British soldiers stationed in the country since 1969. The soldiers had been sent to maintain order after rioting broke out in Londonderry over issues of religious discrimination. Protestant extremists retaliated in similarly violent ways, making it impossible for frequently started negotiations on Northern Ireland's status to succeed. The British government instituted direct rule in 1972, precipitating further violence.

In 1975, Protestant and Catholic voters elected a 78 member convention with the responsibility of drafting a constitution and organizing a government for home rule acceptable to both sides. Unable to reach an agreement, the convention disbanded 10 months later. Although widely publicized, the subsequent struggles of the past two decades have been initiated by extremists on both sides and are not generally supported by either Catholics or Protestants.

In 1985, after talks with the UK, Ireland was awarded a consultative role in the affairs of Northern Ireland. In 1991, talks opened again on the issues of home rule, relations with the Irish republic, and power sharing between Catholics and Protestants. Many hoped that compromises would be reached between Nationalists (those who seek union with Ireland) and Unionists (those who support the current union with the UK). The talks collapsed after only a few months, resumed briefly in 1992 and 1993, and collapsed again.

Near the end of 1993, a framework for peace was jointly announced by Ireland and Britain. Gerry Adams, leader of Sinn Féin, the IRA's political wing, expressed support for the plan. In 1994, the IRA announced a voluntary cease-fire, a gesture soon returned by Protestant paramilitary groups. By 1995, all-party talks on the issue of power sharing between Northern Ireland's political/religious groups were met with optimism on both sides of the border. For the first time, most people believed peace was at hand.

Negotiations continued but stalled in September 1995. Frustrated with British demands for disarmament, the IRA ended its 17-month cease-fire in February 1996 with a bombing in east London. Efforts to revive the peace talks continued despite sporadic violence. Nationalist unrest, the worst in years, flared during the Protestant marching season in July 1997, increasing tension and frustration on both sides. Nevertheless, government leaders from Britain, Ireland, and political parties in Northern Ireland persisted. After months of deliberate negotiations, they reached agreement on a historic peace accord in April 1998. The Good Friday agreement called for an end to direct rule from Britain. Northern Ireland would still remain part of the United Kingdom, but members of an elected Northern Ireland Assembly would be given power to govern locally. The agreement also established a North-South Ministerial Council and a British-Irish Council. Seventy-one percent of Northern Ireland voters approved the accord in June 1998.

Although a deadly market-bombing at Omagh, the assassination of human-rights lawyer Rosemary Nelson, and other sectarian violence complicated matters, many remained hopeful for peace. However, ongoing intensive negotiations for forming the new assembly's cabinet failed after a final 30 June 1999 deadline because of a dispute over IRA disarmament, which Unionists want started before Sinn Féin begins sharing executive power. A last-ditch attempt to devolve power led to a Unionist boycott of the session where Assembly leaders would have been nominated. Beginning in 1999, the Northern Ireland Assembly operated for 10 weeks in a joint sharing of power between Catholics and Protestants but was suspended in February 2000 because of conflict over disarming the IRA. The Assembly resumed operation in June following a pledge from the IRA to put their weapons in arms dumps subject to verification by international inspectors. Continued sectarian violence, IRA and paramilitary disarmament, and other issues continue to complicate chances for lasting peace. Despite the setbacks, negotiators continue their work in the hope that the Good Friday Agreement may yet be salvaged.

In 2001, the highly contagious foot-and-mouth disease presented a grave threat to Northern Ireland's livestock. In response to the rapid spread of the disease, Northern Ireland banned the importation of animal products from other parts of the UK and killed all infected livestock. There is serious con-cern about what impact foot-and-mouth disease will have on the country's agriculture and tourism industries.

THE PEOPLE

Population. The population of Northern Ireland is about 1.7 million and is growing at only 0.25 percent per year. Northern Ireland is basically homogeneous; nearly all inhabitants are Irish, while some have Scottish roots. Belfast is the capital and largest city with about 360,000 people. Good access to health care, education, and economic prosperity affords people opportunities and choices in their own lives.

Language. English is the official language. Although regional accents and expressions may vary, the Irish speak basically the same form of English that is spoken throughout the UK. Also known as British English or Oxford English, it often varies from U.S. American English in spelling, pronunciation, idiomatic phrasing, etc. In recent years, Gaelic, the ancient language of Ireland, has become popular.

Religion. In contrast to the Republic of Ireland (*Éire*), which has a Catholic majority, Northern Ireland (Ulster) has a Protestant majority. There are 950,000 Protestants, compared to some 650,000 Catholics. The largest Protestant churches include the Presbyterian Church, the Church of Ireland, and the Methodist Church. The division between Catholics and Protestants has been a major source of conflict throughout Irish history, not just during the 20th century.

General Attitudes. The Irish believe in hard work, but on the whole the pace of life is more relaxed than in the United States. Religion and politics have long been sources of conflict in this politically troubled nation and generally are avoided as topics of conversation. The Irish are friendly, sincere, and keenly sensitive to the beauties of nature. They appreciate honorable people and those who keep their word. Those loyal to the British Crown are proud of the queen of England. Although Northern Ireland is part of the UK, the people are not English, but Irish. The majority support Northern Ireland's position as part of the UK, and many therefore think of themselves as British in addition to Irish. Being British is not the same as being English.

Despite the political turmoil, the ordinary person in Northern Ireland longs for peace. Daily interaction between both communities is common on a grassroots level. Catholics and Protestants may attend different schools and churches, but most adults work together and shop at the same stores. Government initiatives strive to create a more tolerant and pluralistic society.

The Irish consider their land as one of ancient tales and rich history. They believe this endows their nation with a certain "magic" that is hard to express but easy to feel. Folklore plays an important role in creating that magic.

Personal Appearance. The Irish wear popular European fashions but add their own styles as well. They often wear sweaters in the summer because of the cool climate. Wool clothing is popular. Jeans and sweatshirts are common casual wear. Many tend to dress more conservatively than in the United States. Businesspeople generally dress formally; dark suits with ties are common for men. The youth follow clothing fads in the entertainment industry.

CUSTOMS AND COURTESIES

Greetings.   Handshakes are common during initial meetings. Firm and brief, yet friendly, handshakes are characteristic of the Ulster people. Greetings between people who know each other include *Hello*, *Hi*, and *How are you?* In formal situations or when meeting strangers on the street, one may say *Good morning*, *Good afternoon*, or *Good night*, depending on the time of day. Men who know each other well may greet each other with a hearty slap on the back. People wave at others who are too distant for a verbal greeting. Strangers may offer a brief greeting or wave on uncrowded streets. Rural people often wave to strangers in passing vehicles and expect similar greetings in return. People generally call each other by first name, a practice that is becoming increasingly common even in the business world. Only close friends (particularly those at school) use nicknames.

Gestures.   The Irish do not use hand gestures excessively during conversation, but they do not keep hands entirely still; some gesticulation is common.

The Irish value politeness and generally do not push (even if in a hurry), eat on the street (or on the run), comb hair in public, or otherwise offend those around them. People traveling on buses usually offer their seats to the elderly. Men generally open doors for women. It is polite for drivers to give way to pedestrians and other cars entering from side roads. If one breaches a social norm, an apology is usually in order.

Visiting.   Among good friends, people often drop by unannounced and are always warmly welcomed. If the host is in the middle of something, guests will probably be told to make themselves at home—or be asked to join in. Dinner guests are expected to arrive on time. They usually bring a gift, such as wine or chocolates. It is customary for the hosts to open the gifts immediately in the presence of the guests. People often socialize for a while before dinner is served. Women usually are seated first. When finished eating, one places the utensils together vertically on the plate. Formal rules of etiquette depend largely on the event and the preferences of the hosts; however, many people follow less formal practices.

Hosts nearly always serve refreshments during informal visits, but they do not insist their guests eat. Socializing takes place not only in the home but also in *pubs*.

Eating.   The Irish eat in the continental style, with the fork in the left hand and the knife remaining in the right. They keep the hands above the table. In restaurants, the waiter brings the bill to the table. The bill usually includes a 15 percent value-added tax and a 15 percent service charge. If it does not include the tip, patrons leave money on the table. Families gather on Sunday to enjoy a large, formal meal and to spend time together. The evening meal eaten around 6 p.m. is called *tea*.

LIFESTYLE

Family.   Although the father dominates in the home, the mother exercises considerable influence in family affairs. Women traditionally have played conservative roles by staying at home, but this is changing as many now work outside the home. Men generally do not participate in household chores, and some continue to maintain a separate social life with their male friends after marriage. Still, there is a very low divorce rate in Northern Ireland. Commitment to family ties is important. Visiting one's parents is a popular weekend activity. The elderly often live alone and are proud to be independent as long as possible. However, as fewer adult children can take aging parents into their homes, the number of nursing homes or *shared accommodations* is increasing. Most families, including many newly married couples, own their own homes. Houses typically are two-story buildings made of brick or concrete.

Dating and Marriage.   Teenagers generally start dating between ages 14 and 16. Most either associate with groups of friends or go out as couples. Dancing and going to movies are popular activities. Dating more than one person at a time usually is not accepted. Engagements generally are long and may last two or more years. Women marry at about age 23, men at about 25. Church weddings are still common. Receptions include an elaborate meal (for as many as two hundred guests) often held in a hotel, followed by speeches and dancing. Many couples live together before or instead of marrying. Civil marriages are becoming more common.

Diet.   Mealtime traditionally has been important to the people in Northern Ireland. In the past, this called for large meals and a great deal of preparation. However, as women spend more time working, this is no longer possible and meals are becoming less formal. Fried foods are a traditional favorite, but this is changing also as health issues become more important. Fresh produce, especially vegetables, is readily available. Potatoes have remained an important staple in the Irish diet. With many types of potatoes available, most people eat potatoes in some form every day. Fresh seafood, fish, lamb, pork, and beef are eaten frequently. There are many different bread varieties to choose from, as well as scones and pastries. Irish stew, homemade tarts, and *pasties* (meat pies in the shape of burgers) are traditional dishes.

Recreation.   Soccer, *hurling*, *Gaelic football*, lawn bowling, golf, fishing, cricket, bicycling, sailing, hiking, and rugby are all popular sports in Northern Ireland. *Hurling* is played on a soccer-type field with wooden sticks and a small leather ball. *Gaelic football* is played with a round ball and is like a cross between soccer and basketball. Players can touch the ball with their hands, but they cannot pick it up from the ground. The ball is punched, not thrown, and it can be kicked. Teams score by getting the ball into a soccer-type net but can also make points for putting it over the top of the goal.

Horse, dog, and car racing are also common. The Irish are avid movie fans. Amateur clubs and societies (such as bingo clubs) are enjoyed by some.

The Arts.   The Northern Irish are proud of their cultural heritage. The British government supports efforts to promote and preserve Irish culture, particularly activities related to the Gaelic language. Literature, especially poetry, is quite popular, and Ulster poet Seamus Heaney received a Nobel Prize for his poetry in 1995. Amateur theater companies regularly perform works of contemporary playwrights. Traditional folk music is kept alive by more than 250 organizations, clubs, and schools. Folk instruments (primarily drums and pipes)

▼ EUROPE

are played along with violins and accordions. Festivals are prevalent and typically are held September through April.

Holidays. Official holidays include New Year's Day; St. Patrick's Day (17 Mar.); Easter (Thursday–Monday); Labor Day (1 May); Battle of the Boyne (12 July), a part of Orange Day festivities that can last a full week and consist of parades, speeches, and other celebrations; Halloween (31 Oct.); Christmas; and Boxing Day (26 Dec.). Boxing Day comes from the British tradition of giving small boxed gifts to service workers. It is now a day for visiting friends and relaxing. Fairs that celebrate the harvest, historical figures, or folk traditions are also common throughout the area.

Commerce. Business hours extend from 9 a.m. to 5 p.m., Monday through Friday. Government offices often are closed for an hour at lunchtime and remain open until 5:30 p.m. Banks are open from 9:30 a.m. to 4:30 p.m. Most shops are open from 9 a.m. to 5:30 p.m., Monday through Saturday. Businesses are usually closed on Sundays.

SOCIETY

Government. Northern Ireland comprises 26 districts within the United Kingdom of Great Britain and Northern Ireland. It is represented in the UK's 659-seat House of Commons (Parliament) by 18 elected members. The majority of those seats are held by leaders who support Northern Ireland's union with Great Britain. The UK's head of state is Queen Elizabeth II. A prime minister (Tony Blair) is head of government. The Northern Ireland Assembly has 108 members; the Ulster Unionist Party, the Social Democratic and Labour Party, the Democratic Unionist Party, and Sinn Féin hold the most seats in the Assembly. The first minister is David Trimble. The voting age is 18.

Economy. Farming, fishing, tobacco, shipbuilding, and aircraft manufacturing are the major economic enterprises. Farmers commonly raise cattle, hogs, and sheep and produce dairy products, poultry, and potatoes, among other things. Many farmers suffered in 1996 and 1997 from the European Union's ban on British beef, Northern Ireland's largest export.

Northern Ireland's standard of living is comparable to England's; most people earn an income sufficient to meet basic needs and provide some luxuries. However, continued progress toward peace is needed to create a stable environment that can attract more investment and new industries. Unemployment remains one of Northern Ireland's biggest challenges. However, an educated populace, fine research institutions, and growing high-tech and biomedical manufacturing are opening up the economy. The currency of the UK is the British pound sterling (£).

Transportation and Communications. Transportation is excellent, with buses being the most common and best means of travel within a city. On two-level omnibuses, nonsmokers use the lower level and smokers go to the upper level. On one-level buses, smokers must use the back of the bus. Rail

DEVELOPMENT DATA

Human Dev. Index* rank	10 of 174 countries
Adjusted for women	10 of 143 countries
Real GDP per capita	$20,336
Adult literacy rate	99 percent
Infant mortality rate	6 per 1,000 births
Life expectancy	75 (male); 80 (female)

infrastructure has improved with a high-speed link between Belfast and Dublin, Ireland and a link to Antrim. Taxis are also available. Private cars provide long-distance transportation. Traffic moves on the left side of the road. Communications systems are modern. Private and public television and radio broadcasts are available throughout the nation. All phone calls, including local ones, are billed by the length of the call. Therefore, a person borrowing someone's phone usually offers to pay for the call.

Education. Most children attend either Catholic or Protestant schools; a small number (3 percent) attends integrated schools. Primary school is required for children between ages four and eleven. At age 11, all students take a difficult government-sponsored exam. If they do well, they go to grammar school, which prepares them for a university education. If they fail to score high marks, they go either to a secondary (or intermediate) school or a technical college to prepare for a profession or trade. They can still choose to go to grammar school if the family is able to pay tuition and fees. After this first exam, students must take two more government-sponsored exams to gain admission to a university. Programs of study are much stricter than those in the United States. A bachelor's degree can be obtained in three years, but the exams taken before one is admitted to a university are recognized as being equal to a first-year university exam. The government pays for public education at the university level.

Health. As throughout the UK, the residents of Northern Ireland enjoy relatively good health. Hospital facilities are readily available. Northern Ireland is served by the National Health Service, which provides free or low-cost medical care to all citizens. The individual pays for prescriptions and some dental costs.

CONTACT INFORMATION

Northern Ireland Bureau of the Embassy of the United Kingdom, 3100 Massachusetts Avenue NW, Washington DC 20008; phone (202) 588-7842; Web site www.britainusa.com/nireland/nireland.asp. Northern Ireland Tourist Board, 551 Fifth Avenue, Suite 701, New York, NY 10176; phone (800) 326-0036; Web site www.discovernorthernireland.com/home.asp.

CultureGrams™
People. The World. You.

1305 North Research Way, Bldg. K
Orem, Utah 84097-6200 USA
1.800.528.6279; 801.705.4250
fax 801.705.4350
www.culturegrams.com

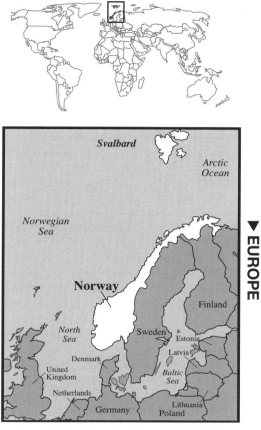

Boundary representations are not necessarily authoritative.

BACKGROUND

Land and Climate. Norway, one of the "three fingers" of Scandinavia, is just larger than New Mexico. It covers 125,182 square miles (324,220 square kilometers). Its coastline, indented with beautiful fjords, stretches more than 1,000 miles (1,600 kilometers) from the North Sea to the Arctic Ocean. *Norway* means "the northern way." In fact, the Arctic Circle crosses the country almost in its middle. Along the fjords on the western coast are numerous small islands. Norway is generally mountainous and has several glaciers. The mountains and high plateaus are interrupted by fertile valleys and small plains, but only about 3 percent of the country is suitable for cultivation.

Norway has many natural resources, including crude oil (in the North Sea), copper, nickel, zinc, lead, and timber. More than one-fourth of the land is forested. The North Atlantic Drift moderates the otherwise cold climate and allows for ice-free harbors and mildly warm summers. Rain is abundant on the west coast. In the interior, winters are colder and summers are warmer than on the coast. Snow lasts for several months of the year. Above the Arctic Circle, the sun shines day and night for part of the summer and does not rise above the horizon for part of the winter. In the absence of the sun, the *aurora borealis* (northern lights) is visible for a period of time.

History. During the Age of the Vikings (800–1050), Vikings conquered many areas in Scandinavia and Europe and even settled briefly in parts of North America. For example, Leifur Eiríksson landed in present-day Canada. In Norway, Viking leader Harald the Fairhead became the first supreme ruler of a unified kingdom around 872. Christianity spread throughout the area by 1030. The country came under Danish domination from 1381 to 1814 before it was given to Sweden as a peace treaty provision to punish Denmark's alliance with Napoleon during the Napoleonic Wars. In reaction to being given to Sweden, Norway declared its independence and drafted a constitution. Still, the Swedish king was accepted as monarch and the two nations were unified. The union was dissolved by referendum in 1905, and a Danish prince (Carl) was chosen to be the constitutional monarch of an independent Kingdom of Norway. He took the name Haakon VII.

Norway was neutral in World War I, but Germany attacked in World War II (April 1940) and held Norway until its liberation in May 1945. During that time, the monarch was out of the country supporting the Allied effort against the Germans. The son of Haakon VII, Olav V, was king of Norway from 1957 to 1991. Upon his death, his son, Harald V, took the throne and is king today.

Norway's postwar period has been marked by political stability, economic progress, and development. The country has good relations with the United States. Norway is a member of the North Atlantic Treaty Organization (NATO), the West European Union, and the European Free Trade Area, but it is not a member of the European Union (EU).

The issue of joining the EU has been fairly sensitive in Norway ever since voters rejected membership in 1972. In 1990, a prime minister (Jan Syse) resigned over the debate. The opposition leader, Gro Harlem Brundtland, replaced him and served until elections in September 1993, when she was reelected prime minister for a four-year term. She and her party (Labor Party) risked her considerable popularity in 1994 to apply for membership in the EU and then to campaign to have voters approve the measure. In a 1994 referendum, held after neighbors Sweden and Finland voted in favor of joining the EU, voters rejected entry into the EU. Many expressed concerns that some autonomy would have to be sacrificed to EU leaders, which is not an acceptable option for most Norwegians. Further, people have enough confidence in Norway's resources and economy remaining strong without membership in the expanding EU.

Thorbjørn Jagland replaced Brundtland as prime minister after she stepped down in October 1996. (Brundtland became director-general of the World Health Organization in May 1998.) While in office, Jagland turned attention away from the EU, focusing instead on budgetary and social issues. A three-party centrist coalition led by Kjell Magne Bondevik took power following general elections in September 1997. Bondevik resigned in March 2000 after losing a landmark environmental vote over whether to build the first gas-powered power plants in Norway. The country's new labor prime minister is Jens Stoltenberg, who, at 41, is Norway's youngest prime minister. Stoltenberg favors EU membership, but no date has been set for a third referendum on the issue. Parliamentary elections are due to be held late in 2001.

THE PEOPLE

Population. Norway's population of 4.5 million is growing at approximately 0.5 percent annually, a rate close to the European average. Norway is one of the most sparsely populated countries in the world. The population is predominantly of Nordic (Scandinavian) descent. Although Norway strictly limits immigration, immigrant workers now number 75,000 since the discovery of oil in the North Sea. A small minority (20,000) of native Sami (pronounced SAW-me) live mostly in the north. Also called Laplanders, their ancestors were the original inhabitants of northern Norway. The two largest cities are Oslo (500,000) and Bergen (225,000).

Language. Norwegian, the official language, has two forms. *Bokmål*, or "book language" is used in most written works and is spoken by more than 80 percent of the people, especially those in urban areas. It is also the main language of instruction and broadcasting, although laws require that the other form, Nynorsk, be used in a certain percentage of schools and broadcasting media. Nynorsk was created in the 1800s as a combination of the many rural dialects then in existence. Bokmål is heavily influenced by Danish, due to four hundred years of Danish rule. The Sami speak Sami (Lappish) but learn Norwegian in the schools as a second language. English is taught in the schools beginning at age seven or eight and is spoken widely as a second language.

Religion. More than 86 percent of the population belongs to the state church, the Church of Norway, which is Evangelical Lutheran. Still, freedom of religion is guaranteed, and many other Christian churches are active in the country. Among them are the Pentecostals, Roman Catholics, and various Protestant groups. Although religion is important to some, less than half the population practices their religion on a daily basis. Most people attend church services only on special occasions or holidays.

General Attitudes. Tolerance, honesty, human kindness, and independence are important Norwegian ideals. Reliability in business and private matters is also valued. Peace and progress are common themes in Norway, the country that sponsors the Nobel Peace Prize. The United Nations is integral to its foreign policy. Norway gives about 1 percent of gross national product in aid to the world's poorest countries. Criticism of other peoples or systems is considered inappropriate. Norwegians take great pride in their individual and national independence. They are very patriotic and feel Norway has developed a superior social system with high standards. Indeed, social equality and a good standard of living are important values that have shaped post–World War II politics. Although the country is rich and has a lot of natural resources, Norwegians tend to be modest about their personal wealth. They also love the outdoors and work hard to protect their environment.

Sincerity in friendship is important, but people show reserve in the expression of personal feelings. Neighbors, even in large cities, get along very well and usually consider each other close friends.

Personal Appearance. Dress generally follows conservative European fashions and is influenced by the necessity to keep warm. Cleanliness and dressing well are important; an unkempt appearance in public is considered inappropriate. Shirt and tie, casual pants, and sweaters or pullovers are appropriate professional attire for men. Suits are worn for business meetings.

Traditional costumes (*bunad*), which are specific to each region, are worn on special occasions, such as weddings and national and local holidays. They are often hand sewn and have elaborate embroidery. For women, these costumes usually consist of a white blouse (often embroidered), a jumper-type skirt, an apron, and a headdress. Men wear knee pants, shirts, and vests.

CUSTOMS AND COURTESIES

Greetings. Norwegians often take the initiative by introducing themselves to strangers. Natural courtesy is important in good relations. Shaking hands is the normal custom. In formal situations, businesslike handshakes are firm and short. In personal situations, handshakes are longer and warmer. Close friends may hug each other while touching opposite cheeks during or after the handshake. Everyday acquaintances greet each other with a casual *Morn* (literally, "Morning"), regardless of the time of day. The term is roughly equivalent to "Hi." *Hei* also means "Hi" and is as common as *Morn*. A slightly more formal greeting is *God dag* (Good day). People greeting others they have not seen for a while often say *Takk for sist!* (Thanks for the last time!).

Traditionally, only close friends addressed each other by first name, but the youth increasingly are using first names once they have been introduced. Older individuals continue to follow the custom of using titles with a family name. When being introduced for the first time, a person addresses the other by both first and last name.

Gestures. Norwegians keep hand gestures to a minimum during conversation. However, people may wave the index finger in the air when warning others or expressing anger. It is impolite to place one's hands in the pockets when standing in front of a large group. Chewing gum is also inappropriate in public and business settings. It is not polite to yawn without covering the mouth. On public transportation, people usually offer their seat to women or the elderly. Courtesy and good behavior are important in all cases.

Visiting. Most Norwegians socialize at home. Friends visit each other regularly, either to maintain friendships or just to socialize. In the past, people visited unannounced, but now a call in advance is appreciated. Guests usually are offered coffee, tea, lemonade, or soda water and cakes or cookies. It is considered rude for invited guests to refuse any refreshments the hosts offer.

When visiting a home for the first time, one customarily brings a gift of flowers, sweets, or another small token of appreciation to the hosts. Traditionally, guests wait to be invited in by the host, who helps them remove their coats as a gesture of hospitality. Guests may also wait to sit down until they are invited to do so. Personal privacy is important; topics such as income and social status are avoided in casual conversation. Punctuality is important. It is considered poor taste to leave directly after dinner.

Eating. In the past, Norwegian families ate breakfast, dinner, and supper together. Today, most families meet together for dinner and sometimes breakfast. Many also enjoy a light evening snack. Norwegians eat in the continental style, with the fork in the left hand and the knife remaining in the right. It is impolite to leave food on the plate. At the end of a meal, whether in casual or formal situations, diners thank the person who prepared or is responsible for the meal. Indeed, children are taught to say *Takk for maten* (Thank you for the food) before leaving the table. Hands are kept above the table during the meal.

Except for special occasions, most Norwegians do not eat out often. In a restaurant, a patron summons the server with a raised hand. The bill usually includes a service fee, but a small tip (5–10 percent) is also customary.

LIFESTYLE

Family. The typical family unit is small, yet important, consisting of a mother, father, and two children. Both parents usually work outside the home, but women still handle most household tasks. Most husbands and wives consider each other equal in authority. In fact, gender equality throughout the country is rather pronounced. Women have a strong presence in politics, holding nearly 40 percent of parliamentary seats and nearly half of cabinet posts. They comprise 45 percent of the labor force. Their influence has helped Norway develop strong child-care, educational, and family programs. After childbirth, parents can take up to 42 weeks of fully paid leave. Fathers are required to take four weeks and mothers twelve.

Many people own their homes or condominiums. More than one-third also own or share a cabin in the mountains or by the sea. Spending time in these cottages is a favorite family activity. Although divorce was once uncommon, a dramatic increase has occurred over the last decade. Still, about half of all adults are married.

Dating and Marriage. Serious dating is discouraged among the youth, but group dating usually starts between ages 14 and 18. Dances, outdoor activities, and movies are favorite pastimes. Most couples live together before or instead of marrying. Men marry around age 25; women marry slightly younger. Weddings take place in churches or before a judge at a public office. Large parties for families and friends include dinner and speeches, followed by refreshments and dancing.

Diet. Breakfast and lunch usually consist of open-face cheese or ham sandwiches and milk or coffee. Meat or fish, potatoes, vegetables, and a soup or dessert generally are prepared for the main meal. A common meal is meatballs with potatoes and brown gravy, served with vegetables. Norwegian specialties include *fish balls* served in a milk sauce, smoked salmon, *lutefisk* (cod or coalfish, soaked in potash lye), *fårikål* (cabbage and mutton), *smalahode* (sheep's head), and a variety of other dishes. Ready-made or frozen foods are popular, particularly for evening snacks. Delis usually have ready-made fried fish, fish cakes, fish pudding, and meatballs. Ice cream and puddings with various toppings are popular desserts.

Recreation. Most Norwegians are physically active. Many Norwegians can ski (cross-country skiing is especially popular), and children learn at a very young age. A saying claims that Norwegians are born with skis on their feet. Norway is one of the world's centers for skiing, both Alpine (downhill) and Nordic (cross-country), and ice-skating. The city of Lillehammer was the site of the 1994 Winter Olympics. Fishing is excellent and popular; trout, pike, and salmon abound in Norwegian waters. People enjoy playing soccer, swimming, and hiking during the summer months. Boating is popular when the frozen lakes and fjords thaw. Sports are not connected to school activities, but each community has its own sports clubs for individual and team competition. Winning is not emphasized as much as participation. Most families are actively involved in these clubs. Reading is a popular leisure activity.

The Arts. Many families participate in the performing arts, either by performing themselves or by attending theater, concerts, and other cultural events. Theater is particularly valued, and permanent theaters are now located in many cities. The Norwegian Opera, the Norwegian National Ballet, and numerous orchestras add to the lively arts scene.

Traditional arts are important to Norwegians. Folk musicians are popular, and festivals feature many types of folk music. The best-known folk dance is the *halling*, in which male dancers perform challenging kicks and leaps. Norwegian folktales are also popular. They often portray animals or mythical creatures such as trolls, pixies, and monsters living in the ocean.

Rock carvings, wooden stave churches, and Viking ships are examples of ancient architecture and craft. Contemporary arts include furniture, jewelry, textiles, and painting. Norwegian mural painting is especially renowned.

Holidays. Official holidays include New Year's Day, Easter (Thursday–Monday), Labor Day (1 May), Constitution Day (17 May), and Christmas (24–26 Dec.). The Norwegian flag is prominent for all holidays; it is even used to decorate Christmas trees. Constitution Day is celebrated much like the Fourth of July in the United States, with parades, flags, family gatherings, and the like. Families often take ski vacations during the Easter holiday. Christmas is the biggest celebration of the year. As in other countries, preparations begin well in advance. At 5 p.m. on Christmas Eve, bells ring and

EUROPE

the holiday officially begins. Stories about *Julenisse* (Father Christmas) are popular among children. Families gather to share a big meal and exchange gifts. Parties are common on Christmas day and thereafter until the new year begins.

Commerce. The average workweek in Norway is one of the shortest in the world, about 37 hours. Office hours are usually from 8 a.m. to 4 p.m., Monday through Friday. Stores open from 9 or 10 a.m. to 4 or 5 p.m. In large towns, stores often stay open as late as 7 p.m. each Thursday. Shops close by 2 p.m. on Saturdays and are closed on Sunday. Shopping centers are now common in cities.

SOCIETY

Government. Norway is a constitutional monarchy. The king has limited authority, except as head of the military and as a symbol of continuity and stability. The leader of the dominant party in Parliament serves as prime minister and has executive power. The *Storting* (Parliament) has an upper chamber (*Lagting*) and a lower chamber (*Odelsting*). Its 165 members are elected every four years. Labor, Progress, and Conservative Parties are the largest in Parliament, but no party has a majority. Hence, the numerous smaller parties, which have substantial followings, can significantly influence political debate. All citizens may vote at age 18. Norway has 19 provinces (*fylker*).

Economy. Norway, which enjoys a strong economy, has one of the highest standards of living in the world, and wealth is, in general, evenly distributed: the poorest 40 percent of households earn 20 percent of the nation's income. Highly developed social institutions are able to provide for general economic prosperity but also result in heavy tax burdens averaging 46 percent. The decision to remain outside the EU has not weakened the economy. In 2000, the economy grew by around 3 percent. Norway remains closely tied to Europe through its trade within the European Economic Area (EEA). Unemployment is low.

Norway is the world's second largest oil exporter, behind Saudi Arabia. Other important exports include natural gas, ships, and fish. Aluminum and some manufactured items, such as furniture, also are exported. Norway is a major producer of aluminum. Oil drilling, commercial shipping, textiles, chemicals, technology, and food processing are among the key industries. The government is attempting to further diversify the economy to reduce its dependence on oil. The services sector of the economy employs 71 percent of the labor force. Agriculture is also important to the domestic economy, employing 6 percent of the labor force in livestock raising, fishing, and crop cultivation. The currency is the Norwegian *kroner* (NKr).

Transportation and Communications. Norwegians depend on cars for personal transportation, particularly due to the length of the country and its sparse population. However, they pay one of the highest prices in the world for gasoline—about 5 dollars per gallon. Trains, buses, and airplanes also connect many cities and towns. Norway has the fourth largest ocean fleet in the world. Ferries, which provide service across many fjords, are vital to infrastructure in western parts of the country. Before cars and airplanes became readily

DEVELOPMENT DATA

Human Dev. Index* rank	2 of 174 countries
Adjusted for women	2 of 143 countries
Real GDP per capita	$26,342
Adult literacy rate	99 percent
Infant mortality rate	4 per 1,000 births
Life expectancy	76 (male); 82 (female)

available, steamboats known as *Hurtitruten*, or coastal steamers, were the main form of transportation for people along the coast. Steamers still transport goods and are popular among tourists. The communications system is highly developed and fully modern. In 1999, the Norwegian and Swedish state-owned telecommunications companies agreed to merge. Norwegians enjoy newspapers; local, district, and national papers are widely read. One state and three private television stations broadcast throughout the country.

Education. Schooling is free and compulsory for all children between the ages of six and sixteen. The first six years constitute primary school, while the last three are lower secondary school. Upper secondary school is open to all, although students usually are between the ages of 16 and 18. It includes both preparation for higher education and vocational training.

After secondary school, many people begin working. Others are admitted to a university or college, and a small number attend the folk high school, a boarding school for teaching liberal arts (after the Danish tradition). Universities are located in Oslo, Bergen, Tromsø, and Trondheim. There are a number of specialized colleges and institutes. Instruction is readily available to most citizens and basically free at all levels, including higher education. Space is limited at universities, however, and many students travel to other countries for their college education.

Health. In keeping with its commitment to social welfare, the government has an extensive system that provides free, high-quality health-care services to all. Health clinics and regional hospitals provide service on a local level, but district and national hospitals are also available. Socialized medicine pays for all hospital charges, although small fees are charged for medicine and some procedures. Costs are shared between the central and local governments. Private doctors, clinics, and hospitals are limited.

CONTACT INFORMATION

Royal Norwegian Embassy, 2720 34th Street NW, Washington, DC 20008; phone (202) 333-6000; Web site www.norway.org. Scandinavian Tourist Board, PO Box 4649, Grand Central Station, New York, NY 10163-4649; phone (212) 885-9700; Web site www.goscandinavia.com. Royal Norwegian Consulate/Information Service, 825 Third Avenue, 38th Floor, New York, NY 10022; phone (212) 421-7333; www.norway.org/embassy/ny.html.

1305 North Research Way, Bldg. K
Orem, Utah 84097-6200 USA
1.800.528.6279; 801.705.4250
fax 801.705.4350
www.culturegrams.com

Boundary representations are not necessarily authoritative.

▼ THE AMERICAS

BACKGROUND

Land and Climate. Panama is a fairly rugged, mountainous country connecting Central and South America. Covering 30,193 square miles (78,200 square kilometers), Panama's total land area is just smaller than South Carolina. Volcanic activity has made the soil very fertile in some areas. About half the country is forested and 6 percent is suitable for cultivation. The Panama Canal, a man-made structure, runs from Panama City to Colón through *Lago Gatún* (Lake Gatún). Areas outside the Canal Zone, which stretches between and includes the two cities, are collectively called *el interior* (the interior). The *Cordillera Central* (Tabasara Mountains) form a spine down the center of the western interior; there are also mountains in the eastern interior. The tropical climate is hot and humid except at higher elevations. The average annual temperature is 80°F (27°C). In the mountains, the average is about 55°F (13°C).

History. The history of Panama has been affected greatly by its strategic location between the Atlantic and Pacific Oceans. Rodrigo de Bastidas, a Spanish explorer, visited Panama in 1501. Columbus claimed the area for Spain the next year. In the 16th and 17th centuries, Panama served as the route for shipping Incan treasures to Spain. In 1821, Spanish rule was overthrown, and Panama became a province of Colombia. During the 1880s, France attempted to build a canal across the narrow isthmus. Planning and financing were poor, and yellow fever claimed more than 20,000 lives. Canal rights were sold to the United States.

On 3 November 1903, Panama declared its independence from Colombia, and the United States sent troops to support the new Panamanian government. Construction of the

Panama Canal began in 1907 under U.S. supervision. The Canal was completed seven years later. It became an important passage for ships traveling between the Atlantic and the Pacific. The United States controlled the Canal, and U.S. citizens worked in most managerial positions. In 1978, the U.S. Senate narrowly ratified a treaty signed by President Jimmy Carter that would allow Panama to assume control of Canal operations in 1999; the United States would continue to guarantee the Canal's neutrality.

Omar Torrijos Herrera, commander of the national guard, seized control of Panama in 1968. He is credited with negotiating the Canal treaty with the United States. Although he ruled as a dictator, most Panamanians now revere him as a national hero. He turned daily government powers over to a civilian administration in 1978 and allowed free, multiparty legislative elections in 1980. After Torrijos died in a controversial 1981 plane crash, his defense minister, Manuel Antonio Noriega, began consolidating power as head of the Panama Defense Forces.

Arturo Delvalle Henríquez became president in 1985; he was ousted in 1988 for trying to fire Noriega, who had effectively suspended the constitution and civil rights in 1987. Noriega ruled under a state of emergency and controlled the national assembly. Following 1989 elections, he refused to allow the new president (who had opposed Noriega) to take office. Noriega's rule became increasingly repressive in Panama, and relations with the United States worsened.

When a 1989 coup attempt against Noriega failed, the United States sent troops to Panama in response to growing concerns about corruption, violence, and Noriega's threats against U.S. interests. Troops loyal to Noriega were defeated and he was taken prisoner. When the elected government was installed, Noriega was extradited to the United States to stand trial for various drug-trafficking charges. Convicted in 1992, he is serving a 40-year prison sentence.

President Guillermo Endara's government struggled to rebuild the nation, but social unrest, poverty, and corruption hindered progress. Free elections prevailed in 1994 and Ernesto Pérez Balladares (known as El Toro) was elected president. Pérez Balladares has been credited with attracting foreign investment, fighting corruption, and stabilizing the economy, but he was constitutionally barred from seeking a second five-year term.

Mireya Moscoso, widow of former three-time president Arnulfo Arias, was elected as Panama's first woman president in May 1999 on promises to fight for the rights of the poor and to slow economic reform and privatization begun by Balladares. On 31 December 1999, Panama assumed full control of the Canal's operations. Moscoso and her administration are evaluating how best to administer the Canal. Expansion of the Canal should be finished by the end of 2001, and should funding permit, further extension projects are planned for 2005.

THE PEOPLE

Population. The population of Panama is 2.8 million, growing annually at 1.34 percent. Next to Belize, Panama has the smallest population in Central America. About 70 percent of Panama's citizens are mestizos. Fourteen percent of the people are black, descendants of laborers from the Caribbean (mostly the West Indies) who came to work on the Canal in the early 1900s. Ten percent of the people are white, having European ancestry. The rest are members of various indigenous groups who have their own rich cultural heritage and often have chosen not to integrate into Panamanian society. The largest groups are the Kuna, Ngöbe-Buglé, and Emberá (or Wounaan). Most of the country's urban population lives in Panama City, the capital, and Colón. The life and culture of the *campesinos* (farmers) in the interior is drastically different from that of urban Panama.

Language. Spanish is the official language of Panama. About 14 percent of the people speak English as a native tongue, and many others speak English as a second language. English is rarely spoken outside of Panama City. Many blacks speak Creole English. Indigenous peoples speak various languages, according to their ethnic background. Most prevalent are Kuna, Ngäbere, and Buglé. Ethnic minorities speak their native tongue and Spanish.

Religion. About 85 percent of the population is Roman Catholic. Another 6 percent belongs to various other Christian organizations. There are small numbers of Muslims, Jews, Hindus, and Baha'i in Panama. Although the Catholic Church has great influence on the lives of the people, Panamanian law maintains freedom of worship and separation of church and state. Many Catholics are critical of local ecclesiastical authorities but remain loyal to the pope.

General Attitudes. Although society is stratified in traditional social classes, Panamanians consider all people to be of worth. They believe people should be treated with dignity and respect, regardless of their class. This value for the individual

is also evident in Panamanians' respect for personal strength and charisma. Tradition, family loyalty, stability, and wealth are all important values in Panamanian society. Men are expected to be polite. However, *machismo*, the defining of a man as forceful, daring, and virile, is a large part of Panamanian culture. Comments by men about women are common. The ideal woman is well-bred, understanding, and feminine. People in large urban areas are more cosmopolitan in their approach to these traditions.

Nationalism is strong in Panama, a reflection of the country's strategic position in the world and the service it provides to all nations. Most citizens, even interior *campesinos*, are well-informed on topics relating to national and international politics. Panamanians are also aware of their country's association with the United States. Many resent the relationship as unequal. Panamanians appreciate their Spanish heritage and, to a lesser extent, their indigenous roots.

Personal Appearance. Most male urban workers wear open-necked shirts called *guayaberas*. Bankers and other executives wear dark suits and ties. Women dress in styles similar to those in the United States. Dress habits are informal, and sandals are common footwear. Nevertheless, Panamanians, especially women, tend to pay careful attention to their public appearance. They admire a polished look and rarely wear sloppy clothing. Traditional costumes are worn on special occasions. For women, this includes a *pollera* (a full-length dress with embroidery). For men, it is the *montuno* (baggy shorts and matching embroidered top), *cutarras* (leather sandals), and palm-fiber hats. Kuna women wear *mola* (appliquéd) shirts, Ngöbe-Buglé women wear *naguas* (colorful dresses), and Emberá women wear skirts but no top. Indigenous men wear Western-style dress.

CUSTOMS AND COURTESIES

Greetings. When greeting, many women (and sometimes members of the opposite sex) give an *abrazo* (hug). That is, they clasp hands as in a handshake, lean forward, and press cheeks. Men shake hands with one another, often while patting the other on the shoulder. *Campesinos* usually only shake hands when greeting. Verbally, they may also "howl" a *grita*, a personally styled cry used to express friendship, break the monotony of fieldwork, and show joy at fiestas.

The most common verbal greetings include *¡Buenos!* (Good day), *¿Cómo está?* (How are you?), *¿Qué tal?* (What's up?), and *¿Qué hay de bueno?* (What's good?). *Buenos días, Buenas tardes*, and *Buenas noches* (Good morning/afternoon/evening) are used more formally or with the elderly. Inquiring about the welfare of one's family members is polite after an initial greeting. For good-bye, one says *¡Hasta luego!* (See you later), or *¡Que le vaya bien!* (May things go well for you). In the cities one says *Chao* (Good-bye). *Adiós* is rarely used because it is considered fairly permanent.

In formal situations among the educated, it is important to address people by educational title, such as *Maestro/a* (teacher), *Ingeniero/a* (person with a bachelor of science degree), or *Doctor/a* (Dr.). These titles usually are followed by the person's given name, not surname. Other titles include *Señor* (Mr.), *Señora* (Mrs.), and *Señorita* (Miss). *Don* and *Doña* are used for respected or elderly men and women. Informally, people often greet one another by given name or nickname. Using someone's nickname is not polite unless the person is a close friend. People often address each other by terms of relationship: *Hermano/a* (brother/sister), *Amigo/a* (friend), *Tío/a* (uncle/aunt), and so forth.

Gestures. People in the interior use nonverbal communication more often than those in urban areas. For example, they pucker their lips to point or to indicate "over there" or "time to go." One might ask "what's up?" by shrugging with the palms facing up. "No" can be expressed by wagging the index finger from side to side. Drawing a circle with the finger in the air means one is coming right back. Wrinkling a nose can mean "I don't understand."

Politeness is important and chivalry common. Men offer their seats on public transportation to women or the elderly. Deference to elders in any situation is important. Personal space generally is small, and people sit or stand close when they converse. Eye contact is important. It is polite to cover the mouth when yawning.

Visiting. Panamanians enjoy hosting others in their homes. They are open, generous, and informal with their guests. Hosts customarily do not establish an ending time to a visit, as that might indicate to the guests that they are not as important as the hosts' schedule. It is polite for guests to allow their hosts to take care of them. That is, guests do not help with dishes, they take any offers of the best seat or food, and they graciously accept any good-bye gifts. When invited to dinner, guests usually do not take gifts to their hosts; this would imply the hosts are not expected to be thorough in providing hospitality. Rather than giving a gift, guests generally expect to return the favor of a dinner invitation.

A visit is a compliment, and friends and relatives visit one another often. Unannounced visitors are always welcome. In the interior, relatives see each other almost daily, depending on their relationship and how far they live from one another. Urban dwellers enjoy Sunday visits. All visitors are offered refreshments, such as a fruit drink (*chicha*). A full meal is also often offered.

Sending (exchanging) gifts is common among friends in the interior, but gifts include items such as food or seedlings, not expensive items. The custom is a way of sharing one's good fortune with friends. It is not commonly practiced in the cities.

Eating. Urbanites generally eat three meals a day. Interior people often have a big breakfast early, a main meal at midday, and a small dinner around 5 p.m. *Campesino* families most often eat two meals: breakfast after 9 a.m. and then dinner around 6 p.m. They may have snacks before or during work. Hands generally are kept above the table during a meal. Conversation is light. The spoon is the most commonly used utensil in the interior.

Any guests present are served first, followed by the men, children, and the women and/or cooks. The cook or hostess usually prepares a plate for each person. Extra food might be put out for second helpings. Guests compliment the cook verbally and by finishing their food. Urbanites eat out often, but *campesinos* rarely do. Urban diners usually leave servers a tip of 5 to 10 percent.

LIFESTYLE

Family. In Panamanian families, the mother generally takes responsibility for the home. This traditional role is still quite admired and respected. Less than 30 percent of the labor force is composed of women. The father's main responsibilities are usually outside the home, but he is still considered the undisputed leader of the family. As in other Latin American countries, the family is the basic unit of society. Due to the changing tempo of modern life, nuclear families are gaining prominence over the extended family. However, adult children expect to care for their aging parents, even if they do not live with them. In such cases, children send money or food, visit them, and arrange for their basic needs to be met. A large number of births take place out of wedlock, but many of these are within stable common-law marriages. Families in urban areas often live in rented apartments, while rural families may own a small home.

Dating and Marriage. Most young women begin group dating around age 14. Compared with girls of other Latin American countries, urban Panamanian girls enjoy a great degree of freedom. However, young women in the interior often are not allowed to date until much later and are subject to parental restrictions. Urban women usually marry in their early twenties; in the interior, women often marry by age 20. In most areas, rural and urban, boys have nearly complete freedom. Although rural boys have farm responsibilities, they receive little supervision outside of school and have no domestic duties. When dating, couples enjoy dancing, going for walks, and watching movies. In the interior, common-law marriages are prevalent and are generally as well accepted and stable as legal marriages performed by the state. Couples desiring a church marriage must obtain a license; a registered religious official can then perform the marriage. Church weddings are common in urban areas.

Diet. In Panama, it is commonly said that one hasn't eaten if one hasn't had rice. Rice is served with nearly every meal, along with a source of protein (eggs, chicken, sardines, meat, fish, or beans). Corn and plantains are also staples. Fish is inexpensive and often made into a soup. People usually eat vegetables as part of the main dish or in a salad. They often eat fruit as a snack. *Chicha*, a popular drink, is made from fresh fruit, water, and sugar. Coffee is usually part of breakfast. Common dishes in the interior include *sancocho* (chicken soup), *guacho* (rice soup), *bollo* (corn mush that has been boiled in the husk), corn tortillas, and *guisado* (stewed meat with tomatoes and spices). *Arroz con pollo* (rice and chicken) is eaten on special occasions. Urban people eat traditional foods as well as a wider variety of international foods.

Recreation. In towns, many participate in team sports. *Futból* (soccer) is the favorite sport. Baseball, boxing, and basketball are also favorites. Panamanians enjoy attending horse races, cockfights, and movies. The national lottery is popular. Socializing on the porch or visiting friends is an important leisure activity. Leisure time for rural women often revolves around domestic events; they may get together to make crafts or to socialize and make *bollos* when the new corn comes in.

The Arts. Native peoples have a special talent for handicrafts (textiles, jewelry, baskets, ceramics, etc.). Kuna women's *mola* shirts are known for their ornate designs. Poetry incorporates indigenous peoples' mythology, and dramatic poetry readings are popular. Panamanians love to dance, especially the *tanborito*, Panama's national dance. Traditional Panamanian music, called *típico*, is played by a band consisting of a singer and players with an accordion, a guitar, and some percussion. Lyrics usually pertain to love and life. *Típico* is more common in rural areas and is joined in cities by salsa, *merengue*, jazz, and reggae. On the Caribbean coast, drumming and singing to an African beat are popular.

Holidays. Official holidays include New Year's Day (1–2 Jan.), Day of the Martyrs (9 Jan.), Easter (Friday–Sunday), Labor Day (1 May), Independence from Colombia Day (3 Nov.), Uprising of Los Santos (11 Nov.), Independence from Spain Day (28 Nov.), Mother's Day (second Sunday in December), and Christmas. Each village or city holds celebrations to honor the local patron saint. *Carnaval* celebrations are always held the Saturday to Tuesday before Ash Wednesday (usually in February or March).

Commerce. The business day begins as early as 7 a.m. and ends by 4 p.m. Many stores stay open until 6 p.m. During holidays, they may remain open until 9 or 10 p.m. Most businesses are open Saturday until 6 p.m., with the exception of government offices, which are closed. Urbanites shop at large grocery stores and open-air markets for most basics. *Campesinos* may shop daily for small amounts of items they need; they also collect from their harvests and exchange produce with friends and relatives. When necessary, they travel to shops and markets in larger interior towns.

SOCIETY

Government. Panama is a multiparty democracy divided into nine provinces. Its president is chief of state and head of government. The 72-seat national assembly has several active parties, including the ruling Arnulfista Party (PA) and the Democratic Revolutionary Party (PRD), originally formed by Torrijos. All citizens are required by law to vote beginning at age 18. At the local level, communities elect a *junta local* (town council) to coordinate town events and functions.

Economy. Panama's potentially strong economy is slowly recovering from years of political instability, authoritarian rule, and U.S. economic sanctions (1988–90). Panama enjoys success in its strong banking industry, financial services, tourism, and trade through the Colón Free Trade Zone. Economic growth was robust in the early 1990s after vital trade relations were restored with the United States. Growth averaged 3.2 percent in 1999, slowed to 2.7 percent in 2000, and is expected to reach 4 percent in 2001. Inflation remains at 1.4 percent. The country faces high unemployment and a shortage of skilled labor.

The economy reflects a growing prosperity for the country but a widening gap between rich and poor; the richest 10 percent of the population owns 49 percent of the wealth. Nearly one-half of Panamanians live in poverty. About 9 percent lack the health care, education, and economic opportunities to rise above human poverty.*

Key exports include bananas, shrimp, coffee, sugar, and clothing. The Panama Canal, a major international trade route, provides vital foreign-exchange earnings. Tourism is

DEVELOPMENT DATA

Human Dev. Index* rank	59 of 174 countries
Adjusted for women	52 of 143 countries
Real GDP per capita	$5,249
Adult literacy rate	91 percent
Infant mortality rate	21 per 1,000 births
Life expectancy	72 (male); 76 (female)

another important sector. About 27 percent of the labor force is employed in agriculture-related industries. The official currency is the *balboa* (B), which consists mostly of coins. Bills are U.S. dollars, which are legal tender.

Transportation and Communications. The highway system is the hub of transportation in Panama. Roads are generally in good condition, especially in and around urban areas. The Inter-American Highway runs from the Costa Rican border through Panama City but stops at the Darien Gap. The capital is linked to Colón by the Trans-Isthmian Highway. Some revenues from the national lottery help build and maintain roads. Domestic airlines and shallow waterways also provide transportation. In cities, buses, *chivas* (minibuses), and taxis are readily available. In the interior, people walk, use *chivas* or buses, or ride horses. The majority of the people do not own cars. Most telephones are owned by people living in urban areas. Centrally located public telephones are available in the interior. Communications facilities are well developed. A free press flourishes and there are many newspapers.

Education. Primary education is compulsory and free between the ages of seven and fifteen. Most school-aged children (72 percent) complete primary schooling and go on to more specialized secondary education. Rural families may have difficulty sending children to secondary schools—usually located in larger towns—because they cannot afford to pay for daily transportation, uniforms and supplies, or room and board in the city. After completing the secondary level, a student may go on to one of several vocational schools or prepare to enter a university. Panama has a national university, established in 1935, as well as a Catholic university and other church-owned schools.

Health. Panama's public health program is part of the national security system. It provides such services as free examinations, care for the needy, and health education and sanitation programs. Most people have access to modern medical care of some kind, although the best facilities and personnel are in Panama City and Colón. Some rural health centers are understaffed or poorly equipped. Malaria and yellow fever are active in the eastern areas near Colombia.

CONTACT INFORMATION

Embassy of the Republic of Panama, 2862 McGill Terrace NW, Washington, DC 20008; phone (202) 483-1407.

1305 North Research Way, Bldg. K
Orem, Utah 84097-6200 USA
1.800.528.6279; 801.705.4250
fax 801.705.4350
www.culturegrams.com

Republic of
Paraguay

Boundary representations are not necessarily authoritative.

BACKGROUND

Land and Climate. Paraguay is a landlocked country in central South America. Covering 157,046 square miles (406,570 square kilometers), it is slightly smaller than California. More than one-third of the country is forest or woodlands, although deforestation is a significant problem. About 20 percent of all territory is suitable for cultivation. There are no high elevations in the country and no real mountains. The *Río Paraguay* (Paraguay River) divides the country into two regions. To the northwest lies the sparsely settled arid region known as the Gran Chaco or simply Chaco. Near the river, the Chaco is mostly wetlands. Southeast of the river is the fertile Paraná Plateau, where the population and agricultural centers are located. The plateau is subtropical and has a hot, humid, and rainy climate. Paraguay is south of the equator; seasonal changes are opposite those in the Northern Hemisphere. Summer is from September to June. The cooler rainy season is from June to September.

History. Spanish explorers came to Paraguay in 1524 and established Asunción in 1537. Colonial rule lasted until the 19th century. Paraguay peacefully gained independence in 1811, and José Gaspar Rodríguez Francia established the first in a long line of dictatorships. He closed the country to the outside world and ruled until 1840. In 1865, Francisco Solano López took Paraguay into the War of the Triple Alliance against Brazil, Argentina, and Uruguay. Ultimately, the war was lost (1870), along with 55,000 square miles (142,450 square kilometers) of territory and 500,000 lives. Foreign troops stayed until 1876, and Paraguay remained politically unstable for another generation.

In 1932, Paraguay waged the three-year Chaco War with Bolivia in a territorial dispute, but gaining two-thirds of the Chaco territory it claimed cost Paraguay a good portion of its male population and did not stabilize the nation. Various dictators and one elected president ruled until 1954, when General Alfredo Stroessner, commander of the army, took control of the Paraguayan government and established a long-term dictatorship. Although his tenure brought some economic development (mainly in the form of three hydroelectric dams), his government was responsible for human-rights violations, corruption, and oppression.

A coup in 1989 ousted Stroessner, who now lives in Brazil. General Andrés Rodríguez Pedotti, who led the coup, was elected president. He restored civil rights, legalized political parties, and promised not to serve past 1993. Rodríguez was the first leader to successfully implement many democratic reforms. A new constitution was ratified in June 1992. Rodríguez's administration helped Paraguay emerge from its isolation under decades of dictatorship to join in regional and international organizations.

Civilian Juan Carlos Wasmosy was elected president in 1993. In April 1996, army chief General Lino Oviedo led an attempted coup against Wasmosy that tested the country's commitment to democracy. In September 1997, a military tribunal sentenced Oviedo to 10 years in prison for holing up in barracks and defying Wasmosy's orders to abandon his command. With strong support from his followers, Oviedo campaigned for president from his prison cell until a Supreme Court ruling forced him to withdraw his candidacy two weeks before the May 1998 elections. Oviedo's running mate, Raul Cubas, won the election in his place and freed Oviedo from prison.

The country plunged into a political crisis in December 1998 when Cubas refused to follow a Supreme Court ruling ordering Oviedo be returned to jail. In February 1999, impeachment proceedings began against Cubas, who refused to bow to pressure from Congress and the Supreme Court. The crisis deepened when Vice President Luis Argaña, a member of the opposing faction within the Colorado Party, was assassinated in late March. Bloody riots broke out as thousands protested Cubas and Oviedo's alleged involvement in Argaña's death and demanded Cubas's resignation. Cubas stepped down, disgraced, and both fled to neighboring countries. Demands for their return and prosecution continue. In April, Senate president Luis González Macchi was sworn in as president under guidelines established by the constitution. The Supreme Court has ruled that President Macchi can finish out Cubas's term until elections in 2003. In August 2000, Julio Cesar Franco of the Liberal Party was elected to fill the vacancy left by Vice President Argaña's death. This major victory for the Liberals comes at a time of growing dissatisfaction with Macchi's administration.

THE PEOPLE

Population. Paraguay's population of 5.59 million is growing annually at 2.64 percent. Paraguay is the most ethnically homogeneous country in South America, partially due to its many years of virtual isolation. As much as 95 percent of the population is of mixed Spanish and native Guaraní heritage. Pure native Guaraní are few in number today; most live around Asunción or in northern Paraguay. Descendants of German and Italian immigrants have assimilated into mestizo society. Some Koreans (who generally are merchants), other Asians, and Arabs also reside in Paraguay, but they have not assimilated into Paraguayan culture. A small number of Mennonites, mostly around Filadelfia, maintain a distinct lifestyle based on their European agricultural heritage. About half of all Paraguayans live in urban areas. Asunción has approximately 800,000 inhabitants. More than 40 percent of the population is younger than age 15.

Language. Paraguay has two official languages: Spanish and Guaraní. Spanish is the language of government, urban commerce, and schooling, but Guaraní is the common language. In rural areas, some people speak only Guaraní, although most also speak or understand Spanish. Portuguese is spoken along the Brazilian border. Paraguay's Spanish is called *Castellano* (Castilian), not *Español*. Paraguayans mix many Guaraní words with Spanish, and many of their vocabulary words differ from those of other Spanish-speaking countries. They generally use the *vos* rather than the *tú* form for informal address.

Religion. About 90 percent of all Paraguayans are Roman Catholic, but most are tolerant of other religions. Catholic holidays play an important role in society. Women tend to be more religious than men. Various Protestant and other Christian churches also have members in Paraguay. Mennonites practice their own religion. Many rural people mix Christian and traditional beliefs of mythical or mystical powers in their worship.

General Attitudes. Paraguayans are proud of being Paraguayan. They often define themselves by three aspects of their culture: speaking Guaraní, drinking *yerba* (herb) tea,

and eating *mandioca* (cassava). Paraguayans say that Spanish is the language of the head, but Guaraní is the language of the heart. Mate (MAH-tay) leaves are made into a mildly stimulating tea. Served cold, it is called *tereré*. Served hot, it is *mate*. *Yerba* tea has been part of the culture for hundreds of years. *Mandioca* is served at nearly every meal.

Paraguay is a traditional society. Large families, property, beauty, virility, money, and status are valued. People are generally concerned with not having problems; an ultimate desire is *tranquilidad* (tranquillity). Deviations from traditional mores and loud, disruptive behavior are not appreciated. Due to generations of isolation, wars with neighboring countries, and other factors, the mestizo population tends to look down on people with darker skin tones, including some foreigners, resident Asians, and dark-skinned or black South Americans.

Paraguayans do not appreciate stereotypes about poverty and inferiority in developing countries; they are proud of their particular heritage. At the same time, they feel other countries take advantage of their nation. As South Americans, Paraguayans do not appreciate U.S. citizens referring to themselves as "Americans." The preferred reference to residents of the United States is *norteamericanos* (North Americans).

Personal Appearance. Western-style clothing is worn throughout Paraguay. Cleanliness is emphasized; even the poorest people have clean clothing and clean shoes. Adults do not wear shorts in public. Men generally do not wear sandals. Urban men wear slacks and a shirt for working, but suits and ties are less common because of the hot climate. Clothing is often lightweight; cotton is a popular fabric. Rural men wear work clothes and a hat when farming.

Women pay particular attention to their appearance, regardless of economic conditions. Styled hair, manicured nails, jewelry, and makeup are all important. Rural women nearly always wear dresses. Women in Asunción are especially fashionable. Society generally considers beauty an important quality in women. The youth enjoy North American fashions.

CUSTOMS AND COURTESIES

Greetings. Spanish greetings, such as *¡Mucho gusto!* (Pleased to meet you), are often used with strangers or for formal situations. Acquaintances might use less formal Spanish, such as *¡Hola! ¿Cómo estás?* (Hi. How are you?), but friends and relatives more often use Guaraní greetings. The most common phrase is *¿Mba'eixapa?* (pronounced m-buy-ay-SHA-pah), which means "How are you?" The reply is almost always *¡Iporã!* (Just fine). In the countryside, it is friendly and polite to call out a greeting (*Adió*, holding out the *o*) to a friend passing one's house.

Except in the workplace, men and women always shake hands when greeting, even if for the second or third time in a day. Friends greeting for the first time in a day (if at least one is a woman) will kiss each other on each cheek as well as shake hands. Rural women are more likely to pat the other's arm than kiss. When departing, most people repeat whatever gesture they used in greeting.

Urban men are addressed respectfully by last name, often accompanied by *Don*. For women, *Doña* customarily accompanies the first name. Using a person's professional title also shows respect. Young people refer to each other by first name. In rural areas, *campesinos* (farmers) commonly address one another by first name, preceded by *Ña* (for women) or *Karai* (for men). Paraguayans often greet a respected elder by holding their hands in prayer position and waiting for the elder to bless them.

Gestures. Perhaps the most common hand gesture is "thumbs up," which expresses anything positive or encouraging. A person uses the gesture when saying *¡Iporã!* or answering a question. Wagging a vertical index finger means "no" or "I don't think so." One beckons by waving all fingers of the hand with the palm facing out or down. Winking has romantic, even sexual, connotations; it is not used as a casual gesture.

Paraguayans are soft-spoken; they do not shout to get someone's attention. If making a "tssst tssst" sound does not work, a Paraguayan might whistle or run after the person. Paraguayan men usually give up their bus seats to older or pregnant women or women with babies. Seated bus passengers usually offer to hold packages or children for standing passengers. To make one's presence known at a home, one claps at the gate. It is impolite to enter the yard until invited.

Visiting. Paraguayans visit one another often. Unannounced visits are common and welcome. Paraguayans enjoy hosting friends and new acquaintances. Guests usually are offered refreshments. If the hosts are eating a meal or drinking *tereré*, they will invite visitors to join in. Otherwise, guests might be offered a soft drink (in the city), coffee, juice, or water. Hosts offer *tereré* to unannounced visitors only if they want them to stay a while. People often drink the tea from a common *guampa* (container, usually made of wood, cattle horns, or gourds) through a *bombilla* (metal straw). The host passes the *guampa* to one person, who drinks and returns the container to the host, who makes another portion for the next person. Participants enjoy this important social custom while relaxing and conversing.

Urban residents like to invite friends to their homes for a meal; rural people generally extend invitations only for special occasions. Guests need not be punctual; being late is accepted and more comfortable for all involved. Invited dinner guests might bring a gift of wine, beer, or a dessert. Guests usually are expected to stay after a meal for conversation and tea.

Eating. Mealtimes and eating habits vary according to region and family. Rather than sit down to a daily family meal, rural people often eat when they can. Farmers might eat lunch in their fields, for example, rather than go home. Urban families usually eat their main meal together.

Children might eat before guests (who are not relatives) arrive or are served. Guests usually receive their plates of food fully served. They may take additional portions from serving dishes on the table. Not finishing one's food is considered an insult to the cook. Hosts usually insist their guests take second helpings. Proper etiquette is important in formal situations, including not placing hands in the lap (they rest on the table edge) and waiting for the hosts to begin eating.

Few people, especially in rural areas, drink during meals. They wait until afterward. At rural parties or celebrations, women eat after men do, or they eat at separate tables. The *asado* (barbecue) is a popular family gathering in many areas.

Street vendors sell a lot of food on urban streets; eating or drinking in public is common. Sharing food or drink is also common. In restaurants, one rarely buys a drink for oneself; one orders a large pitcher for all at the table. Additional rounds are ordered by other diners. When eating a snack or small meal, Paraguayans offer the food to whomever is around. Declining the offer is not considered impolite. In restaurants, service is included in the bill; tips are not expected.

LIFESTYLE

Family. Society centers on the extended family. Three or four generations might live in one home or on one farm. Children are well behaved and polite. They generally show respect to their elders, and adult children expect to care for their aging parents. The father heads the family and the mother takes care of the household. Most rural women, like the men, are involved in agriculture. As much as 40 percent of the urban labor force is female.

Rural families have few modern conveniences. They live in wooden or brick homes with dirt floors and grass or tin roofs. Urban homes are made of concrete and have tile roofs. Nearly all homes in Asunción have running water and electricity.

Dating and Marriage. Most Paraguayan young women have a party at age 15 to celebrate becoming a *señorita*. They are then allowed to go to dances. In traditional homes, they are not allowed to date for another year or two. Young people get to know each other at community *fiestas* (parties), large family gatherings, dances, and so forth. Customarily, a young man must have a young woman's parents' permission to date her. Then he can only visit her on traditional visiting days (Tuesday, Thursday, Saturday, and Sunday). Later in a relationship, the young woman's relative might chaperone the couple. Parents generally expect to approve of any marriage partners. For a marriage to be legal, the wedding must be performed civilly. In addition, couples may have a church wedding. Many couples enter into common-law relationships. Others have children together but do not live together.

Diet. Breakfast usually consists of *cocido* (*mate*, cooked sugar, milk) or coffee, bread and butter, and rolls or pastries. Lunch (the main meal) is eaten around midday and dinner often is served after dark when work is finished. The most important staple foods include *mandioca*, *sopa Paraguaya* (cornbread baked with cheese, onions, and sometimes meat), *chipa* (hard cheese bread), tortillas, and *empanadas* (deep-fried meat or vegetable pockets). Small rural gardens provide *campesino* families with tomatoes, onions, carrots, garlic, squash, watermelon, cabbage, and other produce. Surrounding trees and bushes provide fruit. Beef is very important to the adult diet. Paraguayans also eat chicken and pork dishes.

Recreation. Soccer is the most popular spectator sport, but volleyball is the most common participation sport. Urban men often play volleyball in the evenings. Many enjoy tennis and basketball. Women generally do not play sports. Urban people might go to the theater, the movies, or other cultural events. Rural and urban people alike relax by drinking *tereré* and *mate* and visiting each other.

The Arts. Arts reflect the people's Spanish and Guaraní heritage. Paraguay's famous *ñanduti* lace, known for its intricate and delicate designs, was first introduced by the Spanish. Other popular crafts include wood and stone carving, pottery, and embroidery. Several groups have been formed to preserve Guaraní culture.

Popular music includes Latino polkas and ballads. Music tends to be more Western, and dancing, a popular form of recreation, shows heavy influence from Spain. The youth enjoy music with a distinct beat (disco, rap, etc.). The Paraguayan harp is a famous instrument.

Holidays. Paraguayans celebrate New Year's Day, Epiphany (6 Jan.), *Carnaval* (a week of parades and parties in February), Heroes' Day (1 Mar.), *Semana Santa* (Holy Week before Easter), Labor Day (1 May), Independence Day (14–15 May), Mother's Day (15 May), the Chaco Armistice (12 June), *Día del Amistad* (Friendship Day, 30 July), Founding of Asunción City (15 August, celebrated with large parades), Constitution Day (25 Aug.), Victory of Boqueron (29 Sept.), Columbus Day (12 Oct.), All Saints' Day (1 Nov.), Virgin of Cacupe (8 Dec.), and Christmas. *Semana Santa* is the most important holiday period and is a week for family gatherings.

Commerce. Urban business hours extend from 7 a.m. to noon and 3 to 6 p.m. People in both urban and rural areas take a *siesta* during the three-hour break and eat their main meal of the day. Rural Paraguayans grow much of their own food; they purchase staples and other goods at small neighborhood stores, which are located in homes. People commonly shop on a daily basis due to the lack of refrigeration. Urban people purchase their food from markets or small stores.

SOCIETY

Government. Paraguay is a constitutional democracy divided into 17 *departamentos* (provinces). It is headed by an elected president who cannot serve two consecutive terms. The president is chief of state and head of government. Legislators in the 45-seat Chamber of Senators and 80-seat Chamber of Deputies are elected for five-year terms. The voting age is 18; adults are required by law to vote until age 60. Paraguay's principal parties are the Colorado Party and the Authentic Radical Liberal Party.

Economy. Paraguay's formal economy is based primarily on agriculture; most rural families grow cotton as their primary cash crop. The Mennonites grow soybeans. Other crops include sugarcane, corn, cassava, mate, and tobacco. Beef is an important export; cattle are raised on expansive ranches usually owned by nonresident foreigners. About one-fifth of all workers are employed by industry (meatpacking, textiles, light consumer goods, etc.). Many Paraguayans work in the country's large informal sector, involving imported and reexported consumer goods.

The government has sought ways to decrease dependence on cotton, but little progress has been realized. Rural families commonly send one or more members to Argentina to work. Many farmers must keep their children out of school to help with crop production. Contraband trade is a problem in Ciudad del Este. Political instability, inflation, foreign debt, and lack of infrastructure inhibit economic progress. The country continues to battle a recession. Other challenges include lack of a trained workforce and high unemployment, which is about 17 percent. Deforestation has effectively ruined the potential for a sustainable timber industry. Land redistribution, foreign investment, and economic diversification are needed to improve conditions.

Most of the country's earnings are held by a small wealthy class. Although Paraguay's real gross domestic product has more than doubled in the last generation, about two-thirds of

DEVELOPMENT DATA

Human Dev. Index* rank	81 of 174 countries
Adjusted for women	71 of 143 countries
Real GDP per capita	$4,288
Adult literacy rate	93 percent
Infant mortality rate	31 per 1,000 births
Life expectancy	68 (male); 72 (female)

the population still lives in poverty. Most economic opportunities are available only to urban residents. About 16 percent of Paraguayans lack access to education, health care, and economic opportunities needed to rise above human poverty.* Women earn less than one-fourth of the nation's income. In an effort to strengthen regional economic activity and boost foreign investment, Paraguay joined the Mercosur trade bloc, which includes Brazil, Argentina, and Uruguay. Paraguay's currency is the *guaraní* (G).

Transportation and Communications. Paraguay has some paved highways, but most roads are not paved. Many are impassable during heavy rains. Buses serve as the main form of public transportation in Asunción and throughout the country. Otherwise, rural people walk. Wealthier urban residents have cars. Taxis are available in Asunción. There are two television channels, one government owned and the other private. A private cable company services Asunción. Both AM and FM radio stations broadcast throughout the country. Most people do not have telephones, but public phones are available.

Education. Public education is provided free of charge, but students must buy uniforms and are asked to contribute to the school fund to help buy supplies. Facilities tend to be crowded. Instruction is usually in Spanish, which can be a hardship on rural children. Most children begin school, but less than 40 percent complete all six years of primary school. Less than one-third of eligible children attend secondary school. The school year runs from March to November. Opportunities for those who finish school are limited, and many either work in the fields or migrate to Argentina or other countries to find work. There are some vocational schools and other institutions of higher learning. The official literacy rate does not reflect reality in rural areas.

Health. The health-care system includes hospitals and clinics in major towns. The smaller the town, the smaller the clinic. Rural health posts are staffed a few days a week by a nurse. Rural people use traditional herbs and cures to treat minor ailments. While Paraguayans value cleanliness, many unsanitary conditions (dirt floors, unprotected water sources, poor sewage systems, etc.) contribute to poor health. Malnutrition affects children. Severe dental problems afflict a majority of the population (especially in rural areas).

CONTACT INFORMATION

Paraguay consulate, 300 Biscayne Boulevard Way, Suite 907, Miami, FL 33131; phone (305) 374-9090. Embassy of Paraguay, 2400 Massachusetts Avenue NW, Washington, DC 20008; phone (202) 483-6960.

1305 North Research Way, Bldg. K
Orem, Utah 84097-6200 USA
1.800.528.6279; 801.705.4250
fax 801.705.4350
www.culturegrams.com

Republic of
Peru

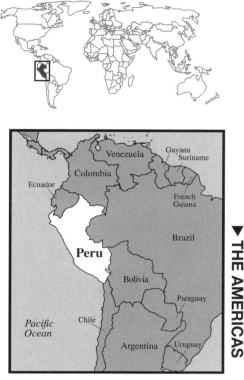

▶ **THE AMERICAS**

BACKGROUND

Land and Climate. Almost the same size as Alaska, Peru is the third largest country in South America. It covers 496,226 square miles (1,285,220 square kilometers). Peru is divided into three distinct geographic regions: the narrow, dry coastal plain (*costa*) in the west; the high Andes Mountains (*sierra*), roughly in the center; and the tropical lowlands of the Amazon Basin (*selva*) to the east. The Andes rise to elevations of 22,000 feet (6,706 meters). Forests, principally in the Andes and Amazon Basin, cover more than half of the country. Only about 3 percent of the land is suitable for farming. The population is concentrated in the west. Mild earthquakes are common; more destructive quakes, like those that killed several hundred people in 1990, also occur. Peru shares with Bolivia the highest navigable body of water in the world—Lake Titicaca. There is little rainfall along the coast, although the winter is foggy, humid, and cool. In the capital city of Lima, the temperature is moderate year-round, averaging 65°F (18°C). Temperatures vary significantly between the rugged Andes and the eastern jungles. The El Niño weather phenomenon periodically has a dramatic impact on Peru, often causing flooding and mudslides. The 1997 and 1998 El Niño pattern killed 200, left some 200,000 homeless, and destroyed hundreds of miles of roads.

History. Several of South America's most advanced cultures lived in pre-Columbian Peru. The last of these groups was the great Incan Empire, which was unsurpassed in the art of stonecutting and also achieved a high degree of economic and political development. Incan and earlier Chimu ruins, notably at Cuzco, Chan Chan, and Machu Picchu, make Peru a favorite destination for archaeologists and tourists. In 1532, the Spanish invaded Peru under the leadership of Francisco Pizarro. They conquered the Incas the next year. The area soon became the richest and most powerful Spanish colony in South America because of its location and many mineral treasures.

Under the leadership of South American liberator José de San Martín, Peru declared independence from Spain in July 1821. With the help of Simón Bolívar, the Venezuelan general who liberated several other countries, the fight for full independence was won by 1826. For a century, Peru worked to secure its territory and build its social institutions.

Peru's 1933 constitution mandated that the country be governed by a president and legislature elected to six-year terms; however, military leaders and dictators dominated Peru until the 1960s. A free multiparty election was held in 1963 and Fernando Belaúnde Terry was elected president. A military junta deposed him in 1968 and ruled for 12 years (a period called *la dictadura*). Belaúnde was reelected in 1980 when the military agreed to return control of the government to civilians.

Economic troubles, which began during *la dictadura*, worsened under Belaúnde and were not resolved during Alán García's presidency (1985–90). In 1980, the Maoist group *Sendero Luminoso* (Shining Path) began a decade of violent guerrilla warfare to overthrow the government. The Shining Path and other terrorist organizations were responsible for some 18,000 deaths during the 1980s. They held power in the Upper Huallaga Valley and were paid by drug traffickers for protection and the right to operate in the region.

Despite these problems, the country maintained democratic institutions and free elections. In 1990, Alberto Fujimori, a son of Japanese immigrants, was elected president. He promised government reform and vowed to overcome economic problems and terrorist violence. Citing factors inhibiting progress, Fujimori suspended the constitution in April 1992, dissolved Congress, took emergency powers, and restricted civil liberties. A 1993 national referendum approved a new constitution that outlined a democratic, albeit more executive-centered, government and a free-market-oriented economy. Fujimori was reelected by a large margin in 1995, and his party gained a majority in Congress. Helping Fujimori to victory was the success of economic reform and the 1992 capture of Shining Path leader Abimael Guzmán Reynoso.

Fujimori also helped resolve Peru's long-standing border dispute with Ecuador. A remote, 48-mile stretch of border, never officially marked after a 1942 treaty, became the subject of fighting in 1981 and 1995. Negotiations led to a cease-fire and demilitarization of the region. A peace treaty was signed between the two countries in October 1998.

In 1997, government troops killed the leader and 14 members of Túpac Amaru Revolutionary Movement (MRTA), the country's second largest guerrilla group, which had held 72 government officials and businessmen hostage for more than four months. With the threat from Peru's two main rebel groups greatly reduced, Fujimori's major challenge lay in making economic reforms effective in the lives of Peru's many poor. Fujimori ran for a third term in April 2000. Before the May runoff, opposition candidate Alejandro Toledo withdrew, citing fraud; election observers also withdrew when they could not guarantee fair elections. The electoral commission declared Fujimori the winner, and the military backed Fujimori.

In 2000, Fujimori fled to Japan after being implicated in scandals concerning the former spy chief, Vladimiro Montesinos. In November, Fujimori resigned but was dismissed from office two days later by Congress. Valentin Paniagua was appointed as the interim president. Although Fujimori has been charged with various crimes, Japan will not extradite him to Peru because he is a Japanese national. Paniagua will rule until the end of July, when he will hand power to the next president, determined by runoff elections in May or June 2001.

THE PEOPLE

Population.   The population of Peru is approximately 27 million and is growing at 1.75 percent annually. Population density is generally low due to the country's large land area. Peru's population is ethnically diverse. About 45 percent is Indian, descendants of the Incan Empire. Many ethnic and linguistic divisions exist among Indians, some of whom are still fairly isolated in the Amazon jungle. Another 37 percent is of mixed European and Indian heritage. Fifteen percent is of European descent (mostly Spanish), and the remaining 3 percent is composed of blacks (descendants of West African slaves), Japanese, Chinese, and other smaller groups. About half of the population is younger than age 20. Lima is the largest city, with more than seven million residents. Seventy percent of all people live in urban areas.

Language.   Spanish and the Indian language Quechua are both officially recognized languages. Aymara, another Indian language, is also spoken widely. Many Peruvians speak both Spanish and one Indian language. About 30 percent of the people speak no Spanish at all; they speak Quechua, Aymara, or another native language. Peruvians with more formal education often are taught English as a second language and can speak it well.

Religion.   The Roman Catholic Church was the state church in Peru until 1979. Although today there is freedom of religion and all churches enjoy equal political status, most people are Roman Catholic and the church continues to play a significant role in their lives. Protestant and Evangelical churches also operate in the country. Many Indians who are Roman Catholic mix traditional indigenous beliefs with Christian values, sometimes calling their gods by Christian names.

General Attitudes.   Peruvians are strong willed and nationalistic. They have been through many trials, politically and economically, but maintain a strong desire to endure and succeed. The people have a good sense of humor and are accommodating and eager to please. Still, they may be sensitive about certain things. Jokes about their lifestyle, especially those coming from foreigners, are offensive. Personal criticism, if necessary, is expected to be expressed in a positive manner. The Peruvian concept of time is more relaxed than in industrialized nations. Appointments and other meetings may not begin on time, and Peruvians generally consider people to be more important than schedules. However, international visitors, to whom punctuality is more important, are expected to be on time for appointments.

Many Indians believe they are discriminated against by Peru's mestizo and European populations. Indians usually are rural people, but even those who move to the city are not accepted. This has fueled resentment among Indians and is one source of the country's social problems. Indians place some hope in promises of increased investment from international organizations and the government. Urban residents, particularly in Lima, are turning their attention to economic progress. People generally are optimistic about the country's future, especially with the return of democracy, the near end of major insurgency movements, and economic reforms.

Personal Appearance.   Western-style clothing is worn in Lima and other urban areas. People dress up when going to public places, such as the *plaza de armas* (town plaza). It is considered bad taste to go out of the home wearing old or dirty clothes. Rural *campesinos* (farmers) often wear traditional clothing related to their ethnic background. Their clothes commonly are made of handwoven fabrics.

CUSTOMS AND COURTESIES

Greetings.   When being introduced or meeting for the first time, members of the opposite sex usually shake hands. Women (and close friends of the opposite sex) commonly kiss each other on one cheek when meeting and parting. Men usually shake hands or pat each other on the shoulder. An arm around the shoulders or a pat on the back is a polite way to greet youth.

Typical greetings include *¡Buenos días!* (Good morning), *¡Buenas tardes!* (Good afternoon), and *¡Buenas noches!* (Good evening/night). Friends address each other by first name. Professionals are addressed by their title

(*Doctor/a*, *Profesor/a*, *Licensiado*, etc.). Older people are addressed as *Señor* (Mr.) or *Señora* (Mrs.), followed by their last name. Women and girls often are addressed by strangers as *Senorita*.

Gestures. Peruvians are often animated and use a lot of hand gestures while conversing. One beckons by holding the palm of the hand downward and waving all of the fingers. Personal space is limited. People stand very close to each other when they talk, often lightly touching the arm or shoulder of the person with whom they are speaking. Constant eye contact is important. On buses, men usually give their seat to women or elderly persons.

Visiting. Peruvians enjoy visiting one another. Most visits between friends and relatives are unannounced. However, when one visits other people, it is polite to make advance arrangements. Visitors are expected to feel at home and be comfortable. The traditional greeting *Está en su casa* (You are in your house) reflects Peruvian hospitality. Hosts always offer their guests drinks (water, juice, soda, etc.) and may offer other refreshments, but declining them is not impolite. In many areas, those visiting around 5:30 p.m. are invited to stay for *lonche*, a light breakfast-type meal served around 6 p.m. Hosts appreciate special acknowledgment of children in the home. It is polite to show concern for the health of the host's family and relatives. When visiting a home, one is not expected to bring gifts, but small gifts such as fruit or wine are welcome on any occasion. Dinner guests commonly bring such gifts.

Eating. Peruvians eat in the continental style, with the fork in the left hand and the knife remaining in the right. They keep both hands (but not elbows) above the table at all times. Proper table manners are important. It is impolite to converse with only one person at the table without including the rest of the group. If this occurs, Peruvians will often repeat the saying, *Secretos en reunion es mala educación* (It is bad manners to tell secrets in gatherings). Guests are expected to eat all of the food that is offered; excuses for not eating something are to be given tactfully. In a restaurant, one summons the waiter by waving. If service is not included in the bill, a tip is expected, and if service is included, a small tip still is given.

LIFESTYLE

Family. The family unit is important in Peru. Nuclear families have, on average, three children. The father is the head of the family. Since the mother usually spends most of her time at home, she is in charge of the children and their day-to-day activities. The father usually is consulted only for major matters. The mother directs and performs household duties. Women occasionally work outside the home, a trend that is more evident in urban areas. About one-fourth of the labor force is female. Most families live in humble circumstances without many of the modern conveniences common in more industrialized nations. Newly married couples often live in their parents' home until they can afford a place of their own.

Dating and Marriage. Urban youth enjoy dancing at *fiestas* (parties) and social gatherings. Dating is exclusive: people do not date more than one person at the same time. Only after a couple breaks up are they allowed to date others. Men usually marry in their late twenties, while women generally marry in their early twenties. People in rural areas often marry at a younger age. Weddings usually include a civil ceremony, a church wedding, and a party for family and friends. The party often includes dancing and a one- or two-course meal. Common-law marriages are prevalent and widely accepted, except among the upper classes.

Diet. The main staples in the diet include rice, beans, fish, and a variety of tropical fruits. Soups are also common. Corn, native to Peru, is the main staple among Indians. Guinea pigs are eaten throughout the country and are raised in nearly all rural homes. *Ceviche* (raw fish seasoned with lemon and vinegar) is popular on the coast. *Papa a la Huancaina* is a baked potato topped with sliced eggs and a sauce (such as hot chili). Highland dishes often include potatoes, onions, and garlic. Fresh vegetables are eaten in season. People purchase most food on a daily basis, either in small corner stores (in cities) or large open-air markets. Bargaining is common in the markets.

Recreation. The most popular sport in Peru is *fútbol* (soccer). Peruvians enthusiastically follow World Cup competitions, especially when their national team is participating. Basketball, volleyball, and gymnastics are also favorites. Families enjoy picnics, and movies provide entertainment. Sunday is a favorite day for outings.

The Arts. Music is important to most Peruvians. International music is widespread, especially with the youth and along the coast, but traditional music is also very popular. Traditional songs often are about Peru, Peruvian culture, people's feelings, or animals. Three instruments used to play traditional music are the *charango*, a small guitar of sorts; the *antara*, an assortment of vertically placed flutes tied together; and the *quena*, which is similar to a recorder. Two types of music from the mountains are *baile de las tijeras* and *huayno*; the *huayno* is also a dance with many jumps. Most cities have their own dances. The *cajón* is an athletic dance that blacks perform in Lima.

Folk arts, especially textiles, are integral to Peruvian culture. Many textiles are made from the wool of the *alpaca* (similar to a llama); clothing is made from this thick wool, along with wall hangings and other decorative art. Motifs that frequent these wall hangings are ruins—especially Machu Picchu—*alpacas*, condors, and people. *Retablos*, another form of folk art, are wooden boxes that feature three-dimensional religious or everyday scenes. Pottery and metalworking are other prevalent crafts; gold is more popular than silver.

Like many other Latin Americans, Peruvians have written about the problems in society, specifically the problems concerning indigenous peoples. Peruvian literature is often romantic, with mythological or fantastical themes. *Indianista*, or the Indian novel, focuses on indignities suffered by native peoples. *Tradición*, a historical anecdote, is a unique Latin American genre.

Holidays. National holidays include New Year's Day, Easter (Thursday–Sunday), Countryman's Day (24 June), St. Peter and St. Paul's Day (29 June), Independence Day (28 July), National Day (29 July), St. Rose of Lima Day (30 Aug.), Navy Day (8 Oct.), All Saints' Day (1 Nov.), Immaculate Conception (8 Dec.), and Christmas. Independence Day is one of the most popular holidays. It is celebrated with fireworks and bands at the local *plaza de armas*. Schools usually take a one-

or two-week break and businesses may close for such celebrations. Many local holidays honor patron saints, celebrate the harvest, or provide recreation.

Commerce. Peru's average workweek is slightly more than 48 hours, one of the longest in the world. Businesses are open at least six days a week. Some small businesses close between 1 and 3 p.m. each day for a *siesta* (break), but this is not as common today as it once was. Many shops remain open late into the evening. Business hours vary slightly according to the season but generally are between 8 a.m. and 5 p.m. Some government offices close as early as 1 p.m.

SOCIETY

Government. Peru is a republic. It is divided into 24 *departamentos* (similar to states). The president holds executive power and serves a five-year term. The 1993 constitution allows a president to serve two consecutive terms, but Peru's Supreme Court ruled that Fujimori could run for a third term in 2000. All citizens age 18 and older are required to vote. The unicameral Congress consists of 120 members, who serve five-year terms. Major political parties include the Change 90–New Majority Party, Union for Peru, the Popular Christian Party, and the Popular Action Party. Several other parties are also active.

Economy. The Peruvian economy faced severe strains in the early 1990s: inflation was high, output was low, and the standard of living was dropping. Fujimori's reforms cut hyperinflation from 7,600 percent in 1990 to 7 percent in 1997, attracted foreign investment, and produced stability and economic growth. However, by late 1998, the effects of the Asian economic crisis and El Niño phenomenon pushed the economy back into a recession. Economic growth in 2000 was about 3.5 percent; 2 percent growth is expected in 2001. Unemployment and underemployment remain high (40–50 percent). More than half of the workforce does not have a full-time job. About half of all Peruvians live in poverty. Nearly 17 percent of the population does not have access to adequate health care, education, and economic opportunities needed to rise above human poverty.*

Peru's natural resources include copper, silver, gold, oil, timber, fish, and iron ore. Peru has a relatively wide economic base with a variety of industries it can depend on for growth. Wheat, potatoes, sugarcane, rice, and coffee are important agricultural products. Agriculture accounts for 36 percent of all employment. Peru's fish catch is one of the largest in the world but recently has suffered a sharp drop because of El Niño. Peru is a member of the Andean Community trade bloc with Bolivia, Colombia, Ecuador, and Venezuela. The currency is the *nuevo sol* (S/.).

Economic dependence on lucrative drug trade has been a challenge. Drug traffickers sell locally grown coca leaf (the basis of cocaine) to Colombian drug cartels for eventual export. Despite the fact that many farmers would prefer to make a living raising crops like coffee or cacao, Peru remains the world's largest producer of the more profitable coca leaf.

Transportation and Communications. Buses are the most

DEVELOPMENT DATA

Human Dev. Index* rank	80 of 174 countries
Adjusted for women	70 of 143 countries
Real GDP per capita	$4,282
Adult literacy rate	89 percent
Infant mortality rate	41 per 1,000 births
Life expectancy	68 (male); 73 (female)

popular form of transportation. Many middle- and upper-class families own a car but regularly use public transportation to get around because gasoline is so expensive. In rural areas, people travel on foot or with the help of animals. Most roads are not paved. Train and air travel are available on a limited basis; some train routes are very scenic. Owning a telephone has become much easier since the telecommunications system was privatized in the early 1990s. Telephone lines are available in most rural areas. Peru has several daily newspapers.

Education. Peruvians are generally well educated. Public education is free and compulsory between ages seven and sixteen. However, schools lack basic materials, and facilities are inadequate. In the 1980s, Peru increased efforts to extend primary schools into remote areas. In some areas, the Shining Path controlled school facilities, so the government has attempted to reestablish control in these areas. Secondary education is also free in Peru. More than two-thirds of eligible children are enrolled in secondary schools. Enrollment in both primary and secondary schools is increasing. The average adult has completed at least six years of school, and more young people are staying in school. The literacy rate is higher among teenagers than adults. Peru has more than 30 universities, including the University of San Marcos in Lima, one of the oldest in South America.

Health. Medical care is adequate in major cities but less so in other areas. Quality care is only available through expensive private clinics. Hospitals are often short on medicine, food, and other supplies and equipment. Many Peruvians are superstitious about health care and are reluctant to use medical facilities. They prefer using home remedies made of herbs and roots before going to a doctor. Many people rely on the treatments of a *curandero/a* as well. Care in small towns is not reliable and not always available. Diseases such as typhoid, yellow fever, cholera, Chagas, and malaria are active in Peru. Water is not always potable. Nearly half of all school-age children suffer from malnutrition.

CONTACT INFORMATION

South American Explorers' Club, 126 Indian Creek Road, Ithaca, NY 14850; phone (800) 274-0568; Web site www.samexplo.org. Embassy of the Republic of Peru, Consular Section, 1625 Massachusetts Avenue NW, Suite 605, Washington, DC 20036; phone (202) 462-1084; Web site www.peruemb.org/main.

1305 North Research Way, Bldg. K
Orem, Utah 84097-6200 USA
1.800.528.6279; 801.705.4250
fax 801.705.4350
www.culturegrams.com

CultureGrams™
standard edition
2002

Republic of
Poland

Boundary representations are not necessarily authoritative.

BACKGROUND

Land and Climate. The name *Polska* (Poland) means "land of fields." The northern and central landscape is dominated by the North European Plain, whose flat expanse extends across the country from Germany to the Ukraine. Impressive mountains run along the southern border: the Tatry (in the Western Carpathians) and the Sudety, which host the country's skiing and resort areas. Forests (both deciduous and coniferous) cover nearly one-fourth of the land. About 47 percent of the total land area is suitable for cultivation. Poland's location and flat terrain has made it vulnerable to territory-seeking armies throughout history, and its borders have changed several times. Covering 120,728 square miles (312,685 square kilometers), the total land area today is about the size of New Mexico.

The climate is temperate, with mild summers; however, it is susceptible to extreme temperature variations within short periods of time. Winters are generally cold and precipitation is common throughout the year. The Poles say one must always carry an umbrella because the weather can change instantly. Poland has important natural resources, including coal, sulfur, silver, natural gas, copper, lead, and salt. The country's natural beauty is challenged by severe air and water pollution, as well as deforestation.

History. The Poles are descendants of a Slavic people who settled between the Oder and Vistula Rivers before the time of Christ. King Mieszko I adopted the Roman Catholic faith in A.D. 966. In the late 14th century, Polish life and culture flourished under King Kasimir the Great. Poland combined with Lithuania in the late Middle Ages, creating a mighty empire that was a major power in Europe. Poland's enlight-

ened 1791 constitution, the second in the world, was patterned after the U.S. Constitution and gave freedom to the serfs. Due to political infighting among the ruling nobles, as well as other factors, the monarchy declined to the point that, in 1795, Poland was invaded and partitioned by Prussia, Austria, and Russia. For the next 125 years, Polish identity and culture were preserved by the Roman Catholic Church and Polish exiles.

Poland became a nation again in 1918, at the end of World War I. Unfortunately, the country had little chance to stabilize, as the German army invaded in 1939. Within days of the German invasion to the west, the Soviets invaded from the east and Poland was again partitioned. More than six million Poles died during World War II, including three million Polish Jews who died in the Holocaust. The Soviets were given administrative control over the regions liberated from German occupation when Germany was defeated. Elections were held, but by 1948 a Soviet-backed communist government was in firm control and the country's political system came to be patterned after that of the Soviet Union, with some exceptions (such as land ownership and matters of religion).

In 1981, following a series of crippling strikes and the formation and activity of the Solidarity Labor Union, General Wojciech Jaruzelski declared martial law. The *Sejm* (Parliament) outlawed Solidarity, and its leaders were jailed. Martial law was lifted in 1983, and Lech Walesa, the leader of the still-outlawed Solidarity union, received the Nobel Peace Prize in recognition of his efforts to win freedom and a better standard of living for the Polish people.

In 1989, the government legalized Solidarity and implemented government changes. Many Solidarity members won parliamentary seats and Solidarity official Tadeusz Mazowiecki became prime minister. The new democratic government began a transition to a market economy. A bold economic program, referred to as "shock therapy," was instituted in 1990. It caused prices to rise sharply and immediately led to high unemployment. Jaruzelski resigned to speed political reform, and voters elected Walesa president in late 1990. After nearly a year in power, Walesa came under increasing criticism for rising unemployment and economic recession. He eventually lost parliamentary support for his economic reforms. Former Communists gained control of parliament in 1993 and have slowed the course of economic reform.

In November 1995, former Communist official Aleksander Kwasniewski narrowly defeated Walesa in runoff presidential elections. Kwasniewski pledged to pursue Poland's goals to join the European Union (EU) and the North Atlantic Treaty Organization (NATO). In March 1999, Poland, Hungary, and the Czech Republic formally joined the NATO alliance. Kwasniewski decisively won a second term in the 2000 presidential election. To prepare for possible EU membership, sustained economic development is Poland's top priority. Key government goals continue to be agricultural reform, privatization of state-run industries, and restructuring of health care, pensions, and finances.

THE PEOPLE

Population. The population of Poland is 38.6 million and is shrinking by 0.04 percent. Urbanization is relatively high; about 65 percent of the population lives in cities. The country is also very homogeneous; almost 98 percent of the people are of Polish origin. Germans living in Silesia (an area bordering Germany) make up 1.3 percent of the population and are the largest minority group. Poland is providing its people more access to resources needed for personal advancement; however, opportunities for some are still limited.

Language. Polish is the official language. Smaller ethnic groups also may speak their own languages. Though a Slavic tongue, Polish uses a modified Latin alphabet; a few unique characters look like Latin letters with accent markings but are distinct letters. Written Polish emerged in the 12th century but did not flourish until the 16th century when it began to overtake Latin, which was used by the ruling class. Although Polish was banned during partition periods, Poles around the world preserved it as a matter of patriotism. Russian was taught until 1989 but is no longer used. English and German are the most popular second languages.

Religion. The overwhelming majority of Poles (around 95 percent) belong to the Roman Catholic Church, which has had great influence in the country since Poland was Christianized in the 10th century. About 75 percent of Poles consider themselves practicing Catholics. Catholic ceremonies (baptism, First Communion, weddings, and funerals) are marked with elaborate family gatherings. Because the Catholic Church is a strong and unified entity, it has played an important political role in the past. The church in Poland historically has been nationalistic and patriotic, championing the cause of the people while under communism. The Catholic pope, John Paul II, is a native Pole.

The issue of Catholicism's influence in Poland is currently being debated. Some people prefer that laws and social customs remain secular, while others would like them to more fully reflect Catholic values. Other churches represented in Poland include the Russian Orthodox, various Protestant faiths, and the Uniate faith (a combination of Russian Orthodox practices and loyalty to papal authority). Foreign missionaries are also present.

General Attitudes. Polish people value individualism, practicality, and self-reliance (exercised on an extended-family level). They place great emphasis on the family, tradition, and education. Poles are generally outspoken, especially in private circles. They are straightforward and realistic, sometimes cynical. People value generosity and do not regard highly those who are not willing to share their time, resources, or power. Poles are proud of their cultural heritage and their ability to survive war, territory losses, and subordination to other nations. During periods of foreign domination, the Poles looked to their heritage as a great power in order to retain a belief that they were not a conquered or subordinate people. Prior to World War II, the Polish noble class considered itself better than the occupying forces, which gave Poles the desire to maintain their culture and language.

Poland's new democracy and transition to a free market have tarnished some hopes. Many people express concern that they did not expect freedom to be so painful. Yet despite the fact that the poor were better off economically under communism, only a minority express a desire to return to the old system. Most recognize the future has greater potential.

Personal Appearance. Men and women like to be well dressed in public. Polish women pay careful attention to their appearance. Polish men generally dress conservatively, while younger women follow European styles. Businesspeople wear conservative suits or dresses. Denim jeans are especially common among the youth and in academic and artistic circles. Jackets and caps with American sports or college emblems are popular. Older rural women continue to wear a scarf around the head, a full skirt, and thick stockings. Clothing is expensive, so some people make their own clothes; secondhand stores are also popular. Children are expected to be clean and well-groomed in school. They celebrate the first spring day or "truant day" outside, wearing funny and odd clothing.

CUSTOMS AND COURTESIES

Greetings. Adult males and teenagers usually shake hands upon meeting. Women greet each other with kisses or handshakes. Close friends greet by kissing the right, left, and then right cheeks. At social and business gatherings, Poles greet each guest personally, women first. A man might kiss the extended hand of an older or younger woman, but not the hand of a woman near his age. When introducing a man, one uses *Pan* before the last name; for a woman, the term is *Pani*. One addresses a professional person by title and last name. The title is used alone in formal conversation or in business. Between adults, first names are used only by mutual consent.

Friends greet each other with *Cześć*, a way of saying "Hi." Common Polish greetings include *Dzień dobry* (Good day), *Dobry wieczór* (Good evening), and *Do widzenia* (Goodbye). *Dziękuję* (Thank you) often precedes an answer about how one is doing. When Poles sign their name, they sign their family name first and then their given name.

Gestures. Poles frequently gesticulate while conversing, whether to emphasize a point or to express emotion. Pointing is not impolite. Poles hold both thumbs in closed fists to wish others good luck. Blinking both eyes can signify romantic interest. Placing an index finger next to the nose indicates that the words just spoken are not quite true or may be a joke. Young females who are best friends often hold hands while walking. Passengers usually help the elderly and mothers with baby carriages get on and off of buses or trams. People are expected to observe public courtesies; those who do not are labeled *primatywny* (primitive).

Visiting. Unannounced visits are common among friends and relatives, particularly in rural areas where telephones are less common. Unarranged visits generally do not last more than a few hours. More formal, longer visits are arranged in advance. Poles often invite friends over for dinner or just for cake and tea. They also like to have formal parties on special occasions. Sunday or weekend family gatherings occur regularly. Weekend visits may last until 6 a.m. in areas where buses do not run between 11 p.m. and 6 a.m.

For even a brief arranged visit, guests customarily give hosts a bottle of wine or vodka or an odd number of flowers (an even number is for sad occasions). They unwrap flowers before giving them to the hostess. Red roses express romantic feelings. White chrysanthemums are reserved for wakes or funerals. Guests nearly always are offered tea or coffee; it is common to politely refuse at first and then accept when the hosts insist. Guests may be entertained at a *kawiarnia* (café), which offers pastries, coffee, and its own specialties. Such visits often last several hours. People more commonly entertain in the home, however, because going out is expensive.

Eating. Although schedules are changing with society, Poles generally eat breakfast between 6:30 and 8 a.m. Many people eat a second breakfast (e.g., a sandwich) around 10 a.m. Some families expect to gather for the main meal at 3 p.m. and enjoy the lighter evening meal (coffee/tea and sweet rolls) between 6 and 8:30 p.m.

Poles eat in the continental style, with the fork in the left hand and the knife remaining in the right. They keep both hands (but not the elbows) above the table during the meal. Conversation during the meal is minimal, but it is polite to sit around the table just after eating to talk.

In restaurants, one requests the bill from the waiter and pays at the table. Tips generally are expected. The host may toast a guest with vodka or wine, served between courses. It is appropriate for the guest to return the gesture later in the meal.

LIFESTYLE

Family. The family is Poland's most important social unit. The average family has one or two children, although rural families often have three or four. The father, traditionally a dominant authority figure, demands obedience yet wants his children ultimately to be independent and have self-discipline. Children are given considerable responsibility from an early age. Because both parents usually work outside the home, children often fix their own breakfasts and go to school by themselves. Older children clean, sometimes cook, and often care for younger siblings. The economic situation of most families demands the equal involvement of both parents in raising the family and working outside the home, although women still bear most responsibility for homemaking. Women comprise nearly half of the labor force. The elderly often live with their adult children and provide child care for grandchildren.

Dating and Marriage. Young people who start working after the minimum required schooling marry earlier than those who continue their education. Women marry between ages 18 and 20; men begin marrying at age 21. Those who go to technical schools and universities usually marry after age 25. Because housing is expensive and in short supply, parents of the couple often give financial assistance and allow the couple to live in their home for the first few years. Poles wed in religious and civil ceremonies and enjoy traditional celebrations. Living together before marrying is discouraged, as is divorce.

Diet. While the early urban breakfast is often light, many rural people eat more substantial food (e.g., hot cereal). The main meal consists of soup, meat or fish, salad, and potatoes. Pastries or ice cream are eaten for a late-afternoon snack. Bread, dairy products, and canned fish are plentiful. People purchase bread several times a week, sometimes even daily. Only those who live far from a store eat bread that is more than two days old. Common dishes include *pierogi* (stuffed dumplings; stuffings vary), *uszka* (a kind of ravioli), *bigos* (sausage, mushrooms, pickled cabbage), braised pork and cabbage, poppy seed desserts, and cheesecake. Pork is more popular than beef. With the switch to a market economy, more food is available in greater variety, but prices are high and many families spend much of their income on food. Gardens often supply a large portion of a family's food.

Recreation. Soccer is popular, but Poles also participate in track-and-field events, cycling, table tennis, skiing, basketball, volleyball, and various individual sports. Bridge is a favorite card game. Attending cultural events and visiting friends are common recreational activities. When Poles go on vacation, it is usually to the mountains, the sea, or the Mazury lake region.

The Arts. Poland has a rich tradition of music, art, dancing, and literature. Romantic composer Frédéric Chopin (1810–48), the country's best-known musician, based many of his compositions on traditional Polish folk music. Classical music of all kinds is performed in Poland. Polish groups also tour regularly on the international scene.

Carved wood sculptures are an important Polish folk art. These painted or stained sculptures made of linden wood depict mythic and biblical themes as well as everyday subjects. Ceramics, embroidery, and painting are other well-known Polish folk arts.

Poles highly value literature as a means of expression. Historically, Polish writers used parables and other symbolic forms as a way to avoid government censure. Parables and fables are still popular today.

The fall of socialism in the 1990s brought about a significant decline in government funding for the arts. Urbanization and the mass media are also transforming Poland's cultural arts.

Holidays. Official holidays include New Year's Day, Easter (two days), Labor Day (1 May), Constitution Day (3 May), Corpus Christi (in May or June), All Saints' Day (1 Nov.),

▼ EUROPE

Independence Day (11 Nov.), and Christmas. On All Saints' Day, cemeteries are decorated with flowers and candles in memory of family, friends, and members of the military. Both the name day (the day assigned to the Catholic saint after whom a person is named) and birthday are celebrated.

Christmas is the most important holiday. On 6 December, children receive small gifts from St. Nicholas. On Christmas Eve, when the first star is sighted, the family gathers for a twelve-course, meatless meal that usually includes fresh fish, dishes featuring poppy seeds or mushrooms, a special compote, and other traditional foods. On the 26th, Poles visit and relax. Nativity scenes and caroling are popular throughout the season. For Easter Saturday, people take a basket of specific foods (ham, eggs, sausages, pieces of bread, etc.) to church to be blessed; they eat the food Sunday after mass. Easter Monday is Wet Monday, a day for young people to squirt or dump water on each other. Other celebrations and local festivals, such as the Folk Art Fair in Kraków, are held throughout the year.

Commerce. Banks generally are open from 8 a.m. until 5 p.m., Monday through Friday, with hours varying on Saturday. Stores generally are open from 7 a.m. to 7 p.m., Monday through Saturday, although hours vary according to location and function. *Kiosks*, small newsstand shops that offer a variety of goods, are common in cities. Supermarkets in large cities carry fresh meat, produce, and other basic foods. In other areas, these goods are purchased in open-air markets and neighborhood stores. Bread is sold in grocery stores; bakeries sell pastries and other sweets.

SOCIETY

Government. Poland's president is head of state and the prime minister is head of government. The president is elected by the people, but he appoints the prime minister, who usually is the leader of the majority party or coalition in parliament. Prime Minister Jerzy Buzek's Solidarity-led government took office following parliamentary elections in September 1997. The country's parliament, or National Assembly, has an upper house (100-seat Senate) and a lower house (460-seat *Diet* or *Sejm*). A new post-communism constitution was approved in May 1997. Poles vote on Sunday. The voting age is 18.

Economy. Poland is progressing in its transition toward a free-market economy. The period of hardships suffered by the people under the 1990 "shock therapy" plan has been followed by steady economic growth. Foreign investment in Poland hit record levels in 1998 and has remained high. However, the privatization of state-owned industries continues to be slow and painful, particularly for the largely inefficient coal industry. Economic reform has led to increased unemployment. However, the country remains committed to becoming a successful free-market economy and joining the EU. Economic growth in 2000 was around 5 percent.

Most people can afford basic needs, but the gap between rich and poor is expanding quickly. This social problem contributes to political instability and general public distrust. In the past, wealth was associated with corruption, because only corrupt Communist officials had wealth. Therefore, today's wealthy, no matter how honest, are viewed with suspicion.

About 28 percent of the labor force is engaged in agriculture, which has always remained in private hands despite Communist-era attempts at collectivization. However, agriculture only accounts for about 5 percent of gross domestic product. Important products include grains, sugar beets, oilseed, potatoes, and pork, as well as dairy products. Poland has a strong industrial sector. Poland is a major producer of minerals and steel. Tourism is growing rapidly. The currency is the *zloty* (Zl).

Transportation and Communications. Public transportation is efficient and inexpensive. An excellent railroad and bus system connects most cities as well as neighboring countries. Travelers purchase tickets from *kiosks*, and on boarding, punch the tickets in machines mounted near the door. Car ownership has continued to rise dramatically in the past few years. As a result, city traffic is difficult and roads are inadequate; transportation infrastructure needs improvement to meet the growing needs of individuals and businesses. Warsaw has a new subway system. Airlines service large cities. Most people have televisions and many have telephones. Access to the Internet in Poland is still limited but is increasing.

Education. Recent educational reforms mandate a free education for children until the age of 18. The restructured system now requires two additional years of education and includes secondary schooling between elementary and high school. Following nine years of basic education, students choose between a three-year high school and a two-year vocational school. Entrance to a university is determined by exam; about 5 percent of all applicants are accepted into the best schools. A university degree takes five to six years to complete. Two-thirds of dental and medical students are women.

Health. The government provides health care to all citizens. Facilities generally are accessible but are not up to Western standards. The poor economy forced hospitals and other clinics to cut some services. However, care is generally adequate. Private care in doctors' offices is better, but one must pay for it. Recent reforms require Poles to see a general practitioner first before going to a specialist.

CONTACT INFORMATION

Embassy of the Republic of Poland, 2224 Wyoming Street NW, Washington, DC 20008; phone (202) 234-3800; Web site www.polishworld.com/polemb. Polish National Tourist Office, 275 Madison Avenue, Suite 1711, New York, NY 10016; phone (212) 338-9412; Web site www.polandtour.org.

DEVELOPMENT DATA

Human Dev. Index* rank	44 of 174 countries
Adjusted for women	40 of 143 countries
Real GDP per capita	$7,619
Adult literacy rate	99 percent
Infant mortality rate	10 per 1,000 births
Life expectancy	69 (male); 78 (female)

People. The World. You.

1305 North Research Way, Bldg. K
Orem, Utah 84097-6200 USA
1.800.528.6279; 801.705.4250
fax 801.705.4350
www.culturegrams.com

Portugal
(Portuguese Republic)

Boundary representations are not necessarily authoritative.

▼ EUROPE

BACKGROUND

Land and Climate.   Portugal is situated on the west coast of the Iberian Peninsula, which it shares with Spain. The Portuguese Republic includes the mainland, the Madeira Islands (west of Morocco), and the Azores (*Açores*) archipelago (about 800 miles or 1,290 kilometers off the Atlantic coast). Formerly part of Portugal, Macau (a small territory near Hong Kong) was turned over to the People's Republic of China in December 1999. Covering 35,552 square miles (92,080 square kilometers), the total land area is about the size of Indiana.

The Tagus (*Tejo*) River, which leads from Spain to Lisbon, divides the country into two zones. In the north, Iberian mountain ranges, such as the Serra da Estrela, extend across the region. The climate is cool and rainy though summers may be warm. Seasonal temperatures vary by elevation. In the south the terrain is less rugged, formed by hills and valleys. The southern climate is warmer and more moderate due to the influence of the Mediterranean Sea. Long dry seasons occur in some southern areas. About 28 percent of the land is suitable for agriculture; 30 percent is forested, some of which has been cultivated for timber. Deforestation has increased from great summer fires and lack of protection.

History.   Portugal has been peopled since Paleolithic times. The Portuguese descend from the Iberians, who first inhabited the peninsula, and the Celts, who had invaded by the sixth century B.C. and mixed with the Iberians. Ancient Phoenicians, Carthaginians, and Greeks also invaded and built colonies on Portugal's coast. In 27 B.C., the Romans took control of the area and made it a province. After the Romans, the Visigoths (who later became Christian) ruled

until they were defeated by the Moors. The Moors (Muslims) governed from the eighth century to the twelfth century. By 1143, Portugal was recognized an independent nation under King Afonso Henriques. In the 14th and 15th centuries, Portuguese explorers claimed a huge overseas empire for Portugal. Global trade routes were established and Lisbon became a key European trading center. Phillip II of Spain ruled Portugal as Phillip I for a short time (1580–98) because Portugal's previous king had left no heirs and Phillip defeated other hopefuls. Phillip's sons also reigned in Portugal but independence was restored in 1640. Portugal's monarchy was eventually overthrown (1910), and a republic was established.

Political rivalries resulted in an unstable regime, and a military coup overthrew the democracy in 1926. From 1928 to 1968, António de Oliveira Salazar led an authoritarian dictatorship, denying the people basic civil rights. When he fell ill, Marcello Caetano succeeded him. Caetano tried to effect some reforms while maintaining the basic authoritarian government. In April 1974, a socialist military group, led by General António de Spínola, took control of the government. Democracy was restored and colonies were granted independence. In 1975, the junta held elections that led to the Third Republic. As politics shifted to the left, key industries were nationalized and some farmland collectivized.

The political situation remained somewhat unstable until the 1985 elections when voters elected Mário Soares (Socialist) president, and Aníbal Cavaco Silva (Social Democrat) became prime minister. Under their leadership, the government began privatization efforts, joined the European Union (EU), and started a series of other reforms aided by EU funding. Prime Minister Silva's popular leadership led to his reelection in 1991. However, the Socialists returned to power in the 1995 parliamentary elections with António Guterres as prime minister. Not permitted to serve a third term as president, Soares stepped down in March 1996; he was replaced by Socialist Jorge Sampaio.

Portugal took over the EU presidency in the first half of 2000, and it was in the first round of EU countries to begin using the euro as its currency. In December of 1999, Portugal ceded Macau back to China, bringing the last remnants of its colonial empire in Asia to an end. Sampaio won a second term in 2000.

THE PEOPLE

Population. Portugal has a population of nearly 10 million, which is currently not growing. In the 1960s and 1970s, Portugal's population declined somewhat due to emigration. Today, many people within the country are moving from the interior to metropolitan areas. Unlike most industrialized countries, Portugal still has a relatively small urban population. Nearly two-thirds of the people live in rural areas or small towns, though migration to urban areas is changing this. Lisbon, the capital, is the largest city, with almost 1.9 million people in the greater metropolitan area. Porto has 300,000 people. Most Portuguese are of ethnic Mediterranean stock; there is not much ethnic diversity. Black Africans, who began migrating to Portugal after decolonization, comprise less than 1 percent of the population. Access to health care, education, and a decent standard of living affords the people many choices in their lives. However, immigrants and gypsies tend to live in poorer conditions.

Language. The official language is Portuguese, which is derived from Latin. Several regional accents can be distinguished on the mainland and in the islands. Many people also understand Spanish due to its similarity to Portuguese. English and French, which are commonly taught in the schools, are understood and spoken by an increasing number.

Religion. Ninety-four percent of the population is Roman Catholic, but most Portuguese consider themselves nonpracticing. People tend to be far more religious in the northern part of the country, where Mass, confession, processions, and religious holidays are participated in more devoutly. Millions of Catholics from around the world make a pilgrimage to a holy site in Fátima, where the Virgin Mary is said to have appeared, to fulfill promises made to the Virgin. Throughout Portugal, Catholic weddings and baptisms are an important tradition. At baptism an infant is given a *padrinho* and *madrinha* (godfather and godmother) who, especially in times past, are responsible for the child were anything to happen to its parents. Approximately 1 percent belongs to other Christian denominations, and some non-Christian religions also are practiced. Freedom of religion is guaranteed.

General Attitudes. The Portuguese generally are traditional and conservative. Most people usually accept change and innovation only after careful consideration, and then quietly. They do not think that protesting or complaining is worthwhile. People and relationships are more important than time, so being late is often acceptable. Punctuality is becoming more important to urban dwellers.

The Portuguese have an open, liberal society but place a greater emphasis on moral values than do those in other European nations. Hospitality, honesty, kindness, and being a good person are highly valued qualities. Many people tend to admire the achievements of others rather than their own. Wealth and power—especially that which shows—is respected. The Portuguese are proud of their cultural heritage (especially its seafaring past), sense of nation, and economic progress. However, most people today avidly discuss soccer results and teams rather than political issues. The Portuguese are open and friendly to people of other nations. They believe friendships should be strong and should last a lifetime.

Personal Appearance. The Portuguese generally dress conservatively. Men wear suits to work, although sport jackets are also popular. Tattered clothing is improper. Leather dress shoes are worn for most occasions; tennis shoes are for recreation, not everyday wear. Clothing is ironed well; wrinkles are considered sloppy. People are careful to be well dressed in public. Youth dress casually and sometimes less carefully.

Each region of Portugal has a distinct costume that residents wear for festivals and special occasions. They often are elaborate and very colorful. For women, most costumes include scarves for the head and/or shoulders and skirts with aprons. Men's costumes usually include a hat, vest, and scarf. After the death of a close relative, people wear black clothing for a certain period of time; it is considered part of the mourning process, particularly in rural areas. Some widows wear black the rest of their lives.

CUSTOMS AND COURTESIES

Greetings. A warm, firm handshake is an appropriate greeting for anyone, although some Portuguese prefer lighter handshakes. Friends often hug. Among relatives and friends, men and women give other women *beijinhos* (little kisses) in which they appear to kiss each cheek, beginning with the right. Actually, they "kiss the air" while brushing cheeks. Children are expected to kiss adults in the extended family when greeting them. Touching is a common part of greeting because it shows friendship. Greeting strangers passing in the street is done in small villages, but not in bigger towns or cities.

The person arriving is expected to greet first. Common greetings include *Olá* (Hello), *Bom dia* (Good day), *Boa tarde* (Good afternoon) and *Boa noite* (Good evening or Good night). *Adeus* (Good-bye), *por favor* (Please), and *obrigado* (Thank you) also are used. People use first names for friends, youth, and children. Otherwise, one addresses an adult by title and surname. Sometimes the title is combined with the first name rather than the last, depending on personal preference and the relationship between the speakers.

Gestures. Although the Portuguese are rather reserved, they use many physical gestures in conversation. To beckon, one waves all fingers with the palm facing up. It is impolite to point directly at a person with the index finger. Pinching the earlobe and shaking it gently while raising the eyebrows means something (a meal, for instance) is really good. Pulling down on the skin just below the eye with the index finger can mean "You are perceptive" or "You are kidding me." Spreading the fingers with palm down and rocking the hand means "More or less." Rubbing the thumb against the first two fingers with the palm facing up is a sign for money. Touching the tips of all fingers to the tip of the thumb with the palm facing up signifies fear or cowardice. Making a "V" sign or "rabbit ears" behind someone's head is a serious insult because it connotes a lack of morals.

Visiting.   When visiting a family, guests wait outside the door until invited inside the home; likewise, guests do not let themselves out when leaving, but they let the hosts open the door. Guests are expected to wipe their feet before entering in order to keep the home clean. Guests usually avoid inquisitive personal questions. Hosts usually offer their guests refreshments; refusing them is impolite. Sincere compliments about the home and its decor are welcome. Most guests express appreciation by inviting the hosts for a visit at their home.

Socializing in the home is common, but business associates usually go to a restaurant. People also enjoy getting together at a café for casual conversation, sweets, and tea or coffee. Visiting relatives, especially those living in one's rural *terra* (homeland), is very popular. Urban people have strong roots to their hometowns or regions and try to visit as often as possible.

Eating.   The Portuguese take time for conversation during the meal. They eat in the continental style, with the fork in the left hand and the knife remaining in the right. When eating fish, one usually uses a special knife and fork. Keeping the hands above the table at all times is important. Stretching, particularly at the table, is impolite and implies one is tired or bored with the company. One covers the mouth when using a toothpick. Unless enjoying ice-cream cones, adults generally do not eat while walking in public.

Breakfast (coffee or milk and toast or a sandwich) might be eaten at home, on the run, or (for children) at day care. Lunch, traditionally the biggest meal, is eaten about 1 p.m., though work pressures and travel are changing that. Dinner is eaten between 8 and 9 p.m. Some people enjoy a snack and coffee break around 4:30 p.m. Lunch and dinner may consist of soup, a main dish that includes meat or fish and vegetables (cooked or in a salad), and fruit or sweets for dessert. *Bica*, a strong espresso-type coffee, is often served after the meal. In some areas of the north, *bica* is called *cimbalino*. On special occasions (or when guests are present) two main dishes may be served, in which case fish is served first.

In restaurants, one summons the server with a raised hand. The bill usually does not include a service charge. People tip what they want to, according to service and the kind of restaurant. Most people do not eat out often.

LIFESTYLE

Family.   The nuclear family is the most common unit in society. Urban couples now tend to have one child. Nuclear families, particularly those in rural areas, are strengthened by a clan spirit that extends to aunts, uncles, cousins, and beyond. Children usually leave home only when they marry; they are expected to care for their parents in their old age. Single parents are becoming more common; divorced people tend to marry again. The husband is head of the family but shares authority with the wife. Women comprise 43 percent of the labor force, but wives still do most of the housework. Families in urban areas enjoy most modern conveniences and have a faster-paced lifestyle, while people living in rural areas still lead fairly simple lives. Rural homes are small, and many luxury items are too expensive to buy.

Dating and Marriage.   Young people often meet at school or college and tend to socialize in groups. Cafés, small parks,

and beaches are popular gathering places. They later pair off in couples and enjoy going for walks and to the cinema. Engagements are usually lengthy while the couple saves money for an apartment. Most people marry between the ages of 25 and 28; having children between the ages of 35 and 40 is not uncommon. Marriage ceremonies generally follow the Catholic tradition. It is not uncommon for urban young people to live together before getting married.

Diet.   Food is extremely important to the Portuguese, whose average caloric consumption is the second highest in Europe. Staple foods in Portugal include meat, bread, fish, cheese, vegetables, and fruits. Soups such as *caldo verde* (made with potatoes, cabbage, and olive oil) are also a staple. One national dish is *bacalhau* (dried salt cod), which usually is served with potatoes and green vegetables and sometimes garbanzo beans and garlic. *Bacalhau* is eaten often and in a variety of ways. *Caldeirada* (fish stew) is a favorite. The traditional Portuguese salad includes dark green lettuce, tomatoes, onions, vinegar, olive oil, and salt. Pork is a typical meat, with most parts of the pig still eaten. *Chouriços*, a salted or smoked sausage made from various meat pieces, is popular. Lamb, beef, chicken, and rabbit are also common. Chicken is eaten in many forms, such as *cabidela* (chicken with rice). Another popular dish is *cozido à Portuguesa*, (a mixture of meats with potatoes, rice, and vegetables). Parsley and garlic are common seasonings. Sweets are popular, and Portugal has many pastry shops. Table wine is inexpensive and consumed by adult family members with their meals. Countless regional varieties of wine and cheese and other foods are available.

Recreation.   Soccer is by far the most popular sport. Running and playing basketball are also favorite activities. During their leisure time, people like to listen to music or watch television, particularly soccer matches or Brazilian and Portuguese soap operas. People also enjoy socializing at sidewalk cafés, going to movies, and dancing at nightclubs or discos. Local recreation clubs offer dances, games, and other activities.

Families like to take walks, go to the park, and have picnics. Going to one of Portugal's beautiful beaches is an essential part of most people's summer. During the summer most people try to spend at least two weeks away from home either visiting relatives or camping.

Portugal is known for its tradition with horses. Portuguese bullfights incorporate the graceful movements of the horse and rider with the charges of the bull; the bull generally is not killed as in other countries.

The Arts.   Portuguese art has a long history and continues to flourish today. The country's architecture features cathedrals, castles, and palaces decorated in various ornamental styles, including the Manueline, a unique baroque style. A notable art is the *azulejo* (glazed tile). *Azulejos*, often cobalt blue and white, decorate many buildings, from palaces to bars. *Fado* (fate) music is very important and is similar to the blues in North America. Accompanied by guitars, it often portrays a sense of loss or sadness.

In recent years, Portuguese literature has gained international recognition. An increasing number of women writers has added variety to contemporary writing. *Revista* is a popular theater where politics or social issues are satirized.

Holidays.   National holidays in Portugal include New Year's Day, Easter (including Good Friday), Anniversary of the

Revolution (25 Apr.), Labor Day (1 May), Corpus Christi (in June), National Day of Portugal (10 June), Assumption (15 Aug.), Proclamation of the Republic (5 Oct.), All Saints' Day (1 Nov.), Independence Day (1 Dec.), Day of the Immaculate Conception (8 Dec.), and Christmas (25 Dec.). On National Day, the poet Luís de Camões is honored and the Portuguese communities scattered abroad are remembered. Throughout the year, local festivals honor patron saints or celebrate such events as the harvest. *Carnaval*, the festivities of the five days preceding Ash Wednesday, includes locally sponsored parades, children dressing up in costumes, and dances at clubs and recreation halls.

Commerce. People in urban areas buy their basic goods from supermarkets or large stores. The number of smaller shops is diminishing due to competition. But most people can still buy fresh food at indoor and outdoor markets and other goods from small shops. Business hours vary from place to place, but the traditional workday is from 9 a.m. to 1 p.m. and 3 to 7 p.m. weekdays and 9 a.m. to 1 p.m. Saturdays. Government offices close around 4:30 p.m. Banks remain open from 8 a.m. to 3 p.m. Shopping centers are open later and do not close for lunch. Many businesses close on Sundays.

SOCIETY

Government. The Portuguese Republic is divided into eighteen districts and two autonomous regions. Portugal's president is chief of state. He can veto approved laws, dissolve parliament, and set the date for new elections, if necessary. The prime minister serves as head of government and is usually the leader of the legislature's dominant party or coalition of parties. Portugal's unicameral Assembly of the Republic has 230 members, all of whom are directly elected. Parliamentary seats are shared between the governing Socialist Party, the opposing Social Democratic Party, the Popular Party, and the Communist Party. The Socialist Party government is serving a second four-year term following its reelection in October 1999. The voting age is 18.

Economy. Although economic development since 1990 has favored urban areas over rural ones, the entire country has benefited from a more stable government and brighter prospects for its future. Economic prosperity is available to a growing number of people. The economy grew by around 3 percent in 2000. Inflation and unemployment are low. Although Portugal remains one of the poorest EU members, joining Europe's monetary union has been a top priority for the country. Government reforms, wide support, and favorable economic trends have enabled Portugal to meet convergence criteria and help launch the euro, Europe's single currency, in January 1999.

However, high interest rates, taxes, bureaucracy, and debt loads in key sectors are obstacles to continued growth. Long-term growth depends on modernization of Portugal's markets, industry, workforce, and infrastructure in order to increase productivity and become competitive in the European market.

Textiles, leather shoes, cork, timber, canned fish, wine, machinery, and tourism are important industries. Fishing and

DEVELOPMENT DATA

Human Dev. Index* rank	28 of 174 countries
Adjusted for women	27 of 143 countries
Real GDP per capita	$14,701
Adult literacy rate	91 percent
Infant mortality rate	6 per 1,000 births
Life expectancy	72 (male); 79 (female)

agricultural sectors are partially subsidized by the EU to lower production. Eleven percent of the labor force is engaged in agriculture, but Portugal still imports much of its food. Main crops include grains, potatoes, olives, and grapes. The currency is the Portuguese *escudo* (Esc).

Transportation and Communications. Automobiles are the main form of transportation for most people. Portugal has a good network of paved roads. Although EU subsidies have led to drastic improvements, few roads are as modern as those in other EU countries. Driving can be hazardous. Traffic accidents are a leading cause of death and injury in Portugal. In urban areas people use buses and trains, which connect most areas, or taxis. Lisbon has a good ferryboat system and a growing subway network; a new beltway and train link to suburbs south of the Tejo are being completed to help resolve serious traffic congestion. The communications system is good, although phone calls are more expensive than in other EU countries. Television is the main source of information, followed by radio. Portugal has four television channels (two are private) and many radio stations. Six major daily newspapers are published countrywide. Seven percent of the population has access to the Internet.

Education. Many children are enrolled in day care from a young age. Education begins at age six and is compulsory through the ninth grade. Private schools and free public schools are available. After elementary school, students may attend three years of high school and three years of college preparation, or two to four years of vocational schooling that also incorporates some college preparatory courses. There are 18 universities in Portugal. Public universities charge a small tuition, but admission is limited and access to vocations such as medicine is highly competitive. The University of Coimbra, founded in the 13th century, is one of the oldest in Europe.

Health. The government subsidizes health care. The national health system includes a network of health centers, hospitals, and private clinics. Public facilities are in high demand and are generally adequate, though service is inefficient. Private clinics provide service for those who are able to pay more.

CONTACT INFORMATION

Embassy of the Portuguese Republic, 2125 Kalorama Road NW, Washington, DC 20008; phone (202) 328-8610; Web site www.portugalemb.org. Portuguese Trade and Tourism Office, 1900 L Street NW, Suite 310, Washington, DC 20036; phone (202) 331-8222; Web site www.portugal.org.

1305 North Research Way, Bldg. K
Orem, Utah 84097-6200 USA
1.800.528.6279; 801.705.4250
fax 801.705.4350
www.culturegrams.com

Commonwealth of
Puerto Rico

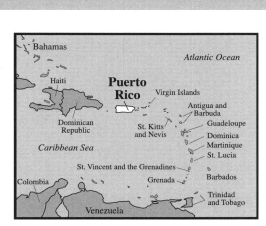

Boundary representations are not necessarily authoritative.

BACKGROUND

Land and Climate. Puerto Rico, covering 3,515 square miles (9,104 square kilometers), is about the same size as Rhode Island and Delaware combined. Its territory includes the islands of Culebra, Vieques, Desecheo, and Mona. The waters between *Isla Mona* (Mona Island) and the capital, San Juan, form a key shipping lane for vessels heading to the Panama Canal. San Juan also has one of the best natural ports in the Caribbean. The island of Puerto Rico is characterized by the *Cordillera Central* (a high central mountain range), a dry southern coast, fertile northern coastal plains, low eastern mountains, and El Yunque rain forest. Relatively little land (8 percent) is available for cultivation. The coastal plains are densely populated.

Puerto Rico's climate is mildly tropical, with warm and sunny weather. Rain falls mainly between May and December; it is moderate in coastal regions and heavier in the mountains. The island often is affected by excessive rains that accompany regional storms. Temperatures average 70°F to 80°F (21–27°C) year-round. Several destructive hurricanes have hit the island, including Hurricane Georges (1998) and Hurricane Hugo (1989).

History. The indigenous Taino people were living on Puerto Rico when Columbus arrived in 1493 and named the island San Juan Bautista. He claimed the island for Spain, and colonizers began building settlements in 1508. Settlers imported African slaves beginning in 1513. The Taino were also enslaved; the men were soon annihilated, but the women remained. Slavery was abolished in 1873.

In 1897, Spain granted self-rule to Puerto Rico under the leadership of Luis Muñoz Rivera. In 1898, as part of the Spanish-American War, the United States invaded the island and conquered its Spanish defenders. Spain ceded the island to the United States that same year. In 1917, Puerto Rico officially became a U.S. territory and its people were granted citizenship. In 1946, President Harry S. Truman appointed Jesus Toribio Pinero as the first island-born governor. Two years later, Puerto Ricans directly elected a governor, Luis Muñoz Marin.

Puerto Rico became a commonwealth of the United States with its own constitution in July 1952. Opposition to commonwealth status has at times erupted into violence. In 1954, militants from Puerto Rico shot several congressional representatives in Washington, D.C., during a session of the House of Representatives. Since then, political groups have occasionally debated the island's status and its relationship with the United States.

Puerto Ricans today are divided by the issue of whether to request U.S. statehood or remain a commonwealth. A small group advocates full independence. Plebiscites in 1967 and 1993 approved commonwealth status, but the margin of victory in 1993 was slim. Momentum increased in March 1998 after the U.S. House of Representatives narrowly passed legislation calling for an official vote on statehood; however, the bill never made it out of the Senate committee. Seeking a mandate from the people to lobby U.S. Congress, Governor Pedro Rosselló (of the pro-statehood New Progressive Party) called for a referendum on the issue in December 1998. In a nonbinding vote, Puerto Ricans were asked to choose among statehood, independence, an associated republic, a territorial commonwealth, or none of the above. Voters again rejected statehood, favoring the current commonwealth status or "none of the above" option (50.3 to 46.5 percent).

Protests against the U.S. Navy's use of its Vieques Island naval base for bombing practice intensified after a 1999 accident killed a civilian. Protests continued throughout 2000, and Sila Calderón, Puerto Rico's new governor, has requested that training activities cease immediately. A referendum will be held in November 2001 to decide whether the U.S. Navy should leave in 2003.

THE PEOPLE

Population. Puerto Rico's population of about 3.92 million grows at an average annual rate of 0.56 percent. Migration rates generally fluctuate relative to the strength of the U.S. economy. People tend to emigrate when there are better work opportunities on the mainland. More than 95 percent of the people are native Puerto Rican, with a mixed Spanish, African, and Taino heritage. Aspects of this mixed heritage are evident in the people's music, arts, food, and traditions. San Juan is the largest city, with a population of about 450,000. However, the largest Puerto Rican community, consisting of nearly one million people, is in New York City, the destination of most emigrants. More than two million Puerto Ricans reside in the United States.

Language. Spanish and English share official status in Puerto Rico. For a short time in the early 1990s, Spanish was declared the only official language, but English has since regained equal status. Spanish is the language of school instruction and daily life. English is required as a second language in school and is used in business. Most people can speak English. The official status of either language often depends on the political climate surrounding Puerto Rico's relationship with the United States.

The close relationship Puerto Rico has with the United States and English has led people to mix many English words with spoken Spanish. Locally, people call this manner of speech *Spanglish*, and it is a comfortable, informal method of communication.

Religion. Roman Catholicism is the major Christian religion in Puerto Rico and claims about 85 percent of the population as members. Approximately 15 percent of the people belong to various Protestant and other Christian churches, and their numbers are growing. Although there is a separation of church and state, Catholic traditions and customs prevail among the people. Puerto Ricans consider themselves to be religious and often attribute their good fortunes to Deity.

General Attitudes. Puerto Ricans are sensitive people, quick to express sympathy and equally quick to resent a slight. They are gregarious and fond of *fiestas* (celebrations). They admire people who are intelligent, hardworking, dedicated, and humble. Puerto Ricans consider open criticism, aggressiveness, and greed offensive. Many believe a person's destiny is God's will, although individuals also must watch for opportunities.

Puerto Ricans value a good education, and a large number of students not only finish high school but also attend college or another institution of higher learning. Gaining a good education is considered a key to a better future. Being able to buy land for a home or business is a universal goal. National and regional pride is strong. Political influence is fairly desirable, and individuals who have such power are admired.

The Puerto Rican concept of time is somewhat relaxed. People are considered more important than schedules. If a friend, relative, or business associate drops in unexpectedly, Puerto Ricans will stop everything they are doing to visit, even if they have other commitments.

Personal Appearance. Puerto Ricans take great pride in what they wear in public. The youth favor popular North American fashions and also like a sporty look. Sloppy, overly casual, or revealing dress is considered inappropriate. Due to the climate, people prefer lightweight fabrics. Jeans are popular at all age levels for informal activities and outdoors work. Tennis shoes and sandals are the most commonly worn footwear. People living in interior towns may wear sweaters and jackets during winter months, as nighttime temperatures can be cool.

Shorts are acceptable casual wear. However, for most parties and social gatherings, formal clothing is expected, including suits with a shirt and tie for men, and dresses or skirts and blouses for women.

CUSTOMS AND COURTESIES

Greetings. People usually shake hands when greeting. Close friends often greet by grasping shoulders and kissing each other on the cheek. Women normally kiss women or men in this manner, but men do not greet other men this way. However, they may embrace a good friend or relative after a long absence. People stand very close when talking, and females often touch each other with their hands. Moving away, even slightly, may be considered an insult.

Although Spanish is most common, both Spanish and English greetings are used. So one might hear *Good morning* or *¡Buenos días!*, *Good afternoon* or *¡Buenas tardes!*, *Good evening* or *¡Buenas noches!*, and *Hi* or *¡Hola!* When one meets a person for the first time, it is polite to say *How are you?* or *¿Cómo está?* Young friends often begin a conversation with *¿Qué tal?*, a casual way to ask "How are you?" Which language speakers use depends on the situation (e.g., on the street, in a business meeting) and the relationship between the two people.

When addressing others in formal situations, one may use titles of respect or profession alone or in combination with a person's surname. These might include *Señor* (Mr.), *Señora* (Mrs. or Ms.), *Señorita* (Miss), *Doctor/a* (Dr.), and so on. One respectfully addresses an older person by combining the title *Don* (for men) or *Doña* (for women) with the person's first name. Friends address each other by given name or nickname.

Most Puerto Ricans have two surnames in addition to one or two given names. The family name is the father's surname; this appears as the second-to-last name, while the mother's surname appears last. Therefore, a person named Victor Arocho Ramos would be called *Señor Arocho*. Women do not change their surnames when they marry.

Gestures. One beckons by waving all fingers with the palm down; beckoning people with the palm facing up is improper. Wiggling the nose can mean, "What's going on?" To point, people often purse or pucker their lips in the direction indicated. One hands, rather than tosses or throws, small items to another person. During conversation, Puerto Ricans might interrupt each other; this generally is not considered rude. Although peers will tease each other in informal situations, such joking is not appropriate in formal settings.

A person can get another's attention by saying "pssst." This is common and not rude, but if a man does it to a woman, she will likely ignore him. Men often smile and stare at women, but it is considered improper for a woman to smile indiscriminately at strangers. It is appropriate for a man to offer his seat to a woman on public transportation. On longer trips, people often share food, and refusing such an offer is impolite.

Visiting. Visiting friends and relatives is considered a social obligation; people expect it as a basic courtesy. While inviting others to the home is not uncommon, most casual visits occur in the early evening without prior arrangement. Visits are relaxed and the entire family participates. Guests are treated to refreshments such as juice, soda, crackers, and cookies. If visitors arrive at mealtime, the hosts generally invite them to join the meal. In most cases, guests politely decline the offer a few times before finally accepting.

Unannounced visits are usually short (one or two hours), but planned activities can last longer. Friends and relatives invited for dinner are expected to stay after the meal to relax and enjoy conversation with the hosts. Invited guests are not expected to bring gifts, except on special occasions. However, hosts may appreciate a gift of flowers, candy, or fruit. If offered, gifts are opened in the presence of the giver.

Eating. Puerto Ricans eat three meals each day, and dinner is the main family meal. The eating atmosphere is relaxed and cordial. Diners keep both hands above the table and do not place them in the lap. Spoons and forks commonly are used; knives are used when appropriate. Some foods are eaten with the hands. Food left on the plate may be interpreted as a sign that the guest did not enjoy the dish. Hosts might offer second helpings when guests finish their food, but guests may decline politely.

People normally eat food near the stand where they purchased it, but it is not uncommon for people to eat while walking in public. At a restaurant, leaving a 15 percent tip is customary when service is not included in the bill.

LIFESTYLE

Family. The Puerto Rican family is close-knit and supportive. Extended families usually do not share a household, but they often live in the same neighborhood or town. This proximity facilitates frequent visits among relatives and allows grandparents to provide child care when both parents work. Children often remain at home until they marry. Families have an average of three children. Parents consider themselves responsible for their children throughout life and expect to give adult children financial or emotional support if needed. Traditionally, children share the responsibility of caring for elderly parents; however, more Puerto Ricans are placing their elderly parents in nursing homes, often due to medical or economic reasons. If families emigrate to New York or elsewhere, one parent may move first and establish a home before the rest of the family joins him or her.

Dating and Marriage. The youth begin dating in groups but eventually pair off into boyfriend-girlfriend relationships. Having a boyfriend or girlfriend is important. Dates may include going to the movies or on a picnic, dancing, or spending time at the beach. In rural areas, the relationship usually does not become serious until the young man has met the young woman's parents. Early dating leads some Puerto Ricans to marry, either formally or in a common-law partnership, at an early age (16–17). The majority of young women prefer marriage at a young age to single motherhood. However, an increasing emphasis on formal education has resulted in more Puerto Ricans marrying at a later age (19–21).

Whether a marriage is performed by a judge or in a church, a wedding is a time of great celebration and family gatherings. Families spend large amounts of money on decorations, food, and music, both traditional and modern.

Diet. Foods in Puerto Rico come from a variety of ethnic backgrounds, reflective of the people's mixed ancestry and colonial associations. Rice and beans is the most commonly eaten main meal. Other popular dishes include *arroz con pollo* (rice and chicken), *bacalao con viandas* (boiled cod with cassava and potatoes), *arroz con gandules y pernil* (rice with roasted pig), and foods made with plantains. Plantains are a starchy banana-like fruit that must be cooked to be eaten. Chicken, pork, and beef are favorite meats. Seafood (shrimp, octopus, clams, fish, etc.) and fruits (pineapples, bananas, mangoes, papayas, grapefruits, and oranges) are also common in the diet. Pasta and fast foods are more popular with younger generations.

Packaged snack foods are as common as in the United States, but people also enjoy locally prepared snacks such as *frituras* (foods fried in oil). Popular varieties of *frituras* include *alcapurrias* (plantains with meat) and *sorullos* (corn flour). The local flat bread typically eaten with meals, *pan sobao*, is made with water, shortening, and flour.

Recreation. Puerto Ricans' favorite sport is baseball, but people also enjoy basketball and volleyball. Families enjoy going to the beach or parks for picnics. In their leisure time, people may visit one another or watch television and videos.

The Arts. The arts enjoy a wide following and reflect both African and Spanish influences. Long before the United States took possession of Puerto Rico, a strong tradition of literature and music, as well as scholarship, had been established. Indeed, art and music are fostered in the home; nearly everyone can play a musical instrument, and a display of musical talent is usually expected at parties. Salsa, *plena*, *bomba*, and *danza puertorriqueña* are the most popular forms of music for dancing and singing. The prestigious Pablo Casals Festival (late May–early June) features special concerts. Latin jazz great Tito Puente died in 2000. Puerto Rican films and other cultural arts are known throughout the world. Among the most common folk arts are the carved religious figurines, called *santos,* which are found in almost every home. They represent the local patron saint or other Christian personages.

Holidays. Puerto Ricans celebrate New Year's Day as part of the Christmas season. The season ends with Day of the Three Kings (6 Jan.), when each child receives a gift. Puerto Rico celebrates both local and U.S. national holidays. Holidays include the Birth of Eugenio Maria de Hostos (11 Jan.), Martin Luther King Jr.'s Birthday (second Monday in January), Presidents' Day (third Monday in February), the Abolition of Slavery (22 Mar.), Easter (including Good Friday), José de Diego's Birthday (third Monday in April), Memorial Day (last Monday in May), U.S. Independence Day

THE AMERICAS

(4 July), Luis Muñoz Rivera's Day (17 July), Constitution Day (25 July), José Celso Barbosa's Birthday (28 July), Labor Day (first Monday in September), All Souls' Day (2 Nov.), Discovery of Puerto Rico Day (19 Nov.), Thanksgiving, and Christmas. An important part of the Christmas season is the *Parrandas*, when groups of friends sing Christmas songs door-to-door. They expect food and drinks in return.

Every town honors its patron saint annually with several days of activities that include going to amusement parks, gambling, singing, dancing, and participating in religious ceremonies. A beauty queen is selected for almost every activity. *Carnaval* celebrations held before Lent (during February or March) are most visible in Ponce. Lively festivities there, as well as in Arecibo and other towns, feature "monsters" (*vejigantes*) who wear bells and elaborate papier-mâché masks with multiple horns. They roam the streets, threatening to "hit" people on the head with a dried pig's bladder, while children try to gather bells from their costumes.

Commerce.   Business hours generally run weekdays between 9 a.m. to 5 p.m., although there are variations. Stores and shops may stay open 24 hours, and many retail outlets are open on Saturday. Some close on Sunday. The same national retail chains found throughout the United States also have stores in Puerto Rico. U.S. companies doing business in Puerto Rico enjoy a tax-exempt status because federal taxes do not apply in a commonwealth. Government offices are open from 8 a.m. to 4:30 p.m.

SOCIETY

Government.   The Commonwealth of Puerto Rico has 78 municipalities. Chief of state is the U.S. president, currently George W. Bush, but the head of government is a locally elected governor. In November 2000, Sila Calderón, San Juan's former mayor, was elected as Puerto Rico's first female governor.

As commonwealth citizens, Puerto Ricans do not vote in U.S. national elections and do not pay federal income tax, but they do elect their own officials. They are subject to the draft and receive partial welfare benefits. They have no voting representation in the U.S. Congress and are restricted by federal controls in managing their territory. A locally elected resident high commissioner represents Puerto Rico in the U.S. House of Representatives. The high commissioner (Aníbal Acevedo-Vilá) cannot vote but can introduce legislation, express opinions, and engage in dialogue on issues that relate to Puerto Rico.

Puerto Rico's Legislative Assembly is composed of a 28-seat Senate and a 54-seat House of Representatives. All citizens age 18 and older may vote. Puerto Rico generally has a very high voter turnout rate. Elections are held on the same schedule as in the United States. The main political parties are the pro-statehood New Progressive Party, the pro-commonwealth Popular Democratic Party, and the Independence Party.

Economy.   Since World War II, industrialization and duty-free trade with the United States have transformed the once-

DEVELOPMENT DATA

Human Dev. Index* rank	NA
Adjusted for women	NA
Real GDP per capita	$8,000 (est.)
Adult literacy rate	89 percent
Infant mortality rate	10 per 1,000 births
Life expectancy	71 (male); 79 (female)

poor agrarian island into a dynamic economy. Annual economic growth is usually around 3 percent.

Only 3 percent of the population is now engaged in agriculture; 17 percent works in the manufacturing sector. The government, services, and tourism provide most employment on the island. Unemployment is considerably higher than in the United States, averaging 10 percent in 2000. Puerto Rico exports sugar, coffee, petroleum products, chemicals, pharmaceuticals, textiles, and electronic equipment. Drawbacks to industrialization include the fact that most food must be imported and is more expensive. But U.S. investment and labor laws have improved the standard of living for most people. The U.S. dollar (US$) is the official currency.

Transportation and Communications.   Roads generally are in good condition, and most families have at least one car. Buses and taxis are available in large urban areas. *Públicos* serve most of the island. These large cars, fitting up to six passengers, travel from a specified terminal to a fixed destination (with no stops in between). Air service operates domestically and internationally. Puerto Rico has numerous radio and television stations and newspapers. Most people have telephones, and they benefit from a modern communications network.

Education.   Education is highly valued and the school system is improving continually. Primary and secondary schooling is the same as in the United States, with children beginning kindergarten at age five or six. A high school diploma, earned upon completion of the 12th grade, is necessary to get a good job or go to college. The drop out rate is very low. Higher education is provided by several universities and colleges, including the University of Puerto Rico, with its nine campuses and 45,000 students. Other institutions include the Inter-American University, Catholic University, Turabo University, Sacred Heart University, and Puerto Rico Junior College. The literacy rate is higher among the youth than adults.

Health.   A network of urban and rural health-care centers and four medical schools (one public and three private) serve Puerto Rico's medical needs. The system of health care is similar to that in the United States, although people are not always eligible for the same federal funds.

CONTACT INFORMATION

Puerto Rico Tourism Company, 666 Fifth Avenue, 15th Floor, New York, NY 10103; phone (800) 223-6530; Web site www.prtourism.com.

Culture Grams™
People. The World. You.

1305 North Research Way, Bldg. K
Orem, Utah 84097-6200 USA
1.800.528.6279; 801.705.4250
fax 801.705.4350
www.culturegrams.com

CultureGrams™
standard edition 2002

Romania

Boundary representations are not necessarily authoritative.

BACKGROUND

Land and Climate. Covering 91,700 square miles (237,500 square kilometers), Romania is about the size of Oregon. The Carpathian Mountains, the country's dominant geographical feature, form half of a crown in the north and central regions, nearly surrounding the Transylvania plateau. The South Carpathians (also known as the Transylvanian Alps) extend westward from the center of the country. Sub-Carpathian hills give way to extended, fertile plains traditionally used for corn and wheat crops. Europe's Danube River runs along Romania's southern border and forms a large delta area in the east before emptying into the Black Sea. Efforts to restore the delta's wetlands and wildlife destroyed in the 1980s are progressing. Low plains lie along the southern and eastern areas.

The climate is temperate-continental. Romanian summers are warm and winters are cold. The average temperature in July is 77°F (25°C); January averages 27°F (-3°C). Natural resources include coal, iron, and timber. Crude oil and natural gas reserves are declining. About 41 percent of the land is arable and 29 percent is forested. Some regions face severe air pollution due to old technology and the environmentally unsafe industrialization policies of past decades. Many cities, rivers, and forests are contaminated. With international support, the government is seeking ways to address the problems. A few cities have begun to develop safer industrial processes and recycling programs that meet European standards.

History. The ancestors of today's Romanians were Geto-Dacians, an Indo-European people. Between the sixth and fourth centuries B.C., the Dacians assimilated surrounding influences to form their own unique civilization. By A.D. 106, the Romans had conquered most of Dacia and made the area a province to supply grain, gold, and cattle to the empire. Roman colonization led natives to assimilate into the Roman culture and adopt their language (Latin). The name *Romania* means "Land of the Romans." With the Roman withdrawal from the region in the late third century, various barbarian tribes (i.e., Goths, Slavs, Bulgars) invaded between 200 and 1100. However, the language and culture remained Latin. In the 14th century, Moldavia (to the east) and Wallachia (in the south) became independent principalities. In 1500, the principalities fell under Turkish control, but they were never an integral part of the Ottoman (Turkish) Empire. Several European wars led to exchanges of Romanian territory among various countries. Complete freedom from Turkish rule was obtained through the Independence War in 1877, after Moldavia and Wallachia had joined together as the state of Romania.

Because of its part in the Allied alliance with France and England in World War I, Romania got back Bessarabia (a Romanian territory that roughly corresponded to present-day Moldova) from Russia and three Romanian-majority provinces (Transylvania, Banat, and Bukovina) from the defeated Austro-Hungarian Empire in 1918; reuniting these areas had been attempted since the 17th century but had never been achieved until then. Romania was occupied by Nazi Germany in 1940. Neutral—but faced with the threat of being divided so that it might not exist—Romania joined the German army in attacking Soviet Russia in 1941. In 1944, however, King Michael arrested Romania's pro-Nazi dictator and Romania switched to the Allied side. Shortly thereafter, Russian troops occupied the country and Romania came under Soviet influence. The monarchy was abolished, King Michael went into exile, and a communist regime was established. Bessarabia was annexed by the Soviet Union as Moldavia. When that area became independent in 1991, ethnic Romanians on both sides initially favored reunification. However, Moldovan desires for independence prevailed.

From 1965 to 1989, Nicolae Ceausescu ruled Romania in a brutal dictatorship, isolated even from its former ally, the Soviet Union. His policies led to grinding poverty for most people. He vehemently resisted Europe's democracy movements in 1989. However, during a popular uprising, he and his wife were executed.

The National Salvation Front replaced the Communist Party and began to govern in 1990 under Ion Iliescu. Initial confidence in his leadership was replaced by more civil unrest in 1991. Following violent repression of the opposition, Iliescu was reelected in 1992. He then sought to improve Romania's international image. Undemocratic laws giving prominence to ethnic Romanians, as well as other nationalist activities, hampered strong regional and European relations for years. In August 1996, Romania and Hungary signed a friendship treaty guaranteeing rights for minorities and quelling fears that Hungary would help ethnic Hungarians in Transylvania secede from Romania. The pact is vital for Romania's ambitions to eventually join the North Atlantic Treaty Organization (NATO) and the European Union (EU).

Fed up with the slow pace of reform, voters elected a strong anticommunist leader as president in November 1996. President Emil Constantinescu (Romanian Democratic Convention) promised to hasten reform. By late 1997, postelection optimism had been dampened by the slow pace of economic reform pursued by Prime Minister Victor Ciorbea. Infighting within the ruling National Christian Democratic Peasants Party (PNTCD) combined with economic and social woes to fuel political instability. Three different prime ministers were appointed in three years.

Leftist Ion Iliescu returned to the presidency in 2000 following a decisive victory over his nationalist rival, and the Party of Social Democracy (PDSR) won in parliamentary elections. Adrian Năstase is the current prime minister. In addition to economic reform, the current government seeks greater integration with Europe, particularly through EU and NATO membership.

THE PEOPLE

Population. The population of Romania is about 22.4 million and currently decreasing by 0.21 percent annually. Officially, ethnic Romanians comprise most of the population (90 percent). A significant Hungarian minority (7 percent), which lives mostly in Transylvania, still identifies with Hungary and the Hungarian culture. Ethnic Hungarians demand more language rights and greater local autonomy, but recent agreements may help resolve some of these issues. The government finances schools where statistically significant minorities can learn in their own language. The government also ensures that funds are given to Hungarian and German theaters to help maintain ethnic identity.

Other minority groups, which comprise around 2 percent of the population, include Germans, Ukrainians, Serbs, Croats, Russians, Turks, and *Romi* (Gypsies). The Romi have never been counted accurately and may comprise up to 8 percent of the total population. They tend to live separately from the

Romanians and generally are not well accepted. Many are poor, undereducated, and underemployed; they do not integrate into mainstream society and are sometimes subject to discrimination. Most Jews and Germans have emigrated to their homelands. More than half of Romania's population (57 percent) lives in cities, largely because of forced urbanization under Ceausescu. About eight million Romanians live outside the country.

Language. The official language is Romanian, a Latin-based language in the same family as Spanish, French, Italian, and Portuguese. Most of the young people speak English, but they may speak German, Italian, or other languages. French is a common second language among older people. Germans, Hungarians, and other minorities speak their native tongues. The Romi speak Romany.

Religion. Nearly all Romanians are Christian. About 70 percent belong to the Romanian Orthodox Church. Six percent of the people are Protestant; 6 percent (mostly Hungarians) are Roman Catholic (of which 1 percent are Uniate or Greek Catholic). Other Christian religions, Islam, and Judaism are also practiced. During the communist regime, religious organizations were persecuted, churches demolished, and clergy imprisoned; however, people are now free to practice religion as they wish. Government and public events often begin with a religious service. Although interest in religion is increasing in all areas, devotion is especially strong in rural areas. About 18 percent of the population claims no religious affiliation.

General Attitudes. Romania is at a crossroads in its history. The euphoric disposition that prevailed after the collapse of Ceausescu's authoritarian regime in December 1989 was replaced by disillusionment. For years, Romanians have not possessed the economic and political freedoms they thought would be theirs. Economic troubles have led to greater poverty, lower living standards, and declining personal wages. Many university-educated youth have emigrated.

Peaceful general elections and a relatively smooth transfer of power have strengthened social stability and given people a little hope for the future. Most people want a way of life built on democratic and liberal principles. Looking to the West, an overwhelming majority favors membership in European organizations. Many claim the country belongs with Europe due to its Roman heritage. They want to change traditional Romanian society to make it more similar to other European societies. Others are willing to accept economic reform, but they do not want radical changes in traditional society. A few remain nostalgic for the days of communism. Organized crime has expanded rapidly due to instability and uncertainty about the country's future. Corruption also remains a challenge.

Personal Appearance. Romanians attach importance to their appearance, although clothing worn in rural areas is often less fashionable. People generally dress conservatively in public. Women wear skirts and dresses. Slacks usually are worn only by younger women and girls. Female office workers may also wear tailored suits. Businessmen wear conservative suits. The youth prize denim jeans, T-shirts, sport jackets, and other Western-style clothing. People do not commonly wear hats, but in rural areas older women wear scarves. The elderly generally wear dark, conservative colors.

In rural areas, colorful folk costumes may be worn on Sundays, at festivals, or on special occasions. Gypsy women wear long, colorful skirts. Family members mourning the death of a loved one may remain in black from six weeks to a year.

CUSTOMS AND COURTESIES

Greetings.   Women greet each other with a handshake, or a kiss on each cheek if they are good friends. Men shake hands with others. A man usually waits for a woman to extend her hand first. When greeting, women often use the phrase *Bună* (Good), while men and young people say *Salut* (Salutation). Young people might also say *Ceau* (Ciao) or *Servus*. In cities, a man might greet a woman by kissing her hand. Even if he does not, he may say *Sărut mâna* (Kiss your hand) as a sign of reverence. Young people also use this greeting with their parents or elders. In rural areas, everyone is greeted individually; people also greet strangers and expect their greeting to be returned.

The most common verbal greeting is *Bună ziua* (Good day). *Bună dimineata* (Good morning) and *Bună seara* (Good evening) also are used. Only close friends and relatives greet each other by first name. However, adults normally address young people by first name. When applicable, people use professional titles ("Doctor," "Professor," etc.) before surnames.

Gestures.   When one sneezes, family or close friends may say *Sanatate* (Good health) or *Noroc* (Good luck). *Noroc* is also used at parties to mean "Cheers." Making eye contact during conversation is a sign of honesty. It is impolite for men to keep their hands in their pockets when speaking to women, officials, older people, or a large audience. People also avoid chewing gum during conversation. Friends often hold hands or walk arm in arm. Gentlemen remove their hats before entering buildings and churches, except stores. Women cover their head when entering a church.

Visiting.   Romanians like to receive and pay visits, which usually are arranged in advance. People often gather for birthdays, anniversaries, holidays, or just to socialize. Hosts generally offer their guests a drink—coffee, tea, brandy, or a popular regional wine—and also offer them fruit preserves (*dulceață*) or other refreshments. It is polite for dinner guests to bring an odd number of flowers (three or more) or a small gift for the hostess. Guests avoid giving red roses or an even number of flowers (often associated with funerals). Guests typically ask the hosts for permission before smoking.

Eating.   Lunch traditionally is the main meal of the day; however, due to work and school schedules, many families can only eat lunch together on Saturday and Sunday. Supper is similar to lunch, but the servings are somewhat smaller. Romanians eat in the continental style, with the fork in the left hand and the knife remaining in the right. They keep both hands (not elbows) above the table during a meal. When beginning to eat, people wish each other *Poftă bună* (Enjoy the meal). If they are at home, after the meal they will thank the person who cooked and served the meal and say *Sărut mâna pentru masă* (kiss your hand for the meal) or *Mulțumesc pentru masă* (Thank you for the meal). Toasting is usually a part of formal and informal lunches and dinners.

LIFESTYLE

Family.   The family has always been important to Romanians, and the father maintains a dominant role. Urban families tend to be smaller than rural families because of a shortage of housing and the high cost of living. Most women work outside the home, but they are also responsible for the upkeep of the home and the children. Men generally are not involved in household chores. Grandparents often live with the family and care for grandchildren.

A private farm includes a two- or three-bedroom home surrounded by a fence, a garden and orchard, and small farm buildings. Ceausescu attempted to destroy these farmsteads—and with them, rural individualism—by tearing down homes and forcing people to move into large housing blocks. These apartments had no running water, bathrooms, or heat, and strictly enforced regulations limited the amount of electricity each apartment could use. While forced urbanization and limits on electricity use are no longer practiced, improvements in living standards have not occurred due to the poor economy. Many urban and rural families still lack proper housing; most go without modern conveniences.

Dating and Marriage.   Young men and women usually begin to socialize in high school. Popular activities include taking walks and going to movies, parties, sporting events, and school dances.

Most adults expect to marry and have a family in spite of economic difficulties. In urban areas, men and women are between 25 and 30 years old when they marry. People in villages still marry at a young age. Local and ethnic customs regarding courtship and marriage vary by region. People in rural areas enjoy engagement ceremonies in which the groom's family brings the engagement and wedding rings to the bride's family. Both families celebrate the event with dinner, singing, and dancing. Before the wedding ceremony, the groom may carry a pine tree on the way to the bride's house as a sign of long life. Most weddings involve church ceremonies. Godparents are expected to take an active part in wedding activities. Most people wish the young couple *Casă de piatră* ("House of stone," meaning a long and durable marriage).

Diet.   Romanian food is characterized by distinctive ethnic specialties including *mititei* (spiced, minced beef/pork/lamb in sausage form), *mamaliga* (cornmeal mush served like mashed potatoes), and *sarmale* (minced meat with rice, rolled in pickled cabbage or grapevine leaves). Breakfast usually consists of eggs, cheese, rolls or other breads, and coffee. Lunch begins with soup, followed by meat, potatoes, and a vegetable. Romanians favor pork over other meats. Most people eat bread with every meal. Wine or beer usually is served as well. A special plum brandy called *tzuica* is also popular. Pastries are popular for dessert. Although food is now more readily available, people cannot easily afford the higher prices. Food in Transylvania has been heavily influenced by Hungarian cuisine. Romanian food in Moldavia and Wallachia is similar to Greek or Turkish food.

Recreation.   Romanians enjoy sports, particularly soccer. Many men spend a lot of time watching soccer matches. Romanian athletes have done well in international competitions, especially in gymnastics, weightlifting, and tennis; however, general participation in such sports is low due to limited facilities. Leisure activities include meeting with friends or family, watching television, taking walks, reading, and going to the movies, theater, or concerts. Swimming, aerobics, and skiing are also popular. Many rural people enjoy folk shows with music and dancing.

The Arts.   There are more than 1,500 museums throughout Romania. Excellent orchestras, theaters, and opera houses are available in major cities. Even in remote areas of the country, performing groups provide access to puppet shows, operas, dance productions, and other arts. Medieval castles, monasteries, and churches are important examples of Romanian architecture.

EUROPE ▼

Romania

Flutes and stringed instruments are common in folk music. The *coboza*, a short-necked lute, and the *tambal*, a stringed instrument played with small mallets, are two folk instruments. Romanian folk art includes wood carving, carpets, elaborate costumes, pottery, and icon paintings. Easter egg painting is celebrated; painted eggs often feature religious symbols and animal designs. Painting religious icons on glass is another notable tradition.

Holidays. Most people celebrate Christian holidays according to the Orthodox calendar. Christmas is a children's holiday and a feasting holiday. Easter services are well attended and are followed by family traditions and feasts. Romania's National Day (1 Dec.) marks the proclamation of Romania as a unified state in 1918. New Year's (1–2 Jan.) is the most popular holiday. For *Mărţişor* (1 Mar.), men give women and girls small brooches. Also celebrated are Women's Day (8 Mar.), Labor Day (1–2 May), and Children's Day (1 June). On certain days (such as Wednesdays and Fridays), on some religious holidays, or before Christmas or Easter, Orthodox Romanians may fast; or they may not eat or cook any animal products, sometimes for as long as 40 days.

Commerce. Factory workers usually work morning, swing, or night shifts. Most factories close on Saturday and Sunday. Government offices are open from 8 a.m. to 4 p.m., while banking offices are open from 9 a.m. to noon and 2 to 4 p.m. A few stores may close around lunchtime but remain open later in the evening. General department stores are open all day. Except for restaurants, coffee shops, and some private shops, most businesses are closed on Saturday afternoon and Sunday. Depending on their seniority, workers enjoy two- to four-week vacations.

SOCIETY

Government. Romania's new constitution established it as a republic in 1991. The president is head of state but also has broader powers. Romania's prime minister is head of government. Parliament has a 143-seat Senate and a 343-seat Chamber of Deputies. The voting age is 18. The most powerful political parties are the governing Party of Social Democracy in Romania, and the nationalist Party of Greater Romania. Several other parties hold blocks of seats in Parliament and are relied on for passing legislation.

Economy. Primarily an agricultural nation before World War II, Romania still suffers from the rapid and forced industrialization policies of former governments. Large state industries with low productivity have drained state finances for decades. Even since the election of noncommunists in 1996, privatization efforts and economic reform have been delayed, hindering the country's transition to a free-market economy. A few foreign companies have been attracted by tax incentives, skilled workers, and Romania's extensive industrial complex; but overall, foreign investment has been minimal.

After three years of recession, the economy grew by around 2 percent in 2000. But inflation was at about 40 percent and unemployment was more than 10 percent. The government's economic goals are to cut inflation, increase economic growth, increase foreign investment, encourage privatization, and hold the budget deficit in check. Most people struggle but are able

DEVELOPMENT DATA

Human Dev. Index* rank	64 of 174 countries
Adjusted for women	55 of 143 countries
Real GDP per capita	$5,648
Adult literacy rate	98 percent
Infant mortality rate	20 per 1,000 births
Life expectancy	66 (male); 74 (female)

to meet basic needs. Food is plentiful but expensive, often consuming up to 70 percent of a family's monthly income. Net monthly income averages about $100.

The most important exports are textiles, metals and metal products, fuels, machinery and equipment, consumer goods, and foods. The country now relies on Russia for much of its energy. Romania's currency is the *leu* (L).

Transportation and Communications. Public transportation in the cities is reasonably efficient and inexpensive. Roads are in poor condition and are not developed to handle an increased number of cars. The train network links major cities, but many trains are poorly maintained and lack heat in the winter. In rural areas, travel by bicycle and horse- or donkey-drawn carts (called *căruţă*) is still common. All major cities have local TV and FM radio stations; many people also have their own telephones. Mobile phone use is developing. Many Romanians have cable television. Communications systems are very limited in some rural areas; some rural areas have no phone service at all. The press is free to print what it wishes.

Education. Education is compulsory and free between the ages of six and sixteen. Students then seek employment, enter vocational training, or prepare for a university education. Most students complete some education beyond the required 10 years. University entrance is determined by entrance examinations and the number of available spaces. University students are among the most vocal supporters of political change.

Health. Many important health problems face the people of Romania. Due to a practice of giving newborn babies blood transfusions if they appeared anemic, many children contracted AIDS from contaminated needles and blood. Many women also have the disease. Hepatitis B and tuberculosis are other dangers. Respiratory and other illnesses associated with heavy pollution and smoking are common. Health facilities are free to all citizens but are poorly equipped and understaffed; some private clinics are available. Large groups of abandoned children in state institutions do not receive necessary attention or care. With the help of Western nations, the government is trying to address these problems.

CONTACT INFORMATION

Embassy of Romania, 1607 23d Street NW, Washington, DC 20008; phone (202) 232-3694; Web site www.roembus.org. Romanian National Tourist Office, 14 East 38th Street, 12th Floor, New York, NY 10016; phone (212) 545-8484; Web site www.romaniatouristoffice.com.

CultureGrams™
People. The World. You.

1305 North Research Way, Bldg. K
Orem, Utah 84097-6200 USA
1.800.528.6279; 801.705.4250
fax 801.705.4350
www.culturegrams.com

Russia
(Russian Federation)

Franz Josef Land

Arctic Ocean

Novaya Zemlya

Kara Sea

Laptev Sea

East Siberian Sea

Barents Sea

Murmansk

SIBERIA

Lena

Vorkuta •

URALS

Ob

Yenisey

St. Petersburg

Nizhniy Novgorod

Yekaterinburg

Angara

Krasnoyarsk

Magadan

Bering Sea

Perm
Kazan

Omsk

Novosibirsk

Sea of Okhotsk

MOSCOW

Ufa

Irkutsk

Lake Baikal

Amur

Petropavlovsk-Kamchatskiy

Pacific Ocean

Kaliningrad

Samara

Chelyabinsk

Volga

Voronezh

Saratov

Khabarovsk

Volgograd

Grozny

Vladivostok

▼ EURASIA

Boundary representations are not necessarily authoritative.

BACKGROUND

Land and Climate. Russia is the largest country in the world. At 6,592,734 square miles (17,075,200 square kilometers), it is nearly twice the size of the United States. Four of the world's largest rivers (Lena, Ob, Volga, and Yenisey) and the world's deepest freshwater lake (Baikal) are in Russia. Much of Russia is covered by great plains, but a large frozen tundra dominates the extreme north. Forests cover much of western Russia. The low Ural Mountains divide Russia's European side from its Asian regions. Siberia is mostly taiga (conifer forests), with tundra (treeless plain characteristic of arctic or subarctic region) to the north, and steppe (dry, treeless grasslands) to the south. Russia's climate varies considerably by region. Russian winters last from November to March except in Siberia, where winter can last nine months.

History. Slavic peoples settled in eastern Europe during the early Christian era. Many converted to Christianity in the ninth and tenth centuries. In 988, Prince Vladimir declared Christianity the state's official religion. Early in the 13th century, Mongols conquered the Slavs and ruled for 240 years. The Slavs finally defeated the Mongols in 1480 to regain their sovereignty. In 1547, Ivan the Terrible (1533–84) was the first Russian ruler crowned czar of Russia. He expanded Russia's territory, as did Peter the Great (1682–724) and Catherine the Great (1762–96). The empire reached from Warsaw in the west to Vladivostok in the east. In 1814, Russian troops that had defeated France's Napoleon marched on Paris, and Russia took its place as one of the most powerful states on earth.

When Czar Nicholas II abdicated because of popular unrest during World War I, Vladimir Lenin, head of the Bolshevik Party, led the 1917 revolt that brought down the provisional government and put the Communists in power. Lenin disbanded the legislature and banned all other political parties. A civil war between Lenin's Red Army and the White Army lasted until 1922, with Lenin victorious.

In 1922, the Bolsheviks formed the Union of Soviet Socialist Republics (USSR) and forcibly incorporated Armenia, Azerbaijan, Georgia, Ukraine, and Belarus into the union. By the time Lenin died in 1924, many people had perished as a result of his radical social restructuring. Lenin was followed by Joseph Stalin, a dictator who forced industrialization and collective agriculture on the people. Millions died in labor camps and from starvation. Germany invaded the Soviet Union in 1941, and World War II (the Great Patriotic War) eventually took more than 25 million Soviet lives.

After Stalin died in 1953, Nikita Khrushchev declared he would build real communism within 20 years. Hard-liners opposed to his reforms and policy of détente with the West replaced Khrushchev in 1964 with Leonid Brezhnev. Before his death in 1982, Brezhnev orchestrated the expansion of Soviet influence in the developing world, ordered the invasion of Afghanistan, and built up the Soviet nuclear arsenal. When the next two leaders died in quick succession, young Mikhail Gorbachev rose to power in 1986.

Gorbachev soon introduced reforms like *perestroika* (restructuring) and *glasnost* (openness). The failure of many reforms exposed inherent weaknesses in the Soviet system. The union quickly unraveled in 1991 after several republics declared independence. Russia's leader at the time was Boris Yeltsin.

In 1993, after Yeltsin dissolved a combative parliament, his opponents voted to impeach him and seized the "White House" (parliament building) in an attempted coup. Following street riots, the militants were forced from the building by tank fire. That victory and the approval of Yeltsin's new constitution were two highlights of an otherwise difficult term in office. Despite poor health and challenges from the Communists and ultranationalists, Yeltsin prevailed in the balloting to become Russia's first-ever freely elected president.

A violent and unpopular war with separatists in Chechnya tarnished Yeltsin's image in 1994. Tens of thousands died before a 1996 cease-fire allowed Chechens to elect local leaders. Although Russian troops withdrew and Chechnya's bid for independence was scheduled for negotiation, troops returned in 1999 after Chechen terrorists allegedly struck Moscow. With public support, military leaders vowed to take control of the republic. While Russian troops captured the Chechen capital of Grozny in early 2000, they have been unable to subdue the rebel resistance. Fighting rages on as both military and civilian casualties mount. The war is a significant drain on Russia's national budget and its resources.

Yeltsin seemed unable to fight rising crime, poverty, corruption, and inflation in the late 1990s. Instead, he fired successive prime ministers and cabinets, only to finally announce his own resignation on New Year's Eve in 1999. Former Prime Minister Vladimir Putin was appointed acting president ahead of March 2000 elections, which he later won decisively. Putin remains popular, largely due to Russia's economic growth. He has continued the war in Chechnya and promised to further economic reform, decrease corruption, and increase security.

THE PEOPLE

Population. Russia's population of 146 million is shrinking annually by 0.5 percent. Of 120 different ethnic groups, most are small. Ethnic Russians form 82 percent of the entire population. Other groups include Tartars (4 percent), Ukrainians (3), Chuvashes (1), Belorusians (almost 1), Udmurts, Kazaks, Buryats, Tuvinians, Yakutians, Bashkirs, and others. The capital and largest city is Moscow, with a population of more than 10 million. Other large cities include Saint Petersburg, Novosibirsk, Nizhniy Novgorod, Yekaterinburg, Saratov, and Samara. More than three-fourths of Russians live in urban areas. Serious gaps between rich and poor, skilled and unskilled, and healthy and ill are widening and threatening Russia's future development.

Language. Russian is the official language. Its Cyrillic alphabet has 33 letters, some of them unlike any letter in the Roman (Latin) alphabet. Non-Russians also usually speak Russian, especially in urban areas. Rural minorities more often speak their own languages at home or within their ethnic groups. For example, Tartars speak Tartar, Chuvashes speak Chuvash, and Udmurts speak Udmurt. After communist rule, these individual languages began to be taught at schools where the ethnic group was prominent. Ethnic Russians are not required to learn other local languages, but students increasingly are studying foreign languages (English, French, German, and Spanish).

Religion. The Russian Orthodox Church is the dominant religion, claiming members totaling half of Russia's population. After the October Revolution (1917), the Communists discouraged all religious worship. Mikhail Gorbachev was the first Soviet leader to officially tolerate—even support—religion. Yeltsin also embraced the church, which rapidly regained its influence. Churches other than the Russian Orthodox are allowed to operate if they have registered with authorities and can prove they have a long-standing presence in Russia. Jewish and Islamic groups do not face these restrictions. Some Tartars and Bashkirs are Muslim, and some Tuvinians and Buryats are Buddhist.

General Attitudes. In Russia's long history of totalitarianism, its inhabitants had few opportunities to make their own decisions, whether ruled by a Czar or the Communist Party. Initiative, personal responsibility, and the desire to work independently were suppressed by the state, and one was expected to conform to official opinion and behavior. Problems were not so much solved as endured or ignored.

After 1991, many Russians were searching for new social values and were optimistic about a future of freedom and opportunity. In reality, Russia's social fabric and economic stability have so deteriorated that Communists and nationalists have regained popularity with people who are tired of Russia's chaos, declining living standards, increasingly violent and rampant crime, and unemployment. Prosperity promised within a few years now seems a generation or more away. Still, social status often is measured by the acquisition of power and wealth. Respect for authority continues. Though frustrated, many Russians seem resigned to their situation and are willing to endure it the best they can. For example, they continue to work when not paid. And, to compensate for the lack of wages, many families feed themselves by gardening. More than half of all fresh produce in Russia comes from private gardens and is consumed by the family. Even urban dwellers have garden plots to sustain themselves.

Friendship is extremely important to Russians, who are warm and open with trusted friends. They rely on their network of friends in hard times and will go to great lengths to help friends whenever possible.

Although intensely proud of Mother Russia and its achievements, Russians are basically pessimistic and usually do not express much hope for a better life in the future. Even generally optimistic Russians might not show their true feelings in public but rather express frustration with everyday life. Still, Russians see their historical heritage and social structure as unique. They desire to be known not for the negative aspects of the Soviet period and its aftermath but for Russian contributions to world literature, art, science, technology, and medicine.

Personal Appearance. Russians, especially women, like to be well dressed in public. Urban people prefer European fashions. More young people are wearing shorts in warm weather; young women like short skirts. Young men wear jogging suits in mild weather. Jeans are popular among most age groups, except older women. The fur hat that many Russians wear in winter is called a *shapka* or *ushanka*.

CUSTOMS AND COURTESIES

Greetings. When meeting, most Russians shake hands firmly and say *Zdravstvuyte* (Hello), *Dobry dien* (Good day), *Dobroye utro* (Good morning), *Dobry vecher* (Good evening), or *Privet* (a casual "Hello"). Good friends say "Hello" with the more informal *Zdravstvuy* or *Zdorovo*. Friends, but not strangers, might also ask *Kak dela?* (How are you?) and wait for a response. Russians are introduced by their full name (given, patronymic, surname). Surnames are not used without titles, such as *Gospodin* (Mr.) and *Gospozha* (Mrs.). The military, police, and some citizens continue to use the Soviet-era title *tovarishch* ("friend" or "comrade"). At work or in polite company, Russians address each other by given name and patronymic (the possessive of the father's first name). This is also the most appropriate form of address for a superior or a respected elder. Close friends use given names alone.

Gestures. Pointing with the index finger is improper but commonly done. It is impolite to talk (especially to an older person) with one's hands in the pockets or arms folded across the chest. To count, Russians bend (close) their fingers rather than open them. It is bad luck to shake hands across a threshold.

Visiting. Russians like to visit and have guests. Sitting and talking for hours is a favorite pastime. One usually removes shoes when entering a home. Hosts generally offer refreshments, but guests may decline them. Friends and family may visit anytime without notice but usually arrange visits in advance if they have telephones. They make themselves at home and generally can expect to be welcomed for any length of time. Visits with new acquaintances are more formal.

Giving gifts is a strong tradition, and almost every event (birthdays, weddings, holidays, etc.) is accompanied by presents. For casual visits, it is common (but not required) for guests to bring a simple gift (flowers, food, or alcohol) to their hosts. The object given is less important than the friendship expressed by the act. Flowers are given in odd numbers; even numbers are for funerals. If friends open a bottle of vodka ("little water"), they customarily drink until it is empty.

Eating. Russians eat with the fork in the left hand and the knife in the right, although many people use only a fork. People keep the hands above the table and not in the lap. Soup is common for lunch or dinner. At lunch or the main meal, people also like *zakuski* (appetizers). When entertaining, Russians put more food than they can eat on the table and may leave some on the plate to indicate there is abundance (whether true or not) in the house. Guests can indicate they have eaten well by leaving a very small amount of food on the plate. Russians generally do not go out to eat in cafés or restaurants because the few that exist are fairly expensive.

LIFESTYLE

Family. The family is the basic social unit in Russia; most people expect to marry and have children. The average urban couple has one child, but rural families are larger. Parents support their children financially until they reach adulthood. Grown children are often expected to help their parents financially because pensions are frequently inadequate. The father is considered head of the family, although many households are led by single mothers. Both husband and wife usually work, but men rarely share in household duties. Women bear the greatest burden in Russia, rarely receiving equal pay, promotions, or leisure time. Women earn only one-fifth of the nation's income.

Child care is available, but few families can afford it. When the elderly live with their children, they often provide child care and do the shopping. Because housing is difficult to obtain, young couples often live with their parents for some time. Urban apartments are small and it is common for a family of three or more to live in a one- or two-room apartment with a kitchen and a bathroom. Rural homes are slightly larger than apartments but often lack running water and central heat.

Dating and Marriage. When young people date, they usually go to a movie or for a walk in a city park. Sometimes they go to bars or cafés, but this is too expensive for many people. Instead, the youth like to have parties in their apartments when their parents are not home. Before 1991, couples could only marry in a "wedding palace." Many people are now also having a traditional church wedding before or after the civil ceremony. The elaborate traditional ceremony is called *venchaniye* (literally "coronation"). The divorce rate is high, as many people do not view marriage as a lasting commitment.

Diet. Although food is plentiful, it is expensive. The average person eats more homegrown produce than imported fruits and vegetables. People on fixed and limited incomes (mainly the elderly) eat more bread and potatoes than anything else. Urban residents more often have meat and dairy products. Traditional Russian foods include *borsch* (vegetable soup), *pirozhki* (a stuffed roll, eaten as "fast food"), *golubtsy* (stuffed cabbage leaves baked with tomato sauce and eaten with sour cream), *pelmeni* (a pasta dish), and *shi* (sour cabbage soup). *Borsch* is still one of the most popular foods in the country. Its ingredients (beets, potatoes, cabbages, carrots, and onions) almost complete the list of vegetables used in everyday life. Pork, sausage, chicken, and cheeses are popular, but they can be expensive. Russians drink coffee, tea, and mineral water; juice and soda are available. Men prefer vodka to wine.

Recreation. Russians have little leisure time because of the hours they devote to getting food, working extra jobs, or taking care of their households. Urban Russians often spend their spare time at their *dachas* (country cottages), if they have them, relaxing and growing fruits and vegetables. In the summer, people like to gather mushrooms. Cities have relatively few nightclubs, but that is changing gradually.

The country's favorite sport is soccer. Winter sports such as ice-skating, hockey, and cross-country skiing are also popular. Most families like to watch television in the evening. People highly appreciate theaters and movies, but these are available only in big cities. Rural people can watch movies at community recreation centers called *dvorets kultury* (palace of culture) or the smaller *dom kultury* (house of culture).

The Arts. Russia has a grand and abiding heritage in cultural arts. Realistic, romantic, political, and psychological themes are common in Russia's world-famous poetry, short stories, novels, and plays.

Russian composers wrote some of the world's most beloved symphonies, ballets, operas, and other musical works. Ballet is an important art form; *Swan Lake* and *Don Quixote* were first performed in Russia. The Bolshoi Ballet, a renowned company, started in 1776. Traditional music and dance is also important to the people. Theater, ballet, symphonic, and folk productions are well attended. Russian folk crafts include nested dolls (*matryoshka*), wood carving, lacquer painting, and lace making.

Holidays. New Year's Day is the most popular holiday in Russia. Almost everyone decorates fir trees and has parties to celebrate the new year. Grandfather Frost leaves presents for children to find on New Year's Day. Easter and Christmas

EURASIA

observances, long interrupted by communism, regained some prominence in 1990. Christmas is on 7 January, according to the Julian calendar used by the Russian Orthodox Church. Women's Day is on 8 March. Solidarity Day (1 May, also known as May Day) is a day for parades. Victory Day (9 May) commemorates the end of World War II and is deeply important to most Russians. Every profession (teachers, miners, police, etc.) has its own special day each year to celebrate.

Commerce. The business week is 40 hours, with Saturdays and Sundays off. Offices generally are open from 9 a.m. to 6 p.m. They close for lunch. Prices in state stores are not negotiable, but prices are flexible on the streets, where an increasing number of items are sold. Wholesale markets (*Melkooptoviye Rynki*), where people can buy everything from food to electronics, are becoming more common. Capitalism boomed for the few people with connections, but newly rich Russian businessmen are generally despised by others and are considered dishonest. Most private businesses pay "protection" money to organized crime groups.

Russians prefer having social interaction before discussing business. Trying to do business on the phone without seeing the prospective business partner is ineffective. One often spends a lot of time in meetings before even a small deal can succeed.

SOCIETY

Government. Russia is a federation of 21 autonomous republics and 49 oblasts, or regions. The constitution provides for a president (Vladimir Putin) as head of state and a prime minister (Mikhail Kasyanov) as head of government. The president is strong and has power to dissolve parliament, set foreign policy, and appoint the prime minister. The Federal Assembly has two houses, a 176-seat Federation Council and the 450-seat State Duma. An array of political parties is represented in the Duma. The actual party names are less important than their alliances. Communists form the largest block, but nationalists and liberals form other substantial voting blocks. The voting age is 18.

Economy. Russia's natural resources give it great potential for economic growth and development. Natural gas, coal, gold, oil, diamonds, copper, silver, and lead are all abundant. Heavy industry dominates the economy, although the agricultural sector is potentially strong. Russia's economy remains weak and unstable for many reasons, including an inefficient distribution system, political uncertainties, declining foreign investment, a crumbling infrastructure, high foreign debt, high interest rates, poor tax laws and collection rates, high inflation (20 percent), low quality production, organized crime, and corruption. Poverty is increasing rapidly; slightly more than one-third of Russians live below the official poverty line. In 1998, the *ruble* (R) nearly collapsed and the economy shrank. The government's strict measures have begun to reverse the downward economic trend. Growth in 2000 was 7 percent. Unemployment decreased to 10 percent. Most transactions are made in cash, which is in increasingly short supply; many communities subsist by bartering goods or services.

DEVELOPMENT DATA

Human Dev. Index* rank	62 of 174 countries
Adjusted for women	54 of 143 countries
Real GDP per capita	$6,460
Adult literacy rate	99 percent
Infant mortality rate	20 per 1,000 births
Life expectancy	59 (male); 72 (female)

Transportation and Communications. Although the number of privately owned cars has grown since the 1980s, most people use public transportation. Major cities have subways, trolleys, trains, and buses. Taxis are expensive and hard to find, but unofficial taxis are increasingly common. Domestic air travel is not always reliable. Railroads are extensive, but service is poor. The telephone system is outdated but has undergone significant changes in the 1990s. Cell phones are increasingly popular, especially in major cities. The press faces challenges to its independence.

Education. Education is free and compulsory between ages six and seventeen. In 1994, new curriculum guidelines were introduced to encourage choice and innovation over previous approaches to teaching, but many public schools are unable or unwilling to implement the reforms due to lack of money, supplies, and clear local leadership. However, a few are embracing new ideas and even teaching basic market economics. Students attend primary, middle, and high school. They can specialize in their last two years. Private schools offer a high-quality education to the wealthy and influential. Education is highly valued; however, economic hardship has seen many preschool closures, declining kindergarten attendance, and teacher strikes. More than five hundred universities, medical schools, and technical academies are found throughout the country.

Health. Medical care is free but of poor quality. Some doctors are well trained, but they lack modern equipment and medicine to adequately treat their patients. Private clinics provide better (but expensive) care. Common major diseases are cancer (especially lung cancer, reflecting a high percentage of smokers), diabetes, and heart ailments. Alcoholism and drug abuse may affect as much as 42 percent of the population, including a large number of teenagers; they are involved in many murders, car accidents, and suicides. Diphtheria, dysentery, tuberculosis, polio, AIDS, and other serious maladies are spreading. The decline in health is reaching crisis proportions. Life expectancy for men is far lower than it is in any other Western country.

CONTACT INFORMATION

Embassy of the Russian Federation, Consular Division, 2641 Tunlaw Road NW, Washington, DC 20007; phone (202) 939-8907; Web site www.russianembassy.org. Russian National Tourist Office, 130 42d Street, Suite 412, New York, NY 10036; phone (212) 758-1162; Web site www.russia-travel.com.

CultureGrams™
People. The World. You.

1305 North Research Way, Bldg. K
Orem, Utah 84097-6200 USA
1.800.528.6279; 801.705.4250
fax 801.705.4350
www.culturegrams.com

Federation of
Saint Kitts and Nevis

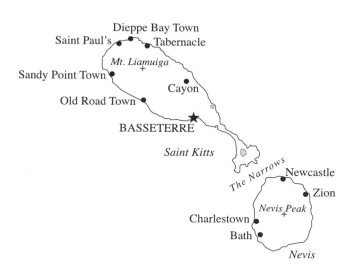

Boundary representations are not necessarily authoritative.

BACKGROUND

Land and Climate.   Saint Kitts, also called Saint Christopher, and Nevis are leeward islands in the Caribbean Archipelago about 200 miles (322 kilometers) southeast of Puerto Rico. The two are separated by a channel called The Narrows that is only 2 miles (3.2 kilometers) wide at its narrowest point. St. Kitts is 65 square miles (168 square kilometers) in size, while Nevis is 36 square miles (93 square kilometers). A mountainous central ridge extends throughout the length of St. Kitts. Its highest peak, Mount Liamuiga, rises to 3,792 feet (1,156 meters). On Nevis, Nevis Peak rises to 3,232 feet (985 meters). Both mountains are long-dormant volcanoes, but there is some evidence of volcanic activity in the form of fumaroles and hot sulfur springs.

Below 1,000 feet (305 meters), St. Kitts is a patchwork of cultivated fields, mostly sugarcane. Above these fields, slopes are covered with tropical rain forests. The peninsula has a number of salt ponds and is quite different from the rest of the island. Nevis is rockier, with clay soils and a higher concentration of natural vegetation. Cultivation is limited to small vegetable and fruit farms. The most valuable natural resources include the islands' beauty, tranquility, and unspoiled natural environment. The climate is dry and tropical, with temperatures ranging from 82°F (28°C) in December to 91°F (33°C) in July and August. The rainy season runs from July to December. Hurricanes are possible between July and November. Hurricane Georges damaged 70 percent of the islands' homes in September 1998.

Nevis's shoreline is ringed by coconut palms. The island is home to goats and donkeys. Deer roam St. Kitts, and West African green vervet monkeys live on both islands. Booby Island, a rocky islet in The Narrows, boasts a large pelican and seagull population.

History.   Prior to the arrival of Christopher Columbus, St. Kitts and Nevis were inhabited by Caribs who had migrated from South America. They called St. Kitts *Liamuiga* (Fertile Island) and Nevis *Oualie* (meaning unknown). Columbus discovered St. Kitts and Nevis on his second Caribbean voyage in 1493. St. Kitts eventually was named *San Cristóbal* (St. Christopher) and Nevis was named *Santa María de las Nieves* (Our Lady of the Snows) because of the cloud cluster lying on Nevis Peak. *San Cristóbal* was later shortened to *St. Kitts* by its English colonists while *Nieves* became *Nevis*.

Sir Thomas Warner colonized St. Kitts (1624) and Nevis (1628). French settlers arrived in 1626 and St. Kitts was partitioned by formal treaty. Despite initial friendly relations with the Carib people and their King Tegreman, the British and French massacred or expelled most Caribs; many leapt from a sea cliff to their deaths.

The English and French coexisted peacefully until war broke out between Britain and France in 1666. The 1713 Treaty of Utrecht ceded the island entirely to the British. Little French presence remains besides historical sites and names (such as the capital, Basseterre).

Sugar production, begun in the 1650s, propelled the islands to 18th-century prosperity. Irish indentured servants, Dutch refugees, and Spanish and Portuguese Jews from Brazil all found their way to the islands. From 1675 to 1730, Nevis was also the headquarters of the African slave trade in the Leeward Islands. The African population eventually outnumbered Europeans ten to one.

The 19th century saw the decline of the sugar industry and the emancipation of the slaves (1833). A subsequent economic downturn was felt acutely by the African population, many of whom emigrated or protested conditions by rioting.

Riots in 1935 were followed by social and political change, including the establishment of trade unions, representative government, and universal adult suffrage (1952). The Crown Colony of St. Kitts-Nevis-Anguilla joined the short-lived West Indies Federation in 1958. In 1967, the three islands were given the status of Associated Statehood, making them responsible for their internal affairs. Anguilla left the union and later reverted to colonial status (1982). Labour Party leader Robert Bradshaw dominated the national political scene from the 1950s until 1980.

St. Kitts and Nevis have not always enjoyed harmonious relations. Independence in 1983 made their association more permanent under the leadership of Prime Minister Kennedy Simmonds. His People's Action Movement (PAM) governed from 1980 to 1995. The Labour Party won 1995 elections and Denzil Douglas became prime minister. He was reelected in March 2000.

The possibility of Nevis's secession from St. Kitts remains at the forefront of relations between the two islands. In October 1997, the five-member Nevis Island Assembly voted unanimously to invoke a constitutional provision allowing Nevis to unilaterally withdraw from St. Kitts. In a 1998 referendum, Nevisians voted for the islands to remain together. Still, independence activists garnered 62 percent of the vote, just short of the two-thirds majority needed for Nevis to secede. The Nevis Reformation Party (NRP) wants to boost the economy before again considering secession. The government is evaluating ways to revise the constitution and grant Nevis greater autonomy.

THE PEOPLE

Population. The islands' total population numbers 38,819 and is shrinking at 0.22 percent. St. Kitts is home to nearly three-fourths of that total; one-fourth lives in the capital, Basseterre. Most inhabitants are of African descent, but a small percentage are European, Lebanese, or East Indian. A large number of St. Kitts and Nevis nationals live in North America, Britain, and other Caribbean nations, but their ties to the nation remain strong. Many European and North American expatriates own vacation homes on Nevis.

Language. English is the official language, although people use a local dialect for daily informal communication. A combination of English and African words and syntax, the dialect is spoken most heavily in rural areas. It is appreciated for its colorful expressions, folk wisdom, proverbs, and riddles.

Religion. Nearly all people on the islands are Christian. The traditionally dominant churches—Anglican, Methodist, Moravian—are being challenged in prominence by a growing number of Pentecostal, Seventh-day Adventist Church, and other Christian congregations. A small number of Rastafarians and Baha'is also live on the islands.

Religious beliefs and values have a noticeable influence on daily life. Not only do people regularly attend church services, but they (especially women) also participate in other church-sponsored activities. Most children are exposed to religious teachings while growing up. Major family events such as weddings, christenings, and burials usually are observed in a church.

General Attitudes. People in St. Kitts and Nevis are sociable, outgoing, and friendly, both among themselves and toward strangers. They are flexible about time and are seldom in such a hurry that they cannot extend a greeting or engage in a conversation. Like members of most small communities, they take a keen interest in one another's affairs, and rumors and gossip are common.

People respect their social institutions, including the law. Therefore, most disputes are settled through litigation. People place considerable emphasis on personal loyalties in politics and on personal relationships with lawyers, priests, doctors, and business and community leaders. They expect equality in social interaction.

Traditionally, people in Nevis are known for their thrift and for valuing land and livestock. In St. Kitts, and generally in urban areas, greater importance is placed on material possessions such as an impressive home or a car. Residents of both islands value financial security and a good education, the traditional route to social mobility.

Personal Appearance. Except when engaged in jobs like farming or fishing that require old clothes or overalls, people are meticulous about their appearance. Women are particularly fashion conscious and they like jewelry. They also pay great attention to the grooming of their hair and that of their children.

Women usually wear dresses or skirts to work, reserving shorts and trousers for casual occasions. Swimsuits are worn only on the beach. Clothes are made of brightly colored, lightweight fabrics. People like colorful T-shirts, embroidered or tie-dyed Caribbean designs, or the latest North American fashions. The latter are popular with the youth. Children generally wear uniforms to school. Men may wear suits on formal occasions but prefer to work in light *shirt-jacs* (a pleated, square-cut shirt with pockets and light embroidery) and trousers. Jeans, shorts, and T-shirts are casual wear.

CUSTOMS AND COURTESIES

Greetings. It is important to greet people with *Good morning*, *Good afternoon*, or *Good night*. Other more informal greetings are *Howdy*, *How you do?* or *Hey, wha'happ'nin'?* When leaving, one might say *Good-bye*, *See you*, or *Take care then till next time*. Older or rural people may still say *See you soon, D.V.* (*Deus Volunte*, or God willing).

Remembering people's names is crucial. One addresses older people, those in important positions, or people one does not know well as *Mr.*, *Mrs.*, or *Miss* with their surname or, less formally, their initial (e.g., *Mr. B.*). Older women may be addressed familiarly as *Auntie*, *Mother*, or *Mama* (e.g., *Mother Saunders*, *Mama Liz*). Informally, one may also be addressed as *Darlin'*, *Me dear*, or *Sweetheart*. Many people have nicknames and seldom are called by their original names. Children are expected to address older people as *Mr.*, *Mrs.*, or *Miss* or as *Auntie* or *Uncle*.

People often touch hands or arms when meeting. A man may put his arm around a woman's shoulder or hold her hand in a friendly meeting. Hugging is more prevalent than kissing, particularly when people meet old friends and children. Formal introductions normally include a handshake.

Gestures. As in the rest of the Caribbean, individuals "talk with their hands," indeed with the whole body. Speaking is accompanied by a variety of hand and arm movements, and the livelier the discussion, the more gestures there are. Women may put their hands on their hips when arguing or as a sign of defiance or aggression. Closely approaching someone during an altercation is also considered aggressive. People shrug their shoulders to indicate uncertainty. They may pucker their mouths, toss their heads, and make a sideways motion with the thumb and hand when humorously mocking someone or indicating real derision. Individuals may purse their lips and make a sound by sucking air through their teeth (known as *sucking the teeth*) to indicate disgust or anger.

Men and younger people are expected to give up public transport seats or offer help to pregnant women, the elderly, and people with young children. Chewing gum during conversation or eating in the street is not well regarded.

Visiting.   People in St. Kitts and Nevis tend to entertain formally for family celebrations like weddings, christenings, or birthday parties or during festive seasons like Christmas. Such occasions feature a great deal of food, drink, music, and perhaps dancing. Gifts are not expected, but for an evening party a guest might bring a bottle of something to drink.

Generally, people "drop in" unannounced for short visits. Hospitality is important; hosts always welcome visitors and usually offer them a cool drink and possibly a slice of cake. On weekends, friends socialize on the veranda or in the garden. When expatriates return to the islands, they spend time visiting family members and old friends.

Eating.   The average family eats three meals a day. Breakfasts are hurried and usually consist of a hot drink, eggs, cereal, or a sandwich. In rural areas where people have been working in the fields for several hours, breakfast may be later and heavier. The main family meal used to be at midday. Increasingly, due to work and school schedules, lunch consists of a snack, and the family eats a substantial cooked meal together in the evening. This meal, preceded by grace, usually takes place around the table, but entertaining is often buffet-style. People eat out much more today than they did 15 years ago. Many eat lunch at restaurants or snack bars.

LIFESTYLE

Family.   The extended family structure is still a feature of life on the islands, but with socioeconomic changes it is gradually being eroded. Families are close-knit. Many households are headed by women who are raising their children, grandchildren, or children of parents who work abroad. Elderly relatives also may live in the home.

Middle-class people are most likely to get married and, at least initially, have a typical nuclear family. Common-law marriages are widespread among lower-income groups, and the children enjoy the same legal rights as do children of formally married couples. Men are encouraged to have contact with their children and are legally required to support them financially, even if they have not married the mother. It is not unusual for an individual, male or female, to have children by two or more partners. Women prize motherhood, while men judge their machismo by their prowess with women and the fathering of children.

In general, women have the greatest responsibility for raising children. They may also be the sole or most consistent breadwinner for the household. Most women work outside the home, traditionally as farmers, domestics, nurses, teachers, or in commercial and administrative jobs. More recently, many have found employment in the light-manufacturing sector or are self-employed in microenterprises.

Grown children are committed to improving their parents' lives by upgrading the family home and contributing to the family income, particularly if they migrate abroad. Unless they work some distance away, young unmarried people, particularly young women, continue to live with their parents.

Dating and Marriage.   Young people go out together, although parents tend to control and supervise the activities of their teenage daughters. Boys and girls meet at school and church functions, at parties, on the beach, during festive occasions, at sporting events, or at a few spots where they simply "hang out."

Older couples may spend a lot of time together, especially on weekends. People generally marry between the ages of 20 and 35. Most weddings are performed in a church. They can be quite elaborate social events with many guests.

Diet.   Popular traditional dishes in St. Kitts and Nevis include salt fish and dumplings (salted, dried codfish prepared as a stew with dumplings—a Good Friday staple), chicken and rice *pelau* with red beans or pigeon peas, and *goatwater* (spicy stew made from goat, breadfruit, and dumplings). *Souse* is prepared from pickled pigs' trotters, cucumbers, and hot peppers. *Black pudding* is made from pigs' blood, rice, and herbal stuffing.

People eat a lot of chicken and fish, both dried and fresh. Pork and mutton are also popular. Peas, beans, and lentils are important sources of protein. Bread is eaten for breakfast and snacks, while cooked staple carbohydrates include rice, breadfruit, yams, cooked cornmeal (usually eaten with steamed fish and okra), dumplings (or the fried version, *johnnycakes*), and macaroni.

Vegetables generally are cooked, although people do eat fresh lettuce and cucumbers or a coleslaw salad. Cabbage, carrots, eggplants, and sweet potatoes are also common. Local fruits include mangoes, sugar apples, soursops, pawpaws, plantains, golden apples, tomatoes, and guavas. The latter are turned into guava jelly or a sweet known as *guava cheese*.

At breakfast, people generally drink tea, coffee, *cocoa tea* (hot cocoa), or *bush tea* (herbal tea). Otherwise, they prefer cold drinks. Lunch and dinner are served with locally made lemonade, ginger beer, or drinks made from fruits like tamarinds or passion fruit. The most popular Christmas drink is *sorrel*, which is made from the petals of a sorrel plant.

Recreation.   Popular team sports include cricket, *football* (soccer), and basketball for men; netball for women; and volleyball for both. Cricket and netball are national sports. Nevis prides itself on being the Caribbean territory that, for its population size, has produced the largest number of cricketers for the West Indies cricket team. Tennis is growing in popularity.

People also go to beaches or organize picnics or hikes. Men get together in bars or elsewhere to talk, drink, and play dominoes or cards. Women meet in their homes, at church-related social activities, or at various leisure spots. People may also belong to community service clubs. Some, especially the youth, seek out nightspots and enjoy themselves at dances. Watching cable television is a favorite leisure activity. People travel frequently throughout the Eastern Caribbean to visit family and to shop. The United States, Canada, and Britain are favorite holiday destinations.

The Arts.   Many are engaged in the development of local music, drama, or folklore. Festivals such as the St. Kitts

▼ **THE AMERICAS**

Music Festival in June bring artists together to compete in reggae, calypso, jazz, *soca* (a mixture of American soul and calypso), gospel, samba, salsa, steel pan, and *merengue*. Nevis's Culturama Day provides opportunities for local artisans to display their crafts. A popular folk troupe named the Masquerades performs dances drawing on both traditional French and African sources.

The massive fortress of Brimstone Hill, constructed in the 17th and 18th centuries and since restored, is an important architectural piece. Slaves laboriously built the citadel and its 7-foot-thick walls over a period of nearly 90 years.

Holidays. National holidays include New Year's Day (1 Jan.), National *Carnival* Day (2 Jan.), Good Friday and Easter Monday, Labor Day (first Monday in May), Whitmonday (seven weeks after Easter Monday), Emancipation Day (first Monday in August), and Culturama Day (an annual August festival on Nevis). Independence Day is 19 September. The Christmas season includes Christmas day and Boxing Day (26 Dec.) and is a time for family gatherings, gift giving, and related activities. The *Carnival* season runs for a week after the 26th and includes street dancing, costumed bands, calypso competitions, beauty contests, and beach parties.

Commerce. Stores generally are open from 8 or 8:30 a.m. to 4 or 5 p.m. Smaller stores may close for lunch at noon. Many are closed on Thursday afternoon but otherwise are open Monday through Saturday. Supermarkets and corner grocery stores may stay open later in the evening. Each island has public markets for vegetables, fruits, meat, and fish. The main market days are Thursday, Friday, and Saturday, but some vendors sell their goods every weekday. Most banks open from 9 a.m. to 3 p.m., Monday through Thursday, and later on Fridays. The National Bank is open Saturday morning.

SOCIETY

Government. The Federation of St. Kitts and Nevis is a parliamentary democracy with a federal constitution. The central government is based on St. Kitts. Nevis has a local government responsible for island administration. The National Assembly has eleven elected members—eight from St. Kitts and three from Nevis. In addition, two senators are appointed by the ruling party and one by the opposition. St. Kitts and Nevis are members of the British Commonwealth. Queen Elizabeth II is head of state but is represented locally by a governor-general, Sir Cuthbert Montraville Sebastian. The voting age is 18; elections are held at least every five years.

Economy. Tourism, agriculture, and manufacturing are the most important sectors of the islands' economy. Hurricanes Georges and Lenny caused hundreds of millions of dollars in damage and slowed down the tourist industry. Sugar is the principal export, but the recent diversification of agriculture has improved domestic self-sufficiency and provided links with the tourist industry. The sugar industry and 85 percent of arable land belong to a state-run corporation. Tourism is becoming important in terms of foreign-exchange earnings and employment. Manufacturing concentrates on textiles, data processing, electronic assembly, and computer software development. More than 20 percent of the labor force is employed in agriculture, another 20 percent in manufacturing,

DEVELOPMENT DATA

Human Dev. Index* rank	47 of 174 countries
Adjusted for women	NA
Real GDP per capita	$10,672
Adult literacy rate	90 percent
Infant mortality rate	17 per 1,000 births
Life expectancy	65 (male); 71 (female)

and 13 percent in tourism. The government also employs one-fifth of the workforce. Inflation is less than 3 percent. The currency is the East Caribbean dollar (EC$).

Transportation and Communications. Cars and buses are the primary forms of transport in St. Kitts and Nevis. Private buses operate routes between main towns and rural areas. There are 190 miles (306 kilometers) of road, including the Kennedy Simmonds Highway, which has opened the southeast peninsula of St. Kitts to general development.

A government ferry operates five days a week between islands. Many private boats also ply the waters with freight and passengers or for fishing and sightseeing. St. Kitts has an international airport and Nevis is expanding its airport.

Most people have at least one radio; 70 percent have access to television. More than half of all households have a telephone. Two national newspapers, *The Democrat* and the *Labour Spokesman*, are owned by the major political parties. Regional newspapers from neighboring islands are also available. One government and one private television station broadcast to the nation. Cable television is also available.

Education. The education system consists of preschool, primary, secondary, and some postsecondary facilities. Education is free and accessible to all. Children are required to attend school between the ages of five and sixteen. A majority of children who enroll in school finish the primary level. About two-thirds of enrolled children pass to the secondary level. The dropout rate is higher among boys. Students who complete their secondary education can obtain vocational and technical education in the country. They also may attend a teacher-training program or study other subjects. For a university degree, students study at the University of West Indies in Jamaica, Barbados, or Trinidad or go abroad elsewhere.

Health. Four hospitals and 17 clinics comprise the national health-care system. There are fewer than 50 doctors. Health care is subsidized by the government, especially for lower-income groups. The government also is upgrading equipment and training to improve care. Hospitals in Jamaica, Barbados, and Guadeloupe take patients whose needs cannot be met on St. Kitts or Nevis. The nation has an excellent child immunization program.

CONTACT INFORMATION

Embassy of St. Kitts and Nevis, 3216 New Mexico Avenue NW, Washington, DC 20016; phone (202) 686-2636; Web site www.stkittsnevis.org.

CultureGrams™
People. The World. You.

1305 North Research Way, Bldg. K
Orem, Utah 84097-6200 USA
1.800.528.6279; 801.705.4250
fax 801.705.4350
www.culturegrams.com

Saint Lucia

Boundary representations are not necessarily authoritative.

▼ THE AMERICAS

BACKGROUND

Land and Climate.   Saint Lucia, often called the Helen of the West Indies for its beauty, lies about 1,300 miles (2,092 kilometers) southeast of Florida. It covers 239 square miles (620 square kilometers) and is about three times as large as Washington, D.C. The Caribbean Sea lies to the west of the island, while the Atlantic Ocean lies to the east. Saint Lucia is a volcanic island with a subtropical climate. As such, it is mountainous and has a lush interior rain forest. The town of Soufrière is near the island's volcanic center. Both black and white sand beaches are found on the island. Saint Lucia's two seasons (wet and dry) tend to be warm, with December to May the driest months and June to August the hottest. The rainy season (and hurricane season) extends from June to November; as much as 160 inches of rain can fall. Constant trade winds moderate the temperatures year-round. The average highs are 80°F to 90°F (26–32°C).

History.   Saint Lucia originally was inhabited by Arawak Indians. By A.D. 800, they were replaced by Carib Indians. Christopher Columbus is said to have "discovered" Saint Lucia in 1498, but that event is now discounted. The first English settlers came in 1605 and the French arrived in 1651. Eight years later, the two groups began fighting over land ownership. Hostilities endured for 150 years and Saint Lucia changed hands between the powers 14 times. The Caribs moved out and African slaves were imported to work on plantations. Saint Lucia finally was ceded to the British in 1814, when France lost the Napoleonic Wars.

Saint Lucia remained a British colony until 1967, when the West Indies Act extended self-rule over internal affairs. Full independence came in 1979, although Saint Lucia remains a member of the Commonwealth.

John Compton's United Workers Party (UWP) prevailed in internal affairs from 1964 until independence, when the opposition Saint Lucia Labour Party (SLP) managed to take office. By 1981, public discontent with the SLP led its leaders to resign, and John Compton became prime minister. The UWP dominated politics during the 1980s and early 1990s. However, the SLP won a landslide victory in 1997 elections, winning 16 of 17 seats in Parliament. Dr. Kenny Anthony is prime minister. The government has promised to diversify the economy, create jobs, and offer tax relief.

THE PEOPLE

Population.   Saint Lucia's population of about 156,260 is growing annually at 1.21 percent. The majority of the people (90 percent) descend from African slaves. Five percent are of mixed heritage. Saint Lucians of East Indian descent (3 percent) live mostly in rural areas; their ancestors came as indentured laborers after slavery was abolished. Many urban merchants are of Syrian origin, and a small number of people with European heritage also live in Saint Lucia. Castries, the capital, is home to nearly 40 percent of the population.

Language.   English is the official language. It is used in school instruction, government, and business. While most people speak English, some rural Saint Lucians are not fluent. Creole or *patois*, an oral language developed during French colonial rule, is the primary tongue for most rural and many urban residents. Except among the upper class, it is the language of daily communication. Urban residents often mix *patois* and

English in conversation. There is a movement to preserve *patois* and develop a written form that could be taught in school.

Religion. Religion plays an important role in the lives of most Saint Lucians. Business meetings, meals, the school day, and other events open with prayer. Most community activities are church sponsored or related. Roman Catholicism is practiced by about 80 percent of the population. Most other Saint Lucians are Christians of other denominations, including Seventh-day Adventist Church (7 percent), Pentecostal (3), and Anglican (2).

General Attitudes. Saint Lucians view themselves as friendly and accepting of others. They tend to be laid-back and make fun of others' perceived pretensions. Saint Lucians can be confrontational at times, quickly engaging in an argument or (more rarely) a fight. But just as harsh words are easily spoken, tempers cool readily and conflicts are soon forgotten. Long-term confrontations are avoided because of local gossip.

While Saint Lucians admire punctuality, they believe the pace of life should not be governed by the clock. Hence, on "Lucian time" everything starts late and no one expects otherwise. People do not like to schedule rigid appointments due to the belief that events occur by the grace of God.

Class divisions cause tension among some Saint Lucians. Prejudices are expressed verbally but rarely rise to a level of hatred or violence. The concept of coexistence prevails, and the country enjoys overall unity. Saint Lucian men express traditional West Indian male dominance over women through macho acts or sexually oriented language. Professional or otherwise economically independent Saint Lucian women are becoming less tolerant of this attitude and are increasingly seeking partnerships based on equality and respect. Saint Lucian women with fewer opportunities in life try to ignore the macho attitude or resign themselves to it as part of life.

Personal Appearance. Saint Lucians try to dress neatly in unwrinkled, modest clothing. Bathing suits, short skirts, and other revealing clothing are not appropriate away from resort areas. Children must be dressed properly for church and social functions.

Attire indicates social status and occupation. Employees of many banks, hotels, and schools wear uniforms. Professional women might wear a skirt and blouse to work. Men often wear a *shirt-jac*: a pleated, square-cut shirt with pockets and light embroidery. The youth prefer U.S. American fashions, especially jeans, denim shirts, shorts, and skirts. Young urban men sometimes wear gold necklaces with medallions. Men also might let their pinkie fingernails grow long.

Some people wear the national costume for cultural events. Men have black trousers, a white shirt, and a cummerbund. Women wear a red-and-orange-checked skirt with a white frill underskirt, a white blouse with a triangle of checked fabric over one shoulder, and a fabric hat that is tied differently depending on one's marital status.

CUSTOMS AND COURTESIES

Greetings. Greeting strangers, acquaintances, and friends is important. Formal greetings include *Good morning*, *Good afternoon*, and *Good night*. Such a phrase is expected when one enters a place of business or boards public transportation. Between people passing on the street, a nod or short greeting (*Alright*, *Morning*, *Afternoon*, *Evening*) is acceptable.

Greetings between friends are less formal. In *patois*, *Sa ka fet?* (What's happening?) is common. In English, an enthusiastic *Alright?* may be exchanged. Among friends, men might high-five, *jam* (lightly touch closed fists), or shake hands vigorously; women pat each other on the shoulder or brush a hand against the other's upper arm.

Nicknames are ubiquitous. In many cases, Saint Lucians are referred to by nickname almost exclusively; one might not even know an acquaintance's given name. Daily radio obituaries list both the given name and nickname of an individual. Nicknames are derived from one's physical appearance, given name, characteristics, or an experience. For example, *Sparks* (meaning intelligent and knowledgeable) may be a nickname for a highly educated man.

Adults often address children as *ish mwe* (my child), *ti ma mai* (my little one), *ti fi* (little girl), or *ti boy* (little boy). Out of respect, younger people call older ones *auntie*, *uncle*, *mummy*, or *daddy*—even if not related. When titles (*Mr.*, *Miss*, *Teacher*, etc.) are used, they often are combined with a given name. Married, divorced, or widowed women may be called *Mrs.* or *Mistress*, followed by their husband's given name or nickname. As a Creole society, Saint Lucians also may address women as *Ma* or *Madam*. Male peers often address one another as *garçon* (*patois* equivalent of "man" or "dude"), tacking the term on to the end of a statement or question.

Gestures. When conversing, Saint Lucians express emotions with their face and hands. Clapping hands to show excitement or while laughing is common. Bending over while laughing is also common. People often nod to show agreement or shake their heads to show disapproval during conversation. Discussions may be punctuated with "eh-eh," which can mean disapproval, concern, or disbelief. People sometimes express extreme irritation by sucking air through closed teeth (known as *choopsing*). Saint Lucians will point to indicate direction, but to get another's attention, they say "pssst."

Visiting. Saint Lucians visit friends and relatives often and unannounced. Visits rarely are the result of a formal invitation. People never seem too busy to stop at a friend's home. When one drops by, it is customary to first call out a greeting from outside the home. The residents may come out and engage in leisurely conversation. The visitors may or may not be invited inside for a drink or snack. The closer the people are, the more likely the invitation will be extended. Guests remove their shoes when they enter the home.

Arranged visits occur most often on weekends. One may be invited to a *fête* (party) or on an excursion to another part of the island. For a *fête*, it is acceptable but not required for guests to bring a beverage or food item to share. Evening parties start late and continue into the early morning hours. If a meal is served, it might be as late as 11 p.m.

Eating. Saint Lucians usually rise early to begin work or chores before the hottest part of the day (11 a.m. to 3 p.m.). Therefore, they may eat breakfast early (before 7 a.m.). Breakfast usually is light, consisting of locally baked bread and butter. It may be accompanied by a hot drink, such as *tea* (green tea), coffee, or *cocoa tea* (Ovaltine).

Lunch (referred to as *dinner* or *the food*) is usually the main meal. Most Saint Lucians begin preparing it in the morning before work. They return home at midday to enjoy the meal, which consists of rice, meat or fish, *peas* (any legume—including lentils, red beans, pigeon peas, etc.), *ground provisions* (foods grown in the ground, such as sweet potatoes or other root vegetables), and locally grown fruit (breadfruit, plantains, and bananas). Unripe bananas might be boiled and put in salads. For people unable to return home for *the food*, the main meal is supper. Otherwise, supper consists of bread and butter, fried fish or tinned meat, sometimes cheese, and tea. On Sundays, people eat a large meal in the early afternoon. It consists of meat or chicken, rice, *peas*, macaroni and cheese, and perhaps a *ground provision*. For special occasions, a goat or sheep may be roasted or stewed.

The spoon is the most common utensil used for lunch and supper. Even in traditional settings, Saint Lucians will make a spoon from a calabash to eat with. Children might eat before the adults, especially when guests are present. To show appreciation for a meal, guests accept offers of second helpings.

LIFESTYLE

Family. Two or more generations often live together, but large traditional families are no longer the trend. Grandparents and other members of the extended family might help raise children and do household chores. Saint Lucia has many single-parent families. Except among the elite and well educated, it is not uncommon to have a female head of household and several generations with no adult men. Men often date even when married; many consider it macho to father babies by different *baby mothers*. Even as a woman's partners change, her children remain with her and are raised together with half siblings. If the mother cannot care for a child, another relative or even a friend might raise it. Saint Lucian society, as well as the law, is pressing fathers to take more financial responsibility for their offspring.

Adult children usually remain home until they marry. If they remain in their parents' home after marrying or having children, they are expected to help maintain the household. While some apartments are found in Castries, most families have their own homes. Private ownership is high (more than 70 percent). The property on which the home sits may have been in the family for several generations. Urban houses are made of concrete and may be built on stilts. Rural houses may be built of concrete or brightly painted wood planks. Both styles have corrugated tin roofs. Around a home, families often plant a small garden with tropical flowers and *ground provisions*. Houses are small and simple, decorated with locally made wrought iron or wooden furnishings, as well as curtains and other accessories made from imported fabric.

Dating and Marriage. Most Saint Lucians date individuals they know from their community. Relationships also may develop through school or church attendance and activities. Men prefer to date several women simultaneously, but more women are demanding monogamous relationships.

While marriage and monogamy are considered important, Saint Lucians often do not get married or commit to one partner. Instead, they may live together in common-law arrangements. More dedicated couples marry after they have built a house, have begun to raise a family, or have lived together for a number of years. Common-law marriages are increasingly being recognized by the legal system for the purpose of child support and other family matters.

Diet. Rice, *ground provisions*, and *peas* are staples. Beef and chicken are both imported and raised locally. Certain fish (red snapper, dolphin, and tuna) are expensive and considered delicacies. Conch, goat, and sheep are eaten for special occasions. Saint Lucians commonly utilize the entire animal in cooking; a favorite dish consists of a pig's feet, snout, and tail simmered in vegetable broth.

Cabbage, tomatoes, peppers, and onions are used in small quantities to garnish a dish. Seasonal fruits include tamarinds, oranges, limes, guavas, mangoes, passion fruits, papayas, and golden apples; they often are made into juice. Mangoes are peeled and eaten whole. Ginger tea is made with fresh ground ginger, sugar, and boiling water. Herbal teas are made from local plants for medicinal purposes. *Coconut water*, drunk from green or immature coconut shells, is available year-round.

Urban residents (in Castries and Vieux Fort) eat more imported foods (like canned fruit juice, frozen chicken, cheese, and canned or powdered milk). They also are more likely to eat in restaurants. Rural people rely on produce grown in their gardens, fruit they pick from local trees, or livestock they raise themselves. Locally caught fish is available near coastal villages. A common rural meal is the *one-pot* stew that is cooked on an outdoor coal pot.

Recreation. *Football* (soccer) is Saint Lucia's most popular sport, closely followed by cricket. Community leagues provide organized competition, but teams also may play against squads from other West Indian nations. Men listen to broadcasts of cricket matches in other nations and World Wrestling Federation events. Saint Lucians love to play dominoes for pleasure or for gambling.

Carnival provides Saint Lucians with a chance to dance, sing, and participate in calypso talent contests. Many people compete for the title of Calypso King and Queen; everyone follows the event closely. Winners are featured at *Carnival* events and hold the title for one year. Several weeks of preparation precede the calypso contests and *Jouvert*, a street parade that begins at sunrise with bands and costumed marchers. Spectators often join the parade.

Most people watch videos and enjoy U.S. American television shows. The island's first cinema opened in Vieux Fort in 1997. Others are planned for Gros Islet and Castries. Saint Lucians go to the local beach for a barbecue or *fête*. Beach parties are usually impressive, with plenty of food served to casually dressed guests. The primary purpose of these events is to socialize and eat, not to swim or play beach sports.

The Arts. As is the case in most Caribbean nations, music plays an important role in society. Local music is heavily influenced by Jamaican reggae. Saint Lucians also enjoy calypso, *soca* (a mixture of American soul and calypso), *dub* (related to rap), U.S. American country, and *cadance* (lively dancing music from the French Antilles). Quadrille dancing is also popular. Saint Lucia hosts a world-renowned jazz festival each May at Pigeon Point.

The French, English, African, and Caribbean influences on Saint Lucia have produced a unique blend of cultural arts. Architecture often follows European designs, although African styles and bright colors are also prevalent.

Holidays. Christmas is the primary religious holiday. The Christmas season begins 13 December, which is also

National Day (previously called Discovery Day for Christopher Columbus). The Christmas Eve midnight mass is widely attended. Special festivities begin after mass and continue into Christmas day. On Boxing Day (26 Dec.), Saint Lucians like to relax and visit. Visitors may come throughout the holiday season, and people save for months to fix up their homes and have special foods to serve their many guests. Visits continue through New Year's. On New Year's Eve (*Old Year's Night*), friends and relatives toast the coming year at each home they visit.

Independence Day (22 Feb.) marks independence from Britain. At Easter, the emphasis is on family and religion. Labour Day is 1 May. *Carnival* takes place in July. Emancipation Day (first Monday in August) commemorates the end of slavery. Thanksgiving is held on the first Monday in October. Local festivals, such as *Jounet Creole* (Creole Day, celebrated 31 October), are held in various communities throughout the year.

Commerce.   Weekday office hours are 8 a.m. to 4 p.m.; banks close an hour earlier. Stores keep the same basic hours but are also open on Saturday until 12:30 p.m. Some local minimarkets or small malls have extended evening hours. Castries has an open-air produce market that stays open until the food is sold or until dusk. Most stores close on Sunday.

SOCIETY

Government.   Saint Lucia is a parliamentary democracy that recognizes Britain's Queen Elizabeth II as head of state. She is officially represented by Her Excellency Dr. Pearlette Louisy, the island's first female governor-general. Prime Minister Kenny Anthony, who leads the SLP, is head of government. In the bicameral Parliament, the House of Assembly's 17 members are directly elected for five-year terms; the Senate's 11 members are appointed. All citizens are required to vote beginning at age 18.

Economy.   Saint Lucia's economy historically has been based on agricultural production for trade with Britain. Bananas are the most important export, but the export of winter vegetables and organically grown produce is expanding. Expecting trends within the European Union to adversely affect Saint Lucia's trading position with Britain, the island has sought since 1990 to develop its tourism industry. New hotels and the supporting infrastructure have been built along the beaches surrounding Castries, Soufrière, and Vieux Fort to attract U.S. American, Canadian, and European tourists.

Saint Lucia does not have the resources to be self-sufficient and must import foods, fuel, and manufactured goods. Unemployment (around 18 percent) and underemployment are serious problems. Inflation remains low, around 3 percent. Although most people have access to education and health care, economic opportunities are limited. Many people go overseas in search of work. Remittances from these workers provide vital income for Saint Lucia. Light manufacturing is controlled mostly by foreign firms. The East Caribbean dollar (EC$) is Saint Lucia's currency.

Transportation and Communications.   Saint Lucia's main paved road runs the perimeter of the island. Several miles of it

© 2001 CultureGrams, a division of Millennial Star Network and Brigham Young University. It is against the law to copy, reprint, store, or transmit any part of this publication in any form by any means without written permission from CultureGrams. This document contains native commentary and original analysis, as well as estimated statistics. The content should not be considered strictly factual, and it may not apply to all groups in a nation. *UN Development Programme, Human Development Report 2000 (New York: Oxford University Press, 2000).

DEVELOPMENT DATA

Human Dev. Index* rank	88 of 174 countries
Adjusted for women	NA
Real GDP per capita	$5,183
Adult literacy rate	82 percent (male); 58 (female)
Infant mortality rate	16 per 1,000 births
Life expectancy	68 (male); 76 (female)

were constructed around Vieux Fort in World War II by U.S. military units wanting easy access to their airport, now Hewanorra International. All towns and villages are connected to the main road. Most urban streets are paved, but rural and other roads are not. Certain remote areas cannot be reached by road. On paved roads, the most popular form of travel is the *transport*. These private minivans run regular routes. They leave from a central location when full and pick up/drop off passengers along the way. They often have a name or slogan painted on them; fares depend on where passengers board and exit. Many Saint Lucians also own cars, and it is common for drivers to stop and offer pedestrians a ride.

Saint Lucians without phones have access to public phones. Radio and television broadcasts reach most people. Radio is the main source of news; people are well-informed on local and regional matters.

Education.   Education, based on the British system, is compulsory for children ages five to fifteen. Uniforms are required. About 80 percent of all eligible children attend school. Children are sometimes taken out of school to work on family banana farms.

At age 11, students take the Common Entrance Exam to determine where they will go to secondary school. The government plans to expand and upgrade the secondary school system to accommodate all who wish to attend. Those who finish secondary school can take the Caribbean Examination Council (CXC) exam to enter Sir Arthur Lewis Community College. To graduate from there, students must take the British "A" level exam in one or more chosen disciplines (arts, science, general studies, teacher education, nursing, technical education, or management studies). To complete a full college degree, students must transfer to the University of West Indies in Jamaica, Barbados, or Trinidad. Some students gain an education abroad. Saint Lucia is proud to have produced two Nobel laureates: Sir Arthur Lewis (Economics, 1979) and Derek Walcott (Literature, 1992).

Health.   Saint Lucia is striving to provide health care to all citizens. Free or low-cost care is available at public clinics and urban hospitals. Rural clinics are staffed by nurses, many of whom live on site; doctors visit weekly. Private doctors serve those who can afford their fees.

CONTACT INFORMATION

Embassy of Saint Lucia, 3216 New Mexico Avenue NW, Washington, DC 20016; phone (202) 364-6792. Saint Lucia Tourist Board, 800 Second Avenue, Ninth Floor, New York, NY 10017; phone (800) 456-3984; Web site www.stlucia.org.

CultureGrams™
People. The World. You.

1305 North Research Way, Bldg. K
Orem, Utah 84097-6200 USA
1.800.528.6279; 801.705.4250
fax 801.705.4350
www.culturegrams.com

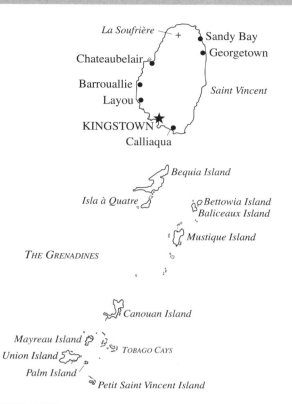

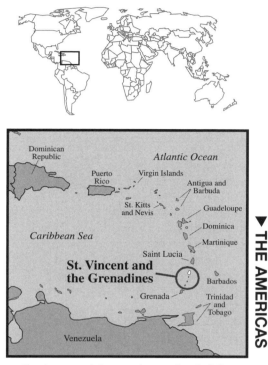

Boundary representations are not necessarily authoritative.

BACKGROUND

Land and Climate. Saint Vincent and the Grenadines consists of a chain of more than 30 volcanic and coral islands. St. Vincent (locally called *the mainland*) is a lush volcanic island with steep mountain ridges, valleys, and waterfalls. Its highest peak, the La Soufrière volcano, rises to 3,864 feet (1,178 meters) at the northern end of its mountain backbone. After an eruption in 1902 that took two thousand lives, La Soufrière lay dormant until the 1970s, when an active phase culminated in an eruption in 1979. No lives were lost and since then the volcano has been relatively stable. From the island's central mountains, numerous streams flow east and west through the valleys to the sea.

The Grenadine Islands, which include many small coral cays, stretch between St. Vincent and Grenada (75 miles to the south). The Tobago Cays are being developed into a marine park. Palm Island and Petit St. Vincent are private resorts. Mustique, home to a number of wealthy foreigners, is owned by the Mustique Company. The combined land area of all the nation's islands is 150 square miles (389 square kilometers).

Temperatures vary according to elevation and time of year, ranging between 64°F and 90°F (18–32°C). The coast is usually warm. The dry season extends from December to June, and the rainy season lasts the rest of the year. Hurricanes can threaten the area between June and October. In 1999, Hurricane Lenny caused widespread damage.

History. Prior to European domination that began in the 18th century, St. Vincent and the Grenadines was home to various Amerindian tribes that had migrated from South and Central America. One early group was the peaceful Arawak, a tribe of skilled potters who also engaged in farming and fishing. By A.D. 1000, the more warlike Caribs overtook the Arawak on islands throughout the Caribbean. The Caribs called St. Vincent *Hairouna* (Home of the Blessed).

The traditional belief that Christopher Columbus landed on St. Vincent in 1498 has been refuted, but the island certainly was known to sailors and traders during his day. The Caribs did not treat well those Europeans who landed there, so sailing vessels avoided St. Vincent for more than two hundred years. The Caribs did welcome other Caribs who had been defeated by Europeans on other islands, as well as escaped and freed African slaves. The Africans mixed with the Caribs and became known as Black Caribs, while the original Caribs were called Yellow Caribs because of their fair skin. Together, they proved nearly invincible to European conquerors. However, when the Black Caribs began to dominate the Yellow Caribs, the latter agreed to let the French build a settlement on St. Vincent in 1719.

The Black Caribs continued to resist the Europeans, and St. Vincent was declared a neutral island in 1748. For years, the French, British, and Black Caribs all struggled to control the island. In 1795, the great Carib chief Chatoyer (the island's first national hero) was killed in battle by the British. His death allowed the British to eventually (in 1797) defeat the remaining five thousand Black Caribs and banish them to the Honduran peninsula. The remnant of the Yellow Caribs retreated to the island's northern tip, where their descendants live today.

For most of the colonial period, sugarcane production was the source of economic wealth. British landowners imported African slaves to work on their plantations. When slavery was phased out between 1834 and 1838, the African-origin population exceeded that of the Europeans, but most freed slaves could do little more than engage in subsistence agriculture. Some became skilled artisans. Gradually, plantation owners brought in Portuguese and Indian indentured laborers, whose descendants live on the island today.

Until 1969, St. Vincent and the Grenadines was part of the Windward Islands colony. It then became an associated state with Britain, meaning it had internal autonomy but not full independence. In 1979, the nation became an independent state within the Commonwealth and improved socially and economically through the 1980s and 1990s.

Economic turmoil increased in the late 1990s as a World Trade Organization ruling favored a U.S. challenge to the European banana regime in the Caribbean. Some farmers have abandoned banana cultivation in favor of tourism and other economic activity. In June 1998, Prime Minister James Mitchell of the New Democratic Party (NDP) was reelected narrowly to a fourth term. In 2000, Mitchell resigned, leaving Arniham Eustace, the former finance minister, as prime minister. In March 2001 elections, the opposition Unity Labour Party (ULP) won with a landslide majority, ending the NDP's 16-year domination of politics. Dr. Ralph Gonsalves was proclaimed prime minister. His government plans to attract more jobs to the islands and encourage foreign investment.

THE PEOPLE

Population. St. Vincent's population of 115,461 includes the 10,000 people who live on various Grenadine Islands. The population is growing at about 0.43 percent annually. Most people are of African descent, either entirely or in part. Many people are also part English, Scottish, Portuguese, East Indian, or Carib. Caribs live mainly at Sandy Bay. A growing number of Syrians live on St. Vincent and are active in the retail clothing industry. Ethnic patterns in the Grenadines are about the same as those on St. Vincent, although Bequia's population is more a mixture of Carib, African, and European peoples.

Language. English is the official language of St. Vincent and the Grenadines, but the French influence of the past has not been lost. Some villages, mountains, and islands still carry French names. A West African influence is also evident in the informal dialect people speak. Words like *boutou* (insult) and *nyam* (eat) stem from African languages, but phrases like *me na able* (I can't cope) illustrate how the dialect is English based.

Religion. Most residents in St. Vincent and the Grenadines are Christians. About one-third of the people belong to the Anglican Church. One-fourth belong to either the Roman Catholic or Methodist faiths. Smaller congregations include Pentecostal churches, the Baptist Church, the Seventh-day Adventist Church, The Church of Jesus Christ of Latter-day Saints, the Salvation Army, Jehovah's Witness, and Baha'i. Nondenominational prayer groups are gaining popularity. Christianity is an important part of daily life. Schools begin and end the day with prayer. Most public and private functions also begin with prayer.

Rastafarians are few in number but have a significant impact on popular Caribbean culture. They are comprised mainly of African descendants who regard Africa as the promised land and Ethiopia's late ruler, Haile Selassie, as "the living God."

General Attitudes. Vincentians are friendly and hospitable by nature. They place great emphasis on family, church, and education. They are known for their honesty, kindness, and willingness to share their resources and time with each other as necessary. Social status often is measured by wealth and family name. People from all classes of society take great pride in the appearance of their homes. Vincentians are relaxed in their approach to time and schedules; therefore, meetings and events do not necessarily begin on time. U.S. American culture and values introduced via television are changing people's lifestyles.

Personal Appearance. Vincentian dress is casual, conservative, and neat. A professional atmosphere prevails in offices and businesses, where women wear dresses or dress suits and men wear shirt jackets and dress pants or suits and ties. In many businesses and in all commercial banks, employees wear uniforms. All primary- and secondary-school students also wear uniforms. In less formal settings, women wear casual cotton tops with slacks or shorts. Men wear jeans or shorts with T-shirts or open-neck shirts. Vincentians do not wear swimwear on the street or in shops and restaurants. Youth dress varies from traditional jeans and T-shirts to U.S. American rapper styles and Jamaican *dance hall* styles.

People buy imported clothing but also favor the creations of the many local tailors and seamstresses. Vincentians dress up for weddings, funerals, and festive occasions. Much emphasis is placed on hairstyling, and the many hair salons offer braiding, perming, cutting, and straightening. Rastafarians, both men and women, wear their hair in dreadlocks. Men also may shave their head or wear *pigtails* (a long, single plait at the back of the head).

CUSTOMS AND COURTESIES

Greetings. Greetings depend largely on the occasion and the relationship between the persons meeting. On the street, people use *Good morning*, *Good afternoon*, and *Good evening* to greet friends and strangers. Friends also might offer an informal *How you do?* or *How things?* to which *Good, good* and *Everything alright* are frequent responses. Friends and youth may use such local informal phrases as *Big up* (Hello), *Respect* (I respect you/It's nice to meet you), *Making a turn* (I am leaving), or *More times* (Until we meet again).

Fisting (hitting fists together) often replaces a handshake or embrace between friends when coming or going. *Fisting* is also typically used by West Indian cricketers (batsman) to congratulate each other on good strokes (scoring a boundary). Men and boys frequently greet with backslapping and a variety of handshakes. Relatives often kiss and hug when greeting.

Elders or authority figures usually are addressed as *Sir*, *Mistress*, or *Miss*. Professional titles are used with surnames when appropriate. Friends usually use aliases (also called *a.k.a.*). For example, West Indies cricketer Nehemiah Perry is *a.k.a. Johnny*. Affectionately descriptive nicknames like *Tall boy*, *Shortie*, or *Yellowman* are also common.

Gestures. Vincentians are usually very demonstrative while speaking. They often use their hands to reinforce an issue, point out a person or object, or show emotion. They may use facial expressions to communicate feelings, shrug their shoulders to express futility, or *stewps* (suck air through their teeth) when exasperated. Friends in casual settings often *stewps*, but it can be considered rude when used as a response or when done in the presence of elders. Staring someone in the eye, called *bad eye*, is used to display anger. Throwing the hand in the air as if brushing the air with the back of the hand is considered a curse gesture. People sometimes hiss "pssst" to get someone's attention. "Excuse me" and "Pardon me" commonly are spoken.

Visiting.   Vincentians enjoy visiting each other on an informal basis. Friends may drop in while passing by, announcing their arrival by calling from the gate or sounding the car horn. Calling in advance is also polite. Sunday afternoons and public holidays are popular times for visiting, and visitors commonly take small gifts of fruit, plants, vegetables, or local preserves. Sunday visiting often includes the whole family.

However spontaneous a visit, guests always are offered some refreshment, including fruit juice, tea, soda, or an alcoholic beverage with perhaps some home-baked cake or pie. In rural areas, people frequently remove their shoes at the front door, but this is rarely done in cities. The custom of frequent visiting is one reason many Vincentians take such pride in their homes.

Eating.   Family members often eat at different times during the week, so lunch on Sunday is an important family meal. Sunday breakfasts also tend to be larger than those served during the week. Sunday evening meals usually are light. Weekday breakfasts are light and often eaten hurriedly. After work or school, people have a snack while waiting for the evening meal, which is served after 6 p.m. Most businesses and schools close for lunch between noon and 1 p.m. However, as life becomes increasingly hectic, more people bring their lunch to work or buy snacks instead of going home to eat. Families usually say a prayer to express thanks and bless the meal.

Entertaining at home continues to be a popular way of getting together with friends. Meals for these occasions range from an informal *cook-up* to very formal dinners with several courses. Unexpected visitors at mealtimes usually are invited to stay and eat.

LIFESTYLE

Family.   The extended family is important to the social fabric in St. Vincent and the Grenadines. Since migration and emigration are primary avenues to financial progress, parents often leave their children in the care of grandparents, aunts, and uncles.

Family ties are usually strong, and families frequently come together on Sundays, holidays, and special occasions. Children often remain at home, regardless of age, until they marry or set up a permanent common-law relationship with someone. Common-law marriages are more prevalent than formal marriages. Many households are headed by single mothers or grandmothers.

Dating and Marriage.   Young teens are not encouraged to date, so serious dating begins around age 17. Youth often mix in family settings, at school and church functions, social events (e.g., fairs and concerts), and through service clubs. Dating couples do not display affection in public. Once parents or guardians accept a relationship, the couple will meet often at each other's homes. Each person comes to be regarded as part of both families. Weddings usually are held on Saturday afternoons at a church, with a formal reception following at the bride's home or at a resort.

Diet.   The main staples are rice, bananas, breadfruit, and ground provisions. Locally grown staple foods include sweet potatoes, yams, pumpkins, and plantains. Legumes and vegetables are also commonly eaten. Much of the country's food is imported, but the government seeks to better use St. Vincent's fertile soil. Fish and shellfish caught by local fishermen complement the diet, as do local or imported meat and poultry. A variety of local fruits (sugar apples, golden apples, *plumroses*, soursops, papayas, mangoes, bananas, and others) are sold at the central market and at occasional roadside stands. Some favorite Vincentian dishes are fried *jack fish* and roasted breadfruit, *pelau* (brown rice cooked with chicken), *boilin'* (fish boiled with green bananas and vegetables), and *boul-joul* (salted codfish sautéed in olive oil with vegetables). Seasonal fruits often are made into nutritious drinks.

Recreation.   Cricket, *football* (soccer), and netball (for girls) are popular spectator sports. Cricket is especially loved, and Sunday village matches are a recreational focal point for men. Many successful Vincentian cricketers first developed their skills at these matches. St. Vincent and the Grenadines has one of the leading netball teams in the Caribbean. Track-and-field meets are held throughout the school system just before Easter break. Table tennis and squash are two indoor sports gaining popularity. On weekends, men gather on porches or in bars to play cards, checkers, or dominoes for hours. Car racing also is becoming increasingly popular.

Friends and relatives of all ages enjoy getting together for beach picnics and river cookouts. In the Grenadines, people like to swim, windsurf, and water-ski. The cinema is popular, but more people watch movies at home. On Friday nights, many Vincentians dance away the stress of the week. Adults also socialize in local bars, restaurants, and nightclubs.

The Arts.   Drama and dance theater receive tremendous support, and music festivals attract individual and choral groups island wide. Reggae and calypso music are popular, and many listen and dance to *soca* (a mix of U.S. American soul and calypso). Festivals often include music and dancing: *Carnival* features street dances and a children's parade of bands, people dance to the music of calypsos and carols at predawn street parties during Nine Mornings (see "Holidays"), and formal dances are held on Old Year's Night.

Holidays.   New Year's Day (1 Jan.) usually is celebrated with family reunions. It follows Old Year's Night (New Year's Eve), a time for *cook-ups* at home and church services. People often spend St. Vincent and the Grenadines Day (22 Jan.) visiting or at the beach. Easter weekend begins with Good Friday, the most important day of the year to attend religious services. It is customary to eat hot cross buns for breakfast and salmon or mackerel for lunch on this day. The weekend, including Easter Monday, offers such festivities as the Easterval water sports on Union Island and the sailing regatta at Bequia. Labor Day is 1 May.

Carnival is the biggest cultural event. Celebrations during the first two weeks in July coincide with Caricom Day (second Monday in July, celebrating Caribbean unity). *Carnival* includes the Miss *Carnival* Show (a beauty pageant) and the *Dimanche Gras*, *J'Ouvert*, and Mardi Gras shows. August Monday (first Monday in August) marks the abolition of slavery. Independence Day (27 Oct.) is observed with an official parade.

Nine Mornings, a uniquely Vincentian celebration, takes place during the nine days before Christmas (25 Dec.). It supposedly originated during slavery when the slaves who drove their masters to early morning *novenas* (nine days of prayer) would spend their time chatting and window-shopping. Nowadays, Nine Morning revelers go walking, swimming, window-shopping, and cycling. Boxing Day (26 Dec.) is a day to relax and visit.

Commerce. Businesses generally open weekdays at 8 a.m. and close at 4 p.m., with an hour break for lunch at noon. Banks usually close at 1 p.m., except on Fridays when they reopen between 3 and 5 p.m. Businesses, but not banks, are open on Saturdays until noon. As commercial activity becomes increasingly centered in the capital, traffic jams are more common and more people are bustling about on Fridays and the days before public holidays.

Most of St. Vincent's retail and grocery businesses are located in or near Kingstown, which also boasts a newly remodeled central market that features fresh produce, boutiques, and specialty shops. Refrigerated fish and meat markets in the area recently have been rebuilt. Local people control most of the food trade, but retailing and wholesale enterprises often have some foreign input or ties.

SOCIETY

Government. As a member of the Commonwealth, St. Vincent and the Grenadines recognizes Queen Elizabeth II of Britain as its nominal head of state. She is represented by a governor-general (Charles Antrobus). The House of Assembly consists of fifteen elected representatives and six appointed senators (two of whom are nominated by the opposition). The ULP gained 12 seats in the 2001 elections, and the NDP took the other 3. The prime minister is head of government. He or she and the cabinet of ministers constitute the country's highest decision-making body. Elections take place every five years. The voting age is 18.

Economy. St. Vincent's economy relies heavily on agriculture, which employs 60 percent of the labor force. Bananas account for nearly three-quarters of the island's export earnings. However, destructive tropical storms such as Hurricane Lenny and increasing competition for global markets have highlighted the need for the islands to diversify their economy. Tourism and light industry are growing with the influx of foreign investment. This is especially true of the large hotels in the Grenadines and the flour and rice mills on St. Vincent. Financial institutions and the retail/wholesale trade also are growing and providing jobs. Despite these advances, the country suffers from high unemployment, which is officially 20 percent but may be closer to 40 percent. The government remains the largest single employer. Most people earn an income sufficient to meet their needs, and economic opportunities are improving. The currency is the East Caribbean dollar (EC$).

Transportation and Communications. Numerous minivans with colorful names such as *Wonder Not*, *Soon Come*, and *Rat Race* provide schoolchildren and workers with commuter service along fixed routes. Taxis are common but unmetered.

DEVELOPMENT DATA

Human Dev. Index* rank .... 79 of 174 countries
    Adjusted for women .... NA
Real GDP per capita $4,692
Adult literacy rate .... 82 percent
Infant mortality rate .... 17 per 1,000 births
Life expectancy .... 71 (male); 74 (female)

Fares are published and usually agreed on before departure. Vincentians use bicycles mainly for recreation. Half of all vehicles (including motorcycles) are privately owned. Traffic moves on the left side of the road.

An efficient ferry service links the Grenadine Islands to each other and to the mainland. Light aircraft provides domestic service and also links the islands to international airports in Barbados, Saint Lucia, Grenada, and Trinidad.

St. Vincent has an efficient postal system and a modern digital telephone service. Both broadcast and cable television are available, as are privately owned newspapers and radio stations.

Education. By the time they enter primary school at age five, many children have had some basic education at a private kindergarten. After six years of primary school, students take a Common Entrance Exam that determines whether and where they will attend secondary school. Children may end their education at age 15 by taking a School Leaving Exam. Some students drop out before this. Education is provided free of charge, but parents must provide uniforms, books, transportation, and lunch.

The Caribbean Examination Council exams (given throughout the Caribbean) are offered in the final (fifth) year of high school. At this level, girls tend to perform better than boys and account for more than double the enrollment of boys. Higher secondary education is available at a grammar school, a technical college, a teacher-training college, and other institutions. There are no four-year universities, but students may pursue further education at a campus of the University of the West Indies or in North America. Local adult education classes have helped Vincentians achieve a high literacy rate.

Health. The government recently has proposed a national health insurance plan. Previously, only the government and some large private enterprises provided coverage. Government health clinics are found in all districts and offer outpatient services and general dental care. Kingstown's General Hospital provides basic surgical, obstetric, and medical care. Three smaller hospitals offer more auxiliary treatment. Private medical care is available to those who can afford it.

CONTACT INFORMATION

Embassy of St. Vincent and the Grenadines, 3216 New Mexico Avenue, Washington, DC 20016; phone (202) 364-6730. St. Vincent and the Grenadines National Tourist Office, 801 Second Avenue, 21st Floor, New York, NY 10017; phone (800) 729-1726.

1305 North Research Way, Bldg. K
Orem, Utah 84097-6200 USA
1.800.528.6279; 801.705.4250
fax 801.705.4350
www.culturegrams.com

Scotland
(United Kingdom)

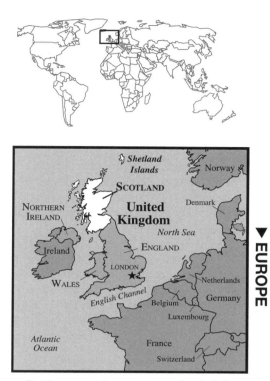

Boundary representations are not necessarily authoritative.

▼ EUROPE

BACKGROUND

Land and Climate. Located north of England on the island of Great Britain, Scotland covers 30,421 square miles (78,789 square kilometers) and is about the same size as South Carolina. Scotland's famous Highlands, which include the Grampian Mountains and the North West Highlands, are in the north. Upland wilderness areas surround the central urban valley, which often is referred to as the Central Belt of Scotland. Mineral wealth has made this region the wealthiest and most populated area. Scotland has more than 800 islands, 130 of which are inhabited.

Throughout the country, rugged mountains, green valleys (*glens*), deep blue lakes (*lochs*), and offshore islands provide beautiful scenery. The climate is generally temperate and wet, although it differs from east to west. Rain falls more than 200 days per year; in the west it falls 250 days per year. The west coast and island areas experience high winds and heavy rainfall and have large areas of marsh and peat bogs. The east, with its fertile agricultural land, is colder, drier, and less windy. Summer temperatures average 60°F to 70°F (15–21°C), while daytime winter temperatures usually remain above freezing (36°F or 2°C).

History. The Scots are descendants of Celtic peoples. Scotland is named after the colony of Scots who came from Ireland in the sixth century and united with the original inhabitants (Picts) in the ninth century. The Scots fought for many years against Vikings from the north and English from the south. Finally, King James VI—son of Mary, Queen of Scots (Mary Stuart)—came to the English throne as King James I of England and united both countries under one monarch in 1603.

Since that time, the histories of Scotland and England have intertwined. In 1707, the Scottish and English Parliaments were united by the Act of Union, which founded the constitutional monarchy of the Kingdom of Great Britain. The kingdom became known as the United Kingdom (UK) in 1801 when Ireland was joined to the union. Scotland shared England's industrial revolution, the great British Empire that spanned the globe, and the trials of the world wars. Despite its close ties with England and its function in the kingdom, Scotland has remained a distinct political and cultural entity. Actually, local histories of the individual cities and towns tell far more about the people of Scotland than does the political history of the UK.

A budding nationalist movement that reemerged in the 1970s gained momentum in the early 1990s. Some Scots wanted outright independence from the UK; most just wanted Scotland to have more control of its own economy and politics. In 1997, the most popular proposal was to avert actual independence by creating a Scottish parliament within the UK with limited tax-raising powers. Supporting this proposal, the Labour Party swept a majority of Scottish seats in May 1997 elections. Soon after taking office, the British prime minister, Tony Blair, and his Labour Party approved constitutional reforms and called for a vote on the matter. In September 1997, Scottish voters overwhelmingly supported a referendum creating their own parliament with tax-raising powers. May 1999 elections for the new Scottish Parliament resulted in Labour forming a coalition with the Liberal Democrats. The Scottish National Party is the opposition. Donald Dewar is the first minister. Parliament opened officially on

1 July 1999, nearly three hundred years since the last Scottish parliament was held.

In February 2001, the highly contagious foot-and-mouth disease broke out among British livestock, prompting bans on British meat imports. Thousands of cattle, pigs, and sheep were slaughtered in an effort to stop the disease. The disease has hurt Scotland's economy, which relies heavily on agriculture and tourism.

THE PEOPLE

Population. Scotland's population of about 5.1 million is decreasing slightly. Most people live in crowded urban areas; only about 350,000 people live in the rugged Highland and island regions. Although roughly 90 percent of the population is of Scottish origin, several small minority groups have immigrated from England, Ireland, India, Pakistan, and Hong Kong and live in larger cities. English settlers make up a substantial part of the population in some rural areas. Scots account for less than 10 percent of the total population of the UK, which also includes England, Wales, and Northern Ireland. Glasgow is the largest city (700,000 people), followed by Edinburgh (443,000), and Aberdeen (200,000).

Language. English is the official language; however, Gaelic (a Celtic language and Scotland's original tongue) and Scots (an English dialect spoken for centuries in the lowlands) also are spoken. Highlanders speak English with a soft, melodic accent, while urban dwellers may have a strong local accent. Gaelic is spoken by about 70,000 people, particularly those living on the Outer Hebrides and in parts of Glasgow. Although Gaelic is the primary language in some areas, people also speak English; shop and street signs are in Gaelic and English. Learning Gaelic has become a popular pastime in many areas. Scots is spoken in Aberdeen and some rural areas.

Everyday conversation includes many terms derived from Gaelic and Scots. For example, the word for dull is *dreich*. A *brae* is a hill; a *bairn* is a baby. Scots also use certain English idioms unique to their culture. *Aye* means "yes." Visitors should be aware that several American English words have different meanings in Scotland.

Religion. The Church of Scotland (or Presbyterian Church) is the official church, but people may worship as they choose. While the Church of Scotland has the most members (about 750,000), Roman Catholics, Baptists, Congregationalists, Episcopalians, Methodists, and other groups are represented. Although Scotland is an increasingly secular society, religion is still very important in the Highlands. Christenings and communions are significant events. Most Scottish youth today have little interest in religion.

General Attitudes. Scots are proud of their heritage. They have a strong sense of their national identity that is expressed in their view of politics and through their traditional culture. Scots are offended by those who refer to Scots as English. They see Scotland as the most independent nation within the UK and will often emphasize its differences. When asked of their nationality, most English will respond "British," while Scots universally identify themselves as "Scottish."

Scots are known for their courtesy and their reserve with acquaintances. Often critical and very independent, the Scottish character has been described as a "combination of realism and reckless sentiment," including rashness, moodi-

ness, and the ability to relentlessly persevere. Honesty, integrity, and generosity are valued. Loyalty to family and friends, the ability to work hard, and a sense of humor are also highly regarded. Scots share a more socialist mindset than other members of the UK. This is reflected in their strong support of left-of-center political parties.

Divisions between the working class and the middle class are present, although they are somewhat less apparent than in England. Social status usually is measured by occupation and education. Education and employment goals usually vary between classes. Land ownership is highly concentrated; relatively few people own the majority of the land. Attitudes also differ between regions. Those on the west coast have a more relaxed view toward life than their eastern counterparts. They are perceived as softer in character and less ambitious. People living on the east coast are considered hardworking, quiet, reticent, and single-minded.

Personal Appearance. Popular European fashions are worn in Scotland. However, climate also influences the choice of clothing. Woolen sweaters are popular during the cooler months. Lighter fabrics are more common in the summer.

Scottish men often wear the traditional tartan kilt on formal occasions, particularly for weddings. The kilt is a heavy pleated tartan skirt worn only by men and accessorized with several traditional items. Tartan patterns (or plaids) originated in the Highlands and gradually became associated with local surnames. Native Scots seldom wear other tartan garments, although women may wear tartan skirts. Women wear long white traditional wedding dresses when they marry.

CUSTOMS AND COURTESIES

Greetings. Scots usually shake hands when meeting people for the first time. However, handshakes are used less often than in other European countries and are generally light and nonaggressive. Scots do not stand close to each other when greeting or speaking. Hugging is reserved for people they know well.

Scots can be somewhat formal, yet friendly, in their greetings. In formal situations, one might say *Good morning/afternoon, Mr./Mrs. . . . How do you do?* In less formal situations, *Hi, Hello,* or *How are you today?* is used. Among friends one might say *Hiya*, or *Aright?* In the northeast, *Fit like?* replaces *How are you?* The Gaelic equivalent is *Ciamar a tha thu* (pronounced KEE-MIR A HA OO). People often use the phrase *Cheers* when leaving. To say good-bye (particularly from a distance), one may lift the hand up to the height of the head while walking away.

Most people address each other on a first name basis; professionals are addressed by their title and surname. Nicknames are used between friends and between husbands and wives. People are referred to as *laddie* (male) or *lassie* (female). The terms *wifey* (female), *mum* (mom), and *chap* (male) may be used also.

Gestures. Scots generally do not use their hands when speaking. A pat on the shoulder may be acceptable when people know each other and want to express appreciation or agreement. It is impolite to pass through someone's line of vision (while shopping, for example). Shouting in public is rude. It is polite to offer the elderly seats on buses and trains.

Visiting. Scots, particularly those in the Highland areas, take pride in their hospitality. Visits to the home are usually prearranged. Only close friends and family drop by unannounced. The custom of enjoying *afternoon tea* around 3 p.m. on a daily basis is no longer common; more common is coffee at 11 a.m. However, friends may be invited to drop by on weekends for an *afternoon tea*. During these short visits, hosts serve a drink and cake or *biscuits* (cookies). Invitations for *tea* in the evening include a formal meal, although most Scots refer to this as *dinner*. Scots are open and candid in conversation and have a keen but subtle sense of humor. Religion, salary, and (less often) politics are topics to be avoided. When formally invited to a home, one customarily brings a small gift, such as flowers, chocolates, or a bottle of wine. Guests usually give their gift to the hosts when they arrive.

Outside of the home, most social interaction takes place in *pubs* (public houses). People go to *pubs* not only for drinks but also for meals and socializing. It is quite common for entire families to go to a *pub*.

Eating. Proper table etiquette is important and admired. Scots use the continental style of eating, with the fork in the left hand and the knife remaining in the right. Asking for and accepting second servings is appropriate. A person indicates that he or she is finished eating by placing the fork and knife together on the plate. Breakfast is usually cereal (sometimes porridge), coffee or tea, and toast. Lunch is a light meal often consisting of sandwiches, soup, and a drink. Dinner is the main meal of the day and is served around 5 or 6 p.m. In restaurants, a common tip is about 10 percent. People do not leave tips in *pubs*.

LIFESTYLE

Family. In urban areas, families are small and tend to keep to themselves. Although relatives visit each other often, families remain separate from each other. The elderly prefer to stay in their own homes and remain independent as long as possible, rather than live with their married children. About half of all families live in rented homes or apartments (*flats*). Scotland is lacking in good family facilities. All Scots value home ownership. While the husband is regarded as the head of the home among older couples, younger couples are more likely to make decisions jointly. A majority of women now work outside of the home and this proportion continues to increase. Women still have a greater share of household responsibilities, although this is changing among younger couples. Children are becoming more independent but also more self-interested.

Early Highland families were loyal to their clan, but contemporary clans are largely irrelevant to national Scots. Clans were originally tribal groups that defended Highland areas until the clan system was destroyed in the early 19th century. Although clans have existed in some form since then, the family has had greater significance. Each clan still is headed by a chieftain whose role is mainly symbolic. Family associations linked to clans are primarily popular with U.S. Americans of Scottish descent.

Dating and Marriage. Dating in Scotland is different from that in the United States. Relationships are formed within a social circle, not as separate couples. Then, rather than dating many different people, Scots date one person at a time. Popular activities include going to discos, the cinema, *pubs*, or just hanging around with groups of friends in town centers.

Little socializing is done within schools. People also enjoy going to dances featuring traditional Scottish music. Living together before or instead of marrying is becoming more common, although it is not always accepted. People usually marry in their mid- to late twenties, but some marry later.

The bride may give sugar almonds or a small posy of dried flowers to special guests or to those who have helped with the wedding. A *scramble* or *pour-out* is a bag of small change that is scattered by the best man onto the pavement or road after the bride and groom have driven away. Small children scramble to get as much of it as possible.

Diet. While daily meals usually are not elaborate in Scotland, many Scottish dishes can be complex and exquisite. The normal diet includes *mince* (ground meat) and *tatties* (potatoes), *fish suppers* (fish and chips seasoned with salt and vinegar), stews, beef, lamb, *neeps* (boiled turnips), and simple vegetables. Baked items, such as cakes and biscuits, are very popular, as well as scones, oatcakes, and *black buns* (a fruit cake on a pastry base). *Haggis* is a national dish. It is made from ground sheep entrails that are mixed with oats and spices, tied in a sheep's stomach, and cooked. *Stovies* (roast beef, onions, and potatoes) are also popular. Fast food and *take-away* (Chinese, Indian, fish and chips) are popular with the younger generation. Scots enjoy sweet desserts. Typical desserts, known as *puddings*, include *crumbles* (fruit pies), ice cream, and trifle. Beer, lager, and Scottish whisky are common drinks.

Recreation. The most popular organized sport is *football* (soccer), followed by rugby. Basketball, volleyball, and badminton are played in the high schools. Swimming, aerobics, fishing, and going to the gym are also popular. The Scots invented golf in the 1500s; it is still one of their favorite games. Scotland's golf courses are spread over the rolling, green countryside and are considered some of the world's best. The Highland Games, which resemble track meets, are held in the late summer. Popular winter sports include *curling* and skiing. *Curling* involves two teams of four players that slide granite stones over ice to reach a target. *Shinty*, a Celtic sport similar to hockey, is popular in the Highlands.

The Highland bagpipe was used throughout Scotland's history as an instrument to inspire warriors. It is used today mostly for ceremonial and sporting occasions, although bagpipe music is enjoyed by many. Watching television, videos, and movies are favorite leisure activities. Social drinking is common, and there are many lounges and *pubs*.

The Arts. Arts festivals, such as Glasgow's Mayfest and the Edinburgh International Festival (one of the largest in the world), are popular. Instruments used in Scottish music include the bagpipes, the fiddle, the cello, and the *clarsach* (a small harp). Folk music is popular; people enjoy writing new folk songs and performing traditional ones.

Scottish dancing is popular in many countries. A *ceilidh* is a type of traditional dance enjoyed by many. Some *ceilidh* dances are the Dashing White Sergeant and the Highland Schottische. The Highland dances, the reel, and Scottish Country Dancing are other prominent types of dance.

Several respected Scottish writers have advanced Scotland's literary tradition. In later years, more women writers have become recognized. Writers are becoming more experimental and developing new styles while continuing to focus much of their writing on Scotland.

▼ EUROPE

Holidays. Scotland celebrates many UK holidays. Official holidays include New Year's Day, Easter, Christmas, and Boxing Day (26 Dec.). New Year's Eve is known as *Hogmanay* and is the biggest holiday of the year; people drink and dance all night long at *ceilidhs*. Virtually everything closes down for Christmas, including restaurants and shops. Boxing Day comes from the old British tradition of giving small boxed gifts to service workers the day after Christmas; it is now a day for visiting and relaxing. Banquets called *Burns Suppers* honor Robert Burns on his birthday (25 Jan.). *Haggis* is always served at these suppers. Other holidays include May Day, celebrated 1 May or the first Monday in May; and Remembrance Day, held the Sunday closest to 11 November. Scots also enjoy local holidays such as a Monday spring holiday and autumn holiday.

Commerce. Businesses generally are open from 9 a.m. to 6 p.m., Monday through Friday. Government offices stay open until 4:30 p.m., Monday through Friday. Small towns have a local half-day during the week when most shops close for the afternoon. Most shops are open Saturdays from 9 a.m. to 6 p.m. Glasgow and Edinburgh are the main centers of business, and major stores often remain open until 8 p.m. at least one night a week. Most large stores open on Sunday from 10 a.m. to 4 p.m.

SOCIETY

Government. The UK's constitutional monarchy, with Queen Elizabeth II as head of state, is a parliamentary system. The House of Lords has limited legislative power, although it is the highest judicial body in the land. Laws are passed in the 659-seat House of Commons, whose members are elected by the people. Scotland has 72 seats in the House of Commons. The leader of the majority party is appointed as prime minister by the queen. The prime minister, currently Tony Blair, selects a cabinet and runs the government. Elections are held at least every five years, but they may be held sooner if called by the prime minister.

Scotland's new Parliament of 129 seats, currently held in Edinburgh, will handle health, education, and local affairs, as well as have a limited role in taxation. Most tax, foreign affairs, defense, and social security issues will remain with the UK. Scotland maintains its own legal system, related to but different from that of England. Police forces are organized regionally. Several other departments are not controlled directly from London. Scotland's two-tier local government system was replaced by a unitary authority in April 1996.

Economy. Many Scots are employed in technology, fishing, manufacturing, forestry, tourism, and textiles. Whisky is also an important industry. Several newer industries, such as chemicals, have taken hold in Scotland. Agriculture is intensive and efficient. Potatoes, vegetables, and grains are among the most important agricultural products. The discovery of oil in the North Sea has brought economic growth to the area. Scotland has many fine ports from which the UK conducts trade. The currency is the pound sterling (£). Scotland also issues its own bank notes.

Real gross domestic product per capita has more than dou-

DEVELOPMENT DATA

Human Dev. Index* rank	10 of 174 countries
Adjusted for women	10 of 143 countries
Real GDP per capita	$20,336
Adult literacy rate	99 percent
Infant mortality rate	6 per 1,000 births
Life expectancy	75 (male); 80 (female)

bled in the last generation. However, there is a larger gap between the wealthy and the poor than in some other European countries. Likewise, the UK's middle class is not as prosperous as its counterpart in other developed nations.

Transportation and Communications. Scotland is linked by international and domestic air services. Railway also connects most parts of the country, except in the northwest. Because of increased traffic, Scotland will invest substantial resources over the next decade in improving its rail network. Most people own cars. Following the British tradition, traffic moves on the left side of the road. Buses, taxis, and underground railways are common in the cities. The public transportation system is excellent. Telecommunications are well advanced, with international fiber-optic cable links and satellite systems. There are a number of daily newspapers and nearly every home has a television. Home computers are commonplace, as is access to the Internet and e-mail.

Education. Education is free and compulsory from ages six to sixteen, although most Scots begin school a bit earlier. Scotland has its own education system. The examinations given at the completion of secondary school are not the same as those in England. Both *state* (public) schools and private schools are available in Scotland. Private schools receive some state funding and are subject to some control. Scotland's first Gaelic-only school opened in 1999. There are various vocational schools as well as 13 universities. University tuition may run £1,000 per term; substantial debate is being applied to the issue because tuition traditionally has been paid by the government. The universities of St. Andrews, Glasgow, and Aberdeen were founded in the 1400s.

Health. The UK's National Health Service provides, on the basis of taxation, free medical treatment and many other social services. Individuals pay only for prescriptions and some dental services. Medical facilities are advanced. Scotland has a high rate of lung cancer and heart disease; the UK has the second worst rate of coronary disease in the Western world.

CONTACT INFORMATION

Scottish Tourist Board, 23 Ravelston Terrace, Edinburgh, Scotland EH4 3TP; phone 44 131 332 2433; Web site www.visitscotland.com. British Tourist Authority, 551 Fifth Avenue, Suite 01, New York, NY 10176; phone (800) 462-2748; Web site www.visitbritain.com. British Information Services, 845 Third Avenue, New York, NY 10022-6691; phone (212) 745-0277; Web site www.britainusa.com.

CultureGrams™
People. The World. You.

1305 North Research Way, Bldg. K
Orem, Utah 84097-6200 USA
1.800.528.6279; 801.705.4250
fax 801.705.4350
www.culturegrams.com

Slovakia
(Slovak Republic)

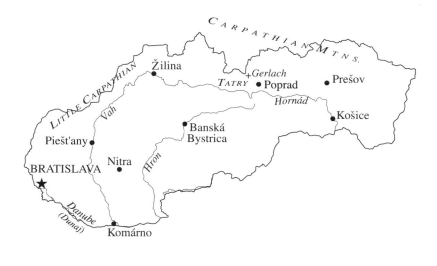

Boundary representations are not necessarily authoritative.

▼ EUROPE

BACKGROUND

Land and Climate. The Slovak Republic is a landlocked country situated in the heart of central Europe. Covering 18,859 square miles (48,845 square kilometers), it is about the size of West Virginia. The land is generally mountainous, with the Tatry Mountains (part of the Carpathian range) dominating the central region. The highest peak is Gerlach at 8,707 feet (2,857 meters). Mountain ridges have inhibited travel at times, preserving Slovakia's variety of dialects and customs. The country's fertile south is part of the Great Hungarian Plain. Slovakia is rich in natural resources such as timber, copper, zinc, mercury, limestone, and iron ore. With a continental climate, summers are warm (especially in southern lowlands) and winters are cold and snowy (especially in northern highlands). Corn, oats, wheat, and potatoes are the most abundant crops. Forests cover much of the central region.

History. Slavic peoples first settled in the area during the fifth century. In A.D. 833, they founded a loose confederation that became the Great Moravian Empire. In 863, the Greek missionaries Methodius and Cyril introduced Christianity and the Cyrillic alphabet. The empire's brief history ended in 907 with the invasion of nomadic Magyars (today called Hungarians). The area came under Hungarian rule. It also adopted Roman Catholicism and the Latin alphabet.

In 1526, Hungary became subject to Austrian Hapsburg rule. Upon its defeat in World War I (1918), the Austro-Hungarian Empire disintegrated. Slovaks joined with Czechs under the leadership of Thomas Masaryk and Milan Rastislav Štefánik in founding the First Czecho-Slovak

Republic (the hyphen was dropped in 1920).

Czechoslovakia became the most democratic of the Hapsburg successor states, although some Slovaks wished for more autonomy within the union. In 1938, the country was not able to withstand Hitler's foreign policy machinations. Even as Germany was annexing Czech lands, Slovakia declared independence in March 1939 and allied with Germany throughout World War II. The move still stirs controversy today. Central and eastern Slovaks staged a revolt in 1944 that was quickly crushed. Upon Germany's defeat, the Soviet Union's Red Army helped install a new unitary Czechoslovak government.

After 1948, Communists seized control of the government, all major institutions, and significant property. Slovaks suffered under forced Stalinization and persecution in the 1950s. During the 1960s, the reform-minded Slovak Communist Alexander Dubček led a movement to create "socialism with a human face." Censorship was relaxed and a spirit of revival and hope swept the country. The experiment met with an abrupt end when Soviet-led Warsaw Pact troops crushed the movement in August 1968. During the 1970s, Gustav Husák's regime attempted to satisfy citizens by making consumer goods more available, but ruthless repression of political dissent continued. Economic stagnation and Mikhail Gorbachev's changes in the Soviet Union laid the foundations for the fall of communism in 1989.

The burst of emotions that accompanied Czechoslovakia's Velvet Revolution soon gave way to the sobering realities of rebuilding democracy. Nationalism reemerged as a major issue. In 1990, Slovaks began pressing for a greater voice in their own affairs. Disagreements over the amount of autonomy for Slovakia and the pace of economic reform led to victory for Slovak nationalists in 1992 elections. When the newly elected Czech and Slovak national governments could not agree about the division of federal powers, Czech Prime Minister Václav Klaus and Slovak Prime Minister Vladimír Mečiar decided to split the state peacefully and fairly.

Mečiar continued some reforms after Slovakia's independence in 1993, but his confrontational style led to political instability. Parliament removed him from office in 1994, but subsequent elections failed to seat a successor and Mečiar returned to office as prime minister. By the time President Michal Kováč's term expired in March 1998, a lack of political reform allowed Mečiar to assume presidential powers as well. However, he lost his seat in parliament in September 1998 elections, and Rudolf Schuster became Slovakia's first elected president in May 1999. Mikuláš Dzurinda is the current prime minister.

The Slovak government continues to focus on economic reform. Joining the North Atlantic Treaty Organization (NATO) and the European Union (EU) is a high priority.

THE PEOPLE

Population. About 5.4 million people live in the Slovak Republic. The population is currently not growing. More than 86 percent of the people are Slovaks. Hungarians (Magyars) constitute the largest minority (10.6 percent) and most of them live in southern Slovakia. The Romany (Gypsy) ethnic group officially accounts for a documented 1.6 percent of the population, but this figure actually may be as high as 9 or 10 percent. The Romany are nomadic and difficult to count, and many listed themselves as Slovaks in the 1992 census. The Romany are not well integrated into mainstream society, especially in rural areas, and struggle against discrimination in many countries.

Smaller ethnic groups that are more integrated into society include Czechs (1 percent), Carpatho-Rusyns (Ruthenians), Ukrainians, Germans, Poles, Moravians, and others. More than 60 percent live in urban areas. Most people have adequate access to health care, education, and a decent standard of living.

Language. Slovaks speak Slovak, a tongue in the Slavic language group that includes Czech, Polish, Russian, and other languages. Slovak uses a Latin script. Literary Slovak is used in official capacities, but numerous dialects exist in various regions. Hungarian is the second most commonly spoken language, especially in the south. Although Slovakia signed a basic friendship treaty with Hungary in 1995, it also passed a law making Slovak the only official language; Hungarians still want their language to have official status. The Romany speak Romany, an unwritten tongue with Indo-Aryan roots, and Slovak.

German is understood widely, while English is the language of choice to study in school. Russian was required before 1989. Other languages also are offered.

Religion. Freedom of worship is guaranteed in Slovakia and many people have deep religious convictions. Of the total population, 60.3 percent is Roman Catholic, followed by Evangelical Lutheran (6.2), and Greek Catholic (4.1). Smaller groups include the Calvinist Reformed (1.6 percent), Eastern Orthodox (0.7), Baptist, and others. Nearly 10 percent of the population is atheist, while the rest either belongs to various smaller groups or has no religious affiliation.

General Attitudes. Slovakia still is adjusting to its newly acquired statehood. Politics is a popular conversation topic. Slovaks are especially interested in how foreigners view them and are anxious to foster a positive image abroad. They are aware that their country is small and often unknown to outsiders; still, they do not like to be mistaken for Czechs, Slovenians, or Yugoslavians.

Although Slovakia has industrialized, particularly since 1948, a romantic attachment to peasant ideals and the countryside remains in the hearts of many Slovaks.

Slovaks value good humor and hard work. Cleanliness and order in the home are also highly valued. Slovaks are generous, especially in the countryside, and will go out of their way to help a stranger. Education, modesty, and honesty are admired. Those who are self-confident or aggressive are often thought to be "too" self-confident or "too" aggressive. Entrepreneurs are considered to be "price gougers" and greedy, especially in rural areas, but this attitude is changing in urban areas with increasing economic development. Also, with the introduction of a free-market economy, social status is becoming more dependent on wealth and material possessions rather than on education or professional achievement.

Personal Appearance. Clothing in urban areas is fashionable, while older, rural people remain more conservative. Most Slovaks are very concerned with their appearance. Professional women dress up for work; businessmen wear suits. Women and girls may wear dresses and skirts or casual attire, depending on the occasion. Jeans and T-shirts are quite popular, and short pants are increasingly common in the summer. Villagers might wear traditional folk costumes for special occasions.

CUSTOMS AND COURTESIES

Greetings. Shaking hands is the most common form of greeting, but one does not cross over another handshake to shake hands in a group. A man usually waits for a woman to extend her hand. Upon parting, men will often hug women or kiss them on both cheeks (sometimes not really touching) and firmly shake hands with men.

Formal titles carry a particular significance. People are addressed as *Pán* (Mr.) or *Pani* (Mrs.), followed by any professional title (doctor, engineer, professor), or the surname, or both. First names are used upon mutual consent among friends and among the youth. More formal greetings include *Dobrý deň* (Good day) or *Veľmi ma teší* (Pleased to meet you). "Good-bye" is *Do videnia*. More casual terms are *Ahoj* (Hi), *Čiao*, and *Servus* (both mean "Hello" or "Good-bye"). Some older villagers still use the traditional *S Bohom* (God be with you). "Thank you" is expressed with *Ďakujem*. The use of *Prosím* (Please) is considered polite before making any requests and for saying "You're welcome."

Gestures. Hand gestures frequently are used to emphasize speech. To wish luck, instead of crossing fingers, Slovaks "hold thumbs." That is, they fold the thumb in and close the fingers on it. Yawning in public is considered improper, and chewing gum is not acceptable during polite social interaction. Smiling is courteous.

Visiting. Impromptu visits are common, but only between close friends and family members. Invited guests, especially those coming from a distance, receive a warm welcome. An invitation to dinner is usually in a home rather than a restaurant. Guests remove hats and shoes in a home; hosts often provide slippers. Visitors wait for hosts to invite them to be seated. Invited guests often present the hosts with a gift, such as flowers, wine, or liquor. Flowers are fresh, unwrapped, and given in odd numbers (three, five, or seven). Even numbers and dried flowers are for funerals; red roses imply romantic intentions. Visitors should not overly admire anything in the home, as the item will be given to them, even if it is a prized heirloom.

Guests are almost always offered something to eat or drink no matter how short or unexpected the visit. Rural Slovaks might serve friends or relatives *slanina* (home-smoked bacon) and bread, as well as a drink; typical is homemade *slivovica* (plum liquor), but beer, coffee, tea, and other drinks also may be offered. Urban hosts tend to serve chips, nuts, and wine rather than homemade refreshments. A tray of ham, cheese, eggs, vegetables, and sweets may be offered. Out of courtesy, guests often politely decline offers before eventually accepting them. Refusing refreshments altogether is impolite, but one may decline liquor or another specific item without offending. An empty cup or glass will be refilled, so guests should leave a little bit of drink when they are finished.

If guests wish to wash up before a meal, they knock on the bathroom door before entering. All doors in a home typically are closed, even if no one is in the room. Newer homes may have the *water closet* (toilet) separate from the bathroom.

Slovaks typically accompany their departing guests outside and then wave to them until they are out of sight. Guests may turn often and return the wave.

Eating. Slovaks eat in the continental style, holding the fork in the left hand and the knife in the right. They eat three meals each day. Breakfast consists of bread and rolls, sliced meat or sausage, and cheese. Soup is commonly served with the main meal at midday, which also consists of meat, dumplings or potatoes, and a vegetable. Slovaks eat a lighter meal of cold cuts, cheese, and bread in the evening. Midmorning and midafternoon snacks are common. Families usually eat together on weekends but not as often on weekdays. Before eating, the head of the home says *Dobrú chut* (equivalent of *Bon appétit*), and others at the table respond with the same. Diners keep both hands above the table but do not rest elbows on the table. They keep napkins on the table, not in the lap. A plate of baked goods often is served before or after the meal.

Women traditionally serve the meal but do not eat at the table when guests are present. Often, only the guests are fed. In some areas it is becoming polite for women to join their guests. Slovak guests wait to be offered second helpings, but it is greatly appreciated if a foreigner asks for seconds. Conversation usually occurs after the meal. Toasting with *Na zdravie* (To your health) is common. When making a toast to someone's health, it is important to look the person in the eye.

Restaurants do not provide water unless requested. Commonly ordered drinks include beer, wine, soft drinks, and mineral water. Slovaks consider milk a drink for children. A small cup of Turkish coffee frequently completes the meal. Tipping is accepted at most sit-down restaurants; it is added to the bill, not left on the table.

LIFESTYLE

Family. Typical Slovak families have two or three children. The state used to provide families with free medical care, schooling, and social security, but budget cuts have resulted in charges for some services. Paid maternity leave for mothers, child-care facilities, and cash allowances for each child until they finish school are still provided. While most women hold jobs outside the home and comprise 47 percent of the labor force, they usually are also responsible for the home and children. However, some men are beginning to share in household duties. Grandparents are usually actively involved in raising their grandchildren.

Most urban families live in small, modest apartments built during the Communist era. Rural inhabitants continue to reside in single-family homes, which usually provide a more pleasant environment.

Dating and Marriage. Popular dating activities include dancing and going to the movies or theater. Festivals are also popular. Men marry between the ages of 23 and 26, and women marry about three years earlier. Most Slovak weddings involve church ceremonies, and brides often are paraded around the village in a traditional procession. The reception afterward lasts until morning, sometimes longer. Inflation has made celebrations lasting several days too expensive for many families. The groom carries his bride over the threshold of their new home. Due to a housing shortage, new couples often must live with parents until an apartment is available.

Diet. Among the most popular Slovak foods are *rezeň* (breaded steak) and potatoes, as well as other kinds of meat served with potatoes, rice, dumplings, or pasta and sauce. Slovakia also has a variety of sweet dishes served as a main course (such as prune dumplings). The national dish is *bryndzové halušky* (small dumplings with processed sheep cheese), but it is not eaten often in the home. Fresh-baked bread and soup are considered staples at the dinner table. Dairy products such as milk, cheese, and butter are widely available. Fresh fruits (apples, plums, and grapes) are abundant and eaten in season. Bananas and oranges are popular for holidays and throughout the year. Potatoes, cabbage, and carrots are the most frequently eaten vegetables. Popular desserts include *koláč* (nut or poppy seed rolls) and *torta* (cake).

Recreation. Soccer, ice hockey, skiing, and tennis are the most popular sports in Slovakia. Other forms of recreation include moviegoing, hiking, camping, swimming, and attending local festivals, cultural events, or art exhibits. Families like to hunt for mushrooms.

Many Slovaks spend weekends or vacations in the beautiful Tatry Mountains, at health spas, or in the countryside. Gardening at summer cottages also is enjoyed. More Slovaks are beginning to tour other parts of Europe.

The Arts. Slovaks are proud of their rich cultural heritage. They celebrate their rural roots through poetry, literature, song, and dance. Slovaks sing with marked enthusiasm at gatherings, and knowing folk songs is considered part of being Slovak. A popular saying is *Kde Slovák, tam spev* (Wherever there is a Slovak, there is a song).

Lace and embroidery are traditional crafts for women. Ceramics (particularly Modra pottery), metalwork, wood

EUROPE ▼

carving, and egg decoration are also valued. Folk art often is given to foreign visitors as a gift.

Slovak folk dance often features couples dancing together or groups of men and women dancing separately or a combination of the two. Most of the movement is concentrated in the legs while the upper torso remains still.

Holidays. Holidays include Sylvester's Day (New Year's Eve), Independence Day and New Year's Day (1 Jan.), Three Kings Day and Orthodox Christmas (6 Jan.), Easter, Labor Day (1 May), Liberation Day (8 May), Cyril and Methodius Day (5 July), Constitution Day (1 Sept.), and All Saints' Day (1 Nov.). Slovak National Uprising Day (29 Aug.) commemorates the 1944 rebellion against the Nazis. Christmas is the most celebrated holiday. Children receive gifts of candy, fruit, and nuts on St. Nicholas Day (6 Dec.). Slovaks celebrate Christmas day with family gatherings featuring ham or poultry, baked goods, and drinking. Following the meal, people decorate the tree and exchange gifts. Church attendance is also traditional.

Birthdays are celebrated more often with family, whereas name days are occasions for parties among friends or colleagues. The name day usually is more important, involving gifts and flowers. People celebrate it on the day commemorating the saint who shares their name.

Commerce. Some grocers open before 8 a.m. Most other businesses and government offices open at 8 a.m. and close by 3 or 4 p.m. Shops are open until at least 6 p.m. weekdays and 2 p.m. Saturdays. Except for a few restaurants and stores, nearly all businesses close on Sunday. Small urban shops and most rural businesses close for lunch. Many people grow their own fruits and vegetables in addition to buying them from markets. Even most urban residents have gardens in the countryside.

Employees typically receive four weeks of vacation each year. Retirement occurs between ages 53 and 60. Friendly social relationships are important between business associates. Foreign business representatives should also have an interest in Slovak culture and accept any offered hospitality.

SOCIETY

Government. Slovakia's president is head of state and serves a five-year term of office. The prime minister is head of government and recommends cabinet members to the president, who makes the appointment. The Slovak National Council has 150 popularly elected members who serve four-year terms. The voting age is 18. Slovakia has four departments (regions) and several smaller districts. Court judges are chosen by the National Council. The current government consists of a coalition of four parties, the largest of which is Dzurinda's Slovak Democratic Coalition (SDK). The Movement for a Democratic Slovakia (HZDS) is the primary opposition. In 2001, the Slovak legislature passed a series of constitutional amendments, including changes that will decentralize power, strengthen the judiciary, and provide greater recognition of minority rights.

Economy. Slovakia has proceeded with market reforms at a slower pace than the Czech Republic. Many large firms

DEVELOPMENT DATA

Human Dev. Index* rank	40 of 174 countries
Adjusted for women	36 of 143 countries
Real GDP per capita	$9,699
Adult literacy rate	99 percent
Infant mortality rate	9 per 1,000 births
Life expectancy	70 (male); 78 (female)

remain in state control. Many of these industries built under Communist rule are inefficient and environmentally unsound. Military-related industries still in operation have the capacity, but not yet the capital, to switch to civilian products. Steel, chemical, textile, cement, and glass factories produce goods and semifinished products that could be globally competitive once the political climate stabilizes.

The economy grew 2 percent in 2000. High unemployment (around 19 percent), inflation (about 10 percent), and deficits hinder progress, but the low level of foreign investment is seen as a more significant problem. Corruption is also a barrier to economic development. Slovaks generally enjoy a good standard of living. Germany and the Czech Republic are Slovakia's biggest trade partners. The currency is the Slovak crown or *koruna* (Sk).

Transportation and Communications. Although Slovak families usually have a car, extremely high fuel prices discourage regular use. Instead, public transportation by bus, streetcar, and train is common. Main roads are paved, but there are only a few good superhighways. However, major north/south and east/west running highways are currently under construction. Railroads link major cities.

Slovakia's press expanded rapidly with the freedom introduced in 1989. More than 120 newspapers, as well as numerous magazines, are published. There are several television and radio stations. The use of cable TV is increasing. Some Slovaks who still lack phones in their homes are purchasing cellular phones instead.

Education. Education, which is free at public institutions, begins at age six and is compulsory for 10 years. Education and research have a high priority. Although public universities charge no tuition, admission is limited and highly competitive. The oldest of Slovakia's 13 universities is Comenius University in Bratislava. Those who do not attend college can obtain work skills through vocational schools.

Health. Slovakia's national health-care system, anchored by state-run hospitals, is undergoing change. Nearly all people have access to physicians, and medical advances have lowered the infant mortality rate. Health spas service patients from around the world. Pollution poses serious health hazards in both rural and urban environments. Funds are lacking to clean the water and air and to restore decimated forests.

CONTACT INFORMATION

Embassy of the Slovak Republic, 2201 Wisconsin Avenue NW, Suite 250, Washington, DC 20007; phone (202) 965-5160; Web site www.slovakemb.com.

1305 North Research Way, Bldg. K
Orem, Utah 84097-6200 USA
1.800.528.6279; 801.705.4250
fax 801.705.4350
www.culturegrams.com

Republic of
Slovenia

▼ EUROPE

BACKGROUND

Land and Climate. Slovenia covers 7,820 square miles (20,253 square kilometers) and is slightly smaller than Massachusetts. The Karawanken and Julian Alps, the Adriatic seacoast, and rolling gentle plains give Slovenia diverse climates, from alpine to continental to Mediterranean. Dynamic geographic formations include some six thousand limestone caves, natural bridges, sinkholes, springs, waterfalls, and thermal springs. Half of Slovenia is forested and supports rich animal and plant life. Wildflowers adorn the fields, hills, and mountains. The Slovene national flower, the red carnation, is a traditional motif that appears in many different forms, as does the leaf symbol for the national tree, the linden. The highest peak, Mount Triglav (9,396 feet or 2,864 meters) in the Julian Alps, is portrayed on the national flag. The three major rivers are the Sava, Drava, and Soča. The alpine lakes of Bled and Bohinj are well-known, as is the disappearing Lake Cerknica in southern Slovenia. The average temperature range in January is 35°F to 39°F (2–4°C) and in July, 68°F to 75°F (20–24°C).

History. Slovenia was inhabited by ancient Illyrians and Celts, followed by Greeks and Romans. Slavs, including Slovenes, began settling the Balkans in the sixth century A.D. The Slovenes enjoyed brief independence in the state of Carantania from 620 until 745 when they recognized Bavarian supremacy. The Carantanian constitution was one model referenced in preparing the U.S. Constitution. The Bavarian state submitted to the Franks in 788 and eventually (in 963) became part of the Holy Roman Empire. Slovene territory later fell under Hapsburg domination.

During the Bavarian period, Slovenes began to accept Christianity. Later it was embraced more fully when Cyril,

Methodius, and others taught the faith in Slavic languages. In addition to continuing pressures of Germanization, the Slovenes suffered terribly from Turkish raids in the 15th and 16th centuries. Peasant uprisings against feudal masters began at the end of the 15th century and lasted almost 250 years.

For a short time (1809–13), much of Slovenia was under French rule as the province of Illyria. This furthered the rise of nationalism and the use of the Slovene language. The Hapsburgs regained control of Slovene territory, but the spirit of a national consciousness continued to grow. The enlightenment of 1830 to 1848 further promoted the development of Slovene language and literature. At the beginning of the 20th century, hopes for a South Slav state that would include Slovenia under a Viennese crown were never realized, and Slovenia continued as part of the Austro-Hungarian Empire until it collapsed at the end of World War I. Slovenia then joined the Kingdom of Serbs, Croats, and Slovenes (renamed Yugoslavia in 1929) under a Serbian monarch. Italy and Germany occupied Slovenia during World War II. Some Slovenes allied themselves with fascist forces, but others joined partisan (communist) fighters to resist the Germans and wage a civil war for control of the region. The partisans were helped to victory by Allied forces. After World War II, Slovenia became one of the six republics of the Socialist Federal Republic of Yugoslavia, a communist state ruled by partisan leader Josef Broz Tito.

When democracy began sweeping through Eastern Europe, the Slovenes voted for self-determination and proclaimed independence in 1991. This move prompted an attack by the

Yugoslav army. A 10-day war in the summer of 1991 was resolved peacefully, and the last Yugoslav soldier left Slovenia in October 1991. In 1992, Slovenes elected Milan Kučan to be president; he was reelected in 1997. Together with other leaders, he has worked to stabilize society and build the economy, now one of the strongest among former communist-bloc nations. Prime Minister Janez Drnovšek's center-left government was ousted in April 2000 after the People's Party, junior partner in his coalition government, withdrew from the cabinet to form an alliance with the Christian Democrats. After two months of political uncertainty, Slovenia's parliament approved a new government led by Prime Minister Andrej Bajuk, deputy president of the People's Party. However, following October elections, Drnovšek returned to power at the head of a four-party center-right coalition.

Integration into the European Union (EU) and membership in the North Atlantic Treaty Organization (NATO) are key government goals. Slovenia is now among the first group of countries expected to join the EU, possibly as early as 2003.

THE PEOPLE

Population. Slovenia's population of 1.9 million is declining slightly. Most people are native Slovenes, except for small Hungarian and Italian minorities. Other groups living in Slovenia are Croats (3 percent), Serbs (2 percent), Muslims, Montenegrins, and Albanians. The capital, Ljubljana, has 330,000 residents. It was first inhabited some five thousand years ago. In Roman times, it was a major settlement called Emona.

Between the 1880s and 1920s, more than 75,000 Slovenes migrated to the United States. Later immigrants went to Canada, South America, Australia, and western Europe.

Language. Slovene, the official language, is a Slavic language. On top of the singular and plural, Slovene uses the dual, a special language construction referring to two persons or things. Like Croatian, Slovene uses Roman letters but excludes *q*, *w*, *x*, and *y* and incorporates the letters *š* (sh), *č* (ch), and *ž* (zh). The oldest preserved documents written in Slovene, the Freising Fragments, date to A.D. 1000. The first book was printed in Slovene by Primož Trubar in 1550. In 1584, Adam Bohorič produced a grammar book. Starting around 1774, elementary school students were taught in their native language. Despite pressures to Germanize, Slovene became widely used in all spheres of life. Many Slovenes speak a second language, most often English, followed by German, Italian, French, Croatian, and Serbian. Hungarian and Italian have official status for use in border areas.

Religion. Slovenes are predominantly Roman Catholic (70.8 percent). A few are Protestant. Serbs tend to be Orthodox Christian. Muslims and Jews also have small congregations in Slovenia. Many buildings neglected under communism are being restored to their former glory. In the countryside, small churches dot the mountaintops, and small shrines (*kapelica*) are found along roadways.

General Attitudes. Slovenes are proud of their country and heritage. They are reserved initially but are warm in relationships with family and friends. In conversation, people maintain a certain distance from each other, even if they are long-time acquaintances. Slovenes do not admire people when they are late, untruthful, rude, boastful, unreliable, aggressive, fearful of change, pessimistic, or xenophobic.

When they receive a compliment, Slovenes smile and say, "I invite you for a drink," meaning they gracefully accept the compliment. Motherhood is greatly respected and children are cherished. People treat pets with affection and kindness.

Slovenes are industrious and hardworking. They may spend their free time working in the garden or building their own homes over a span of several years. A clean, neat, and attractive home and garden are important. People's respect for the land is reflected in relatively clean streets and parks and well-tended rural fields. Many city dwellers have a small plot of arable land where they plant vegetables, fruits, and flowers. Homegrown foods are regarded as a precious commodity. People often place flowers on sunny windowsills to grow throughout the year, especially in the countryside.

Personal Appearance. It is important to be well-groomed, clean, and neat in public. Contemporary European styles are popular. People wear furs in the winter to protect against the cold. A traditional fur hat (*polhovka*), made from the skins of the dormouse, is worn in southern regions. People's daily dress reflects their occupations. Village women working in their homes and on the land wear work dresses covered with a full-length apron. When visiting, they may wear a dress and sweater or a skirt and blouse. Village men wear coveralls or heavy trousers with a blue coat and heavy boots during the day. Young people usually attend secondary school in the cities and live there in dormitories during the week, so they become acquainted with the dress of the city youth.

In cities, men wear suits or sport coats and slacks with a shirt and tie to work. Urban women wear suits, dresses, slacks, jackets, and other cosmopolitan fashions. Urban youth wear blue jeans and adopt fashions from abroad.

CUSTOMS AND COURTESIES

Greetings. Upon meeting, people smile, shake hands, and greet each other with *Kako se imate?* (How are you?). Informally, the term is *Kako se imaš?* Some people kiss on both cheeks when greeting. "Hello" is expressed with *živijo* or *Zdravo*. *Dobro jutro* (Good morning), *Dober dan* (Good day), *Dober večer* (Good evening), or *Lahko noč* (Good night) are also common. Some Slovenes bow their heads slightly when shaking hands. If the hand is soiled, they will bow slightly and greet the person verbally while offering an apology for not using the hand. Urban residents rarely greet strangers on the street. In the countryside, people look at strangers directly and may offer a greeting.

Women are addressed as *Gospa* (Madam) or *Gospodična* (Miss), and men as *Gospod* (Sir). The use of titles shows respect. Only close friends use first names, usually after many years of acquaintance. This formality is also reflected in the Slovene use of the formal pronoun for "you" (*vi*). Only relatives and close friends use the informal *ti*. Likewise, verb forms can be more formal. The youth usually do not observe these formalities. When parting or exiting a room or an elevator, people customarily say *Na svidenja* (Good-bye) or *Adijo* (Adieu) even if they do not know the others present.

Gestures. Hand movements emphasize conversation. Holding hands and other displays of affection usually are seen only among young people. Two girls or women, especially older women, may walk along the street arm in arm. When conversing with another person, one stands straight and does not place the hands in the pockets. It is customary to adhere to good manners, i.e., hold the door for other persons, avoid chewing gum in public and during conversation, cover the mouth when coughing, and avoid conversation with food in the mouth. Slovenes remove their hats when they reach their destination and prepare to sit down.

Visiting.   Family and friends enjoy visiting each other. They usually call ahead, as spontaneous visits are not frequent. It is also common to invite friends to one's home. Visiting is more common on Sundays and holidays but also occurs during the week. Invited guests take a bouquet of flowers to the hostess, a bottle of wine to the host, or a small gift for the children. Hosts offer guests refreshments such as coffee, juice, cookies, or pastries. Visitors take care not to stay for a long period of time. Shortly after the meal, once coffee is served, guests take their leave. Hosts will accompany guests to the door and sometimes to the street or car if appropriate.

Many Slovenes remove their shoes in the home and wear slippers. Thus, it is impolite for guests to pass a home's entryway without first offering to remove their shoes.

Slovenes enjoy eating at local inns called *gostilne*, where the atmosphere is warm and the food is well prepared. They also enjoy meeting acquaintances at indoor or outdoor cafés for coffee or a drink.

Eating.   Slovenes traditionally eat in the continental style, with the fork in the left hand and the knife in the right. Daily meals usually include *zajtrk* (breakfast) early in the morning, *malica* (midmorning snack), *kosilo* (main meal) in the midafternoon or after work, and *večerja* (light supper) in the evening. Families usually eat the main meal together. These patterns are changing in the face of modern lifestyle factors such as more women in the workforce, greater access to convenient and fresh foods, and improved cooking facilities.

When drinking together, all persons raise the glass and toast each other with *Na zdravje* (To your health) or *živijo* (Long live). A customary toast of wine precedes a meal when guests are present. After serving the food, the host nods and offers all present the wish *Dober tek* (the equivalent of *Bon appétit*). Members of the group then offer each other the same greeting. Diners follow the host's lead to begin eating. Guests are always served first and later are offered additional food and drink. Glasses and plates are refilled continually.

LIFESTYLE

Family.   Family size and living arrangements are changing. The average family has one or two children, but couples might also choose to remain childless. Ten years ago, it was not unusual for two or three generations to live in the same household. Now young couples move out on their own. However, family ties remain strong. Both parents work outside the home and share child raising and housework. Most urban people live in apartments, while small private homes are common in rural areas. City dwellers may own a small weekend house in the country to which they retreat on weekends and holidays.

Dating and Marriage.   Dating takes place throughout the teenage years. Young people attend movies and fairs, dance, visit museums and other historical places, visit friends, gath-

er in groups in cafés, enjoy outdoor sports, travel, walk in the hills or the town, and people-watch from some vantage points. A large number of young people live in the Ljubljana area, attending high school or university.

Marriages usually occur after schooling is completed. Civil ceremonies and church weddings are common. There are more church weddings now than in the past, even in the cities. Rural weddings are elaborate and incorporate more of the old customs. For instance, a bridal carriage bedecked with flowers may transport the bride and her party to the ceremony. In the *šrange* custom, the bride is detained by young men in her village until the groom ransoms her. Old castles, such as Castle Snežnik near Kozarišče in the Notranjska region, are now being used as wedding sites.

Diet.   Slovene cuisine has been influenced by Austrian, Italian, South Slavic, and Hungarian kitchens and is therefore a mix of tastes and textures. However, a typical main meal includes meat (beef or chicken), beef or chicken soup, green salad, and apple, cherry, or cheese strudel with coffee.

Pork, veal, chicken, and turkey commonly are served. Organ meats also appear often on the dinner table. No matter the season, Slovenes serve a daily green salad with vinegar-and-oil dressing. Potatoes, onions, cabbage, celery, carrots, bananas, apples, and walnuts round out the dietary staples. The forests provide a variety of mushrooms, berries, and nuts.

People traditionally produce homemade wine, fruit brandies, sauerkraut, pickled foods, sausages, dried fruits, canned fruits and vegetables, and fruit juices. Households now have better access to fresh fruits and vegetables, frozen foods, and seasonal specialties.

A hearty autumn meal may consist of blood sausage, braised potatoes, pickled turnips, and dark bread; *jota*, a hearty soup of kidney beans, sauerkraut, and bacon; or *kurja obara*, chicken stew with buckwheat groats. On New Year's Day, roasted pork and sauerkraut brings good luck. Slovenes celebrate spring with a salad of dandelion greens or *motovilec* (a green called "corn salad" or *mâche* in English).

Slovenes enjoy sweets, pastries, cakes, and chocolate candy. *Potica* is a traditional nut roll served during Christmas and Easter. Slovenes also drink a variety of coffees. In the past, they drank tea only as a medicinal remedy, but now they accept it as an alternative to coffee. Many people still grow herbs used to make teas for treating a variety of maladies. Wine, beer, and mineral water are all produced locally.

Recreation.   Slovenes of all ages enjoy sports and outdoor activities. The major winter sport is skiing. Popular team sports include hockey, basketball, volleyball, and soccer. A walk along city streets, through the parks, or in the hills is a daily regimen considered essential for health. Bicycling is a popular means of transportation as well as exercise. Hiking is a very popular recreational activity. In the country, a *veselica* (summer picnic) may be sponsored by a firemen's group or other local groups. A revered pastime is picking berries, mushrooms, and nuts in the forests. During July or August, families usually vacation in the mountains, at a health spa, at a family farm adapted for tourism, by the seaside, or in another country. Movies are especially popular.

The Arts.   The arts are well developed, and many Slovenes attend the theater, opera, ballet, and concerts. A significant number also participate in amateur choirs, dance groups, and

EUROPE ▼

theater troupes. Art galleries and museums are common even in smaller cities and towns in Slovenia.

Slovenes also enjoy poetry and literature. The country's most revered poet is France Preseren. Preseren authored the lyrics of the Slovenian national anthem. People like to listen to folk music, sing in choirs, and play the national instruments: the button box accordion and the zither. The traditional handicraft of lace making remains popular, and Cipka lace is known for its unique patterns.

Holidays. Official holidays are New Year's Days (1–2 Jan.), National Culture Day (8 Feb.), Day of Uprising against the Nazi Occupation (27 Apr.), Labor Days (1–2 May), National Day (25 June, for independence in 1991), Reformation Day (31 Oct.), and Independence Day (26 December, for the 1990 plebiscite to form an independent state). Easter, Assumption Day (15 Aug.), Day of the Dead (1 Nov.), and Christmas (25 Dec.) are also holidays.

Slovenes celebrate seasonal events such as the harvest and grape-picking days. Farmers celebrate *Koline* by sharing newly butchered pork and special sausages with neighbors. *Pust* is the Slovene equivalent of Mardi Gras. The eve of a holiday is also celebrated. The name for such evenings is suffixed with *-ovanje*: *Silvestrovanje* (New Year's Eve), *Miklavžovanje* (St. Nicholas Eve), *Kurentovanje* (the evening before *Pust* when the *Kurent*, demon figure, appears to chase away the winter), *Kresovanje* (Midsummer's Night Eve), and so on.

Commerce. Offices are open from 8 a.m. to 4 p.m. Shops open from 8 a.m. to 7 p.m. during the week and sometimes on Saturday until noon or 1 p.m. Kiosks and private shops are open longer in the evenings, on weekends, and on holidays. Twenty-four-hour gas stations have small shops, too. Ljubljana's large farmers' market is open weekdays and Saturdays. Other towns also have smaller open markets. Slovenia is in the process of privatizing state grocery stores, and many new private businesses are being established.

SOCIETY

Government. Slovenia is a democratic republic. All citizens age 18 and older have the right to vote for members of the National Assembly and for the president, who is head of state. Parliament is a 90-member National Assembly. One seat each is reserved for an elected representative of the Italian and Hungarian minorities. The president, elected for a five-year term, appoints the prime minister with approval of parliament. Several major political parties are represented in parliament, but the largest are the Liberal Democracy of Slovenia, the Social Democratic Party of Slovenia, and the Associated List of Social Democrats.

Slovenia is a member of the United Nations and the Council of Europe, as well as many other international organizations. In 1998, Slovenia began negotiations for full membership in the EU, along with Hungary, the Czech Republic, Poland, Estonia, and Cyprus.

Economy. Slovenia has worked diligently to create a strong market economy through privatization, attracting foreign investment, and promoting international trade. Gross domestic product growth in 2000 was around 4 percent. Inflation is

DEVELOPMENT DATA

Human Dev. Index* rank	29 of 174 countries
Adjusted for women	28 of 143 countries
Real GDP per capita	$14,293
Adult literacy rate	99 percent
Infant mortality rate	5 per 1,000 births
Life expectancy	71 (male); 79 (female)

less than 10 percent, down from 207 percent in 1992. All workers belong to a union that negotiates labor contracts with the Chamber of Economy (representing employers) and the government. The EU receives nearly 70 percent of Slovene exports. Key economic sectors include manufacturing and mining. Slovenia's monetary unit is the *tolar* (SIT).

Transportation and Communications. Public rail, bus, and highway systems are well developed and linked with other European cities. Many persons own cars but may prefer public transportation in cities where parking is a problem. Adria Airways is the national airline. The port of Koper provides full cargo services for central Europe. Slovenia enjoys a free and active press with six daily newspapers and a large variety of periodicals. One state-owned television/radio enterprise and several private television and radio stations operate throughout the country.

Education. Children begin primary school at age six and must attend for at least eight years. Thereafter, they may attend *gymnasium* (an academic high school that prepares students for university) or a vocational school to learn a trade or crafts. After the eighth grade, students must pass the *matura* exam to get a workbook. Without it, one cannot get a job. Maribor and Ljubljana each have a university, with the larger one in Ljubljana (founded in 1919).

Health. Slovenia continues to have the best medical facilities of all the former Yugoslav republics. Its network of public health centers, hospitals, and pharmacies was gradually developed in the Austro-Hungarian period and maintained in the Yugoslav years. The quality of care has kept pace with that in western Europe.

Legislation in 1992 provided that physicians and other health workers may work in public or private practices. Health-care facilities and pharmacies may also operate under private ownership. All Slovenes have basic health insurance. Workers and employers contribute to a fund, and the unemployed are covered by public money. People may purchase additional insurance to cover services not provided in the basic package.

CONTACT INFORMATION

Embassy of the Republic of Slovenia, 1525 New Hampshire Avenue NW, Washington, DC 20036; phone (202) 667-5363; Web site www.embassy.org/slovenia. Slovenia Travel Board, 345 East 12th Street, Suite 27, New York, NY 10003; phone (212) 358-9024.

CultureGrams™
People. The World. You.

1305 North Research Way, Bldg. K
Orem, Utah 84097-6200 USA
1.800.528.6279; 801.705.4250
fax 801.705.4350
www.culturegrams.com

Kingdom of
Spain

Boundary representations are not necessarily authoritative.

BACKGROUND

Land and Climate. Spain occupies most of the Iberian Peninsula in Europe. Covering 194,897 square miles (504,782 square kilometers), it is nearly as large as Nevada and Utah combined. Much of central Spain is a high plateau surrounded by low coastal plains. The famous Pyrenees Mountains are in the north. Other important mountain ranges include the Iberians in the central part of the country and the Sierra Nevada in the south. The northern coasts enjoy a moderate climate with frequent rainfall year-round. The southern and eastern coasts have a more Mediterranean climate, with long, dry summers and mild winters. Spain has many natural resources, including coal, iron ore, uranium, mercury, gypsum, zinc, copper, and potash. About 32 percent of the land is forested. Spain's territory also includes the Balearic Islands and the Canary Islands (a popular tourist retreat), as well as the cities of Ceuta and Melilla, both located on the northern coast of Morocco.

History. Civilization on the Iberian Peninsula has been recorded as far back as 2000 B.C. Various peoples migrated over the centuries to populate the area. Rome began to exercise its influence around 218 B.C. and controlled the entire peninsula by the time of Christ. In the centuries after the Roman Empire fell, Spain was first ruled by the Visigoths, Germanic tribes who invaded in the fifth century, and then by the Muslim Moors, who invaded from North Africa in 711. Christians began to fight the Muslim Empire and finally defeated the Moorish king. The area gradually emerged into two Christian kingdoms: Castile and Aragón. The marriage of Isabella I (Queen of Castile) to Fernando II (King of Aragón) united the kingdoms in 1469. In 1492, Christopher Columbus

sailed under the Spanish flag to the Americas. That same year, most Jews and Muslims were expelled from Spain.

During the 16th century, Spain was one of the largest and most powerful empires in the world. Its territories in the Americas were extensive and wealthy. One of Spain's most famous rulers was Philip II (1556–98), who fought many wars in the name of the Roman Catholic Church. Spain began to lose territory and influence in the 18th century, beginning with the War of the Spanish Succession (1701–14) and continuing through the Napoleonic Wars, which ended in 1815. By 1850, Spain had lost most of its overseas possessions, including the Philippines, Cuba, and other territory, to the United States in 1898.

King Alfonso XIII abdicated his throne in 1931 when the people called for a republic. Unfortunately, civil war erupted in 1936 between the Nationalists (led by Francisco Franco) and the Republicans. After a brutal war, Franco's forces were victorious in 1939. Franco ruled as a dictator until 1975. In 1969, Franco named Juan Carlos de Borbón y Borbón as his eventual successor. When Franco died in 1975, Juan Carlos restored the monarchy and became King Juan Carlos I. He also instituted a democratic constitutional monarchy, and he remains popular today. Prime Minister Adolfo Suarez helped implement many government reforms until he stepped down in 1982.

The Spanish Socialist Workers Party, led by Felipe González, came to power after elections in 1982. Despite numerous political and economic problems, González served in office until 1996. Spain joined the European Union (EU) in 1986. Relations with Europe and the United States were stormy during the 1980s but improved in the 1990s. The government also struggled with the Basque separatists' drive for independence in northern Spain. Violent terrorist attacks by the ETA (Basque Homeland and Freedom) escalated. Nearly eight hundred people have been killed since 1968 as a result of the conflict. Allegations that the government had killed Basques during the 1980s sparked a political crisis in 1994. Already under pressure from many fronts, González lost a majority in parliament and was forced to call early elections; some of his ministers resigned or were arrested.

Conservative José María Aznar (Popular Party) defeated González in the March 1996 elections. Aznar's minority government implemented strict austerity measures, liberalized employment policies, and began to address escalating ETA violence. The ETA called a voluntary cease-fire in September 1998 but ended the cease-fire in December 1999 and renewed its bombing attacks in 2000. A peaceful resolution has not yet emerged. In January 1999, Spain joined with other EU nations in completing the first phase of economic and monetary union. The Popular Party was reelected in March 2000, winning an absolute majority for the first time. The margin of victory means that Aznar will be free to govern without the support of regional parties. The government's primary concerns are dealing with the troubled Basque region, creating jobs, and helping keep Spain on target for full monetary union by 2002.

THE PEOPLE

Population.   The population of Spain is around 40 million and is growing annually at 0.11 percent. The Spanish are a composite of Mediterranean and Nordic ancestry but are considered a homogeneous ethnic group. A small portion of the population is composed of immigrants from Latin American nations, other European countries, Africa, and Asia. More than three-fourths of the population lives in urban areas. Madrid, the capital, has the largest population—about four million people. Barcelona is the next largest urban area with 1.8 million (3 million including suburbs). Low birthrates stem in part from extremely high unemployment, which causes many couples to marry later because of the difficulty of finding work. Then, to hold on to those jobs, couples tend to have smaller families.

Language.   Spain has four official languages. Castilian Spanish is the main language of business and government. The other official languages include Catalan (spoken by 17 percent of the population), Galician (7 percent), and Basque (2 percent). Catalan is spoken mostly in the northeast corner, down the coast to Valencia, and on the Balearic Islands; Galician is spoken in the northwest; and Basque is common in the Basque provinces in the north (near the border with France). Spanish is the language of instruction throughout the country, except in Catalonia where Catalan is used. English is the most common foreign language, followed by French.

Religion.   Spain is largely a Roman Catholic nation; 99 percent of the people are baptized members. Catholic traditions (baptisms, weddings, funerals, and family ties) remain an integral part of society even though many people do not consider themselves religious. Personal devotion often varies by generation. Freedom of religion, granted in the 1970s, opened the way for Spaniards to join other churches. One percent of the population is involved with other (mostly Christian) religious groups. Some Muslims and Jews also reside in Spain.

General Attitudes.   Spaniards place a high value on what others think of them. Peer and family pressure are strong in conditioning individual behavior. Personal pride and appearance—making a good impression and meeting social conventions and expectations—are extremely important. People seek to project an impression of affluence and social position. Regional identities and devotions are strong and increasingly expressed. Personal honor is highly valued: keeping one's word and commitments is an expression of that honor.

The Spanish are generally sociable and helpful people. Many are quite talkative and enjoy giving advice. They consider it their duty to correct "errors" they see in others; however, rules and punctuality tend to be interpreted in a relaxed way. Silence is uncomfortable, so people commonly address complete strangers.

Personal Appearance.   Style and quality of clothing are important indicators of a person's status and respectability. Men usually dress conservatively, avoiding flashy or bright colors. Women like to be stylish, and children are dressed as nicely as possible. People tend to dress up when going out in public. Colorful regional costumes sometimes are worn for festivities.

CUSTOMS AND COURTESIES

Greetings.   Men usually greet each other with a handshake. Good friends often add a pat on the back and, if they have not seen each other for some time, an *abrazo* (hug). Women may greet other women by giving one kiss on each cheek. Such kisses are also very common between a man and a woman when a friend introduces them for the first time, if they haven't seen each other for some time, or if they are bidding farewell. When parting, women give each other a slight embrace and kiss on the cheek. Typical greetings include *¡Buenos días!* (Good day), *¡Buenas tardes!* (Good afternoon), *¡Buenas noches!* (Good evening), and the more casual *¡Hola!* (Hi). Friends or young people may ask *¿Cómo estás?* (How are you?) rather than the more formal *¿Cómo está?*, which is used with older people to show respect. Other local greetings vary according to the language of the region.

People may address professionals or older persons by family name and title, such as *Señor* (Mr.), *Señora* (Mrs.), and *Señorita* (Miss). The titles *Don* and *Doña* are used with the first name to show special respect. Close friends and young people call each other by first name.

Gestures.   Social space is quite close. Spaniards stand close and frequently touch one another on the arm while conversing. Eye contact is also important and often maintained longer than what would be comfortable in other cultures. One indicates "yes" by nodding the head up and down and "no" by moving it side to side. Spaniards often use exaggerated hand gestures and facial expressions to support what they are saying. They may also speak loudly, laugh, and smile a lot. Pointing at others is impolite. Showing emotion in public is acceptable for women but not for men. It is common for men to open doors for women.

Visiting.   Spaniards enjoy visiting, often doing so for hours at a time. Visits are arranged in advance, usually by telephone; arriving unannounced is impolite. It is understood that an invitation to visit someone's home may only be given as a polite courtesy. Ignoring such invitations is acceptable and sometimes even expected. One may accept if the host insists. However, openly declining an invitation is offensive. Guests are expected to stay at least one to two hours, often longer. It is polite for guests to bring a bottle of wine, flowers, or a special dessert (often cake or ice cream), particularly if they are invited to dinner or if someone is ill; a guest would never take back what is left over. Hosts usually serve coffee or refreshments. Light snacks (cheese, chips, olives, etc.) are common before the main meal. On formal occasions, hosts might give gifts to guests, who open the gifts immediately in the hosts' presence.

Eating. People eat at least three meals a day: *el desayuno* (breakfast), *la comida* (lunch), and *la cena* (dinner). Lunch, the most substantial meal, is eaten at about 2 p.m., while dinner is usually at 9 or 10 p.m. Some Spaniards also enjoy a *merienda* (a small snack) between 5 and 6 p.m. The *merienda* usually consists of a *bocadillo* (sandwich), sweet bread, or crackers served with coffee or hot milk. Schedules make it difficult for families to eat together, but many still try to gather for lunch, particularly on weekends.

Spaniards eat in the continental style, with the fork in the left hand and the knife remaining in the right. The knife or bread (in less formal situations) is used to push food onto the fork. Accepting a second serving is one of the best ways to show appreciation to the cook. Upon finishing the meal, one places the knife and fork side by side on the plate; leaving them crossed or on opposite sides of the plate indicates one wishes to eat more.

During the meal, people always keep their hands (but not elbows) above the table. If a person enters a home or room when others are eating, he or she will be invited to join in eating. The invitation usually is extended out of courtesy, and the person generally refuses politely, saying *¡Que aproveche!* (Enjoy your meal). It is considered bad manners for adults to eat while walking down the street.

In restaurants many people enjoy *tapas*, a typically informal meal where guests take small bites from shared dishes. One summons the server by raising a hand. The bill, which is paid to the server, usually includes a service charge, although it is also customary to leave a small tip (5–10 percent of the bill). Compliments or friendly remarks to waiters or other workers are generally appreciated.

LIFESTYLE

Family. The family is important in Spain. Divorce rates are relatively low but are increasing, particularly among young couples. The average family has two children. The father is traditionally the undisputed head of the home. Generally the wife is responsible for caring for the house and children, although many women living in urban areas also work outside the home. About one-third of the labor force is female. Grandparents, aunts, uncles, and cousins commonly maintain close relations with the nuclear family. Men are expected to be strong and masculine, while women are expected to be understanding and feminine. These attitudes are changing in urban areas but still play a key role among rural peoples. In such cases, men enjoy more social freedom than do women. Children usually live with their parents until they marry, regardless of age.

Dating and Marriage. The youth usually begin dating in groups around age 14 and as couples at age 18. In some areas, couples only date if they plan to marry; otherwise, group activities prevail. Rather than call on a girl at her home, a boy often meets a girl at a prearranged site. Couples normally are engaged for a long time while they work and save money to pay for an apartment. Usually parents must approve potential spouses. Most people marry in their late twenties or early thirties. Weddings are followed by a banquet and a dance. Presents often are given in cash to help compensate for expenses.

Diet. Spanish cuisine is typically Mediterranean. Fresh vegetables, meat, eggs, chicken, and fish are common foods. Most fried foods are cooked in olive oil. Meals often include two courses: rice or pulse (e.g., lentils, peas, beans), followed by fish or meat, served with potatoes. Each region also has its own specialties, including seafood, ham and pork sausages, lamb stew, roasted meats, *gazpacho* (cold vegetable soup), *paella* (rice with fish, seafood, and/or meat), *arros negre* (rice with calamari ink), and *cocido* (Castilian soup). Breakfast is generally a light meal of coffee or hot chocolate, bread and jam, or sometimes *churros* (a batter made of flour, salt, and water, deep-fried, and sprinkled with sugar). Lunch usually includes soup, salad, a dish consisting of some kind of fish, a main dish, and fresh fruit. Soup and a *tortilla española* (omelette with potatoes and onions) are common for dinner. Fresh bread, purchased daily from the *panadería* (bread shop), is eaten with every meal. Adults enjoy coffee and wine while children drink mineral water or soft drinks. *Sangría* (a drink made with wine, fruit, and soft drinks) is also popular.

Recreation. Soccer is the most popular spectator sport. Fans often crowd local bars and their homes to watch important matches. Bull fighting (*corrida de torros*), a popular attraction, usually is considered more an art than a sport. Team sports are not part of school programs, so those interested in participating in sports (soccer, tennis, basketball, swimming, and others) join private clubs. Hunting, skiing, and fishing are favorite activities in some areas.

Going to movies or watching television is a popular pastime. People also enjoy taking walks, particularly along the seashore or on main streets, often stopping to greet acquaintances. *Tertulias* (social clubs) meet regularly in cafés to discuss ideas, events, and politics. Men play dominoes, cards, or other games in bars. Bingo parlors and lotteries are also popular. People typically vacation for three to four weeks in July or August. Those living in central Spain go to the beaches or mountains to escape the heat.

The Arts. Music and dance play an important role in the lives of Spaniards. Some common instruments in Spanish music include guitars, *castañuelas* (castanets), tambourines, and *gaitas* (bagpipes). Each region has its own folk dance, music, and dress. Probably originating with Gypsies in southern Spain, flamenco dance is world famous. Many enjoy contemporary music and dance as well.

The Spanish appreciate the performing arts and are proud of their international achievements. World-famous opera tenors Placido Domingo and José Carreras are Spaniards.

The visual arts boast such world-renowned painters as Velázquez, Goya, Picasso, and Dalí. Spain is also rich in folktales and legends, one of which is the story of Don Juan. For hundreds of years, the story has been represented in poetry, plays, movies, and music. Women writers have been

EUROPE ▼

recognized more recently as making vital contributions to Spanish literature.

Holidays. National holidays (both customary and voluntary) include New Year's Day; the Day of the Three Kings (6 Jan.), when Christmas gifts are opened; Holy Week and Easter; Labor Day (1 May); National Day (12 Oct.); All Saints' Day (1 Nov.); Constitution Day (6 Dec.); Immaculate Conception (8 Dec.); and Christmas. Local celebrations can replace voluntary holidays. Each city and region has its own special *fiesta* (festival), usually in honor of a patron saint. Most are held in the summer. People eagerly await these *fiestas*, planning them well in advance. Activities include processions, fireworks, bullfights, amusement attractions, dancing, and wearing regional costumes.

Commerce. Businesses are traditionally open six days a week, from about 9 a.m. to 1:30 p.m. and from 5 to 8 p.m. Banks are open from 9 a.m. to 2 p.m. The midday break traditionally allowed families to be together for the main meal and take a *siesta* (afternoon rest). However, this practice is disappearing, particularly in urban areas. Many businesses stay open all day or have a shorter meal break. Business is not conducted as usual during July and August because many people are away on vacation. Supermarkets gradually are replacing many traditional markets and small family shops.

SOCIETY

Government. Spain is a parliamentary monarchy. King Juan Carlos I is Spain's chief of state, but the prime minister is head of government. Spain's bicameral legislature (*Las Cortes Generales*) consists of a 256-seat Senate and a 350-seat Congress of Deputies, the latter having the greater power. Elections are scheduled every four years but can be held earlier. The voting age is 18. The primary political parties are the Popular Party and the Spanish Socialist Workers Party.

Spain is divided into 17 autonomous communities (regions). Each region has its own rights, elected officials, and justice system. The constitution recognizes the Catalan, Galician, and Basque nationalities as having distinct historic and cultural heritages.

Economy. Economic conditions have improved substantially since Spain joined the EU. Economic opportunities are now available to the majority of the population and most people earn a decent income. Government austerity measures adopted since 1996 enabled Spain to qualify for the European Monetary Union launched in January 1999. The economy grew about 3.2 percent in 2000 and inflation increased 3.7 percent. Economic growth has brought down Spain's unemployment rate to around 14 percent, the lowest rate in 20 years but still the highest in the EU. Efforts to lower unemployment and reduce the deficit are hampered by political opposition to changes in labor laws and pension plans.

Although industry, which employs 29 percent of the labor force, is vital to the economy, the services sector (including tourism) now employs 62 percent. Tourism is increasingly important to economic development, especially in coastal regions. Tourists enjoy visiting Spain for its climate; it is a popular destination for many other Europeans. Agriculture

DEVELOPMENT DATA

Human Dev. Index* rank	21 of 174 countries
Adjusted for women	21 of 143 countries
Real GDP per capita	$16,212
Adult literacy rate	97 percent
Infant mortality rate	5 per 1,000 births
Life expectancy	75 (male); 82 (female)

employs 9 percent of the labor force. Agricultural products include grains, citrus and other fruits, vegetables, and wine grapes. The country exports some food as well as live animals. Spain is a world leader in the production of wine and olive oil. Trade and investment in Latin America also are expanding Spain's economy. The currency is the *peseta* (Pta) until the euro takes its place sometime before July 2002.

Transportation and Communications. Efficient air and rail service is available throughout the country. Trains connect most cities; a high-speed train (AVE, short for *alta velocidad* or "high speed") connects Madrid and Sevilla. Private bus companies serve rural areas. Buses are also common in large cities, but most people prefer to use private vehicles. Madrid, Barcelona, Bilbao, and Valencia have subway systems. The telecommunications system is modern. Half of the adult population uses mobile phones regularly. Dozens of radio and television stations serve the country.

Education. School is compulsory between the ages of six and sixteen, the legal age for starting work. Education for children older than three is available in some areas but does not meet demand. Many schools are operated by the Roman Catholic Church or by private organizations. Middle- and higher-income families spend a good share of their income on private education. Most students attend school until they are 18; some continue their education through vocational training while others prepare for a university education. A general restructuring of education (known by the acronym LOGSE) began in the 1990s and recently was completed. Some of the goals of the restructuring were to increase vocational training, improve the quality of teaching, and better help students with special needs. More women are currently enrolled in Spain's universities than men.

Health. The Spanish enjoy a good system of medical care that is coordinated by the government; private doctors are also available. Spaniards generally enjoy good health, although increasing levels of smoking in youth may affect life expectancy in the future. About 40 percent of Spaniards between the ages of 17 and 24 are smokers. Spain has Europe's highest prevalence of AIDS.

CONTACT INFORMATION

Embassy of the Kingdom of Spain, 2375 Pennsylvania Avenue NW, Washington, DC 20037; phone (202) 452-0100; Web site www.spainemb.org/ingles/indexing.htm. Tourist Office of Spain, 666 Fifth Avenue, 35th Floor, New York, NY 10103; phone (212) 265-8822; Web site www.okspain.org.

1305 North Research Way, Bldg. K
Orem, Utah 84097-6200 USA
1.800.528.6279; 801.705.4250
fax 801.705.4350
www.culturegrams.com

Kingdom of
Sweden

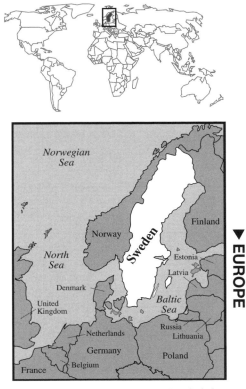

Boundary representations are not necessarily authoritative.

BACKGROUND

Land and Climate. Sweden, one of the "three fingers" of Scandinavia, is just larger than the state of California. It covers 173,732 square miles (449,964 square kilometers). From the northern tip to the southern tip it is about 1,000 miles (1,600 kilometers). Thousands of tiny islands line the coast. Mountains form much of the northwest, but most of Sweden is relatively flat with some rolling hills. Many rivers flow from the mountains through the forests and into the Baltic Sea. Sweden is dotted with lakes, which, with the rivers, provide ample water for the country. More than half of the land is forested. North of the Arctic Circle, winters are long and relatively cold while summers are short and pleasant. But summer's "midnight sun" makes the days long. Although Sweden is located far to the north, most of the country has a relatively temperate climate, moderated by the warm Gulf Stream. July temperatures in Stockholm average 64°F (18°C); January temperatures average 27°F (-3°C), with snow remaining on the ground about one hundred days each year. Important natural resources include timber, silver, zinc, lead, iron ore, and copper. Rivers in the *Norrland* region (roughly the country's northernmost two-thirds) provide most hydroelectric power.

History. Sweden has been inhabited for nearly five thousand years and is the home of the Gothic peoples who battled the Roman Empire. In the ninth century, Rurik, a semilegendary chief of the Swedes, is said to have founded Russia. Christianity was introduced in the 11th century and adopted by the monarchy. Queen Margrethe I of Denmark united Denmark, Norway, and Sweden in the Union of Kalmar in 1397. Sweden remained fairly autonomous and even had its own parliament in 1435. It became an independent kingdom in

1523, with Gustaf I Vasa as ruler. The kingdom fought wars with Denmark and Russia in the 16th and 17th centuries, and by the 17th century, Sweden was one of the Great Powers of Europe. It acquired Norway in 1814 through the Napoleonic Wars. Swedish power declined in the 19th century. Finland was an integral part of Sweden until 1809, when it briefly became an archdukedom of Russia. Norway became independent in 1905. The Frenchman Jean Baptiste Bernadotte was elected Sweden's crown prince in 1810 and became king in 1818 as Karl XIV Johan. His dynasty continues today.

During the 20th century, neutrality and nonalignment were cornerstones of Sweden's foreign policy, keeping it out of both world wars and allowing it to transform its rather poor society into a prosperous social welfare state. The Social Democratic Party dominated politics and led every government until 1976, when its rule was interrupted until 1982. With the end of the Cold War, and increased European integration, Sweden joined the European Union (EU) in 1995.

Sweden's image as a peaceful, egalitarian society, with relatively low crime, was shaken in 1986 when Prime Minister Olof Palme was assassinated on the streets of Stockholm. Palme was succeeded by Ingvar Carlsson of the Social Democratic Party. After the rejection of his austerity package in 1990, Carlsson resigned and led a minority government until elections in 1991. The new prime minister, Carl Bildt of the Moderate Party, formed a coalition government. Bildt's administration concentrated on economic challenges and negotiated Sweden's entry into the EU.

The Social Democrats won the 1994 elections, and Ingvar Carlsson returned to power. Carlsson retired from the party leadership in November 1995 and was replaced by his finance minister, Göran Persson. A fiscal conservative, Persson continued austerity measures aimed at improving the country's finances. Although a member of the EU, Sweden opted out of joining Europe's Economic and Monetary Union (EMU) in 1999 due to voter opposition to welfare service cuts. More recent polls indicate that Swedes remain ambivalent about adopting the euro.

Persson became prime minister after September 1998 elections, in which his Social Democratic Party lost substantial ground, and currently governs in a coalition with the ex-communist Left Party and the Greens. Employment, EMU, and taxes are all issues being debated in Parliament. Sweden took over the six-month presidency of the EU in January 2001.

THE PEOPLE

Population. Sweden's population of 8.9 million is growing at 0.02 percent per year. More than 80 percent of Swedes live in the southern third of the country. At least 85 percent of the people are ethnic Swede. Finns compose about 5 percent of the population; most of them are immigrants from Finland, but some are native to northern Sweden. A small indigenous minority (up to 20,000 people), the Sami (pronounced SAW-me), live in the north. Traditionally, they herded reindeer for a living. While some continue that occupation, most are involved in other fields. The Sami are known to some as Lapps, but this is a derogatory term and therefore not used in Sweden. Immigrants have added to Sweden's population since the 1960s; Swedish immigration laws are some of the most liberal in Europe. One-eighth of the population is immigrants or has at least one immigrant parent. Many immigrants recently have come from the former Yugoslavia, Greece, Turkey, and Latin American or African countries.

An extensive social welfare system provides for most of the people's needs and affords them many choices in their lives. Swedish men and women, whose earned income share is the highest in the world, enjoy equal access to opportunities for personal advancement.

Language. Swedes speak Swedish—a Germanic language related to Danish, Norwegian, and Icelandic. Swedish emerged as a distinct language around the 10th century. The Sami speak their own language and the Finnish minority speaks Finnish. Most immigrants speak their native tongue in the home. Many people speak English, which is also taught in the schools.

Religion. Sweden, like most of Europe, is a highly secular society. Freedom of religion is guaranteed by the constitution. Most Swedes (about 87 percent) are members of the Evangelical Lutheran Church but rarely attend church services. The Lutheran Church is supported by the state; however, plans to largely separate church and state began in 1995. Membership is growing in other religious organizations. Most of these are various other Christian churches, such as the Roman Catholic faith, which has a following of about 1 percent of the population. Other groups, such as Muslims and Jews, also are expanding, primarily due to the immigrant population.

General Attitudes. Swedes are somewhat more reserved than people in the United States. Friendships are important but take time to develop. Swedes are proud of their nation, as well as their regions and towns. Visitors who recognize this pride are careful not to praise another area over the one being visited. Swedes value modesty and material security. Punctuality also is emphasized in various aspects of daily life.

Sweden has built one of the most egalitarian societies in the world and has managed to develop a strong capitalist economy. Swedes can rely on a generous social welfare system to provide health, education, and retirement benefits. While public sentiment in the early 1990s led to some cuts in the system, most people oppose deep changes in what are called "cradle-to-grave" benefits.

With the exception of the Nobel Peace Prize, which Norway sponsors, Sweden awards the Nobel Prizes each year. These prizes are given to significant contributors in the areas of chemistry, literature, medicine, and physics. Alfred Bernhard Nobel (1833–96), the inventor of dynamite and a wealthy businessman, was born in Sweden.

Personal Appearance. General European fashions are common. However, because of the country's cooler climate, Swedes wear warm clothing more often than other Europeans. People generally dress conservatively; it is important to be neat and clean in public. Swedes may not dress up as much as people in other countries when they go out. They prefer to avoid glamorous clothing but are still fashionable. Traditional costumes, which vary by region, are worn on special occasions.

CUSTOMS AND COURTESIES

Greetings. Swedes commonly shake hands when meeting. Most adults will shake hands with each person in the room when entering or leaving a social setting. From a distance, one may nod the head or raise the hand to greet another person. People usually address each other by first name; they use titles only in very formal situations. More formal greetings include *God dag* (Good day) or *God morgon* (Good morning). However, most people are more casual and say *Hej* (pronounced HEY, meaning "Hi"). One answers the phone with *Hallå* (Hello) and clearly identifies oneself. "Good-bye" is *Adjö* or, more casually, *Hej då*.

Gestures. Eye contact is important during conversation. Swedes avoid excessive hand gestures when speaking. Chewing gum, yawning, or having one's hands in the pockets when speaking to another person is considered impolite. Although in the past people seldom embraced in public or put their arm around another's shoulder, the population in general is becoming more casual and such displays of friendship are increasing.

Visiting. Swedes enjoy visiting one another, but they do not often visit without prior arrangement. Hosts usually offer guests coffee or something else to drink. People most often entertain in the home; it is popular to invite friends over for an evening meal. Guests are expected to arrive on time. In bad weather, they usually bring an indoor pair of shoes to wear after entering the home. An odd number of flowers or a box of chocolates are common gifts for the hosts. Sweets for the children are appropriate if the parents approve. Guests unwrap flowers before giving them to the hostess. If they do not give a gift, guests usually send a thank-you card later in the mail. It is also customary to thank the host or hostess for their hospitality the next time a guest sees them.

It is impolite to "eat and run." Swedes expect guests to

stay for coffee and conversation, even as late as 11 p.m. Conversation, ranging over a wide variety of topics, is a popular pastime. When leaving, guests say good-bye before they put on their coats.

Eating. Swedes eat a light breakfast around 7 a.m. and might have a coffee or tea break at midmorning. The main meal (*middag*) traditionally was eaten at midday. This is still the case in most rural areas, but urban residents eat only a light lunch at noon and then have their main meal around 6 p.m. Swedes eat in the continental style, with the fork in the left hand and the knife remaining in the right. A dinner knife is not used as a butter knife, since separate butter knives usually are provided. Diners keep hands, not elbows, above the table during the meal. When finished eating, a person places the utensils side by side on the plate. Leaving any food on the plate is impolite. Guests usually wait for the hosts to offer second helpings. Declining is not impolite, but guests may take more if they desire. Food is placed in serving dishes on the table, so if they are empty there is usually no more food and asking for more would be impolite.

For some occasions, the host makes a welcome speech at the beginning of the meal. The host then makes a toast (*skål*) and all dinner guests taste the wine. The guest of honor makes a speech during the dessert, elaborating on the meal and the charm of the hostess. Each guest personally thanks the host directly after the meal.

LIFESTYLE

Family. The structure of the family in Sweden has changed over the years. Extended family relationships are maintained through gatherings and holiday visits. The nuclear family is the basic social unit and is usually strong and close-knit. Most families have only one or two children. Many women work outside the home; they comprise nearly half of the labor force. Young children are cared for during working hours at day-care centers. Adult children are expected to be independent. Elderly individuals generally rely on the social system or themselves for their care and support.

Many urban families live in apartments, but most people in smaller towns and rural areas have single-family dwellings. Sweden is known for its red wooden houses built in the 18th and 19th centuries that still dot the countryside.

Dating and Marriage. Although serious dating is reserved for older teens, Swedes start to date early. They enjoy going to movies, eating out, having parties, and dancing. Many people choose to live together before or instead of marrying. Often, a couple marries when they have a child. Divorce and single-parent homes are on the rise. Unmarried couples who live together have nearly the same rights and obligations as married couples. That is, cohabitation is nearly the same as marriage under the law.

Diet. Health concerns have affected eating patterns in Sweden in much the same way they have in other industrialized countries. Once heavy in meat, fish, and cheese, the diet now includes many fresh vegetables and fruits. Common foods include potatoes (eaten a few times a week), cheeses of many types, seafood, and other fresh foods. For breakfast, one might eat *fil* (a kind of yogurt), *knäckebröd* (crisp bread) with margarine, and coffee. Open-face sandwiches (*smörgåsar*) are also popular. Some favorite main-meal dishes include *Köttbullar med kokt potatis, brun sås och lingonsylt* (meat-

balls with brown sauce, boiled potatoes and lingonberry jam); *Stekt falukorv med senap och potatis* (fried slices of thick German sausage with mustard and boiled or fried potatoes); *grillad lax med spenat, citron och potatis eller ris* (grilled slices of salmon with spinach, slices of lemon, and potatoes or rice); and *Pytt i Panna* (potatoes, leftover meats, and onions, fried with an egg on top and served with pickled beets).

The *smörgåsbord* is a lavish buffet eaten (mostly at restaurants) on holidays or special occasions. It is not an everyday meal. A *smörgåsbord* includes warm and cold dishes, meat, fish, and desserts. Some families have a special type of *smörgåsbord* on Christmas Eve.

Recreation. Swedes are sports enthusiasts. Popular sports include soccer, skiing, tennis, golf, swimming, ice hockey, bandy (a game related to hockey), and orienteering races (using a map and compass to cross an area). Ice-skating and other winter sports are common. Physical fitness is particularly important to Swedes. Most towns have lighted exercise trails for jogging/walking (in the summer) or cross-country skiing (in the winter).

Even more popular than sports are activities such as hiking, fishing, and bird-watching. Swedes love nature and spend as much time as possible outdoors. For many, the ideal is owning a summer cottage for weekends and vacations. Sweden's mountains and fells are popular destinations. Favorite leisure activities also include reading, attending cultural events such as the theater or concerts, and watching movies and television. Singing in choirs is by far Sweden's most popular hobby, with 1.5 million participants.

The Arts. Because the arts in Sweden receive substantial public and private funding, cultural activities are accessible throughout the country. People enjoy traditional music by singing, playing instruments, or attending festivals. Common types of music are the *polksa* (polka) and the *vals* (waltz). The fiddle, wind instruments, and accordion are prominent instruments. The *nyckelharpa* (key fiddle) is a Swedish invention.

Swedish filmmakers and actors are known worldwide. Ingmar Bergman is recognized as a major figure in contemporary filmmaking. Perhaps the most acclaimed Swedish writer is August Strindberg.

Common crafts are tiled stoves, wood carvings, ceramics, textiles, and stainless steel. Swedish design and architecture are recognized for their simplicity and functionality.

Holidays. Sweden's national holidays include New Year's Day, May Day (1 May), and National Day (6 June). Other holidays often are associated with the season or a religious event. At *Påsk* (Easter), children dress up like old witches with brooms and go door-to-door (among friends and neighbors only) to collect candy. Colored Easter eggs are also common at this time.

Midsommar (Midsummer) celebrations are held in late June (usually around the 20th) when the summer days are much longer than the nights. Festivities include dancing around the maypole and having picnics. In contrast, *Lucia* coincides with the longest night of the year. On the morning of 13 December, a girl in the family (or school or town) assumes the role of St. Lucia (the "light queen") and dresses in white with a crown of candles in her hair. She sings a special song and serves coffee and *lussekatter* (Lucia cats), a type of roll. This often marks the beginning of *Jul* (Christmas) season. The climax is Christmas Eve, when a

▼ **EUROPE**

family *smörgåsbord* is accompanied by gift giving. The *Jultomte*, which was once a Christmas gnome who lived under the house, is now the Swedish Santa Claus who brings gifts to the door for the children. A Christmas tree is placed in the house only a few days before Christmas Eve. Christmas day is spent relaxing, while 26 December is for visiting family and friends.

Commerce. Business hours generally run from 9 a.m. to 5 p.m., with some variations. For example, many businesses (but not shops) close by 4 p.m. in the summer. Banks usually close at 3 p.m. People buy their food and other goods from supermarkets and department stores, as well as smaller neighborhood shops. Open-air markets operate in some places on Wednesdays and Saturdays; they usually only sell fresh produce.

Swedes enjoy one of the shortest workweeks in the industrialized world. They receive at least five weeks of vacation each year, along with other benefits. Some benefits recently were cut to reverse a trend toward lower productivity and absenteeism.

SOCIETY

Government. Sweden is a constitutional monarchy. King Carl XVI Gustaf, a descendant of the Bernadotte Dynasty, has ruled since 1973. His duties are mostly ceremonial. The head of government is the prime minister. Members of the 349-seat Parliament (*Riksdag*) are elected for four-year terms. The voting age is 18. Municipal councils handle local affairs. Immigrants must reside in the country three years before they can vote in local elections. Citizenship is required to vote in national elections.

Economy. Sweden has one of the most prosperous economies in the world. It is highly industrialized, has a modern distribution system, and boasts a skilled and educated labor force. Only around 2 percent of the workforce is engaged in agriculture, while 21 percent labors in mining and manufacturing. Sweden is a major producer of automobiles (such as Volvo and Saab) and exports machinery and steel products. Timber exports (mostly pulp for paper products) are also important. Lacking indigenous fossil fuels, which must be imported, Sweden depends on nuclear and hydroelectric power for 90 percent of its energy needs.

In spite of its strengths, Sweden's economy was hampered in the early 1990s by budgetary difficulties, inflation, unemployment, and a gradual decline in global competitiveness. Fortunately, recent austerity measures have boosted confidence in the economy, inflation is at a record low, and the government budget has yielded surpluses in recent years. The economy grew by 4 percent in 2000. Unemployment is currently about 4 percent. Membership in the EU is expected to provide greater opportunities for trade and economic growth.

Although salaries are high, the cost of living is high, too. An income tax funds the country's extensive welfare system. Tax rates peaked at 70 percent in 1989 but dropped to 51 percent in 1991 due to demands for change. Private alternatives and other cuts have encouraged greater productivity and reduced overall costs. Preserving key elements of the

DEVELOPMENT DATA

Human Dev. Index* rank .... 6 of 174 countries
   Adjusted for women .... 6 of 143 countries
Real GDP per capita $20,659
Adult literacy rate .... 99 percent
Infant mortality rate .... 3 per 1,000 births
Life expectancy .... 77 (male); 82 (female)

country's welfare system remains important to most Swedes. The currency is the Swedish *krona* (SKr).

Transportation and Communications. Only one in four households does not own a car. Although private cars provide important transportation, public transport is well developed, punctual, and frequently used. Trains, buses, subways, and streetcars are common. There are three international airports. Most roads are paved and in good condition. The Øresund Link, a combined motorway and railway link between Copenhagen, Denmark, and Malmö, Sweden, opened in July 2000. The telecommunications system is excellent. Sweden relies heavily on mobile phone service. The Swedish Broadcasting Corporation, which used to have a legal monopoly on television broadcasting, now faces competition from other broadcasters. Cable and satellite television are available. Many Swedes use the Internet; Sweden has a high density of Web servers.

Education. Illiteracy is virtually unknown. The Swedish government spends more money per pupil than most other countries. The public school system is a comprehensive nine-year program that children begin at age seven. All education is free, and one free hot meal is provided each day. Immigrant children have the right to some instruction in their native language. When compulsory education ends at age 16, students have several choices. About one-fifth start working. The others choose between a three-year high school (with a focus in either the social or natural sciences) and a three-year vocational school. There are more than 30 institutions of higher learning. Tuition is free and loans are available for living costs. Adult education programs are extensive.

Health. All Swedes are covered by national health insurance. The government pays nearly all fees incurred for medical care. At least 85 percent of day-care costs also are covered. Dental fees are shared by the individual. While basic health care is readily available, elective surgery must often wait several months before being approved. In response to public demand, private health-care options are now more widely available, as are private child-care facilities. The government pays an ill person's wages for an extended period. Parents share a total of 12 months' leave when a child is born. The infant mortality rate is one of the world's lowest.

CONTACT INFORMATION

Embassy of Sweden, 1501 M Street NW, Washington, DC 20005; phone (202) 467-2600; Web site www.swedenemb .org. Scandinavian Tourist Board, PO Box 4649, Grand Central Station, New York, NY 10163-4649; phone (212) 885-9700; Web site www.goscandinavia.com.

1305 North Research Way, Bldg. K
Orem, Utah 84097-6200 USA
1.800.528.6279; 801.705.4250
fax 801.705.4350
www.culturegrams.com

Switzerland
(Swiss Confederation)

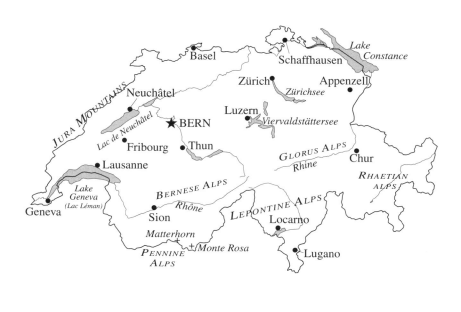

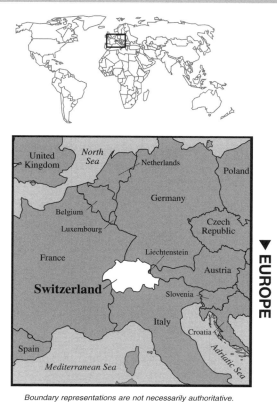

▼ EUROPE

Boundary representations are not necessarily authoritative.

BACKGROUND

Land and Climate. Covering 15,942 square miles (41,290 square kilometers), Switzerland is just smaller than Denmark or about twice the size of New Jersey. Switzerland is sometimes called the "roof of Europe" because of its towering Alps, which cover more than half of the country, running east to west. The Jura Mountains extend across another 10 percent of the territory. The highest mountain peaks include Monte Rosa at 15,209 feet (4,635 meters) and the Matterhorn at 14,691 feet (4,478 meters). Numerous lakes and large flat green valleys are interspersed throughout the majestic Alps. Swiss waters drain into five key European rivers: the Rhine, Rhône, Po, Adige, and Danube.

The climate varies according to elevation and region but is generally temperate. In major cities, daily summer temperatures average 77°F (25°C), while winter temperatures range between 27°F and 32°F (-3–0°C). Winters tend to be long and snowy, especially in mountainous areas, while the valleys are frequently foggy and rainy. Switzerland's diverse landscape and distinct seasons make it one of the most beautiful places on earth.

History. The Celtic tribes that occupied the area of present-day Switzerland were part of the Roman Empire for five centuries. Later, Burgundian tribes settled in the west and Alemannians in the east; both were Germanic tribes, but they developed along different lines. During most of the Middle Ages, Switzerland was part of the Holy Roman Empire.

Switzerland is one of the world's oldest democracies. The founding of the Swiss Confederation took place on 1 August 1291, when the mountain cantons of Uri, Schwyz, and Unterwalden began a revolt against Austrian Hapsburg control by signing the Perpetual Covenant of 1291. Through a series of military victories, Swiss soldiers gained a reputation for their fighting prowess. The confederation later grew more powerful by adding other cantons (Luzern, Zürich, Bern). After withstanding the turmoil and war of the 16th and early 17th centuries, Switzerland received official recognition as an independent nation in the 1648 Treaty of Westphalia.

In 1815, because of a brief invasion by Napoleon, Switzerland became permanently neutral. Early in the 19th century, Switzerland became a centralized nation-state. In 1848, it adopted a constitution, making it a federal state. In 1874, direct democracy by the people became an integral part of the constitution. During the 19th century, Switzerland became industrialized and urbanized. While other neutral European nations fell to attacking armies during World Wars I and II, Switzerland, aided by natural geography, remained neutral and was not invaded.

As part of its neutrality, the Swiss Federation is not a member of the United Nations (it has observer status), the North Atlantic Treaty Organization (NATO), or the European Union (EU). However, it maintains solid relations with many nations. Switzerland serves the world by sponsoring the International Red Cross, hosting some UN offices, and acting as an impartial location for peace conferences and summits.

Switzerland's image was tarnished in 1996 after Jewish groups and others alleged its status in World War II was not entirely neutral. Millions of dollars belonging to European

Jews were deposited in Swiss bank accounts before or during the war and then "lost" or used to fund Nazi activities. Several years of negotiations led to an August 1998 settlement by the two largest Swiss banks to pay a $1.25 billion sum to cover losses from Holocaust survivors during World War II.

In April 1999, the Swiss approved several constitutional amendments, including changing the requirement that the currency be backed by gold, granting the right to strike, and giving equal opportunity to the handicapped. Currently, one of the government's foreign policy priorities is to strengthen ties with the EU. Domestic objectives include reducing the budget deficit, reforming the state pension plan, and determining the future of Switzerland's nuclear power stations.

THE PEOPLE

Population. The population of Switzerland is almost 7.3 million and is growing at 0.3 percent annually. Switzerland is made up of a variety of ethnic groups. Germans, who account for 65 percent of the total population, dominate in the east and central cantons. The French are located mostly in the west and comprise 18 percent of the population. In parts of the south, most people are of Italian descent and make up 10 percent of the total population. One percent of the population has Romansch ancestry. About 6 percent of the people who live in Switzerland have come from the Middle East, the former Yugoslavia, Spain, Greece, Italy, and other countries. Most of them are guest workers and do not have Swiss citizenship. The largest cities are Zürich (500,000), Geneva (300,000), and Basel (250,000). Switzerland affords its people a high standard of living and excellent access to health care, education, and economic opportunities.

Language. Four official languages are spoken in Switzerland: German, French, Italian, and Romansch. Each canton has the right to declare which language it will use. All street signs are in that language only. In the schools, all the languages are available for study, but the language of instruction is that of the canton. Most Swiss can understand at least one of the other official languages of the confederation, and many speak English, which is also offered in the schools. Although French and Italian are basically spoken as written, there is a difference between written German (standard German) and what is spoken every day by the German Swiss. Their dialect (Schwiizertütsch) is rather unique and difficult for other German-speaking peoples to understand. Protection of minority languages and relations between the different language groups continue to be important political issues.

Religion. Close to half of the people are Roman Catholic and the other half belong to various other Christian churches, mostly Protestant. There is a small Jewish minority (0.3 percent of the population). Switzerland was the center of the Zwingli and Calvin Protestant Reformations of the 16th century and has produced important modern theologians. Swiss Protestant churches are locally controlled and democratic. Both Catholic and Protestant churches have generally worked toward greater harmony. Switzerland is a secular society and participation in religion often is reserved for special events and holidays. As elsewhere in Europe, religion has greater influence in rural areas than in the cities.

General Attitudes. The Swiss value nature and beauty and are proud of their efforts to protect the environment. Their attitudes have been influenced by the majestic mountains and beautiful lakes found throughout Switzerland. Recycling is widely practiced. The Swiss also value hard work, sobriety, thrift, and independence. They prize tolerance, punctuality, and a sense of responsibility. A favorite saying claims that if people are late, they are either not wearing Swiss watches or not riding Swiss trains.

The Swiss are proud of their political and social system, which is unique in Europe. One of its key elements is the federal system that unites different groups into one country. The motto is "Unity, yes; uniformity, no." Each canton is highly autonomous, but all citizens participate in national civic affairs. For example, every physically fit male serves in the Swiss Army. They train regularly and keep their guns and uniforms at home—always ready to form a militia to defend the country. There are only a few professional officers; most serve part-time. While this structure has been challenged recently, it remains intact.

Switzerland's self-confidence recently has been tested by domestic social problems, its decision to forego European integration, questions about its political neutrality, and immigration debates. Redefining its role in a new Europe and determining how best to adapt its grassroots form of democracy to the 21st century are challenging tasks. These tasks are further complicated by an intense national pride in the Swiss way of life and by political disagreements between the French- and German-speaking populations, especially where European integration issues are concerned.

Personal Appearance. People dress conservatively and well, following modern European fashions. The Swiss place a high value on cleanliness, neatness, and orderliness. Suits and ties are required for businessmen. Some people may wear casual clothing to work, depending on the situation. Traditional costumes are reserved for special occasions.

CUSTOMS AND COURTESIES

Greetings. A handshake is appropriate for men and women. When entering or leaving an elevator or a store, most Swiss exchange simple greetings, even with strangers. People in small villages exchange greetings on the street. Because the Swiss Confederation is a multilingual society, actual verbal greetings may vary. German greetings include *Guten Morgen* (Good morning), *Guten Tag* (Good day), *Guten Abend* (Good evening), and *Auf Wiedersehen* (Until we meet again). *Grütsie* (Hi) is a typical Swiss German greeting used throughout the day. In formal situations, French speakers often say *Bonjour* (Good day) or *Bonsoir* (Good evening). Friends may greet each other with *Salut* (Hello) or *Tchao* (Hi). It is most polite to address others by their title and surname. Although the youth use first names, adults generally reserve first names for close friends and family members.

Gestures. People generally avoid speaking with their hands. Chewing gum or attending to matters of personal hygiene in public is not appropriate. Talking to an older person with one's hands in the pockets is generally considered disrespectful. However, people usually place their hands inside their coats to keep warm during winter. Legs generally are crossed with one knee over the other. When one is entering or leaving a building, it is polite to hold the door for the next person.

Visiting. Visits, particularly those on weekends, are planned in advance. Many people belong to sports, religious, or cultural associations. People may get together with their families on special occasions (Christmas, Easter, etc.), or they may meet friends in their associations; otherwise, people tend to keep to themselves. Being at home is important and enjoyed by most adults.

The Swiss are hospitable to guests and expect courtesy in return. Dinner guests often bring chocolates or a bottle of wine for the host and flowers for the hostess. Flowers generally are presented in odd numbers and are unwrapped before being given. When one leaves a home, it is customary to shake hands with all members of the family or group.

Eating. Lunch, which is heavier than dinner, usually is eaten at 12:30 p.m. Dinner is eaten around 6:30 p.m. The Swiss use the continental style of eating, with the fork in the left hand and the knife remaining in the right. Soft foods, such as potatoes, are cut with a fork, not a knife. Cutting such foods with a knife implies they are improperly cooked. The best compliment one can give is to take additional helpings. Asking for salt or pepper is often considered an insult because it implies the food is improperly spiced. When finished eating, a person places the utensils side by side on the plate. If they are placed another way, it may indicate the person wants to eat more. During a meal, hands (not elbows) are always kept above the table. In restaurants, service charges usually are included in the bill, which is paid at the table.

LIFESTYLE

Family. The nuclear family is the most important social unit in Swiss society. Families are generally small, with only one or two children. Family privacy is important. The man is traditionally the head of the household. An increasing number of women work outside the home, although still fewer than in many other European countries. Maternity benefits for working women are limited. Children of working parents are sent to day care and schools. Women gradually are taking a greater part in political life. Only in 1971 did women receive the right to vote in national elections and in most cantons. By 1990, only the Appenzell canton of Inner-Rhoden continued to deny women the right to vote on local issues.

About 70 percent of the people rent their housing. Most urban families live in three-bedroom flats or apartments; houses are more common in rural areas. Housing is built in harmony with the environment. Switzerland is known for its chalet-style homes in rural areas.

Dating and Marriage. Youth as young as 14 often socialize in groups and begin dating a few years later. Going to nightclubs (discos), restaurants, pubs, and the cinema are popular activities. The legal age for marriage is 18 for women and 20 for men. Most adults marry in their mid- to late twenties. Many couples prefer to live together for several years before or instead of marrying. It is often important to finish one's education or become financially established before getting married. Church weddings are popular and typically followed by a dinner with dancing. There are no obligations between families; the newly married couple usually finances their own marriage.

Diet. Meat, potatoes, and milk products (cheese, yogurt, creams, etc.) are the main foods. Potatoes are prepared in a variety of ways, such as *Röstis* (grated, pan-fried potatoes) or *Gratin* (potatoes sliced and baked with white sauce and cream), french fries, or boiled potatoes. Grilled sausage, known as *Bratwurst* (in German) or *saucisse* (in French), is popular. Regional specialties include various sausages, rich cheeses, special wines, fish, leek soup, and pork. Each canton has its own specialty bread. *Fondue* (melted cheese on a piece of bread) and *Raclette* (melted cheese on a piece of potato) are popular cheese dishes. Fruit pies and cakes are enjoyed also.

Breakfast is light and might include various types of fresh breads, cheeses, and coffee. Lunch usually consists of a main dish with meat, some form of potatoes, and a salad. Open-faced sandwiches commonly are eaten at dinner. In major urban areas, the trend is to have the main meal in the evening.

Recreation. The Swiss enjoy vacationing, either within their own country or abroad. They love nature and the outdoors and enjoy hiking, skiing, and other such activities. Mountain climbing is a favorite for some. Soccer and cycling are the most popular sports. A small number enjoy traditional Swiss games, such as *schwinger*, a type of wrestling that is similar to Graeco-Roman wrestling but does not have weight classifications. The Swiss also enjoy taking walks, watching movies, and attending cultural events.

The Arts. Swiss visual arts have increased in stature in the 20th century. Paul Klee, Alberto Giacometti, and Jean Tinguely have all achieved international reputations. Photography and graphic arts are prominent. A variety of excellent museums, both large and small, provide access to the work of artists around the world.

Prominent Swiss writers include Nobel Prize winner Carl Spitteler, as well as contemporary dramatists Friedrich Dürrenmatt and Max Frisch. Le Corbusier was an important figure in developing the International Style, a major architectural influence in the 20th century.

Swiss folk music is famous, particularly yodeling and alpenhorn blowing. The alpenhorn, up to 12 feet long, is used for communication and to provide music for ceremonies and other events. Other popular folk art forms are wood carving and embroidery.

Holidays. Major holidays include New Year's Day, Easter (Friday–Monday), Labor Day (1 May), Ascension, Whitsunday and Whitmonday, National Day (1 Aug.), Federal Day of Prayers (a thanksgiving holiday in mid-September), and Christmas. Christmas is the biggest celebration of the year. Gifts are exchanged on Christmas Eve, when the family gathers for a large meal. The family relaxes on Christmas day and visits friends on 26 December. New Year's Eve is a time for parties and fireworks.

Commerce. In general, business hours are from 8 a.m. to noon and from 2 to 6 p.m., Monday through Friday. Government offices close between 2 and 4 p.m.; banks close at 4 p.m. Large stores do not close at midday. Some stores remain open later in the evening on certain nights, and hours vary between the different cantons. All cities and villages have supermarkets.

▼ EUROPE

SOCIETY

Government. Switzerland is a highly decentralized federal state; most political power resides in the 26 cantons, as well as local communities. Constitutional amendments can be initiated by popular initiative, and virtually all important legislation is subject to popular referendums. Each community has its own constitution and laws but is under the supervision of the canton. Each canton also has its own constitution and control over such things as school systems, police, welfare, and local issues. At these two levels, decisions are made by the people.

At the federal level, democracy becomes more representative. The Federal Assembly has two houses, one with representatives of the people (200-seat National Council) and one with representatives of the cantons (46-seat Council of States). Members of both bodies are directly elected to four-year terms. Several political parties have legislative representation, including the Radical Free Democratic Party, Social Democratic Party, Christian Democratic People's Party, and Swiss People's Party. Following elections at the end of 1999, the Social Democratic Party maintained its majority of seats in the National Council, and the Radical Free Democratic Party won a majority in the Council of States.

A Federal Council constitutes the executive branch; it has seven members elected to a four-year term by the Federal Assembly. Each year, the council selects one council member to serve as its president. That person is then technically the president of Switzerland for a calendar year because that is the highest office in the land. A vice president is also chosen for a year. Switzerland's current president is Adolf Ogi. The federal government is responsible for foreign policy and matters affecting all cantons.

Economy. Despite a lack of natural resources, Switzerland has one of the strongest and most stable economies in the world. Its people enjoy a high standard of living and have the highest rate of job satisfaction in Europe. Its economy has high standards of performance and a strong middle class; poverty is nearly nonexistent. The economy is slowly recovering from a six-year recession. Growth in 2000 was around 3 percent. Unemployment and inflation remain low.

Switzerland is known as the banking and finance capital of the world. Changes to its banking laws have been made to prevent the opening of accounts by corrupt sources. Its finance industry has fueled economic success. Tourism is a vital and driving force in the economy; industrial production is equally important. The Swiss produce not only fine watches and cheeses but also machinery, chemicals, textiles, and various precision instruments. They are known for their excellent quality and craftsmanship. Switzerland donates money to various development projects around the world.

The Swiss people have not wanted to join the EU (against the advice of Swiss business and political leaders). In a 1992 national referendum, voters rejected a proposal to join the European Economic Area (EEA). Many fear this will further isolate Switzerland from the European economy.

DEVELOPMENT DATA

Human Dev. Index* rank	13 of 174 countries
Adjusted for women	13 of 143 countries
Real GDP per capita	$25,512
Adult literacy rate	99 percent
Infant mortality rate	5 per 1,000 births
Life expectancy	77 (male); 83 (female)

Switzerland's currency is the *franc* (SFR).

Transportation and Communications. Due to Switzerland's small land area and high population density, the country has a very well-developed public transportation system. Buses, streetcars, and trains form the backbone of the transportation network. Still, most families have cars, and private transport is common. Voters have banned heavy truck traffic from Swiss roads, causing large transportation problems for other European nations. Recent negotiations between the EU and the Swiss have not been successful at resolving the dispute. A new high-speed rail link between Geneva and Brussels began operating in May 2000. Communications systems are excellent and completely modern. Numerous television and radio stations broadcast throughout the country, and daily newspapers are available everywhere.

Education. Education is the responsibility of the individual cantons. Education is free and compulsory until age 15. There are three basic levels: primary, secondary, and *gymnasia* (high school). The high schools provide preparation for a university education. Many students choose to enter a vocational school after their secondary education. There are a number of private schools in addition to the state schools. Seven cantonal universities, two federal institutes of technology, a college of education, and a university for economic and social sciences are available. Many students travel abroad for advanced training. Switzerland spends a slightly lower percentage of its income on education and has a lower enrollment rate than many other industrialized countries.

Health. Both private and public hospitals exist. Medical facilities offer efficient care, and personnel are well trained. While the government provides benefits for the elderly and social welfare, it does not have a uniform system of health insurance. Each canton has different laws regarding insurance, but most people must purchase private insurance. The Swiss generally enjoy good health, a fact reflected in their high life expectancy. Switzerland, which has one of the highest rates of drug addiction in Europe, voted against a proposed 1998 amendment to legalize heroin and other narcotics.

CONTACT INFORMATION

Embassy of Switzerland, 2900 Cathedral Avenue NW, Washington, DC 20008; phone (202) 745-7900; Web site www.swissemb.org. The Swiss National Tourist Office, 608 Fifth Avenue, Swiss Center, New York, NY 10020; phone (212) 757-5944; Web site www.myswitzerland.com.

CultureGrams™
People. The World. You.

1305 North Research Way, Bldg. K
Orem, Utah 84097-6200 USA
1.800.528.6279; 801.705.4250
fax 801.705.4350
www.culturegrams.com

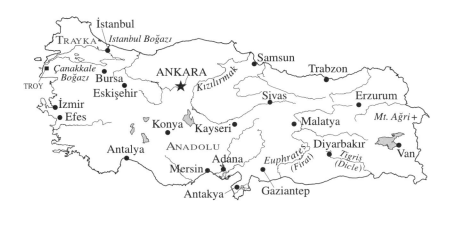

▼ EURASIA

Boundary representations are not necessarily authoritative.

BACKGROUND

Land and Climate. Turkey is located at the juncture where Europe meets Asia, forming a bridge and a link to each continent. Covering 301,382 square miles (780,580 square kilometers), Turkey is about the size of Texas. The northwestern portion is called Thrace (*Trayka*), while the remaining area is known as Anatolia (*Anadolu*) or Asia Minor. Two-thirds of Anatolia is a plateau that becomes more mountainous to the east. Mountains are also found along the Black Sea. Both the Euphrates and Tigris Rivers flow through Turkey. The coastal regions are generally low. Winters can be very cold in some portions of the country, although they are mild along the coasts. Summers are pleasant but can be hot in some areas.

History. Modern Turkey is the most recent in a series of important states and empires that have inhabited the Anatolian peninsula since the beginning of history. The oldest known site of human urban habitation is located in central Turkey at Çatalhöyük (6500 B.C.). The great Hittite Empire (1750–1200 B.C.), which dominated much of the Middle East, was centered east of Ankara. Ancient Troy, the scene of much of Homer's *Iliad*, was located near the Dardanelles (*Çanakkale Boğazı*). Alexander the Great captured Anatolia in the fourth century B.C., and the Romans followed three centuries later, establishing important cities, such as Ephesus (*Efes*) and Antioch (*Antakya*), as major provincial capitals.

In A.D. 330, Emperor Constantine of Rome founded the city of Constantinople, which later became the center of the Byzantine Empire. This great state dominated eastern Europe for one thousand years. The Muslim Seljuk Turks entered Asia Minor in the 11th century and began the long process of Islamization and Turkization. In 1453, the successors of the Seljuks, the Ottoman Turks, captured Constantinople and went on to create a vast empire, stretching beyond the bounds of the Byzantine Empire into the Balkans, the Middle East, and North Africa. The Ottoman Empire survived until World War I when it allied itself with the Central Powers. With the defeat of the Central Powers, the empire was dismembered.

In 1923, out of the ruins of the Ottoman Empire, General Mustafa Kemal (known as Atatürk) fashioned the Republic of Turkey. Under Atatürk, the nation was reformed from an empire to a secular state with an Islamic majority. A series of reforms abolished the sultanate and caliphate, proclaimed the republic, and adopted Western civil law code, the Gregorian calendar, the Latin alphabet, and modern Western dress. Although most of Turkey is in Asia, it has always had important European ties. In 1952, Turkey joined the North Atlantic Treaty Organization (NATO) and provided land for a U.S. military base. Turkey's application to the European Union (in 1987) is pending the fulfillment of certain economic and political requirements.

Over the next three decades, the country went through various cycles of political turmoil. In the late 1970s, serious economic problems and political upheaval led the military to seize control in 1980. The military restored stability, called for elections in 1983, and withdrew from power. The military commander responsible for these actions, Kenan Evran, was elected president. His prime minister, Turgut Özal, became the dominant political figure in the 1980s.

In 1989, Özal was elected president. Parliamentary elections in 1991 brought Özal's rival to power as prime minister. Süleyman Demirel had been prime minister before and was twice (1971 and 1980) ousted in coups. When Özal suddenly died in 1993, Demirel was elected by parliament as the new president. Mrs. Tansu Çiller replaced Demirel and became Turkey's first female prime minister. Her government faced economic challenges and the ongoing insurgency by the Kurdistan Workers Party (PKK). The Turkish government does not recognize the Kurds as an ethnic minority and refuses to negotiate with the PKK, which fights for an independent state. Thousands of lives have been lost in the struggle; PKK leader Abdullah Öcalan was captured in March 1999 and sentenced to death, although the case is being reviewed by the European Court of Human Rights.

Following the collapse of several governments, President Süleyman Demirel appointed Bülent Ecevit to form a new government following early elections held in April 1999. Ecevit of the Democratic Left Party (DSP) leads a coalition government with the National Movement Party (MHP) and Motherland Party (ANAP).

In August 1999, a devastating earthquake struck İstanbul and neighboring regions, killing more than 17,000 people and causing billions of dollars in damages to homes, infrastructure, and the economy. A second quake hit the same area in November. In spite of government efforts and international assistance, many still remain homeless. In May 2000, parliament elected the reformist judge Ahmet Necdet Sezer as president. A 2001 row between Sezer and Ecevit created a financial crisis that destabilized the currency and weakened the country's ability to bring about economic reform.

THE PEOPLE

Population. Turkey has 65.67 million inhabitants, a population that is growing at 1.3 percent annually. Ankara, the capital, has more than 3.5 million people. İzmir has about 3 million. İstanbul (10 million), formerly called Constantinople, is still the industrial, commercial, and intellectual center of the country. About 80 percent of the people are Turkish, 17 percent are Kurdish, and 3 percent belong to a variety of smaller groups. Kurds live mostly in the southeast. Nearly 64 percent of Turkey's population lives in urban areas. People in rural areas tend to be more segregated. About 1.3 million Turkish workers live abroad, mostly in Europe and Saudi Arabia.

Language. Turkish, the official language, is related to the Ural-Altaic languages spoken across Asia (from Finland to Manchuria). Arabic script was used during the Ottoman Empire period, but a Latin-based alphabet has been used since 1928. Most of the Kurdish minority speaks Kurdish. However, Kurdish was banned for many years and some people forgot how to use it. Bans on its use in education and domestic broadcasting are still in effect, but Kurdish can be used in some publications and public speaking. Arabic is also spoken. English is increasingly important in school instruction.

Religion. Although 98 percent of Turkey's population is Muslim, the government makes it clear that Turkey is a secular state with freedom of religion. Islam's status as the state religion was abolished in 1923. Still, Islam maintains an important influence on society.

Muslims believe in one God, *Allah*, and that his will was revealed to the prophet Muhammad through the angel Gabriel. These revelations were recorded in the *Kur'an* (Koran), the holy book of Islam. Muslims accept many Judeo-Christian prophets but proclaim that Muhammed was the last and greatest. Throughout life, they strive to live the five pillars of Islam: professing *Allah's* name and Muhammed's role as prophet; fasting during the holy month of *Ramazan*; giving aid to the poor; making a pilgrimage to Mekke, Saudi Arabia; and praying daily at five specific times.

General Attitudes. Turkey is often described as a bridge between East and West. Due to centuries of interaction with Europe and Asia, Turks have incorporated features from both areas into their lifestyle and thinking. At the same time, they are patriotic and have developed a unique society. The people are proud of the achievements of their modern state as well as the accomplishments of their ancestors, who ruled great empires. Turks consider their society to be progressive, Europe-leaning, and strongly influential in the region. They often feel misunderstood by European and other Western nations because of the often publicized Kurdish rebellion. Turkey is known in the United States, Turks believe, mostly for its past and the terrorist violence; Turks emphasize another side of the country, one that is modern and ethnically diverse but tolerant and democratic.

Individually, Turks prize a good sense of humor; it is considered a sign of intelligence. Group orientation is valued over personal assertiveness or aggression, and honesty and cleverness are admirable qualities. People also value a good education, secure employment, wealth, social status, and an honorable heritage. Bravery and loyalty also are prized.

Personal Appearance. Western-style clothing is most common. European fashions are especially popular among the youth. Some Muslim women may wear a scarf to cover their hair. Military-led governments have sought to impose a controversial ban on head scarves in high schools and universities. Some traditional costumes still are worn in rural areas or for special occasions. The design of a costume's headdress and the type of material used signify a person's social status.

CUSTOMS AND COURTESIES

Greetings. When greeting friends or strangers, one shakes hands and says *Nasılınız?* (How are you?) or *Merhaba* (Hello). A typical response to *Nasılınız* is *İyiyim, teşhekur ederim* (Fine, thank you). Greetings among friends are followed by polite inquiries about one's health, family, and work. Among close friends of the same (or sometimes the opposite) gender, Turks clasp hands and kiss on both cheeks when greeting. The hands of an older person may be kissed and touched to the greeter's forehead to show respect. The youth often greet each other with *Selam* (Salute). Someone entering a room, office, or teahouse might say *Günaydın* (Good morning) or *İyi günler* (Have a nice day). When parting, people customarily wish for blessings from *Allah* (*Allahaısmarladık*) and respond agreeably (*Güle güle*).

Upon joining a small group, one greets each person in the group individually. When addressing others formally, one uses professional titles. Otherwise, the title *Hanım* is used for women and *Bey* for men among peers or with younger persons. These follow the given name: *Leyla Hanım* or *Ismail*

Bey. With older people, one uses *Abla* for women (*Fatma Abla*) or *Ağabey* for men (*Ahmet Ağabey*). These terms mean "sister" and "brother." When greeting someone much older, one uses *Teyze* (aunt) and *Amca* (uncle) after the first name.

Urban people generally do not greet strangers when passing on the street; rural people are more likely to greet strangers.

Gestures. Turks generally use their hands a great deal during conversation, forming gestures that add meaning and emphasis.

Social courtesies are valued in Turkey. One does not put feet on a desk or table, point the sole of the foot toward another person, smoke without asking permission, or cross the legs while in the presence of an older or superior person. In rural areas it is not proper for adults to eat on the street. It is not rare for members of the same sex to hold hands while walking or to kiss on the cheeks. Public displays of affection between men and women are not acceptable. Passing an item with the left hand may be an insult among more traditional people. "No" can be expressed by either shaking the head or lifting it up once quickly.

Visiting. Turks enjoy visiting one another in their homes, and hospitality is an integral part of the culture. Friends, relatives, and neighbors visit often. In large cities, people call ahead, but this is not practical in smaller villages, where unexpected visits occur more frequently. Guests always are invited in and offered refreshments. This usually involves something to drink (tea, coffee, soda) and sometimes something to eat (crackers and cookies). It is impolite to decline these refreshments. Many Turks remove their shoes when entering a home and replace them with slippers. Guests are expected to do the same at homes where this custom is followed. Visitors are expected to bring a pleasant presence to the home; bad news or accounts of problems are saved for other occasions and locations. It is not polite to ask personal questions of hosts. First-time visitors to a home may bring a small gift, such as candy, fruit, or flowers. Turks strive to make their guests feel comfortable. For example, even if the hosts do not think smoking is appropriate, they may allow visitors to smoke in their homes.

Eating. Breakfast usually is eaten around 7 a.m., or earlier in rural areas. Lunch is at midday and dinner is around 7 p.m. Dinner is the main meal and the family generally expects to sit down together for this meal.

Eating habits vary with the region and the food being eaten. Turks generally observe the continental style of eating, with the fork in the left hand and the knife remaining in the right. Some foods are eaten with the hand. To begin or end a meal, one might say *Afiyet Olsun* (May what you eat bring you well-being). One may compliment the cook on the meal by saying *Elinize sağlık* (roughly "Bless your hand"). Meals can be lavish, and Turks are quite proud of their rich cuisine. Restaurants range from those offering fast food to international cuisine; the most common is the Turkish kebab restaurant. Some restaurants include a service charge in the bill (about 10 percent), in which case a 5 percent tip is customary. If no service charge is included, a 15 percent tip should be given.

LIFESTYLE

Family. The primary social unit in Turkey is the family. In rural areas, traditional, patriarchal values prevail. An individual is loyal to and dependent upon the family. The Turkish household often consists of an extended family: a mother and father, their unmarried children, and in some cases, married sons with their families. The married sons remain until they are financially independent. In urban areas, nuclear families are the standard and traditional authority structures are less pronounced. It is uncommon for a person to live alone, mostly for economic reasons. Polygamy, as permitted by Islamic law, was abolished in 1930. Women gained the right to vote in 1927 and the right to divorce in 1934 when civil marriage contracts were introduced. Urban women frequently work outside the home. Thirty-three percent of the labor force is female.

Dating and Marriage. Except perhaps at universities or in large urban areas, dating in the Western sense is not common. Young people associate more in groups. In the cities, this association is generally open and casual. In rural areas, chaperones are common. Rural families are heavily involved in deciding who a person will marry, but the choice is generally the couple's in urban areas. It is against the law for women to marry before age 15 and men before age 17. In the cities, many wait to marry until they have completed their education and sometimes military service. Hence, the average age for marriage is 22 for women and 25 for men. Most Turks expect to marry and have children.

Traditional wedding celebrations last three days and still are practiced by some in rural areas. Urban couples often follow more European traditions when marrying. Traditional festivities begin with the *Kına Gecesi* (henna evening), an event only for women. They decorate the hands and fingers of the bride with henna leaf dye and dance and sing. On the second day, both sets of parents serve lunch and dinner to their guests. On the third day, the bride is taken to the groom's home on a horse after folk dances are performed. This tradition is increasingly rare because of the time and expense involved.

Diet. Turkish cuisine is among the finest in the world. Lamb and rice are served with many meals. Seafood is more abundant along the coast. The famous *kahve* (Turkish coffee), a thick brew served in very small cups, is served with nearly every meal. Breakfast is usually light, consisting of tea, white cheese, bread, butter, marmalade or honey, and olives. The main meal of the day is eaten in the evening and may consist of several courses. Turkish cuisine is famous for many things, among them the *meze*, a tray or table of hors d'oeuvres including stuffed grape leaves, salads, shrimp, and a variety of other items. There are also many unique Turkish soups. Shish kebabs (chunks of lamb on a skewer) are a favorite, as are vegetables prepared in olive oil. Rice *pilav* is common. Turkish desserts are famously sweet, including *baklava* (syrup-dipped pastry) and *muhallebi* (milk pudding). Turkish coffee and tea are the most common drinks.

Recreation. The most popular sport for both spectators and participants is soccer, which was introduced by the British in the 19th century. Volleyball, basketball, cycling, grease wrestling, traditional wrestling, swimming, and a variety of other sports also are enjoyed. Picnics are common family activities. August is the month for most vacations. During their leisure time, urban residents may watch television, eat

▼ **EURASIA**

out, visit others, or attend movies. Women often do volunteer work. Rural women visit one another in their homes or watch television. Men throughout the country gather at teahouses (like cafés) to socialize. When at home, they also watch television. Folk dancing and other cultural arts are popular.

The Arts. Theater, both contemporary and traditional, is popular. *Karagöz* (a shadow play) is created by casting shadows of puppets on a curtain. Other types of theater are village shows and *orta oyunu*, a type of comedy.

Turkish music varies widely by ethnic group, region, and religious orientation. The most common folk instrument is the *saz*, a kind of long-necked lute, but countless varieties exist, from bagpipes to fiddles and drums. Dance often accompanies music at festivals and important events ranging from weddings to circumcisions.

Turkey is recognized for handicrafts, especially carpets, renowned worldwide for centuries. Other crafts include weaving, metalwork—especially copper and brass—woodwork, musical instruments, glassware, stonework, and jewelry.

Historically, the banning of the Kurdish language forced many arts underground but made Kurdish arts, especially music, integral to the passing on of traditions. The music relies heavily on vocals and follows traditional rhythms. Instruments vary, from the *oud* (lute) to various reeded flutes.

Holidays. The ninth month of the Muslim lunar calendar is *Ramazan*, during which practicing Muslims fast from dawn to dusk. People celebrate the end of *Ramazan* by eating sweets during a three-day holiday called *Seker Bayramı* (sugar holiday). A second Muslim holiday is *Kurban Bayramı* (sacrifice holiday), which marks the season of pilgrimage to Mekke. It also commemorates Abraham's willingness to sacrifice his son. An animal usually is sacrificed and the meat distributed to the poor. Other official holidays include New Year's Day, National Sovereignty Day and Children's Day (23 Apr.), Atatürk's Memorial Day and Youth Day (19 May), Victory Day (30 Aug.), and Republic Day (29 Oct.).

Commerce. Businesses are generally open from 9 a.m. to 5 p.m., Monday through Friday. Some are open for a half day on Saturday. Most people buy fresh produce at open-air markets but get other goods from supermarkets (in large cities) or neighborhood shops.

SOCIETY

Government. Turkey is a constitutional republic with a multiparty parliament. It is divided into 73 provinces. The president is head of state; the prime minister is head of government. The Grand National Assembly (parliament) has 550 members and elects the president, who serves a seven-year term. Major parties include the Motherland Party, the Virtue Party (the main opposition), the Democratic Left, the True Path Party, and the Republican People's Party. The Islamist Welfare Party was outlawed in January 1998 for threatening the state's secular order. The voting age is 18.

Economy. Agriculture is the traditional backbone of the economy, once providing the bulk of all exports. Today, it still employs half of the labor force but accounts for one-fifth of all exports. Chief agricultural products include cotton,

DEVELOPMENT DATA

Human Dev. Index* rank	85 of 174 countries
Adjusted for women	69 of 143 countries
Real GDP per capita	$6,422
Adult literacy rate	92 percent (male); 74 (female)
Infant mortality rate	49 per 1,000 births
Life expectancy	69 (male); 73 (female)

tobacco, fruit, cereals, nuts, and opium for medicine. Manufacturing employs 15 percent of the labor force but accounts for nearly 60 percent of all exports. Its success is therefore vital to the economy. Mining and tourism are also important.

Global recession, the 1999 earthquakes, and a serious of financial and political crises have hampered growth. High inflation (currently 30 percent) and a large budget deficit remain challenges. Income distribution is unequal: urban residents enjoy far higher incomes than rural people or migrants. The currency is the Turkish *lira* (TL).

Transportation and Communications. Around major urban areas, the roads are paved and in good condition. In rural areas, infrastructure is generally adequate but not always well maintained. Taxis, buses, streetcars, and *dolmuş* (shared taxis) provide public transportation. The railroad is used for travel between cities, as are the airways. Turkey is connected with other countries by international air links. The overall communications system is fairly good; several television and radio stations broadcast throughout the country. The press is free and active. Telephone service is best in urban areas.

Education. Primary and secondary education is free and coeducational. Primary schooling lasts five years and secondary education lasts three. Additional years are possible to about age 17. Nearly all children complete the primary level, and about half go on to the secondary level. A foreign language is required. Exams determine university entrance. There are more than 70 universities in Turkey, the oldest of which was founded at Istanbul in 1453. Some 250 specialized colleges and institutions offer vocational and other training.

Health. Basic health care is provided but is not sufficient to meet the country's needs. Urban facilities are generally modern and adequate, but rural facilities are not as well equipped. Institutions, such as the military and state-owned enterprises, provide additional care to their personnel. Turkey's relatively high infant mortality rate is attributed to poor education about child care and the lack of family planning. The government seeks to reduce the figure through improved child immunizations, prenatal care, education, and other programs.

CONTACT INFORMATION

Embassy of the Republic of Turkey, 2525 Massachusetts Avenue NW, Washington, DC 20008; phone (202) 612-6740. Turkish Government Tourist Office, 821 United Nations Plaza, Fourth Floor, New York, NY 10017; phone (212) 687-2194.

CultureGrams™
People. The World. You.

1305 North Research Way, Bldg. K
Orem, Utah 84097-6200 USA
1.800.528.6279; 801.705.4250
fax 801.705.4350
www.culturegrams.com

Ukraine

Boundary representations are not necessarily authoritative.

▼ EUROPE

BACKGROUND

Land and Climate. Ukraine, located in southeastern Europe, covers 233,090 square miles (603,700 square kilometers) and is slightly smaller than Texas. Forests cover some 13 percent of territory, chiefly in the Carpathian Mountains and in the northern regions. Southern Ukraine is dominated by large plains (*steppes*) with fertile soil. One-third of the world's black soils are in Ukraine, giving it great potential as a food producer. The Crimean Peninsula extends into the Black Sea, with its northeastern coast on the Sea of Azov and its southern coast marked by the Crimean Mountains. Europe's largest wetland (Pripiyat Marshes) is located in a forested northern basin of the Dnipro and Pripiyat Rivers. Ukraine has cold winters and warm summers, although a Mediterranean climate prevails in the Crimea.

History. Ukraine has been inhabited continuously since about 1500 B.C., but the Slavic ancestors of today's Ukrainians did not begin to settle the region until the seventh century A.D. In the eighth and ninth centuries, seven Slavic tribes merged under the leadership of a Norse tribe (Varangians) to form the state of Kievan Rus'. A prominent early leader, Volodymyr I (ruled 980–1015), converted to Christianity and established close ties with the Byzantine (Eastern Orthodox) church. Kievan Rus' weakened in the 12th and 13th centuries to the point that Mongol invasions in 1220 and 1240 destroyed the state. Despite some independent principalities, the Ukrainians were without unity and autonomy for many centuries. The Mongols held the east even as expansionist Poland and Lithuania controlled the west. The Mongols were eventually forced out, and by the mid-1500s, Poland and Lithuania (which had merged) controlled most Ukrainian lands. The Poles introduced Western Christianity, which clashed with the traditional Eastern Christianity of the people and embittered them against their rulers.

Rebellion soon followed, most notably from a self-governing group called *Kozaks* (Zaporozhian Cossacks). They functioned with autonomy because of their military capacity and soon challenged Poland and, by extension, the Roman Catholic Church. The Kozaks waged a national liberation war (1648–54) under the leadership of Kozak *Hetman* (military chieftain) Bohdan Khmelnitsky. In 1654, he signed an alliance with Russia against the Polish-Lithuanian Kingdom. A Kozak state was carved out of the east (the west remained with Poland), and it prospered for a century. During the reign of Russia's Catherine the Great, Russia defeated the Kozaks (1775) and took control of the east. Control over the west was gained that same year by partitioning Poland. Ukraine became a Russian province and so remained until the monarchy fell in 1917.

Ukraine declared independence but was occupied by Germany in World War I and then forcibly incorporated into the Soviet Union in 1922. Communist repression was greatest under Stalin, who collectivized farms and thereby caused a 1933 famine (*holodomor*) that took seven million lives. Dissidents were imprisoned or executed, and use of the Ukrainian language was limited.

Independence became increasingly desirable, even as the Union of Soviet Socialist Republics (USSR) added territory (Crimea) to Ukraine and developed its industry to further integrate it into the Soviet system. Language restrictions and repression eased after Stalin's death. Disaster struck the republic in 1986 with the meltdown of a nuclear reactor at Chornobyl (north of Kyiv). Radioactive contamination caused by the explosion killed many people, ruined the surrounding land, and affected much of eastern Europe. In June 2000, the government announced that the Chornobyl nuclear power plant would be closed down on 15 December.

Hopes for independence strengthened as the Soviet empire weakened, and local elections in 1990 paved the way for official independence in August 1991. Leonid Kravchuk became the first president. Ukraine's possession of nuclear weapons and poor relations with Russia hindered progress on some economic and social fronts. In 1993, however, Ukraine ratified the first Strategic Arms Reduction Treaty (START), agreeing to destroy the bulk of its nuclear warheads. Elections in 1994 brought Leonid Kuchma to office as president. Declining living standards led Kuchma to slow economic liberalization, but he reinstated reform programs in 1996 to obtain vital International Monetary Fund (IMF) loans. In May 1997, Kuchma and President Boris Yeltsin of Russia signed an agreement settling disputes over the former Soviet Black Sea fleet in Crimea. Russia has agreed to pay rent for access to Ukraine's Sevastopol port for the next 20 years.

The Communists returned to power in March 1998 parliamentary elections. Kuchma was reelected in November 1999 despite criticism of his plans for economic reform and privatization. Recently, Kuchma and several other government leaders have been rocked by allegations of corruption. Because of these scandals and continued opposition to its economic measures, the government lost a no-confidence vote in April 2001. A coalition government is expected to replace the outgoing cabinet until 2002 elections.

THE PEOPLE

Population.   The population of Ukraine, about 49.1 million, is decreasing annually by 0.83 percent. Ethnic Ukrainians comprise 73 percent of the population. Ethnic Russians (22 percent) live mainly in the east and in Crimea, where they comprise two-thirds of the population. Despite recent agreements between Russia and Ukraine, ethnic Russians are expected to continue pressing for autonomy in Crimea. Smaller groups include the Jews, Tatars, Poles, Germans, Hungarians, Romanians, and Greeks. Tatars live in Crimea but lack citizenship rights. They were expelled by the Soviets in 1944 but have returned in small groups since 1989. More than seven million ethnic Ukrainians reside in western Europe, North America, and other areas. More than two-thirds of all people live in urban areas. Kyiv, the capital, is the largest and oldest city; its population is more than 2.8 million.

Language.   Ukrainian is a Slavic language written in the Cyrillic alphabet of 33 letters. It is the official and most commonly spoken language. During the Soviet period, Russian was also official and was the language of instruction in secondary schools and universities. Russian is no longer as prominent, but it is the primary language of ethnic Russians, many Ukrainians in Kyiv and cities east of the Dnipro, and other ethnic groups. More than half of the population is bilingual. Minorities also speak their respective languages, including Polish, Hungarian, and Romanian. New language laws guarantee ethnic minorities the right to use their native language for public and judicial business.

Religion.   Christianity is the dominant religion of Ukraine, represented by Orthodox (Russian and Ukrainian), Greek Catholic (Uniate), and Roman Catholic churches. The Ukrai-

nian Orthodox Church split from its parent Orthodox church in Russia in 1992; it has no official status. Catholicism is found mostly in the west. Communism led many people to abandon their beliefs. As a whole, however, Ukrainians maintained their religious heritage. When religious freedom was allowed in the late 1980s, Christianity began to revive. This intensified with independence, and today Christians also include small but growing groups of Protestants and other denominations. Jews now represent only 1 percent of the population, but their numbers were much higher prior to World War II. Ukraine is home to many sacred Jewish sites.

General Attitudes.   Ukrainians consider themselves a merry people, prone to singing and dancing. They appreciate openness and wit, as well as humor. Individualism is also valued, although it was somewhat muted during the Soviet era. Friendships play an important role for most Ukrainians, and neighbors are generally supportive of each other.

The nationalism and euphoria of independence has waned. Many Ukrainians are nostalgic for the poor but stable way of life they had under the Soviet regime.

Ukrainian society is in great transition. Those accustomed to Soviet work patterns are learning the meaning and value of private enterprise, individual labor, and personal initiative. At the same time, Ukrainians have been faced with economic hardships and other problems that have led to cynicism toward the ruling elite and disenchantment with reform and democracy.

Personal Appearance.   Most fashions are similar to those in other European countries. Professional men wear suits, ties, and hats. Women wear pantsuits, dresses, or skirts. Clothing is often imported and is quite expensive, but many women have sewing machines and make clothes for their family. They also knit sweaters, hats, and scarves for the winter. Taste and tidiness are important; it is improper to wear wrinkled or soiled clothes.

The older generation dresses more conservatively; elderly women in rural areas usually wear dresses and cover their heads with scarves. On special occasions (e.g., weddings, festivals, and religious holidays), people in Western Ukraine often wear the national outfit. The most traditional item is *vyshyvanka*—a shirt or blouse embroidered in one of several regional patterns that have not changed for centuries.

CUSTOMS AND COURTESIES

Greetings.   When meeting informally, men and women usually wave the hand and give a verbal greeting like *Pryvit* (Hi) or *Dobryj den'* (Good day). *Dobryj den'* is also appropriate in formal situations, in which case people often shake hands. Men wait for women to extend their hand first. Titles are used in official situations, including professional titles and *Pan* (Mr.), *Pani* (Mrs.), *Panna* (Miss), or *Panove* (Sirs or Gentlemen).

Relatives and close friends often kiss cheeks and hug when greeting. They address each other by first name. A respectful form of address is using the first name followed by the patronymic, which is the father's given name and a gender-specific (for son or daughter) suffix.

Gestures.   Hand and body gestures are used only moderately in daily conversation. It is important to establish eye contact a few times (but not constantly) during a conversation. Facial expressions are reserved. Smiling at strangers is rare. Approval is expressed by nodding the head. Pointing with the index finger is considered uncultured, but some people do it anyway. To speak to a superior (teacher, boss, official, or senior) with one's hands in the pockets or arms folded across the chest is viewed as disrespectful and cause for reprimand. Chewing gum is also improper.

Women expect some chivalry from men. It is rude for a man to not open a door for a woman. Men commonly help women carry heavy items or at least offer to do so. When on public transportation, men usually offer their seats to women.

Visiting. Because of the Ukrainian tradition of hospitality, people welcome both expected and unexpected guests. Still, visits arranged in advance are preferred whenever possible. Friends, neighbors, and relatives often visit just to socialize. In these cases, guests are always offered tea or coffee and some refreshments. Guests invited for dinner are offered a meal that is more than abundant and are expected to stay for a while afterward. They commonly present their hosts with flowers (only in odd numbers), cake, a bottle of liquor, or candy or toys for the children. Guests do not sit on the floor or put their feet on furniture. It is polite to stand when a woman enters the room.

Eating. People eat a light *snidanok* (breakfast) in the morning before leaving for school or work. The main meal, eaten in midafternoon, is called *obid*. It consists of two main courses, the first being some kind of soup, the second containing meat or fish. Working people usually bring food from home or go to *canteens* (cafés) for *obid*. The third meal, *vecheria*, is eaten at 6 or 7 p.m. and is usually the time when family members eat together. When eating, Ukrainians usually keep hands (not elbows) on the table. It is improper to place them in one's lap. Ukrainians eat with the fork in the left hand and the knife remaining in the right. Leaving food on the plate is considered wasteful. Guests honor the hosts when they ask for or accept second helpings. Due to the difficult economic situation, most people eat out only for special occasions.

LIFESTYLE

Family. The family unit is important in Ukraine, and extended family ties are valued. The average family has two children and is led by the father. Both parents usually work outside the home. Child care is expensive and in short supply. Many elderly parents live with their adult children, and they often assume responsibility for daily child care. Women perform most household chores.

The elderly are treated with love and respect. It is a common practice for parents to support children until they reach adulthood and even after they are married. In turn, children expect to care for aging parents when it becomes necessary. When parents live in the country and adult children live in the city, the latter may send their children to live with the grandparents for several weeks during the summer.

Most urban families live in a small one- or two-bedroom apartment. Many in large cities now own their apartments due to recent privatization programs. Some affordable apartments still are leased from the government; to rent from a private owner is expensive. Suburban families have most modern conveniences (electricity, gas, and water); rural people have much simpler houses.

Dating and Marriage. Young people meet at discos and concerts, in school and at work, and through friends. When dating, they usually visit friends, go to bars or movies, or dance at discos. From April to October they spend a lot of time in parks, engaging in a variety of outdoor activities. Young couples usually marry in their early twenties. A marriage is legal

only if performed in a city hall or in a "wedding palace." Most couples today also have a religious ceremony.

Urban wedding parties are fancy but do not involve much tradition. On the other hand, rural weddings are big events that usually last for three days. Such weddings resemble a combination of a grand party and a performance, since many people are responsible for completing traditional acts. For example, at some point the bride must be "stolen." The successful thieves "demand" a ransom for her return.

Diet. Vegetables, breads, dairy products, and starchy foods are basic staples. Ukraine is one of the few areas in Europe where corn-on-the-cob is eaten. Pork and beef are the most loved meats. Poultry, sausages, and preserved meats are also widely available. The most popular Ukrainian dishes are made of cereal grains and flour pastes. Common grains include buckwheat, oats, and millet. Rice is imported. Popular dishes include *varenyky* (dumplings), *holubtsi* (cabbage leaves stuffed with ground meat and rice), and *kasha* (cooked or baked cereal). *Kasha* is served with either meat or poultry. Chicken Kyiv is known worldwide. Soup is essential; *borsch* is the most popular. *Borsch* usually contains cabbage, beets, potatoes, and carrots; meat is optional. It can be served hot or cold, with or without sour cream, and there are several varieties according to locality and season.

Ukrainians enjoy such seasonal fruits as apples, pears, plums, berries, and melons. Fresh produce is available but very expensive in the winter, so in summer and autumn people make numerous preserves for the winter months.

Recreation. On weekends, young people enjoy leaving the city and camping on a riverbank or in the woods. Hiking and skiing are also popular activities. In the summer, people enjoy swimming, volleyball, soccer, and table tennis. Fishing and soccer are especially popular with men. Watching television or visiting friends is a typical leisure activity.

Urban people with *dachas* (country houses) spend much time there tending a garden, making preserves, and relaxing. People without *dachas* often have a small plot of land near the city on which to grow a garden. Theaters and musical concerts are available in cities. Rural people get together on weekends to play music, sing, and dance. Literature is important to Ukrainians, and most avidly read.

The Arts. During the Soviet era, the fine arts often were used by the government as propaganda, but Ukrainian culture was preserved through folk songs and legends, which are now highly treasured. Folk songs are sung a cappella or are accompanied by instruments such as the *sopilka* (flute), *volynka* (horn pipe), and stringed *bandura*, Ukraine's national instrument. The *hopak* is a showy Ukrainian folk dance in which men jump, twirl, and kick, and women perform more simple movements. Ukrainian folk dance groups are very popular and perform all over the world.

Ukraine is known worldwide for the delicate art of Easter-egg painting (*pysanka*), which is still practiced with great skill today. Embroidered clothing and tapestries are also appreciated.

Ukraine's independence has meant greater artistic freedom, but government funding for the arts also has been drastically reduced.

Holidays. New Year's is the most popular holiday. On New Year's, people decorate fir trees and have parties that often last through the night. Religious holidays are regaining prominence. Christmas, celebrated on 25 December by Catholics and

EUROPE

on 7 January by Orthodox Christians, is particularly popular in Western Ukraine and rural areas. During the Christmas season, children go door-to-door to receive candies and cookies in exchange for *koliadki* (Christmas carols) and jokes. Easter is observed throughout the country. Family and friends gather to visit and prepare painted eggs and *paskha* (special cakes).

National holidays include International Women's Day (8 Mar.), Solidarity Day (1 May), Victory Day (9 May), and Independence Day (24 Aug.). An old holiday, Soviet Army Day (23 Feb.), is unofficially celebrated as a sort of Men's Day. On Women's Day, women receive flowers and gifts, household help from husbands, and a day off from work. Special attention is paid to mothers, and girls are congratulated as future women. Victory Day marks the end of World War II and is extremely important to most families.

Commerce. Offices are open weekdays from 8 or 9 a.m., closed for an hour lunch break around 2 p.m., and open again until 5 or 6 p.m. Grocery stores usually open at 8 a.m.; other stores (clothing, department, etc.) open at 9 or 10 a.m. but stay open later. A banking system has not yet fully developed; most stores and individual consumers use only cash.

Prices are fixed in stores, but people bargain in the markets. Due to recent economic changes, the variety of goods available in state and private stores has improved significantly, but prices are relatively high. Small street boutiques offer many imported goods. The old business structure is being replaced by a capitalist market; the transitional period has produced some inconsistencies and difficulties for entrepreneurs. The younger generation is more business oriented than those who were used to the communist system.

SOCIETY

Government. Ukraine is a parliamentary democracy led by a strong executive president, who is elected for a five-year term. Parliament (*Verkhovna Rada*) has 450 directly elected members. A large number of political parties are represented. The prime minister, who is appointed by the president, is the head of government. All citizens may vote at age 18.

Economy. Ukraine was the Soviet Union's "breadbasket" because it produced more than one-fourth of the USSR's agriculture. The potential for agriculture to be the basis of Ukraine's growing economy exists, but it cannot be tapped without significant reform. Farms must be modernized and laborers must adjust to wage work; however, government privatization has been slow. Large coal and iron deposits contributed to the development of a large industrial base that produced goods for many other republics. In fact, Ukraine was the second most productive Soviet republic (behind Russia). But industry also requires materials from outside Ukraine, and these can now be purchased only with hard (convertible) currencies that are in short supply. The country also has a large defense industry (space and nuclear) that must be converted into consumer-oriented firms before it can be useful.

Corruption, political opposition, and continued state subsidies to unprofitable industries and collective farms have hindered growth and foreign investment in recent years. Reforms and improvements in infrastructure are needed to

© 2001 CultureGrams, a division of Millennial Star Network and Brigham Young University. It is against the law to copy, reprint, store, or transmit any part of this publication in any form by any means without written permission from CultureGrams. This document contains native commentary and original analysis, as well as estimated statistics. The content should not be considered strictly factual, and it may not apply to all groups in a nation. *UN Development Programme, Human Development Report 2000 (New York: Oxford University Press, 2000).

DEVELOPMENT DATA

Human Dev. Index* rank	78 of 174 countries
Adjusted for women	63 of 143 countries
Real GDP per capita	$3,194
Adult literacy rate	99 percent
Infant mortality rate	22 per 1,000 births
Life expectancy	60 (male); 72 (female)

stabilize the cash-strapped economy and overcome large public debts. Many goods and services are bartered or traded informally; in fact, the size of Ukraine's unofficial economy rivals the official economy. The government reports that the economy experienced positive growth in 2000. High inflation and unemployment are ongoing problems. In 2000, the government avoided defaulting on 2.6 billion dollars in loans by negotiating with investors to postpone repayment, but foreign debt continues to be a significant problem. Ukraine's currency is the *hryvnia* (UHR).

Transportation and Communications. Urban public transportation is efficient. Street cars, buses, and trolleys are the main means of transport, but major cities also have subways. Most families do not own cars. Roads are extensive but are often in poor repair. Fuel is expensive. This makes taxis expensive and not always easy to find. Unofficial "taxis" often pick up people who ask for a ride.

Rural people get around on bicycles; buses or trains take them to nearby towns. The railroad network is developed, although trains are in need of modernization. Air Ukraine is the domestic airline. Telephone and postal services have improved but are still inadequate. The press is active, but newspapers and television are tightly controlled by different political groups, both in the government and the opposition. Many local radio and television stations are private.

Education. Education is highly valued in Ukraine. Children begin attending elementary school at age six and must attend until age fifteen, when they finish middle school. Most teenagers prefer to go to high school for two more years and prepare to enter a university. Others choose to work in the day and attend evening school, train at schools specializing in certain careers, or enter job-training programs. Universities are located in major cities. Entrance exams are required by all institutions of higher education.

Health. Medical care is free, but service is poor. Although medical advice is available, treatment is often inadequate because facilities frequently experience basic supply shortages and lack modern equipment. Pollution levels are high and tap water is not safe to drink. Cancer and other problems stemming from the Chornobyl nuclear accident continue to afflict a large portion of the population.

CONTACT INFORMATION

Embassy of Ukraine, 3350 M Street NW, Washington, DC 20007; phone (202) 333-0606; Web site www.ukremb.com. Continent, 1800 Connecticut Avenue NW, Washington, DC 20009; phone (202) 232-4377.

CultureGrams™
People. The World. You.

1305 North Research Way, Bldg. K
Orem, Utah 84097-6200 USA
1.800.528.6279; 801.705.4250
fax 801.705.4350
www.culturegrams.com

United States of America

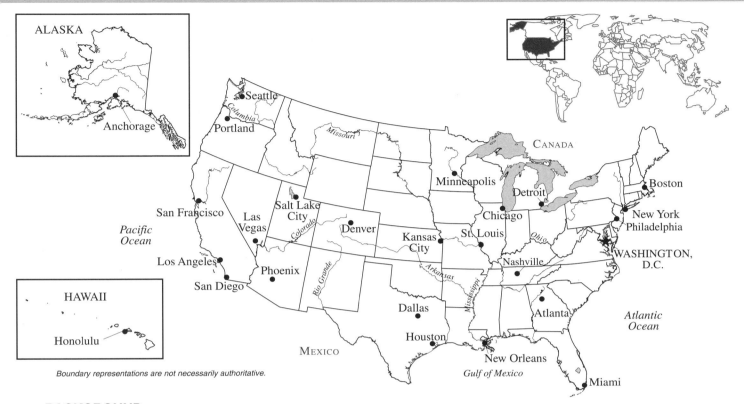

ALASKA

Anchorage

HAWAII

Honolulu

Seattle
Columbia
Portland
Missouri
CANADA
Minneapolis
Detroit
Boston
San Francisco
Salt Lake City
Chicago
New York
Philadelphia
Pacific Ocean
Las Vegas
Colorado
Denver
St. Louis
Kansas City
Ohio
WASHINGTON, D.C.
Los Angeles
Phoenix
Rio Grande
Arkansas
Nashville
San Diego
Mississippi
Atlanta
Atlantic Ocean
Dallas
Houston
New Orleans
MEXICO
Gulf of Mexico
Miami

Boundary representations are not necessarily authoritative.

▼ THE AMERICAS

BACKGROUND

Land and Climate. The United States covers the central portion of North America and includes Alaska and Hawaii. Covering 3,618,765 square miles (9,372,558 square kilometers), it is the fourth largest country in the world. Because of its size and location, the United States has a variety of geographical features and climates. Large mountains, vast deserts, wide canyons, extensive coasts, subtropical forests, wetlands, rolling hills, prairies, frozen tundra, and more features can be found. Beyond the beaches and mountains of California, the Rocky Mountains in the west give way to a vast central plain, which merges with the rolling hills and low mountains of the east. Hawaii's rugged volcanic topography is lush and green year-round. Alaska has towering mountains, broad valleys, glaciers, and a varied landscape.

Climates throughout the country are as varied as the terrain. Natural resources include coal, copper, lead, uranium, bauxite, gold, phosphate, iron, mercury, nickel, silver, petroleum, natural gas, timber, and much more. Natural disasters, such as droughts, floods, hurricanes, tornadoes, earthquakes, and severe winter storms, affect various regions.

History. North America's history before Europeans arrived is incomplete, but the original inhabitants had advanced civilizations. From the 17th century on, Native Americans were displaced by European settlers who came for riches, territory, and religious freedom. Disease brought by the settlers decimated the Native American population. Thirteen British colonies were established on the east coast. The American Revolution (1775–83) led to independence from Britain and a loose confederation of states. A constitution was created, which set up a system of government, balanced the rights of the states and federal government, and protected free speech and other civil liberties. Explorers and pioneers headed west and settled large areas of land. The United States acquired territory from France, Mexico, Russia, and Spain throughout the 19th century, expanding its borders from the Atlantic to the Pacific Ocean.

In 1861, civil war broke out between Union states in the north and Confederate states in the south over issues of slavery, states' rights, and economic differences. Under President Abraham Lincoln, Union forces defeated the Confederates in 1865. Slavery was abolished and the Union was restored, although it took many years for the nation to heal from the conflict. Legal discrimination based on race continued until the civil rights movement of the 1950s and 1960s prompted legislation ending such discrimination.

In the late 19th and early 20th centuries, immigration boomed, the economy grew substantially, and government policy focused on finding world markets. Initially wary of involvement in European affairs, the United States provided troops during the final year of World War I. By 1942, it was a major combatant in World War II and emerged as the strongest economic and military power in the world. The United States became a principal donor of financial and technological aid to developing countries in an effort to spread U.S. American values (which were not always welcome) and stop the spread of Soviet-sponsored communism. With the U.S. defeat in Vietnam, American influence declined, although this trend seemed to reverse in the 1980s and 1990s. U.S. leadership was pivotal in the 1991 Gulf War, in Bosnia, Somalia, and Kosovo and is currently vital to ongoing peace talks and negotiations around the world. President Clinton was especially active in Middle East peace negotiations. In the 2000 presidential elections, George W. Bush was declared the winner over Al Gore after numerous vote recounts and court decisions. Bush hopes to reduce taxes, reform education, and reduce government involvement in citizens' lives. The United States is an active member of the United Nations and a key donor of international aid.

THE PEOPLE

Population. The population of the United States (about 281 million) is the third largest in the world, following China and India, and is growing at a rate of 0.9 percent per year. People of European, Latin American, and Middle Eastern origin (also known as whites) comprise 75.1 percent of America's population. Other groups include those of African descent (12.3 percent), Asian descent (3.6 percent), and Native American descent (0.9 percent). People of Latin American descent, who may be of any race, comprise the fastest-growing minority group. Often referred to as Hispanics or Latinos, they constitute about 12.5 percent of the total population.

Although members of any ethnic group can be found anywhere in the country, populations vary by region. For example, Hispanics reside mostly in the west and southwest, while African-Americans live mostly in the east and southeast. In Hawaii, 51 percent of the people are Asians or Pacific Islanders. Minority populations also tend to be concentrated in urban areas. About one-fourth of the population is younger than 18 years of age, and nearly 80 percent of all Americans live in metropolitan areas. (*American* is the term most often used to describe a citizen or product of the United States, even outside of the country.)

Language. English is the predominant language and is spoken by most citizens. The English spoken in the United States is referred to in other English-speaking nations as American English. It is characterized by unique idioms and spelling and pronunciation variations from British English. Spoken English is very flexible, while written communication is more formal and standardized. Many first-, second-, or even third-generation immigrants also speak their native tongue. In fact, one in seven Americans speaks a language other than English in the home. Spanish is spoken in many communities. Native Americans speak a variety of Amerindian languages.

Religion. Although the United States has never had an official state church, about 95 percent of the population professes some religious belief. Most Americans (80–85 percent) are Christians. Early European settlers were primarily Christian, and the Constitution and Bill of Rights are based, in part, on Christian values and principles. However, the Constitution dictates that church and state remain separate. Scores of different Christian churches exist throughout the country. About 24 percent of the population is Roman Catholic. Baptists, Methodists, and Lutherans are the largest Protestant groups; more than half of all Americans belong to these or other Protestant organizations. Other Christian denominations account for another 3 to 5 percent of the total. There are also substantial numbers of Jews (2 percent), Muslims, Buddhists, and other non-Christians. Between 40 and 50 percent of Americans attend religious services weekly. About 10 percent of all Americans have no religious affiliation but may still have spiritual convictions. Religion is generally a personal matter for Americans, but some openly discuss their beliefs with others.

General Attitudes. Americans tend to be frank and outspoken. They voice their opinions and share their views on a variety of subjects. In general, they appreciate people who are candid. There are few subjects an American will not discuss. Of course, there are exceptions, and religious values may keep some from discussing certain issues. Those who are not close friends avoid extremely personal questions. Americans value innovation, industry, and integrity. They enjoy a good sense of humor, including sarcasm. Americans have the ability to laugh at themselves as well as at others. Even though they may criticize the government, most are patriotic and believe the United States is one of the greatest countries in the world. Americans consider their country to be a guardian of democracy and freedom and a promoter of peace worldwide. They strongly value their freedom and independence, as a nation and as individuals. Individualism, as opposed to conformity, is often cited as an American characteristic. Even when working as a team, Americans usually think in terms of several distinct individuals blending their efforts rather than a group working as one unit.

Personal Appearance. Although fashion trends affect how people dress, Americans generally feel free to wear whatever they please. Some use clothing to make a social or personal statement. Americans emphasize cleanliness but may purposely wear tattered clothing or casual attire in public. Dressing "down" (casually) is a trend in the workplace; still, suits for men, and pantsuits, dresses, or skirts for women are standard attire in many offices. Formal clothing is worn for certain social occasions. Appearance, in general, is important to the individual American.

CUSTOMS AND COURTESIES

Greetings. Both men and women usually smile and shake hands when greeting. The American handshake is often firm. Good friends and relatives may embrace when they meet, especially after a long absence. In casual situations, people may wave rather than shake hands. Friends also wave to each other at a distance. Americans may greet strangers on the street by saying *Hello* or *Good morning* (in Spanish, *Hola* or *Buenos días*), although they may pass without any greeting. Among the youth, verbal greetings or hand-slapping gestures are common. Except in formal situations, people who are acquainted address one another by given name. Combining a title (*Mr.*, *Ms.*, *Dr.*, for example) with a family name shows respect. When greeting someone for the first time, Americans commonly say *Nice to meet you* or *How do you do?* A simple *Hello* or *Hi* is also common. Regional variations exist, such as *Aloha* in Hawaii. Friends often greet each other with *How are you?* and respond *Fine, thanks*. Americans do not really expect any further answer to the question.

Gestures. When conversing, Americans generally stand about 2 feet away from each other. However, they may spontaneously touch one another on the arm or shoulder during conversation. Members of the opposite sex may hold hands or show affection in public. To point, a person extends the index finger. One beckons by waving all fingers (or the index finger) with the palm facing up. Direct eye contact is not necessary for the duration of a conversation, but moments of eye contact are essential to ensure one's sincerity. Winking to children is a gesture of friendliness; when adults wink it usually means that they or someone else is kidding or joking. People may prop their feet on chairs, place the ankle of one leg on the knee of the other, cross legs at the knee (more common for women), or sit with legs spread apart. Poor posture is not uncommon. People often hand items to one another with one hand and may even toss something to a friend. Holding up one's hand, palm in, with only the middle finger extended, is an offensive gesture.

Visiting. Although Americans are informal, they generally are conscious of time. Appointments are expected to begin promptly. Guests invited to a home for dinner should arrive on time because the meal often is served first. Hospitality takes many forms: a formal dinner served on fine dishes, an outdoor barbecue with paper plates, or a leisurely visit with no refreshments. Most events are casual. Guests are expected to feel comfortable, sit where they like, and enjoy themselves. It is not unusual for either guests or hosts to agree on a reasonable limit of time for the visit if schedules are pressing. Guests are not expected to bring gifts, but a small token such as wine, flowers, or a handicraft might be appreciated. Hosts inviting close friends to dinner may ask them to bring a food item to be served with the meal. Americans enjoy socializing; they gather in small and large groups for nearly any occasion, and they enjoy talking, watching television or a movie, eating, and relaxing together.

Eating. Eating styles and habits vary among people of different backgrounds, but Americans generally eat with a fork in the hand with which they write. They use a knife for cutting and spreading. Otherwise they lay it on the plate. When a knife is used for cutting, the fork is switched to the other hand. People eat some foods, such as french fries, fried chicken, hamburgers, pizza, and tacos, with the hands. They generally place napkins in the lap. Resting elbows on the table usually is considered impolite. Dessert, coffee, or other after-dinner refreshments frequently are served away from the dining table. Guests are expected to stay a while after the meal to visit with the hosts. In restaurants, the bill usually does not include a service charge; leaving a tip of 15 percent is customary.

LIFESTYLE

Family. The American family is the basic unit of society, but it has been changing. A generation ago, the average family consisted of a mother, father, and two or more children. This nuclear family often maintained important ties to members of the extended family. Today, only about one-fourth of all households consist of a mother, father, and one or two children. Other family structures are more common, including families with a single parent and unmarried couples with or without children. One-third of all children are born out of wedlock. Children may live with or be cared for by grandparents, especially if the parent is young and not married.

A generation ago, men were the traditional breadwinners. Today, nearly half of all working Americans are women. In homes where both the husband and wife work, men are now expected to share household chores, although women still perform most domestic duties. Men often play an important role in raising children as well. With both parents working, the use of day-care facilities is increasing. Single-parent families also rely heavily on day care. Elderly individuals who cannot care for themselves live in retirement communities or other institutions; many live with their adult children. Otherwise, the elderly live in their own homes and comprise a rapidly expanding segment of the population. More than half of all young, unmarried adults (ages 18–24) live with their parents. The American family is mobile. People frequently move from one region of the country to another for education, employment, or a change in living conditions.

Dating and Marriage. Dating is a social pastime. Youth may begin dating in couples as early as age 13, although group activities are more common at that age. More serious dating begins around age 15. Going to movies, dancing, having picnics, participating in sports, and eating out are popular activities. Casual sexual relationships are common. Many couples choose to live together before or instead of marrying. Still, many consider marriage to be the preferred living arrangement. Weddings can be either lavish or simple, depending on the region, the family's economic status, and their religious affiliation. The age for marriage averages 26 for men and 24 for women.

Diet. It is difficult to name a national dish. The abundance of fast-food restaurants in the United States would seem to indicate that the national foods are hamburgers, french fries, pizza, and chicken. While these foods are popular among most segments of the population, they reflect a busy lifestyle as much as preference. The majority of popular "American" foods are adopted from the national cuisines of immigrants; this includes Mexican, Chinese, Italian, and myriad other nations. Americans eat beef, pork, chicken, and turkey in fairly large quantities, although eating habits have changed with health concerns. Fresh vegetables and fruits are available year-round. Americans consume large amounts of candy, ice cream, and other sweets. Most Americans will readily try any food, and the culture easily adapts to new tastes.

Recreation. Basketball, American football, and baseball are the most popular spectator and participation sports. Public schools and local organizations provide team sports for the youth. Professional sports are an important part of the culture. Americans also enjoy soccer, cycling, racquetball, hockey, tennis, swimming, golf, bowling, jogging, and aerobic exercise. The U.S. Women's Soccer Team won the 1999 Women's World Cup. Leisure activities include watching television, going to movies, surfing the Internet, spending time with friends, attending music concerts, and traveling.

The Arts. Galleries and museums nationwide exhibit many art styles and mediums. Government and private organizations provide financial support to artists and art education programs. Larger cities usually have a professional orchestra, and most have at least one theater. Broadway musicals are quite popular, and the best tour the nation. The U.S. entertainment industry, including movies and music, is known worldwide. Pop music is the most common form of music. However, jazz, blues, country, bluegrass, and several rock and roll styles all originated in the United States and have large followings. Realistic fiction is the most popular literary form in the United States.

Holidays. Each state has its own public holidays and each city may have celebrations. National public holidays include New Year's Day, Martin Luther King Jr.'s Birthday (third Monday in January), Presidents' Day (third Monday in February), Memorial Day (last Monday in May), Independence Day

▼ **THE AMERICAS**

(4 July), Labor Day (first Monday in September), Columbus Day (second Monday in October), Veterans' Day (11 Nov.), Thanksgiving (fourth Thursday in November), and Christmas. Although they are not holidays, other observances include Groundhog Day (2 Feb.), Valentine's Day (14 Feb.), St. Patrick's Day (17 Mar.), Easter, Mother's Day (second Sunday in May), Father's Day (third Sunday in June), Flag Day (14 June), and Halloween (31 Oct.).

Commerce.   Business office hours usually extend from 8 or 9 a.m. to 5 or 6 p.m. However, retail and grocery stores often remain open until 9 or 10 p.m., and many are open 24 hours a day, seven days a week. Suburban Americans shop for groceries and other goods in supermarkets, large enclosed *malls* with department and specialty stores, smaller open-air *strip malls* that feature specialty shops, and chain discount stores. Urban residents shop in many of the same stores but also might buy goods at small neighborhood shops that are part of large office or apartment buildings.

SOCIETY

Government.   The United States is a democratic federal republic guided by a constitution. Individual states hold sovereignty over their territory and have rights that are not reserved by the federal government. Each state has its own legislature for enacting local laws. Free elections have always determined the country's leadership, and citizens may vote at age 18. The U.S. president (currently George W. Bush) is elected by an electoral college, which represents the vote of the people in each state. Presidential elections are held every four years; the next will take place in November 2004. The bicameral legislature (Congress) has two houses: the 435-seat House of Representatives, whose members serve two-year terms, and the 100-seat Senate, whose members serve six-year terms. Congress is dominated by the Republican and Democratic Parties. Smaller parties are active throughout the country and a few have seats in the House of Representatives, but most act as pressure groups rather than viable election contenders. The government also has a separate judicial branch.

Economy.   The United States has the largest, most diverse, and technically advanced economy in the world. Inflation remains low, but the economy is showing signs of slowing. While American society as a whole is prosperous, there is a widening gap between the wealthy and the poor, and even between those who earn a comfortable income and those who struggle to meet basic needs.

The country's economic strength is based on diversified industrial and service sectors, investments abroad, the dollar as a major world currency, a demand-driven consumer society, and exports. The service sector employs more people than manufacturing, but the United States remains a world leader in industry and high technology. It exports capital goods, cars, consumer goods, food, and machinery. It also exports pop culture (e.g., movies, music, television, fashion, sports), which can fuel demand for American goods. The United States is a key world financial center, and its economic fortunes affect global markets and international economic

DEVELOPMENT DATA

Human Dev. Index* rank	3 of 174 countries
Adjusted for women	4 of 143 countries
Real GDP per capita	$29,605
Adult literacy rate	99 percent
Infant mortality rate	7 per 1,000 births
Life expectancy	74 (male); 80 (female)

growth. The currency is the U.S. dollar (US$).

Transportation and Communications.   The United States has an extensive network of paved highways, and the private car is the chief form of transportation. In large cities, urban mass-transit systems are common. In many areas, however, public transportation systems are not well developed. Many people travel by air, and the United States has the largest number of private airline companies in the world. Passenger train travel is limited to short commuter distances and relatively few cross-country routes; trains more frequently transport goods. The communications network is extensive and modern. Most households have a telephone (and often a cellular phone, too) and one or more television sets. Most homes have cable or satellite television. There are thousands of radio and television stations in operation throughout the country; most are privately owned. Freedom of the press is guaranteed. Although newspapers are available everywhere, only about half of all Americans read one every day. Others watch television or use the Internet for news. More than 40 million households have Internet access.

Education.   Each state is responsible for its educational system. Education is free and compulsory for ages five through sixteen. Most children attend public schools, but a growing number attend private schools or are schooled at home. Most students complete their high school education at grade 12 (at age 17 or 18). Many enter the labor force at that age or seek vocational and technical training. Others enter a university or college to pursue higher education degrees. Although nearly all Americans can read, functional illiteracy is a problem for many adults.

Health.   The health problems facing Americans are different from those in some other countries in that a sedentary lifestyle and risky physical behavior are the two greatest causes of adult health problems. The United States is the only industrialized country in the world without a national (public) health-care system. Most people must have private insurance to receive medical care without paying very high prices. The health network is extensive and modern, except in some rural areas. Each state has its own regulations regarding health care, and there are some national standards as well. Public and private reform movements are changing how health care is provided and paid for. The United States is a world leader in medical research and training.

CONTACT INFORMATION

U.S. Department of State, 2201 C Street NW, Washington, DC 20520; phone (202) 647-4000; Web site www.state.gov.

1305 North Research Way, Bldg. K
Orem, Utah 84097-6200 USA
1.800.528.6279; 801.705.4250
fax 801.705.4350
www.culturegrams.com

Oriental Republic of
Uruguay

▼ THE AMERICAS

Boundary representations are not necessarily authoritative.

BACKGROUND

Land and Climate. Uruguay covers 68,039 square miles (176,220 square kilometers) and is about the same size as Washington state. Bordered by the Atlantic Ocean, Río de la Plata, and two rivers (Uruguay and Cuareim), the country is nearly enclosed by water. Rolling lowland plains covered with prairie grass extend across most (about 78 percent) of the country. These plains provide excellent pastures for stock raising and agriculture. Forests and hills dominate the northeast region. Uruguay's coastline has several fine beaches. Free of many natural disasters, the land has remained relatively unchanged over time, providing a constant and stable environment. The climate is temperate and the seasons are opposite those in North America. Fahrenheit temperatures in July average in the 50s (10–14°C); January is the warmest month, with temperatures in the 70s (22–25°C).

History. Originally, Uruguay was home to small groups of native Indians, including the Guaraní and Charrúas. Spanish explorers first landed in the area in 1516. The Portuguese founded Colonia del Sacramento in 1680 and maintained a presence in the area until 1726, when the Spanish drove them out and pursued colonization, founding Montevideo. The Banda Oriental del Uruguay became part of the Spanish viceroyalty of Río de la Plata in 1776. During European colonization, nearly all of Uruguay's indigenous population was conquered, killed, or driven out.

A war of independence began in 1811 in conjunction with a general uprising throughout South America. Under the leadership of José Gervasio Artigas, Uruguayan Orientales joined forces with Buenos Aires to make significant gains against the Spanish, even gaining de facto independence for a time. However, Artigas and his forces could not halt the 1816 invasion of Portuguese forces from Brazil and fled to neighboring Paraguay. Even so, Artigas is considered the Father of Uruguay. His efforts inspired another uprising in 1825, when a group of patriots known as the Thirty-Three Immortals rebelled against Brazilian domination and declared independence. Three years later, Brazil granted Uruguay full independence.

Civil war raged between conservative landowner *Blancos* (Whites) and liberal urban *Colorados* (Reds) from 1839 to 1851; these two groups would dominate Uruguayan politics for much of the 19th and 20th centuries. War with Paraguay (1865–70) was followed by a period of dictatorship. A president, José Batlle y Ordóñez, was finally elected in 1903. Ordóñez controlled national politics for two decades but laid the groundwork for a modern democracy. Throughout the first part of the 20th century, liberal governments applied socialist principles to the political and economic systems. Uruguay was among the first South American countries to legalize divorce (1907), give women the right to vote (1932), and recognize the rights of trade unions.

Severe economic problems in the 1950s and 1960s led to unrest and urban terrorist violence. In the early 1970s, under pressure from the military, President Juan María Bordaberry attempted to restore order by suspending the constitution, dissolving the legislature, and banning all political activity. By 1976, the military had ousted him from power. A decade of brutal military rule followed, during which thousands were detained and tortured. A 1980 referendum determined that the military should relinquish control of the government, but the military nullified the results and appointed General Gregorio Alvarez president in 1981.

Public pressure paved the way for general elections in 1984. The military stepped down when the elected president, Julio María Sanguinetti of the Colorado Party, took office in 1985. The new government restored basic human rights, and to avoid clashes with the military, granted amnesty to personnel suspected of human-rights violations.

Elections in 1989 marked the first democratic transfer of power from one elected government to another since 1971. Luis Alberto Lacalle Herrera of the Blanco Party was elected president. Lacalle encouraged market-oriented solutions to Uruguay's economic troubles, but his plan was not popular with the public. He did not run for reelection due to a constitutional ban on consecutive presidential terms. In 1994 elections, his party was defeated by Sanguinetti, who returned to office as president for another five-year term. Sanguinetti's top priorities were to reduce inflation and government spending.

Jorge Batlle won the Colorado Party's presidential nomination in April 1999. Batlle was narrowly elected president in a second round of voting in November 1999; he has determined to promote trade and resolve issues surrounding 160 people who disappeared during the 1970s and 1980s. In 2000, a special commission was formed to investigate their disappearance.

THE PEOPLE

Population. Uruguay has a population of 3.33 million. Unlike most other nations in South America, it has a low annual growth rate of 0.77 percent. People of European descent, mostly Spanish and Italian, account for 88 percent of the total population, a figure also dissimilar to other South American countries, where mestizos usually are the majority ethnic group. In Uruguay, mestizos comprise only 8 percent of the population. Four percent of the people are black (descendants of slaves who were imported by the Spanish). More than 85 percent of the people live in urban areas. Montevideo (MOAN-tay-vee-DAY-oh) is the capital and largest city, with about 1.5 million people. It is the country's financial, political, and cultural center.

Language. Spanish is the official language of Uruguay and is spoken by nearly the entire population. People in northern border towns often speak a mixture of Spanish and Portuguese known as *Portuñol* or *Brazilero*. Uruguayans speak with an accent quite different from that heard in other Spanish-speaking countries. Most notable is the Uruguayan "sh" pronunciation of *y* and *ll*. For instance, *yo* (I) is pronounced more like "show" than "yoh." Portuguese and English are common second languages. Small minority groups speak Italian and other languages.

Religion. Uruguay is perhaps the most secular of Latin American countries. Although 65 percent of the population belongs to the Roman Catholic Church, less than half regularly attends services. There is no official religion, and church and state are strictly separated. Religious freedom is guaranteed. About 2 percent of the population is Protestant and roughly the same percentage is Jewish. The rest, about 30 percent, belongs to various other Christian or non-Christian organizations or professes no religion at all.

General Attitudes. Uruguayans have retained a European bias in their culture and often view Uruguay as one of the more culturally advanced countries in South America. They are also proud of their country's cultural traditions, such as the *gaucho* (a cowboy-like figure), which is regarded as a symbol of the country's rugged independence. People are conservative and often distrustful of change. While Uruguayans generally are pessimistic, opinionated, and individualistic, they do not appreciate aggressiveness or arrogance. Occupation, power, and money may grant social status, but ostentatious displays of wealth or power are frowned upon. Education is held in high esteem. The democratic view that *Nadie es más que nadie* (No one is better than anyone else) is shared by most. Although the government is considered bureaucratic and inefficient, many people prefer it to run the economy as opposed to foreign companies, which are not trusted.

Punctuality is admired but not always practiced. Arriving later than a scheduled time is not improper. However, the more formal a meeting, the more important it is to be on time. Uruguayans are extremely proud of their country, but they are also aware of its problems. They do not appreciate individuals who praise other countries over Uruguay—not because they do not appreciate other countries but because they do not want to be treated as inferior.

The immediate family is close-knit and members are devoted to each other, but not to their community. Uruguayans value education highly and parents often will go to great lengths to ensure their children have good schooling. The elderly are respected and adult children often care for aging parents.

Personal Appearance. Conservative, well-tailored clothing is the general rule. Subdued colors (blue, brown, and gray) are pervasive. Fashion generally indicates a person's social status. European fashions are common. Women do not wear much makeup or jewelry, but they wear dresses more often than do U.S. American women. Businessmen wear conservative suits. Popular casual clothing includes jeans and T-shirts. In interior (rural) areas, some men wear *bombachas* (loose-legged trousers) with wide belts, boots, and hats or Basque-style caps.

CUSTOMS AND COURTESIES

Greetings. Men usually greet others with a warm, firm handshake. They use an *abrazo* (hearty hug) and occasionally a kiss with family or close friends. Women (and sometimes men) appear to kiss one cheek when they greet each other. Actually, they only brush cheeks and "kiss the air." If a woman greets a person with an *abrazo*, it is always accompanied with a "kiss." Verbal greetings depend on the time of day or situation. *¡Hola!* (Hi) and *¿Cómo estás?* (How's it going?) are common casual greetings. Especially popular in the morning is *¡Buen día!* (Good day). The Usted form of greetings (*¿Cómo está?*) is used for someone older than yourself or to show respect.

People generally do not greet strangers when passing on the street, particularly in cities. The other person might misunderstand if one were to extend a greeting or even a smile. Rural people are more open and more likely to greet passing strangers with *¡Chau!* (Good-bye). They use *¡Chau!* because they are passing (not stopping) and therefore saying good-bye more than hello.

One greets all individuals in a small group when one arrives at a social function. Group greetings and farewells are considered impolite. In general, people address each other by an appropriate title and surname. For example, *Señor* (Mr.), *Señora* (Mrs.), or *Señorita* (Miss) is used with the family name. Only close friends and family members address each other by given name.

Gestures. To beckon, one snaps the fingers or makes a "ch-ch" sound. The "ch-ch" sound is used for many purposes, such as getting someone's attention or stopping a bus. People use hand gestures often in conversation. One avoids hiding the hands or fidgeting with them when conversing because such actions can convey unintended messages. Forming a zero with the index finger and thumb is extremely rude. Brushing the back of the hand under the chin means "I don't know." Raising one's shoulders quickly can mean "What's up?" Placing the thumb and index finger on the upper lip in an upward "V" is called *bigote para arriba* (upward mustache) and means "Everything is all right." People do not sit on tables or ledges or rest their feet on objects in a room. On public transportation, it is polite for a man to offer his seat to a woman.

Visiting. Uruguayans commonly visit for hours at a time in cafés and bars. Visiting friends and relatives at home is important, but busy schedules make this increasingly difficult. People in rural areas often visit in the late afternoon or early evening. It is impolite to visit unannounced during regular mealtimes. Invited guests are not expected to bring gifts to their hosts, but flowers or chocolates are considered a nice gesture. Guests invited to a meal may bring wine or a dessert. Hosts always offer their guests refreshments (soft drinks, tea, coffee, etc.). The length of a visit often depends on the familiarity between host and guest, but a guest may comfortably leave after having eaten and had coffee or tea. It would be rude for a host to suggest that a guest leave. On weekends or during the summer, hosts may invite lunch guests to stay for the afternoon *siesta* (rest) and a round of *mate* (pronounced MAH-tay) afterward.

Many Uruguayans, particularly men, appreciate having friends come by to socialize and share a round of *mate*. *Mate* is a strong, bitter herb tea that is drunk from a gourd through a silver straw (*bombilla*) that has a screen at the bottom. The gourd is filled almost to the brim with *mate* and is repeatedly filled with hot water for each person to finish and pass on to the next. Holding on too long to a passed *mate* is impolite. Men like to share *mate* when discussing sports, politics, or family matters. Women commonly share *mate dulce* (*mate* with sugar) but men do not. Sharing *mate* with someone is a sign of acceptance, and strangers are seldom invited to participate in a round. The activity has become a cultural ritual for many. Uruguayans drink *mate* at any time and any place (in a park, walking on the street, etc.).

Eating. Uruguayans eat in the continental style, with the fork in the left hand and the knife remaining in the right. During the meal, they keep the hands (not elbows) above the table rather than in the lap. People often wipe their plates clean with bread as they finish eating. Taking second helpings indicates one likes the food. When finished, one places the utensils side by side on the plate. Dinner guests remain at the table until all have finished eating. Using a toothpick in public or reading a newspaper at the family table is impolite.

Although habits in urban areas are changing to accommodate schedules, Uruguayans traditionally eat a light breakfast of coffee and bread. They have their main meal at 1 or 2 p.m. When possible, workers go home for this meal. Supper is lighter and later in the evening (8 or 9 p.m.). Children usually have a snack when they get home from school, and adults may snack around 5 p.m.

LIFESTYLE

Family. Strong ties traditionally unite the family. The average family has two children, and nuclear families are the norm. Although extended families do not live together, they play a significant role in the social lives of Uruguayans. The father presides in the home. This patriarchal order is still predominant, but the role of women is increasing in significance. A large percentage of women work or study outside the home. Uruguay has more professional women than men; however, men are still expected to earn the better salary. Many couples today share family responsibilities more evenly. Nannies or family members often care for children while the mother is at work. Due to housing shortages, children remain at home until they marry, regardless of their age. Young university students from the interior may stay with relatives in Montevideo while attending college.

A small number of wealthy families generally control politics and the economy. The majority of families live in more humble circumstances, although few are without basic modern conveniences. Most rent their home or apartment because of the difficulty and cost involved in purchasing a home.

Dating and Marriage. Dating customs are similar to those in the United States, although young people usually date only one person at a time. Some rural families have retained traditional European customs in which the young man asks the parents' permission to date the young woman for the first time. He must also request her hand before getting engaged. Young people enjoy dancing, eating out, going to the beach, and watching movies. Men and women usually marry in their mid- to late twenties. Both families play a large role in preparing for the wedding and often associate closely after their children are married. The marriage reception usually includes a formal, catered party, from which the couple generally leaves early.

Diet. Uruguay produces most of its own food. Wide varieties of meats, fish, vegetables, and fruits are available. Wheat and rice are the principal grains. Beef is consumed in some form almost daily. Pasta usually is served with the main meal. Families often eat roasts and stews served with potatoes and carrots. Meat pies are popular menu items. Traditional dishes include *asado* (grilled beef), *chivito* (steak and egg with cheese and mayonnaise), *milanesa* (fried breaded steak), and *guiso* (ground beef with rice, onion, egg, etc.). Homemade pasta is also common: *tallarines* is like spaghetti, and *ñoquis* is gnocchi.

Recreation. *Fútbol* (soccer) is the national sport. Uruguayans closely follow the country's national team in World Cup competitions. Basketball, volleyball, cycling, swimming, and other water sports are also popular. Young urbanites like rowing. *Asados* (barbecues) are popular social events. Beaches in the southeast are popular summer (January) vacation destinations. Uruguayans enjoy watching movies or television and attending cultural events.

The Arts. Uruguay has a rich national tradition in the arts and literature. Painting is influenced by international trends but often focuses on local themes like rural life, history, and the *gaucho*. Carved *mate* gourds are an indigenous craft, and crochet and textiles are also made.

▼ **THE AMERICAS**

Tango, the dance and the music, is very popular. The *milonga* and the *vidalita* are other traditional dances. The *candombe*, an African-influenced rhythm, is played with three *tambores* (drums) and is often performed at *Carnival*. *Carnival* theater productions are performed on *tablados* (stages) throughout Montevideo. Especially popular are *las murgas*, small groups of singers and actors who present parodies of the year's main events.

Holidays. The most important holidays are New Year's Day, Children's Day (6 Jan.), *Carnival*, Easter (including Holy Thursday and Good Friday), Landing of the Thirty-Three Patriots (19 Apr.), Labor Day (1 May), Constitution Day (18 July), Independence Day (25 Aug.), Christmas Eve, and Christmas. Most Catholics have celebrations to honor local patron saints, and some celebrate name days (a day honoring the saint for whom one is named). Christmas Eve and New Year's Eve are celebrated with large family parties and midnight fireworks. The week preceding Easter is also known as *Semana de Turismo* (Tourism Week), when people travel throughout the country and participate in a variety of local festivals.

Commerce. Business hours are from 9 a.m. to 7 p.m., Monday through Friday. Businesses in interior towns often close for a *siesta* at midday; a *siesta* may last two to four hours depending on the season (longer in summer). Government hours vary between the seasons, running primarily in the morning during the summer and in the afternoon and evening during the winter.

SOCIETY

Government. Uruguay is a democratic republic divided into 19 *departamentos* (provinces). The executive branch is headed by the president and vice president. The legislature, or *Asamblea General* (General Assembly), has two houses: a 30 seat Chamber of Senators and a 99-seat Chamber of Representatives. Uruguay's major political parties include the Colorado Party, National (Blanco) Party, and Broad Front Coalition. All three parties won an almost equal number of legislative seats in 1994 elections. A few smaller parties also have legislative representation. Uruguayan parties held presidential primary elections for the first time in April 1999. Beginning at age 18, all citizens are required to return to their place of birth to vote.

Economy. Uruguay's greatest natural resource is its fertile land. More than 80 percent of the land is used for agriculture and livestock production. Agriculture employs about 20 percent of the labor force. Uruguay is a world leader in the production of cattle and wool. Other products include wheat, rice, corn, and sorghum. The industrial sector is tied to agriculture as well, with the chief industries being meat processing, wool and hides, footwear, leather apparel, and fish processing. The services sector is growing in importance. Uruguay has been a member of *Mercosur* (Southern Common Market) since 1995.

The economy grew under Lacalle, but inflation remained high (130 percent in 1990), and poor labor relations resulted in long and frequent strikes. Sanguinetti successfully lowered inflation to 11 percent in 1998 and 6 percent in 1999. Under Batlle, inflation remains at about 5.5 percent. The economy

DEVELOPMENT DATA

Human Dev. Index* rank	39 of 174 countries
Adjusted for women	37 of 143 countries
Real GDP per capita	$8,623
Adult literacy rate	97 percent
Infant mortality rate	15 per 1,000 births
Life expectancy	70 (male); 76 (female)

slid into a recession, shrinking by 1.7 percent in 1999 and 1.2 percent in 2000. The government is trying to strengthen the economy through economic reforms and austerity measures and predicts positive growth in 2001. Unemployment is about 14 percent.

Incomes are modest but sufficient to meet basic and other needs. Uruguayan women earn 34 percent of their nation's income, the largest share among Latin American countries.

People enjoy access to education, health care, and a standard of living sufficient for them to make choices in their lives; only 4 percent of the population (the lowest percentage in South America) lives in human poverty.* The country's currency is the Uruguayan *peso* ($Ur).

Transportation and Communications. Buses are the primary form of public transportation. Many Uruguayans also travel in private automobiles. Taxis are readily available in the cities. Roads are generally good around major urban areas but are less developed in rural areas. Key highways are paved and well maintained. Uruguay has international airway links. The communications system is developing rapidly; the best facilities are in Montevideo. Private telephone lines are becoming increasingly accessible. The country has a national radio relay system and a number of radio and television stations. Most people own a radio and television. Newspapers are widely circulated.

Education. Uruguay has one of the highest literacy rates in South America at 97 percent. Primary schooling is compulsory for nine years. Afterward, students may choose to enter a government-subsidized *liceo* (secondary school) or receive technical training at a vocational school. While the government provides education free of charge through postgraduate studies, general economic conditions do not allow everyone to continue their studies. Still, Uruguay boasts a large percentage of professionals (lawyers and doctors, for example). The University of Montevideo, founded in 1849, and the Catholic University have fine reputations throughout South America.

Health. Health care is free and available to all citizens. Uruguay has good health standards, and modern facilities are available in Montevideo. Health and other social programs are highly valued. Private health organizations also provide care for those who can afford it. Sanitation is good.

CONTACT INFORMATION

Consulate of Uruguay, Tourism Office, 1077 Ponce De Leon Boulevard, Suite B, Coral Gables, FL 33134; phone (305) 443-9764. Embassy of Uruguay, 2715 M Street NW, Third Floor, Washington, DC 20007; phone (202) 331-1313; Web site www.embassy.org/uruguay.

1305 North Research Way, Bldg. K
Orem, Utah 84097-6200 USA
1.800.528.6279; 801.705.4250
fax 801.705.4350
www.culturegrams.com

Bolivarian Republic of
Venezuela

Boundary representations are not necessarily authoritative.

BACKGROUND

Land and Climate. Venezuela is a tropical land located in northern South America. Covering 352,143 square miles (912,050 square kilometers), it is slightly larger than Texas and Oklahoma combined. The country is divided roughly into four geographic zones: west, central, east, and south. The Andes Mountains dominate the west, where Pico Bolívar rises 16,427 feet (5,007 meters) above sea level. The central zone includes the northern coast and Venezuela's largest cities. To the east of the Orinoco River is a *llano* (large plain). The south is dominated by high plateaus and jungle. Angel Falls, the highest waterfall in the world at 3,212 feet (979 meters), displays its beauty in the southeast. In the far south is a reserve for the country's 14,000 Yanomami Indians. Covering 32,000 square miles (almost 83,000 square kilometers), the area is off-limits to farmers, miners, and all non-Yanomami settlers.

The rainy season is from May to November. Temperatures average between 70°F and 85°F (21–29°C), but the mountains can experience cool temperatures, and some Andean peaks are snowcapped year-round. Earthquakes are not infrequent. Torrential rains in December 1999 caused flooding and mudslides in the coastal state of Vargas, which left more than 20,000 people dead and 100,000 homeless.

History. Before the arrival of Columbus, Venezuela was inhabited by a number of indigenous groups, including the Caracas, Arawak, and Cumanagotos. Columbus discovered the area in 1498. The Spanish soon began conquering offshore islands and coastal regions. They named the area *Venezuela* (little Venice) because the coastal homes were built on stilts,

reminding them of Venice, Italy. Caracas, the capital, was founded in 1527. The Spanish Crown, which claimed the territory, controlled Venezuela through the 18th century. After various failed revolts, a congress formed and declared independence in 1811. This began a 10-year struggle to achieve the desired freedoms. Finally, in 1821, the forces of Simón Bolívar were victorious at the Battle of Carabobo, and a republic was established. The republic (Greater Colombia) contained Venezuela, Ecuador, and Colombia. It dissolved in 1830 and Venezuela became independent.

Venezuela experienced instability and dictatorships for many years. The 20th century began under a dictator (Cipriano Castro). He was deposed by his vice president, Juan Vicente Gómez, who ruled as a brutal dictator until 1935. More political instability and military coups followed.

A freely elected president came to power in 1958, and democratic elections have been held since. For a time, Venezuela was the most stable South American country and was also one of the wealthiest in the region. Its oil reserves are the largest in the world outside of the Persian Gulf area, and it benefited from high oil prices in the 1970s and 1980s. Carlos Andrés Pérez, who took office as president in 1989, introduced a controversial economic austerity plan to address the plummeting price of oil and rising foreign debt. The reforms boosted gross domestic product, but the wealth was concentrated in the hands of a few. Poverty, inflation, and unemployment increased, and violent opposition soon rose to challenge Pérez. He was nearly overthrown by two coups in 1992. Pérez was impeached in 1993 and later imprisoned for misusing government security funds.

December 1993 elections brought a former president, Rafael Caldera, to office. He promised to slow privatization begun under Pérez, end corruption, and stabilize the economy. In 1994, Caldera implemented price and market controls, but public pressure forced him to reverse his policies. Austerity measures and high inflation sparked public protests, as the standard of living for most Venezuelans declined dramatically under Caldera's leadership.

Record-low oil prices in the late 1990s deepened Venezuela's economic crisis. Discontentment with poverty and corruption spread. Claiming to represent the needs of the poor, Hugo Chavez Frias was elected president by a large majority in the December 1998 elections. Chavez, who had led a coup attempt in 1992, has transformed Venezuela's political system since coming to office, promising complete social reform. A referendum to change the constitution was passed in December 1999. The new constitution dissolved the bicameral parliament, established a single National Assembly, allows a second presidential term, and gives greater powers to the president. In July 2000, elections were held for nearly every official except local ones. Chavez was returned to office until 2006, and his supporters won a majority in congress. In November 2000, the National Assembly passed a bill giving Chavez power to pass laws in certain areas by decree for the space of one year; Chavez maintains this is necessary to deliver much-needed economic and social reforms.

THE PEOPLE

Population. Venezuela has a population of 23.54 million, which is growing at 1.6 percent annually. The country is the most urbanized in South America; more than 90 percent of the people live in urban areas. Caracas has 3.3 million inhabitants. The majority of the population (67 percent) is of mixed Amerindian and Spanish heritage. Twenty-one percent is either of European descent (mostly Italian or Spanish) or *mulatto* (mixed European and black); many of these people live in coastal regions. About 10 percent of the population is black and 2 percent is Amerindian.

Language. Spanish is the official language and is spoken by all, except some Amerindians living in remote areas. These indigenous groups speak a variety of native languages. The Spanish spoken in Venezuela is known for its many colloquialisms. *Chevere* means "very well" or "cool." *Estar pelado* (to be bald) and *estar limpio* (to be clean) can also mean "to be broke," or out of money. *Ponerse las pilas* (to insert batteries) means "to be aware or watch out." Students are required to take English courses in high school.

Religion. Religious freedom is guaranteed by the constitution. Still, 90 percent of the population is Roman Catholic. While many Catholics do not attend church services regularly, the majority profess some faith in God, the Catholic Saints, and the Virgin Mary. Protestant and other Christian faiths are becoming more prevalent. In general, Venezuelans are somewhat less religious than other Latin Americans. Rural people tend to be more devoted to their faith than urban residents.

General Attitudes. Venezuelans take great pride in their country and the heroes of the independence movement. The South American liberator Simón Bolívar was Venezuelan. While he is honored in many other nations, he is a national treasure to Venezuela. Most cities have a *Plaza Bolívar* that occupies a block near the city center. It is rude to behave disrespectfully in that plaza or to refer negatively to Bolívar.

Venezuelans admire honesty, generosity, and a good sense of humor. Their penchant for talking, joking, laughing, and spontaneity often creates a party-like atmosphere wherever they happen to be. Venezuelans feel that the joy of an event or the needs of an individual are more important than the demands of a time schedule. Therefore, they may be late for appointments, and scheduled events may last longer than expected. Venezuelans are proud of the beauty of their country and of Venezuelan women; they proudly point out that winners of international beauty contests are frequently from Venezuela. Loss of prosperity over the last decade has affected the outlook of many, as Venezuela's once relatively large middle class now focuses on making ends meet. Still, many are optimistic that they can work out their current problems.

Personal Appearance. In all areas and at all levels of society, it is important to look one's best and be groomed properly. Professional men and women wear suits or more casual clothing, which is always neat and clean. Venezuelans are quite fashion-conscious; urban people wear the latest European styles. In the summer, cotton clothing is the most common and comfortable. Shorts and swimwear are worn only in urban recreation areas and at the beach. Native peoples may wear European or traditional dress or a combination of both.

CUSTOMS AND COURTESIES

Greetings. Men greet close friends with an *abrazo* (a full embrace, while patting each other on the back); women greet and part with an *abrazo* and a kiss on the cheek. Usually a man and a woman exchange an *abrazo* only if they are close friends or relatives. A firm handshake is a common greeting and parting gesture among acquaintances and strangers. It may be accompanied by a pat on the back, or among closer acquaintances, an *abrazo*.

During conversation, people stand much closer than they do in the United States. Backing away is improper. Common greetings include *¡Buenos días!* (Good morning), *¡Buenas tardes!* (Good afternoon), and *¡Buenas noches!* (Good evening). The youth generally use the more casual *¡Hola!* (Hi). Greetings generally include polite inquiries about a person's health. Common parting phrases might include *Hasta luego* (Until later), *Nos vemos* (We'll see you), and *Chao* (Good-bye).

Friends often address one another by nickname. Acquaintances and professionals are addressed by title (*Doctor*, *Señor*, *Señora*, etc.), usually followed by the surname. Elderly, respected people may be addressed as *Don* (for men) or *Doña* (for women), followed by the first name.

Gestures. Venezuelans generally use their hands during conversation to communicate or emphasize a point. They may also use a gesture to communicate without speaking. For example, one can ask the price of an item or request payment by rubbing the thumb and index finger together while rotating the palm up. People normally stand close to each other during conversation; however, those in the Andes prefer some distance. It is courteous to maintain eye contact while conversing. When sitting, a person does not slouch or prop the feet up on any object. Pointing with the index finger is considered rude; motioning with the entire hand is more polite. Passing between conversing individuals or interrupting a conversation is also rude; in such circumstances, one is expected to say *Con permiso* (With permission). People often offer their seats to the elderly on public transportation.

Visiting. Venezuelans enjoy visiting friends and relatives. Friends may visit unannounced, but such visits generally are short and not at mealtimes. People typically only invite close friends to their homes; business contacts and other visitors usually are invited to dine at a restaurant. Venezuelans are hospitable and careful to provide for their guests. When visitors arrive at a home, business, or office, they often are served *un cafecito* (a thick black coffee) in a very small cup. This is a symbol of hospitality and a way of extending friendship. Polite discussion usually precedes any business matters. In the home, hosts may offer guests refreshments in addition to coffee. It is polite for guests to inquire about the health of the host's family members. Hosts generally do not expect gifts from visitors.

Eating. Lunch is the main meal of the day. Families traditionally eat together for midday and evening meals; however, this varies by region. Families in big cities no longer eat midday meals together. The parents usually sit at the head and foot of the dinner table. Some Venezuelans eat in the continental style, with the fork in the left hand and the knife remaining in the right. Others use the style more common in the United States, with the fork in the right hand, unless the knife is picked up to cut something. Both eating styles are accepted. When a person is finished, he or she places the utensils together or in an "X" at the center of the plate. It is inappropriate for adults to eat on the street. In restaurants, the bill usually includes a service charge (10 percent), but patrons are expected to leave a small additional tip.

LIFESTYLE

Family. Family ties are strong and most families are close-knit. However, about half of all births in Venezuela are out of wedlock or in common-law marriages. Households commonly include members of the extended family, usually grandparents. The father dominates in the home, but the responsibility for raising the children and managing the household traditionally rests with the mother. More couples are sharing responsibilities as an increasing number of women work outside the home, especially in Caracas. Women comprise about one-fifth of the labor force. If members of a family are affluent, they customarily share their wealth with less-fortunate relatives.

Dating and Marriage. Dating and courtship traditions are similar to those in other Western countries. Young people enjoy socializing and choosing their own companion. Weddings are social events for many Venezuelan families. Most weddings include two marriage ceremonies: a civil ceremony for legal recognition and an optional religious ceremony. Religious ceremonies are an important part of the Venezuelan culture due to the Roman Catholic tradition. Parties usually are held after the religious ceremony.

Diet. Common foods in Venezuela include pasta, rice, beans, plantains, white cheese, chicken, potatoes, and fish. Corn is the basis of many dishes, and fried foods are popular. One favorite is the *arepa*, a deep-fried thick pancake made from white corn flour and sometimes filled with butter, meat, and cheese. *Hallacas* are similar to *arepas* but are stuffed with stewed meat, potatoes, olives, raisins, and other spices; they are especially popular at Christmastime. Casseroles, meat pies, meatloaf, and stews are popular, although rising prices have diminished meat's popularity somewhat. *Puntatrasera* is a favorite tender steak. *Pabellón criollo* consists of black beans, rice, shredded meat, plantains, and *arepas*.

In most cities, open-air markets provide a large variety of tropical fruits and fresh vegetables. Popular fruits include mangoes, *lechoza* (papaya), bananas, and watermelon. These may be eaten or made into *batidos de fruta* (fruit shakes), which are sold on the street at *refresquerias* (fruit-and-drink stands). *Raspaitos* (shaved ice) are another common treat. Although soda and coffee are favored drinks, hot chocolate is also popular, particularly in the cooler Andean states.

Recreation. The most popular sports in Venezuela are baseball and basketball. Venezuelans also enjoy watching horse racing and bullfighting. Fishing, swimming, cycling, and tennis are popular participation sports. Many women enjoy walking, cycling, and playing softball. For entertainment, Venezuelans like to go dancing, to movies, or to cultural events. Playing dominoes and visiting are favorite leisure activities. *Telenovelas* (nighttime soap operas) have a large following, particularly among women. Going to the beaches and the mountains are popular vacation activities.

The Arts. *Llaneros* (like cowboys) have a great influence on Venezuela's arts. *Joropo* (traditional music of *los llanos*) is the national dance. *Maracas* (rattles made of gourds) and the *cuatro* (a small guitar) often accompany it. Annual music festivals feature such popular music as salsa, *merengue*, *gaitas* (traditional Christmas music), and *aguinaldos* (traditional Christmas songs). Classical music is appreciated, and there is an orchestra in many cities.

Literature developed substantially in the 20th century. Much literature is characterized by nationalism. Some Venezuelan sculptors are involved in kinetic art, which has movable parts. Many people produce crafts such as canoes, saddles, and musical instruments.

Holidays. Official public holidays include New Year's Day, *Carnaval* (two days before Ash Wednesday), Ash Wednesday, Easter (Thursday–Sunday), Declaration of Independence Day (19 Apr.), Day of Workers (1 May), Battle of Carabobo (24 June), Independence Day (5 July), Simón Bolívar's Birthday (24 July), Columbus Day (12 Oct.), Christmas Eve, Christmas, and New Year's Eve.

Many families vacation at the beach or in the mountains during *Semana Santa*, the week preceding Easter. *Carnaval* is most celebrated in eastern Venezuela, where water fights, parades, dancing in the streets, and other activities are common. Towns and cities hold annual *ferias* (festivals), honoring the local patron saint. Festivities include bullfighting, street dances, craft exhibits, and beauty contests. Flowers are important in Venezuelan celebrations. During each holiday, statues of Simón Bolívar, the father of Venezuela, are decorated with colorful wreaths.

Commerce. Business hours generally extend from 8 a.m. to 6 p.m. (with a one- or two-hour break), Monday through

Friday. Government offices maintain similar hours, with regional variations. Standard banking hours are from 9 a.m. to 3:30 p.m. Urban dwellers purchase basic goods from larger stores and shopping centers, while rural residents rely on local markets, small specialized shops, and their own labor for these basics.

It is customary for service personnel, such as garbage collectors and postal carriers, to present a calling card requesting a *regalo* (gift) in the form of money at Christmastime. The expediting of needed services or supplies sometimes requires a tip in advance.

SOCIETY

Government. Venezuela is a republic, headed by a president who serves a six-year term. As chief of state and head of government, he or she governs with a Council of Ministers. The new constitution abolished the 52-seat Senate and 207-seat Chamber of Deputies and replaced it with a single National Assembly. The December 1998 elections transformed Venezuela's political party system. Two new parties, Movement for a Fifth Republic (MVR) and Proyecto Venezuela, defeated several traditional parties, most notably the Democratic Action Party (AD) and the Social Christian Party (COPEI). The MVR, the party currently in power, was created by President Hugo Chavez. The voting age is 18.

Economy. Venezuela is a member of OPEC (Organization of Petroleum Exporting Countries) and petroleum is the cornerstone of the economy. It accounts for nearly 80 percent of all export earnings and more than half of all government revenues. Those revenues have allowed the country to develop a modern infrastructure. However, oil has also made Venezuela subject to market fluctuations. When the price of oil drops, the entire economy suffers. Therefore, the government stresses economic diversification. Tourism, petrochemical, and gas sectors are potential sources of revenue. The country also exports some minerals and other raw materials. Agriculture employs about 10 percent of the population and produces grains, sugar, fruits, coffee, and rice.

Economic growth has been somewhat erratic in the 1990s. Years of negative or low growth commonly have followed years of strong growth. Several major banks went bankrupt in 1994, which led to a severe currency devaluation of the *bolívar* (Bs) and added to concerns about economic stability. Low world oil prices in the late 1990s plunged the economy into a deep recession. The economy shrank in 1998 and shrank a further 7 percent in 1999. However, the economy recovered in 2000, recording growth of around 3 percent. A similar rate is expected for 2001. Unemployment is about 11 percent. Inflation reached 30 percent in 1998 but dropped to about 13 percent in 2000. Low oil prices, a large external debt, and the loss of foreign capital remain serious problems for the economy.

The standard of living of most Venezuelans is falling. Nearly 80 percent of the people now live in poverty. The gap between rich and poor is widening as Venezuela's middle class continues to shrink. Benefits from Venezuela's oil wealth have eluded a significant proportion of the population.

DEVELOPMENT DATA

Human Dev. Index* rank	65 of 174 countries
Adjusted for women	56 of 143 countries
Real GDP per capita	$5,808
Adult literacy rate	92 percent
Infant mortality rate	26 per 1,000 births
Life expectancy	70 (male); 76 (female)

Access to health care, education, and a decent standard of living is somewhat limited for the general population.

Transportation and Communications. Most people use public transportation; few Venezuelans can afford to own a private car. Buses and taxis are common, but the *Por puesto* is the most popular and cheapest form of transportation. It features a system of taxi-like automobiles that travel a regular route throughout the city, picking up and letting off passengers at any point. The cost is less than a taxi but more than a bus. Highways are excellent in Venezuela, but driving is often hazardous. Railroads generally are not used for passenger travel.

The communications system is modern and expanding. Private phones are expensive, but public phones are readily available. Several radio and television stations broadcast in Venezuela. A number of daily national and regional newspapers (including one in English) also service the country.

Education. Education is compulsory (though not enforced) from ages seven to fourteen. All education, including university level, is free in public institutions. The government has taken great strides in improving the literacy rate. About three-fourths of all students complete primary school (nine years), and most of those children go on to secondary school (two years). Secondary school tracks are available in the sciences, humanities, or technical fields. About two-thirds of the overall school-age population does not attend a secondary school. Many families are unable to afford the necessary books and transportation. After secondary school, students may choose from a variety of three-year vocational schools or take an aptitude test to enter a university.

Health. Good medical facilities can be found in urban areas, but the best are private and very expensive for the average citizen. Many facilities, particularly in rural areas, lack staff, equipment, and supplies. Strikes involving medical-care personnel are relatively frequent. The National Health System is being restructured; some seek to have part of it privatized. Only about two-thirds of all infants are immunized against childhood diseases, but the government is trying to improve this percentage. Malnutrition now affects some 40 percent of the population. Malaria is active in some rural areas, and cholera outbreaks occurred in the 1990s.

CONTACT INFORMATION

Embassy of the Republic of Venezuela, 1099 30th Street NW, Washington, DC 20007; phone (202) 342-2214; Web site www.embavenez-us.org.

1305 North Research Way, Bldg. K
Orem, Utah 84097-6200 USA
1.800.528.6279; 801.705.4250
fax 801.705.4350
www.culturegrams.com

U.S. Virgin Islands

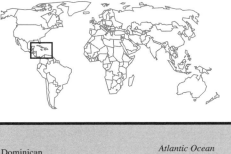

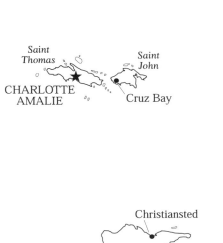

Boundary representations are not necessarily authoritative.

BACKGROUND

Land and Climate. The U.S. Virgin Islands (USVI) comprise 68 islands in the Greater Antilles, a total of 135 square miles (349 square kilometers). The three largest islands are Saint Croix (83 square miles), Saint Thomas (31 square miles), and Saint John (20 square miles). St. Thomas is about 40 miles from Puerto Rico. The remaining islands are small and mostly uninhabited.

USVI's highest point is Crown Mountain (1,550 feet or 368 meters), located on rugged St. Thomas. This island is also home to Charlotte Amalie, a natural port and the territorial capital. St. John is characterized by moderately sloping mountains that meet the shorelines. St. Croix is dry and windswept in the east and lushly tropical in the west. Central high pastures are favorable to agriculture.

The subtropical climate is moderated by constant trade winds; the temperature averages 79°F (16°C). About 43 inches (109 centimeters) of rain fall each year, although droughts are possible. Hurricanes occur periodically and can inflict serious damage. Hurricane Georges battered the islands in 1998, and in 1999 Hurricane Lenny caused more than $30 million in damage, mostly on St. Croix.

History. The Virgin Islands have a long and active history. Artifacts show the Igneri or Ancient Ones (A.D. 50–650) preceded the peace-loving Arawak tribes who were eventually dominated by the fierce Caribs. It was the Caribs who greeted Christopher Columbus with arrows at the Salt River on St. Croix. Columbus named this island *Santa Cruz* (Holy Cross). Sailing north, he compared the other islands to St. Ursula's 11,000 virgins (hence, the name Virgin Islands).

Spain made little effort to colonize the Virgin Islands, and for the next two hundred years, the French, Dutch, and English traded them back and forth. By the 1700s, Denmark had planted its flag on St. Thomas, adopted St. John, and purchased the now-designated St. Croix from the French. Britain secured the islands from the Dutch that are the British Virgin Islands today.

Denmark went on to promote the islands as thriving sugarcane and trading centers. By the late 18th century, St. Croix had 264 sugar mills (many of which remain as ruins) and more than 24,000 African slaves. The sugar-based economic system began to decline when the European sugar beet was introduced and when the Danes proclaimed slave trading (but not slave labor) illegal in 1803. In 1848, Governor Peter von Scholten promised emancipation for all "unfree" persons after an organized slave protest. The Danish government then enacted harsh labor laws that provoked eventual conflict. This climaxed with the Great Fire Burn of 1878. Laborers destroyed or burned more than 40 estates and miles of plantations, ultimately putting an end to the sugarcane industry.

The United States decided to buy the Danish Virgin Islands in 1917 to block any enemy approach to the Panama Canal during World War I. In 1927, the territory's residents were granted U.S. citizenship. The U.S. Navy administered the islands until 1931, when the Department of the Interior assumed jurisdiction. The first 11-member legislature was locally elected in 1954, but it was not until 1970 that a governor was popularly elected. In 1972, the U.S. Virgin Islands received a nonvoting seat in the U.S. Congress. Charles

Turnbull was elected governor in the November 1998 elections. Turnbull wants to reduce the public debt, secure more rights for his territory, and stimulate growth in the private sector. He managed to reduce public spending by 10 percent in 1999 and continues to cut government expenditures.

THE PEOPLE

Population. The estimated population of the U.S. Virgin Islands is 120,917, with more than 60,000 residing on St. Croix, 50,000 on St. Thomas, and 3,000 on St. John. The annual growth rate is 1.07 percent. Charlotte Amalie is the largest city on St. Thomas. Cruz Bay is home to most of St. John's population, and St. Croix's residents are spread across the island. Approximately two-thirds of the population is of African descent, one-fourth is from Puerto Rico, and one-tenth is from the continental United States and Europe.

When new industries were created in the 1960s, a severe labor shortage brought thousands of workers from surrounding islands—nearly tripling the population. In 1985, Congress passed legislation that offered legal status to these individuals. As a result, the Virgin Islands's strong inherent culture is influenced by a number of other Caribbean cultures.

Language. English is the official language, but Virgin Islanders converse with one another in a local dialect (English Creole) that incorporates many languages. For example, *Man, yoh overtake meh* (Friend, you surprised me) has its roots in English, but *What a pistarkel* (What a spectacle) stems from the Dutch Creole *Spektakel* or the Danish *Spetakel* meaning "noise" or "din." St. Thomians, St. Johnians, and Cruzians speak the same dialect but have slightly different accents. A St. Thomian would say *Com hare* (Come here) and a Cruzian would say *Com yah* or *Com heh*.

On St. Croix, 45 percent of the population speaks Spanish. French Creole (*Patois*), Dutch Creole (*Papiamento*), East Indian, and Arabic also are spoken in smaller communities.

Religion. Religion is important to Virgin Islanders. Most people are Christians. Of the 35 different Christian denominations active in the Virgin Islands, the Baptist (42 percent), Catholic (34 percent), and Episcopalian (17 percent) faiths are the largest. One Jewish synagogue serves the small Jewish population. Most people attend church services. To be honest and considered a good Christian is highly regarded. Many native islanders often carry scriptures with them and read them in spare moments or while waiting for buses and taxis. Non-Christian communities (including Rastafarians, Muslims, and Hindus) also have a presence on the islands.

General Attitudes. Virgin Islanders have a tradition of being gracious and somewhat conservative. They enjoy their privacy and strive to be morally respectable. Many social values were adopted from other West Indian islands, but current ones are coming more from the United States. For example, women are now less tolerant of the classic West Indian male-dominant relationship. Also, events that begin on time rather than on "island time" or "Cruzian time" (i.e., late) are viewed as more professional than other events.

Islanders vote regularly and show great interest in current affairs as reported in the local media. Whether heated or light-hearted, daily discussions about politics and the economy are prevalent. It is acknowledged that an educated person will have more opportunity to progress in today's society.

Therefore, children are encouraged to go to school, and parents do their best to provide the means.

Each island prides itself on something different. St. Thomas accommodates tourism, St. Croix highlights private industry, and St. John values its natural beauty. The three sister islands engage in a sense of good-natured competition.

Personal Appearance. Islanders wear conservative clothing that is pressed and clean. Children wear cotton school uniforms with shoes or sneakers. Men wear shirts and long pants with shoes or sandals. Traditional men often wear *guayabera* shirts; these short-sleeved, cotton shirts are square cut, pleated, and lightly embroidered with four pockets on the front. Women dress in stylish skirts, dresses, or pantsuits with sandals or high heels. Hats or umbrellas are donned by those walking or sitting in the sun. The youth prefer U.S.-mainland styles such as jeans, shorts, or T-shirts. Gold jewelry is popular, especially with younger people. Islanders wear formal, even elegant clothing to church services, graduations, funerals, and weddings.

CUSTOMS AND COURTESIES

Greetings. Courtesy is essential to greetings in the Virgin Islands. People say *Good morning*, *Good afternoon*, and *Good night* when greeting a stranger or a group. These formal greetings also precede daily conversations. It is considered rude, for example, to not say *Good morning* before asking a store clerk a question or upon entering a waiting room containing several people. Islanders shake hands, particularly when being formally introduced. Formal titles are used more often in professional situations rather than for social introductions.

Greetings between friends are more casual, with *Hi, Hello, Ya alright?* or *Hey, how's it going?* being typical. Male friends shake hands or may say the other's nickname while tapping fists. Women commonly refer to each other as "dear" or "sweetheart." A casual *pssst* will get another person's attention. The older generation usually addresses strangers or acquaintances as "Miss" or "Mister." Traditionally, but now less often, children have been taught to use "Miss" and "Mister" plus the person's first name.

Gestures. Gestures of courtesy—such as holding a door open for someone or covering one's mouth when yawning or coughing—are important to Virgin Islanders. It is considered improper for a woman to drink directly from a bottle or can; she usually asks for a cup or straw.

Hand gestures and facial expressions are used often during conversation. Men, especially those of Spanish descent, tend to be the most animated in their discussions. To widen the eyes and raise the eyebrows with a slight nod of the head indicates surprise or disbelief. This is often accompanied by *Whaaa?* The act of sucking one's teeth to make a mild noise, called *chuups*, is used to express annoyance (e.g., as when waiting in a long line). Patting the air several times with a flat hand is the symbol for "stop." Islanders use this to hail taxis or to tell traffic behind them to slow down or stop, usually to avoid a collision.

Visiting. People usually visit one another at home on weekends and holidays. The visits typically are prearranged, and guests will *carry* something to give to the host, such as fruit or pastries. When arriving, guests knock on the front door and wait to be invited in. Guests rarely wander through a home unless invited to do so by the hosts. Children formally greet the adults and then go off to play. Guests are offered something cool to drink. If a meal is to be served, the hostess usually serves each seated guest after offering to *fix a plate* for him or her. Departure courtesies are drawn out and it can take up to an hour to actually leave: guests get up to leave, talk with the hosts, walk together over to the door and talk some more, then walk out to the car and chat some more before finally leaving.

Unannounced visits normally involve close neighbors or family and usually have a purpose, such as to borrow something or to discuss a bit of news. Friends commonly drop in just to *check on* each other and see how each is doing. In the summer, friends and families often spend the day picnicking at the beach. Many of the young people socialize in the evenings at clubs or music events. *Hey de mon, leh we go limin* is a typical invitation between male friends to go out on the town.

Eating. A typical workday begins with an early breakfast consisting of foods like eggs, cereal, and toast. Many people drink a cup of hot *bush tea* in the morning. This is an infusion of basil leaves, mint, lemon grass, or a combination. *Bush tea* is also said to have medicinal value when blended in certain ways. Lunch is traditionally the main meal and people try to go home to eat lunch if their work schedules allow. Otherwise, people meet friends for lunch at local restaurants and eat their main meal in the evening. For the rural worker, privately owned food vans or women carrying baskets come around at lunchtime selling meat, fish *pates* (similar to turnovers), or other hot entrées.

Evening meals usually are eaten at home, since this is the time the family can sit at the table and eat together. The atmosphere is casual. It is generally acceptable to eat certain foods with the fingers, although utensils are used for most dishes. Special occasions, holidays, or Sunday afternoons call for roasted goat or pig with all the trimmings. Such meals are served in buffet style, although the hostess may *fix a plate* for special guests.

LIFESTYLE

Family. Families are large and play an important role in the lives of Virgin Islanders. In a two-parent family, the woman is expected to raise the children and handle household responsibilities. The father is expected to support the family, although more women are now earning an income. Grandmothers often take care of their grandchildren while parents are working or living off-island (usually in the United States) for economic reasons. Elderly people often live with a daughter's family rather than in a retirement home.

It is not unusual for a woman to be the head of household. Young single mothers are also not uncommon and they rely on their families for support. Half-siblings live together with their mother. Children tend to maintain friendships and socialize with their cousins and other family members close to their age. It is common for close friends to participate within a family as godparents.

Dating and Marriage. Young people meet and socialize at school, church, beach outings, music events, movies, and holiday affairs. Dating habits are about the same as those in the United States. Weddings are formal and elegant. One tradition unique to the Virgin Islands is the *black cake*. This is prepared by soaking a heavy cake, consisting mostly of raisins and currants, in brandy for several days until it turns dark. The cake is then cut into small pieces, each of which is nicely wrapped and placed in a small box as a gift for each wedding guest.

Diet. The Virgin Islands import a wide variety of food from the mainland United States. However, many locally produced foods and drinks are also available. Traditional dishes include chicken, conch, goat, fish, and pork. These are served with seasoned rice, rice and pigeon peas, sweet potatoes, or plantains. Okra, eggplant, pumpkin, or dumplings are often added to a stew or sauce. Nutmeg, thyme, and cloves are standard seasonings. Johnnycakes (deep-fried, dumpling-like bread) are popular; they are sold regularly on the street or at festivals and are prepared for any gathering or special occasion.

Kallaloo, a special dish of African origin, traditionally is made with pig tail, conch, blue fish, land crab, salt beef, or ox tail. It gets its name from the *kallaloo* bush, which seasons this elaborate stew. Today, some of the ingredients are hard to find, so canned crab may be substituted for land crab and spinach often is used instead of the *kallaloo* greens. It is not uncommon to find a modern version of *kallaloo* on the menu in local restaurants. *Fungi*, cooked cornmeal with okra, is usually served with *kallaloo*. Other favorite foods include red kidney bean soup, curried goat or chicken, and salt fish. Local fruits like mangoes, guavas, papayas, soursops, bananas, and smooth-skinned avocados (called *pears*) are seasonally abundant.

Recreation. Fishing is a passion among Virgin Islanders. USVI waters are considered some of the best for sportfishing (tuna, sailfish, marlin, wahoo), and they host annual fishing tournaments. Most fishermen stay offshore trolling in small motorboats.

Friends and relatives like to gather on the many public beaches to relax and socialize. Large sound systems are set up right on the beach and the music is played quite loudly. Islanders picnic in this festive atmosphere, but they do not usually go swimming. West Indians, including Virgin Islanders, generally do not know how to swim. If they go in the water at all, it is to stand shoulder deep and chat in a group; this is called *coolin' out*. Hanging out with friends is called *limin* or *out on a lime*.

The Arts. Virgin Islanders love music. *Soca*, which has a Latin reggae beat, is a favorite at parties and on festive occasions. Reggae, calypso, and other forms of contemporary music are also popular. Musicians often use unconventional instruments, like washboards, to make their music more lively. Older people still enjoy *quadrille* dancing, which is similar to square dancing, only with an island beat. Artists and musicians draw on plant, animal, and ocean life for inspiration. The North Shore Shell Museum has a large collection of shells and handicrafts.

Holidays. The Virgin Islands celebrate all U.S. federal holidays and a few of their own. These include Transfer Day (31 Mar.), which celebrates the transfer from Danish rule to U.S. rule; Organic Act Day (21 June), the day when the Virgin Islands were granted local rule; Emancipation Day (3 July), honoring freedom from slavery; Hurricane Supplication Day (29 July) at the beginning of the hurricane season; Hurricane Thanksgiving Day (21 Oct.) at the end of the hurricane season; and Boxing Day (26 Dec.), or

▶ **THE AMERICAS**

U.S. Virgin Islands

Christmas Second Day as it is sometimes called. In July, St. Thomians celebrate French heritage week in conjunction with Bastille Day (14 July). Columbus Day (second Mon-day in October) is also called Virgin Island/Puerto Rico Friendship Day.

Carnival holidays are the happiest of times in the Virgin Islands. The days are filled with crowded food fairs and parades that feature costumed dancers, music, and elaborate floats. At night, people enjoy calypso contests and more food and music at the *Carnival* Village. St. Thomas holds its *Carnival* at the end of April; St. John's is on 4 July. Three Kings Day, or the Cruzian Christmas Festival (6 Jan.), marks the climax of St. Croix's *Carnival*.

Commerce. Downtown shops have normal business hours, but these stores attract mostly tourists. Virgin Islanders do most of their shopping at *plazas* (large parking areas that have supermarkets, banks, department stores, post offices, fast-food restaurants, and so on). At Saturday-morning markets, local farmers sell fresh vegetables and fruits. Many well-trafficked corners have roadside stands where vendors sell fresh local fish, fruits, and vegetables, as well as charcoal, sweets, and cold drinks.

SOCIETY

Government. The U.S. Virgin Islands are governed by the Revised Organic Act of 1954. This document allows for executive, legislative, and judiciary branches of government that function similarly to state governments on the U.S. mainland. The government is free to make laws that do not conflict with the U.S. Constitution. Ultimate jurisdiction resides with the U.S. Congress. The governor and lieutenant governor are elected to serve four-year terms and are limited to two terms.

The territory is grouped into two legislative districts: St. Thomas/St. John and St. Croix. Each district elects seven senators and all three islands elect a senator-at-large from St. John. Senators serve two-year terms with no term limit. Islanders also elect a delegate to the U.S. House of Representatives. Although they are U.S. citizens, Virgin Islanders have no vote in national elections, and the delegate to Congress votes in committees only (not on the floor). In the judiciary branch, the Territorial Court tries most local cases and a federal judge handles all matters involving violations of federal law.

Economy. Tourism is the largest sector of the economy and employs more than half of the labor force. Cruise ship arrivals are increasing steadily, offsetting a decline in air arrivals. In 2000, 25 percent more people visited the islands than in 1999. The government employs one-third of the population. Unemployment is a persistent problem, causing many to leave the islands.

Industry is dominated by the Hess Oil Refinery, the largest in the Western Hemisphere, which employs 10 percent of St. Croix's workers. The islands are also an important tax haven for U.S. American and other corporations. In 2000, the Organization for Economic Cooperation and Development cited the islands as one of several Caribbean tax havens with

DEVELOPMENT DATA

Human Dev. Index* rank	NA
Adjusted for women	NA
Real GDP per capita	$12,500
Adult literacy rate	NA
Infant mortality rate	10 per 1,000 births
Life expectancy	74 (male); 82 (female)

little accountability. Hurricane reconstruction has become a significant component of the economy because of major destruction from hurricanes Hugo (1989), Marilyn (1995), Georges (1998), and Lenny (1999). The currency is the U.S. dollar (US$).

Transportation and Communications. The Virgin Islands have more than 530 miles of roads, many of which are paved and in good condition. All vehicles (except public buses) are designed for right-hand driving; however, traffic moves on the left. Under these circumstances, it becomes faster and safer for drivers on the straightaway to yield to side-street traffic.

The public bus system services St. Thomas. Private taxi vans stop and pick up passengers on the side of the road and run unscheduled service between main towns. The seaplane and a handful of commuter airlines offer regular flights between St. Thomas and St. Croix. St. John can only be reached by sea; it is linked to St. Thomas by a comprehensive ferry system.

There are two local newspapers, one of which (*The Virgin Islands Daily News*) won a Pulitzer Prize in 1995 for public service journalism. There are twelve radio stations, two television stations, and two cable companies. The phone company offers good service; a call between islands is considered a local call. USVI is part of the U.S. domestic postal system.

Education. Education is mandatory and free for all children between the ages of 5 and 16. There are 35 public schools (elementary to high school) and many private ones. Public schools require uniforms; private school students wear street clothes. Many St. John students take a daily ferry to attend high school on St. Thomas. The University of the Virgin Islands has campuses on St. Thomas and St. Croix. Many of its 3,200 students come from other Caribbean islands.

Health. Local hospital boards, together with the U.S. Department of Health and Human Services, operate the territory's hospitals. St. Croix's hospital was destroyed by Hurricane Hugo in 1989 but reopened in 1994. St. Johnians needing hospitalization are ferried to the hospital on St. Thomas. All three islands have ample outpatient facilities. The Department of Health administers home care, diagnostic clinics, specialized programs, and free immunizations.

CONTACT INFORMATION

U.S. Virgin Islands Department of Tourism, PO Box 6400, Charlotte Amalie, St. Thomas, USVI 00804; PO Box 200, Cruz Bay, St. John, USVI 00831; or PO Box 4538, Christiansted, St. Croix, USVI 00822; phone (800) 372-8784; Web site www.usvi.org/tourism.

CultureGrams™
People. The World. You.

1305 North Research Way, Bldg. K
Orem, Utah 84097-6200 USA
1.800.528.6279; 801.705.4250
fax 801.705.4350
www.culturegrams.com

Wales
(United Kingdom)

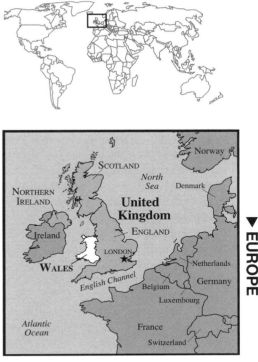

Boundary representations are not necessarily authoritative.

► EUROPE

BACKGROUND

Land and Climate.   Situated in the west of Britain, Wales has an area of 8,019 square miles (20,769 square kilometers), which is slightly larger than New Jersey. Wales is bounded by more than three seas: the Irish Sea to the north; St. George's Channel to the west; the Bristol Channel to the south; and the Celtic (or Cambrian) Sea to the southwest. The land is largely mountainous; the Cambrian Mountains dominate the central upland region. Snowdon, at 3,560 feet (1,085 meters), is the highest point in England and Wales. The coastline is varied with bays, beaches, cliffs, and peninsulas. Wales has many national parks.

The climate is temperate but it is also often unpredictable and wet. Frequent rainfall makes the landscape generally green and picturesque, particularly in the countryside. Still, the soil is relatively poor and less than 5 percent of the land is tilled. Grasslands cover nearly 38 percent of the land, making livestock the largest agricultural sector. Wales is the largest region for rearing sheep in Europe.

History.   The Welsh are descendants of the ancient Britons, who inhabited the British Isles when the Romans first arrived in the first century B.C. After the Romans withdrew in the fifth century A.D., Britain was invaded by Saxons who remained in the southeast. The Saxons gradually absorbed the British population and then extended their dominion over what later became England. The Welsh, under their native princes, preserved their independence in the western part of the island until long after the Norman Conquest of England in 1066, even though William the Conqueror proclaimed himself Lord of Wales in 1071. The Welsh eventually were defeated when Llywelyn ap Gruffydd, known to the Welsh as

the Last Prince, was killed by the English under King Edward I in 1282. In 1301, King Edward named his firstborn son the Prince of Wales, and since then that title has been given to the eldest son of the British monarch (Prince Charles is the current Prince of Wales).

The national hero of the Welsh, Owain Glyndwr, rose against the English in 1400, but without success. Wales was formally incorporated with England by the Act of Union in 1536; this gave the Welsh the same rights as the English, but it outlawed the Welsh language (which survived anyway). The Welsh were early converts to Protestantism, but they broke away from England's established church, leading to the development of separate religious traditions. After the addition of Scotland (1707) and Ireland (1801), the Union was called the United Kingdom of Great Britain and Ireland (UK). Northern Ireland remained after Ireland's independence in 1921.

With the creation of the University of Wales toward the end of the 19th century there was a renaissance in Welsh culture that has continued to the present day. Indeed, since 1950 there has been a growth in Welsh nationalism and in calls for greater Welsh autonomy. Still, when a 1979 referendum gave the Welsh the chance to have limited self-government, the people chose to maintain their existing ties with England. The Labour government held a similar referendum in November 1997. This time, Welsh voters on a very low turnout—equaling roughly one-quarter of the electorate—narrowly approved the creation of a 60-seat Welsh Assembly with limited powers over health, education, and local affairs. Elections in May 1999 saw Labour take 28 seats and opt for minority rule. The primary opposition is the nationalist Plaid

Cymru party, which took 17 seats. The Conservative Party took nine seats and the Liberal Democrats took six. The Assembly formally assumed powers on 1 July 1999.

In February 2001, the highly contagious foot-and-mouth disease broke out among British livestock, prompting bans on British meat imports. Thousands of cattle, pigs, and sheep were slaughtered in an effort to stop the disease. Although not a threat to human health, foot-and-mouth disease may have a substantial economic impact on agriculture and tourism in Wales.

THE PEOPLE

Population. The population of Wales is about 3.5 million. Nearly two-thirds lives in the industrial urban areas of the south—mainly in Cardiff, the capital city, and valleys in its hinterland to the north. The rest of Wales is sparsely populated; people live mostly in small market towns and villages. The majority are ethnic Welsh, but recently many English have settled in Wales, particularly along the northern coast. Many people of Irish descent live in the industrial valleys. Immigrants from former British colonies are found mostly in Cardiff, Newport, and Swansea. Wales has suffered from emigration, many of its people having left in search of work. It is not known exactly how many Welsh live in England.

Language. English is spoken throughout Wales and has official status. About 18.5 percent of the population (around 500,000 people) also speak Welsh (*Cymraeg*), a Celtic language related to Breton but different from Irish and Scottish Gaelic. Welsh uses the same alphabet as English, but its letters are often pronounced differently. For example, *dd* is pronounced like an English *th*, and *f* is pronounced like *v*.

Welsh now has official status throughout Wales and can be seen, for example, on road signs and public buildings. Some Welsh is spoken in all parts of Wales; however, most Welsh speakers live in the northwest and southwest areas. It is taught in schools and also used extensively in cultural affairs. Several organizations encourage its use, and a number of magazines and books are published in Welsh. The Welsh Language Society (*Cymdeithas yr Iaith Gymraeg*) campaigns for official status for the language in such areas as law, education, and local government. The Welsh name for Wales is *Cymru* (the land of compatriots); *Wales* is the English name for "the land of the foreigners."

Religion. Like the rest of the UK, Wales is mostly a secular society. Only 11 percent of the population attends any form of religious worship. Most Welsh people who are members of a religious organization belong to the nonconformist traditions (of Christian Protestant stock). This means they are affiliated through faith or family tradition to the Presbyterian Church of Wales (Calvinistic Methodists), Welsh Baptist Union, Methodist Church (Wesleyans), Union of Welsh Independents (Congregationalists), or the Church in Wales. The Church in Wales is a sister organization to the Church of England; it has its own archbishop. Catholicism (among Irish populations) and other religions also are represented, particularly in larger towns.

General Attitudes. The Welsh regard themselves as a people who are different from the English. However, as descendants of the original Britons who first inhabited the island of Britain, many also think of themselves as British. The Welsh have a reputation for being warmhearted, gregarious, articu-late, and democratic. They also are emotional, inquisitive, quick-tempered, and individualistic. The Welsh generally are more outgoing and open than the English. It is possible to strike up a conversation in the street with a Welsh man or woman and expect a reply.

Local pride is well developed; every Welsh person feels a strong attachment to a particular place. Some differences can be observed between northerners and southerners, but they have much more in common. Traditionally, the Welsh have a keen interest in genealogy. Education is also important; status is usually gauged by one's level of education. Standards of living differ between those of working- and middle-class backgrounds. Famous Welsh people include David Lloyd George (former prime minister of Great Britain), Dylan Thomas (poet), Richard Burton and Anthony Hopkins (actors), and Tom Jones (singer).

Personal Appearance. Fashions do not vary from those in the rest of Britain, although some clothes are made from Welsh materials. The national costume is seen only on ceremonial occasions. On Sundays, people tend to dress in their best clothes—suits for men and more expensive dresses for women. It often is possible to distinguish, say, a farmer from an office worker by their style of clothes. High fashion is seen only in the larger towns.

CUSTOMS AND COURTESIES

Greetings. The Welsh are known for their friendliness and hospitality. If practical, it is polite to introduce each person in the company (including children and youth). People may shake hands when first being introduced but usually do not thereafter unless they have not seen each other for a while. A firm handshake is preferred. Women who are close friends may embrace, kissing each other once lightly on the cheek; men may also greet women this way. Women remain seated when being introduced and shaking hands, while men stand up.

When meeting for the first time, people may say *How d'you do?* or *Pleased to meet you* or even *How are you?*, but not *Hi!* Good friends greet each other with *Hello* and *Hi*. In informal social gatherings, the Welsh use first names. In business or on public occasions, titles and surnames normally are used. Gentlemen may stand when a woman or unknown man enters the room and sit down only after the other person is seated.

Gestures. The Welsh often use their hands to express themselves when speaking. Maintaining eye contact is important. During conversations it is acceptable to cross the arms, but it is rude to whisper or chew gum. Keeping one's hands in one's pockets while conversing is impolite; people also are careful not to rattle loose change in their pockets. Legs may be crossed at the knees, but it is not acceptable to place the ankle of one leg on the knee of the other. Holding the door for the next person or not passing between people who are conversing is appreciated. A gentleman may give up his seat on a train or a bus to a woman.

Visiting. The Welsh enjoy good company. They like visiting friends and neighbors in their homes for a chat and a cup of tea or coffee. Although it is wise to call ahead to make sure the person is at home, it is appropriate for friends to drop by during daylight hours. It is best to call the elderly before visiting, particularly at night. Hosts usually offer their guests a drink (coffee or tea), perhaps with *cakes* or *biscuits* (cookies).

Friends who have traveled a long distance are offered a meal; otherwise, lunch or dinner is usually by invitation. At more formal meals, old friends often bring a bottle of wine and sometimes a delicacy. Strangers are not expected to bring a gift, although the hostess will appreciate flowers. It is considered impolite to arrive late for a meal. Wine may be served with the meal unless the hosts do not drink.

After the meal, guests are invited to sit in a comfortable place, perhaps to have a cup of coffee or a brandy. It is polite to offer to help with clearing the table or washing the dishes; declined offers are accepted gracefully. Lunch guests usually stay for the afternoon. Dinner guests often stay until about 11 p.m., except on weekends when they may stay later. Guests usually take their cue on when to leave from the host but otherwise stay as long as they feel comfortable. It is considered good manners to call the hosts within a day or two after the meal to thank them for their hospitality, or more formally, to write a note, especially after visits of a few days.

Eating. Most people eat only two meals a day, breakfast and an evening meal. Midday or late night snacks are common. Typical breakfasts include toast, marmalade, cereal, bacon and eggs, sausages, and coffee, eaten between 7 and 9 a.m. Lighter breakfasts (cereal, toast, and tea or coffee) are also common. Dinner (meat, vegetables, and sometimes dessert) is usually at 6 or 8 p.m. The terms *lunch* and *dinner* are interchangeable; *tea* is also sometimes used to mean a cooked evening meal. Guests sometimes are invited for coffee at about 11 a.m. Family members usually eat when it is convenient for them. However, when guests are present families will make the effort to sit down and eat together. Lunch on Sunday tends to be an important meal.

On special occasions the meal is served from serving dishes on the table. For common family meals, the food is dished up in the kitchen and the guest is served first. It is polite to wait for all members to have their food before starting to eat. The Welsh follow the European style of eating, with the knife in the right hand and the fork remaining in the left. The knife is not ever used to put food in the mouth. It is acceptable to use the fingers to pick up pizza or bones. The napkin is placed on the lap; elbows are not placed on the table. Guests are expected to talk at the table and to share the conversation with the persons sitting next to them. The hostess likes to be complimented on the meal, and second helpings show an appreciation for the food.

With more family *pubs* catering for children, it is becoming more common for families to eat out. At the end of the meal, the server gives the bill to the person who requests it. A service charge is often added to the bill, so tipping is only given for exceptional service. If a charge has not been added, a 10 percent tip is acceptable.

LIFESTYLE

Family. The Welsh usually live in houses rather than *flats* (apartments), which are more common in the cities. Houses may be detached, semidetached, or in terraces (row houses). Terrace houses are most prevalent because they are the least expensive. Seventy-one percent of homes are owner-occupied. Families usually are close-knit. The nominal head of the household is the father, but the mother plays an equally important role in all family affairs. Many women work outside the home when their children are older. Elderly grandparents sometimes live with the family. Unmarried children live at home or move into their own apartment. Single-parent families are becoming more common. The average family has two or three children.

The main family celebrations occur at Christmas and Easter or for birthdays and weddings. There are special celebrations for a person's 18th birthday, when he or she comes of age, is eligible to vote, and gains other legal rights.

Dating and Marriage. Young people socialize through school activities. They also meet at discos or the local *public houses* when they are old enough to go to them. Dating usually begins by the age of 15 or 16. Going to clubs, movies, and parties are also popular activities. Young people also spend a lot of time in each other's homes. Marriage is legal at 16, but most marry in their mid-twenties. Civil weddings are as common as weddings in churches or chapels. It is possible to get married in hotels, palaces, and other special interest sites that are licensed for this purpose. About half of young couples live together before or instead of marrying. Although many couples remain married for life, the divorce rate is high.

Diet. The Welsh enjoy a variety of foods common throughout Europe, from fish-and-chips to Chinese and Indian cooking to the cuisine of France and Italy. Traditional Welsh dishes include *cawl* (a soup), *bara brith* (currant cake), and *Welshcakes*. Other common foods are *bara lawr*, or *laver bread* (a mixture of seaweed and oatmeal that is fried and then served with bacon), and *Glamorgan sausages* (a meatless dish made with cheese, bread crumbs, herbs, and leeks). Meat and potatoes are considered staple foods. Beer, wine, and other alcoholic drinks are sold in *pubs*. Snacks, tea, coffee, and sandwiches are available in cafés. People drink wine on special occasions or when entertaining guests. A dessert, often referred to as a *sweet* or *pudding*, may be served after the main meal.

Recreation. The national sport of Wales is rugby (or rugby football). Wales hosted the Rugby World Cup in Cardiff in 1999. People also enjoy *football* (soccer), England's most popular sport; however, professional rugby teams far outnumber professional soccer teams. Cricket, tennis, and other sports are also popular. Most people enjoy watching television or listening to the radio. Most large towns have movie theaters and arts centers. *Pubs* are popular places for socializing. The Welsh people are more conservative in their holiday destinations. On the whole, they are less widely traveled than the Irish, Scots, and English.

The Arts. Choral and folk music are popular in Wales. The Welsh enjoy singing in public places (sporting events, *pubs*, etc.). The Welsh National Opera Company and the Welsh Theater Company have an excellent reputation in Britain. People continue to play the harp, Wales's national instrument. Much literature is written in the Welsh language. Some successful writers, such as poet Dylan Thomas, have written in English. Government funding helps sustain literary efforts in both Welsh and English.

The National *Eisteddfod* is held every year during the first week of August, alternately in the north and south of Wales. It features competitions in music, drama, literature, and art. The festival is conducted in Welsh. There also is an annual weeklong *Eisteddfod* for youth.

Lovespoons, intricately carved wooden spoons that people traditionally gave to their loved ones, still are made today.

▼ **EUROPE**

Wales

Holidays. England and Wales share the same national holidays, including New Year's Day, Good Friday (before Easter Sunday), May Day (1 May), the spring and summer bank holidays, Christmas, and Boxing Day (26 Dec.). Boxing Day comes from the tradition of giving small boxed gifts to service people. It is now a day for relaxing and visiting friends. The Patron Saints Day (1 Mar.), also known as St. David's Day (in honor of Wales's patron saint), is not an official holiday but is celebrated in schools with music festivals. Also on St. David's Day, people wear a leek or daffodil (national emblems) on their clothing.

Commerce. Factory hours are from 8 a.m. to 4:30 p.m. and office hours are from 9 a.m. to 5 p.m. Banks are open between 9:30 a.m. and 4:30 p.m., Monday to Friday; some banks and businesses are open Saturday morning. Offices and smaller shops close for an hour at lunchtime. Although some shops close for a half day during the week, shopping hours generally are more flexible. Supermarkets are open from 8:30 a.m. to 8:30 p.m. Supermarkets and large stores now are permitted to be open on Sunday until 5 p.m. Small towns have market days for vendors to sell items from outdoor *stalls* (booths).

SOCIETY

Government. The Principality of Wales has 22 counties, each governed by a local council. The Labour Party, the largest party in Wales, usually dominates in urban areas and ex–coal mining areas. The nationalist party, *Plaid Cymru*, is popular in the northwest. The Conservatives and Liberal Democrats also field candidates in parliamentary elections. A 60-member Welsh Assembly (*Senedd*) was elected for the first time in May 1999. Welsh Labour leader Alun Michael is the new Welsh Secretary.

Britain has a constitutional monarchy, with Queen Elizabeth II as head of state. The Parliament consists of two houses. The 1,200-member House of Lords (with noblemen, life appointees, and Church of England bishops) has no legislative power. Laws are passed by the 659-seat House of Commons whose members are elected by the people. There are 40 members of Parliament sitting for Welsh constituencies in the House of Commons. The leader of the majority party (currently the Labour Party) is appointed by the queen as prime minister (currently Tony Blair). Elections are held at least every five years but can be called sooner.

Economy. Steel and coal, the traditional heavy industries of Wales, largely have been replaced by light industries, agriculture, business, and service industries. Still, 30 percent is employed by industry. Many computer-based industries are located in the southern coastal strip. Banks and insurance companies moving into the south are improving the southern economy. The manufacturing sector is highly productive but wages are still low. Wales has attracted a significant amount of foreign investment (three times the UK average per capita); many manufacturing plants are foreign-owned. Farming (primarily livestock) and tourism are the main occupations in rural areas.

Unemployment in Wales is usually higher than it is in England. Income is slightly lower. Most people have access to a decent income, although there is a larger gap between the wealthy and the poor than there is in other European countries. Likewise, the middle class is not as prosperous as its counterparts in other European nations. The currency is the pound sterling (£).

DEVELOPMENT DATA

Human Dev. Index* rank	10 of 174 countries
Adjusted for women	10 of 143 countries
Real GDP per capita	$20,336
Adult literacy rate	99 percent
Infant mortality rate	6 per 1,000 births
Life expectancy	75 (male); 80 (female)

Transportation and Communications. Although most parts of Wales are accessible by road, travel can be difficult in mountainous terrain. Private cars are the main form of transport; most homes have at least one car. Public transportation between small towns is improving. Train services in many areas of Wales are among the best in Britain. Ferries regularly cross from Wales to Ireland. Cardiff is two hours away by rail from London and has its own international airport. Most homes have telephones. Television and radio are provided by the British Broadcasting Corporation (BBC) and several independent companies. Channel S4C operates in Welsh. Postal service is reliable; collections are made from red *letterboxes*.

Education. Schooling is free and compulsory between ages four and sixteen. The school system is divided into infant/junior schools and secondary/comprehensive schools. Although the education system is connected to that of England, many schools teach in Welsh. At age 16, students take the General Certificate of Secondary Education exam. Some may attend school for two more years before taking the advanced level exams required to enter universities. The University of Wales has campuses in five cities. The University of the Air, called the Open University, offers degree courses throughout Britain. The Polytechnic of Wales recently became the University of Glamorgan. Many Welsh students attend universities in England.

Health. Britain's National Health Service, based on taxation, provides free universal health coverage. There is a small charge for prescriptions, eye tests, and dental treatment. Health standards are comparable to those in England, although Wales has had more industry-related illnesses. There are also concerns that the health-care system in Wales is underfunded and that the quality of care in rural areas is sometimes lower.

CONTACT INFORMATION

The British Embassy, 3100 Massachusetts Avenue NW, Washington, DC 20008; phone (202) 462-1340; Web site www.britainusa.com/consular/embassy/embassy.asp. British Tourist Authority, 551 Fifth Avenue, Suite 701, New York, NY 10176; phone (800) 462-2748; Web site www.travelbritain.org. British Information Services, 845 Third Avenue, New York, NY 10022-6691; phone (212) 745-0277. Wales Tourist Board, Brunel House, 2 Fitzalan Road, Cardiff CF24 0UY, Wales, UK; phone 44 29 2049 9909; Web site www.tourism.wales.gov.uk.

1305 North Research Way, Bldg. K
Orem, Utah 84097-6200 USA
1.800.528.6279; 801.705.4250
fax 801.705.4350
www.culturegrams.com

◄ **EUROPE** ►

Boundary representations are not necessarily authoritative.

BACKGROUND

Land and Climate. Yugoslavia covers 39,518 square miles (102,350 square kilometers)—about the same area as Kentucky. Serbia accounts for 34,136 square miles; Montenegro, 5,382. Several major rivers flow through this region, including the Danube, Sava, Tisa, Morava, and Drina. Vojvodina (in the north) is part of the Danubian plain and contains fertile agricultural land. The North Albanian Alps (*Prokletije*) and Šar Mountains are in the southwest, and the Balkan Mountains are in the east. *Montenegro* (literally "black mountain") is mostly mountainous and consists of the Zeta Valley, Dinaric Alps, and Skadarsko Lake (shared with Albania). Montenegro also has a coastline on the Adriatic Sea that includes the picturesque Bay of Kotor and Saint Stefan Island.

The climate is central continental; Montenegro experiences more severe weather and colder temperatures than Serbia. Serbian winters are cold, averaging 32°F (0°C) in January; summers are warm, averaging 75°F (23°C) in July. Central Serbia is susceptible to strong winds (*košava*) that pick up speed on the plain of Vojvodina. Belgrade is the federal capital as well as Serbia's capital. Podgorica (Titograd until 1992) is Montenegro's capital.

History. Slavic peoples settled on the Balkan Peninsula in the seventh century and for several generations were organized by clans rather than in a united state. In the 11th century, Serbs united and consolidated territory that eventually became the empire of Tzar Dušan. Montenegro was incorporated in the 12th century. In 1346, Tzar Dušan's rule included Albania, Epirus, and northern Greece. Serbian power began to decline with the Battle of Kosovo (1389), when Serbs were defeated by the Turks. For the next five hundred years, Serbians were ruled by the Turkish Ottoman Empire and still consider the era one of bondage. Montenegro remained independent.

Serbia rebelled under the leadership of Karageorge (1804) and Obrenovic (1815), both of whom formed ruling dynasties. Serbia achieved full independence in 1878. Other Balkan Slavs had been subjugated to both the Turkish and Austro-Hungarian Empires, and Serbia determined to rid the Balkans of these forces. In the first Balkan War (1912), it defeated Turkey with the help of neighboring nations. The second Balkan War (1913) brought victory over a former ally Bulgaria. In 1914, a Bosnian Serb assassinated Austrian Archduke Franz Ferdinand in the effort to liberate Serbs in Bosnia. Austria declared war, regional alliances formed, and the conflict quickly became World War I. The Austro-Hungarian Empire lost the war and was broken into several new states. At that time, Serbia led the move to unite Slavs under one government, becoming the principal power in the Kingdom of Serbs, Croats, and Slovenes in 1918. The name was changed to the Kingdom of Yugoslavia in 1929.

When Germany invaded Yugoslavia in 1941, Croatian leaders sided with the Fascists against Serbia. At the same time, a bloody civil war was being waged in Yugoslavia between communists and monarchists. Fighting on both fronts, many Serbs lost their lives in battle and at the hands of fellow Slavs. Thousands of civilian Jews, Gypsies, and Serbs were killed in Croatian concentration camps, a fact not easily forgotten by Serbs who later (1990) came under Croatian domination.

The civil war ended when World War II did, and the communist partisan fighters emerged victorious. They formed, under the leadership of Josip Broz Tito, a federal socialist state. Its politics were more liberal and economics more progressive than other socialist countries.

Tito died in 1980 and the federation weakened. Ethnic tensions and a deepening economic crisis led Croatia and Slovenia to demand secession in 1990. Slovenia's independence proceeded smoothly, but Croatia's was resisted by resident Serbs who wanted to remain united with Serbia. A war ensued (1991) in which the Yugoslav army helped Croatia's Serbs gain control of Croatia's Krajina region (which Croatia regained in 1995). Serbia also supported Serbs in Bosnia-Herzegovina in their war against Muslims and Croats but eventually urged Bosnian Serbs to cooperate with international peace efforts. The 1995 Dayton Peace Accord formally ended the war.

Before 1990, Serbia was a republic that incorporated two autonomous provinces, Kosovo and Vojvodina. Since the breakup of the former Yugoslavia, those regions have been reincorporated into Serbia (as they were before 1974). In 1992, Serbia and Montenegro declared themselves the Federal Republic of Yugoslavia.

After completing his second and final term as president of Serbia, Slobodan Milosevic won parliamentary support from Serbia and Montenegro to serve as the president of the Federal Republic of Yugoslavia. Massive protests erupted against Milosevic in November 1996 after his party, the Socialist Party of Serbia (SPS), failed to recognize local election results. The SPS reinstated election results three months later, but divisions between opposition groups stalled further change.

Tensions between ethnic Albanians and Serbs in the province of Kosovo erupted into fighting. By September 1998, Serbs had forced several hundred thousand Albanians to flee the area, which, though 90 percent Albanian, Serbs regard as the cradle of their culture. Negotiations and international sanctions failed to deter Yugoslav forces. In March 1999, the North Atlantic Treaty Organization (NATO) began intensive air strikes on targets throughout Yugoslavia, especially Belgrade and Kosovo. Meanwhile, Serb forces systematically destroyed Albanian property and also used torture, rape, and mass executions to "cleanse" the province of Albanians. Nearly a million refugees fled to Albania, Macedonia, and other states for safety, straining those states and the international community's ability to cope with the numbers. After 78 days of air strikes, Milosevic agreed to withdraw his forces. An estimated ten thousand Kosovar Albanians were killed in the Serbian campaign; more than three thousand Albanians, Serbs, and Roma are missing. The conflict also caused billions of dollars in war damages and devastated the economy. A large multinational peacekeeping force was deployed to protect civilians and establish order as the refugees are repatriated. Serbian and Gypsy residents of Kosovo are now targets of retaliation.

Following defeat in September 2000 elections and mass demonstrations, Milosevic was ousted and Vojislav Koštunica became president. Milosevic has since been arrested and faces charges of misappropriation of funds and abuse of power. Many in the international community also are pressing to have Milosevic tried for war crimes. International sanctions against Yugoslavia have been lifted.

Pro-independence forces narrowly won parliamentary elections in Montenegro in 2001. It is unclear when or if a referendum on independence from the Yugoslav federation will take place, but there are fears that independence in Montenegro could further destabilize the region by encouraging other ethnic separatists in the Balkans.

THE PEOPLE

Population. Serbia's population of 10.6 million people is growing at 0.74 percent. Montenegro's population of 680,000 is shrinking at about 12 percent annually. Most Serbians are urban dwellers, while Montenegrins tend to be more rural. Similarities between the two groups are great and differences are found mostly in historical experience. Prior to the end of World War II, Montenegrins were counted as Serbs in the census.

Most people in Serbia are ethnic Serbs (66 percent). Ethnic Albanians (17 percent) dominate Kosovo but only settled the region in large numbers in the past 50 years. Hungarians (4 percent) are concentrated in Vojvodina. Serbia is also home to smaller numbers of Romanians, Croats, Ruthenians, Turks, and Slovaks. In Montenegro, most people (62 percent) are ethnic Montenegrin, but there are also Slavic Muslims (12.5 percent), Serbs (9.2 percent), Albanians (6.2 percent), and Croats (1 percent).

Language. The principal language is Serbian, a Slavic tongue virtually identical to Croatian. In fact, before 1990, the language of Yugoslavia was Serbo-Croatian. Serbian can be written in both Cyrillic and Latin scripts. Cyrillic is the official script, but schoolchildren are required to learn both. In 1974, Albanians and Hungarians won the right to use their language in local government, media, and education.

Religion. Serbs and Montenegrins are Serbian Orthodox Christians. The Serbian Orthodox Church was formed in 1221 by St. Sava and is similar to the Greek and Russian Orthodox Churches in practice and doctrine. It has strong ties to these churches but distinguishes itself from them in some respects. For example, it teaches that each family is protected by a specific patron saint. On each saint's day, relevant families prepare large amounts of food for anyone who enters their homes. Hosts serve these guests a spoonful of *zito*, a mush made of wheat, sugar, and nuts.

The Serbian church follows the Julian calendar, which is 13 days behind the Gregorian calendar. Patriarch Pavle is the current head of the church.

Religion was neglected during the communist period, but activity has surged since 1990, as evidenced by growing numbers of baptisms and religious wedding ceremonies. Religious freedom allows for the current proliferation of Muslim mosques and Catholic churches. Other Christian denominations are small, as is the Jewish community.

General Attitudes. Serbs consider themselves principally to be a heroic and proud people. Likewise, Montenegrins value their heroic traits above all else. Based on a history of resisting Turks, Austrians, and Germans, Serbs view themselves as liberators. Both Serbs and Montenegrins are warrior peoples who honor the memory of military conquests. The Battle of Kosovo has been ingrained in the national consciousness as the time when the Christian Serbs tragically but heroically chose death at the hands of Muslim Turks rather than surrender.

Serbs are openly emotional and are not a very private people. They share their lives with extended family, neighbors,

bors, and friends. They tend to be pessimistic and sometimes fatalistic about events that surround them. They value family, country, and honesty. Serbs also have a sense of humor that allows them to laugh at their own faults.

Montenegrins, while sharing many Serbian traits, tend to be more traditional and patriarchal. Men still dominate society and women are considered subordinates.

Personal Appearance. People are concerned with their public appearance and take care to look well dressed and groomed. Most wear Western clothing styles, except in a few rural areas where older people wear *nošnje*. This traditional attire varies by region but tends to include long skirts and cotton shirts for women; men wear wide pants, vests over shirts, and *opanke* (leather shoes with upturned toes). Older urban men wear hats. Women often dye their hair (gray hair is seldom seen); red and auburn shades are popular among younger women. Western-style running shoes and jeans are popular throughout the country.

CUSTOMS AND COURTESIES

Greetings. When people are introduced, they shake hands and say their last name, followed by *Drago mi je* (I am pleased). If people already know each other, they shake hands or kiss (often three times on alternating cheeks) and say *Zdravo* (Hello) or *Dobar dan* (Good day). In greeting an older person, a younger one must rise. Men always rise when greeting women.

Adults are addressed by professional (i.e., Dr., Professor) or conventional titles and their last names. *Gospodin* (Mr.), *Gospodja* (Mrs.), and *Komšija* (neighbor) have reemerged to replace "comrade" as conventional titles. *Tetka* (auntie) and *Čika* (uncle) are reserved for older people who are not family but for whom "Mr." and "Mrs." are too formal. People never refer to others, except close friends and family, by their first names. Likewise, they use *vi* ("you" formal) to address others, especially initially. Moving from *vi* to *ti* ("you" informal) must be initiated by the older person, or if two people are the same age, by the female, but this practice is changing with the younger generation.

Gestures. Serbs do not use hand gestures much when speaking. It is impolite to stretch, yawn, or crack one's knuckles in public. It is also impolite to point with the index finger. Smoking in public used to be considered rude, but it is increasingly common in both urban and rural areas. Eye contact is valued and is expected when people are raising glasses in a toast prior to drinking.

Visiting. People spend a lot of time visiting and entertaining. Sitting for hours over cigarettes and a cup of coffee or some *rakija* (alcoholic drink usually made from plums) is common. The length of visits reflects a leisurely pace of life. Most visiting is on an informal, unannounced basis; people simply drop in. Sometimes people prearrange socializing but usually not far in advance. Guests often bring gifts such as flowers, coffee, wine, or a box of chocolates; if one is visiting for the first time, a gift is nearly obligatory. Flowers are given in odd numbers, as even numbers are reserved for funerals. Guests bring relatively expensive gifts when visiting on special occasions, particularly for weddings.

Eating. Since the workday usually begins at 6 or 7 a.m., people wait until 10 a.m. for their breakfast (*doručak*), which can be a substantial meal. The main meal of the day is *ručak*, eaten after work around 4 p.m. This is a heavy meal that includes soup and a meat dish. Dinner is a light snack.

Guests invited to dinner are served *meze* (an antipasto of cheese, sausages, etc.) before the meal. When entertaining, hosts offer more food than can be eaten; this is a sign of hospitality and wealth. Indeed, hosts consistently urge guests to eat more during the meal and guests customarily decline several times before accepting. The host or hostess often places more food on the guests' plates despite protests. As times change, people are declining only once or twice before accepting; further protests are taken seriously by a growing number of hosts. Guests are expected to finish all food on their plates. Meals are times for family conversation and social interaction.

LIFESTYLE

Family. The family is highly valued; nearly everyone expects to marry and have children. Divorce and remarriage are common. Rural families tend to have more children than urban ones. The father is the head and backbone of the family; in rural areas, male children are valued more highly than females. Rural households include three generations. Upon marriage, a couple moves in with the groom's parents. Due to a housing shortage, urban couples might also live with parents for a while, but this is seen more as an economic necessity than a desirable tradition. Throughout the country, both husband and wife usually work outside the home. Children are cared for primarily by grandparents or other relatives, and less commonly in child-care facilities.

Dating and Marriage. When dating, young people tend to go out with one steady partner. They go for walks, to cafés and parties, and to each other's homes. Civil wedding ceremonies are most common, but religious ones are on the rise. Rural weddings are more elaborate than urban ones; they include several days of drinking, dancing, and eating that often force the family into debt. The groom's family usually pays most wedding expenses, except in less traditional urban areas where costs are split more evenly. Rural brides often have a dowry (home furnishings or cash), and they usually are given a piece of jewelry by the groom's family. Among Albanians, the groom's family pays a bride-price to the woman's family and the bride has no dowry.

Diet. The cuisine is influenced by Turkish, Austrian, Hungarian, and Greek cultures. The most common foods include *pasulj* (beans), *sarma* (cabbage leaves stuffed with minced meat and rice), *roštilj* (grilled meats), *ćevapčići* (small, elongated minced meatballs eaten with chopped onions), and *punjene paprike* (stuffed peppers). Roasted pork or lamb, served with potatoes, is favored on special occasions. Montenegrins are known for their smoked meats. Coastal Montenegrins eat more seafood.

Typical cheeses include *kajmak* (consisting of the accumulated skim of boiled milk) and *sjenički sir* (a soft and fatty cheese often crumbled on *sopska*, a Greek-like salad). Locally grown produce includes cabbage, lettuce, tomatoes, potatoes, carrots, apples, pears, watermelons, strawberries, plums, and raspberries. Bread (usually white) is eaten with each meal, and wine is served at the main meal. People also drink coffee and juices; they drink tea more during illness.

Recreation. Visiting and talking are favorite leisure activities, but people also enjoy watching television. In small towns, residents walk the main streets in the evening. Soccer is the most popular sport, followed by basketball, volleyball, swimming, and skiing. Sports are stressed in school, so

▼ EUROPE

young people tend to be more enthusiastic about them. Some people enjoy boating on lakes and rivers.

The Arts.   Music is popular throughout the country, but folk music (*narodna muzika*) is especially favored in rural areas. People perform folk dances such as the *kolo*, consisting of small movements by dancers sometimes linked in a long line or circle. The *gusle*, a small traditional stringed instrument, is played in rural areas. Traditional music, dance, and costume vary from one region to another. *Turbofolk*, dance music popular with young people, is a mixture of folk tunes and rock instruments and is prevalent in larger cities.

Most theaters are state run and have permanent acting troupes. Yugoslavians enjoy native and foreign movies, and Belgrade's annual film festival shows works from all over Europe. Visual arts are strongly supported through museums and galleries, especially in Belgrade. Government aid to preserve the country's cultural heritage has been more forthcoming in recent years.

Holidays.   Yugoslavians celebrate Orthodox Christmas (7 Jan.) and New Year's Day (14 Jan.). The International New Year (1 Jan.) is celebrated also. Women's Day (8 Mar.) honors women in the home and at work. Easter is in the spring. Workers' Day (1 May) is a major holiday for all. *Vidovdan* (28 June) commemorates the Battle of Kosovo. Four times throughout the year, Orthodox Serbs mark *Zadushnice* (a day to honor the dead). One such day is in early November soon after Catholics and Protestants have their day (1 Nov.) to visit the graves of family and friends.

Commerce.   Public offices are open from 7 a.m. to 3 p.m. Private businesses and kiosks tend to have longer, more flexible hours. Food shops and large department stores remain open until 8 p.m. Some urban *dragstors* (drugstores) that sell basic foods are open 24 hours. Outdoor food markets open around 6 a.m. and close in the afternoon so the vendors can return to their villages.

SOCIETY

Government.   The federal president is elected by the people for a four-year term. Zoran Zizic is the prime minister. The Federal Assembly consists of a Chamber of Republics and a Chamber of Citizens. The former has 40 seats split equally between Serbs and Montenegrins. The Chamber of Citizens has 138 members. Both Serbia and Montenegro have presidents. Milan Milutinovic is the president of Serbia. The president of Montenegro is Milo Djukanovic. The voting age is 18.

Economy.   The economy is in shambles; few accurate statistics are available. Long-lasting problems stem from 1990 when the government first began dismantling its market socialism system. Significant funds were spent in supplying ethnic Serbs in warring areas and in housing refugees from Bosnia and Croatia. International sanctions blocked external trade and froze foreign assets until 1996, suffocating the economy and precipitating hyperinflation.

Although UN sanctions were lifted in 1996, the economy did not grow as hoped. The average per capita income has been estimated at roughly $1,500, but most people earn closer to $150. One-third of the population lives in poverty.

DEVELOPMENT DATA

Human Dev. Index* rank	NA
Adjusted for women	NA
Real GDP per capita	NA
Adult literacy rate	NA
Infant mortality rate	20 per 1,000 births (Serbia)
Infant mortality rate	11 per 1,000 births (Montenegro)
Life expectancy	69 (male); 76 (female) (S)
Life expectancy	71 (male); 80 (female) (M)

Unemployment is about 50 percent. Inflation was brought under control in 1994 with the introduction of the new *dinar* (YD) currency but remains high. International sanctions banning foreign investment and freezing state assets abroad were imposed again in 1998 due to escalating violence in Kosovo. Slow reform, lack of privatization, an expanding trade gap, and a "brain drain" of skilled labor—as well as extensive damages to infrastructure from air strikes—are hindering progress. Also, some international reconstruction aid for Kosovo has not been delivered as promised.

Serbia produces fruit, vegetables, wheat, corn, oats, and livestock. Natural resources include lead, zinc, copper, and lignite. Manufacturing plants are located in Serbia, while Montenegro has aluminum and steel factories. Montenegro also has tourism, shipping, and agricultural potential.

Transportation and Communications.   A well-developed public transportation system serves most of the population. Air travel connects major cities, as do rail and bus service. Rural areas are reached by bus and private vehicle. Most roads are paved. Most newspapers and magazines receive some government support and are under pressure to accept certain controls. The state controls television and radio stations but some private stations also broadcast. Some urban residents have access to satellite television.

Education.   Free schooling begins at age seven with eight mandatory years at the basic (*osnovna*) level. Optional middle school (*srednja* or *škola*) includes grades nine through twelve. Graduates can then go to a two-year technical college, called *viša škola* (higher school), or to a university. Entrance to the four state universities is determined by examination. Ethnic minorities have the right to education in their language: Albanians, Hungarians, Ruthenians, Slovaks, Romanians, and Turks have schools through high school. The one Albanian-language university has been closed due to secessionist activity.

Health.   There is an extensive national health system. Private practice was legalized in 1990, but most people cannot afford it. Public hospitals suffer supply and equipment shortages, and health standards are deteriorating. Food shortages prior to 1996 caused some nutritional deficiencies in children.

CONTACT INFORMATION

Permanent Mission of the Federal Republic of Yugoslavia to the United Nations, 854 Fifth Avenue, New York, NY 10021; phone (212) 879-8700.

1305 North Research Way, Bldg. K
Orem, Utah 84097-6200 USA
1.800.528.6279; 801.705.4250
fax 801.705.4350
www.culturegrams.com

The following is a list of some common concepts found in CultureGrams. These are not necessarily definitions; they are explanations of how the terms are used in the series, what significance they hold in regard to understanding cultures, and often how they are calculated. For explanations of international organizations (United Nations, European Union, and others), please refer to reference sources in a library.

Cash Crops. A cash crop is an agricultural product that is grown for sale, not for the farmer's consumption. It is often a crop (coffee, cotton, sugarcane, rice and other grains) that requires manufacturing or processing. It also may be a crop (oranges, potatoes, bananas) that can be consumed upon harvest but is cultivated primarily to be sold. Cash crops are produced most effectively on a large scale, but they can be grown on small plots of land. When grown on a large scale, the crops are more likely to be exported than consumed locally, although small growers in developing countries may sell to a local buyer who then sells larger quantities domestically and abroad. The economies of many countries depend heavily on the sale of cash crops.

Diversified Economy. An economy is considered diversified if its stability relies on a variety of industries rather than one or two commodities. For example, oil-rich countries that rely almost solely on the petroleum industry for their income are vulnerable to changes in the price of oil on the world market. When the price drops significantly, the countries are suddenly unable to pay debts or finance social development projects. The same is true for countries that rely on agricultural products such as coffee or on minerals such as copper for their income. Countries whose economies are based not only on agriculture but also manufacturing, services, and technology are better able to withstand global price changes. Thus, the more diversified a country's economic base, the better.

Expatriate and Repatriate. A person is an expatriate if he or she is working, studying, or living in a foreign country. For example, an oil company executive from the United States working in Saudi Arabia is an expatriate resident of Saudi Arabia. A Chinese student attending an Australian university is likewise an expatriate resident of Australia. Tourists are not expatriates. Expatriates are not permanent residents, but they usually are long-term residents. They have no citizenship rights in their host countries, and it is assumed they eventually will return to their home countries. *Expatriate* also can be a verb referring to the process of forcing citizens or permanent residents, such as refugees, to leave their own country. *Repatriate* refers to the process of returning people (usually refugees or other immigrants) to their home countries.

Extended Family. As used in CultureGrams, this term refers to a family unit that includes parents, their children, and one or more relatives. The relatives most often include grandparents and sometimes cousins, aunts, and uncles. Some extended family units are organized with older parents, their married sons (and occasionally daughters) and their families, and all unmarried sons and daughters. Extended families may share a single household or live in a compound that includes living structures for each nuclear unit, in which case families share work and other responsibilities. When a CultureGram states that the extended family is the basic unit of society, it means households generally are composed of the extended family or the extended family network, both of which are essential to personal and social security.

Foreign Language Phrases. Most CultureGrams contain phrases and words in the target culture's official or common language. In general, CultureGrams do not provide a pronunciation guide for these phrases, due to limited space. Also, including pronunciation and a translation tends to interrupt the flow of the text. CultureGrams are not designed to teach foreign languages. Rather, the phrases contained in CultureGrams are there to facilitate the description of how people interact with one another. Their translation often provides insights about the culture, but pronunciation is not necessary to gain that insight. In the few cases where pronunciation hints are provided, they are necessary for English speakers to pronounce a word properly. For instance, the country Lesotho is not pronounced as it would seem. Instead of saying "le-SO-tho," one should say "le-SUE-too."

Free and Compulsory Education. Most countries provide free education to their citizens, meaning the government operates a public school system open to all children who are in a certain age group. It does not necessarily mean there are no costs involved in attending school. Students may be required to wear uniforms (which must be purchased), might live far from the nearest school (and transportation must be paid for), or may need to supply their own books, pencils, and other basic items. In addition, having a child in school can cost a rural family one laborer on the family farm. This can become such a burden to poorer families that free education is still not accessible to them.

Compulsory education refers to the fact that the law requires children to attend school for a certain number of years. In many countries this rule is seldom enforced. Therefore, it may reflect the government's target for how long children should remain in school to obtain a basic education rather than how long they actually are required to attend. Compulsory education usually encompasses six to nine years, and optional schooling usually continues for three or more years.

Gross Domestic Product (GDP) Per Capita. This economic statistic refers to the value of all goods and services produced annually in an economy per person. Naturally, not every person produces goods and services, but the total is averaged for the entire population. If the term is expressed as "gross national product" (GNP), it is essentially the same statistic except for the addition of income earned abroad minus the income earned in the country by noncitizens. This is significant when part of the population works in other countries and sends back money to their families. It is also significant for countries that have substantial investments abroad. For most countries, the two statistics, GDP and GNP, are almost interchangeable.

In the past, GDP was calculated in terms of the U.S. dollar after conversion from the local currency at official exchange rates. This caused accuracy problems because of artificially set exchange rates and because a dollar may not buy the same amount of goods in the United States as it does in another country. Social scientists recently have developed the concept of Purchasing Power Parity (PPP), a measurement that tries to account for the inconsistencies of the past. When GDP is figured in terms of PPP, an international dollar not affected by exchange rates is used. Likewise, PPP attempts to express the relative ability of a person to purchase goods with the local currency. Therefore, measured with PPP, five hundred dollars will buy essentially the same things in the United States as it will in Brazil or Japan. For many countries, PPP data does not yet exist, and only estimates are available for others.

Most CultureGrams use PPP with GDP, as expressed by the phrase "real gross domestic product." When the word "real" is absent, only the GDP has been calculated. The real GDPs in CultureGrams usually are taken from the *Human Development Report 2000* (New York: Oxford University Press, 2000). In cases where the real GDP is low (less than one thousand dollars, for example), one can assume that people have very little disposable income. But one should also remember that rural families may grow their own food and therefore need less disposable income to meet basic needs. In other cases, such a low figure indicates people indeed may be without food, shelter, clothing, or other necessities.

Hard Currency. Many countries have currencies that are not acceptable as currency for international purchases or exchanges. These currencies are considered inconvertible (not a medium of exchange) outside of their sponsoring nation. Such countries must pay for imports with a convertible currency that is accepted as a medium of exchange among countries. A convertible currency often is called hard currency because it is worth something outside its own borders. The U.S. dollar, Japanese *yen*, British pound, German *Mark*, and a few others are global hard currencies. The currencies of most advanced economies are also convertible. Regional hard currencies also exist, such as the *CFA franc*, a French-backed currency used in many West African nations (former French colonies) as both a domestic and regional exchange currency. However, the *CFA franc* would not be accepted as a global hard currency. Developing countries without convertible currencies use hard currencies to import goods and services.

They obtain hard currency through their goods and services exports, their expatriate workers, tourism, and international lending or aid.

Human Development and Gender-Related Development Indexes. Originating with the United Nations Development Program, the human development index (HDI) and gender-related development index (GDI) attempt to compensate for the inability of traditional economic indicators to portray accurately the environment in which people live—whether that environment nurtures personal development or hinders it. The project functions under the assumption that human development is "a process of enlarging people's choices" (UNDP 1997, 15). The three essential choices that people must have in order to access others include the ability to "lead a long and healthy life, to be educated and to enjoy a decent standard of living" (15). Accordingly, the basis of the HDI and GDI is statistics related to infant mortality, life expectancy, literacy, and real GDP. If people have access to adequate education, health care, and wages, they are more likely to be involved in community affairs, join the middle class, and contribute skills and time to society. Such societies are more often democratic and respectful of human rights.

Each country is ranked in relation to the others according to an index value that falls between 0 and 1. The HDI "shows how far a country has to travel to provide . . . essential choices to all its people. It is not a measure of well-being. Nor is it a measure of happiness. Instead, it is a measure of empowerment" (UNDP 1995, 12). The GDI measures progress in the same way as the HDI, but it is adjusted to account for inequality between men and women. It is common for women to lag behind men in having access to the same basic resources and choices. Only 143 nations have been ranked for the GDI, whereas 174 have been listed for the HDI. Each CultureGram for which HDI and GDI data are available lists the country's rank. For more detailed analysis and additional data, refer to the entire *Human Development Report*, which is updated annually.

Income Distribution. This phrase generally is used in connection with the gap between what the poorest people in a country earn and what the richest earn. If income distribution is highly unequal, a small wealthy class generally controls the economy (and often the government) and owns most property. The much larger poor class is often landless, which is significant since the people are probably farmers who must rent property and receive only a small share of the benefits from their labor. An unequal, but not highly unequal, income distribution often indicates that a middle class is beginning to grow. When the distribution is fairly equal, as is the case in a minority of countries, it is due mostly to a large and prosperous middle class. However, it also can indicate the presence of a broad poor class and absence of a wealthy elite. Generally, having a highly unequal income distribution means the economy is unhealthy, whereas the existence of a strong middle (consumer) class is good for an economy.

Infant Mortality Rate. This statistic is expressed as the number of children per 1,000 live births who die before their first birthday. It is an important indicator of the overall health of a population, since infants who die at this age usually are subject to preventable diseases or birth defects related to the mother's health. Those who die at birth often do so because of a lack of prenatal care and medical attention at birth. People who have access to health care, clean water, nutritious food, and education are more likely to have a low infant mortality rate than people without such access. Industrialized countries generally have a low rate (fewer than 10 per 1,000), while developing countries usually have a higher rate (averaging more than 30). The poorest countries may have rates exceeding 100.

Life Expectancy. This measurement refers to how long a person can expect to live from birth if mortality patterns remain unchanged. Someone born today may be expected to live 80 years if living in some European countries but only 58 years if living in parts of Africa. However, since mortality patterns do change throughout a person's lifetime, the statistic is really a better reflection of how long an adult who is currently living can expect to live. So a person who is 50 today can expect to live until 80 in some countries or only a few more years in others. Women live longer than men in most countries, and people in industrialized countries live longer than those in developing countries. People in countries with high pollution have lower rates of life expectancy.

When a CultureGram lists only one average age, it is the average of the male and female averages. This statistic, like infant mortality, helps the reader understand the overall health of a population and whether the people have access to nutritious food, clean water, health care, and proper sanitation.

Literacy Rate. CultureGrams list a literacy rate for the general adult population. These data usually are taken from the *Human Development Report*, which defines literacy as "The percentage of people aged 15 and above who can, with understanding, both read and write a short, simple statement on their everyday life" (UNDP 2000, 280). This is the global standard for reporting literacy, although a few countries will certify persons literate if they can write their name or if they have ever been enrolled in school. Most educational experts agree that such definitions are misleading, since being able to write a name or a short sentence does not imply a person can understand such things as a ballot, a newspaper, or work instructions. Were it possible to report functional literacy, many countries would have far lower literacy rates than are presented. Unfortunately, no uniform standard exists for reporting functional literacy. Therefore, readers should keep in mind that an official literacy rate is only one indicator of a nation's overall educational level.

On the other hand, many developing countries report their literacy rates based on an official language that a majority or significant group of people does not even speak, let alone read. In these cases, people may be functional in a local language or an oral language but not functional in the "official" language. Although one cannot read and write an oral language, one can use it to recount history, calculate numbers,

share information, relate instructions, and so on. In some areas, the ability to read may not be considered a necessary life skill. In other words, readers cannot equate intelligence or skill with literacy.

Nuclear Family. As used in CultureGrams, this term refers to a family unit that includes one or two parents and their children. The nuclear family usually lives in a single-family dwelling. When CultureGrams state the nuclear family is the basic social unit, it means the average household is composed of a nuclear family.

Population and Population Growth Rate. The population listed for each country in CultureGrams is an estimate for the year previous to publication (i.e., 2000 population for text published in 2001). The estimate is based on the actual population at the last census, multiplied by an annual growth rate. The estimate may seem to conflict with other sources, since other sources often only print the population as of the latest census (whenever it may have been taken) or an estimate made in a base year (e.g., 1990). CultureGrams estimates are in keeping with figures in U.S. government publications, but they sometimes are modified by information from the target culture's government. Each population estimate is revised on an annual basis.

The population growth rate is an estimate based on the previous year's difference between births and deaths and the net number of migrants leaving or entering the country. The growth rate may change substantially in a single year if there is a large influx of immigrants, a massive emigration, a natural disaster, or an epidemic. Growth rates tend to be low in industrialized countries because families are small, averaging one or two children. Growth rates are generally high in developing countries, especially in areas where subsistence farming is the primary economic activity. These cultures require large families to help farm the land, but they often have a high infant mortality rate; many children are conceived to ensure that enough will survive into adulthood. In small nations, the growth rate may be low due to emigration, as people must go elsewhere to find work.

Poverty. Poverty is noted in CultureGrams in two ways. Sometimes poverty is described in general terms to indicate a low standard of living according to various governmental or societal criteria. Other references to poverty (those marked by an asterisk) are based on the Human Poverty Index (HPI) from the *Human Development Report 2000*. The HPI measures more severe deprivation in four main areas—"a long and healthy life, knowledge, economic provisioning, and social inclusion" (UNDP 2000, 150). These figures, expressed sometimes as percentages and sometimes as fractions, indicate what portion of a population not only lives in poverty but also lacks access to adequate education, health care, safe water, and economic opportunity to escape the poverty they face.

Staple Food. Staple foods are those foods that supply the majority of the average person's calories and nutrition. A people's primary staple food is usually starchy, such as cassava (manioc), corn, rice, millet, or wheat. Staple foods also include any meats, fruits, and vegetables eaten in large quantities or on a frequent basis.

Subsistence Farming. Subsistence farming refers to farming as the main source of a family's livelihood. That is, a family will grow its own food, raise its own livestock, build its own home, and often make its own clothing. Members of such a family generally do not earn a wage by working at a job, but they usually are not entirely without a cash income. Family members might sell surplus produce or livestock, or make crafts or other items (blankets, baskets, etc.), in order to buy things they cannot provide for themselves. These usually include items such as sugar, cooking oil, clothing, rice or another staple food, and so forth. Subsistence farmers also may set aside part of their land to grow cash crops in order to earn money. Subsistence farmers generally do not grow an abundance of anything. They often live on small owned or rented plots of land, and they seldom enjoy the luxuries of running water or electricity.

Underemployment. Underemployment refers to when workers are not officially unemployed but either are not able to find enough work in their profession or are working in jobs below their skill level. For example, if a country's universities graduate many people in engineering or other professional fields but the economy is not diversified or well developed, those people may find themselves underemployed, working in jobs that do not take advantage of their skills, or only working part-time in their field of study. In the latter case, they may return to farming or local retailing. In too many cases, the most educated people simply emigrate to another country to find work, resulting in what is called a "brain drain."

Government unemployment figures generally do not include underemployment; it must be estimated. However, when unemployment is high (more than 10 percent), one usually can assume that underemployment affects at least as many or more workers. This condition reflects an economy that is not growing, and it can lead to social unrest. High underemployment (more than 40 percent) often leads to political turmoil and violence. Employing and paying people according to their skill level helps secure social stability and encourage economic growth.

Western/Western-style. This term usually refers to the dress, eating customs, culture, and traditions of Western Europe, the United States, and Canada. This culture often is referred to as Western because of its common ancient (primarily Greek and Roman) philosophical, legal, political, and social heritage. The term *Western* can also refer to cultures that have a Judeo-Christian value system and religious orientation.

Suggested Reading

It is impossible to list all the available sources on the many cultures represented in this series. Many libraries have information on each country. However, the following sources are recommended because they provide information on most countries or regions of the world.

Background Notes. A publication of the U.S. Department of State that provides historical details, a map, and other valuable information about individual countries. Series updated periodically. Available through the Superintendent of Documents, U.S. Government Printing Office, PO Box 371954, Pittsburgh, PA 15250-7954; or at Web site www.state.gov/www/background_notes.

Current History. An excellent world affairs journal with articles that describe and analyze current political, economic, and social trends in selected countries. Subscriptions available at 4225 Main Street, Philadelphia, PA 19127; or at Web site www.currenthistory.com.

Human Development Report. An annual statistical report by the United Nations Development Program (UNDP) used to measure countries' abilities to offer people essential life choices related to health, education, and prosperity. Published by Oxford University Press, 198 Madison Avenue, New York, NY 10016; or at Web site www.undp.org/hdro.

The Statesman's Year-Book. A statistical and informational guide to all countries and many of their provinces and territories. Updated regularly. Available at most libraries and through most bookstores. Published by St. Martin's Press, 175 Fifth Avenue, New York, NY 10010.

World Factbook. An annual statistical publication of the Central Intelligence Agency. Designed for use by government officials. Available on CD-ROM through National Technical Information Service, 5285 Port Royal Road, Springfield, VA 22161; or at Web site www.odci.gov/cia/publications/factbook.

World Development Report. An annual publication of the World Bank that discusses salient issues, provides economic analysis, and presents data for developing countries. Available through World Bank Publications, PO Box 960, Herndon, VA 20172-0960; or at Web site http://publications.worldbank.org/ecommerce.

World Tables. Statistical data on most countries, focusing on economic indicators and trends for the past 20 years. Available from World Bank Publications (see address above). Other excellent resources also available for purchase. Free catalog from World Bank Publications.